Corel® WordPerfect® Suite 8 Professional: The Official Guide

Alan Neibauer

Osborne/**McGraw-Hill**

Berkeley   New York   St. Louis   San Francisco
Auckland   Bogotá   Hamburg   London
Madrid   Mexico City   Milan   Montreal
New Delhi   Panama City   Paris   São Paulo
Singapore   Sydney   Tokyo   Toronto

Osborne/**McGraw-Hill**
2600 Tenth Street
Berkeley, California 94710
U.S.A.

For information on translations or book distributors outside the U.S.A., or to arrange bulk purchase discounts for sales promotions, premiums, or fund-raisers, please contact Osborne/**McGraw-Hill** at the above address.

Corel® WordPerfect® Suite 8 Professional: The Official Guide

1234567890 AGM 901987654321098

ISBN 0-07-882439-7

Publisher: Brandon A. Nordin
Editor-in-Chief: Scott Rogers
Acquisitions Editor: Megg Bonar
Project Editor: Jennifer Wenzel
Associate Project Editor: Cynthia Douglas
Editorial Assistant: Gordon Hurd
Technical Editor: Corel
Copy Editor: Ann Spivack
Proofreaders: Pat Mannion and Karen Mead
Indexer: Valerie Robbins
Computer Designer: Roberta Steele
Illustrator: Leslee Bassin
Series Design: Michelle Galicia

To Barbara

PART I

Guide to Corel Office 8

PART II

Corel WordPerfect

PART III

Corel Quattro Pro

PART IV

Corel Presentations

PART VI

Corel Bonus Applications

Corel WordPerfect Suite 8 Professional: The Official Guide is the latest title in the CorelPRESS™ series of books dedicated to you, the users of Corel® software. The author, along with the staff at Corel, have spent many hours working on the accuracy and features included in this book to present you with this powerful overview of Corel's new WordPerfect® Suite 8 Professional product.

Corel® WordPerfect® Suite 8 Professional offers users leading-edge collaboration and productivity tools and the advanced Web technology that let you connect to the world. The power of Corel's new Suite unleashes your full productivity potential as it delivers a powerful ensemble of applications— intuitive word processing, powerful spreadsheets, captivating presentations and an efficient information manager, for starters. The products in the Suite offer a seamless integration among the Suite's core applications and boost efficiency to allow you to design and create documents with ease, and to take advantage of the product's powerful features.

The CorelPRESS series represents a giant step in the ability of Corel to disseminate information to our users through the help of Osborne/McGraw-Hill and the fine authors involved in the series. Congratulations to the team at Osborne, and the staff at Corel who together have created this excellent book.

Dr. Michael C. J. Cowpland
President & CEO
Corel Corporation

FOREWORD

ACKNOWLEDGMENTS

My thanks to everyone who worked on this project, especially acquisitions editor Megg Bonar, project editor Jennifer Wenzel, editorial assistant Gordon Hurd, copy editor Ann Spivack, proofreaders Pat Mannion and Karen Mead, and indexer Valerie Robbins.

Thanks also to the Osborne production team of Marcela Hancik, Jani Beckwith, Roberta Steele, Michelle Galicia, Sylvia Brown, Peter Hancik, and Lance Ravella, all of whom worked marvelously on this project.

Special thanks to the staff at Corel Corporation for technically reviewing the book; specifically the members of the WordPerfect Suite 8 Professional documentation group, without whose help technical accuracy would not be complete.

I am also in dept to the Corel staff that supported me, and numerous other users through the beta cycle, including J'Lene Willes, Chris Wilford, Michael Scott, Brian Prothero, Leonard Shoell, Gary Gibb, Jackie Brinkerhoff, and Wade Brown.

Working alongside of me throughout this entire project has been a remarkable woman, my wife Barbara. She was always there with a helping hand, a kind word, a gentle nudge, and a captivating smile. We're working on our fourth decade as a couple, and I'm still looking forward to her surprises.

In what now seems like the dinosaur days of personal computers, a handy little program called WordPerfect came out of Utah, and it quickly pushed the leading word processing programs off the top of the hill.

What was so remarkable about this upstart? It ran nicely on a computer with just two floppy disks (the huge 5.25" ones), could work with a variety of printers, and would even underline without the need to type special codes.

A lot has happened since then, but WordPerfect continues to evolve and improve with each incarnation. For proof, just consider Corel WordPerfect Suite 8 Professional. Suite 7 combined the power of Windows 95 with the versatility and integration of the Corel applications to make an unbeatable combination. So, what could they have added now?

Consider Corel WordPerfect. Not only does it check your spelling as you type, but it suggests synonyms and checks your grammar. The interface has been enhanced with dynamic property bars that change as you work, always offering useful tools and other features for the job at hand. Want to connect to the Internet? Just type a Web address (for example www.my_favorite_site.com) and click on it. Want to send e-mail? Type an e-mail address in your document and click on it. Have to create equations? Now you have two equation editors to choose from. Need to create Web documents? With Internet Publisher you can now create interactive forms.

Did they forget about Corel Quattro Pro? No way. The new QuickCell feature may be worth the price of admission alone. Drag a cell down to the application bar on the bottom of the window, then watch how it is recalculated as you work. There's no more scrolling back and forth.

Still not enough? Corel Presentations has been revamped with a new look, new features, and easier animations. Publish the shows to the Web complete with framed pages of hypertext links. Web surfers can even download your entire presentation, with sounds, graphics, and slide transitions and animations.

How about Corel Paradox? It now has two HTML Publishing Experts for moving your database to the Web, a totally revamped project viewer, thorough integration with the rest of the suite, and dynamic hyperlinks to the Internet.

If you are still not convinced, then just imagine all those features along with:

- Designing, managing, and publishing complete Web sites with Corel WEB.SiteBuilder.

- Keeping track of your calendar, address book, card files, and Internet mailbox with CorelCENTRAL.

INTRODUCTION

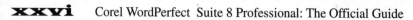

- Planning and managing projects with Corel® Time Line®.

- Publishing your work to Barista™, Corel's powerful JAVA implementation

- Designing Web pages with Corel® WordPerfect®, Corel® Quattro Pro®, and Corel® Presentations™

- Accessing ten thousand clipart images and graphics

- Selecting from 150 fonts

- Using Bitstream Font Navigator for managing all these fonts

You can get all this, and more, in one tightly integrated package. It is a lot of computing power, and you have this book to help you make sense of it all.

The Official Guide to Corel® WordPerfect® Suite 8 Professional covers all of the Suite's key features with enough detail and illustrations so you'll be using the software almost as fast as you can install it. As a Corel "Official Guide," every instruction in the book has been checked and approved by the experts at Corel Corporation; and just like the Suite itself, this book packs quite a punch.

In the first two chapters you will learn to use the common elements that run through the Suite's major applications—including the Corel Address Book, file management with QuickFinder, the Scrapbook for inserting clipart, and writing tools such as Spell Check, Thesaurus, Grammatik, and QuickCorrect. You will learn to use the Desktop Application Director (DAD) and the Accessories, Setup & Notes, and Tools menus to work with the Suite. You will find special features for using templates and other time-saving tools. Because the Suite is integrated with the Net, in Chapter 3 you will learn how to use Netscape Communicator that is integrated with CorelCENTRAL for electronic mail, discussion groups, and surfing the Web.

Chapters 4 through 13 are all about Corel WordPerfect, the powerhouse word-processing program praised by millions of devoted users around the world. In Chapter 4, you will learn how to create, save, and print documents, as well as how to check your spelling as you type, insert and delete text, and change the view and magnification of text and graphics on the screen. Chapter 5 is all about editing documents, and teaches you how to perform tasks such as moving and copying text, finding and replacing text, inserting comments and bookmarks, working with multiple windows, and revising documents. Formatting characters, lines, and paragraphs is covered in Chapter 6. In Chapter 7, you will learn how to create professional-looking Web pages, complete with hyperlinks, and how to use templates and styles. Templates let you create completely formatted documents, such as newsletters, with a few clicks of the mouse.

In Chapter 8, you will learn how to format pages by changing margins and page size, set up pages for binding and printing on both sides, and print booklets, envelopes, and labels. Creating tables and working with columns are covered in Chapter 9. You will learn how to create and format tables, even adding formulas and functions to perform math, and how to create multiple-column documents.

If you want to customize Corel WordPerfect or create macros to save you from repeating keystrokes, then check out Chapter 10. Here, you will also learn how to create custom toolbars and menus, and how to assign key combinations to your favorite tasks.

Creating form documents is covered in Chapter 11. In Chapter 12, you will learn all about Corel WordPerfect's graphics features, which includes sections about adding pictures and charts, formatting equations, and creating special effects with text. Finally, you will learn how to share information between applications in Chapter 13, so you won't have to retype any information to use it in another program.

Corel Quattro Pro is the focus of Chapters 14 through 21. This powerful program lets you create worksheets, graphs and maps, databases, and even slide shows. After learning what the program is all about in Chapter 14, you will learn how to create worksheets in Chapter 15. Then, Chapter 16 teaches you how to edit and format worksheet contents.

Chapter 17 explains how to work with blocks of information, use multiple windows, and manipulate entire notebooks. In Chapter 18, you'll learn how to work with formulas and functions. Adding maps, charts, and graphics to worksheets is discussed in Chapter 19, along with combining graphics and bullet charts into slide shows. Using the map feature, for example, you can show a map of the United States, along with major highways, illustrating the geographic distribution of your company's sales or organization's membership.

In Chapter 20, you will learn how to use sophisticated but easy tools to analyze the information in your worksheet. In Chapter 21, you'll learn how to create macros and share information with other applications.

Corel Presentations is covered in Chapters 22 through 24. You will learn how to create slides of all types in Chapter 22, add eye-catching graphics in Chapter 23, and then build complete slide shows in Chapter 24. You'll even learn how to take your slide show on the road, and how to publish it to the Internet completed with framed pages.

Corel Paradox is covered in Chapters 25 through 27. In Chapter 25, you'll learn how to create a database using the Database Expert and Table Expert, and how to create forms, queries, and reports. Chapter 26 shows you how to create custom tables, work with database objects, and protect your database with passwords. In Chapter 27,

you'll learn powerful database features, such as creating lookup tables, using referential integrity to avoid errors, and how to design custom forms and reports.

Finally, Chapters 28 through 33 cover the bonus applications.

Chapters 28 and 29 are all about Corel Time Line. In Chapter 28, you'll learn how to create a project by adding tasks, estimating their effort and duration, and setting relationships between them. You'll also learn how to work with Gantt and PERT charts, and view the Critical Path. Chapter 29 shows you how to set up and manage resource calendars and costs, and to track your progress.

Corel WEB.SiteBuilder is covered in Chapter 30. SiteBuilder lets you create and manage complete Web sites, including designing individual Web pages, linking pages together, and publishing the site to the Internet or an intranet using the software provided in the Suite.

Chapter 31 covers CorelCENTRAL, a personal time and contact management program. You'll learn how to schedule events, and to create and use card files for storing information. CorelCENTRAL also serves as your central mailbox for e-mail and discussion group messages, so you can send events to the calendars of other CorelCENTRAL users.

In Chapter 32, you'll learn that with Envoy you can convert your documents to a format that anyone can read, annotate, and print — even if they do not have the Corel WordPerfect Suite.

Finally, Chapter 33 is a little gift for those who also have the standard version of the Corel WordPerfect Suite. The standard version comes with Corel Photo House that lets you customize and add pizzazz to photographs and other graphics. You'll learn how to use Photo House in this chapter.

Because this book is organized by Suite application, you do not have to read it from cover to cover. You should read the first two chapters to get acquainted with the Suite, but then you can jump ahead to the section or chapter you are most interested in. You can read the other sections later to learn how the remaining applications and features work, so you can take full advantage of the Suite. You'll find easy-to-follow, step-by-step instructions and clear but complete details on the features that you'll want to use.

You'll also find some helpful elements along the way. Look for these tips to learn how the features of the Suite applications are integrated:

NOTE: *Here you'll find some additional bits of information about the topic being discussed.*

TIP: *Look here for shortcuts or special techniques.*

CAUTION: *Keep an eye out for these warnings about potential problems.*

The Corel WordPerfect Professional Suite is perfect for use in the office, home, classroom, or dorm. The more you use it, the more features you'll find, and you'll grow to love its ease and versatility. You will especially like its integration with the Internet, and the many ways that you can take advantage of the vast world of resources on the World Wide Web. In fact, once you get on-line, drop me a line describing what you like best about the Suite. You can reach me at alann@worldnet.att.net.

About the Author...

Alan Neibauer is the best-selling author of Osborne's wildly successful *Corel WordPerfect Suite 8: The Official Guide*, as well as over 20 other computer book titles, including *The Official Guide to Corel WordPerfect Suite 7 for Windows 95*, *Word for Windows 95 Made Easy*, and two editions of *Access for Busy People*.

A graduate of the Wharton School, University of Pennsylvania, Neibauer has taught at the high school, college, and corporate levels for 14 years, and is a popular corporate trainer on WordPerfect and Quattro Pro.

PART

I

Guide to Corel Office 8

The Corel WordPerfect Professional Suite

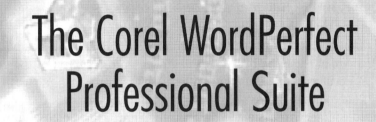

Corel WordPerfect Suite 8 is a complete set of desktop applications and tools for creating, publishing, and distributing documents of all types. The applications are integrated to provide stand-alone and workgroup solutions and easy access to the Internet and online services.

Integration means convenient flow from one application to another. It also means that you can use the best features of each program to build *compound documents*—documents that can combine text, tables, charts, and graphics—without worrying about compatibility between file types and program features.

Included with the Professional version of the Suite are these programs:

- Corel WordPerfect 8

- Corel Quattro Pro 8

- Corel Presentations 8

- Corel Paradox 8

- Corel WEB.SiteBuilder

- CorelCENTRAL

- Corel Time Line

You also get Corel Address Book to store addresses of persons and organizations, a wide selection of fonts, Bitstream FontNavigator, Envoy for viewing and sharing documents, thousands of clipart images, and useful utilities for working with and sharing information. For communicating over the Internet you get Netscape Communicator.

Integrate IT! *Corel WordPerfect Suite applications and utilities are designed to work together. So, for example, you can easily insert a Corel Quattro Pro worksheet into a Corel Presentation slide and into a Corel WordPerfect document. You can also publish a document to Envoy by just choosing an option from an application's File menu.*

To make the Corel WordPerfect Suite easy to use, the applications are installed directly on the taskbar, and you can access them from the Start menu. Click on the Start button, and point to Corel WordPerfect Suite 8 to see the applications that you've installed and the Accessories, Setup & Notes, and Tool options. Figure 1-1 shows the programs included with the Suite, as well as the accessory utilities and applets. These will be discussed later. To start a Corel WordPerfect Suite application or accessory, just click on the program name in the Start menu or use the Desktop Application Director.

 NOTE: *Although Corel Photo House comes only with the Standard Suite and not the Professional Suite, we've included it later in this book for the convenience of Standard Suite users.*

Now, before looking at the individual parts of the Suite, let's look at the interface that binds them together.

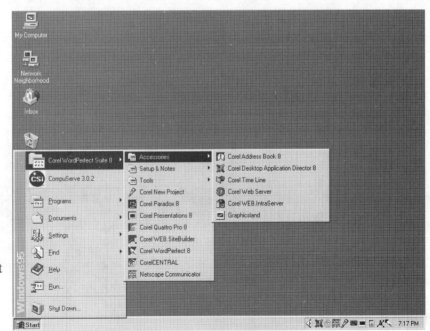

Corel WordPerfect Suite Start menu and accessories

FIGURE 1-1

Desktop Application Director

Buttons to start the Corel WordPerfect Suite applications and special features have been placed on the taskbar, in the *Desktop Application Director* (DAD) toolbar, as shown in Figure 1-2.

Click on the button for the program you want to run.

You can also right-click on the buttons to launch one of the features from a menu, to Exit (remove) the bar, or to display the Properties dialog box to remove specific items from the bar.

Corel WordPerfect Suite Accessories

In addition to the major applications and the Desktop Application Director, the Corel WordPerfect Suite includes some useful accessories. To access them, click on the Start button, point to Corel WordPerfect Suite 8, and then point to Accessories, Setup & Notes, or Tools to see a menu of additional items.

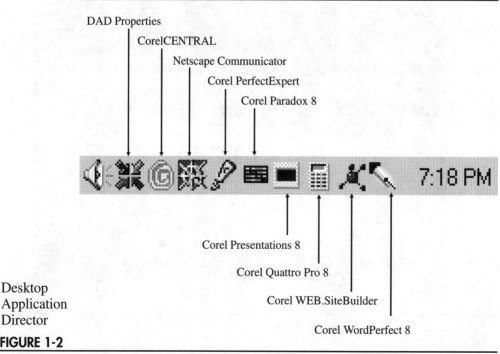

DAD Properties
CorelCENTRAL
Netscape Communicator
Corel PerfectExpert
Corel Paradox 8

7:18 PM

Corel Presentations 8
Corel Quattro Pro 8
Corel WEB.SiteBuilder
Corel WordPerfect 8

Desktop
Application
Director

FIGURE 1-2

Accessories

The Accessories submenu contains these items:

- *Corel Address Book 8* lets you maintain an Address Book of contacts. You'll learn about the Address Book later in this chapter.

- *Corel Desktop Application Director 8* opens the DAD taskbar if it is not already displayed.

- *Corel Time Line* is a project management program for organizing, tracking, and reporting on projects.

- *Corel Web Server* is a full-featured Web server that handles requests between Web browsers and compatible applications.

- *Corel WEB.IntraServer* lets your computer act as a server on an intranet.

- *Graphicsland* launches an application for transmitting files to a service bureau to create slides from Corel Paradox slide shows.

Setup & Notes

The items in this menu help you find information or set up the Suite and its applications. The options are as follows:

- *Corel Approved Partners Help* lists the names, addresses, and telephone numbers of authorized trainers and service bureaus around the world.

- *Corel Remove Program* removes the Corel suite from your system.

- *Corel WordPerfect Suite 8 Setup* lets you modify your installation by adding or deleting components.

- *Paradox Technical Support Help* explains how to get customer support on Corel Paradox.

- *Reference Center* provides access to detailed onscreen documentation.

- *Release Notes* displays last-minute information about the Suite.

- *Technical Support Help* explains how to get customer support on the Suite applications.

Tools Menu

The Tools menu offers useful applications and programs, including the following:

- *Corel PerfectScript* records macros that open Corel WordPerfect Suite applications and perform tasks.

- *Corel Settings Editor* is an advanced tool for working with the Windows 95 Registry.

- *Corel Time Line Import-Export* lets you share information with and from Corel Time Line databases.

- *Corel Time Line Reports* lets you prepare reports from Time Line databases.

- *CorelCENTRAL User Profile Manager* allows several users to share Corel Netscape.

- *Data Modeling Desktop* lets you create reports including cross-tabulations and subtotals from Quattro Pro worksheets.

- *Database Desktop* lets you work with database and SQL files.

- *Database Engine 4.0* is used to configure ODBC, a method for sharing information between databases and other programs.

- *Envoy 7 Viewer* lets you read, print, and annotate Envoy files, such as those found in the Reference Center.

- *QuickFinder Manager 8* allows you to quickly search frequently used files and folders.

- *QuickFinder Searcher* launches QuickFinder to locate a file or folder.

QuickFinder Searcher

Even with the Windows Explorer, finding the correct file on your hard disk can be difficult. The Suite can help you, though, with QuickFinder Searcher. Not only is *QuickFinder Searcher* available in the Tools menu, but it is integrated into most Corel WordPerfect Suite file management dialog boxes. For example, when you open or save a document using Open and Save, you have full access to the QuickFinder Searcher system.

Because QuickFinder Searcher is a common utility found in all Corel WordPerfect Suite applications, we'll discuss it in Chapter 2.

Corel Address Book

Use the *Corel Address Book* to store names, addresses, telephone numbers, e-mail addresses, and other useful information about the people you contact. You can also store information about organizations, grouping your contacts according to their company or other affiliation. The Address Book is fully integrated into the Corel WordPerfect Suite; you can access it directly from Corel WordPerfect when creating letters, envelopes, and labels. You should add your own information to the Address Book—for example, to use with Corel WordPerfect templates, so your name and address appear on fax cover pages and letters.

Here's how to use the Address Book:

1. Select Corel Address Book 8 from the Corel WordPerfect Suite 8 Accessories menu. You can also start it from within Corel WordPerfect. The book comes with two pages, My Addresses and Frequent Contacts, as shown in Figure 1-3. You may see other pages if you've created an Address Book in Microsoft Exchange, and you can create additional pages or books. The Frequent Contacts page stores addresses that you contact often. When you first access an address, either from Corel WordPerfect or by dialing it, the address is copied into Frequent Contacts. The Address Book then keeps a count of the number of times you access the address, and records the last contact date.

2. To add a person or organization to the Address Book, click on Add. A dialog box will appear with three choices, Person, Organization, and Resource. When you add an organization, you'll be asked to enter its name, telephone number, address, fax number, and comments. You can then insert the organization's name into a person's personal record. A resource includes a telephone number, e-mail address and type, owner's name, and comments.

3. To add information about an individual, click on Person and then on OK. You'll see the dialog box shown in Figure 1-4.

4. Enter information into the Address Book, and then click on OK.

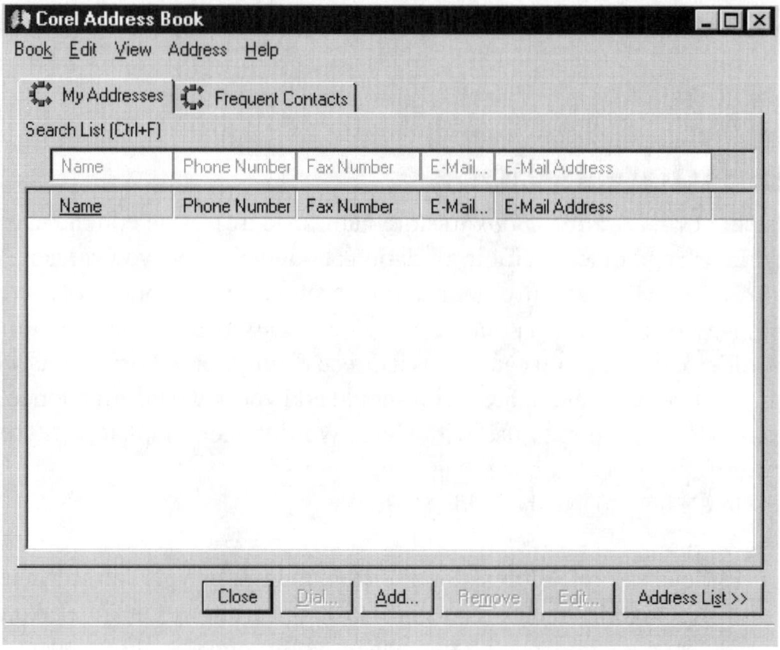

Corel
Address
Book

FIGURE 1-3

As you type the first and last names, they also appear in the display name section. The Address Book will use the full display name in its list, and you can access it for use with templates.

On the Phone Numbers tab you can enter up to five telephone numbers: one for the office, home, cellular, home fax, and office fax. You have to select one of the numbers as the default that will be listed in the Address Book and automatically dialed. Just click the Option button next to the phone number.

On the Security tab you can designate the listing as hidden or read-only.

When you've completed the entry, click on New to add another without having to close the dialog box first, or click on OK. Names and organizations will be listed in the Address Book, with a small icon designating organizations.

Working with Address Books

TIP: *Using the buttons on the bottom of the Address Book, you can add, edit, delete, and dial the phone number of the selected contact.*

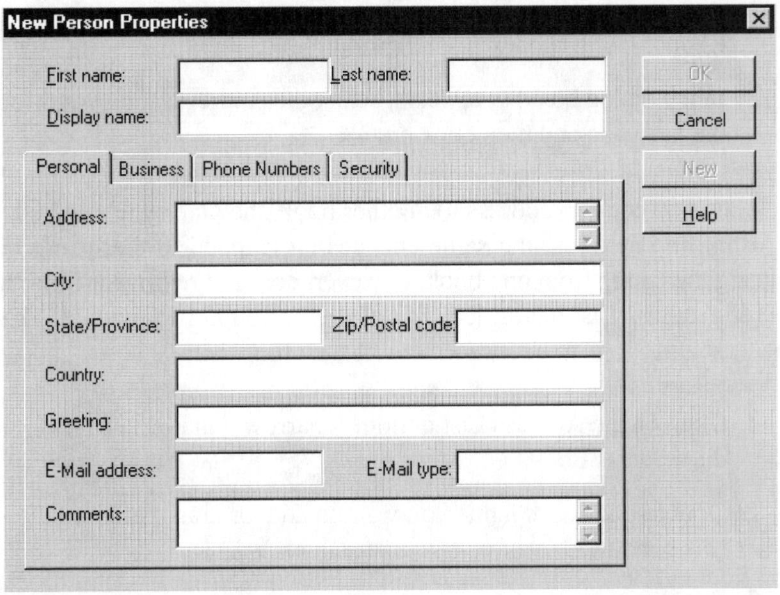

Adding an entry for an individual to the Address Book

FIGURE 1-4

To create another Address Book, select New from the Book menu and enter a name. A page for the book will appear in the dialog box. Click on the tab to access it. To close an Address Book, click on its tab and then select Close from the Book menu. To open the book, use the Open command.

You can also make a copy of an existing Address Book, using these steps:

1. Click on the Address Book tab to open it.

2. Select Save As from the Book menu.

3. Type a name for the Address Book.

4. Click on OK.

When you have more than one book, you can copy and move addresses between them. To move a name from one to the other, use the Edit Cut and Edit Paste commands. Cut the name from one Address Book and paste it in the other. To copy a name from one to the other, use these steps:

1. Select the name in the Address Book.

2. Choose Copy Names from the Edit menu.

3. In the dialog box that appears, select the Address Book you want to place the names in and then click on OK.

When you copy an address to another book, they are synchronized. If you edit the listing in one book, the same changes are applied to the listing in the other. Deleting the listing from one book, however, does not remove it from the other.

The Address List button lets you create a group of individuals. You can then broadcast a message to every member of the group. Here's how:

1. Click on the Address List button. A narrow window appears to the right of the Address Book.

2. Double-click each name you want to add, or drag them into the Address List window.

3. Click on the Save Group button.

4. In the dialog box that appears, type a group name and an optional comment, and then click on OK.

5. The group will be added to the Address Book, with an icon indicating that it is a group entry.

You can double-click on a name in the address list to remove it from that window, or right-click on it and select Remove from the QuickMenu that appears.

Sorting Addresses

Your addresses appear in the same order that you entered them. When you're scanning the book to find a particular contact, however, it would be easier if the addresses were sorted in some other order, such as by name or organization. Sorting the addresses also helps you draw some conclusions about your contacts, such as how many are in a particular organization or live in the same city.

If you want to sort on a particular field, right-click on the column heading for the field to see the QuickMenu shown here. The Sort All option sorts all of the addresses by the values in the first column, either ascending or descending. Choose to sort on the selected column to order the records by the values you see here.

✔ Sort All Ascending
  Sort All Descending
  Sort on 'Phone Numb...' First

  Name
  First Name
  Last Name
  Organization
  Phone Number
  E-Mail Address
  Address
  City
  State
  Zip Code
  Country

  More Columns
  Sort

You can also sort on a specific column, even one not displayed, by choosing Sort from the QuickMenu to see the dialog box shown in Figure 1-5. Choose the column and the order, and then click on OK. For example, use the Column Sort dialog box to sort the listing by last name, even though the column is not on the default view. An alternative is to add the column and then sort by it.

Changing the Address Book Display

The default display shows the most frequently used fields. You can change the order of fields, adjust the width of columns, and decide which fields are displayed, much as you can with a database or spreadsheet program.

To change the width of a column using the mouse, point to the line on its right and drag. To change the position of a column, drag its name to the left or the right.

You can make additional changes using the QuickMenu. Right-click on a column heading to see the QuickMenu that lists the names of most-often-used fields. The fields already displayed will be dimmed, so click on one of the others to display it.

For even more choices, click on More Columns in the QuickMenu to see the dialog box shown in Figure 1-6. Select the columns you want to add or remove. To change a column's width, click on it in the list and then click on the <<, smaller, larger, and >> buttons. These will be dimmed if you select more than one column. Use the move to left (up) and move to right (down) buttons to change the order of columns.

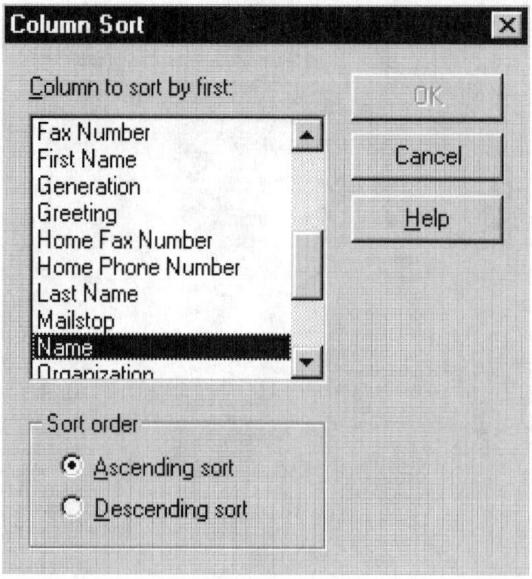

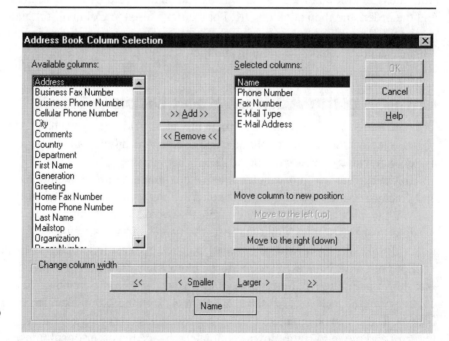

Sorting an
Address
Book

FIGURE 1-5

Selecting
columns to
display

FIGURE 1-6

Searching for Addresses

If you do not have many addresses in your book, you can locate one by scrolling the list. However, this becomes tedious as your Address Books grow. Rather than scrolling, you can use either of two techniques to locate an address—searching and filtering.

You search the Address Book using the search list above the first address. Here's how:

1. Click in the box representing the information you want to search for. To locate a record by the person's name, for example, click in the Name box. You can also press F2 and click on OK from the box that appears to enter the Name box, and then move to others by pressing the TAB key.

2. Type the information you are looking for.

As you enter information into the row, the address list scrolls to highlight a matching listing in that column. (It does not scroll until you stop typing.) For example, if you are looking for a person named George Jones, click on the Name field and type the name. The list will scroll to the first person with that name. Enter additional information on other columns to further refine your search.

Using a Filter

While searching scrolls the listing, a filter determines which addresses are shown. It filters out those addresses that don't meet the criteria that you create, displaying only those that do match.

A *filter* is a logical statement, such as "Zip Code Equals 94501." It includes a column name (Zip Code), an operator (Equals), and a condition (94501). The statement means "show only addresses that have the value 94501 in the Zip Code field." You can combine several statements in logical AND and OR operations for more exact searching, and you can even group the conditions for a precise selection.

To create a filter, follow these steps:

1. Select Define Filter from the View menu to see the dialog box shown in Figure 1-7.

2. Pull down the list in the first column, and choose the column you want to filter by.

3. Pull down the list of operators and choose from these options:

= Equal To
! Not Equal To
< Less Than
<= Less Than or Equal To
> Greater Than
>= Greater Than or Equal To
[ ] Contains

4. Enter the value in the condition field.

You can include wildcards in the condition, using an asterisk to represent any number of characters and the question mark for a single character. For example, to locate all persons whose last name begins with "G," use the Equal operator and enter **G*** in the condition field. This tells the filter to locate all persons whose last name begins with the letter "G," regardless of how many characters are in the name.

To further narrow the search, pull down the list by clicking End and choosing a compound operator. Select the AND operator to match persons who meet more than one condition. Use the OR operator to find persons who meet one or the other condition but not necessarily both. There will be a separate row for each condition. Use Insert Row and Delete Row as needed to add and remove statements. For example, Figure 1-8 shows a filter that locates all persons in California, as well as those whose last name begins with the letter "G."

To delete a group, just delete the individual rows in it. Choose End to designate the last condition.

TIP: *Use Reset to remove the filter.*

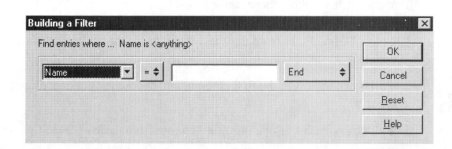

Defining
a filter

FIGURE 1-7

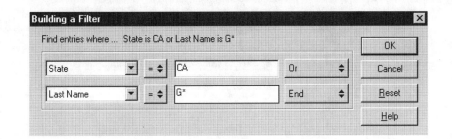

A
compound
filter

FIGURE 1-8

When you close the dialog box, the filter will be applied, listing just those records that match the conditions. You'll see a small icon next to the Search List that shows that there is a filter and that it is enabled. To display all of the addresses without removing the filter, select Filtering Enabled from the View menu. The icon next to Search List changes its appearance to remind you that a filter is still defined.

To edit the filter, select Define Filter from the View menu, or click on the icon next to Search List. To remove the filter, not just disable it, click on Reset in the Define Filter dialog box.

PerfectScript

PerfectScript is a macro creation tool that you can use from the Accessories menu. Using PerfectScript, you create a macro that opens one or more Corel WordPerfect Suite applications and performs functions within them. It also gives you a common way to make a macro regardless of the application. PerfectScript does not replace the macro functions in the individual programs. Rather, it provides another layer of utility to access the applications from the DAD bar.

Creating macros from within applications is discussed in Chapters 10 and 21. To create a macro from the desktop, pull down the Tools menu, and click on Corel PerfectScript to display the dialog box shown in Figure 1-9.

To record a macro using PerfectScript, first make sure one of the Corel WordPerfect Suite applications, such as Corel WordPerfect or Corel Quattro Pro, is open. Then follow these steps:

1. Pull down the Tools menu from the Corel WordPerfect Suite 8 option in the Start menu and click on Corel PerfectScript to start PerfectScript.

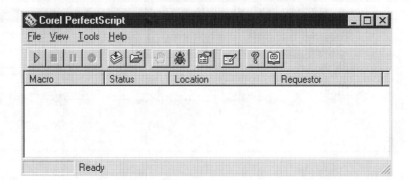

PerfectScript
dialog box

FIGURE 1-9

2. Open the Corel WordPerfect Suite application that you want the macro to work with.

3. Click on the Corel PerfectScript button in the taskbar to switch to the PerfectScript dialog box, and then click on the Record button or select Record from the File menu. The Record Macro box appears.

4. Type a macro name, and then click on Record.

5. Switch to the Corel WordPerfect Suite application. The application will appear with its own record macro mode. With Corel WordPerfect, for example, you'll see its macro feature bar on the screen.

6. Record the keystrokes or menu selections that you want in the macro.

7. Click on the Stop button in the application's macro toolbar, or switch to PerfectScript and click on the Stop button.

The four most recent PerfectScript macros you created or edited will be listed in the PerfectScript File menu. To run the macro, pull down the File menu and click on its name. The macro will switch to or open the application and repeat the keystrokes and menu selections.

Editing and debugging macros requires knowledge of the PerfectScript macro language and a basic understanding of programming. You can see a list of all PerfectScript macro commands, for example, by clicking on the Macro Command Browser button in the PerfectScript toolbar. You can also click on the Debug button on the toolbar to step through your macros command by command, and to look at the value of your variables. For more information on PerfectScript, search Corel WordPerfect Help and the Corel WordPerfect User's Guide in the Reference Center.

To edit macros, you must first select a macro editor. Choose Settings from the Tools menu, and click on the Edit tab. Enter the path and filename, choose the word processing program you want to edit the macro in, and then click on OK. You can now select Edit from the File menu and choose a macro to edit.

TIP: *Use the Dialog Editor option from the Tools menu to create custom dialog boxes for a macro. See Chapter 10 for more information on creating dialog boxes.*

Bitstream Font Navigator

Corel WordPerfect Suite includes over 100 fonts, and you probably have other fonts already installed on your system. To help manage and organize your fonts, Corel has provided Bitstream Font Navigator.

To run the program, click on Start in the Taskbar, point to Programs and then to Bitstream Font Navigator, and then click on Font Navigator 2.0. The first time you run the program, you'll see the Font Navigator Wizard that lets you locate all of the fonts on your system. Click on Next to see a tree-diagram of your system. Click on the hard drive containing your fonts, and then click on Finish. The program searches your disk, creating a database of the fonts, and then displays them as shown in Figure 1-10. To see what a font looks like, click on it in either list. A sample of the font appears in the Font Sample panel.

Use the toolbar buttons and menu to work with the fonts. For example, the toolbar contains these features:

- *Folder List* lets you navigate through your system, much like the Explorer. Pull down the list to select drives and folders.

- *Up One Level* moves to the next-highest folder level.

- *View All Fonts* displays all of the fonts in your system.

- *View by Format* displays all fonts, or just True Type or Postscript fonts.

- *View by Style* displays all fonts, or those categorized as decorative, monospaced, sans serif, script, serif, or symbol.

- *Create New Font Group* creates a group in which to store similar fonts.

- *View Properties* displays detailed information about the selected font.

- *Print Sample* prints a sample of the selected font. You can choose a one- or two-line sample, a sample of the font family, or a chart of the characters in the font.

- *Help* displays information about the item you click on.

The View menu offers additional features. For example, you can change the size and text that appears in the Font Sample panel, and the size of the panels within the windows.

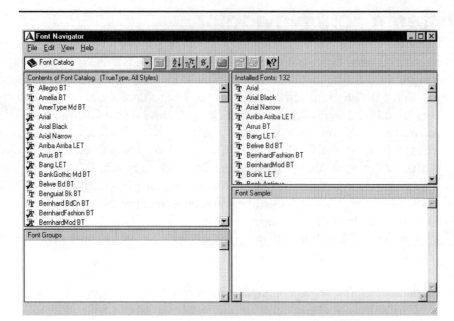

Bitstream
Font
Navigator

FIGURE 1-10

Using Corel Tools and Utilities

2

The integration of Corel WordPerfect Suite components gives us the advantage of a common set of tools. Features such as Help and Spell Check and processes such as file handling work the same way in Corel WordPerfect, Corel Quattro Pro, and Corel Presentations. (Corel Paradox uses the same Help system but different file management techniques.) Thus, once you learn the basics of these features, you don't have to retrace your steps with every application. In this chapter, you'll learn how to use the tools that are common to all three major applications.

When You Need Help

All Windows applications come with an onscreen help system. Although each Corel WordPerfect Suite application and accessory has its own help information, the interface works the same in all of them.

 REMEMBER: *You can access the Reference Center from the Setup & Notes menu to read detailed documentation on most of the Suite applications.*

To start Help from within an application, pull down the Help menu in the menu bar to see these options:

- *Help Topics*—Get help by topic, search for keywords, and see interactive demonstrations.

- *Ask the PerfectExpert*—Enter a keyword or phrase, or ask a question, such as "How do I print in landscape?"

- *PerfectExpert*—See a panel of interactive options on the screen.

- *Corel Web Site*—Connect online to Corel via the Internet or online services such as CompuServe or America Online.

You may see some other options, depending on the application. These additional help choices will be discussed in later chapters.

Help Topics

Help Topics is perhaps the most comprehensive way to find information. The Help Topics dialog box contains up to four pages (Contents, Index, Find, and Ask the PerfectExpert). Each page gives you a different way to search the Help database for the information you want. If you have trouble finding what you need on one page, try another.

Contents Page

The Contents page works just like a table of contents in a book. You'll see a list of major topics, each with an icon of a book. Clicking on the icon opens the book to display other topic areas, with their own book icon, or specific help topics indicated by the Help icon. Continue opening books until you see a listing for the exact information you need, and then double-click on the topic to display a Help dialog box.

In some of the help systems you'll see a Showcase option, such as Showcase Corel WordPerfect. Clicking on that option displays a help topic illustrating several samples of documents that can be created with the application. One of the samples will be selected, and an enlarged version of it appears with triangles marking parts of the document for which help is available. Click on the sample that you are interested in, and then click on a triangle to read instructions on how to create that effect.

Index Page

The Index page works like an index at the back of the book. It is an alphabetical list of the keywords in all of the Help topics. Rather than manually scrolling through the list, however, type the first few characters of the subject you need help with to automatically scroll the list to that part of the index. If the exact topic isn't shown, type a few more characters of the topic or scroll the list manually using the scroll bar. When you see the topic, double-click on it.

Find Page

You can also locate a help topic using the Find page. This makes available a database of all of the words in the help system.

The first time you select Find in each application, you'll be given a choice of the type of database you want to create. Choose Minimize Database Size for a simple search of words and phrases as they appear in Help windows. Select Maximize Search Capabilities to be able to look up subjects with similar concepts. Choose Customize Search Capabilities to specify which Help files you want to search. You can later rebuild your database to choose another option.

Once the database is created, you enter a word or phrase that you are looking for. Help displays two lists, as shown in Figure 2-1. One list shows matching words that it found in the database, and the other shows Help topics containing those words. To narrow your search, click on each of the matching words to see which topics it is found in. When you see the topic in the second list, double-click on it, or select it and then click on Display.

The Find page of the Help dialog box

FIGURE 2-1

If you chose to maximize your search capabilities, each of the Help topics will have a checkbox. To locate related information, click on the checkboxes for the topics you are interested in, and then click on the Find Similar button.

The number of matching topics and the Help settings appear at the bottom of the Find dialog box. The default setting is All Words, Begin, Auto, Pause. Here's what that means.

- *All Words* means that the Help topic must contain all of the words that you type in any order. If you type "settings environmental," for example, only topics containing both words will be listed.

- *Begin* means that it will look for words that begin with the same characters that you typed.

- *Auto* means that Find will start searching for words after each of your keystrokes.

- *Pause* means that Find will wait until you stop typing before it searches.

You can change these settings by clicking on Options to see the Find Options dialog box. There you can choose to match all or at least one of the words. If you selected Maximize the Search Capabilities, you can also choose to search for the words in the exact order you typed them and to display matching phrases.

The Show Words That option lets you find words that begin or end with, contain, or match those that you've typed.

In the Begin Searching section, choose to start the search only after you click the Find Now button, or immediately after each keystroke. The Files button lets you choose which Help files to search.

Ask the PerfectExpert

Ask the PerfectExpert is the same option that is listed on the Help menu. Ask the PerfectExpert allows you to type a word, a phrase, or even a question, such as "How do I indent a paragraph?" You'll get a list of topics, and perhaps projects, that relate to the question—just double-click on the one you want to read about. If you ask "How do I create a memo?", for example, the Corel WordPerfect 8 Memo project will be launched.

Help Windows

When you select a topic, a window will appear onscreen with information about it. A typical Help window is shown in the following illustration. This particular screen shows you how to create a header or footer in Corel WordPerfect. It contains a series of steps to follow and a few tips. This box also contains the Related Topics and About options that explain more about the topic. Click on one of the buttons to learn more.

You might also see words or phrases underlined with a series of dashes. These are called *jump terms* or *pop-up terms*. Click on the term to display a box with a definition or explanation. Click elsewhere in the Help window when you have finished.

You may also see a series of topics, each following a small square. These are additional topics that relate to the subject. Click on a topic or the square to display its Help page.

Click on Help Topics in the Help window toolbar to return to the Help Topics dialog box. Click on Back, if it is not dimmed, to return to the previously displayed Help window. Click on Options and you'll see a menu with several choices, described here:

■ *Annotate* lets you type a note, message, or reminder and "attach" it to the Help page. When you close the Annotate window, an icon of a paper clip will appear next to the topic. Double-click on the icon to read or edit the note.

- *Copy* places a copy of the text in the Help window in the Clipboard. You can then paste the information into a program. Only the text in the window is copied, not any graphics.

- *Print Topic* prints the contents of the Help window.

- *Font* lets you choose the size of the text in the window. Options are Small, Normal, and Large.

- *Keep Help on Top* controls how the Help window appears when you click on another window. You can choose to keep the Help window on top, displayed in the foreground, rather than moved into the background when you switch windows.

- *Use System Colors* applies the same colors that you see in the Application window to the help system.

- *Open a file* lets you open the Help files that are available on your system, even if they are on the network.

- *Exit* closes the help system.

- *Define a Bookmark* lets you mark a page in the help system. Use it to mark a topic that you refer to often.

- *Display a Bookmark* lets you go directly to one of your defined bookmarks.

- *Version* reports the version of your help system.

Corel Web Site

The Corel Web Site option on the Help menu will launch your Internet account, if you have one, to link directly into Corel Corporation's Web site. When you select this option, your Web browser will start automatically; you'll be connected to the documentation page on the Web for the application that you used to launch Help.

 TIP: *You can also access Corel from the Corel Internet Namespace button in an Open or Save dialog box. You'll learn more about this feature later.*

You can then get help or other information about Corel WordPerfect and other products, and even download a user manual. You can also find additional help demonstrations and tips and access customer support.

Using Corel PerfectExpert

Corel's PerfectExpert does more than just answer your questions. PerfectExpert is also a menu of options, which take you step-by-step through many Corel functions; it's a perfect aid for users new to the Corel WordPerfect Suite applications. To display PerfectExpert, select it from the Help menu. For example, Figure 2-2 shows the PerfectExpert that appears in Corel WordPerfect. The PerfectExpert makes it easy to perform typical WordPerfect tasks by choosing options from the panel.

You use the buttons on the top of the PerfectExpert panel to navigate through its menus. The panel contains a series of buttons, and a text box with some useful or interesting information. Clicking on a button may display additional options in the panel, open a dialog box, or perform some action in the application you have open. For example, clicking on the Set Up the Document button in Corel WordPerfect displays buttons for changing the page size, margins, font, and justification; for adding page numbers, and headers and footers; for performing merges; for creating labels and envelopes; and for creating HTML Web pages.

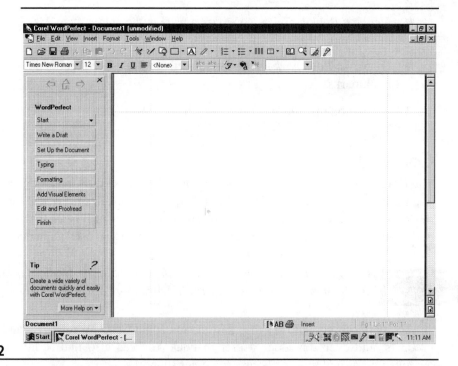

Perfect-
Expert

FIGURE 2-2

Quick Help

The help system is comprehensive, but it often requires negotiating through a series of help topics to find just what you are looking for. There are several shortcuts to getting help that bypass the Help menu.

Many dialog boxes have a Help button—click on it to go directly to the help system pages for that dialog box. If there is no Help button, press F1—the application will display a Help screen explaining that option in the box. If a dialog box is not displayed, pressing F1 shows the Help Contents page.

To find out about a specific item in a dialog box, right-click on the option. Read the information that appears, and then click the mouse. You can also click on the What's This? button in the box's title bar. The mouse will change to an arrow with a question mark. Point and click on the option you need help with.

You will also see a What's This? option on all QuickMenus. A QuickMenu appears when you right-click on an object. Choose the What's This? option to read a brief description of the selected object.

Managing Files

Windows 95 offers several ways to locate files and folders. You can use the Explorer, the Find command from the Start menu in the taskbar, or just surf through your folders starting with the My Computer icon. The Corel WordPerfect Suite incorporates its own file management capabilities directly in dialog boxes, such as Open, Insert File, Save As, and New, that let you access files. You can locate files based on their names through these dialog boxes, and you can index commonly used files and folders for even faster searches.

NOTE: *The main Corel applications now let you choose between the Corel file management dialog boxes and the Windows 95-style boxes.*

Figure 2-3 is an example of a file management dialog box, the Open File box from Corel WordPerfect. The dialog box has a toolbar, as well as a menu bar of options.

TIP: *You can display the QuickFinder file management box by selecting QuickFinder Searcher from the Corel WordPerfect Suite Tools menu.*

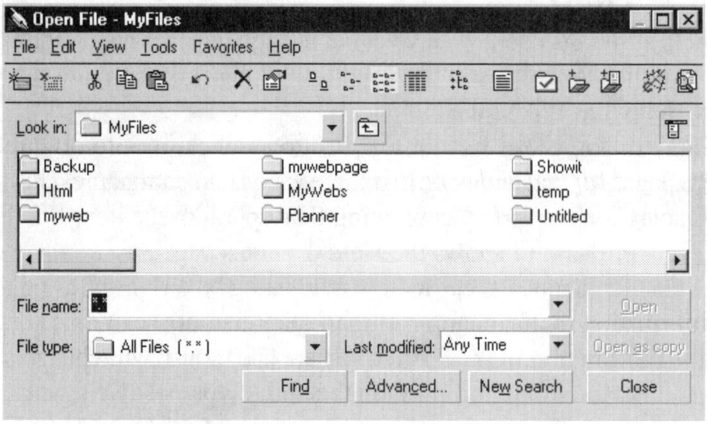

Corel
WordPerfect's
Open File
dialog box

FIGURE 2-3

Browsing Through Folders

The dialog box lets you list files by the folder in which they are stored. First, select the folder that you want to look in. The current folder being displayed appears in the Look In list.

To move up one level at a time, click on the Up One Level icon next to the Look In list. For example, suppose you are viewing the Template folder in the path c:\Corel\Suite8\Template. The large list is displaying the folders and files within the Template folder. Here's what selecting Up One Level will display:

1st click	Suite8 folder
2nd click	Corel folder
3rd click	C: drive
4th click	My Computer, including all of your drives
5th click	Desktop

Rather than clicking, however, you can just pull down the Look In list and choose the disk drive that you want to search. For example, suppose you want to find a file on drive C, but located in some entirely different path than the current folder.

1. Pull down the Look In list and click on [C:]. All of the folders in the drive will appear in the large list box, along with files on the drive's root directory.

2. In the large list box, double-click on the folder in which the file is stored. This will display all of the folders and files in that folder.

3. Continue opening folders in the same way until you see the file you are searching for.

 TIP: *If you know the full path and name of the file you want to locate, you can just type it in the File Name box.*

Changing the Default Folder

Corel applications are set up to display a default folder when you first open a file management dialog box. This default will be used each time you start the application, unless you change it using the application's Settings or Properties commands.

During a work session, however, the application remembers the last folder selected in the dialog box. So the next time you open the box in that session, the same folder will appear. If you do not want the application to change the folder during a session, pull down the Edit menu and deselect the Change Default Folder option.

 NOTE: *If the menu bar is not displayed in the dialog box, click on the Menu On/Off button on the right of the dialog box under the toolbar.*

The Favorites Folder

Chances are there are certain files and folders that you use often. Rather than search for them each time you want to access one, you can store a shortcut to each file in the Favorites folder. You can then open the Favorites folder and click on the folder or file that you want to open.

Go to/From Favorites	Add Current Location to Favorites	Add Selected Item(s) to Favorites

To add a file to the Favorites folder, click on it in the file list, and then click on the Add Selected Item(s) to the Favorites button in the toolbar. To add the current or selected folder to your favorites list, click on the Add Current Location to Favorites button.

When you want to open the file or folder, click on the Go To/From Favorites button in the toolbar or select Go To/From Favorites in the Favorites menu. The folder will open, displaying the shortcuts. Click on the folder shortcut to open the right folder, or click on the document shortcut to open the document.

 TIP: *Select Go To/From Favorites again to return to the previous folder.*

Displaying Files

Once the correct folder is displayed, you'll need to display the files. You can do this in either the File Type list or the File Name text box.

The File Type list will offer some preset choices. Pull down the list and select All Files (*.*) if you want to see every file in the folder. The other options will depend on the application you are using. In Corel WordPerfect, for example, you can choose to see templates, macros, or text files. In Corel Quattro Pro, you can select from a list of common spreadsheet program formats.

If none of the choices in the File Type list are appropriate, you can use a wildcard pattern in the File Name box. Use the asterisks to represent any number of unknown characters. For example, typing **report*.*** and pressing ENTER will list only files starting with the letters "report", and with any extension. To list just files with the DOC extension, type ***.DOC** and press ENTER.

 TIP: *In the Open dialog box in Corel WordPerfect, pull down the list at the end of the File Name text box to see a list of recently opened files.*

Viewing Files

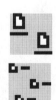 By using the buttons in the toolbar and the View menu, you can select how the folders and files are displayed in the list box. All of the options display an icon along with the filename. The shape of the icon indicates its type.

Select *Large Icons* to display each filename under a large icon that is easy to see.

Select *Small Icons* to display each filename to the right of the icon. When there are more files than can be displayed, a vertical scroll bar will appear.

Select *List* to display each filename to the right of the icon, but with a horizontal scroll bar to scroll left and right.

Select *Details* to display a list with four columns—the file icon and name, its size, type, and the date it was created or last modified.

Arranging Icons and Files

By default, all items are listed in alphabetical order by name, but with all folders first, and then the files. You can change the order of the files to arrange them by their size, type, or date, as well. Pull down the View menu, point to Arrange Icons, and select the desired order. If you are displaying the files in the Details view, you can click on the column heading. Click on Type, for example, to sort the list by type in ascending order.

TIP: *Click on the heading in which the list is already sorted to change between ascending and descending order.*

In addition to the folder and file lists just described, you can display two other windows—Tree View and Preview. Here's how to use Tree View:

1. Click on Tree View to display the complete structure of your system in a list on the left, with the folder and files on the right, as shown in Figure 2-4. Unlike the Look In list, Tree View lets you expand or collapse the

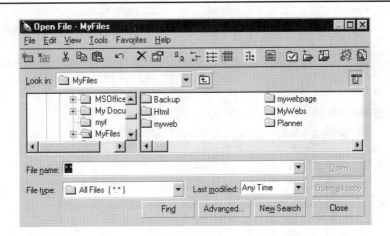

Using Tree View to display the structure of your computer folders

FIGURE 2-4

folder structure. A small plus sign next to a Drive or Folder icon means that it contains an additional folder.

2. Click on the plus sign to expand the drive or folder so you'll be able to see the other folders contained within it. The icon will then be marked with a minus sign—click on it to collapse the display.

3. To see the contents of a drive or folder in the list on the right, click on the Drive or Folder icon itself.

The Preview button opens a viewer window in which the Corel file management dialog box will display the contents of a selected text or graphic file. You can control how the file appears using the Preview option in the View menu. Pull down the View menu, point to Preview, and then select one of these options:

■ *No Preview* closes the Preview window.

■ *Content* displays the contents of the file in readable form.

■ *Page View* displays a thumbnail of the page.

■ *Use Separate Window* displays the preview in a separate window, outside of the dialog box.

Working with Folders and Files

You can use the file management boxes not only to display and open or save files, but to delete, move, copy, and rename them as well. So you can perform many of the same functions as you can in Windows Explorer right within the Corel application.

 To delete a file or folder, for example, select it in either the tree diagram or file list, and then click on the Delete button in the toolbar or press the DEL key.

A dialog box will appear asking you to confirm that you want to delete the item into the Windows 95 Recycle Bin. Click on Yes or No.

To rename a folder or file, use these steps:

1. Right-click on the folder and select Rename from the QuickMenu. You can also click two separate times—not a double-click—on the name. The name will appear in reverse in a dotted box.

2. To delete the current name, press DEL or start typing a new name.

3. To edit the name, press the LEFT ARROW or RIGHT ARROW key to remove the highlight, and then proceed with the edit.

You can move or copy a file or folder to another location. When you move or copy a folder, all of the folders and files located within it move as well. To use drag-and-drop to move a folder, follow these steps:

1. Display the Tree View.

2. Expand the drive or folder so you can see the location where you want to insert the folder.

3. Display the icon for the folder you want to copy or move.

4. Click on the folder you want to move, and then drag it to the location in the tree diagram where you want to place it. The destination location will become highlighted.

5. To move the folder, just release the mouse. To copy the folder, hold down the CTRL key and release the mouse.

To move or copy a file, use a similar technique:

1. Display the name of the file in the list box on the right.

2. Expand the tree diagram on the left to see the drive or folder where you want to insert the file.

3. Drag the file to the drive or folder and release the mouse. Hold down CTRL as you release the mouse to copy the file.

If you prefer not to use drag-and-drop, you can use the File menu. Follow these steps:

1. Select the folder or file you want to move.

2. Pull down the File menu. Select Move to Folder or Copy to Folder, depending on what you want to do. Corel will display another Browse dialog box.

3. Select the destination location in the Browse box.

4. Click on the Move or Copy button at the bottom of the dialog box.

TIP: *You can also use the Cut, Copy, and Paste options from the Edit menu or the QuickMenu.*

Printing Files and Directory Listings

You can print a file, or a listing of a folder's contents, from the file management dialog boxes. To print a file, however, it must have an extension that is associated with an application already installed on your computer. For example, the extension WPD will be associated with Corel WordPerfect, and WB3 with Corel Quattro Pro. You can print a Corel Quattro Pro worksheet directly from the file management box because Windows 95 associates the extension with the application.

To print a file, right-click on it in the file list, and then choose Print from the QuickMenu. You can also select Print from the File menu.

To print the contents of a folder, click on the folder, and then choose Print File List from the File menu.

TIP: *The options in the QuickMenu depend on the type of file you click on. If you click on a sound file or a Corel Presentations run-time slide show, for example, the menu will include the option Play Slide Show as well as Print.*

QuickFinder

If you don't know where the file is that you are looking for, you can spend a great deal of time surfing your disk. Corel WordPerfect Suite provides a faster alternative: QuickFinder.

With QuickFinder, you can locate files by their name or contents. For example, you could list all files that contain the word "budget," or just files with a certain extension.

Access QuickFinder in any file management dialog box, such as Save As and Open, or by selecting QuickFinder Searcher from the Corel WordPerfect Suite 8 Tools menu.

To start a search, type a word or characters that you are looking for in the File Name box. You can use wildcards to help narrow the search. Then click on the Find button. Corel will locate the files whose title or contents contain the word and display them in the QuickFinder Search Results folder, along with their locations, as shown here.

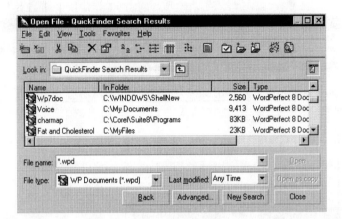

You can change the view and manipulate the files just as you can files in any folder. To start a new search, click on the New Search button, and then enter the new file name or pattern. Click on the Goto/From Search Results button to toggle between the current location and the QuickFinder Search Results.

Performing an Advanced Search

Searching for files by entering text in the File Name box is useful, but WordPerfect will only look for one word or phrase. For even more search options based on the content, file name, or date of a document, click on the Advanced button in a file management box to see the dialog box shown in Figure 2-5.

 NOTE: *The dialog box contains any search criteria already entered in the File Name box.*

To search for a file by its contents or name, double-click on the *Filename contains words* prompt to see these pull-down lists:

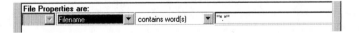

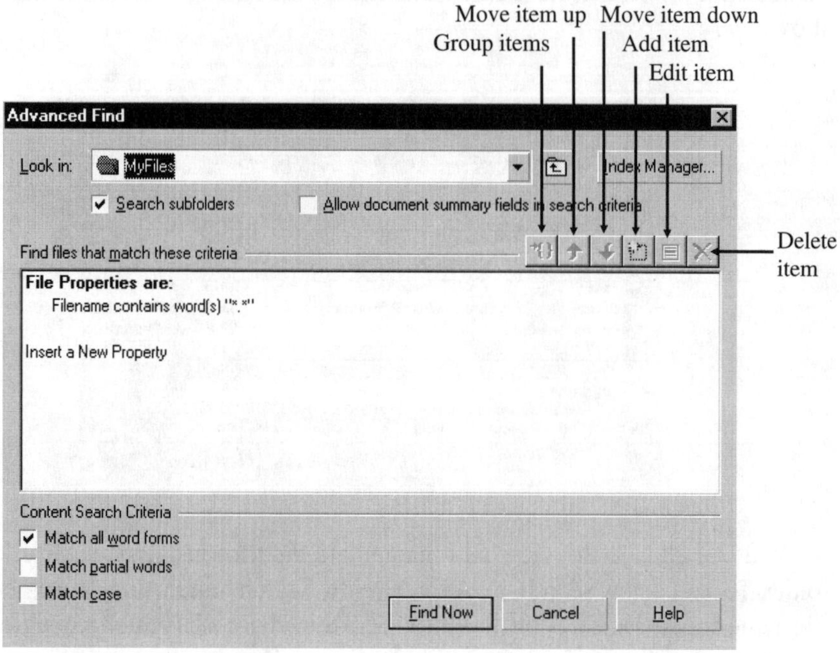

Move item up   Move item down
Group items   Add item
Edit item

Delete item

The dialog box you use for performing an advanced search

FIGURE 2-5

- To search for the same text in either the filename or contents of the document, pull down the first list and choose Filename or Content. To locate a file by its date, choose Last Modified Date from the list.

- If you are searching based only on the filename, choose either *contains word(s)* or *does not contain word(s)* from the second list, depending on how you want to search. If you are searching for files based on their date, the second list contains options such as these:

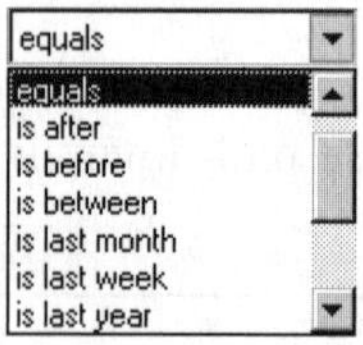

2

■ Enter the text you are searching for in the last text box, or the date, then press ENTER.

To search for a file based on its contents, double-click on the prompt *Insert a New Property* to see these lists:

Choose And or Or from the first list, then pull down the third list and choose from options such as those shown here (scrolling the list for even more choices):

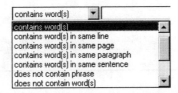

Enter the text you are searching for in the last text box, then press ENTER.

To enter additional search criteria, click on *Insert a New Property* again and repeat the process. Use the buttons to the right of the Find Files That Match These Criteria box to organize your criteria—adding and deleting criteria, combining them into groups, and changing their position.

Finally, select options from the checkboxes at the bottom of the dialog box, and click on Find Now.

Using QuickFinder Manager

When you perform a search for contents, QuickFinder has to look at every word in all of the files specified in the Look In box. If you are searching through many files, this may not be so quick.

To make QuickFinder quicker, you can create an index of the files that you search often. The index is an actual listing of every word in the files, so QuickFinder can locate contents by scanning through the index rather than the documents themselves.

To access QuickFinder Manager, select QuickFinder Manager 8 in the Corel WordPerfect Suite 8 Tools menu. The QuickFinder Manager dialog box is shown in Figure 2-6. You can set up two types of indexes. A Standard Fast Search searches a

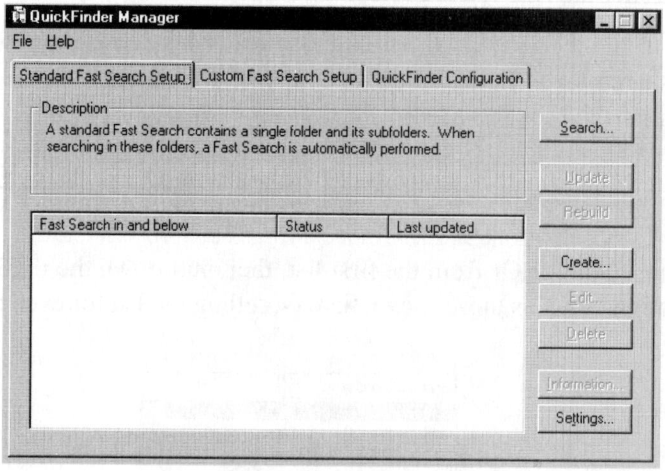

QuickFinder
Manager

FIGURE 2-6

single folder and all of its subfolders. A Custom Fast Search can include one or more folders, with or without their subfolders. Let's look at Standard Search first.

Creating a Standard Fast Search

If you want to create an index of the documents in a single folder, including its subfolders, display the Standard Fast Search Setup page of the QuickFinder Manager dialog box. Then create a search using these steps.

1. Click on Create to display the QuickFinder Standard Fast Search dialog box.

2. Specify the folders or path you want to include in the index.

3. Select the updating method. When you select automatic updating, QuickFinder Manager will periodically—every time period that you specify—reindex the files. This means that your searches will be more up to date, but the reindexing may occur when you are performing other tasks and may slow the system response. If you select manual updating, you will have to tell QuickFinder Manager to update the index.

You can now specify options to customize the index. Follow these steps:

1. Click on the Options button to display the dialog box shown in Figure 2-7.

2. Choose an option in the Include For Search section to determine what parts of the documents to include in the index.

3. Choose options in the Other Settings section. By default, the search includes only document files—not graphics files and program files with extensions such as EXE, COM, and DLL—and it indexes numbers as well as words.

4. Set the Search Level. Drag the slider to choose between Low and High. As you drag, the label under the slider changes to reflect where word patterns must be located—sentence, paragraph, page, or document.

5. Choose an Extended Characters option.

6. Select where to store the index file.

7. Select where to store temporary files generated during the index's operations.

8. Click on OK to return to the previous dialog box.

9. Click on OK to begin the indexing.

Using a Standard Search is automatic. Just open QuickFinder and perform a search that includes the folder specified. QuickFinder will automatically use the index.

If you selected to manually update the index, you should perform an update after you change the files in the folder. To do so, display the QuickFinder Manager dialog box, click in the index you want to update, and then click on the Update button. Use the Rebuild button to reindex the files from the beginning.

TIP: *Use the Edit button to change the specification of a search; click on Delete to remove a search; or click on Information to see details about the index. Use Preferences to set options for all searches.*

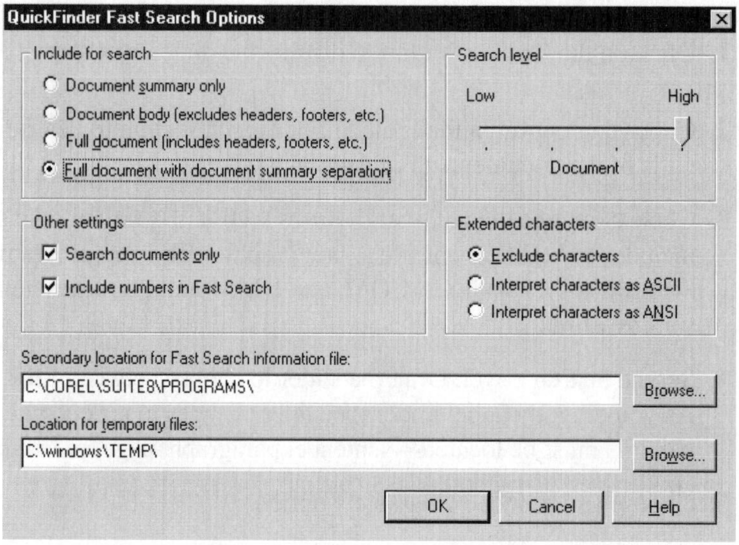

QuickFinder Fast Search Options

Include for search
- ○ Document summary only
- ○ Document body (excludes headers, footers, etc.)
- ○ Full document (includes headers, footers, etc.)
- ● Full document with document summary separation

Search level
Low   High

Document

Other settings
- ☑ Search documents only
- ☑ Include numbers in Fast Search

Extended characters
- ● Exclude characters
- ○ Interpret characters as ASCII
- ○ Interpret characters as ANSI

Secondary location for Fast Search information file:
C:\COREL\SUITE8\PROGRAMS\   Browse...

Location for temporary files:
C:\windows\TEMP\   Browse...

OK   Cancel   Help

QuickFinder
Fast Search
Options
dialog box

FIGURE 2-7

Creating a Custom Fast Search

Creating a Custom Fast Search is similar to a Standard Search, except you can select more than one folder, and you can choose to not index the subfolders. In the QuickFinder Custom Fast Search dialog box, type the path of each of the folders, or select them from the browse list, and then click on Add.

Reaching Corel

You can reach Corel on the Internet while you are working with the Open or Save dialog box. Click on the Goto/From Corel Internet button to launch your browser and connect to Corel. The Corel Web site will appear directly in the dialog box window, as shown in Figure 2-8, and you can use the Back, Forward, Reload, and Stop buttons in the dialog box toolbar to help you navigate around the site.

Using Writing Tools

Features such as the spell checker, thesaurus, grammar checker, and QuickCorrect are also common to the Suite applications, although not every tool is available in

The Corel
Internet
Namespace

FIGURE 2-8

each program. Although only Corel WordPerfect provides special Spell-As-You-Go and Grammar-As-You-Go features to check your spelling and grammar automatically, the Spell Check feature can be used in Corel WordPerfect, Corel Quattro Pro, and Corel Presentations, but not in Corel Paradox. Access these utilities from the program's Tools menu. In this section, you'll review how to use these powerful tools.

 NOTE: *Spell Check, Thesaurus, and Grammatik (the grammar-checking program) are listed in the tabs in the same dialog box, so you can easily switch between them.*

Checking Spelling

The Spell Check feature compares every word in a document with those in a built-in word list. If a word is not found in the list, it is reported as a possible misspelling. To start the spell checker, pull down the Tools menu and click on Spell Check. Some applications also have a Spell Check button in the toolbar.

NOTE: *In Corel Presentations, a text box must be selected to access Spell Check, Thesaurus, and Grammatik. You can also spell check your Web pages in Corel WEB.SiteBuilder.*

Spell Check starts comparing the words in the document, the slide, or the selected cells of a worksheet with those in the dictionary. When it finds the first possible error, it displays the word and a list of alternative spellings, as shown in Figure 2-9.

If the Word Is Spelled Incorrectly

If the word is spelled wrong, look for the correct spelling in the list. If it is there, double-click on it to replace the misspelled word. To retype the word correctly yourself, type the correct spelling in the Replace With text box, and then click on Replace. Click on Auto Replace to replace the same word with the corrected one throughout the entire document, and to create a QuickCorrect entry so the word will be corrected for you when you next type it.

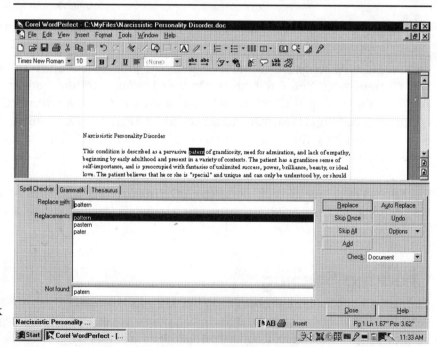

Spell Check dialog box

FIGURE 2-9

If you are not sure of the correct spelling, try typing an alternate in the Replace With text box—as you type, Spell Check will look up and display words in the Replacements list. If you just want to skip the word and correct it later, click on Skip Once.

If the Word Is Spelled Correctly

If the word is spelled correctly but is not in the dictionary, you have several choices. You can click on Skip Once to accept the word as it is in this instance—however, Spell Check will stop at the same word later in the document. Click on Skip All to ignore the word in the remainder of the document.

You can also click on Add to insert the word into a supplemental dictionary so Spell Check does not stop at it again.

Depending on the application, you also may be able to choose from other options. Pull down the Check list, for example, to select how much of the document is checked.

Using the Thesaurus

When you just can't think of the correct word, use the thesaurus. This will display a list of synonyms for the word at the position of the insertion point. In Corel WordPerfect, the Prompt-As-You-Go feature displays synonyms for words as you type. Here's how to use the thesaurus:

NOTE: *Corel Quattro Pro and Corel Paradox do not have access to the thesaurus.*

1. Pull down the Tools menu and click on Thesaurus to display the Thesaurus dialog box. The box has two lists, as shown in Figure 2-10. On the right are definitions for the word at the insertion point; on the left are synonyms for the selected definition.

NOTE: *The definitions will only appear if you selected to install them while doing a Custom installation of the Corel WordPerfect Suite.*

2. Scroll the list of definitions and select the one that best suits your meaning.

3. Scroll the list of replacements and select the one you want to use.

4. Click on Replace.

If none of the suggested synonyms seem appropriate, click on one that is the best possible and then on the Look Up button to see additional choices. Continue looking up words until you find one that you want to insert.

Checking Your Grammar

Grammatik is a program that checks your grammar, looking for words, phrases, and sentence structure that just don't agree with the program's grammatical rules.

 NOTE: *Corel Quattro Pro does not have access to Grammatik. Corel WordPerfect can check your grammar for you with Grammar-As-You-Go.*

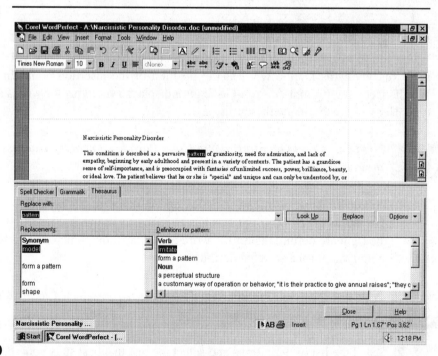

Thesaurus

FIGURE 2-10

To start the program, pull down the Tools menu and click on Grammatik. When it finds the first possible error, it displays it in a dialog box, such as the one shown in Figure 2-11, along with the following:

"If the suggested correction is acceptable, click on Replace. You can also click on Skip Once or Skip All to leave the text as it is and to continue to the next problem. If you want to ignore the grammatical rule that is being violated for the remainder of the process, click on the Turn Off button."

You can also evaluate your writing by clicking on the Options button and selecting Analysis to choose from the options shown in Table 2-1.

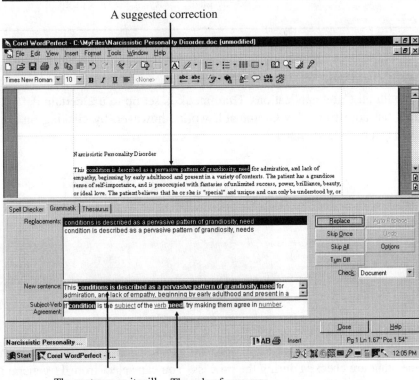

A suggested correction

Grammatik dialog box

The sentence as it will appear corrected

The rule of grammar being violated

FIGURE 2-11

Option	Description
Parse Tree	Displays a tree diagram of the grammatical structure of your text, including the parts of speech
Parts of Speech	Displays its usage under each word
Basic Counts	Shows the number of syllables, words, sentences, paragraphs; short, long, and simple sentences; big words; and the average syllables per word, words per sentence, and sentences per paragraph
Flagged	Shows the number of each type of error detected
Readability	Shows the reading level, the use of passive voice, and the complexity of your document

Grammatik
Options

TABLE 2-1

Customizing Grammatik

As with all Corel applications, Grammatik is set up to use certain default values. You can adjust the way Grammatik works, however, by clicking on Options to display a pull-down menu.

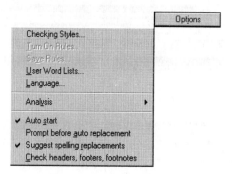

Use the Checking Styles feature, for example, to choose the range of grammatical rules that are checked during the process. You can select from 11 general types of documents or sets of rules, such as formal letters or technical documents. The style you select will determine which grammatical rules are applied and how strictly your text must conform to them. You'll be given more latitude, for example, in informal letters than you will on student compositions.

The Options menu also lets you determine whether Grammatik also checks spelling, prompts you before performing an automatic replacement, and in Corel WordPerfect also allows you to check headers, footers, and footnotes.

Streamlining Your Work with QuickCorrect and Format-As-You-Go

It is easy to get spoiled with Corel. Not only will it check your spelling—even as you type with Corel WordPerfect—but it can correct mistakes and insert special symbols and characters as you type. This magic is performed by two special features: QuickCorrect and Format-As-You-Go.

Using QuickCorrect

QuickCorrect can expand an abbreviation and fix your mistakes automatically as you type. In fact, QuickCorrect can correct over 125 common misspellings and typographic errors as you type. For example, if you type "adn," QuickCorrect will automatically replace it with "and." If you forget to capitalize the first letter of the sentence, QuickCorrect will do that also. It will change two spaces following a sentence to one space, and correct two irregular capitals (such as changing "WHen" to "When"). In addition, QuickCorrect will automatically make the following replacements for you:

Replace	With
(c	©
(c)	©
(r	®
- -	—
1/2	<EQUATION VENTURA FORMAT:> 1/2

In addition to the built-in corrections, you can add your own. Pull down the Tools menu and click on QuickCorrect to see the dialog box shown in Figure 2-12. The two-column list box shows QuickCorrect entries that are already defined for you. In the Replace text box, type the abbreviation that you want to use, or a word as you usually misspell it. In the With box, type the expanded word or phrase, or the correct

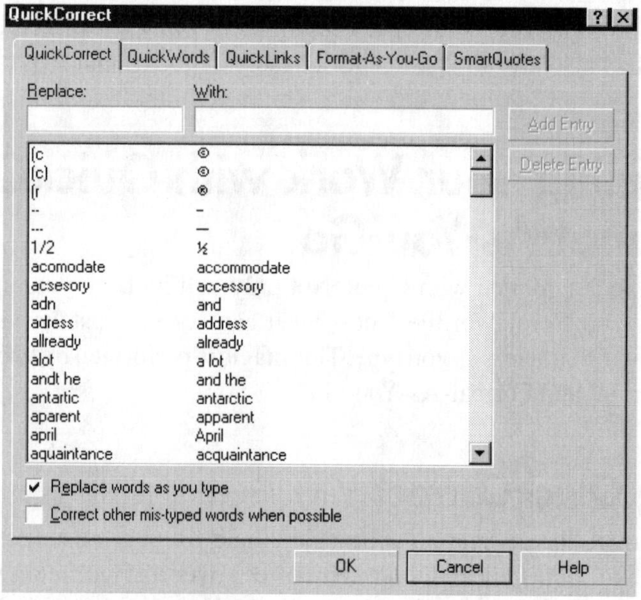

Creating
QuickCorrect
entries

FIGURE 2-12

spelling of the word. Then click on Add Entry. Your abbreviation will be added to the list, in alphabetical order. Close the dialog box. Now whenever you type the abbreviation, or misspell the word, QuickCorrect will expand or correct it for you.

TIP: *If you select text before opening the QuickCorrect box, the text will appear in the With box—just enter the abbreviation for it.*

If you do not want QuickCorrect to replace words for you, deselect the Replace Words As You Type checkbox. You'll need to do this, for example, if you want to type (C) and not change it into the copyright symbol. To delete a QuickCorrect entry, select it in the list and then click on Delete Entry.

TIP: *Select the Correct Other Mis-Typed Words When Possible option to have Corel WordPerfect automatically correct other words when there is only one possible suggested replacement for it in the dictionary.*

QuickCorrect entries are not case sensitive. If you already have an abbreviation "pc," then creating one called "PC" will replace it.

Watch Your Case with QuickCorrect

When you create a QuickCorrect entry, pay attention to the case of your characters. If you enter the Replace and With text in lowercase characters, QuickCorrect will automatically insert text based on the case of the abbreviation, as shown here:

You Type	QuickCorrect Inserts
tlc	tender loving care
TLC	TENDER LOVING CARE
Tlc	Tender loving care

If you use any other combination of cases, such as "tLC," QuickCorrect will match the first letter. So "tLC" and "tlC" will both be replaced by "tender loving care."

If you type the With text in all uppercase, it will always appear uppercase. If you type it with an initial capital letter, QuickCorrect will match the case of the abbreviation.

Format-As-You-Go

A special feature of Corel WordPerfect, Format-As-You-Go, can adjust sentence spaces and create lines, lists, and other formats automatically as you type. To access these features in Corel WordPerfect, select QuickCorrect from the Tools menu, and then click on the Format-As-You-Go tab to see the options shown in Figure 2-13.

The Sentence Corrections section determines the capitalization and spacing within a sentence. It will capitalize the first letter of a sentence, fix two initial capitals, and replace two spaces between words with one space.

The End of Sentence Corrections section determines the spacing between sentences. You can select to leave your sentences as you type them (none), or to replace a single space with two, or vice versa.

The Format-As-You-Go choices section determines what special formats Corel WordPerfect applies for you as you type.

- *CapsFix* corrects improper capitalization and turns off the CAPS LOCK key if you type text after accidentally clicking on it.

- *QuickBullets* starts the automatic numbering or bulleted list feature. If you start a paragraph with a number or letter followed by a period and a tab, or a special character at the beginning of a line followed by an indent or tab, Corel WordPerfect will continue numbering, lettering, or bulleting subsequent paragraphs.

- *QuickIndent* lets you indent a paragraph from the left margin. If you press the TAB key at the beginning of any line but the first, Corel WordPerfect will indent the entire paragraph.

- *QuickLines* draws a horizontal line on the screen when you start a line with three or more hyphens, or a double line when you type three or more equal signs and press ENTER.

- *QuickOrdinals* replaces the characters "st," "nd," and "rd" with superscripts behind numerals such as in "1st," "2nd," and "3rd."

- *QuickSymbols* replaced two hyphens with an en-dash, and three hyphens with an em-dash.

SmartQuotes

SmartQuotes are the curly types of apostrophes and quotation marks that you see in published documents. By default, Corel WordPerfect replaces the straight quotes

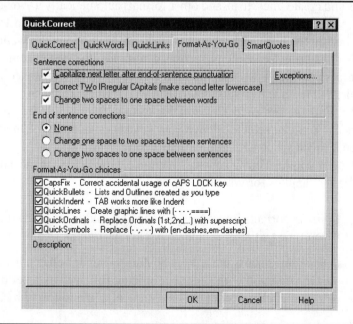

Format-As-You-Go settings

FIGURE 2-13

that you enter from the keyboard with their curly equivalents. Use the SmartQuotes page of the QuickCorrect dialog box to turn off this feature, or select another curly quote character to insert in its place.

You can also choose to leave plain straight quotation marks that follow numbers. This is useful when you want to indicate inches.

 NOTE: *In Chapter 5 you'll learn about QuickWords and QuickLinks, two other time-saving features available in Corel WordPerfect.*

Publishing Document to Barista

All Corel WordPerfect suite applications let you print documents. You can also, however, output your work to other sources as well. Using the Send To option in the File menu, you can output a document to a floppy disk, to a briefcase, or to a mail recipient through your local e-mail system or the Internet. Using Send To, you can also "send" the document to these three options:

- HTML
- Envoy
- Corel Barista

 TIP: *The Envoy option will be dimmed if you're not using the Professional version of the Corel Suite.*

Sending the file to HTML converts the document into a form readable by Web browsers, such as Netscape Navigator and Microsoft Internet Explorer. You'll learn more about publishing your document to HTML and creating Web pages in later chapters.

Barista is Corel's Java technology. Java is a programming language designed to create applications that run on Web pages. Programmers use Java to create Web pages that do things other than solely display information. Although you can use Java to simply create professional-looking Web pages, it's capabilities go far beyond this.

With the Corel WordPerfect Suite, you can display WordPerfect documents, Quattro Pro spreadsheets, and Presentation slides and slide shows in a Java window on the Web by publishing them to Barista, Corel's Java technology.

To publish a document to Corel Barista, select Send To from the program's File menu, and choose Corel Barista to see the dialog box shown in Figure 2-14. Choose the options as described here, and then click on Send.

- Choose the folder and file name in which to store the resulting files. Use the default folder shown in the box so your browser can access the necessary Barista files.

- Choose to launch your Web browser and display the Java window after the document is saved in Corel Barista format.

- In the Advanced tab of the dialog box, choose if you want to embed the path to Barista classes.

When you click on Send, Corel will launch the Web browser that is registered on your system for Internet shortcuts.

NOTE: *If Netscape Communicator is the registered browser, you may see a dialog box reporting that you must establish a profile. A profile contains information that Communicator needs to work with e-mail, newsgroups, and other Internet features. If you share your version of Communicator with other users, you can create a profile for each. Follow the instructions in the dialog boxes that appear onscreen, entering the information required.*

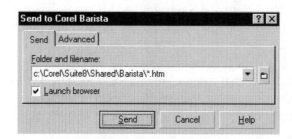

Publishing
to Barista

FIGURE 2-14

Using Corel Projects

A *project* is a formatted document linked to a custom PerfectExpert panel—all you need to do is enter your own information. If you need to send a fax, for example, you can choose a fax cover page project. Need to create a budget in Corel Quattro Pro? Select a budget project. Want to develop a presentation of your business plan? Select a business plan project.

You access the projects in any of three ways:

■ Clicking on the Corel PerfectExpert in the DAD bar in the taskbar

■ Selecting Corel New Project from the Corel WordPerfect Suite 8 menu

■ Selecting New from the File menu in Corel WordPerfect, Corel Quattro Pro, Corel Paradox, and Corel Presentations

In the dialog box that appears, click on the Create New tab to see the options as shown in Figure 2-15.

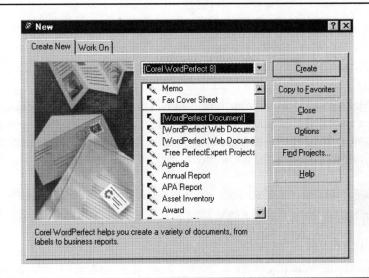

Projects to automate your work

FIGURE 2-15

If you display the box from within a Corel application, you'll see projects for that application. Otherwise, pull down the list on the top of the box to select another Corel application or to choose from groups of projects, as shown here.

```
[Corel Address Book 8]
[Corel CENTRAL 8]
[Corel Paradox 8]
[Corel Photo House]
[Corel Presentations 8]
[Corel Quattro Pro 8]
[Corel Time Line]
[Corel WEB.SiteBuilder 8]
[Corel WordPerfect 8]
[CorelCENTRAL 8]
[PaperDirect]
Auto
Budget, Business
Budget, Personal
Business Accounts
Business Finance
Business Forms
Business Reports
Correspondence, Business
Custom QP Templates
Custom WP Templates
Education
Hobbies
Home and Family
Home Management
Inventory
Investment
Job Search
Legal
Marketing
Mortgage
Publish
Retirement Planning
Sales
Slide Shows
Time Management
Web
Web Publishing
```

Make your selection from the pull-down list, and then double-click on the project you want to use. If you are in the application that uses the project, the project document will open and appear onscreen. If you select a project from another application, the program starts and displays the project. It's that easy.

 NOTE: *In Chapter 7, you'll learn how to use Corel WordPerfect templates to automate your work.*

Many projects have places for your name, address, phone number, or other information. You designate a listing from the Address Book as your personal information listing, and Corel WordPerfect uses it for projects. If you have not yet selected your personal listing, a dialog box will appear reporting that fact, and you'll be given the opportunity to select a listing from the Address Book. Once you do so, information from that listing will appear automatically in the project or in dialog boxes prompting you for information. In the example shown in Figure 2-16, the dialog box appears after clicking on Fill in Heading Info in the PerfectExpert panel for the Memo project.

NOTE: *Although initial releases of Corel WordPerfect do not allow you to create your own projects, you can add documents to the project list, and you can create additional groups in which to store them. Pull down the Options list to access these features.*

Clipart and the Scrapbook

The three major Corel applications share a common resource—the Scrapbook. The Scrapbook is a handy location to store clipart and other graphic files that you find useful in your publications. Access the Scrapbook by clicking on the ClipArt button in the application's toolbar, to see the dialog box shown in Figure 2-17.

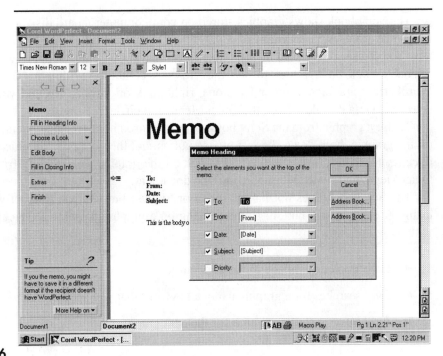

Using a
Project

FIGURE 2-16

The
Scrapbook

FIGURE 2-17

The Scrapbook shows graphics stored on your computer's hard disk. To access additional graphics, insert your Corel CD in the CD drive and click on the CD Clipart tab. You'll see a series of folders representing various categories of graphics —double-click on a folder to see the graphics contained within it. To locate WordPerfect graphics in other locations, right-click on the background window, select Set Default Folder from the QuickMenu, and click on Browse.

To use a graphic from the Scrapbook, drag-and-drop it into the document. Click on the graphic, hold down the left mouse button and then drag the graphic to the document window. You can also right-click on the graphic, select Copy from the QuickMenu, and paste the graphic into the document.

The Scrapbook does not have a menu or toolbar, but you can interact with it using the right mouse button. Right-clicking on a graphic presents a QuickMenu with these options:

- *Copy* copies the image to the clipboard.

- *Find* searches for a graphic using a keyword that you specify.

- *Find Next* repeats the search for the next graphic.

■ *Set Default Folder* designates the current folder as the default for the Scrapbook.

■ *Properties* displays the name and size of the graphic, and its keywords.

When you right-click on the Scrapbook background, the QuickMenu contains the Find, Find Next, Keep on Top, and Set Default Folder options as well as View. The Keep on Top option keeps the Scrapbook in the foreground of other open windows. The View submenu lets you choose to see graphics as large or small icons, as their filenames, or with their keywords.

NOTE: *To insert graphics other than those in WordPerfect's WPG format, select Graphics from the application's Insert menu, and choose From File.*

Corel and the Internet

3

The *Internet* is an informal network of computers around the world. There are thousands of companies, educational institutions, associations, and other organizations, along with millions of individuals connected to "the Net" in one way or another. Some people access the Net through their school or company while others have individual accounts with Internet Service Providers (ISPs) or online services such as AT&T, CompuServe, or America Online.

The *World Wide Web*, or "the Web" as it's affectionately known, is one interface to the Net. The Web can be seen as a series of documents, all dynamically linked so you can move from one to another, no matter where they are actually located in the world, simply by clicking the mouse, or by typing the document's address and name.

The address of a computer on the Web is referred to as the computer's *Web site*. Again, you don't have to worry about the geographic location of the site, just its address. As far as you are concerned, you can be connected to a site on the other side of the world or across the street with equal ease.

Integrated Internet

Internet access is integrated directly into the major applications of the Corel WordPerfect Suite. For example, Corel WordPerfect features QuickLink. Need to send an e-mail? Just type an e-mail address in the format "xxx@xxxx.xxx" as in alann@compuserve.com, and press SPACEBAR or ENTER. Corel WordPerfect converts the address into an underlined link; clicking on it will launch your browser and display a mail window already addressed. Corel WordPerfect will also create a link when you type any Web site URL, such as www.corel.com

The major applications in the Corel WordPerfect Suite can create Web documents. Corel WordPerfect can also read Web documents.

The Internet is integrated into the Suite in many more ways, which you'll learn about in later chapters. Here I'll summarize some of the ways that you can take advantage of this wonderful resource.

- *Creating Web pages*—You can format and publish your own Web pages directly from Corel WordPerfect through Internet Publisher.

- *Publishing presentations*—With a few clicks of the mouse, you can publish an entire Corel Presentations slide show on the Internet, and even add a button that readers can click to download the slide show to their computer.

- *Browsing the Web*—You can launch your Web browser from almost anywhere in the Corel WordPerfect Suite by clicking on a Toolbar button.

- *QuickLink*—You can create hypertext links to Web pages and sites in your Corel WordPerfect document, Corel Quattro Pro worksheets, and Corel Presentations slides. Use the links to launch your Web browser and jump to a site. You can also use them to make documents available on your Web server by placing linked files in a public access directory.

- *Working with Web pages*—You can open HTML files—the source code for Web pages—directly into Corel WordPerfect 8, and you can save your documents, spreadsheets, and presentations in HTML format.

Making the Connection

There are several ways to initiate the connection to the Internet. To launch Netscape Communicator, which is included in the Corel WordPerfect Suite, just click on its icon in the Corel DAD bar. Netscape Communicator will also start if you click on a hyperlink in a Corel application.

What happens when you first make a connection to the Internet depends on your system and your ISP. If you have a dial-up account and you're not yet online, you may see the Windows 95 Dial-Up Networking Connect To dialog box. Make sure the information in this box is correct—it should be if you set up everything correctly—and then click on Connect. Your modem will dial your ISP, and your browser will download and display a Web page.

 NOTE: *If you see a message that your Web browser is no longer registered to handle Internet Shortcuts, just click on No.*

The actual information in the browser window depends on how you launch your browser. If you select Corel Web Site from the Help menu, for example, you'll see the Corel home page, where you can access information about Corel products. In other instances, you may see your ISP's home page.

The Corel WordPerfect Suite applications let you make the connection, but you must have a Web browser already installed on your system. A *Web browser* is a program that communicates with the Internet, letting you move about the Web, send and receive messages, and search for information.

Corel WordPerfect Professional Suite 8, and newer releases of the standard Suite, come with the Netscape Communicator browser that is integrated with CorelCENTRAL, Corel's calendar and scheduling program that you'll learn about in Chapter 31. When you use certain functions of Netscape Communicator, it will automatically start CorelCENTRAL to access its features, and visa versa. When you use the Mailbox feature of Netscape Communicator, for example, CorelCENTRAL will start and you'll have access to its mailbox feature for sending and receiving e-mail.

 NOTE: *The first release of the standard version of Corel WordPerfect Suite 8 included Netscape Navigator 3.0. However, it also included a coupon that could be redeemed for CorelCENTRAL and Netscape Communicator.*

It takes some time for information from the Internet to be displayed on your monitor. Sometimes text appears first with icon boxes showing where graphics will appear; then the graphics are downloaded and displayed. As the information is being transferred to your computer, you'll see a message in the progress bar at the bottom of the window reporting the percentage of the information that is being transmitted, along with a moving bar to its left. Most pages will be too large to appear on the screen, so you'll see a vertical scroll bar. The information is actually both displayed and saved into a temporary file on your disk called a *cache*. The cache enables the browser to quickly redisplay the information without having it transmitted all over again. The message Document Done will appear when all of the information has been received.

 TIP: *If you get tired of waiting and change your mind, click on the Stop button. If your previous page doesn't appear, click on Back.*

The process of moving from one place to the other on the Internet is called *navigating* or *surfing*. One way to do this is to click on *hypertext links*. These may be underlined words, text in a different color than other text, or even icons, buttons, and graphics. When you point to a hypertext link, the mouse pointer will change to look like a small hand. Just click on the link to connect to another location in the same document, another document on the same computer, or another location in the world. You don't have to worry about where it takes you because you can always return to your previous location by clicking on the Back button in the toolbar.

If you return to the previous page, you'll notice that the color of the links that you've used has changed. This indicates that you have already used the link, but you can still click on it again to return to the page.

Web pages can contain several types of elements—text, links, inline images, and frames. You already know that a link lets you move to another location. A *frame* is a smaller, independent section within the window. Sometimes the contents of a frame can change automatically as you are connected to the site. A Web page may also have inline images—graphics that are dynamically linked to locations on the page and that are transmitted separately. In many instances, the text of the page will appear first so you can start reading and clicking on links right away, with the inline images being added after.

Profiles

The first time you start Netscape Communicator or CorelCENTRAL you'll be asked to create a user profile. The *profile* contains information about your e-mail account, bookmarks, address book, stored messages, and settings.

Corel lets you create more than one profile to share Netscape Communicator or CorelCENTRAL with other users—such as other family members who also have e-mail accounts. You can also create multiple profiles for yourself if you have multiple e-mail accounts or want to use more than one set of preferences.

 NOTE: *You must create a profile even if you are the only person using Netscape Communicator on your computer.*

Click Next when the box appears reporting that you must create a profile, then click on Next again to go to the next message. In a series of dialog boxes, you'll be asked to enter information or select options. If you do not know any of the information requested, such as your incoming and outgoing mail servers, ask your ISP. Complete each box, clicking next after each, until you've finishing giving this information:

■   Enter your name and your e-mail address.

- Enter a profile name and directory to store your profile information. The defaults shown will be your user name from your e-mail address, and Corel's default folder for profiles. Use the default directory, and if this is your only profile, use the default profile name—otherwise enter another unique profile name.

- Enter your name, e-mail address, and outgoing SMTP mail server.

- Enter your incoming mail server and designate the type—either POP3 or IMAP.

- Enter your NNTP news server and port. Accept the default port if you're not sure.

- Click on Finish.

You can later edit the profile settings or create additional profiles for yourself or other users. You edit a profile from within Netscape Communicator or CorelCENTRAL. You'll learn more about this in the "Customizing Netscape Communicator" section later in this chapter.

To create a new profile, click on Start, point to Corel WordPerfect Suite 8, Tools, and then click on CorelCENTRAL User Profile Manager to see a dialog box listing your current profiles, as shown in Figure 3-1.

Click on New to create a new profile, using the same series of dialog boxes that you did the first time. To change the default profile, select it in the list, then click on Start.

Netscape Communicator Basics

Netscape Communicator is more than just a Web browser. In addition to the browser function, the program offers these features:

- A *mailbox* for sending and receiving e-mail and schedule information from CorelCENTRAL.

- A *group discussion* manager for sending and receiving messages from Internet discussion groups.

- A *page composer* for creating Web pages and e-mail messages in HTML format.

- A *conference* program for real-time online discussions and white-boarding across the Internet. (White-boarding means that all persons in the conference can see what you're writing or drawing on the screen.)

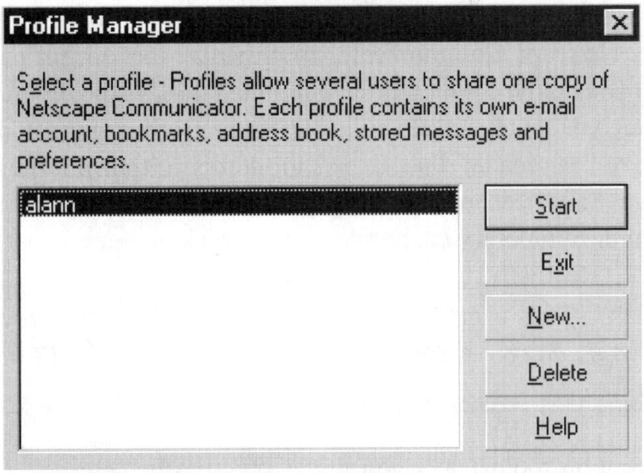

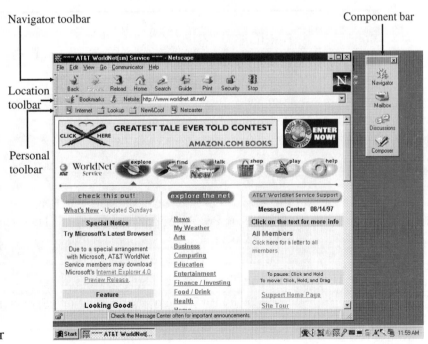

Create or edit profiles in the Corel-CENTRAL User Profile Manager

FIGURE 3-1

A typical Web page displayed in Netscape Communicator is shown in Figure 3-2, using AT&T as the ISP and connecting to the AT&T WorldNet home page.

Web page in Netscape Communicator

FIGURE 3-2

The purpose of the Navigator toolbar buttons, as described in Table 3-1, is relatively straightforward, but the Reload button may need further clarification. This button tells Netscape Communicator to redisplay the current page. If you view a page long enough, the computer that generated it may actually make changes to the page. When you click on Reload, Netscape Communicator determines if any changes have been made; if so, it asks the server to transmit the entire page again. If no changes have been made to the page, then Netscape Communicator reloads the image from the temporary cache file on your disk.

TIP: *If you want Netscape Navigator to have the file transmitted again even if changes were not made, hold down the SHIFT key when you click on Reload.*

The Location toolbar lets you go to sites on the Internet. The bookmark list contains the name of sites that you use often. Corel starts you out with bookmarks for many popular sites, and you can add your own sites as you find them. The location

Button	Function
Back	Redisplays the previous Web page
Forward	Returns to the previous page after using the Back command
Reload	Redisplays the current page
Home	Displays the designated home page
Search	Displays a page of search engines to find information on the Internet
Guide	Displays a pop-up menu of areas to search, including the Internet, People, Yellow Pages, What's New, and What's Cool
Print	Prints the displayed page
Security	Lets you display and change security settings
Stop	Stops the transmission of the page to your computer

Navigation Toolbar Buttons

TABLE 3-1

text box shows the URL of the current site, and you can enter the URL of a site that you want to go to.

The Personal toolbar contains buttons that let you quickly move to or find interesting sites. You can use the default buttons on the bar as well as add your own.

The Component bar lets you open windows for Netscape Communicator's major components—the Navigator for browsing, the Mailbox for e-mail messages, Discussions to subscribe to news groups, the Composer to create Web pages.

NOTE: *If your close the Component bar, its buttons appear in the lower right of the Netscape window. To restore the bar, drag the lines on the leftmost part of the buttons to another position on the screen.*

Many Web pages are interactive. They offer forms that you can complete to send mail or even to purchase items through your credit card. In general, most of the information you send via the Net is relatively safe. However, no system is foolproof and burglar-proof. The security button in the toolbar, and the security icon at the lower left of the Netscape window, let you display and change security settings for the page being displayed, and give you some guidance regarding the security of your transmission, as shown in Figure 3-3. Security means that the information you are sending is being encrypted so only the receiver can use it. When the security icon appears as an open padlock, the site is not secure.

Using the QuickMenu

One other way to control Corel Netscape is by using the QuickMenu that appears when you click the right mouse button on an object. As with all QuickMenus, the items on it depend on the object you click on. For example, here are some of the QuickMenu items that may appear depending on where you right-click:

- *Back* displays the previous Web page.

- *Forward* returns after you select Back or use the History list.

- *Reload* updates the page.

- *Stop* ends the transmission of the page.

- *View Source* displays the HTML tags for the page.

- *View Info* displays detailed information about the objects on the page, such as its background and other graphic image files.

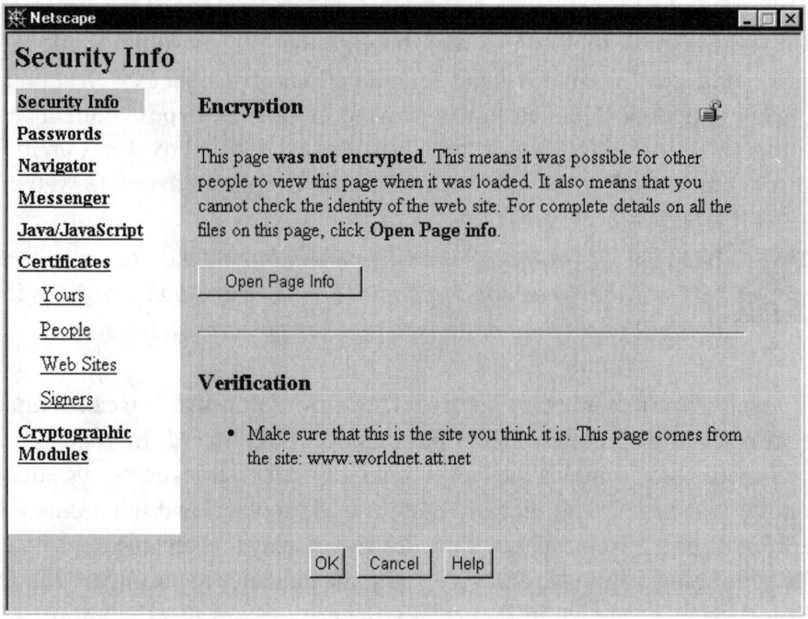

Displaying
security
information
for the
current site

FIGURE 3-3

- *View Image* displays the selected graphic in a separate window.

- *Set as Wallpaper* uses the image as the Windows 95 wallpaper.

- *Add Bookmark* creates a bookmark of the address of the link being clicked on.

- *Create Shortcut* creates a shortcut to the current Web page on the desktop—double-click on the shortcut to launch Netscape Communicator and jump to the site.

- *Send Page* opens a mail window that includes the current page as an attachment.

- *Save Image As* lets you save the selected image to your disk.

- *Save Background As* lets you save the page background to your disk.

- *Copy Image Location* saves the URL of the selected image to the Windows clipboard.

- *Save Link As* saves the linked page on your disk.

- *Copy Link Location* saves the URL of the link to the Windows clipboard.

Jumping to a Known Site

You can go to a specific site if you know its address. Web pages are identified by a *Uniform Resource Locator* (*URL*) address. An URL (pronounced "Earl") is much like your own street address in that it tells the browser exactly where to locate the information. You'll find lists of useful or interesting addresses in magazines and newspapers, advertisements—almost anywhere these days. Type the address in the Location box at the top of the window and press ENTER.

NOTE: *When you click on a link, Netscape Communicator inserts the URL into the Location box and moves to it automatically.*

The syntax of the URL depends on the type of protocol it uses or its interface. Some of the most common are these:

- *http* for Web pages that use HyperText Transfer Protocol

- *ftp* for transferring files through the File Transfer Protocol

- *news* for Usenet newsgroups

- *gopher* for a menu-driven interface

Following the protocol is the identifier of the computer system that contains the information. For example, the URL for WorldNet is http://www.worldnet.att.net/.

Use the pull-down list on the right of the Location box to select from the ten most recently used sites. The list is remembered even after you close Netscape Navigator, so you can quickly return to the sites during the next session. During a session, however, you can also view a history of the locations you visited. Pull down the Communicator menu and click on History to see the URLs of the sites that you visited. To go back to a site, double-click on it in the History list, or right-click on it and select Go To Page. Right-click on the page and choose Add to Bookmarks to add the site to your bookmark list.

Saving Web Pages

When you find a Web page that you are interested in, you can save it on your disk. You can even save a page before you display it, either as a formatted HTML file or as plain text. To do so, follow these steps:

1. To save the displayed page, pull down the File menu and click on Save As.

2. Pull down the Save as Type list and select either HTML Files (*.htm, *.html) or Plain text (*.TXT).

3. Type a name for the file.

4. Click on Save.

Source HTML files will contain the text and background of the page just as it appears on the Net, but without the inline graphics. You can later open it into Netscape Communicator to display it on the screen. To do so, use these steps:

1. Pull down the File menu.

2. Click on Open Page to see the dialog box shown in Figure 3-4.

3. Enter the path and filename, or use the Choose File button to select the file.

4. Select to display the file in either the Composer or Navigator windows. Choose Composer if you want to edit the page.

5. Click on Open.

NOTE: *You can also open an HTML-formatted file directly into Corel WordPerfect and other Suite applications.*

If you save the page using the Plain Text option, you can open the file into any word processing program. It won't have any of the formats or graphics—just the text of the page.

NOTE: *If you are viewing a page with frames, choose Save Frame As from the File menu to save the contents of the current frame.*

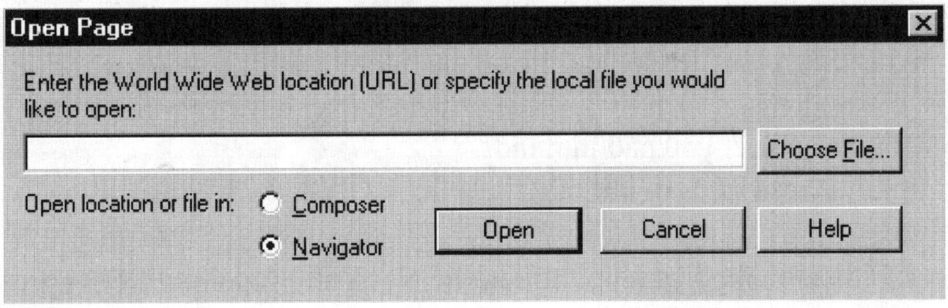

Opening a
Web page
from the
disk

FIGURE 3-4

You can also save a page directly from the link to it before you actually display it. Point to the link with the mouse and click the right mouse button to see a QuickMenu. Choose Save Link As to jump to the link, but save it on the disk rather than displaying it on the screen.

Printing Web Pages

In addition to saving a Web page, you can also print it. Click on the Print button on the toolbar, or pull down the File menu and click on Print to see a dialog box, and then click on Print.

If you are displaying a page with frames, the Print option in the File menu is replaced with Print Frame.

To adjust the format of the printout, pull down the File menu and click on Page Setup to see the Page Setup dialog box. Select options from the box, and click on OK. Use the Page Preview command from the File menu to see onscreen how the printed page will appear.

Searching for Information

One way to locate information is to follow the trail of links, clicking on them to move from site to site on the Internet until you find the information you are looking for. You can also search for the information using a keyword or phrase. You will be amazed at the breadth of information and services available on the Internet.

Before you go surfing around the Internet using search tools, however, keep in mind that much of the information there may not be useful, valuable, accurate, or socially acceptable. The Internet is just a ragtag network of millions of computers. No one controls, polices, or censors it—which is actually one of its greatest strengths. Searching for something on the Internet using a word or phrase may reveal a list of hundreds of locations, some of which may have very little—or nothing—to do with the subject you had in mind.

Follow these steps to initiate a search:

1. Click on the Search button in the Navigation toolbar. Netscape Communicator will open a search page, as shown in Figure 3-5.

Near the top of the page is a series of buttons for companies that provide directories of the Internet. They all offer similar types of service, although you may eventually find some better than others depending on your own preferences. Click on a button to change search companies.

2. Type the keywords or phrase that you want to find—such as a company name or topic.

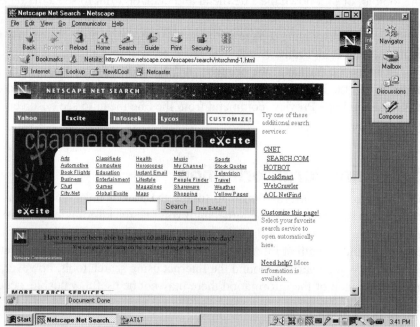

Netscape Communicator's Search page

FIGURE 3-5

3. Click on the Search button to begin the search. The name of the button may vary with search companies.

After a while, you'll see a screen reporting the number of matches and a list of the sites. The appearance of the screen will depend on the search directory you used. Figure 3-6, for example, shows the results of searching for "soap operas" using the Excite service — complete with any typographical errors that exist in the references! You may also see a list of categories, followed by actual sites. You can select a category and begin another search, or scroll the list looking for a location of interest. Click on the site that catches your attention, and continue surfing.

In most cases, the list will only include a first set of the locations. When you get to the end of the list, there will be a button to display additional sites.

Using Bookmarks

Once you find an interesting site, you don't want to have to surf the Web to find it later on. You could write down the URL address that appears in the Location box. Better yet, save the address as a bookmark.

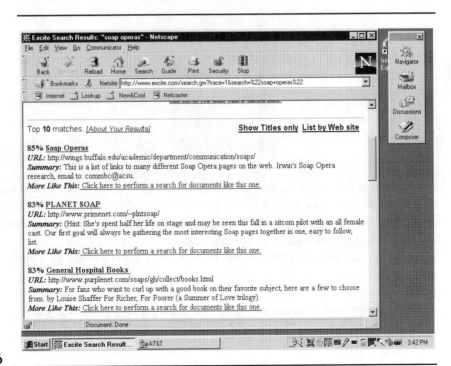

Search
results

FIGURE 3-6

You use a bookmark when reading a book so you can quickly return to the page you were on. That's exactly how bookmarks work in Netscape Communicator. You save the URL as a bookmark so you can simply click on the bookmark name to move to that site.

If you pull down the Bookmarks menu in the Netscape Communicator Location toolbar, you'll see any bookmarks you've already added, or bookmarks that Netscape Communicator has already created for you, as shown here:

The bookmarks are collected in folders around a common theme, with those that you've added, but not inserted in a folder, listed at the bottom. To move to a bookmark, just click on that item in the menu. Clicking on a category displays a menu of related bookmarks that you can select.

You can add your own sites to the Bookmarks menu to return to them quickly. Here's how:

1. Launch your browser and go to the page that you want to add as a bookmark.

2. Pull down the Bookmarks list and click on Add Bookmark.

The title of the displayed page, or its URL, will be added to the end of the Bookmarks menu. To later return to that site, just click on it in the menu.

To add a page to a category of bookmarks, follow these steps:

1. Launch your browser and go to the page that you want to add as a bookmark.

2. Pull down the Bookmarks list and point to File Bookmark to see a list of bookmark categories.

3. Click on the category you wish to add the bookmark to.

TIP: *You can also create a bookmark by right-clicking on the link and selecting Add Bookmark. Choose Internet Shortcut in the QuickMenu to add a shortcut to the link on the Windows 95 desktop.*

You can edit, delete, or change the order of bookmarks in the menu by displaying the Bookmarks window. Display the window by choosing Edit Bookmarks from the Bookmarks list.

The Bookmarks window, shown in Figure 3-7, displays bookmarks listed in a tree diagram, much like files on your disk. To delete a bookmark, click on it in the list and choose Delete from the Edit menu.

You can also use the Edit menu to cut, copy, and paste a bookmark to another location in the tree, or you can use drag-and-drop—drag the bookmark to where you want it to appear. To change the bookmark name or URL, right-click on it and choose Bookmark Properties from the QuickMenu, then make your changes in the dialog box that appears.

You can also insert a bookmark without logging onto the Web as long as you know its URL. Select New Bookmark from the File menu. In the dialog box that appears, enter a bookmark name, enter its URL location and optionally a description, and then click on OK.

Use the New Folder option from the File menu to create a new category.

TIP: *Use the View menu to change the order in which categories and bookmarks are displayed—by name, location, the date created, or the date the site was last visited.*

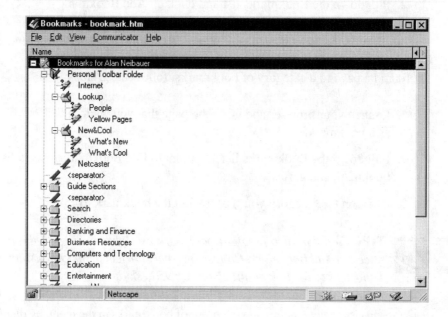

Working
with
bookmarks

FIGURE 3-7

Using the Address Book

Netscape Communicator Navigator uses the same address book that you learned about in Chapter 2. When you compose a message, you can either type the recipient's address directly into the mail form, or you can select it from the Address Book. You can select multiple recipients, and you can even broadcast the message to everyone in a group.

To access the Address Book, pull down the Communicator menu and click on Address Book to display the Corel Address Book 8 window. See Chapter 1 for information on creating a group of addresses to broadcast a message to multiple recipients.

Using E-Mail

Electronic mail is built into Netscape Communicator, but you may also have a special mail program that your company or organization uses. There are mail programs that you access directly from the Windows 95 desktop without needing to launch a Web browser. In this chapter, however, we'll discuss the e-mail system that is supplied with the Netscape Communicator browser.

NOTE: *In order to use the e-mail features of Netscape Communicator, you must have e-mail service through your ISP, company, or organization that supplies your Internet service. The e-mail servers must be specified in the Mail Servers page of the Preferences dialog box. See the section on "Customizing Netscape Communicator" later in this chapter.*

To read or send mail, click on the Mailbox button in the Component bar, or select Messenger Mailbox from the Communicator menu. (You can also access e-mail services from directly within CorelCENTRAL, as you'll learn in Chapter 31.) The CorelCENTRAL program will start and load its mailbox feature. (Just be patient if the CorelCENTRAL Card File window first appears.) If a box appears asking for your e-mail password, enter the password then click on OK. Mailbox will then check for new messages. If there are messages, they will be downloaded automatically and saved in your Inbox.

TIP: *To check for mail later in the session, click on the Get Messages toolbar button.*

The Mailbox window, shown in Figure 3-8, has three main parts—Mail folders, Message header list, and Message window. The tools in the window are described in Table 3-2.

NOTE: *You'll learn all about the CorelCENTRAL program and interface in Chapter 31.*

You use the Mail folders to organize your incoming and outgoing mail. You can create your own folders to store groups of messages, and Netscape Communicator can manage these folders for you:

- *Inbox* contains messages that you received.

- *Unsent Messages* contains messages that you've created but not yet sent.

- *Drafts* contains messages that you have started but that are not yet completed or are ready to send.

- *Sent* contains messages that you have sent.

- *Trash* contains messages you are deleting.

Message headers

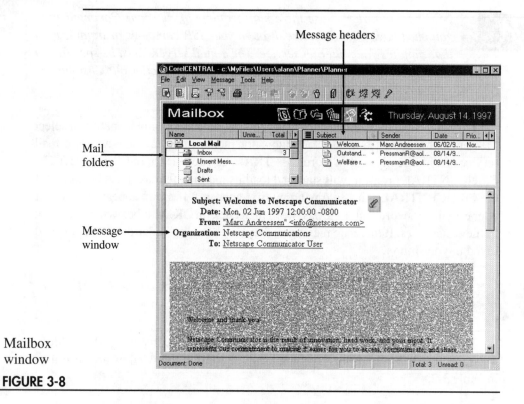

Mail folders

Message window

Mailbox window

FIGURE 3-8

- *Event* contains events accepted into CorelCENTRAL.

- *To Do* contains To Do items created in CorelCENTRAL.

Double-click on a folder to see its contents.

To create your own folder, pull down the File menu and click on New Folder. Type a name for the folder in the box that appears, and then click on OK.

The Folder window has several columns. The Unread column will list the number of messages that you have not yet read, and the Total column shows the number of messages in each folder.

TIP: *Drag-and-drop to rearrange the columns.*

Tool	Function
Get Messages	Inserts any unread mail into your Inbox
Show/Hide Messages	Opens or closes the message window
New Message	Opens the Message Composition window to create a new message
Reply to Message	Lets you choose to reply to just the sender, or the sender and all recipients of the messages, then opens the Message Composition window, with the sender's address of the current message in the To text box
Forward	Opens the Message Composition window for a new message, using the current message as an attachment
Print	Prints a copy of the selected message
Cut	Deletes the selected text to the clipboard
Copy	Copies the selected text to the clipboard
Paste	Inserts the contents of the clipboard
Accept	Accepts an event sent to you from another CorelCENTRAL user and inserts it into your CorelCENTRAL calendar
Decline	Rejects an event sent to you from another CorelCENTRAL user
Delete	Inserts the current messages into the Trash folder, creating the folder if necessary
Address	Opens Corel Address Book 8
Conference	Begins Netscape Conference
Web page composer	Lets you create an HTML document
Browse the Web	Launches the Netscape Communicator browser
PerfectExpert	Displays the PerfectExpert panel

Mailbox
Toolbar

TABLE 3-2

Reading Mail

To read mail, follow these steps:

1. If it is not already selected, double-click on the Inbox icon in the Mail folder. A list of your messages will appear to the right. The list is divided into columns that include:

   - The subject of the message

   - A Read icon indicating if you've read the message

   - The name of the sender

   - The date and time the message was inserted into your Inbox

   - The priority assigned to the message
     You can scroll the columns, using the arrows to their right, to display fewer columns, or to display more information, such as a flag for marking the message for future reference and the size of the message. Click on a heading to sort the list by it.

 TIP: *Drag-and-drop, or use the File Message or Copy Message options from the Message menu, to move a message to another folder.*

2. Click on the message you want to read in the Message header list. Netscape Communicator will display the message in the bottom pane of the window.

 TIP: *Double-click on a message header to display the message in a separate window.*

3. To add the address of the message's sender to your Address Book, pull down the Message menu, point to Add to Address Book, then choose to add just the sender's address or the address of all recipients of the message.

Reading Attachments

A mail message may also include an attachment. An *attachment* is a separate document or file that was transmitted along with the message. This can be a formatted Web page or a file. The attachment either will appear as text along with the message, or you will see an icon following the message.

If the attachment is readable, such as a text file, it may appear following the text of the message. You can switch between displaying the text of the message or an icon representing it by pulling down the View menu then choosing either Inline or As Links from the Attachments option. If the attachment cannot be displayed in line, it will remain shown as a link. As a link, an attachment will appear like this:

| Part 1.2.2 | **Name:** Neibauer incomplete discovery
 Type: unspecified type (application/octet-stream)
 Encoding: base64 |

When you click on the attachment link, Netscape Communicator will open the attachment in a separate window. If the attachment cannot be displayed on a window, the Save As dialog box appears so you can save the attachment to your disk, then open it later with the appropriate application.

 You can also choose to display the attachment as a single icon. Click on the Display Attachments button in the message to display a symbol like this for every file that has anattachment :

vcard.vcf

Double-click on the icon to open it, or right-click and choose Save Attachment As to save the attachment to your disk.

Sending and Replying to Mail

Creating and sending mail is a snap from within Messenger Mailbox. You can create mail online or offline. *Offline* means that you create the mail before actually connecting to the Web, so you won't waste your connect time and charges.

To create message online, just follow the steps below from within Messenger Mailbox. To create a message offline, refer to the "Going Offline" section coming up later in this chapter.

 TIP: *You can also send mail, reply to mail, and perform other functions by right-clicking on the message and choosing options from the Quickmenu.*

To send mail, follow these steps:

1. Click on the New Message button, or pull down the Message menu and click on New Message. The Message Composition window appears as shown in Figure 3-9.

2. Type the recipient's e-mail address in the Mail To box. If the recipient is in your Address Book, click on the Address button in the toolbar to open the Address Book. Double-click on the listing for each person you want to send the message to then click on OK.

3. To send a copy of the message to others, click on the next blank line under the recipient and pull down the To list to see the options shown here. Choose an option, then enter the recipient's e-mail address or select it from the Address Book.

Message
Composition
window

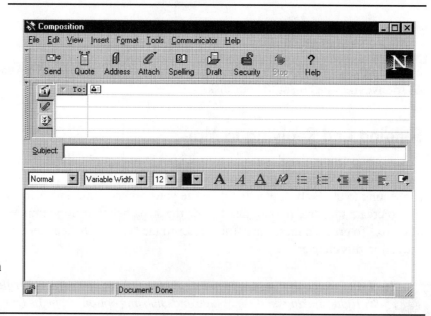

FIGURE 3-9

4. Type a subject.

5. Click in the large text box and type and format your message, as you'll soon learn how to do.

6. Click on Send. If you are offline, choose Send Later from the File menu. The next time you go online, send the message by selecting Send Unsent Messages from the Message menu.

You write and format the message in the large text box, using the buttons shown here to compose a message in HTML format.

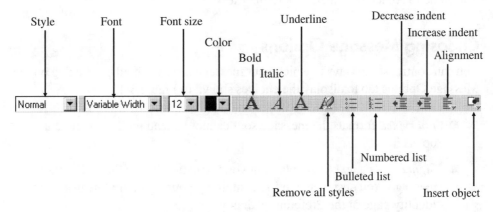

The font size list, by the way, lets you choose a size relative to the current font, such as -2, -1, 0, +1, +2. You can change Netscape Communicator's settings to choose fonts by their point sizes. See the "Customizing Netscape Communicator" section later in this chapter.

 TIP: *For more information on HTML formats, see the section "Entering and Formatting Text" in Chapter 7.*

Sending an Attachment

To send an attachment with your message, click on the Attach button in the toolbar to see these options:

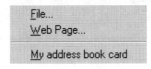

If you select File, a dialog box appears for you to enter or select the file to attach. If you choose Web Page, a box appears asking for the URL. Choose My Address Book Card to send your name and address information from the Address Book. An address book card in a message appears as shown in Figure 3-10.

You can also click on the Attachment tab, shown here:

The address lines will be replaced by a large box. Click on the box to display the Enter File to Attach box, then choose the file.

Choosing Message Options

 You can control some ways in which your message is transmitted by clicking on the Message Options tab to display the choices shown in Figure 3-11.

- *Encrypted* formats the message so it cannot be read until the recipient opens it.

- *Signed* adds a text file containing your signature line to the end of the message. You designate the file containing your signature line using the Identity page of the Preferences dialog box.

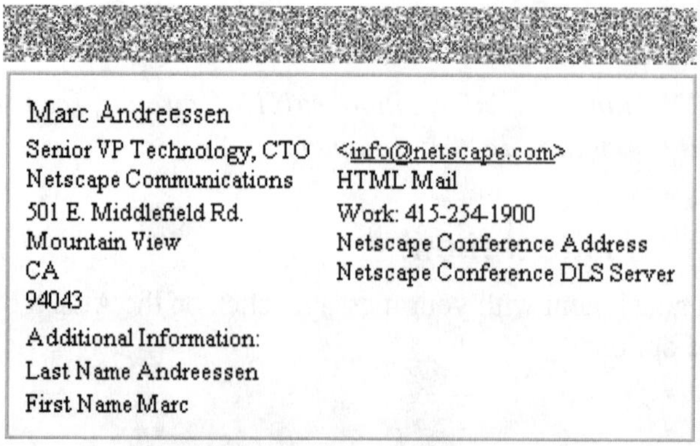

Marc Andreessen
Senior VP Technology, CTO   <info@netscape.com>
Netscape Communications   HTML Mail
501 E. Middlefield Rd.   Work: 415-254-1900
Mountain View   Netscape Conference Address
CA   Netscape Conference DLS Server
94043
Additional Information:
Last Name Andreessen
First Name Marc

Address
book card

FIGURE 3-10

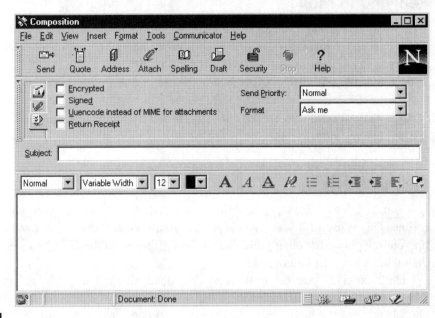

Message
options

FIGURE 3-11

■ *Uuencode Instead of MIME for Attachments* determines the format of
non-text messages.

■ *Return Receipt* will send you an e-mail when your message has reached
the recipient's mail service—not when the message has actually been read
by the recipient.

Send Priority marks the message so the recipient knows its priority. The options
are lowest, low, normal, high, and highest. The setting does not affect the actual
delivery of transmission.

Format lets you determine the format if your message. The options are Ask Me,
Plain Text Only, HML Text Only, and Plain Text and HTML. Choosing Plain Text
will remove any HTML formats you applied in the composer window. If you are
unsure whether your recipient can read HTML messages, choose either Plain Text
Only or Plain Text and HTML.

Replying to Mail

To reply to the message you are reading, click on the Reply to Message button, then select to reply to just the sender, or to the sender and all recipients of the original message. The Compose window will appear with the text of the original message. Type your reply, and then click on Send.

TIP: *If you selected New Message instead of Reply to Message, click on the Quote button to insert the text of the message selected in the Mail window.*

Going Offline

If you have a lot of messages to write or respond to, you may want to write them offline. This is useful if you are charged for your connect time, or just want to free up your telephone for other calls. Select Go Offline from the File menu to see the dialog box shown in Figure 3-12.

The box gives you the options to download all mail and discussion group messages and to send all unsent mail that you've already composed. You can also choose to select which discussion group messages to download. Make your selections from the box, then click on the Go Offline button to send and receive mail as you've selected.

Offline
dialog box
for
downloading
messages

FIGURE 3-12

Using Composer

Netscape Composer lets you create Web pages in HTML format. It gives you many of the capabilities that you'll find in the Corel applications discussed in the following chapters.

Click on Composer in the Component Bar, or select Page Composer from the Communicator menu to see the window shown in Figure 3-13. Use the buttons in the Formatting Toolbar to format text, just as you learned to format an e-mail message earlier in this chapter.

The functions of most of the toolbar buttons are rather straight forward, although several may be new to you:

- *Publish* lets you upload the Web page to a remote server. You'll need to know the HTTP or FTL location to which you want to upload the file.

- *Link* creates a hypertext link of the selected text. You'll be asked to specify the Web page URL or the local file to jump to when the link is clicked.

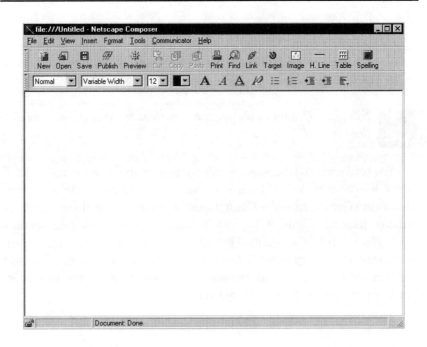

Page
composer
for HTML
files

■ FIGURE 3-13

- *Target* lets you create a bookmark that you can jump to when clicking on a link.

- *Image* inserts a graphic into the Web page.

When you're done creating the page, click on Save to save the page to your disk. Click on Publish if you're ready to upload the page to your Web server.

Using Collabra Discussion Groups

A discussion group (commonly called a *newsgroup)* is a group of people that share a common interest. Members of a newsgroup can be spread out around the world. By joining a newsgroup, you can send mail to every member of the group, and you can receive mail sent by all of the members.

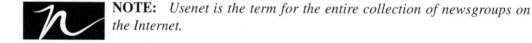 **NOTE:**   *You must have newsgroup access through your ISP, company, or organization that supplies your Internet service. The newsgroup server must be specified in the Group Server page of the Preferences dialog box. See the "Customizing Netscape Communicator" section later in this chapter.*

Sending a message to the newsgroup is also called *posting.* It is similar to sending e-mail, except that your message will automatically be sent to every member of the group; so if there are 1,000 members of the group, your message will go to all of them. You can also choose to send a message to a single member of the group.

NOTE: *Usenet is the term for the entire collection of newsgroups on the Internet.*

You read and send messages to newsgroups in the News window. To display the News window, click on Discussions in the Component bar, or select Collabra Discussion Groups from the Communicator window. You'll see the message center window shown in Figure 3-14, with the name of your newsgroup server selected.

If you've already subscribed to newsgroups, there will be a plus sign in the icon next to the newsgroup server. Click on the icon to display the groups, and to display the number of messages as shown here. Discussion groups shown in boldface contain messages that you have not yet read.

netnews.worldnet.att.net		
corel.printhouse		3
compuserve.general	**31**	**36**
net.com.netcruiser.general		
usc.org.tsa		1

Subscribing to Groups

You have to subscribe to groups that you want to send messages to and receive messages from. Click on the Subscribe to open the Describe to Discussion Groups dialog box. Netscape Communicator will download and then display a list of newsgroups that your server handles, as shown in Figure 3-15. Be patient—it may take some time when you first click on Subscribe to download the list of groups.

The check mark next to the items in the Newsgroup pane means that you are subscribed to the newsgroup. This means that messages posted to the group will also

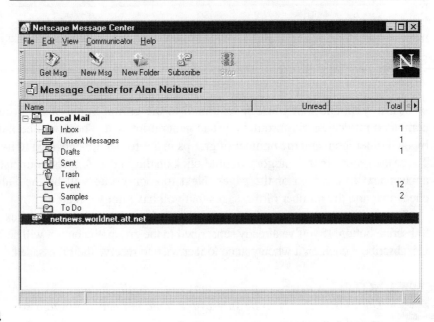

Message
Center

FIGURE 3-14

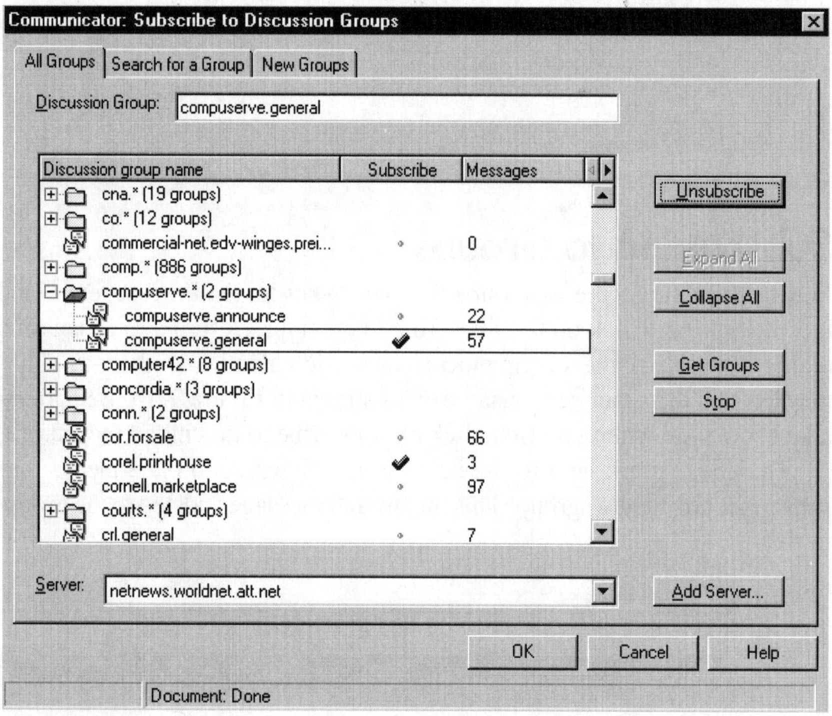

Communicator: Subscribe to Discussion Groups   [×]

All Groups | Search for a Group | New Groups

Discussion Group: compuserve.general

Discussion group name	Subscribe	Messages	
⊞ 📁 cna.* (19 groups)			
⊞ 📁 co.* (12 groups)			
📰 commercial-net.edv-winges.prei...	∘	0	
⊞ 📁 comp.* (886 groups)			
⊟ 📂 compuserve.* (2 groups)			
📰 compuserve.announce	∘	22	
📰 compuserve.general	✔	57	
⊞ 📁 computer42.* (8 groups)			
⊞ 📁 concordia.* (3 groups)			
⊞ 📁 conn.* (2 groups)			
📰 cor.forsale	∘	66	
📰 corel.printhouse	✔	3	
📰 cornell.marketplace	∘	97	
⊞ 📁 courts.* (4 groups)			
📰 crl.general	∘	7	

Buttons: Unsubscribe | Expand All | Collapse All | Get Groups | Stop

Server: netnews.worldnet.att.net   Add Server...

[OK]   [Cancel]   [Help]

Document: Done

List of available newsgroups

FIGURE 3-15

be sent to you, and that you can send mail to the group. Some of the groups are combined into categories around a broad general interest. These will be indicated by the Folder icon, and the number of groups in the folder appears next to its name. To see the groups in the category, double-click on the folder. A newsgroup itself will appear next to the icon of the pages. Next to each group will be the Subscribe checkbox, and the number of messages that you have not yet read.

To subscribe to a group, click on the listing for it in the box, then click on the Subscribe button. If you've already subscribed to the group, the button will be labeled Unsubscribe—click on it when you no longer wish to receive their messages.

NOTE: *A newsgroup name may not actually indicate its interest area. The only real way to be sure of the topic is to read through some of the posted messages.*

Use the Search for a Group tab to look for a newsgroup using keywords, and use the New Groups tab to list groups recently added by your ISP.

To read an item, follow these steps:

1. Switch to the CorelCENTRAL Mailbox window if it is already open, or double-click on the name of a newsgroup in the Netscape Message Center window.

2. Double-click on newsgroup name in the folder pane. The message's headers for the group will be downloaded and will appear in the Message Header pane, as shown here:

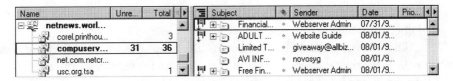

3. Click on the message you want to read in the Message Header pane.

4. Read the message.

Double-click on a message header in the Message Header pane to display the message in its own window.

 TIP: *The message headers (not the messages themselves) are downloaded and added to the CorelCENTRAL mailbox. To download the messages themselves so you can read them offline, use the Go Offline option from the File menu.*

Sending newsgroup mail is similar to sending regular e-mail, except you are sending a message or a reply to the entire group. Sending a new message begins a new *thread*, a series of messages on a specific theme or topic. Replying to a message adds to the current thread. The icon in the Message header illustrates if there are multiple messages in the thread, such as replies to the original message. You can expand the thread to show the replies, as seen here:

When you're reading a discussion group message and choose to send a new message, the composer window opens with the name of the group as the recipient. If you click on Reply to a displayed message, you can then choose from these options:

> Reply to Sender
> Reply to Sender and All Recipients
> Reply to Group
> Reply to Sender and Group

Customizing Netscape Communicator

Netscape Communicator is installed using certain default values, such as the home page. All of the default Netscape Communicator settings are stored in a series of dialog boxes called *preferences panels*.

Although you cannot change some of these settings because they are required by your ISP, you can modify most of them. Select Preferences from the Edit menu to see the dialog box shown in Figure 3-16.

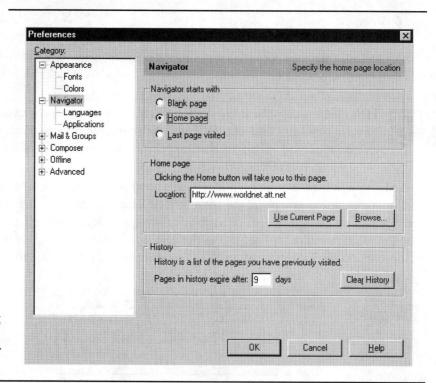

Customizing
Netscape
Communicator

FIGURE 3-16

Each item on the left controls another category of settings. If the item is preceded with a plus sign, click on the sign to display items in the category. There will be a page of options for the heading, such as Appearance, as well as pages for each item under the heading, such as Fonts and Color. The completely expanded list of preferences is shown here:

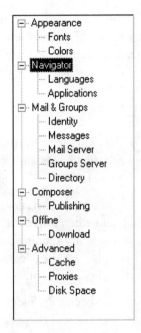

Appearance

The Appearance options affect the way the Netscape Communicator window appears when you start it, including the initial window and the appearance of the toolbar. The Fonts option determines the font used to display and encode text; this is also where you determine whether you want to include dynamic fonts that are downloaded when the page appears. The Colors options let you set the colors of links, backgrounds, and text.

Navigator

The initial Navigator page determines if Netscape Communicator starts with a blank page, home page, or last page visited, and the URL of the home page. It also can be directed here as to the number of days you want it to retain the history page of sites last visited. The Languages settings are used by Netscape Communicator to tell computers what language you are using. The Applications setting specifies the locations of some supporting Netscape Communicator applications.

Mail and Groups

These settings control the look of the Mail and News windows, and general ways in which these features operate. The initial page determines the style of quoted text, the manner in which messages and message lists are displayed, and whether a sound is played when new messages arrive.

The option has five subcategories:

■ Use the *Identity* page of the dialog box to store your name, e-mail address, an alternative reply-to address, and the name of a file storing your signature (closing) to add to the end of mail and news postings.

■ Use the *Messages* page to choose HTML default format, to quote original messages when replying, and when to tell the system your preferences for wrapping long lines; automatically sending copies of your messages to yourself or other user; you also use the Messages page to determine the folder in which to insert copies of sent messages.

■ Use the *Mail Server* page to specify the incoming and outgoing mail server. If you are unsure about any of these settings, check with your ISP.

■ Use the *Group Server* page to specify the newsgroup server.

■ Use the *Directory* page to specify the directories to search when looking for addresses.

Composer Page

These options determine how often Page Composer automatically saves your work, the external HTML and graphic editors, and the way font sizes are selected.

The Publishing page determines how to maintain links and keep images with pages when saving remote pages, and the default publishing location.

Offline Page

This page determines if Netscape Communicator starts online, offline, or asks you which you'd prefer when you start.

The Download page determines if you download only unread messages, download messages by their date, or select messages to download.

Advanced

The options in these pages are for more advanced users. The initial page determines if Netscape Communicator automatically loads images, enables Java, Java Script, and other elements; or accepts, disables, or warns you when cookies are detected. A *cookie* is special code that allows the remote Web site to gather information about your computer.

The Cache page determines the size of memory and disk caches, lets you empty the caches, choose the default disk cache location, and lets you tell the system how often to compare the cache file with the document on network—once per session, every time, or never.

The Proxies page lets you choose advanced options for additional security.

Use the Disk Space page to save space on your disk. You can select not to download messages over a certain size (the default is 50 KB), to make folders compact when they reach as certain size (the default is 100 KB), and when to clean up (erase) old discussion messages.

Using Conference

Netscape Conference lets you communicate by voice in real-time over the Internet —just like making a call on the telephone. Just click on Conference in the Component bar.

NOTE: *Your computer must be equipped for sound, with speakers and a microphone.*

The first time you run Conference, you'll be told that you have to set it up for your system. In a series of dialog boxes, you'll be asked to enter or select information. Click on Next after each box.

- Enter your e-mail address and the type of network you are using for Internet connection.

- Enter name and address information, as well as the filename of a photograph that you want to appear online while you are speaking. The information is used for your "business card"—a panel of information that appears on the screen of the person receiving your call.

- Designate the service that you want to use to manage your communications when online, as shown in Figure 3-17. Netscape Conference includes default server information that you should use, unless you have another server. You can also choose not to list your name in the phonebook maintained by the server.

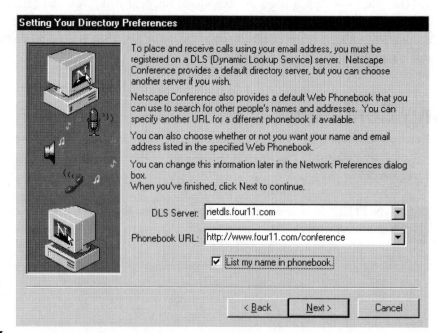

Server
information
for a
conference

FIGURE 3-17

- Select your modem speed or indicate if you are using an ISDN or local area network.

- Specify the microphone and speaking drivers being used by your system —it is usually best to accept the default drivers shown.

Check your recording level, as shown in Figure 3-18. Click on the Microphone icon then speak into the microphone. As you speak, a green line should extend to its right. If the line does not appear, drag the blue control in the dialog box, called the Silence Sensor, to the right.

The next time you start Conference you'll see the dialog box shown in Figure 3-19. Enter the e-mail address of the person you want to speak with, select the person's name from the address book, or click on Web Phonebook to find a person in your conference server's directory. The person must be connected to the same conference server as you. Click on Dial to make the connection.

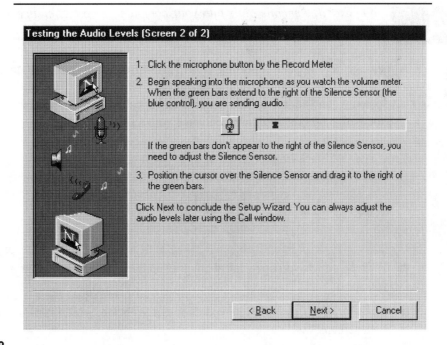

Testing your audio level

FIGURE 3-18

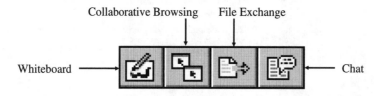

Making a
conference
call

FIGURE 3-19

 NOTE: *If someone dials into your computer for a conference, click on the large button next to e-mail address box to answer the call.*

A message will appear reporting if the person accepts your call, then their business card and photograph (if available) appears. Click on the Microphone button to start speaking, and adjust the microphone and speaker levels.

Use the buttons on the toolbar to enhance your call:

- *Whiteboard* lets you open and share graphic files or create drawings as you speak.

- *Collaborative Browsing* lets you choose a Web site, which appears on both screens.

- *File Exchange* lets you download files.

- *Chat* lets you communicate by writing, rather than voice, as in a chat line on AOL and other online services.

If the person is not available, the Voice Mail box appears, as shown here. Click on the Record button, record your message and then click on Send. Your recording will then be sent to the recipient in the form of an e-mail with the voice recording as an attached file.

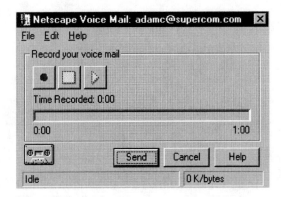

 NOTE: *Use the Speed Dial list to enter and later access up to six e-mail numbers for conference calls.*

PART
II

Corel WordPerfect

Creating Documents with Corel WordPerfect

4

Corel WordPerfect is the flagship of the Corel Office suite for a very good reason. It is known around the world as an outstanding word processing program, with millions of dedicated users. Corel WordPerfect 8 is the next generation of this legacy, bringing new, powerful, and timesaving features to this landmark program.

Starting Corel WordPerfect

To start Corel WordPerfect, click on the Start button, point to Corel WordPerfect Suite 8, and click on Corel WordPerfect 8. You'll see the Corel WordPerfect screen shown in Figure 4-1.

At the top of the screen are the title bar, menu bar, toolbar, and property bar. Corel WordPerfect gives the name "Document1" to the first document window during the session, "Document 2" to the second, and so on. The word "unmodified" in the title bar means that you have not changed the document since it was started or opened. That word will disappear as soon as you start typing to indicate that you must save your work if you want to use it again. When you do save your document, the name you give it will appear on the title bar.

NOTE: *If the ruler does not appear on your screen, select Ruler from the View menu to display it.*

The property bar has pull-down lists and buttons for performing common functions, such as changing the type size or centering text on the screen. The items on the property bar depend on the task you are performing. There are over 30 property bars in Corel WordPerfect. Each is named according to its function, such as the Outline bar and the Header bar. The one displayed by default is called the Main property bar. You'll learn each of the functions of the toolbar and property bar throughout this book.

The blank area under the property bar is the typing area where your document will appear. The dotted lines around the typing area are the margin guidelines. They not only show you where your page margins are, but you can drag them to change the margins. The blinking vertical line is the insertion point where characters appear

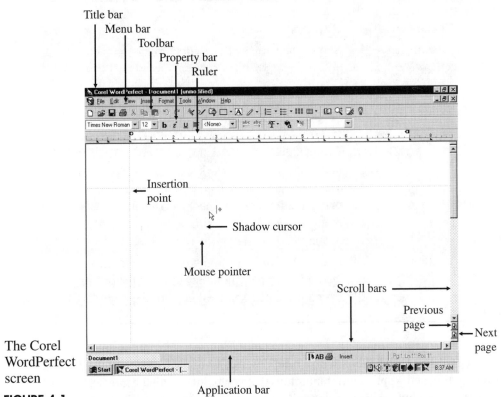

Title bar
Menu bar
Toolbar
Property bar
Ruler

Insertion point

Shadow cursor

Mouse pointer

Scroll bars

Previous page

Next page

The Corel WordPerfect screen

Application bar

FIGURE 4-1

as you type. Next to the mouse pointer is the *shadow cursor*. This shows where characters will be inserted when you click the mouse, and the alignment that has been applied to the text. You'll also see the horizontal and vertical scroll bars. Use the vertical scroll bar to scroll lines up and down, the horizontal scroll bar to scroll right and left. At the bottom of the vertical scroll bar are the Previous Page and Next Page buttons, which you can use to move from page to page through your document.

Finally, at the bottom of the screen, just above the Windows 95 taskbar, is the *application bar.* This bar shows the names of the documents that you have open and gives you information about WordPerfect and your position in the current document, as shown in Table 4-1. You can use the application bar to move and copy information between documents without having both appear onscreen at the same time.

What you don't yet see on the screen are four helpful, timesaving features: QuickTips, QuickMenus, QuickStatus boxes, and QuickLinks.

Section	Displays
Document	Shows the names of open documents.
Shadow Cursor	Toggle shadow cursor on and off.
Caps Lock	Toggle CAPS LOCK on and off.
Printer	Click to display the Print dialog box.
Insert	Insert means that as you type new characters within a document, existing text moves over to make room. As you work with Corel WordPerfect, other messages will appear in this section indicating that some feature is turned on, or that the insertion point is in a table, column, or other special formatted section of text.
Position	Location of the insertion point in the document, including the page number (Pg) and the distance from the top (Ln) and left edge of the page (Pos).

Application Bar

TABLE 4-1

A *QuickTip* is a small box with a brief description of the function of the Toolbar, Property Bar, and Application Bar buttons that you point at with the mouse. If you're not sure what a button does, point to it and read the QuickTip, as shown here.

A *QuickMenu* is a list of items that will appear when you right-click on an object. Which menu items will show depends on where the mouse is pointing. It is usually faster to display and use the QuickMenu than it is to perform the same functions with the menu bar or toolbar, since you don't have to slide the mouse to the top of the screen. Every QuickMenu has the "What's This?" option. Click on it to read about the object you are pointing to.

QuickStatus boxes will appear when you change the sizes of margins, columns, and table cells, showing their exact dimensions. As you drag the mouse, watch the QuickStatus box—release the mouse button when the dimension is what you want:

TIP: *You'll also see special symbols indicating where you changed tab stops or applied certain combinations of formats and styles.*

QuickLinks are words that have been associated with sites on the World Wide Web. Corel has defined a number of QuickLinks for you. QuickLinks start with the @ symbol. If you type @Corel, for example, WordPerfect will automatically display the word in color and underlined, indicating it is a QuickLink. When you point to the link, the mouse appears like a pointing hand, and clicking on the word launches your Web browser and connects to http://www.corel.com. If you type @Netscape, WordPerfect creates a QuickLink to http://www.netscape.com. In fact, when you type anything in the format www.xxxx.xxx (such as www.MyWebSite.com), WordPerfect automatically converts it to a QuickLink.

From time to time, Corel WordPerfect will also display other small icons in the left margin indicating that some object has been inserted or that a special format has been applied. When you change tab stops, for example, an icon appears showing that new tab stops are in effect. If more than one icon should appear, Corel WordPerfect displays a special icon showing that multiple formats exist in that paragraph. Click on that icon to see the icons for the individual objects. This icon, for example, indicates two tab formats, a comment, and a sound file:

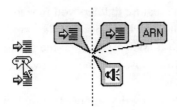

Typing a Document

You type a document in Corel WordPerfect just as you would in any other word processing program, and almost the same as on a typewriter. The letter and number keys insert exactly what you see on the keys; just remember to press SHIFT to get uppercase letters and the punctuation marks shown on the top part of the key. Press the CAPS LOCK key or click on the CAPS LOCK button on the application bar to type uppercase letters without holding down the SHIFT key. You can use the keypad to enter numbers, but you must first press the NUMLOCK key—otherwise, you will move the insertion point.

TIP: *Remember to use the PerfectExpert to help you create and format documents of all types.*

Press the BACKSPACE key to erase your mistakes. Each time you press BACKSPACE, Corel WordPerfect deletes a character to the left of the insertion point. Indent the first line of a paragraph by pressing the TAB key, and press the ENTER key to insert a blank line or to end a paragraph. Do not press ENTER, however, when the insertion point reaches the right margin; just keep on typing. Corel WordPerfect will sense that the word you're typing will not fit on the line and it will automatically move it to the next.

When your typing reaches the bottom of the screen, just continue. The text at the top will scroll up and out of view, but it will not be deleted. You can always scroll the screen back to see it.

And don't worry about where the page ends—just keep on typing. Corel WordPerfect will automatically end the page when it is full and start a new one. If you want to end a page before Corel WordPerfect does, press CTRL-ENTER.

Using the Shadow Cursor

WordPerfect offers a unique feature that lets you type anywhere in the typing area. As you move the mouse in the white space of the typing window, you'll see the shadow cursor moving with it. When you click the mouse, the insertion point will appear at the tab stop position closest to the shadow cursor. (The default tab stops are set every half inch.)

You can click anywhere in the document, even in the middle of the page, and start typing. For example, you do not need to press ENTER to insert blank lines into a document, or press the TAB key to indent a line. Just point to the location where you want to type, and then click.

Along with the shadow cursor is an arrow indicating the alignment of the text. When the arrow points to the right, the text will be left-aligned at the tab stop position, with characters moving to the right as you type.

If you point the mouse at the exact middle of the screen, the shadow cursor will appear with a two-pointed arrow. Click when the two-headed arrow appears to type text centered between the margins. As you type, characters will move alternately to the left and right.

If you point at the far right margin, the arrow points to the left. Click there to right-align the text, so it shifts to the left as you type.

Hard Versus Soft

When Corel WordPerfect moves the insertion point to the start of a new line, it is called a *soft return*. When it ends one page and starts another, it is called a *soft page break*. When you press ENTER to end a line, it's a *hard return*. When you press CTL-ENTER to end a page, it's a *hard page break*.

Why bother with hard versus soft? As you insert, delete, and format text within a document, Corel WordPerfect can automatically adjust the other text on the page. If you add text to a paragraph, for example, the other text in the paragraph and on the page will move over and down to make room. If you delete text, it may move text up from the next page, always ending pages when they become full.

If you pressed ENTER to end each line at the right margin, as you do with a typewriter, then each line would be considered a separate paragraph. Text would not flow neatly to adjust to your changes. Likewise, if you press CTRL-ENTER to end a page, a new page will always start at that location, even if you delete some text from the page before.

You cannot delete a soft page break; it will adjust automatically as you work. You can delete a hard page break by pressing DEL or BACKSPACE.

CAUTION: *Never end a page of continuous text by pressing ENTER until Corel WordPerfect inserts a soft page break. If you later insert or delete text, the extra blank lines will end up where you don't want them.*

Spell-As-You-Go

Corel WordPerfect automatically checks your spelling as you create your document using its Spell-As-You-Go feature, placing a wavy red line under words it cannot find in its dictionary, as shown here (the wavy line will appear red on your screen):

The Three Stoges are my favorite actors. I think they are very funy.

You can leave the wavy lines where they are and correct your errors later on, or you can fix them as you work. If you know the right spelling, and the mistake was just a typo, you can press the BACKSPACE key to erase the mistake, and then type the word again.

You can also let Corel WordPerfect correct the word for you. Point to the word and click the right mouse button to see the Spell-As-You-Go QuickMenu, shown here:

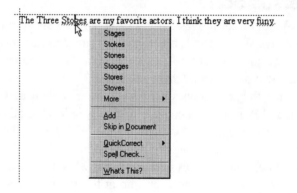

At the top of the menu are some suggested spellings. Just click on the correct word to insert it in place of your own. The word "More" means that Corel WordPerfect has found more suggested spellings than will fit on the menu—point to "More" to see these other choices.

Here are the other options on the QuickMenu:

- *Add*—Select this if the word is spelled correctly and you want to add it to Corel WordPerfect's dictionary. The word will not be flagged with a wavy line again in any Corel WordPerfect document.

- *Skip in Document*—Choose this if you want to ignore the word only in this document. It will be flagged in other documents, however.

- *QuickCorrect*—Pick this to create a QuickCorrect entry for the word.

- *Spell Check*—Use this to start the Spell Check feature.

 NOTE: *The QuickCorrect option only appears when Corel WordPerfect has suggested spellings.*

You can turn off the Spell-As-You-Go feature if you don't like all of the wavy lines. Pull down the Tools menu, point to Proofread, and click on Off.

Grammar-As-You-Go

Corel WordPerfect also includes Grammar-As-You-Go. With this feature turned on, you'll see wavy blue lines under possible grammatical errors. Right-click on the error to see the rule of grammar being violated and a suggested correction.

To turn this feature on or off, pull down the Tools menu, point to Proofread, and click on Grammar-As-You-Go.

Prompt-As-You-Go

The list box at the far right of the property bar is called *Prompt-As-You-Go*. This option will display alternate words from the dictionary for misspelled words, and will display synonyms for words in the Thesaurus.

When you click on a word in your document, or immediately after you type a word, the word will appear in the Prompt-As-You-Go box. Pull down the list associated with the box to display alternate words, as shown here:

Click on a word in the list to insert it in place of the word in your document.

When you misspell a word, a suggested spelling will appear in the box. Move the insertion point back over the word, and then pull down the list to see suggested spellings. Suggested spellings will also appear if you click on a word that Spell-As-You-Go has underlined.

Inserting and Deleting Text

If you don't catch a mistake until you are past it, you don't have to press BACKSPACE to delete all of the text back to that point. Instead, move the insertion point and then make your changes to the text. To do this, move the mouse and point to the area where you want to insert or delete characters.

You can also use the keyboard to move the insertion point by pressing the arrow keys. Press HOME to quickly move to the start of a line, and END to move to the end of the line.

Before trying to insert text, look at the application bar. If it says "Insert," you are in Insert mode. As you type, existing text will move over and down as necessary to make room. You can switch out of Insert mode by pressing the INS key, or by double-clicking on Insert in the status bar. This display will change to Typeover—now each character that you type will replace an existing one.

To delete text, press the BACKSPACE key to delete characters to the left of the insertion point, and DEL to delete characters to the right.

Scrolling the Screen

How do you move the insertion point to a place in the document that has already disappeared off the screen? The answer is *scrolling*. Scrolling means to bring into view text that has disappeared off the top or bottom, or the left or right, of the document window.

The simplest way to scroll the window is to use the arrow keys. When the insertion point is at the top line of the document window, pressing UP ARROW will scroll a new line into view—if there are any. When the insertion point is on the last line in the window, pressing DOWN ARROW will scroll a new line into view—again, if there are any.

If you have to move a great distance through a long document, however, using the arrow keys is certainly not very efficient. Instead, use the vertical scroll bar on the right of the screen to scroll up and down. Use the horizontal scroll bar at the bottom of the window to scroll left and right.

To scroll through your document line by line, just as you would by pressing the arrow key, click on the up or down triangles on the ends of the scroll bar. To scroll screen by screen, click above or below the scroll box—the box within the bar. Each time you click, Corel WordPerfect scrolls the window about the same number of lines that you can see. You can also drag the scroll box to scroll to a relative position in the document. If you drag the box to the middle of the scroll bar, Corel WordPerfect will display page five of a nine-page document, for example.

To move page by page through a document, click on the Previous Page and Next Page buttons on the bottom of the scroll bar.

Keep in mind a very important point. Scrolling with the scroll bars and with the Previous Page and Next Page buttons does not move the insertion point, it only changes the part of the document being displayed on the screen. You'll notice that the position indicators in the status bar will not change as you scroll, so if you don't click first, the screen will scroll back to its previous location when you begin typing or press an arrow key. To insert or delete text in the displayed area, you must first click where you want to type.

To go to the start of a specific page, double-click on the position indicator on the status bar to see the Go To dialog box, shown in Figure 4-2. Type the number of the page you want to move to, and then click on OK. You can also click on Position and select the location from the list:

- Last Position

- Previous Table

- Next Table

- Reselect Last Selection

- Top of Current Page

- Bottom of Current Page

Using the
Go To box
to move
within the
document

FIGURE 4-2

To scroll the screen and move the insertion point with the keyboard, use these shortcuts:

Press	To Move
PGUP	Up one screen
PGDN	Down one screen
CTRL-HOME	To the start of the document
CTRL-END	To the end of the document
ALT-PGUP	To the previous page
ALT-PGDN	To the next page

Selecting Text

When you want to perform a Corel WordPerfect function on more than one character or word at a time, you need to select them. You can select text using either the mouse or the keyboard. Selected text appears highlighted—light letters over a dark background.

n   **NOTE:**   *When you select text, the property bar will change. The Insert Symbol and Prompt-As-You-Go items are replaced by four new buttons: Protect Block, New Comment, QuickWords, and Hyperlink. You use Protect Block to keep a section of text from being divided into two pages. You'll learn how to use the other buttons in later chapters.*

It is easy to select text with the mouse by dragging. Here's how:

1. Move the mouse so it is at one end of the text that you want to select. It can be at either end, in front of the first character or following the last character.

2. Press and hold down the left mouse button. Make sure the pointer appears like the I-beam. If the pointer is an arrow, you'll draw a box to hold clipart or another object, as you'll learn in Chapter 12.

3. Keep the button down as you drag the mouse, until the pointer is at the other end of the text. Drag straight across the line, not up or down, unless you want to select more than one line of text.

4. When you reach the end of the text, release the mouse button. The selected text will appear highlighted. Click the mouse to deselect the text, removing the highlighting.

TIP: *The Reselect Last Selection option in the Go To dialog box will automatically move to and highlight the last text selected with the mouse.*

Corel WordPerfect uses QuickSelect, an intelligent selection system. If you start dragging in the center of a word, the program will select the entire word when you get to the next one. If you drag to select the space before a word, Corel WordPerfect automatically selects the whole word to the right as you drag onto its first characters. Similarly, when you select the space after a word and the one following, Corel WordPerfect selects the whole word to the left as you drag onto its last character.

Something similar occurs when you drag the mouse up or down. When you drag to the line above, Corel WordPerfect automatically selects everything to the left of the original line and to the right of the new line. If you drag down to the next line, Corel WordPerfect selects everything to the right of the original and to the left of the next line.

As long as you do not release the mouse button, you can drag as much or as little text as you want. If you drag too far to the right, for example, just keep the mouse button down and drag back toward the left.

If you want to delete text quickly, select it with the mouse and then press the DEL or BACKSPACE key. You can also point to the selected text, click the right mouse button, and choose Cut or Delete from the QuickMenu that appears when you right-click on selected text.

CAUTION: *Before going any further, here's a word of warning. Selected text will be deleted if you press any number, letter, punctuation key, the SPACEBAR, or the ENTER key. Corel WordPerfect uses this technique to make it easy for you to replace characters with something else. If you do not want to replace text, make certain that no text is selected before you start typing.*

Just as there are many ways to scroll the screen and move the insertion point, there are many ways to select text. Double-click to select a word, click three times to select the sentence, or click four times to select the entire paragraph.

If you double-click on a word and then delete it, Corel WordPerfect will also delete the space following the word. Corel WordPerfect figures that if you want to delete the word, you don't want to leave an extra space between the words that remain.

If you want to select a portion of text without dragging, use the SHIFT key. Place the insertion point at one end of the text, hold down the SHIFT key, and then click at the other end of the text.

You can also select text by clicking on the left margin. When you place the mouse pointer in the left margin, the pointer will be shaped like an arrow. Click the left mouse once to select the sentence of text to the right of the pointer; click twice to select the entire paragraph. If you hold down the mouse button and drag in the left margin, you will select multiple lines.

 TIP: *Right-click in the left margin to see a QuickMenu with the options Select Sentence, Select Paragraph, Select Page, and Select All. Choose the amount you want to select.*

You can also select text using the Edit menu. Point to Select on the menu and choose to select the sentence, paragraph, page, or the entire document.

If you want to select text using the keyboard, remember these two important keys: F8 and SHIFT. To simulate dragging, press the F8 key. Now text becomes selected as you move the insertion point using the arrow keys, other key combinations, and even by clicking the mouse. For example, if you press F8 and then RIGHT ARROW, text becomes selected as the insertion point passes over it. To stop selecting text, press the F8 key again.

 TIP: *You can also select text using SHIFT. When you hold down SHIFT, all of the insertion point movement keystrokes also select text.*

Using Undo and Redo

It would be nice if we never made mistakes, but unfortunately, life just isn't that perfect. It is all too easy to delete characters you really want, or type characters and then change your mind about them. Because Corel WordPerfect knows we are not always perfect, it gives us a quick and easy way to correct our mistakes using the Undo and Redo commands:

Undo Redo

The Undo command reverses changes that you make in your document. Delete a paragraph by mistake? Use Undo to return it to the document. Type a sentence and then change your mind? Use Undo to remove it from the document. There are two ways to use Undo—from the Edit menu or from the toolbar.

CAUTION: *Not every action that you perform can be undone. For example, you cannot undo saving or printing your document.*

To reverse the change you just made to the document, pull down the Edit menu and click on Undo, or click on the Undo button in the toolbar. Corel WordPerfect will reverse the last action you took—whether it's restoring deleted text or undoing your last typing. Corel WordPerfect "remembers" the last ten actions that you performed, even when you save and close the document. Once you undo the very last action, Corel WordPerfect will be prepared to undo the one before that; just click on Undo again or select it from the Edit menu.

Corel WordPerfect remembers not only the action you took, but also the ones you undo. So if you undo something and then change your mind, you can redo it using any of these techniques:

- Pull down the Edit menu and click on Redo.

- Click on the Redo button on the toolbar.

Undo/Redo History

If you do make a lot of changes to your document, you can forget which action will be undone or redone when you click on the button. To see a list of your last actions, and to increase the number of actions that Corel WordPerfect remembers, choose Undo/Redo History from the Edit menu. You'll see a dialog box like the one shown in Figure 4-3.

Undo/Redo
History
dialog box

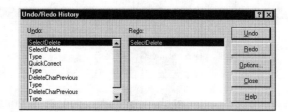

■ **FIGURE 4-3**

Your last actions are listed with the most recent on top. To undo or redo the last action you took, just click on Undo or Redo. To reverse more than one action at a time, click elsewhere on the list. You cannot, however, delete a specific action other than whatever is listed on top. If you click on the third in the list, for example, Corel WordPerfect will automatically select all of the actions above it as well. So to undo your last five actions, click on the fifth item in the list and then on Undo.

To change the number of items that Corel WordPerfect remembers, click on Options in the dialog box. You can tell Corel WordPerfect to remember up to 300 actions, and to remember or forget them when you close the document.

Saving a Document

You should get in the habit of saving your documents, even if you think you may not need them again. You might not find a typo or other mistake in a printed copy until a later time. If you didn't save your document, you'd have to type it all over again. To save a document, follow these steps:

1. Click on the Save button in the toolbar, or choose Save As from the File menu to display the Save As dialog box.

2. Type the document name, and select the folder where you want to store it.

3. Click on Save. The word "Modified" will appear after the filename in the title bar.

NOTE: *By default, Corel WordPerfect saves documents with the WPD extension in the MyFiles folder.*

When you've finished working with your document, look for the word "Unmodified" in the title bar. If it is not there, it means that you've changed the document since you last saved it, and you must save the document again. When you click on Save this time, Corel WordPerfect saves the document immediately without first opening the Save As dialog box.

 TIP: *Remember, use Save As from the File menu to save the document with a new name.*

 In Chapter 13, you'll learn how to save your documents so you can share them with other programs.

Closing a Document

When you have finished working with your document, clear it from the screen by closing it. Click on the Close box on the right of the menu bar, or choose Close from the File menu. If you did not save your document since last changing it, a dialog box will appear asking if you want to save it now—select Yes or No.

If you are only working with one document at a time, a new blank one will appear when you close it. If you have more than one document open, closing one document will display another open document.

Printing Documents

To print your document using all of the default printing settings, click on the Print button in the toolbar. To choose printing options, follow these steps:

1. Click on the Print button in the application bar, or choose Print from the File menu to display the Print dialog box shown in Figure 4-4.

2. Choose Options from the box.

3. Click on Print.

Pull down the list box in the Print section and choose to print the entire document, the current page, a range of pages, or multiple pages. To print just a range of pages,

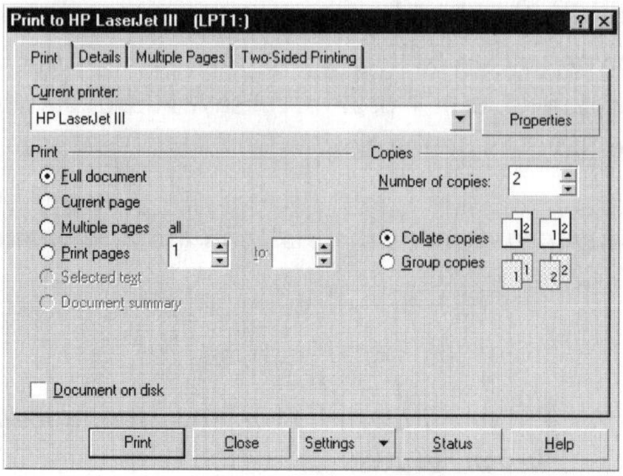

Print
dialog box

FIGURE 4-4

enter the page numbers in the From and To boxes at the Print Range option. You can automatically select to print a range of pages simply by entering numbers in the box.

You can also print sections of multiple pages, or chapters and volumes, depending on how you laid out your document. Pull down the list box in the Print section and choose Multiple Pages, and then click on the Multiple Pages tab of the dialog box. In the box that appears, specify the pages in the Multiple Page(s)/Label(s) text box. Use a hyphen to represent a range of pages, as in 1-6, and a comma to separate individual pages 4, 6, 9. To print from one page to the end of the document, end with a hyphen, such as 10-. Begin with a hyphen to print from the first page to a specific page, as in -5.

To print more than one copy of the document, set the Number of Copies option. If you are printing more than one copy, select how they are collated. Choose Collate when you want each complete set of the document to print separately. Choose Group to print multiple copies of the individual pages.

Select a resolution setting if your printer has more than one setting available. The resolution will have an effect on graphics, but not much on text.

Click on Status to see a list of the documents you printed during the current session, along with the time and date you sent them to the printer and when they began to print, as shown here.

Document	Status	Printed From	Printer	Submit Time	Begin Time
A:\chron.doc	Complete	Corel WordPerf...	HP LaserJet III	2:04:12 PM ...	2:04:12 PM ...
A:\chrono.doc	Complete	Corel WordPerf...	HP LaserJet III	2:00:04 PM ...	2:00:04 PM ...
A:\chrono.doc	Complete	Corel WordPerf...	HP LaserJet III	1:56:37 PM ...	1:56:38 PM ...
Corel Office Document	Complete	Corel WordPerf...	HP LaserJet III	12:11:48 PM...	12:11:48 PM...
Corel Office Document	Complete	Corel WordPerf...	HP LaserJet III	12:07:55 PM...	12:07:56 PM...

The Document Summary option will be dimmed if you do not have a summary attached to the document.

4

NOTE: *You'll learn about the Two-Sided Printing part of this dialog box in Chapter 8.*

If your document does not print accurately, you may have the wrong printer selected. Pull down the Current Printer list and choose your printer. If your printer is not listed, click on the Details tab of the dialog box, click on Add Printer to start the Windows 95 Add Printer Wizard, and follow the directions on the screen.

Starting Another Document

To start a new document when you're still working with another, click on the New Blank Document button—the first button on the left side of the toolbar.

If you already have one document open, it will move to the background. You'll learn how to use multiple document windows in Chapter 5.

Quitting Corel WordPerfect

When you are finished using Corel WordPerfect, choose Exit from the File menu, or click on the Close box on the right of the Corel WordPerfect title bar. If you made any changes to the document since you last saved it, a dialog box will appear asking if you want to save the document before closing. Select Yes to save the document, No not to save it, or Cancel to remain in Corel WordPerfect.

Opening Existing Documents

To edit an existing document that is not already on the screen, you must first open it. When you open a document, Corel WordPerfect recalls it from the disk and displays it in a document window. Opening a document does not remove it from the disk, it just places a copy of it in your computer's memory. If you already have a document on the screen when you open another, Corel WordPerfect opens another window for the new document. The window will appear in the foreground, showing the document you just opened. The other document window will move into the background. The names of both documents appear in the application bar. See Chapter 5 for more information on working with multiple documents.

Because you often work on a document in more than one session, Corel WordPerfect gives you two ways to easily reopen the last documents that you worked on. Once a document is open, you can edit, print, or just read it.

Pull down the File menu. At the bottom of the menu, Corel WordPerfect lists up to the last nine documents that you've opened or saved (see Figure 4-5). Click on the name of the document you want to open.

You can also select New from the File menu, and then click on the Work On tab of the dialog box to display the documents you most recently used. Click on a file

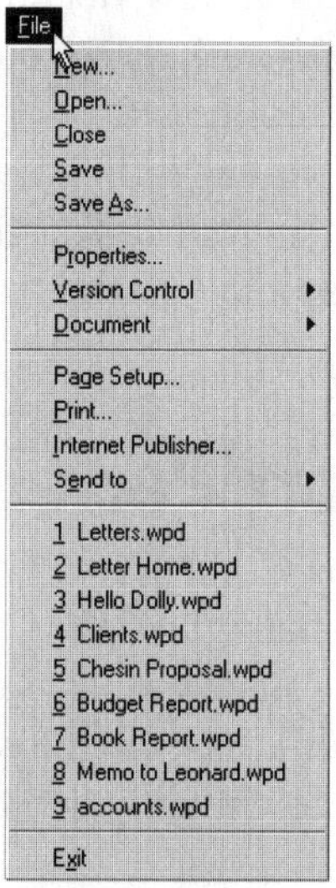

Your last nine documents listed in Corel WordPerfect's File menu

File
New...
Open...
Close
Save
Save As...
Properties...
Version Control ▶
Document ▶
Page Setup...
Print...
Internet Publisher...
Send to ▶
1 Letters.wpd
2 Letter Home.wpd
3 Hello Dolly.wpd
4 Clients.wpd
5 Chesin Proposal.wpd
6 Budget Report.wpd
7 Book Report.wpd
8 Memo to Leonard.wpd
9 accounts.wpd
Exit

FIGURE 4-5

to see a preview of it, or set its checkbox to mark it as a work in progress. Click Open to work on the selected file.

Using the File Open Dialog Box

To open a document not listed in the File menu, you can either click on the Open tool in the toolbar or select Open from the File menu. The Open dialog box will appear. Corel WordPerfect lists files in the MyFiles directory. Double-click on the document you want to open, or highlight its name and then click on Open. Use the navigation tools in the dialog box to find files in other folders and disks.

If you make changes to a document, you must save it again to record the changes to the disk. Click on the Save button in the Standard toolbar or select Save from the File menu. Corel WordPerfect will save it without displaying the Save dialog box. If you want to change its name or folder, select Save As from the File menu.

 In Chapter 13, you'll learn how to open documents created with other programs.

Changing the Document View

When you start Corel WordPerfect, it will be in Page view. This means that you'll see your document as it will appear when you print it. The margin guidelines will show the size of your margins, and you'll see headers, footers, page numbers, graphics, and other elements of your layout.

While Page view shows how your document will look when printed, it has some disadvantages, so Corel WordPerfect gives you three other views: Draft, Two Page, and Web Page. To change the view, pull down the View menu and choose the view you want.

In Draft view, you'll see fonts, graphics, and the left and right margin guidelines, but not headers, footers, page numbers, and the top and bottom page guidelines. It lets you see more lines on the screen than Page view, while still showing most elements of your layout.

Two Page view displays two complete pages onscreen at one time, a useful preview of side-by-side pages. You can still edit and format text in Two Page view, but the text will probably be too small to read.

You use Web Page view to create HTML documents for publishing to the Web. You'll learn more about that in Chapter 7.

Changing the Display Magnification

By default, Corel WordPerfect displays your document about the same size it will be when printed. Changing to Two Page view will reduce the size of the document to two complete pages. If you are in Draft or Page view, you can adjust the magnification as you wish. If you have trouble reading small characters, you can enlarge the display. For example, set magnification at 200% to display your document at twice the printed size. You can also reduce magnification to display more text on the screen than normal, and you can display a full page or more at one time! Changing magnification does not actually change the font size, just how it appears onscreen.

TIP: *You can edit and format your document no matter what magnification you select. And you can change to any view regardless of the magnification.*

There are two ways to change magnification: with the toolbar and the View menu. To select a magnification, pull down the zoom list in the toolbar. You can choose 50%, 75%, 100%, 150%, 200%, Margin Width, Page Width, Full Page, and Other—to set a custom magnification. The Margin Width option sets the magnification so that the lines of text fill the width of the window. Choose Page Width so the full width of the page, including margins, fills the screen.

TIP: *You can access the same options, or enter a specific magnification up to 400%, by selecting Zoom from the View menu.*

Displaying Guidelines and Toolbars

You have several ways to change what appears on the screen. If you want to see as much text as possible, you can remove the toolbar, property bar, and application bar from the screen. Here's how:

1. Pull down the View menu, and click on Toolbars. A dialog box will appear with checkboxes for the toolbar, property bar, and application bar.

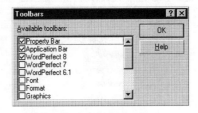

2. Deselect the items you do not want to appear.

3. Click on OK.

To remove all of the bars at one time, select Hide Bars from the View menu, and then click on OK in the dialog box that appears. WordPerfect will remove everything—the menu, scroll, ruler, property, application, and toolbars—except the Windows 95 taskbar. Redisplay all of the bars by pressing ESC.

You can also turn the guidelines on and off. Select Guidelines from the View menu, and then select the view guidelines for tables, margins, columns, and headers and footers.

To quickly show symbols indicating spaces, carriage returns, tabs, centered text, indentations, flush right alignment, and some other formats, choose Show ¶ from the View menu. Select the option again to turn off the display.

NOTE: *In Chapter 6, you will learn how to reveal all of the format codes, and in Chapter 10, you will learn how to further customize the look of Corel WordPerfect.*

Working with Toolbars

Corel WordPerfect comes with 15 different toolbars. Most contain a set of common buttons, such as Save and Print, as well as buttons for performing special functions. To display a different toolbar, point the mouse on the toolbar already on the screen, and then click the right mouse button. You'll see the QuickMenu listing the toolbars that Corel WordPerfect makes available, shown in Figure 4-6. The check mark next to a toolbar name means that the toolbar is being displayed. Click on the name of another toolbar to display—you can only display one at a time.

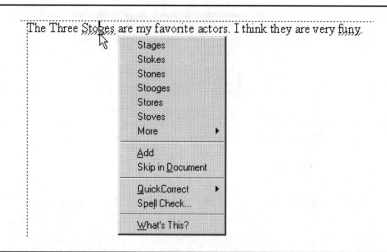

Selecting
a toolbar
from the
QuickMenu

FIGURE 4-6

   **TIP:**   *To hide a toolbar, select Hide Toolbar from the QuickMenu.*

Moving a toolbar is as easy as dragging. Point the mouse to one of the vertical lines between buttons on the toolbar so the pointer appears like a hand. Do not point to a button on the toolbar. Hold down the mouse button and then drag the mouse. As you drag, a gray box representing the toolbar will move along with the pointer. Release the mouse button when the box is where you want the toolbar to appear.

If you drag the toolbar somewhere above the text area, or to the bottom of the screen above the status bar, the buttons on the toolbar will appear in one row, just like the default layout. If you drag the toolbar to the far left or right of the screen, the buttons will be in one column. If you drag the toolbar into the typing area, however, the toolbar will appear as a small window, complete with a title bar and control box, as shown here:

You change the size and shape of the toolbar by dragging one of its borders, just as you can change the size and shape of any window in Windows. Click on the control box to turn off the toolbar. To turn it back on, you'll need to display the Shortcut menu and select the name of the toolbar.

The Edit option on the QuickMenu, by the way, lets you add or delete features from both the toolbar and property bar. The Settings option lets you customize menus, toolbars, and property bars, and even create new ones. Using Settings, for example, you can choose to show icons or text (or both) on the face of buttons, change the type and size of the text, and even create your own toolbar.

You can also right-click on the menu bar and property bar. From the menu bar, you can select from six different menu bars and choose Settings. The QuickMenu from the property bar includes the Edit and Settings options, and you can choose to hide the property bar from display.

 NOTE: *In Chapter 10, you'll learn more about customizing toolbars, menus, and property bars.*

Editing Documents

5

Y ou already know how to edit documents by inserting and deleting text. However, sometimes you have to make major changes, such as moving text from one location to another, or changing a word or phrase that appears several times in the document.

In this chapter, you will learn editing techniques to make your work time as efficient as possible.

Moving and Copying Text

Sometimes you type text only to discover it would be better in a different location in your document. One of the great advantages of Corel WordPerfect is that you can easily move text from one place to another. You can even make a duplicate copy of text in another location. When you *move* text, you delete it from one place in your document and insert it into another location. When you *copy* text, you make a duplicate of selected text and place the copy in another location—the text in the original location is not affected.

 In Chapter 13, you will learn how to share Corel WordPerfect text with other applications.

Moving and Copying Text with Drag-and-Drop

Using the mouse, you can easily copy and move text using a method called *drag and drop*. This means that you drag the selected text to where you want to insert it, and then release the mouse button to drop it into place.

 NOTE: *Later in this chapter you will learn how to drag and drop text between open documents using the application bar.*

Use the mouse to select the text you wish to move, and then point anywhere in the selected area. Press and hold down the mouse button, and then drag the mouse to where you want to insert the text. As you drag the mouse, a small box and the insertion point will accompany the pointer:

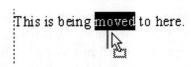

Release the mouse button when the dotted insertion point is where you want the text to appear.

If you want to *copy* text rather than move it, press and hold down the CTRL key while you release the mouse button. When you hold down CTRL, a plus sign will appear with the pointer, confirming that you are making a copy of the text:

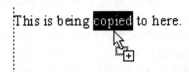

 NOTE: *You do not have to hold down the CTRL key while you are dragging, only when you release the button.*

You can use drag and drop to move or copy text anywhere in the document, even in areas that have scrolled off the screen. When you drag the pointer past the top or bottom of the window, the screen will scroll automatically.

If you change your mind about moving the text while you are dragging, just move the pointer back to the selected text and then release the button. If you've already dropped the text and then change your mind, use the Undo command from the Edit menu, or click on the Undo button in the toolbar.

Dragging with the Right Button

If you drag selected text with the *right* mouse button instead of the left, you'll be able to make some decisions about the effects of drag and drop. When you release the mouse, you'll see these options:

■ Move Here

■ Copy Here

■ Move Here without Font/Attributes

■ Copy Here without Font/Attributes

You can then choose to either move or copy the text—without worrying about the CTRL key—and whether you want to insert the text without its formats. Normally when you insert text, it retains the same formats it had in its original position. If you choose to insert it without its fonts and attributes, the text takes on the same formats of the text where you insert it.

Moving and Copying Text Through the Clipboard

The *Clipboard* is an area in the computer's memory where Windows 95 temporarily stores information. You can place text into the Clipboard and later take it from the Clipboard to insert elsewhere. When you move text using the Clipboard, it's called *cut and paste*—you cut the text from one location and paste it elsewhere. When you copy text with the Clipboard, it's called copy and paste—you make a copy of the text and then paste it elsewhere.

To move text using cut and paste, first select the text you want to move. Then cut the text into the Clipboard by clicking on the Cut button in the toolbar. The selected text is now in the Clipboard. You can also cut text to the Clipboard by using one of these techniques:

- Select Cut from the Edit menu.
- Press CTRL-X.
- Select Cut from the QuickMenu that appears when you click the right mouse on the selected text.

Next, place the insertion point where you want to insert the text. Then paste it into the document by clicking on the Paste button. Word will insert whatever is in the Clipboard into the document. You can also paste the contents of the Clipboard using one of these techniques:

■ Select Paste from the Edit menu.

■ Press CTRL-V to insert the text with its fonts and attributes.

■ Press CTRL-SHIFT-V to insert the text without its fonts and attributes.

■ Select Paste or Paste without Font /Attributes from the QuickMenu that appears when you right-click.

 TIP: *The Paste option will be dimmed in the Shortcut menu if no text is in the Clipboard.*

To *copy* text rather than move it, follow the same steps as above but click on the Copy button. You can also select Copy from the Edit menu, press CTRL-C, or select Copy from the QuickMenu.

Normally, Windows can store only one thing at a time in the Clipboard. So think about the consequences. If you cut some text in preparation for moving it, and then absentmindedly cut or copy something else, the text you want to move is erased from the Clipboard. Click on the Undo button twice to restore both cut portions of text, and then start over. If you do want to add text to what is already on the Clipboard, select the text and then choose Append from the Edit menu.

The contents of the Clipboard will remain there until you cut or copy something else, or until you exit Windows. This means that you can insert the same text over and over again in your document, as long as you do not cut or copy something else. To insert the Clipboard contents in multiple locations, just position the insertion point and select Paste at each spot.

Inserting with QuickWords

In Chapter 2, you learned how to use QuickCorrect to quickly insert text or expand abbreviations. QuickCorrect is useful because sometimes you find yourself writing the same word or phase over and over again. You may repeat it several times in one document, or use the same phrase in a number of documents that you write. It's not bad if you have to repeat a small word several times. But imagine having to repeat a complex scientific or medical term, or the full name of some company or government agency. Sure, you could copy the word and then paste it where you want it. But then the word would be deleted from the Clipboard if you had to cut or copy something else.

While QuickCorrect is handy, however, it does have two drawbacks.

First, QuickCorrect always inserts text in the same format as the text it is expanding. Suppose you create a QuickCorrect entry by selecting a boldfaced underlined phrase. When QuickCorrect later inserts the phrase for you, it will take on the current format.

Second, QuickCorrect is always automatic. Suppose you create a QuickCorrect entry to replace the state abbreviation CA with California. Just imagine your chemistry teacher's response when every reference to calcium (which is abbreviated CA) in your report is printed as "California" instead. You can turn off QuickCorrect, but then it wouldn't make any of the corrections for you.

You can solve both of these problems by using QuickWords. With QuickWords you have the option of inserting any amount of text, formatted or plain, automatically or manually. Use QuickWords when you frequently use a word, phrase, or even a long section of text in a specific format, but you do not want it to be replaced automatically. You can then insert a word, phrase, or entire section of text by typing the abbreviation. You can use QuickWords to insert your name and address, for your telephone number, for standard closings, or for anything that you want to insert easily and quickly.

To create a QuickWord, first type, format, and select the text you want to assign to an abbreviation, and then click on the QuickWords button in the property bar (it only appears when text is selected), or choose QuickWords from the Tools menu. Try it now by typing your full name in a new document window. Select your name, and then choose QuickWords from the Tools menu to display the dialog box shown in Figure 5-1, listing any QuickWords that you've already created.

In the Abbreviated Form box, type your initials—the abbreviation you want to represent your name.

Notice the checkbox labeled "Expand QuickWords when you type them." When this box is checked, WordPerfect expands your QuickWords just as it does QuickCorrect entries. If you deselect this box, you have the option of expanding the word when you type it.

Click Add Entry to add the abbreviation to the list and close the dialog box.

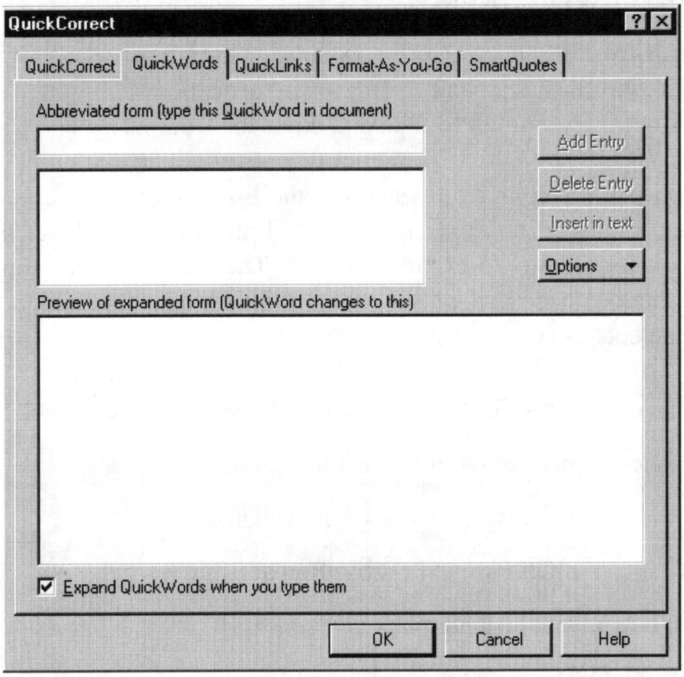

QuickCorrect   ? X

QuickCorrect | QuickWords | QuickLinks | Format-As-You-Go | SmartQuotes |

Abbreviated form (type this QuickWord in document)

[   ]   [Add Entry]

[   ]   [Delete Entry]

                                              [Insert in text]

                                              [Options ▼]

Preview of expanded form (QuickWord changes to this)

[   ]

☑ Expand QuickWords when you type them

[OK]   [Cancel]   [Help]

The
QuickWords
dialog box

■ **FIGURE 5-1**

If you set QuickWords to expand words as you type them, it will automatically expand the abbreviation when you press ENTER, the SPACEBAR, or TAB, just as QuickCorrect does. If you deselected the checkbox, when you want to enter the word, type the abbreviation for it and press CTRL-SHIFT-A. Corel WordPerfect will replace the abbreviation with the complete word or phrase. If you did not deselect the box, QuickWords will expand it automatically.

NOTE: *QuickWord names are not case sensitive.*

If you forget what abbreviations you used, or you want to delete one, select QuickWords from the Insert menu, and click on it in the list. The full text will appear in the Preview panel. To add the word to the document, click on Insert in Text.

NOTE: *Refer to Chapter 2 to refresh your memory about QuickCorrect and Format-As-You-Go.*

QuickWord Options

By default, WordPerfect inserts the expanded QuickWord in the same format it was created in. This is the Expand as Text With Formatting setting. If you want to insert QuickWords in the current format, pull down the Options list and choose Expand as Plain Text.

When you select an abbreviation in the list, you can also choose the Rename Entry and Replace Entry options. Rename Entry lets you change the abbreviation that you want to enter to expand the item. The Replace Entry command lets you change the expanded text that is associated with an abbreviation. Here's how to replace an entry:

1. Select the new text you want the abbreviation to represent.

2. Select QuickWords from the Tools menu.

3. Click the abbreviation you want to change.

4. Pull down Options and choose Replace Entry.

5. Click Yes in the dialog box that appears.

6. Click OK to close the QuickWords dialog box.

Inserting QuickLinks

A QuickLink is a word or phrase that Corel WordPerfect automatically converts into a hyperlink to a site on the World Wide Web. When you click on a hyperlink, Windows starts your Web browser, makes the connection, and opens the site named in the link.

To see the QuickLinks already defined, select either QuickCorrect or QuickWords from the Tools menu, and then click on the QuickLinks tab to see the dialog box in Figure 5-2.

The list shows the QuickLink words, along with the Web sites they are linked to. You can insert the link into your document by choosing it in the list and then clicking on the Insert Entry button. You can also simply type the QuickLink word into the document, starting with the @ symbol. If you type @yahoo, for example, QuickLinks converts the word into a link to http://www.yahoo.com. When you point to the link, the mouse pointer appears like a pointing hand, and a QuickStatus box appears showing you the Web address. Click on the link to make the connection.

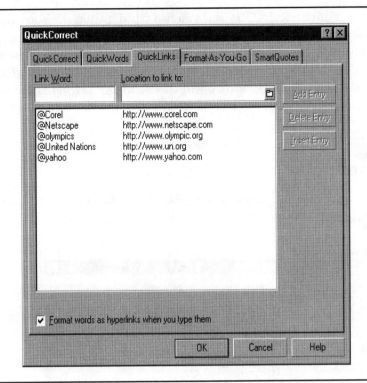

QuickLinks
to the
Internet

FIGURE 5-2

You can also add your own QuickLink words and Web sites. In the appropriate text boxes in the QuickLink tab, type the link word and the location to link it to, and then click on Add Entry.

TIP: *Corel WordPerfect will convert any text in the format, www.something.something, into a QuickLink.*

Inserting the Date and Time

You probably add the date to letters, memos, and faxes. You might even add the time to faxes, logs, journals, messages, and other documents when the time of distribution or printing is important. Rather than manually typing the date or time, have Corel WordPerfect do it for you.

You can enter the date and time in two ways—as text or as a code. When you have Corel WordPerfect insert the date or time as *text*, Corel WordPerfect enters it as a series of characters, just as if you had typed it yourself. You can edit or delete individual characters, just as you can edit any text that you've typed.

When you have Corel WordPerfect insert the date or time as a *code*, however, you will see the date or time appear on the screen, but Corel WordPerfect has actually entered a code. The date or time will change to the current date or time whenever you open or print the document. You can't edit the date or time itself.

    TIP: *Press CTRL-D to insert the date as text, or SHIFT-CTRL-D to insert it as code.*

To insert the date or time, select Date/Time from the Insert menu to see this dialog box:

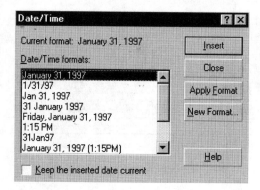

Scroll the Date/Time Formats list and click on the format for the date or time you want to insert. To insert the date or time as a code, check the Keep the Inserted Date Current checkbox. Finally, click on Insert to add the date to the document.

Changing Date Formats

Once you enter the date as text, you have to edit it yourself or reinsert it if you want to use a different format. If you change your mind about the format of a date code, however, you can have WordPerfect change it for you.

Place the insertion point just before the date, and then display the Date/Time dialog box. Choose the new format that you want and click on the Apply Format button. WordPerfect automatically reformats dates entered as codes that follow the insertion point.

Custom Date Formats

If none of the formats suits your tastes, you can create your own. Click on New Format in the Date/Time dialog box to see the options in Figure 5-3.

The currently used format will appear in the Edit Date/Time Format text box, shown as a series of codes. A sample date in that format is displayed. To change a format, you must enter codes that represent the year, month, day, and time. All of the possible codes are shown in the list boxes in the four pages of the dialog box. Select a code from the list, and then click on Insert to add it to the Edit Date/Time Format text box. A preview of how the format displays a date appears in the Date/time sample box.

Inserting Other Useful Objects

In addition to inserting the date, you can insert the name of the file and other items into a document. These may not be used as often as the date, but they are handy when you need them, even in headers, footers, and captions. Pull down the Insert menu and point to Other to access these options:

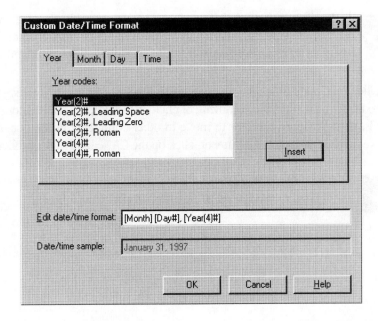

Creating your own date or time format

FIGURE 5-3

- *Filename* inserts the name of the current document. Nothing will appear if you have not named it yet—the default Document1 name, for example, will not be inserted.

- *Path and Filename* inserts the complete path as well as the name. The path is the location of the folder in which the document is stored, starting from the root directory of the disk drive.

- *Counter* inserts codes to consecutively number figures, tables, and other objects.

- *BarCode* inserts a POSTNET bar code. A dialog box will appear for you to enter the ZIP code.

Inserting Comments

A *comment* is an annotation, a note, reminder, or reference that you want to place in the document but not print along with it. It is a handy way to record reminders to yourself and explanations to others who may be reading or editing your document. To insert a comment, pull down the Insert menu and point to Comment to see the options Create, Edit, and Convert to Text.

 TIP: *To convert existing text into a comment, select the text, and then click on the New Comment button in the Selected Text property bar. The text will be removed from the document and inserted into the comment.*

Click on Create to display the Comment window, shown in Figure 5-4. Now type the text that you want in the comment, or click on the Property Bar buttons to add your initials, name, date, or time, or to move to other comments in the document. When you've finished writing the comment, click on the Close icon in the property bar.

 NOTE: *Corel WordPerfect will only display your initials or name if they are defined as part of the Corel WordPerfect environment.*

Comment window

Comment property bar

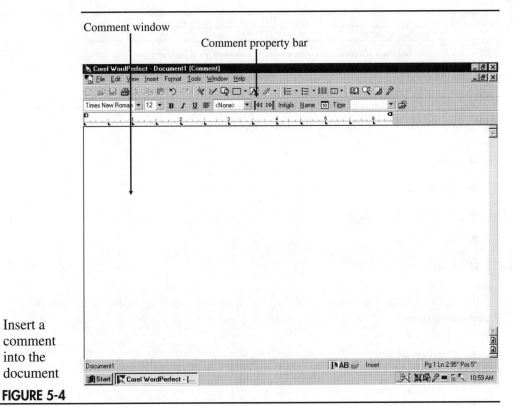

Insert a
comment
into the
document

FIGURE 5-4

You'll see your initials in a small box in the margin, or a Comment icon if your initials are not in the environment:

Comment initials

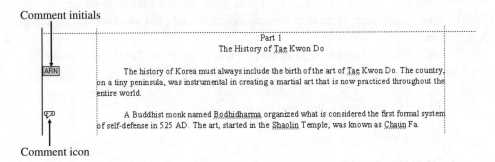

Comment icon

To read a comment, click on it with the mouse. The comment will appear as a balloon near the text.

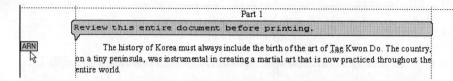

There are two different comment QuickMenus. The menu that appears when you right-click on the Comment icon has these options:

- Cut

- Copy

- Delete

- What's This?

- Edit

The QuickMenu that appears when you right-click on the displayed comment has these options:

- Convert to Text

- Delete

- What's This?

- Edit

To edit a comment in its own window, double-click on the icon, or display the QuickMenu and click on Edit. Edit it as you wish, and then click on Close.

To print a comment, open it in the Edit window and click on the Print button in the toolbar.

To convert a comment to regular text so it appears normally in your document, use the following steps:

1. Place the insertion point after the comment.

2. Pull down the Insert menu.

3. Point to Comment.

4. Click on Convert to Text.

You can also click on the comment to display it, and then right-click on the displayed comment and select Convert to Text.

To delete a comment, right-click on it and select Delete from the QuickMenu.

Setting Bookmarks

A *bookmark* marks your place in the document. Like a bookmark in a book, it allows you to quickly return to a specific location. You can add any number of bookmarks in a document, giving each a name, so you can return to a specific location later on. You can also create a QuickMark, which lets you return to a position with two clicks of the mouse, and you can set up Corel WordPerfect to automatically set a QuickMark at the last position of the insertion point when you save the document.

To create a bookmark, place the insertion point where you want the bookmark to be set. Corel WordPerfect will associate the bookmark with that location of the insertion point. If you want the bookmark to be linked to text, select the text before creating the bookmark. Then pull down the Tools menu and click on Bookmark to display the dialog box in Figure 5-5. Click on Create. In the box that appears, type a name for the bookmark and click on OK.

 TIP: *When text is selected, set a bookmark by pulling down the Hyperlink button in the property bar and selecting Insert Bookmark.*

To return to a bookmark position, select Bookmark from the Tools menu, click on the bookmark name in the list, and then click on Go To. If the bookmark is associated with selected text, click on Go To & Select. Corel WordPerfect will move to the text and select it.

You can also set one QuickMark in a document. This is a bookmark that you do not have to name. Use these steps:

1. Place the insertion point at the position you want to mark—or select the text.

2. Display the Bookmark dialog box.

3. Click on Set QuickMark.

4. To return to that position, select Find QuickMark from the dialog box.

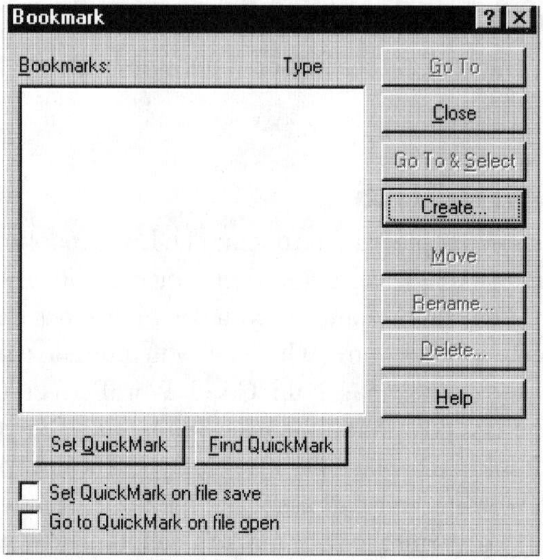

Creating a
bookmark

FIGURE 5-5

One of the best uses for a QuickMark is to set your place when you save the document, so you can start where you left off when you next open the document. To have WordPerfect do this automatically, select the two checkboxes at the bottom of the Bookmark dialog box. One box sets the QuickMark when you save the document, while the other sets WordPerfect to move to the bookmark position when you open the document.

Other options on the dialog box let you delete, rename, and move a bookmark. Moving a bookmark associates an existing bookmark with a new location or selected text.

We'll look at inserting sounds and other items in later chapters.

Finding and Replacing Text

The Find and Replace command can be a real time-saver. Suppose you're looking for a specific reference in your document but you're not sure exactly where it is. Instead of scanning through the entire document, with a chance that you'll miss it, let Corel WordPerfect locate the text for you. The Replace part of the command can even replace text that it locates, so you can quickly correct an error in several locations, or change one word to another every place it is used.

You can also find a word by example, a new feature of Corel WordPerfect 8. Let's look at that option first.

Using QuickFind

QuickFind lets you place the insertion point in a word that's already in the document, then quickly move to the next or previous occurrence of the same word. You can use this technique to simply find a word, or to move through a document applying the same formats or style to each occurrence of a word.

TIP: *To use QuickFind to locate the first occurrence of a word, just type the word at the start of the document, and then use the Find Next command.*

Here's how to use this new feature.

1. Click anywhere in the word that you want to locate. To locate an entire phrase, select the phrase first.

2. Click on the QuickFind Next button.

Corel WordPerfect locates and highlights the next occurrence of the word or phrase. You can now edit, delete, or format the word as you want. Click the button again to find the next occurrence, or click the QuickFind Previous button to locate words toward the start of the document.

Finding Text

Both the Find and the Replace functions are in the same dialog box (Figure 5-6), displayed when you select Find and Replace from the Edit menu.

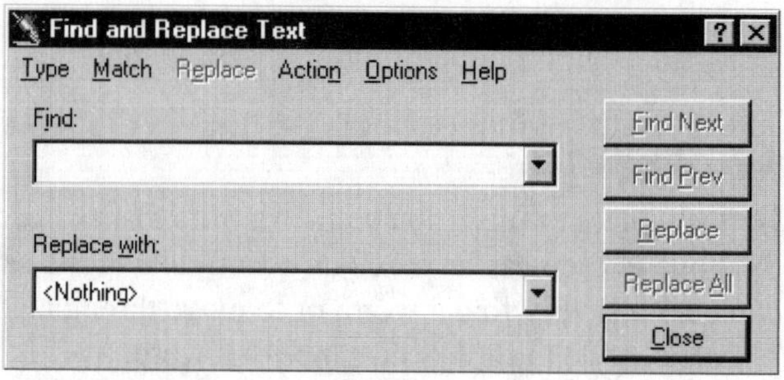

Find and
Replace
dialog box

FIGURE 5-6

The Find command scans your document looking for the first occurrence of the word or phrase that you specify. After it finds the word or phrase, you can repeat the command to find the next occurrence, and so on, until your entire document has been searched. It is similar to using find-by-example, except you can also specify formats in order to find text that's in a specific font, size, or style.

Corel WordPerfect starts looking for text at the current location of the insertion point. If you want to make sure that the entire document is searched, move to the start of the document. Pull down the Edit menu, and select Find and Replace to display the dialog box. In the Find What box, type the characters you want to locate. Corel WordPerfect saves your last ten search phrases. To select one, pull down the list on the right of the Find text box, and click on the word you want to locate.

NOTE: *If you performed a find-by-example, the searched text will appear in the Find What text box of the Find and Replace Text box.*

Then click on Find Next. Corel WordPerfect will select the next occurrence of the text following the insertion point. To locate text above the insertion point, click on Find Prev. The Find dialog box will remain on the screen so you can find the next occurrence by clicking on Find Next again. If the text is not found, a dialog box appears with the message "Not Found." Select OK or press ENTER to remove the message, leaving the insertion point in its original position.

Corel WordPerfect will locate the characters you search for even if they are part of another word. Searching for the word "love," for example, will select the characters in the word "lovely." You can customize how Corel WordPerfect locates text using the Find and Replace menu bar.

The Match menu, for example, determines what is considered a match. The options are

- *Whole Word* locates just whole words that match the text you are looking for. If you are looking for "love," it will not match with "lovely."

- *Case* matches only characters in the same case. By default, searches are not case sensitive, so looking for *love* will locate *LOVE*.

- *Font* lets you choose a specific font, so you can look for a word only if it is in Times Roman, for example.

- *Codes* lets you search for a formatting code, or a specific format of text. Use it, for example, to locate any text that is centered, or a specific centered word.

The Action menu determines what happens when Corel WordPerfect locates a match. The options in the menu are

- *Select Match* highlights the located text.

- *Position Before* places the insertion point before the text.

- *Position After* places the insertion point after the text.

- *Extend Selection* selects all of the text from the current location of the insertion point to the located text.

The Options menu determines the way the search operates. The options are

- *Begin Find at Top of Document* starts searching from the beginning of the document regardless of the insertion point position.

- *Wrap at Beg./End of Document* continues at the beginning of the document when Corel WordPerfect reaches the end and you did not start at the beginning. If you search using Find Prev, Corel WordPerfect will wrap to the end when it reaches the start.

- *Limit Find Within Selection* searches only the currently selected portion of text.

- *Include Headers, Footers, etc. In Find* searches for the text in headers, footers, and all document elements, even those not displayed.

- *Limit Number of Changes* will make only a specific number of replacements that you specify, when using the Replace All command.

The Type menu determines what Corel WordPerfect looks for. The default setting is Text. You can also select Word Forms and Specific Codes. If you want to locate all forms of a word, such as "drink," "drank," and "drunk," pull down the Type option and click on Word Forms. Type one form of the verb and then click on Find Next. For example, searching for "sing" with this option selected will locate "sing," "sang," and "sung." The Specific Code option lets you search for a code that has specific settings, such as a certain indentation or margin.

Replacing Text Automatically

Making a mistake is only human, but making the same mistake more than once is downright annoying. Have you ever typed a document only to discover that you've made the same mistake several times? The Replace part of Find and Replace will search your document to find text automatically and replace it with something else. You can use it not only to correct errors, but also to recycle documents. Perhaps you created a sales proposal that mentions a person's name in several places. You may be able to modify the proposal for another prospect by changing just one or two words several times. You can have Corel WordPerfect scan the entire document, automatically replacing "Mr. Smith" with "Mrs. Jones." It just takes a few keystrokes.

To replace text automatically, use these steps:

1. Move the insertion point to the location where you want the replacements to begin.

2. Choose Find and Replace from the Edit menu.

3. In the Find box, enter the text that you want to replace.

4. In the Replace With box, enter the text that you want to insert. When you click in the Replace With box, the notation <Nothing> will disappear.

CAUTION: *Selecting Replace or Replace All when <Nothing> is in the Replace With box will delete the located text.*

The Replace operation will first locate the text that you want to replace, so you should select options from the menus to specify how you want the Find part of the operation to proceed. In fact, the options and the Find What text will be the same as you selected in the last Find operation. If you only want to replace the text when it appears as a whole word, for example, pull down the Match list and select Whole Word. The Match list will only be selectable when you are in the Find text box.

When you are in the Replace With text box, you can pull down the Replace list to select these options:

- *Case* toggles case-sensitive replacing on and off.

- *Font* replaces text formatted a specific way.

- *Code* lets you choose a code to insert.

Confirming Replacements

You might not want to replace every occurrence of the text in the document. For example, suppose you refer to the titles of two persons in your document. You call Mrs. Jones the President, and you refer to Mr. Smith as Vice President. After completing the letter, you learn that Mrs. Jones's correct title is Chairperson. Can you use Replace All to change every occurrence of President to Chairperson? Not really. If you do, you would change Mr. Smith's title to Vice Chairperson.

When you do not want to replace every occurrence of the text, use the Find Next and Replace buttons. Click on Find Next to locate and select the next occurrence of the text following the insertion point. (Use Find Previous to locate text above the insertion point.) To replace the selected text, click on Replace. Corel WordPerfect will make the replacement and then automatically locate and select the next occurrence. If you want to leave the text as it is and locate the next occurrence, click on Find Next again.

Automatic Replacements

If you feel confident that you want to replace every occurrence of the text, click on the Replace All button. Corel WordPerfect will scan the document making the replacements for you. Use this option with caution. Remember, the default Find and Replace settings ignore case and locate characters even if they are part of another word. With these settings, replacing every occurrence of the text could unintentionally change parts of other words. Changing "his" to "her" would also change "history" to "hertory" and "Buddhism" to "Buddherm."

To safeguard against these types of errors, either confirm each replacement or use the Match Case and Match Whole Words options.

Finding and Replacing Formats and Codes

Sometimes you want to find information that you cannot type into the Find What box. For example, suppose you want to find a word, but only when it is in italic format. You must tell Corel WordPerfect not only what text to locate but also its format.

 NOTE: *You will learn about codes in Chapter 6.*

In the Find text box, enter the text that you want to find. Then, pull down the Match list and click on Font to display the dialog box shown in Figure 5-7. To search for text in a certain font and style, pull down the Font list and choose the font, and then select the style in the Font Style list. To search for text in a specific point size,

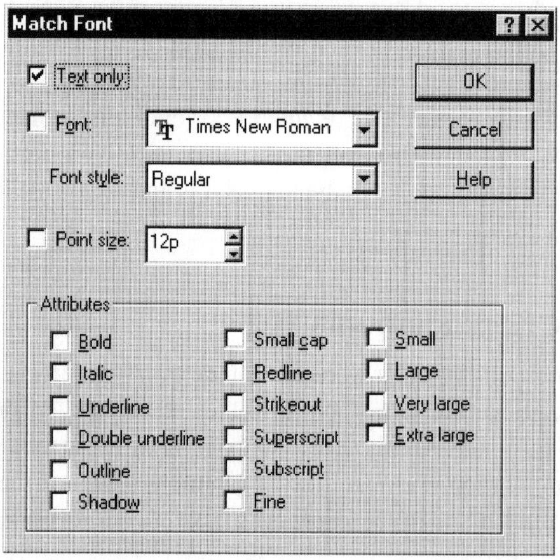

Selecting
formats and
codes to
locate

FIGURE 5-7

choose the size in the Point Size list. In the Attributed section, choose any other font formats that must be applied to the text.

 TIP: *To later search for text without considering its format, click on Text Only.*

When you replace the text, it will appear in the same font as that replaced. To apply other formats to the replaced text, click on the Replace With box, pull down the Replace list, and click on Font. Now select the formats that you want applied to the new text. The dialog box shows the formats you are locating and replacing, as follows:

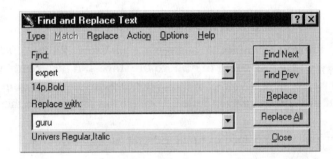

To find just a code, such as a tab or paragraph mark, click on the Find text box, pull down the Match menu, and click on Codes to see this dialog box:

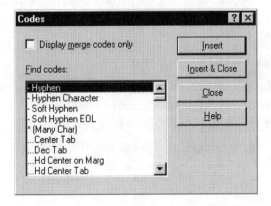

Scroll the list and choose the code that you want to locate. (Codes that cannot be inserted in place of others will be dimmed.) If you do not want to replace the code with another, click on Insert to add the code to the Find text box, and close the dialog box. If you want to replace the code with another, click on the Replace With text box. Then choose the code in the dialog box and click on Insert & Close.

 TIP: *If you are not sure what code to select, use the Reveal Codes feature to see how the code is named for the format you want to find or replace.*

There are other codes that have specific settings. For example, if you choose to replace a Margins code, you have to designate the margin settings. In either the Find or Replace With box, pull down the Type menu, and click on Specific Codes. In the box that appears, select the code you want to find or replace, and then click on OK. A dialog box will appear where you can select or set the exact value.

Replacing All Word Forms

The Word Forms feature will locate and replace all forms of a word. For example, suppose you typed **He was going to walk to the store, but he already walked ten miles**. You now realize that you want the sentence to read **He was going to run to the store, but he already ran ten miles**. To make the changes, use these steps:

1. Select Find and Replace from the Edit menu.

2. Type **walk** in the Find text box.

3. Pull down the Type menu and click on Word Forms. If the word in the Find box cannot be found in Corel WordPerfect's dictionary, a warning box will appear. Click on OK to clear the warning box and enter another word or turn off Word Forms.

4. In the Replace With box, type **run**.

5. Click on Replace All. Corel WordPerfect will highlight the word "walk" in the sentence and display this dialog box asking which form of the replacement word you want to insert:

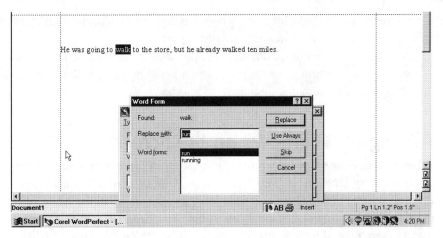

6. Click on Replace With to use the suggested "run." Corel WordPerfect will select the word "walked" and display the Word Form dialog box with the choices "run" and "ran."

7. Click on "ran" and then on Replace With.

8. Click on Close to close the Find and Replace dialog box.

NOTE: *The Use Always button in the Word Form dialog box will automatically use the same selection for all replacements. The Skip option leaves the work unchanged.*

Using Multiple Documents and Windows

Corel WordPerfect lets you have more than one document open at the same time, so you can move and copy text between documents as easily as you can within a document. For example, suppose you are on a tight deadline and you are trying to complete an important report. You realize that you need to refer to a letter that you wrote last month. With Corel WordPerfect, there's no need to rummage through your file cabinets. Just open the letter in its own window on the Corel WordPerfect screen so you can refer to it as you work on your report.

Because the names of all documents appear in the application bar, you can tell at a glance what documents are open, switch between them with a click, and even drag and drop text from one document to another.

Arranging Windows on the Screen

When you open a second document, it appears in the foreground and its name is added to the application bar. The first document is moved into the background behind the new document window. To switch from one document to the other, just click on the document's name in the application bar. You can also pull down the Window menu to see a list of the documents, and click on the one you want to display.

It is much easier to work with multiple documents, however, when you can see them both on the screen. To arrange windows on the screen, pull down the Window menu. Select Cascade to display all open windows overlapped, as shown in Figure 5-8. Select Tile Top to Bottom to display each window stacked vertically, one above

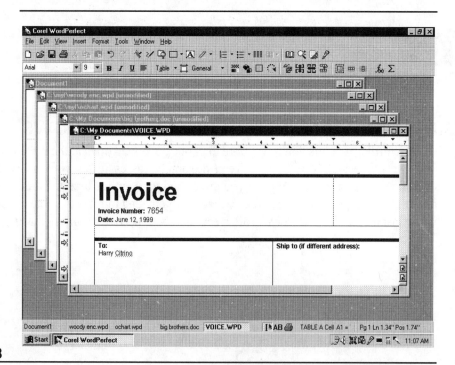

Cascaded
windows

FIGURE 5-8

the other. Choose Tile Side to Side to arrange the windows horizontally, next to each other. To edit or format the text in a window, click in it to make it active. The active window will contain scroll bars and the ruler, if it is turned on. Inactive windows do not have scrolls or rulers, and their title bars are dimmed.

When you want to display a window full screen, click on its Maximize button. To close a window, click on its Close button. The active window will be the one affected by options you select in the menu bar and toolbar. If you click on the Print button, for example, only the document in the active window will be printed.

Moving Text Between Documents

You can move and copy text from one open document to another whether or not they are displayed at the same time. Because of the application bar, you can drag and drop text between documents even when both are not displayed.

To drag and drop text from one displayed window to another, select the text, point to it with the mouse, hold down the mouse button, and drag the selected text to the other window. When you release the mouse button, the window to which you dragged the text will be active. Remember to hold down the CTRL key if you want to copy the text rather than move it.

To drag and drop text to a document in the background, use this technique.

1. Select the text that you want to move.

2. Drag the text to the name of the other document on the application bar. The document will open.

3. Continue dragging in the now-open document to the location where you want to place the text.

4. Release the mouse. Remember, hold down the CTRL key when you release the mouse to copy the text rather than move it.

If you have difficulty dragging text between windows, you can also move and copy text using the Clipboard. Switch to the window containing the text you want to move or copy. Select the text and then click on either the Cut or the Copy button in the toolbar. Switch to the window containing the document where you want to place the text, and then click on the Paste button in the toolbar.

You can also use the Clipboard to copy or move text to a new document, or to an existing document that you have not yet opened. After you cut or copy the text to the Clipboard, click on New to start a new document or open an existing one. Then position the insertion point and click on the Paste button.

Once you cut or copy text into the Clipboard, you can close the document that it came from. The document does not have to be open for you to paste the Clipboard contents elsewhere. If you forget what you've placed in the Clipboard, open a new document and click on Paste to display the contents of the Clipboard.

Inserting a File into a Document

Use drop and drag, or the Clipboard, to move or copy text from one document to another. You don't really even have to open a document if you want to copy all of it into another document.

To insert one entire document into the open document, place the insertion point where you want to insert the contents, and then select File from the Insert menu. Corel WordPerfect will display the Insert File dialog box, which is similar to the Open dialog box. Select the document that you want to insert, and then click on OK. Corel WordPerfect inserts the document using the page layout setting of the active document. You can now edit the inserted text, just as if it were originally part of the document.

Changing the Case of Characters

Did you type a title and then decide it would be better all uppercase? Pretty annoying, isn't it? Rather than retype everything, quickly change the case of existing characters using the Edit menu. To change the case of text, start by selecting the text, and then point to Convert Case in the Edit menu. Click on Uppercase, Lowercase, or Initial Capitals. The Initial Capitals option, by the way, changes the first letter of every word to capital except articles, prepositions, and certain other words when they do not start or end the sentence.

Repeating Actions

Sometimes you want to repeat an action a specific number of times in succession. For example, suppose you want to insert a row of 78 asterisks across the screen, or paste 10 copies of the contents of the Clipboard. The Repeat Next Action option from the Edit menu lets you repeat one action the number of times you specify. It will repeat a single keystroke, cursor movement, or a selection from the toolbar or power bar that is activated by a single click of the mouse.

When you want to repeat a keystroke, pull down the Edit menu and select Repeat Next Action to display this dialog box:

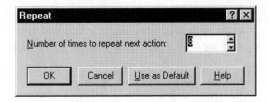

By default, your next keystroke after closing the box will be performed eight times. To repeat it a different number of times, enter the number in the text box. If you want that number to be the new default, click on the Use as Default button.

Then click on OK, and enter the keystroke or use the command that you want to repeat, such as typing an asterisk or clicking on the Paste button.

Highlighting Text

You've no doubt seen, or used, those transparent highlighting pens. When you want to mark an important word or phrase in a textbook, for example, you draw over it with a colored highlighting pen. This emphasizes the text, so you can quickly find it when scanning over the pages. You can use the Corel WordPerfect Highlight tool to do the same thing. You can even choose a color and print the highlight with the document.

To highlight text, select it and then click on the Highlight tool in the toolbar. You can also click on the Highlight tool first, before selecting text, so the mouse pointer changes to the same icon that is on the face of the button. Then drag over the text you want to highlight. When you release the mouse button, the text will be covered with the highlighting color. The Highlight function will remain on after you release the mouse button, however, so you can continue highlighting other text. This way you can scan through a document, highlighting text as you find it. To stop highlighting, click on the Highlight tool again.

Corel WordPerfect gives you several ways to remove highlighting from text. To quickly do so, click anywhere in a section of the highlighted area and click on the Highlight tool. If you want to remove the color from just part of a highlighted section, such as one word in a highlighted sentence, select the text first and then click on the Highlight tool. To remove the highlight from nonconsecutive highlighted areas, select all of the text, and then pull down the Tools menu, point to Highlight, and click on Remove.

By default, the highlight color is yellow. To select another color, pull down the list associated with the Highlight button and select from the color palette that appears. You can also pull down the Tools menu, point to Highlight, and click on Color to see this dialog box:

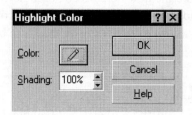

Click on the box containing the color sample to display a palette of 256 colors. Click on the color you want to use. You can also choose a shading for various degrees of the selected color. Choosing 50%, for example, prints the color in half of its intensity.

For even more choices, click on the More button at the bottom of the color palette to see the dialog box shown in Figure 5-9. Use this box to create custom colors by mixing red, green, and blue. If you pull down the Color Model list, you can also choose HLS to mix by hue, lightness, and saturation, or choose CYMK to mix cyan, yellow, magenta, and black.

TIP: *You can also display this dialog box to select colors for other Corel WordPerfect formats.*

The color you choose will now be used as the default when you click on the Highlight tool—until you select another color. However, the color on the Highlight tool itself will remain yellow.

When you print your document, what you see is what you get. If you have a color printer, the highlight will print in the same color it is on the screen. If you have a

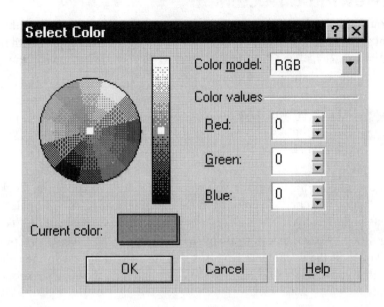

Creating
custom
highlight
colors

FIGURE 5-9

monochrome printer, highlights will print in shades of gray. To hide the highlighting
so it does not appear onscreen or when printed, pull down the Tools menu, point to
Highlight, and click on Print/Show Highlighting. Use the same options to later
redisplay the highlight.

Tracking Document Revisions

If you are working on a document with other authors, or editors, you can keep track
of revisions. You'll be able to see at a glance the text that someone else added or
thinks should be deleted. The changes each person makes are shown in a different
color, so you can tell who made the changes. This is especially helpful when you
use the Workflow feature to transmit your document across the network. You can
then go through the document, quickly moving to each edited section, and accept or
reject individual edits, or all that appear.

How you use this feature depends on whether you are the author or a reviewer.

Reviewing a Document

If you are reviewing a document written by someone else, pull down the File menu, point to Document, and click on Review. A dialog box will appear with two options: Author and Reviewer. Click on Reviewer to display the Reviewer pane at the top of the document, as shown in Figure 5-10.

 NOTE: *If you have not yet entered your name or initials into the Corel WordPerfect environment, a dialog box will appear that gives you the opportunity.*

First, choose the color that you want your editing to appear in. Click on the Set Color button and choose a color from the palette that appears. (The palette also has a Palette button that you can click on to mix your own personal colors.) The name and colors used by other reviewers, if any, will be listed in the Other User Colors box.

Now edit the document. Text that you insert will appear in the selected color. Text that you delete will change to the color and appear with a strikeout line.

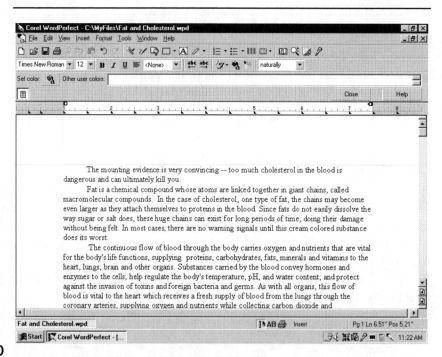

Reviewing
a document

FIGURE 5-10

NOTE: *Click on the Show/Hide Changes button on the lower left of the Reviewer pane to temporarily remove text you deleted and show your inserted text in the normal text color.*

When you have finished reviewing, click on the Close button in the Reviewer pane. Corel WordPerfect will display all of the text in the normal color, leaving the deleted text onscreen with the strikeout lines.

Reviewing Changes as the Author

When reviewers send back the document to you, the author, you want to review the changes and decide which ones should be made. Pull down the File menu, point to Document, click on Review, and then click on Author. The Author pane will appear as shown in Figure 5-11, with the first change in the document highlighted.

Use the review buttons in the pane to look at the changes and decide which should be saved or deleted.

5

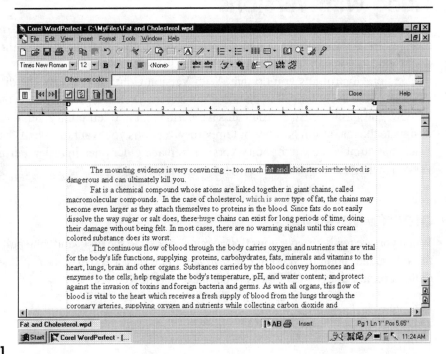

Reviewing changes as the author

FIGURE 5-11

- *Show/Hide Changes* temporarily hides deleted text and shows all text in the normal color.

- *Next Annotation* moves to and highlights the next change.

- *Previous Annotation* moves to and highlights the previous annotation.

- *Insert Current Annotation* accepts the highlighted change, either removing deleted text or changing inserted characters into regular text.

- *Insert All Annotations* accepts all of the changes to the document.

- *Delete Current Annotation* rejects the highlighted change, replacing text that was marked for deletion, or deleting text that was added.

- *Delete All Annotations* rejects all of the changes that were made.

 NOTE: *The options in the Review pane do not affect text marked separately by the Redline or Strikeout font attributes discussed in Chapter 6.*

Working with Versions

As you edit a document, you may not be sure that you want to keep all of your changes. In fact, sometimes you may even want to store several versions of the same document, so you can select between them as the need arises.

Version Control lets you do that. With Version Control, you save the different versions of the document all in one file. You can then select which version you want to view, edit, print, or save. You can save permanent and temporary versions. You designate the maximum number of temporary versions you want to save. When you reach that number, new temporary versions replace older ones in order. Permanent versions will not be replaced.

Saving Versions

When you are ready to save your first version, save it to the disk, and then pull down the File menu, point to Version Control, and click on Save Current. You'll see the dialog box in Figure 5-12. Use the dialog box as shown here:

- Select *Make First Version Permanent* to mark this first version as permanent so it will not be replaced.

- Choose *Use Compression* to store documents in a compressed format.

- Deselect *Save Version to Single Location* to save the versions in a file separate from the original document.

- Set the maximum number of temporary versions you want to save.

- Click on OK to save the version information. You do not have to resave the document.

Now when you are ready to save an edited version of the document, pull down the File menu, point to Version Control, and click on Save Current again. This time you'll see the Version Properties box shown in Figure 5-13. The box lists the version number and gives you the opportunity to mark the version as permanent. Add a brief description of the version in the Comments box and then click on OK to save the version.

IP: *After saving the version, you do not have to save the document itself.*

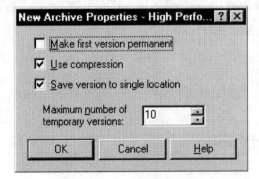

Saving the
first version

FIGURE 5-12

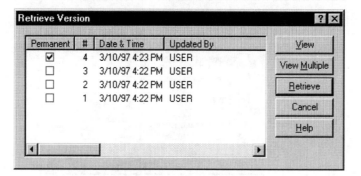

Saving
additional
versions

FIGURE 5-13

Retrieving Versions

When you want to see, edit, or print a version of the document, open the file, and then choose Retrieve Current from the Version Control menu. You'll see a dialog box listing all of the versions and showing which are permanent:

To see what a version looks like, click on it and then on the View button. The document appears in a viewer window showing its name and version number. The viewer window menu bar has three commands—File, Edit, and Options. Use the File menu to print the displayed version, and use the Edit menu to copy text that you select in the viewer window. Use the Options menu to choose how viewed versions are displayed onscreen, select printing options, and choose how selected viewer objects are inserted into the Clipboard. To see the first version and one other at the same time, click on the other version and then on the View Multiple button. The multiple view window does not have a menu bar. Close the viewer window to return to the Retrieve Version dialog box.

Click on the version you want to open and then click on Retrieve. A box will appear asking if you want to replace the currently displayed version with the one you selected. Click on Yes.

To open a version as a separate file so you can save it independently of the others, click on NO when you are asked if you want to replace the current version. A box will appear reporting that the document will be saved under its version name—click on OK.

If you want to open a version without first opening the original file, select Retrieve Document from the Version Control menu. In the box that appears, double-click on the name of the document for which versions have been saved. WordPerfect displays the Retrieve Version dialog box, so choose the version you want to open. You'll get an error message if you try to open a document that does not have any versions associated with it.

n **OTE:**   *When you choose not to save versions in a single location, they are stored separate from the original document in a file named with this syntax:* C$$DIRECTORY$FILENAME$WPD. *For example, for a document named* LETTERS *in the* MYFILES *directory, the versions are in* C$$MYFILES$ LETTERS$WPD. *You cannot open this file or retrieve versions from it directly.*

Using Explorer

You can work with Corel versions directly from Explorer, the Windows 95 desktop, and the Open or Save dialog box. When you right-click on a filename, the QuickMenu will now include the option Corel Versions. Point to Corel Versions to choose from these options:

- *Save* displays the dialog box so you can save the document you are pointing to as the first version.

- *History* displays a list of versions in the selected document, and lets you copy, delete, and view versions; print the version's history; and change the number of temporary versions. This option will be dimmed if you do not select a WordPerfect document that contains version information.

- *File* lets you delete, move, or copy the document, and all of its versions.

Formatting Text

6

hen you edit a document, you change its content. When you format a document, you change its appearance. As with editing, you can format text as you type it or any time after, so you don't have to worry about the format when you're struggling to find the right words. In this chapter you will learn how to format characters, lines, and paragraphs.

Character formatting affects the shape, size, and appearance of characters. Use these formats to make your document visually appealing and to emphasize important points. Formatting lines and paragraphs adjusts their position on the page.

Working with Corel WordPerfect Codes

Before learning how to format, you should get a basic understanding of Corel WordPerfect's codes. Every format that you apply to text, as well as noncharacter keys such as TAB and ENTER, is inserted as invisible codes into the document. The codes tell Corel WordPerfect when to turn formats on and off, insert a tab, end a paragraph, end a page, and perform every other Corel WordPerfect function. Knowing that all formats insert codes into the document will help you later understand how formats affect text.

As long as you have no problems inserting and deleting text and formatting your document, you may never have to worry about the codes. But sometimes, especially when you just can't seem to format the text the way you want, it pays to reveal the codes on the screen so you can see exactly what's happening. You may find that you accidentally pressed the wrong function key, or applied and then forgot about a format.

You reveal the codes in a separate window at the bottom of the screen. The quickest way to reveal codes is to drag one of the Reveal Codes lines, the small black rectangles at the top and bottom of the vertical scroll bar. As you drag the top line down, or the bottom line up, a bar will appear across the screen showing the size of the Reveal Codes window. When you release the mouse, you'll see a window that shows your text, as well as symbols that represent the codes, as shown in Figure 6-1.

The insertion point is seen as a red rectangle, while codes appear in boxes. Hard carriage returns (created by pressing the ENTER key) are represented by HRt, soft carriage returns (added by word wrap) are shown as SRt, tabs are Tab, and spaces are diamonds.

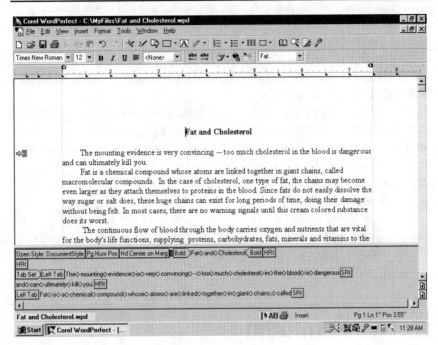

The Reveal
Codes
window

FIGURE 6-1

Codes that format text will surround the characters that they affect. The shape of the box indicates if it is an On code or an Off code, as you can see in these bold codes:

Other codes appear abbreviated when the insertion point is not immediately to their left. For example, the Tab Set code indicates that you've made a change in the tab stops. If you place the insertion point just before the code, it will be expanded to show the full tab settings:

TIP: *You can also reveal codes by pressing ALT-F3, or selecting Reveal Codes from the View menu.*

If you want, you can leave the codes revealed as you continue writing. To remove the code window, drag the dividing line off the top or bottom of the screen, or select Reveal Codes from the View menu, or press ALT-F3 again.

If a code is associated with a dialog box, open the dialog box by double-clicking on the code. For example, double-clicking on a character format code, such as bold, will display the Font dialog box.

Not all codes appear at the location in the text where you applied them. A code that affects the entire page, such as changing a page size, will be placed near the start of the page, before any codes that only affect paragraphs. Corel WordPerfect will also delete duplicate or redundant codes. If you select one page size and then change your mind and choose another, Corel WordPerfect will replace the first Page Size code with the other.

You can view, delete, move, and edit codes in the Reveal Codes window. To delete a code from the document, and thus remove its format, drag it off of the Reveal Codes window. You can also delete a code by pressing DEL or BACKSPACE, as you would delete other characters.

Character Formatting

There are literally thousands of combinations of formats that you can apply to your document. You can access all of these formats using the Format command from the menu bar. Some of the most common formats used in documents are also provided as buttons on the property bar.

Applying Bold, Italic, and Underline Formatting

Three of the most popular character formats are bold, italic, and underlining, by themselves or in combination. These are quick and easy to apply because buttons for them are on the property bar, as shown here.

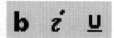

 TIP: *Shortcut key combinations for the three most used character formats are CTRL-B for bold, CTRL-I for italic, and CTRL-U for underlining.*

To format text as you type it, just click on the appropriate button and then type. Try it now using the following example:

1. Type **Your bill is** and then press SPACEBAR.

2. Click on the Underline button in the property bar and then type **seriously overdue**. Corel WordPerfect underlines the words and the spaces between them as you type.

3. Now turn off underlining by clicking on the Underline button again. This stops the formatting and changes the button so it no longer appears pressed down. This type of action is called a *toggle,* named after a toggle switch that turns a light on and off.

 TIP: *Not all property buttons act as toggles.*

6

4. Press SPACEBAR, type **and we will be forced to take**, and then press SPACEBAR again.

5. Click first on the Bold button and then on the Italic button in the property bar. To use a combination of the formats, click on each button that you want to apply.

6. Type **legal action**, and then click on the Bold and Italic buttons again. You can click the buttons in any order.

7. Type a period and then press ENTER. Your sentence should look like the one shown here.

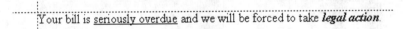

Your bill is <u>seriously overdue</u> and we will be forced to take *legal action*.

To format text that you've already typed, first select the text, and then click on the button. You can format a single word by clicking anywhere in the word and then choosing the button from the toolbar—you do not have to select the word first.

If you format characters by mistake, or just change your mind, select the text. The formats applied will appear as depressed buttons. Click on the button representing the format you want to remove.

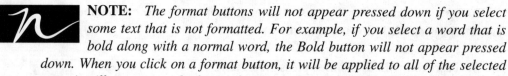

NOTE: *The format buttons will not appear pressed down if you select some text that is not formatted. For example, if you select a word that is bold along with a normal word, the Bold button will not appear pressed down. When you click on a format button, it will be applied to all of the selected text—it will not remove the format from text already in that style.*

Selecting Fonts and Sizes from the Property Bar

The property bar contains drop-down lists for selecting the font and size of characters. You can set the font and the size of text as you type it, or you can change the font and size of text—even a single character—by selecting it first. To change the font and size of a single word, however, just place the insertion point in the word before selecting the formats.

The Font box on the property bar will display the font being used at the location of the insertion point. To select another font, pull down the list associated with the box to display the fonts that are installed on your system. When you point to a font on the list, a sample of it appears enlarged under the property bar:

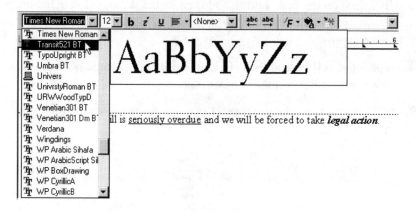

The fonts are listed in alphabetical order. However, after you start using Corel WordPerfect to select fonts, you'll see several fonts at the beginning of the list, separated from the rest by a line. These are the fonts that you've used recently. Corel WordPerfect places them first to make it easy for you to select the fonts that you use most often. To select a font, click on its name in the list and scroll the list as needed.

If you select text first, your choice will only affect that text. Otherwise, it will affect all text from the position of the insertion point to the end of the document. Its effect will end, however, when you choose another font, and it will not change text to which you already applied another font.

This is an important concept that affects many formatting commands, so make sure you understand it before going on. Let's say that you typed an entire document with the default font that Corel WordPerfect uses automatically. If you then move the insertion point to the start of the document and choose a font, all of the text in the document will change to that font.

Now suppose again that you typed an entire document in the default font. You then selected the third paragraph and chose a font from the property bar. Only that text will be affected. But now you move to the start of the document and choose a font. This time, your selection affects every paragraph except the third because it has a font already applied to it on its own.

You change the size of text using the Font Size list in the property bar. It affects text just like the Font command.

6

Font Color

With color inkjet printers becoming increasingly popular and affordable, Corel WordPerfect has made it easy for you to change the color of text. Pull down the Font Color list in the property bar to display a palette of colors, as shown here.

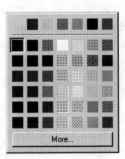

Click on the color that you want to apply to the selected text, or to all next text starting at the location of the insertion point.

To mix a custom color, click on the More button in the palette to see the dialog box shown here:

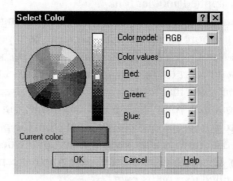

You can select a color model (RGB, HLS, or CMYK), enter amounts of the colors shown, or click in the color wheel and intensity bar to select a custom color. Click on Select when you've finished.

 NOTE: *If you do not have a color printer, Corel WordPerfect will print colors in corresponding shades of gray.*

Using QuickFonts

As you use Corel WordPerfect, you'll find combinations of fonts, sizes, styles, and colors that you'll want to use often. To reselect one of the last 20 combinations you used, pull down the QuickFonts list in the property bar, as shown here.

Each item in the QuickFonts list includes the combination of typeface, font size, font colors, and attributes. Choosing an item from the list applies to all of the formats. For example, if you click on an item that says Arial 18, and that appears underlined and bold, all four attributes will be applied to selected text, or the text that you are about to type.

Use the QuickFonts list to format selected text, or the word in which the insertion point is placed. QuickFonts will not affect any other text on the page.

TIP: *The Font option at the bottom of the QuickFonts list will display the Font dialog box.*

Formatting with the Font Dialog Box

The formatting options in the property bar offer only a sampling of Corel WordPerfect's formats. For a full range of choices, display the Font dialog box shown in Figure 6-2. Display the box using any of these methods:

- Select Font from the Format menu.

- Right-click on the text window, and select Font from the QuickMenu.

- Pull down the QuickFonts list and click on Font.

- Double-click on the QuickFonts, Font, or Font Size button in the property bar.

Make your choices from the dialog box, watching the preview panel to see their effects, and then click on OK to apply the settings to your text.

You can select a font, size, style, and appearance. When you close the dialog box, the font and size you select will be shown in the font and size boxes in the toolbar. The appearance options you select will be reflected in the look of the Bold

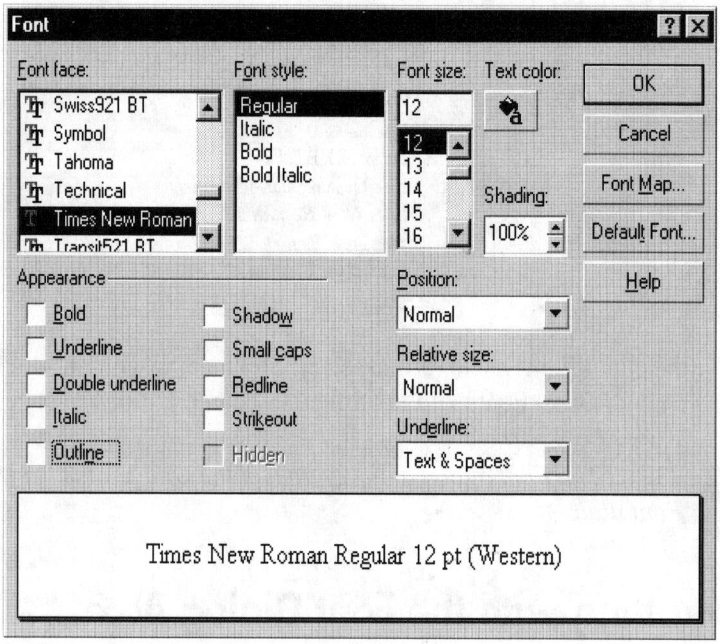

Font
dialog box

FIGURE 6-2

and Italic buttons in the toolbar. If you choose the Bold appearance option, for example, the Bold button in the toolbar will appear pressed down. You can later change the font, size, and appearance using either the toolbar or the dialog box.

A font style, on the other hand, will not be reflected in the toolbar. Choosing the Bold option in the Font Style list will not press down the Bold button in the toolbar, and you won't be able to remove the style using the toolbar. This actually changes the font to a bold font, rather than applying the bold attribute. To remove the style, you must return to the Font dialog box and select Regular from the Font Style list.

Here are some other options in the dialog box:

- Select a Position option to create superscripts and subscripts.

- Choose to underline the spaces between words, the spaces inserted by pressing TAB, or just the words themselves.

- Pick a color and shading for the text. If you do not have a color printer, Corel WordPerfect will substitute an appropriate shade of gray.

■ Use the Default Font button to change the default font that Corel WordPerfect uses for every new document. Click on the Default Font button to see the dialog box shown in Figure 6-3. Choose a font, size, and style. Setting the Default Font will not affect existing documents you've already saved, or text in the current document formatted with font codes.

NOTE: *The Font Map command lets you change what appears when you change font attributes and sizes. For example, you can use one set of attributes on the screen and another when printed. You can also specify the font to use when you select one that is not available.*

Selecting a Relative Font Size

When you choose a font size using the property bar, or the Font Size list in the Font dialog box, you are selecting a specific point size. Sometimes, however, you may want to format text in relation to the text around it. You might want a headline, for

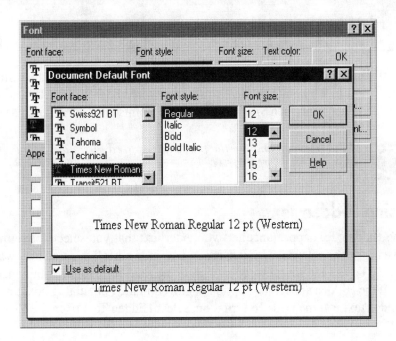

Selecting an
initial font

FIGURE 6-3

example, to be twice the size of the text in the paragraph, or a portion of legalese fine print to be half the size.

To format text in a relative size, follow these steps:

1. Select the text you want to format.

2. Open the Font dialog box.

3. Pull down the Relative Size button in the Font dialog box to see the choices Fine, Small, Normal, Large, Very Large, or Extra Large.

4. Click on OK.

Each of the relative size choices are defined as a percentage of the current font:

Option	Percentage of Current Font
Fine	60%
Small	80%
Normal	100%
Large	120%
Very Large	150%
Extra Large	200%

If you are using the default 12-point font, for example, choosing Small would format text in 9.6 points, while Extra Large would be 24 points. If you were using a 10-point text font, then Small would be 8.1 points and Extra Large 20 points.

TIP: *You can change the percentages used for relative fonts by running the macro SETATTR.WCM.*

Using Hidden Text

The Hidden Text appearance lets you enter text that you selectively either hide or reveal, print or not print. Use it to create notes to yourself that you may want to print in draft copies for your review but not on the final copy for distribution.

If the Hidden appearance option is grayed in the Font dialog box, the display of Hidden text is turned off. To turn it on, select Hidden Text from the View menu.

When you select the Hidden appearance, just enter text as you would normally. When you want to hide it, so it does not appear onscreen or print with the document, deselect Hidden Text from the View menu.

Using Redline and Strikeout

In Chapter 5, you learned how to add, reject, or accept reviewers' comments. Text that a reviewer inserts appears in a different color than other text, and text that is deleted appears with strikeout.

You can also mark inserted and deleted text using the Redline and Strikeout appearance options in the Font dialog box. Strikeout text to show that you'd like to delete it, and redline text that you'd like to add. Redline text appears in a different color than other text; strikeout text has lines through it. You have to apply these formats yourself; Corel WordPerfect will not do it for you automatically as you edit. Either select the text first and then choose the Redline or Strikeout appearance, or choose the format first and then type the text.

To accept or reject the changes, pull down the File menu, point to Document, and click on Remove Compare Markings for two options:

- *Remove Redline Markings and Strikeout Text* removes the color from redlined text and deletes the strikeout text from the document.

- *Remove Strikeout Text Only* deletes strikeout text but leaves the redline color on inserted text.

The Redline Method option on the Document menu lets you choose to indicate redlined text with a marker in the margin. You can choose to place a vertical line either in the left, right, or alternating margins next to redlined text, and you can change the marker to some other character.

Using Special Characters and Symbols

Most fonts usually contain symbols and accented characters in addition to the characters shown on your keyboard. These characters and symbols are useful when you are composing scientific or technical documents, or writing in a language other than English or in British English—an American might, for example, need to enter the currency symbol when writing to England. Corel WordPerfect lets you access these characters, as well as hundreds of other foreign language, mathematical, and scientific characters, and graphic symbols.

These characters are collected in 15 character sets. When you want to insert an international character or symbol in your document, use this procedure:

1. Select Symbol from the Insert menu, or click on the Insert Symbol button in the property bar, to see the dialog box shown in Figure 6-4.

2. Pull down the Character Set list box and select the character set. The characters in that set are displayed in the Characters box. The character sets are ASCII, Multinational, Phonetic, Box Drawing, Typographic Symbols, Iconic Symbols, Math/Scientific, Math/Scientific Extended, Greek, Hebrew, Cyrillic, Japanese, User-Defined, Arabic, and Arabic Script.

3. Click on the character that you want to insert, and then click on the Insert and Close buttons.

Corel WordPerfect will insert the character at the position of the insertion point, in a size that matches the surrounding text. So if you are typing a headline in 24 points, for example, the special character will appear in 24 points. If the character is one that appears on the keyboard, Corel WordPerfect will also match the current font.

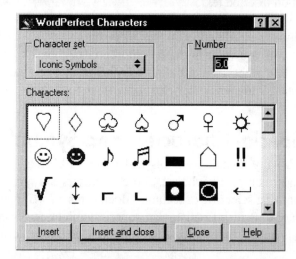

Inserting
special
characters
and symbols

FIGURE 6-4

If you want to insert a number of characters, leave the dialog box on the screen and move back and forth between your document and the dialog box. Drag the dialog box out of the way, and then double-click on the character you want to insert, or choose the character and then click on Insert. Corel WordPerfect will insert the characters but leave the dialog box open so you can insert additional characters. Click in the document window to position the insertion point where you want to insert another character—even to add or edit text if you want—and then click back in the dialog box when you want to insert a different character.

The sets are numbered from 0 to 14, and each character is numbered within the set. You'll notice that when you click on a character, its set and character numbers appear in the Number box, such as 7,2 to represent the second character in set seven. If you know the set and number, you can enter them in the Number box yourself. When you type the character number, the set will appear in the dialog box with the character selected.

NOTE: *Remember that QuickCorrect will automatically insert some special characters for you, such as the copyright and registered symbols.*

Duplicating Formats with QuickFormat

With all of the format options that Corel WordPerfect makes available, there are certainly a large number of possible combinations. If you've gone to the trouble of selecting a combination that you like for one section of text, you do not have to make the selections all over again for some other text. Just apply the same combination using QuickFormat.

When you want to copy a format, use these steps:

1. Place the insertion point in the text that uses that format.

2. Click on the QuickFormat button in the toolbar to see a dialog box with four options. The table options will only be available when the insertion point is in a table.

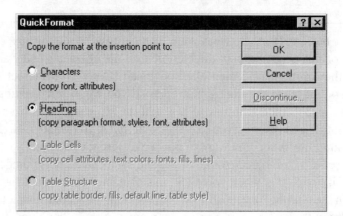

 TIP: *You can also choose QuickFormat from the Format menu or from the QuickMenu.*

3. Select the Characters option in the dialog box if you only want to copy the font and character formats of the text. Select the Headings option in the dialog box if you want to copy all of the formats, including the font, line, and paragraph formats.

4. Click on OK. The shape of the mouse pointer will depend on your selection—a paintbrush if you choose characters, a paint roller if you choose Headings or either of the table options.

5. Drag over the text that you want to apply the format to. When you release the mouse button after selecting the text, Corel WordPerfect will apply the formats. It will leave QuickFormat on, however, so you can apply the same formats to other sections of text.

6. To turn off the feature, click on the QuickFormat button again.

Formatting Lines and Paragraphs

When you want to add some style and flair to your document, apply *line* or *paragraph* formats. These formats affect the alignment of text on the page. Probably the first two formats that you'll want to learn are centering text between the margins and changing the line spacing. Again, Corel WordPerfect offers much more. As with character formats, you can format paragraphs as you type them or anytime afterward.

There are several ways to apply formats. You can use the property bar, the menu bar, or the QuickMenu.

Using the QuickMenu

Before discussing the formats that you can apply, take a look at the QuickMenu that appears when you right-click in the typing area (when no text is selected):

NOTE: *The QuickMenu shown here will not appear if you right-click on a word that Spell-As-You-Go has marked as a possible error.*

You'll learn how these options work as I discuss the formats, but here's a summary of the QuickMenu options.

- *Center* lets you center text, either between the margins or at the location of a tab stop.

- *Flush Right* aligns text along the right margin.

- *Indent* lets you indent a paragraph from the left margin.

- *Default Tab Settings* restores the default tab stops, deleting custom tabs that you created.

- *Paste* inserts the contents of the Clipboard.

- *Paste without Font/Attributes* inserts the contents of the Clipboard in the same fonts and attributes as surrounding text.

- *Properties* displays summary information and the word, sentence, and character count for the current document.

- *What's This?* displays a brief explanation about the area you are clicked in.

- *Font* opens the Font dialog box.

- *Symbols* displays the WordPerfect Characters dialog box.

- *Shadow Cursor* toggles on and off the shadow cursor.

- *QuickFormat* toggles on and off the QuickFormat feature.

- *Reveal Codes* displays or hides the reveal codes area.

Changing Line Spacing

The line spacing command affects text in the same way as changing a font. If you select text first, the line spacing will only be applied to that text. If you did not select text, it will affect all of the text from the location of the insertion point, up to any text that has another line spacing applied to it.

To change the line spacing, choose Line from the Format menu and then click on Spacing. In the dialog box that appears, type the line spacing number or click on the up or down pointers to increment or decrement the setting in intervals of one-tenth line with each click. Click on OK to return to the document.

Aligning Text Between the Margins

Probably the first paragraph format you'll want to use is centering. You may need to center your address on a letterhead or a title on a report. Corel WordPerfect provides six options for aligning text between the margins.

- With *Left alignment,* lines of text align evenly at the left margins, with an uneven right margin.

- *Center alignment* centers the text between the left and right margins, with uneven left and right margins.

- *Flush Right alignment* creates even right margins, with an uneven left margin.

- *Flush Right with Dot Leaders* inserts periods in the blank space to the left of right-aligned text.

- *Full* adds spaces to the lines of text, except lines ending with hard carriage returns when you pressed ENTER, so they are aligned evenly on both the left and right. This option does not affect the last line of a paragraph.

- *All* extends every line between the margins, including the last line of paragraphs, titles, and other single-line paragraphs.

You can select alignment options using the property bar and menu bar, but there are two general ways: line formatting and justification.

Line formatting affects individual lines or paragraphs. If you turn on the format and type text, the format ends when you press the ENTER key. If you place the insertion point in existing text and select a line format, only the current paragraph is affected. Text following the current paragraph will not be changed.

The *justification* commands, on the other hand, insert codes that affect all of the text starting in the paragraph where the insertion point is located—up to the first other justification code. If you are typing new text, the format remains on when you press the ENTER key. So if you use the line center command to center text, the insertion point returns to the left margin when you press ENTER. If you use the justification center command, the insertion point moves to the center of the screen when you press ENTER. You have to choose another justification command when you no longer want centered text.

 NOTE: *If you select text first, both methods only affect the selected text.*

If you apply a justification format to text, you cannot change its format with a line formatting command. You can only change it by applying another justification. The justification commands take precedence over line formatting. If you already applied a line format to text, applying a justification format will change it. A line format command, however, will not affect justified text.

Centering Text

To center a single paragraph or selected text, choose Center from the QuickMenu, or pull down the Format menu, point to Line, and click on Center. To center existing text, however, make sure you first place the insertion point at the start of the line or paragraph. If you start with the insertion point within the text, only text in the paragraph following the insertion will be centered.

 TIP: *To center a new line of text using the shadow cursor, point to the middle of the page so the cursor includes a two-directional arrow, and then click.*

To turn on centering for all text from the insertion point to the next justification code, or for all selected text, pull down the Justification button in the property bar and click on Center. You can also pull down the Format menu, point to Justification, and click on Center. To turn off centering, pull down the Justification list and choose Left, or choose Left from the Format Justification menu.

Aligning Text on the Right

To align a single paragraph or selected text so it is flush with the right margin, select Flush Right from the QuickMenu, or pull down the Format menu, point to Line, and click on Flush Right. To align text on the right and insert periods in the blank space before the text, select Flush Right with Dot Leaders from the Format Line menu. Start with the insertion point at the start of the line to format all of the text.

 TIP: *To right-align a new line of text using the shadow cursor, point to the right margin of the page so the cursor includes a left-pointing arrow, and then click.*

To turn on the flush right format for all text from the insertion point to the next justification code, or all selected text, pull down the Justification button in the property bar and select Right. You can also pull down the Format menu, point to Justification, and click on Right.

Justifying Text

To justify text on the left and right, pull down the Justification button in the property bar and select Full or All. You can also select Full or All from the Format Justification menu. Remember, All justifies every line of text, even those ending with a hard carriage return. This can result in some strange effects by spacing out words in the last line to reach the right margin.

Enhancing Text with Borders

When you want to draw attention to a paragraph or section of text, enclose it in a border, or fill in the background with a color, shading, or pattern. It's an easy way to add a little pizzazz to a document without going all the way to graphics.

To add a border to a single paragraph, place the insertion point anywhere in it. To enhance more than one paragraph, follow these steps:

1. Select all of the paragraphs you want to enhance.

2. Pull down the Format menu, point to Paragraph, and click on Border/Fill to see the dialog box in Figure 6-5. The box has three pages.

6

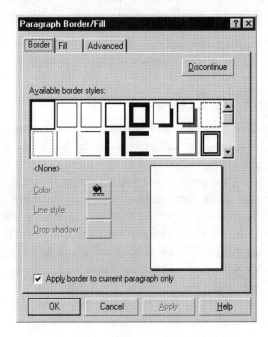

Adding a
border or
shading

FIGURE 6-5

On the Border page, you choose the color and style of lines that will surround the text. You can also choose to place the border around all of the remaining paragraphs in the document by deselecting the Apply Border to Current Paragraph Only checkbox.

On the Fill page, you select a color or pattern to print in the background behind the text. If you select a pattern rather than a solid color, you can also choose a background and foreground color for two-tone patterns.

On the Advanced page, you customize your selected border and fill patterns. You can adjust the distance between the border lines and text, pick a drop shadow color and width, round box corners, and adjust the gradient pattern. Experiment with the options to discover how they work.

 NOTE: *In Chapter 8, you'll learn how to add other types of lines and borders, including a border around the entire page.*

If you just want to draw a line on the screen, remember the QuickLines feature of QuickCorrect Format-As-You-Go. Type four or more hyphens or equal signs, and then press ENTER. Corel WordPerfect will draw a single or double line across the page.

Introducing the Ruler

You usually want to change margins, set tabs, or indent paragraphs specific amounts. You can set all of these formats using dialog boxes, where you can enter the measurements in inches, millimeters, or other unit of measurement. If you want to use the mouse to create these formats, it will help if you first display the ruler. In fact, to set tabs and indent paragraphs by dragging the mouse, you must display the ruler. The ruler is an onscreen object that indicates the positions of tabs, margins, and indentations, just as if you actually held a ruler against the screen.

To display the ruler, pull down the View menu and click on Ruler. The Corel WordPerfect ruler, shown here, has three parts.

Margin and indentation indicators

Ruled line

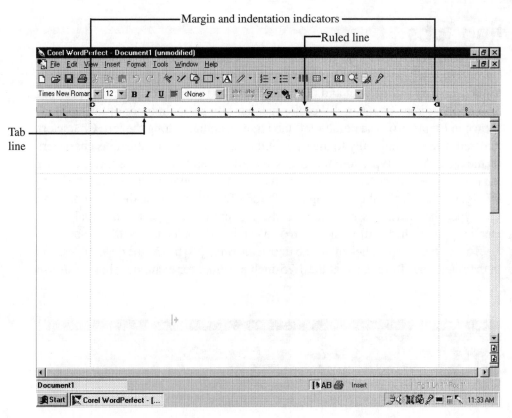

Tab line

The middle section of the ruler is a ruled line in inches. (You can change the units of measure using the Settings dialog box that you'll learn about in Chapter 10.) Use the ruled line to place objects in exact positions in your document.

Above the ruled line are the margin and indentation indicators, which you use to set the left and right page margins, and to indent paragraphs.

Below the ruled line is the tab line, which you use to set, delete, and change tab stops. The triangles on the tab line show the position of the default tab stops, set every half inch.

NOTE: *Because the ruler represents the spacing of your page, it will scroll as you scroll your document horizontally.*

Setting Tabs

Tab stops not only control the distance moved when you press the TAB key, but they affect how paragraphs are indented, as you will learn later in this chapter. You can use the mouse to quickly set and delete tab stops on the ruler, or you can work with tabs using a dialog box. Corel WordPerfect lets you set eight types of tab stops, as shown in Figure 6-6. The default left tab aligns a column along the left. Characters that you type shift normally to the right of the tab stop. A right tab aligns characters on the right. As you type, your text shifts toward the left of the tab stop. Use a center tab to center text at the tab stop. As you type, text shifts alternately to the left and to the right. Use a decimal tab to align a column of numbers on the decimal point. As you type, the characters shift toward the left until you type the decimal point. Decimal values then shift to the right. You can insert dot leaders with all tab types.

To set a tab, simply click in the tab line of the ruler, just below the desired position in the ruled line. To set a tab at the 1.75-inch position, for example, click as shown here:

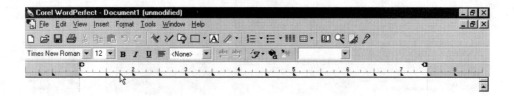

LEFT	CENTER	RIGHT	DECIMAL
One	One	One	1.00
Two	Two	Two	22.00
Three	Three	Three	333.00
.. One	One	.. One.	... 1.00
.. Two.	Two	.. Two.	.. 22.00
.. Three.	Three.	... Three.	.. 333.00

Types of
tab stops

FIGURE 6-6

Left-aligned tabs are set by default. To choose another type of tab stop, right-click on the tab line to see the QuickMenu shown here.

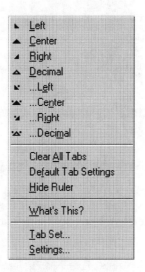

You can also display this menu by clicking the left mouse on the tab indicator on the far left of the ruler. You won't see this indicator, however, unless you reduce the magnification to at least 90%:

Tab indicator

Click on the tab type that you want to set, with or without dot leaders. The shape of the button changes to illustrate the type of tab that you set:

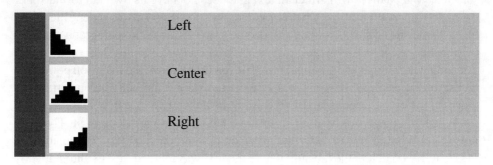

Decimal

Left (left tab with leaders)

Center (center tab with leaders)

Right (right tab with leaders)

Decimal (decimal tab with leaders)

You can also move and delete tabs using the mouse and the ruler. To delete a tab stop, use these steps:

1. Point to its marker in the ruler.

2. Drag the mouse down into the typing area.

To move a tab stop to a different position, drag its indicator to a new position on the ruler. As you drag the tab indicator, a dotted line will appear down the screen showing where text will align. To delete all of the tab stops, right-click on the tab line and select Clear All Tabs—click on Default Tab Settings to reset to Corel WordPerfect's default tabs every half inch.

Be careful when setting, deleting, or moving tabs. If you do not have any text selected, your changes will affect all text that does not have its own tab formats. For example, suppose you type several paragraphs, pressing TAB to indent their first lines. At the end of the document, you decide you want a special paragraph indented 0.75 inches, so you drag the tab stop at the half-inch position to 0.75 on the ruler. The indentations of every other paragraph, even those above the insertion point, will adjust to that position. If you just delete the tab stop at the half-inch position, the indentations of the existing text will shift to the next tab on the right.

When you press TAB, you are inserting a tab code into the document. The code tells Corel WordPerfect to move the insertion point to the next tab stop position on the right. If you delete the tab stop where the text was aligned, it will automatically move to the next tab stop. If you insert a tab stop prior to that position, the text will shift to that new tab stop.

NOTE: *When you click to the right of the left margin with the shadow cursor, Corel WordPerfect inserts a series of tab codes between the left margin and the position where you clicked.*

To change the tab stops for just a portion of the document, select it first. This will only affect the selected text. If you later change tabs elsewhere in a document, all text except it will be affected.

Using the Tab Bar

When you change the tab stops in a paragraph, Corel WordPerfect will display the Tab icon in the margin, as shown here.

Why Women Should Study Tae Kwon Do

For weeks I had contemplated visiting the gym where my eight year old nephew Adam studied Tae Kwon Do. For more than twenty years I have wanted to learn a martial art but those years were devoted to earning college degrees and establishing myself in my chosen profession of Medical Technology. In addition, I believed that "sports" did not come easy to me. I was really just inventing excuses for not signing up and thought that being a woman, thin and weak, was a legitimate reason why I could only fail in pursuing Tae Kwon Do.

The icon indicates where the code was inserted that affects tab stops. If you click on the icon with the left mouse button, Corel WordPerfect will display a tab bar just above the paragraph showing the tabs applied to the text:

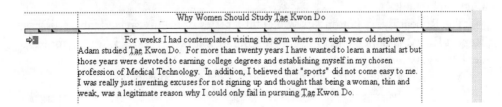

Why Women Should Study Tae Kwon Do

For weeks I had contemplated visiting the gym where my eight year old nephew Adam studied Tae Kwon Do. For more than twenty years I have wanted to learn a martial art but those years were devoted to earning college degrees and establishing myself in my chosen profession of Medical Technology. In addition, I believed that "sports" did not come easy to me. I was really just inventing excuses for not signing up and thought that being a woman, thin and weak, was a legitimate reason why I could only fail in pursuing Tae Kwon Do.

You can use that tab line to add, delete, or change tab stops in the text, just as you can by using the ruler. To remove the tab line from display, click elsewhere in the document.

If you select text and change the tabs, Corel WordPerfect will insert a Tab icon in the margin of the edited text, as well as at the start of the next paragraph. This shows that different tab settings apply at those locations. What happens if you change tabs within a section that has already had a different set of tabs applied?

Corel WordPerfect will display a special icon showing that multiple formats exist in that paragraph, such as the end of one tab setting and the start of another. When you click on that icon, you'll see two or more icons representing the different tab settings. Click on each of those icons to show the tab bar for the format.

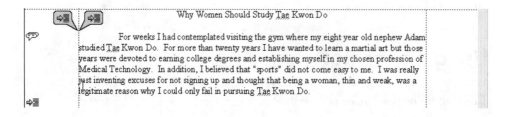

Setting Tabs with the Dialog Box

The Tab Set dialog box, shown in Figure 6-7, gives you even greater control over tab stops, although it may not be as easy to use as clicking the mouse. To adjust tabs, right-click on the ruler and select Tab Set from the QuickMenu, or pull down the Format menu, point on Line, and click on Tab Set.

To set a tab, pull down the Type list and choose a tab type. Enter the location of the tab in the Position text box, and then click on the Set button. To delete a tab, type its location in the Position box and click on the Clear button. Click on Clear All to delete all of the tabs. If you want to restore all of Corel WordPerfect's default stops, click on Default.

The Repeat Every button lets you enter a series of evenly spaced tabs. Click on Repeat Every, and then enter the spacing in the text box. Type **.75**, for example, to set tabs every 3/4-inch across the ruler.

You can also change the character that is used as the dot leader.

Relative Versus Absolute Tab

When you type a position setting for a tab, Corel WordPerfect sets it relative to the left margin. A tab set at 1.25, for example, will be 1.25 inches from the left margin, or 2.25 inches from the left edge of the paper using the default 1-inch margin.

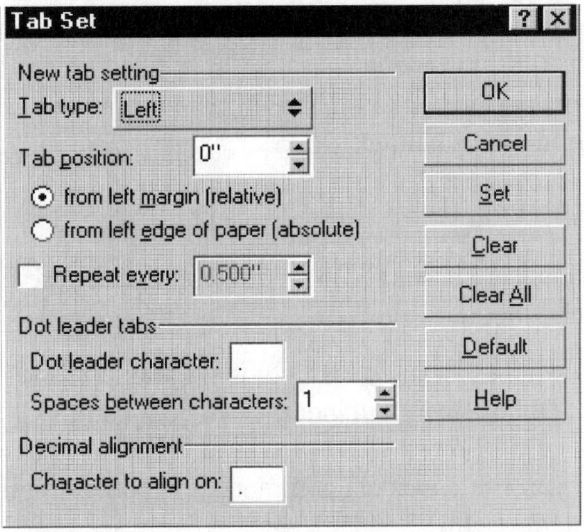

Tab Set

New tab setting
Tab type: [Left]
Tab position: [0"]
⦿ from left margin (relative)
○ from left edge of paper (absolute)
☐ Repeat every: [0.500"]

Dot leader tabs
Dot leader character: [.]
Spaces between characters: [1]

Decimal alignment
Character to align on: [.]

OK
Cancel
Set
Clear
Clear All
Default
Help

Tab Set
dialog box

FIGURE 6-7

Because the tab is relative, it will remain at that distance from the margin even if you change the left margin setting. So if you change the margin to 1.5 inches, the tab stop will still be 1.25 inches from it, but now 2.75 inches from the edge of the page.

If you want a tab stop to remain at a fixed position, regardless of the margins, click on the Left Edge Of Paper (Absolute) option in the Tab Set dialog box. Now, changing the left margin will not affect the position of tab stops from the edge of the paper. The position of tabs will be set at a distance from the edge of the paper, rather than the margin.

Indenting Paragraphs

If you want to indent the first line of a paragraph, just press the TAB key. But you might want to indent every line of a paragraph from the left margin or from both the right and left margins. You might also want to automatically indent the first line of every paragraph to save yourself the trouble of pressing TAB. You can control paragraph indentations using the ruler, the QuickMenu, or the Paragraph dialog box.

NOTE: *You can also indent text using the margin settings. See Chapter 8 for more information on this method.*

Corel WordPerfect gives you a variety of ways to indent text from the left. The quickest ways are to either press the F7 key or pull down the Format menu, point to Paragraph, and click on Indent.

To indent existing text, place the insertion point at the start of the paragraph, and then use any of these techniques:

- Press F7.

- Right-click at the start of the paragraph and choose Indent from the QuickMenu.

- Pull down the Format menu, point to Paragraph and choose Indent, or choose Double Indent to indent from both margins.

Each time you use an Indent command, the paragraph is indented another tab stop position to the right.

 NOTE: *If you use the Indent command when the insertion point is not at the start of the paragraph, Corel WordPerfect will shift the following text to the next tab stop and create the hanging indentation at that position.*

To indent new text as you type it, use the Indent command to move the insertion point where you want the paragraph to start, and then type. Each line of the paragraph will begin at the tab stop position. When you press ENTER after the paragraph, Corel WordPerfect ends the indentation and moves the insertion point back to the left margin.

You can also indent text from the left with a dialog box. Pull down the Format menu, point to Paragraph, and then click on Format to see this dialog box:

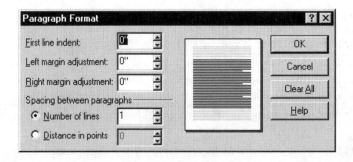

Enter the amount of left indentation in the Left Margin Adjustment box, and the amount of right indentation in the Right Margin Adjustment box. To automatically indent the first line of every paragraph, so you do not have to press TAB, enter a setting in the First Line Indent option.

Use the Spacing Between Paragraphs option to automatically add space between paragraphs. For example, if you want to double-space between single-spaced paragraphs, set the option at 2.

Hanging Indentations

You can also create a hanging indentation, where the first line extends to the left of the remainder of the paragraph. There are two general uses for hanging indentation, as shown here:

VLDL   Very Low Density Lipoprotein --The largest of the lipoproteins, these contain mostly triglycerides and are about 10 percent protein. They are usually not reported in typical lipid profiles because they only transport through the bloodstream from 5 to 12 percent of the cholesterol. Too many VLDL's make the plasma appear cloudy.

Low Density Lipoprotein -- Commonly called the "bad cholesterol", these tend to promote deposits of plaque in the arteries. They are made up of about 50% cholesterol and carry from 60% to 70% of your total cholesterol through the bloodstream. Your LDL level should be less than 130 mg/dl. Your diet should be aimed at lowering LDL's.

In one case, some text stands by itself to the left of the paragraph. In the other, the text is continuous. To create a hanging indentation with continuous text that you've already typed, move the insertion point to the beginning of the paragraph, and then choose Hanging Indent from the Format Paragraph menu. To type a hanging indented paragraph, select Hanging Indent before you start typing.

Creating a hanging indentation with text that stands by itself is just as easy.

1. Type the text that you want to stand by itself.

2. Use the Indent command—by either pressing F7 or selecting Indent from the QuickMenu or Format Paragraph menu.

3. Continue typing the remainder of the paragraph.

You can also create a hanging indentation using the Paragraph Format dialog box. Set the Left Margin Adjustment to where you want the remainder of the paragraph to be, and enter a negative distance for the First Line Indent.

Indenting with the Ruler

You can also create indentations—from the left, from the right, for the first line, and hanging—using the ruler. To indent text from the right, drag the Right Indent marker, which is the small triangular object at the right end of the ruler, to the position at which you want to indent the text.

To indent text from the left, use the left section of the ruler. There are actually two separate indentation controls.

First Line Indent marker

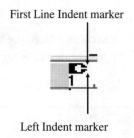

Left Indent marker

The First Line Indent marker controls the position of the first line of every paragraph. To indent just the first line of the paragraph, drag the top triangle on the left side of the ruler.

To indent every line of a paragraph on the left, drag the Left Indent marker, the bottom triangle on the left of the ruler, to the right.

When you drag the Left Indent marker, the First Line Indent marker moves also in order to always remain at the same relative distance. If you want to set both, set the left indentation first and then the first line indentation. So if you want to create a hanging indentation, first set the left indentation where you want remaining lines to appear, and then drag the First Line Indent marker to the hanging position of the first line.

Creating Lists

Another way to enhance text is to format it as a list. A list makes it easy to read a series of related items, and helps to organize your points. There are two types of lists, bulleted and numbered. A bulleted list has a small graphic object, such as a circle or diamond, at the start of each paragraph. A numbered list looks like an outline, with numbers or letters.

When you begin a list, Corel WordPerfect automatically turns on the outlining feature and displays the Outline property bar. I discuss how to create the lists first, and then explain about outlining.

Using the Toolbar

The toolbar provides two buttons to help you create lists and outlines:

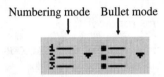

To begin a numbered list, pull down the Numbering Mode list and select the type of numbering you want from these options:

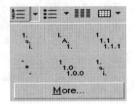

Corel WordPerfect will now automatically number paragraphs like an outline, using indentations to correspond to outline levels, and creating a hanging indentation when text wraps to the next line. To stop numbering, press ENTER after the last line and then BACKSPACE to delete the last number inserted.

To create a bulleted list, pull down the Bullet Mode button and choose from these options:

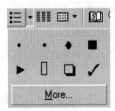

The symbol you select will be inserted at the start of each line. Press ENTER and then BACKSPACE to stop inserting bullets.

Using Format-As-You-Go

The QuickBullet feature of QuickCorrect Format-As-You-Go will sense when you are starting a list and take over from there. To create a list, follow these steps:

1. Type an asterisk or a lowercase **o** and press TAB.

2. Type the first paragraph. When you press ENTER, Corel WordPerfect changes the asterisk to a bullet and inserts another bullet on the next line.

3. Continue typing the items for the list.

4. Press ENTER after the final item and then BACKSPACE to delete the bullet.

In addition to the small bullet, you can insert these other bullet characters by using these keys:

To Use This Bullet	Start With This Character
▸	>
◆	^
★	+
▪	0
●	O
—	-

You can number lists in the same way, with QuickNumbers, using these steps:

1. Type the first number, letter, or roman numeral.

2. Type a period and press TAB.

3. Type the paragraph—Corel WordPerfect creates a hanging indentation when text wraps to the next line.

4. Press ENTER and Corel WordPerfect will insert the next-highest number or letter in the series and indent the insertion point at the indented position of the line above.

5. Press ENTER and BACKSPACE to stop numbering.

The Bullets and Numbering Dialog Box

For more bullet and list options, use the Bullets and Numbering dialog box—either before typing the list or to format existing paragraphs. Select Outline/Bullets & Numbering from the Insert menu to display the dialog box shown in Figure 6-8.

The Options list lets you choose the template in which to save the format. You'll learn about these options in Chapter 7. The Text tab of the dialog box lets you create custom list formats to use for standard types of text, such as heading, quotations, and definitions.

If you already have a list in the document before the insertion point, you can choose to resume numbering where you left off, or start a new number sequence.

You can choose or edit the standard numbering and bullet formats, or create your own. When you choose to Create or Edit a style, you'll see a dialog box like the one shown in Figure 6-9. If you are editing a format, its name and other specifics will appear in the box.

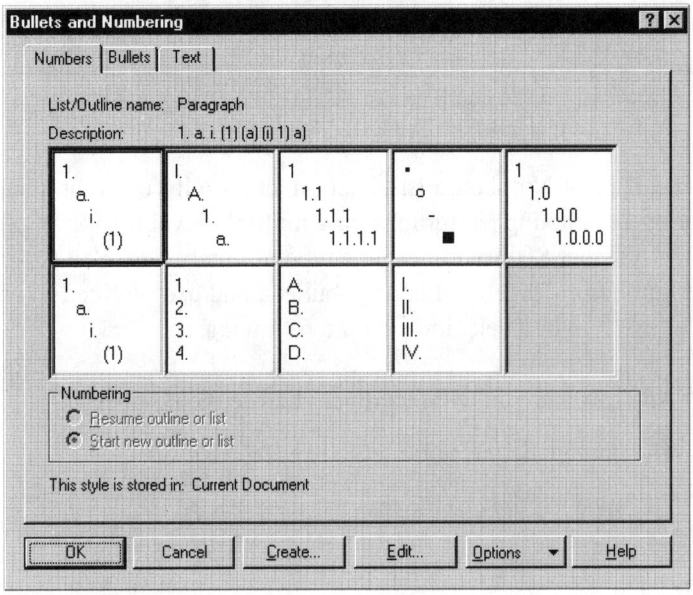

Bullets and Numbering dialog box

FIGURE 6-8

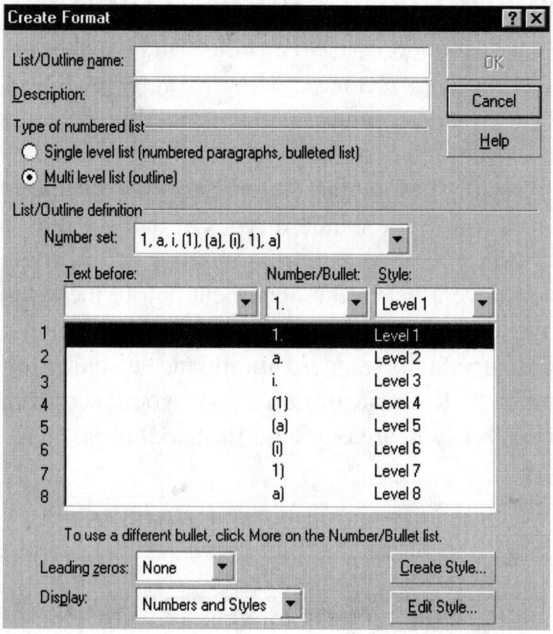

Creating a
custom
format

FIGURE 6-9

In the Type of Numbered List section, choose if you want a single list for just numbering or bulleting paragraphs, or a multiple-level list for an outline.

In the Number Set list, choose the type of numbering. You can choose standard outline numbering, legal numbering, bullets, and user defined to create your own. Then for up to eight levels, indicate the following:

- Any text that you want to appear before the number

- The number, letter, or bullet to use for the level

- The style to apply to the text

Outlining

When you are in a list, Corel WordPerfect displays the property bar shown in Figure 6-10, with the new buttons labeled. Use the buttons on the bar to create your outline.

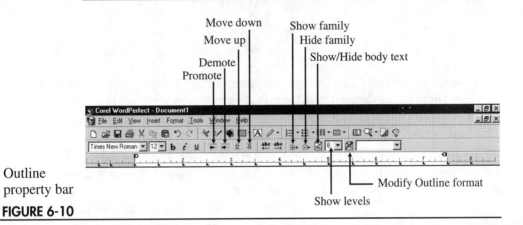

Outline
property bar

You can press TAB or click on the Demote button to move to the next-lowest outline level (such as from I to A, and from A to 1). Press SHIFT-TAB or click on the Promote button to move to the previous highest.

Body Text

Body text is text that is not numbered as part of the outline, but appears between outline entries. To type body text, press ENTER twice at the end of an outline entry. When you press ENTER the second time, a blank line appears between the two outline levels. Now each time you press ENTER, another blank line is inserted. Move up to the blank line and type the body text. When you're in the body text line, by the way, the Outline property bar is replaced by the Main property bar.

NOTE: *To continue adding to the outline, move the insertion point down to the numbered lines and begin typing.*

If you just want to view the outline itself, with the narrative of body text, click on the Show/Hide Body Text button in the Outline property bar. Corel WordPerfect removes the body text from display. Click on the button again to redisplay the body text.

Moving Outline Families

The arrangement of outlines in families make them easier to work with. An *outline family* consists of a heading at any level and all of the subheadings and text under it. You can move outline families by clicking on these buttons:

Move Up   Move Down

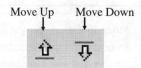

To move just an individual line in the outline, click anywhere in it and then click on Move Up or Move Down. Corel WordPerfect moves the text and renumbers the outline levels depending on where you insert the line. Moving just the line does not affect any sublevels that may have been under it.

To move an entire family, select the family and then click on the Move Up or Move Down button. To select the family, point to anywhere in the heading line and drag to the end of the section you want to move.

 TIP: *When you select a family, make sure the Outline property bar still appears. If the Main property bar appears, select the family again, making sure that the start and end of the selection are within outline levels.*

Collapsing and Expanding Outlines

One of the advantages of working with an outline is that it lets you visualize the organization of topics and subtopics. You can see at a glance how subjects are related. When you have a long outline, however, headings may be too far apart to show the structure. To solve this problem, you can collapse and expand outline families.

When you collapse a family, you hide its sublevels, displaying just the heading that you select. To collapse a family, click in the heading and then click on the Hide Family button in the Outline property bar. To collapse more than one family, select them first.

To expand the family, click on the Show Family button.

 TIP: *To collapse the entire outline to a specific level, pull down the Show Levels list in the property bar, and select the lowest level to display.*

Hyphenating Text

When you justify text on both the left and right, Corel WordPerfect inserts extra space to fill out the line, but sometimes the extra space is just too obvious. You hyphenate text to reduce these extra spaces. Hyphenation will divide some words between lines, adding enough characters at the right to avoid large blank spaces between words. You can have Corel WordPerfect hyphenate automatically as you type, or you can have it hyphenate a selection of existing text. To turn on hyphenation, pull down the Tools menu, point to Language, and click on Hyphenation to display the dialog box shown in Figure 6-11. Click on Hyphenation On, and then select OK.

Corel WordPerfect will automatically insert a hyphen based on certain rules. If its rules cannot be applied to the end of a line, you'll see a dialog box such as this:

Press the RIGHT ARROW or LEFT ARROW to place the hyphen where you want it to appear, and then click on the Insert Hyphen button. You can also choose to insert a space at that location or a Hyphenation SRt code—a position where Corel WordPerfect divides a word without a hyphen character.

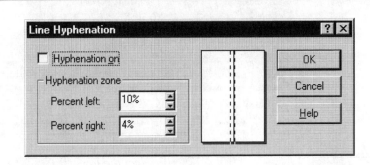

Turning on
automatic
hyphenation

FIGURE 6-11

You can always hyphenate words yourself, but don't just press the hyphen key. Pressing the hyphen key actually inserts a hyphen code that should only be used for hyphenated words such as "mother-in-law." If the word must be divided between lines, Corel WordPerfect will use one of the hyphen positions. If you later add or delete text, the hyphen may be moved to another line so it always appears between the words. If you press the hyphen to simply hyphenate a word, later editing may move the hyphen to another line, separating the word incorrectly with a hyphen character.

If you want to hyphenate a word only when it must be divided between lines, press CTRL-SHIFT- (the CTRL and hyphen keys together, and then the SHIFT and hyphen keys together) to enter a soft hyphen code. The hyphen will only appear when Corel WordPerfect must divide the word between lines.

If you want to hyphenate a word or other text, but do not want to divide it between lines, press CTRL- (the CTRL and the hyphen keys together). Use this for minus signs in formulas, or for hyphens in phone numbers that you do not want divided.

Inserting Other Codes

There are other hyphenation styles available, and other special formatting codes. To access these, pull down the Format Line menu and click on Other Codes to display the Other Codes dialog box, shown in Figure 6-12. The Other Codes dialog box includes some useful features. You may not need them often, but it pays to be prepared just in case.

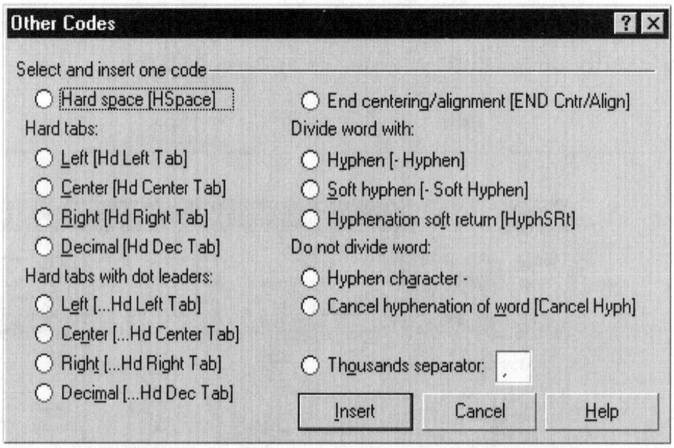

Other Codes dialog box

FIGURE 6-12

A *hard tab* is a tab code that moves the insertion point to the next tab stop position on the right, just like pressing the TAB key. But unlike a tab inserted with the TAB key, a hard tab will not be affected if you change the tab type. Use this type of code, for example, to set a different tab type without affecting other lines. If you set a hard center tab at two inches, for example, the tab indicator will not change, but text at that location—for that line only—will be centered. The Other Codes dialog box lets you enter hard left, right, center, and decimal hard tabs, with and without dot leaders.

The dialog box also includes the Hard Space and the End Centering/Alignment codes. Use a hard space when you want to put a space between words, but do not want them ever divided between lines. Corel WordPerfect treats the hard space as a real character and will not wrap the two words at that point.

The End Centering/Alignment code stops the current centering or alignment. For example, suppose you want to type text so the first character starts at the exact center of the screen. Start by centering the insertion point with the Center command, and then select the End Centering/Alignment code from the dialog box. Your text will now move to the right as you type, rather than being centered.

The dialog box contains these five options:

- *Hyphen [- Hyphen]* will let Corel WordPerfect divide the word between lines at the hyphen position.

- *Soft Hyphen* only displays the hyphen if the word is wrapped at that location.

- *Hyphenation Soft Return* will divide a word at that location without displaying a hyphen character.

- *Hyphen Character* prevents Corel WordPerfect from dividing the word between lines.

- *Cancel Hyphenation of Word* moves the word to the next line, rather than hyphenating it.

Changing Character Spacing

The spacing of characters and lines are set by the font, font size, and line spacing commands. But sometimes you may want to make minor adjustments to spacing to fit text into a certain space or create a special effect. Book and magazine publishers do this all the time when they compose pages for publication. Corel WordPerfect gives you some of the same capabilities in the Typesetting options in the Format menu. Use these commands when your document requires precise spacing.

Printing Text in Specific Positions

Sometimes you need to print text in an exact position on the page. When filling in a preprinted form, for example, a word or phrase must appear on a line or in a box already printed on the paper. To specify an exact position, use the Advance command. It doesn't even matter where on the page you enter the code, because the text will print at the designated location regardless of where it appears on the screen.

Select Advance from the Typesetting menu to see the dialog box shown in Figure 6-13. You can set a horizontal or vertical position relative to either the current location of the insertion point or the edges of the paper. To set an exact position on the paper, set it relative to the left edge and the top edge of the page. Use positions relative to the insertion point to create custom subscripts or superscripts.

When you do set a position relative to the top of the page, Corel WordPerfect places the baseline of the text at that location so characters appear above it. This

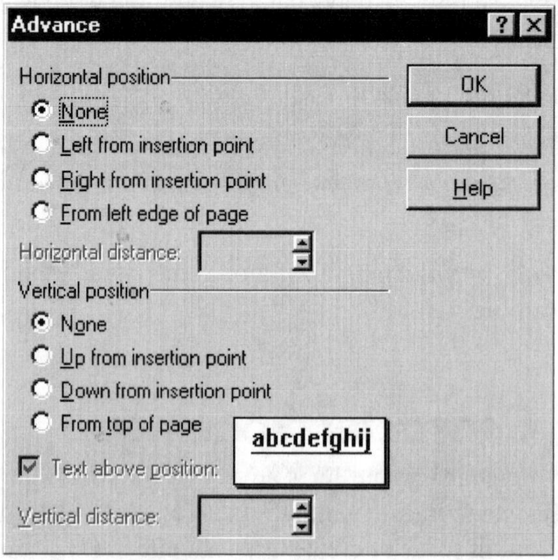

Advance
dialog box

FIGURE 6-13

means that if you set a position two inches from the top of the page, the bottom of the text will be two inches from the top. If you want the top of the text to be two inches from the top, deselect the Text Above Position checkbox.

Overstriking Characters

When you overstrike, you print two or more characters in the same position. Use this command to create special effects, such as slashed zeros or combinations such as shown here:

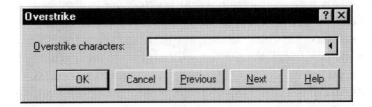

Select Overstrike from the Format Typesetting menu to see the dialog box shown here. Type the characters that you want to superimpose. To change the style or relative size of the characters, click on the left-pointing triangle at the end of the text box to select a style or size from the list. Click on OK to see the characters onscreen.

Spacing Between Words and Characters

To customize the spacing between characters and words, select Word/Letter Spacing from the Format Typesetting menu to see the dialog box shown in Figure 6-14.

Use the Word Spacing option to set the spacing between words. Normal is the spacing determined by the font; Optimal is Corel WordPerfect's default spacing. To change the spacing, select Percent of Optimal and enter a percentage of the default spacing. Use values less than 100 to reduce the spacing between words, over 100 to increase the spacing. Print a specific number of characters per inch by entering the number in the Set Pitch text box.

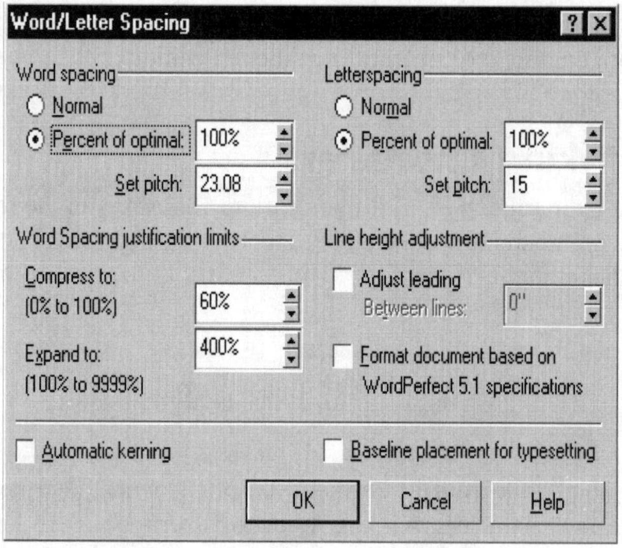

Word/Letter Spacing   ? ✕

Word spacing
- ○ Normal
- ⦿ Percent of optimal: 100%
- Set pitch: 23.08

Letterspacing
- ○ Normal
- ⦿ Percent of optimal: 100%
- Set pitch: 15

Word Spacing justification limits
- Compress to: (0% to 100%)   60%
- Expand to: (100% to 9999%)   400%

Line height adjustment
- ☐ Adjust leading   Between lines: 0"
- ☐ Format document based on WordPerfect 5.1 specifications

☐ Automatic kerning   ☐ Baseline placement for typesetting

[OK]   [Cancel]   [Help]

Customizing
space
between
characters
and words

FIGURE 6-14

The Word Spacing Justification setting controls the spacing between words in fully justified text. Use the Compressed To and Expanded To settings to control the minimum and maximum amount that words can be spaced as a percentage. For example, by default, Corel WordPerfect will only reduce the spacing between words to as little as 60 percent or increase it by as much as 400 percent. If your justified text appears packed too close, increase the Compressed To setting. If words appear spaced too far apart, reduce the Expanded To setting.

The Letterspacing options control the spacing between letters. Change the spacing if fonts appear too tight or too loose.

Kerning

Kerning is the process of moving together certain pairs of characters that have opposite slants, such as *A* and *V*, to create a smoother appearance with less space between them. To have Corel WordPerfect automatically kern a default set of letter combinations, check the Automatic Kerning option in the Word/Letter Spacing dialog box.

To control the spacing between two characters yourself, place the insertion point between them and select Manual Kerning from the Format Typesetting menu to see the dialog box shown next. Click on the UP and DOWN ARROWS at the Amount text box to adjust the space between the characters.

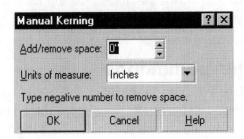

Adjusting Line Spacing

The Line Spacing command is just one way to control the spacing and position of lines. You can create special effects and customize line spacing in a variety of ways.

The distance between lines of text in a paragraph is determined by the size and style of the fonts. Corel WordPerfect automatically spaces lines based on the font settings. To increase or decrease the spacing, select Height from the Format Line menu, click on the Fixed option button, and enter a specific line height in the text box. This sets the baseline-to-baseline distance at a specific size regardless of the font size.

You can also adjust line height in the Word/Letter Spacing dialog box. Click on the Adjust Leading box in the dialog box, and then enter any extra spacing you want in points between lines in the Between Lines text box. If you enter 6p, for example, Corel WordPerfect will add an additional 6 points between lines. Enter a negative number to bring your lines closer together.

If you are using a document written with Corel WordPerfect 5.1, you can maintain the spacing set with that version by clicking on the Format Document Based on Corel WordPerfect 5.1 Specifications checkbox.

Setting the Baseline

The *baseline* is the imaginary line on which characters sit. The position of the first baseline on the page is determined by the size of the top margin and the font. For example, if you are using a 12-point font, and the default one-inch (72-point) margin, the first baseline is 84 points from the top of the page. The position of the first baseline will affect the location of other text, such as where characters appear using Advance up and down commands.

To set a specific location for the first baseline, display the Word/Letter Spacing dialog box and click on Baseline Placement for Typesetting. This tells Corel WordPerfect to position the first baseline at the top margin, so it is in the same position on every page regardless of the font or font size being used.

Giving Printer Commands

Corel WordPerfect and Windows 95 should be able to take advantage of all of your printer's special features. If your printer has a feature that is not supported, however, you can still use it by entering printer codes. These are special commands that turn on and off printer features, such as condensed or other types of printing. Your printer's manual should include a complete list of commands.

Select Printer Command from the Format Typesetting menu to see the Printer Command dialog box. Enter the codes between angle brackets, as in <18>. The Escape character is <27>. You can also specify a file that you want downloaded to the printer.

If you have an old-fashioned daisy wheel printer, you can also pause it to change print wheels or the ribbon color. To pause the printer, place the insertion point where you want to make the change, display the Printer Command dialog box, and click in the Pause Printer checkbox.

Controlling Widows and Orphans

You know that as you type, Corel WordPerfect divides your document into pages. As one page becomes full, Corel WordPerfect adds a soft page break and begins a new page. Sometimes, however, Corel WordPerfect may divide text in a way that creates widow or orphan lines. A *widow* is the first line of a paragraph that appears by itself at the bottom of a page. An *orphan* is the last line of a paragraph that appears by itself on the top of a page. With Corel WordPerfect you can avoid these undesirable situations and control how text is divided between pages.

To avoid widows and orphans, pull down the Format menu and select Keep Text Together to see the dialog box in Figure 6-15. Click in the checkbox in the Widow/Orphan section to prevent the first and last lines of paragraphs from being divided between pages.

Widow and orphan control, however, affects just one line of a paragraph. It will not, for example, move a two-line widow to the next page, nor will it prevent a title or subtitle from appearing at the bottom of the page, with the first paragraph relating to that title starting on the next. If you want to keep a section of text on the same

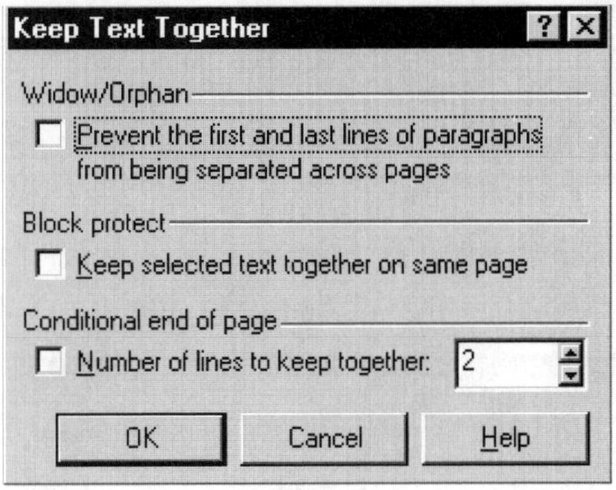

Keep Text Together dialog box

Keep Text
Together
dialog box

■ **FIGURE 6-15**

page—such as a title with the first paragraph in its section—select the text, display the Keep Text Together dialog box, and then click on the box in the Block Protect section. Corel WordPerfect will keep all of the selected text on the same page.

TIP: *You can keep text together by selecting it and then choosing Block Protect from the QuickMenu.*

If you just want to keep a specific number of lines at the end of a paragraph together, place the insertion point in the last line of the paragraph, and display the Keep Text Together dialog box. Click in the checkbox in the Conditional End of Page section, and then enter the number of lines that you want to keep together in the text box.

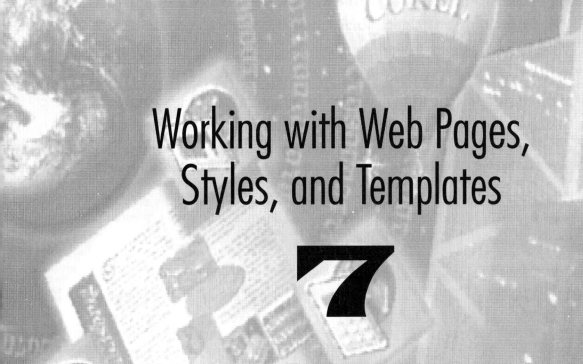

Working with Web Pages, Styles, and Templates

7

There are many ways to make your documents look good. Formatting characters, lines, and paragraphs is just the start. If you don't want to spend a great deal of time with formatting, but still want your documents to look great, then use a few of Corel WordPerfect's special helpers. In this chapter, you'll learn three powerful ways that you can create terrific-looking documents.

Using Internet Publisher, you can create eye-catching pages for the World Wide Web without worrying about special codes and complex commands. Using templates, you can start with a completely formatted document and then just add your own text. And with styles, you can apply sets of formats with a single click of the mouse.

Web Pages

If you're unaware what the Internet is, or have never heard of the World Wide Web, then you must have been living in a cave. The World Wide Web ("the Web" for short) is a graphic interface to the Internet, an informal network of computer systems around the world.

If you subscribe to an online service such as America Online, CompuServe, or Prodigy, then you have access to the Web and the Internet. You may have access to the Internet through your company's network, your school, or through any one of thousands of service providers around the world. The Web is one way that you connect to and share information across the Internet. It's now the most popular method because of its graphic capabilities, which allow you to see pictures and hear sounds as you move easily to Web sites all over the planet.

 You can also create Web pages directly from Corel Presentations and Corel Quattro Pro by saving documents in HTML format.

When you connect to a site on the Web, you are looking at a Web page. This is really just a special document that contains information, as well as hypertext links to other documents and other places on the Web. A *hypertext link* (hyperlink) is a graphic or piece of text that you can click on to move to another Web location.

For a document to be used as a Web page, however, it must be written using special format codes. These codes tell the *Web browser,* the program that lets you contact the Web, how to display the document on the screen, and what to do when you click on a hypertext link. These formats are known as *HTML* (HyperText Markup Language), and the codes are called *HTML tags.* You can create a Web document using any word processing program by typing in the HTML tags. However, trying to visualize how a Web page will appear from just looking at the tags is difficult. Since the tags must use specific formats, it is all too easy to make a mistake and get a terrible mess when you view it on the Web page screen.

Rather than type the tags, you can use Corel WordPerfect in several ways to create a Web page graphically—by selecting formats, styles, and page elements from the menus, the toolbar, and the power bar. You can only select Corel WordPerfect formats that have corresponding HTML tags, so your document will resemble how it will look on the Web. When you are satisfied with the look of your document, Corel WordPerfect converts its format codes to their equivalent HTML tags. Not all Web browsers support the same set of HTML tags, so Web documents may appear slightly different to some Web surfers.

NOTE: *Internet Publisher supports HTML version 2.0. You can insert some codes from version 3.0 and 3.2 using the Custom HTML command.*

Using the Web Page Expert

The Web Page Expert is a series of dialog boxes that lead you step-by-step through the process of creating a Web document. You can even add a background graphic, as well as a menu of links that lets you move among any number of additional Web documents.

To start the Expert, select New from the File menu, then click on the Create New tab of the New dialog box. Pull down the list at the top of the dialog box and select Custom WP Templates. In the list of templates that appears, click on <Web Page Expert> and then on Create.

The Expert creates a basic Web document and displays a dialog box asking for the name of a new folder where the page should be stored. Type a new folder name—you cannot use an existing folder—and then click on the Next button to see the dialog box in the next illustration. In this dialog box, you enter a name, e-mail address, and a title for the Web page, and then click on Next.

Web Page Expert

Enter a title for your web page. Also enter
the name and e-mail address of the person
who will maintain this web page.

We_b page title:

N_ame:

E_-mail address:

Ne_xt >

< P_revious

Cancel

T_ip...

The default Web page has three hypertext links: My Hobbies and Interests, My
Personal Background, and My Professional Information. When you later click on
My Personal Background in your Web browser, for example, another page appears
where you've entered information about yourself. The default Web page serves as
your *home page,* sort of a table of contents for the other pages. In this Expert you
check the boxes for the pages that you want, and you can create other linked pages,
or delete the three default ones. To create another page, click on Add, enter a title
for the page, and then click on OK. The title will be used as the hypertext link in the
home page.

When you've specified the pages, use the following steps to choose a color
scheme and background wallpaper:

1. Click on Next to display a dialog box that shows 15 color schemes and 25
   wallpaper backgrounds.

2. Choose a color scheme that you find pleasing.

3. Choose a wallpaper. Corel WordPerfect will display it in the background
   so you can see how it looks before accepting it. If you don't like it,
   choose another before going on.

4. Choose a justification style for the text—the options are Left, Right, and
   Center—and then click on Next.

5. When you're satisfied, click on Finished. A message will appear
   reminding you that you must select the Publish to HTML feature to
   actually use the Web page on the Internet.

6. Click on OK to clear the message and to display your Web page, as
   shown in Figure 7-1.

TIP: *If your Web page appears like a regular WordPerfect document, click on the Change View button on the toolbar, and then click on OK in the message that appears.*

Next you can add and format text, graphics, and sounds, and create hypertext links using the menus, toolbar, and property bar—as you'll learn in this chapter.

 TIP: *After designing a Web page, you must choose the Publish to HTML option from the Internet Publisher toolbar or dialog box.*

Creating a New Web Page

You can also create a Web page without using the Web Page Expert. This is useful if you've already designed some of the page as a regular WordPerfect document, or if you just like doing it all from scratch.

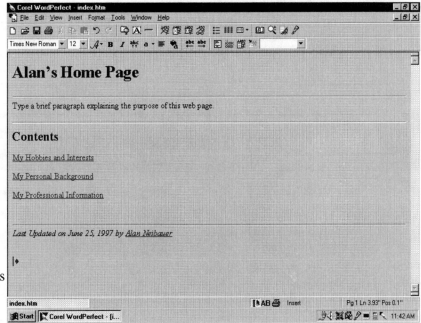

A Web page created by Corel WordPerfect's Web Page Expert

FIGURE 7-1

If you have a blank document onscreen, or a document that you want to use as your Web page, use any of these techniques:

■ Click on the Change View button in the toolbar.

■ Select Web Page from the View menu.

■ Start Internet Publisher and click on Format as Web Page.

When you use Internet Publisher, you'll see the dialog box shown in Figure 7-2. You have four options:

■ *New Web Document* lets you design a new Web page from scratch or use the Web Page Expert.

■ *Format as Web Document* modifies or deletes the WordPerfect codes in the current document so they can later be converted into HTML tags.

■ *Publish to HTML* converts the Corel WordPerfect format codes in the document into HTML tags and saves the Web page on the disk.

■ *Browse the Web* launches your Web browser.

Click on New Web Document; in the dialog box that appears, double-click on Create a Blank Web Document.

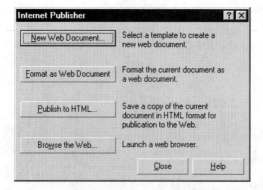

Internet
Publisher
dialog box

FIGURE 7-2

Corel WordPerfect will change to the HTML view and display the Internet Publisher toolbar and property bar.

If you're using an existing document, a message will appear reporting that only those formats that have HTML-equivalent tags will be retained. Click on OK. Retained formats include bold, italic, underline, color, subscript, superscript, hypertext links, bullets, and numbers (but not QuickBullet). The shadow attribute will still appear onscreen, but will be changed to blinking when saved in HTML. The redline and strikeout formats will also be retained, although some Web browsers will not display them. Footnotes are converted to endnotes and appear at the end of the document.

All other formats are deleted, such as drop capitals, headers and footers, and watermarks. Tabs and indentations are converted to spaces.

 TIP: *If you want to change HTML tags to Corel WordPerfect formats, open the Web page in Internet Publisher, choose Internet Publisher from the File menu, and then click on Format as WP Document.*

The Web Page toolbar contains the standard first nine buttons, the ClipArt and Text Box buttons, as well as those shown here.

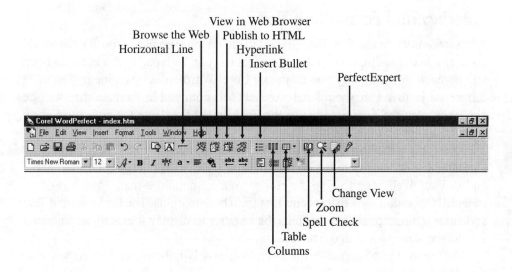

The Internet Publisher property bar contains the Font Face and Font/Size lists, the Prompt-As-You-Go list, as well as these options:

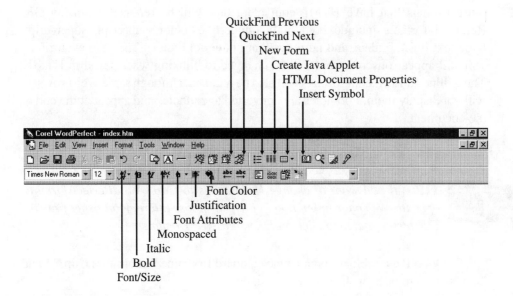

Entering and Formatting Text

Whether or not you use Web Page Expert to create the Web page, you'll want to add your own text, headings, and other elements to your Web page. You enter and edit text in much the same way you do in any Corel WordPerfect document. The main difference is that you should only use HTML-compatible formats that will be available from the Font/Size list or the Font dialog box. Use the styles to format selected text or text you are about to type.

The styles in the Font/Size list include the normal default text, six heading styles, and three list styles. There is also the Address style, which is typically used at the end of your Web page to give the reader your name and e-mail address, and an Indented Quotation style that indents text from both margins. The Preformatted Text style uses a monospace font that tells the browser to display it exactly as you enter it, with the same spaces and line breaks.

You use the Font/Size list, or the Insert Bullets & Numbering command, to create three types of lists:

- A *Bullet list* inserts a round bullet at the start of each line—the Web browser will determine the bullet size.

- A *Numbered list* numbers consecutive paragraphs—use the TAB key to create multiple levels.

- A *Definition list* uses no numbers or bullets, but uses indented paragraphs following a name or title at the left margin. With all multiple-level lists, press TAB to move to the right, SHIFT-TAB to move to the left.

The Font Attributes list contains the character styles that HTML can display. In addition to the usual bold, italic, and other styles, you can select Blink, which will flash the text on and off when in the browser.

The Justification list lets you align text on the left, center, or right. Use the Font Color list to choose the text color, and the Align Text list to position text on the left, center, or right of the screen.

Use the Table button in the toolbar to insert a table, and the Columns button to arrange text in columns.

When you have finished creating your Web page, click on the Publish to HTML button on the toolbar. Corel WordPerfect will convert its formatting codes into HTML tags and save the document with the HTML extension. You can also click on the View in Web Browser button to see how the document will appear on your Web browser.

Inserting Interactive Forms

With Corel WordPerfect you can also create interactive forms as part of your Web page. Users will be able to enter passwords and text, choose option buttons and checkboxes, select from lists and combo boxes, and submit and reset forms.

You'll need to know a bit about HTML and more advanced Web page techniques to take advantage of interactive forms, but we'll look at the fundamentals of adding forms to your Web pages.

When you want to add a form field, click on the New Form button in the Internet Publisher property bar. Corel WordPerfect will display icons representing the start and end of the form area, and the property bar shown here.

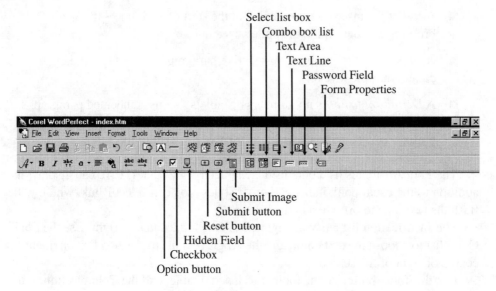

Click on the button for the type of field you want to insert. You can type text before or after the fields to use as labels.

Next set the properties for each field. Properties determine the field's name and its initial state, such as the items in a list or whether a checkbox is selected by default. Place the insertion point immediately after the field, and click on the Form Properties button in the property bar. Which properties appear depends on the type of field.

For example, the options for a list box are shown here:

Enter a name for the field that you can use to identify it in your scripts or Java programs. To add an item to the list, click the Add button. In the box that appears, enter the text for the item in the list, the value that it represents, and if the item will be initially selected in the list. Click OK to see the item in the list. Figure 7-3 shows an example of a Web page form in the Internet Explorer browser.

NOTE: *If you select Form Properties when the insertion point is at the start of the form, you can set overall form properties, such as the Include Action URL and MIME Script, as well as select either the GET or POST methods.*

Creating Hyperlinks

Hyperlinks are really what make the Web so powerful. They let you move from site to site—surfing the Web by clicking on keywords or graphics. There are basically three ways to use hypertext links:

- To move to another location in the same document—up or down to another paragraph or page, for example.

- To move to another HTML document on your disk. Clicking on the link will open the HTML document and display it in the browser or in Internet Publisher.

- To move to another Web site, anywhere in the world.

When you use Web Expert to create a Web page, you can create any number of additional Web documents. These documents, such as My Personal Information, are separate files on your disk. To create additional links from within the Internet Publisher, you use the Hyperlink button in the Internet Publisher toolbar.

CREATING LINKS WITH THE DOCUMENT   If you want to create a link to a location in the current Web page, you must first set a bookmark. A *bookmark* gives a name to a specific location or block of text. To go to that location, you use the name in the link.

To create a bookmark, use these steps:

1. Place the insertion point where you want the hyperlink to take you.

2. Click on the Hyperlink button in the toolbar, and click on Insert Bookmark.

3. Type the bookmark name.

4. Click on OK.

Once the bookmark is set, you have to create the link to it, as follows:

1. Type and format the text that you want to click on to move to the bookmark. It can be before or after the bookmark, depending on if you need to jump up or down.

2. Click on the Hyperlink button in the toolbar, and click on Create Link to display the Hyperlink Properties dialog box shown in Figure 7-4.

3. In the Bookmark text box, enter the bookmark name, or select it from the drop-down list.

4. Decide if you want the link to appear as text or a button. By default, the text will appear in blue or some other color, indicating it is a link. If you select the Make Text Appear as a Button checkbox, the text will appear on the face of a button:

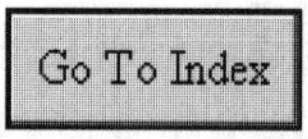

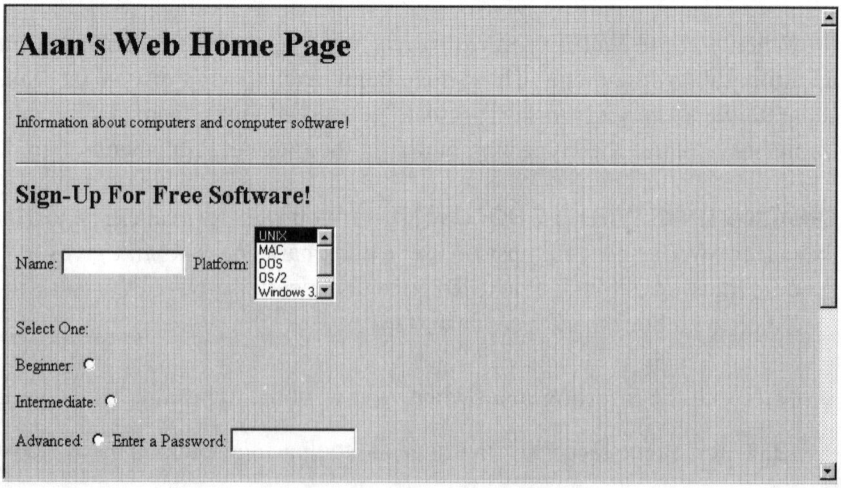

Web page
form

FIGURE 7-3

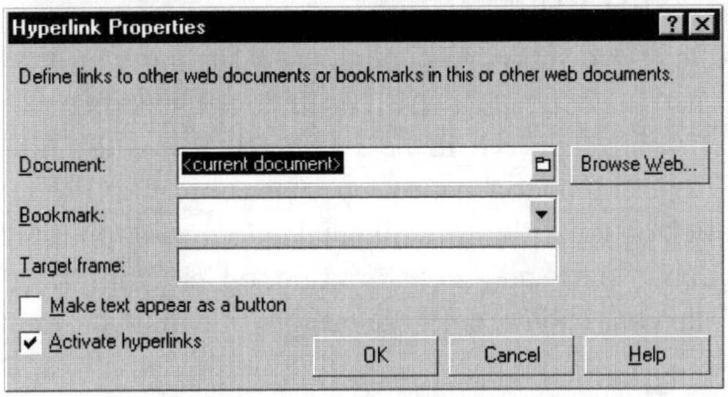

Creating a
hypertext
link

FIGURE 7-4

You also can use the Hyperlink Properties dialog box to create links to other
HTML documents on your disk, and to Web sites. To open another document as the
link, enter its path and name in the Document text box, and click on the Document
option button. To move to a bookmark in the document as soon as it opens, type the
bookmark name in the Bookmark text box under the document name.

To jump to another site on the Web, enter the desired site's Web address in the
Document text box. If the Web page consists of frames, you can also indicate
the frame to display. If you do not know the correct address, you can surf the Web
to find it, using these steps:

1. Click in the Document text box.

2. Click on the Browse Web button in the toolbar to launch your Web
   browser. Corel WordPerfect will launch your Internet browser. As you
   surf the Web, the address of the Web page being displayed will also
   appear in the Document text box.

3. When you find the correct location, switch to the dialog box and click
   on OK.

4. Exit your browser when you have finished browsing.

NOTE: *If you think you know the address, enter it into the Document text
box and click on Browse Web. Netscape will attempt to connect to that site.*

Creating Web Page Titles

Corel WordPerfect displays the document's filename on the title bar, but a Web browser displays a document's title. If you do not specify a title, Corel WordPerfect will use the first heading style in the document. To create a title, click on the HTML Document Properties button in the property bar, or select Properties from the Format menu and click on the Title tab in the dialog box that appears.

You can choose to enter a custom title, or let Corel WordPerfect use the first heading. Make your choice, enter the custom title that you want, and then click OK.

Changing Colors and Wallpaper

By default, hypertext links are displayed in blue. When you click on a link, it temporarily changes to a color called the *Active Link* color. When you return to the Web page, the link appears in what's called the *Visited Link* color to indicate that you've already jumped to that hypertext location. You can change the colors used for text and links, and select a wallpaper background, by clicking on the HTML Document Properties button in the property bar, and then clicking the Text/Background Colors tab to see the dialog box shown in Figure 7-5.

 NOTE: *The Advanced tab in the HTML Document Properties dialog box lets you enter a Base URL and Meta information.*

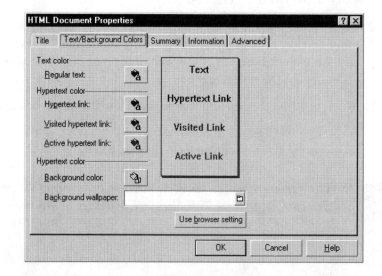

Changing
the
hypertext
colors and
wallpaper
background

FIGURE 7-5

To change the default color for text, pull down the Regular Text list and choose the color from the palette that appears. Change the colors used for default hypertext links, visited hypertext links, and active links by choosing colors from their palettes.

Filling in the background with an attractive graphic or color adds a finishing touch to a Web page. If you did not select a wallpaper with Web Page Expert, you can add a background at any time, or change the background in the Text/Background Colors dialog box. Select a background color from the palette or choose a wallpaper. Clicking on the folder icon next to the Background Wallpaper text box will display a list of graphic files. You can choose one of these files, or select any other file that's on your system.

NOTE: *You will learn in Chapter 12 how to insert graphics into your Web pages and other documents, and in Chapter 13 you will learn how to insert sound and other multimedia files.*

Uploading Web Pages

Once you have your Web page designed, you have to upload it to your system so others can see it. The exact instructions for uploading Web pages depend on your Internet service provider or on your organization's policies. You generally have to copy all of the HTML files to your Web server.

All of the major commercial online services let you upload your own personal Web pages, although the procedures vary greatly. America Online, for example, has several Web publishers that you can select from that help you design a Web page and upload it to the system.

CompuServe includes the Publishing Wizard, which leads you step-by-step through the process. It will let you select all of the Web pages that you created and pick one of them as the home page. It will then ask for your CompuServe password, connect to the service, and upload the Web pages.

Ask your Web provider how to upload a Web page on your system.

Creating Java Applets

In Chapter 2, you learned that Corel applications can create Java applications by publishing Web pages to Corel Barista. To review, select Send To from the program's File menu, and choose Corel Barista. Choose options from the dialog box and then click on Publish.

Internet Publisher offers other Java tools for advanced users. From the View menu, for example, you can select Java Applets to see what Java applications are currently running. If you have the Java development software installed on your computer, you can also choose to create or modify a Java applet by clicking on the Create Java Applet button in the property bar, or by selecting Java from the Insert menu. Corel WordPerfect will display the dialog box in Figure 7-6.

When you create a Java applet, you can specify class information, including the class name and code base. You also specify the width, height, spacing, and alignment of the Java window, as well as the Java applet parameters.

Styles

When you selected an option from the Font/Size list in Internet Publisher, you applied a combination of formats at one time, such as a font, font size, and character style. With one selection you applied several formats, because they were combined into one option, or style.

A *style* is just a collection of formats that you can apply to text. Remember QuickFormat? With QuickFormat you apply the formats in one paragraph of text to another paragraph. A style is a place to store the formats before you apply them. You can store many different styles and then apply them to text whenever you want.

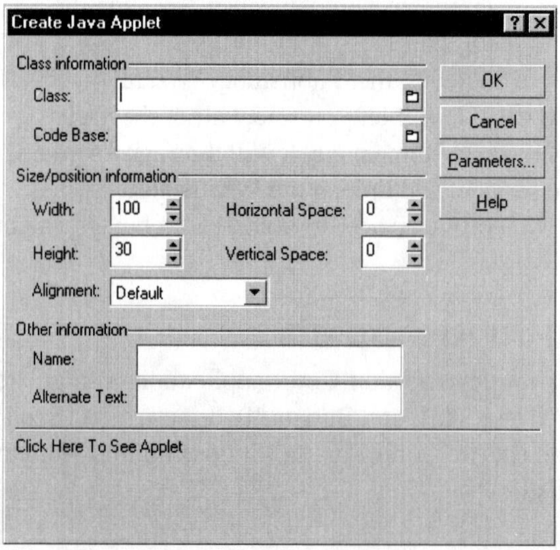

Creating a
Java applet

FIGURE 7-6

Styles provide two benefits: consistency and flexibility. By defining a set of formats in a style, you can easily apply the formats to similar portions of text. Using a headline style, for example, will ensure that all headlines use the same format. It is easier than having to apply multiple formats individually.

However, one of the greatest benefits of styles is their ability to change text. If you edit a style, all of the text formatted by it will change automatically. For example, suppose you type a long document with 20 subtitles formatted the same way. If you want to change the format of the headings, you'd need to reformat each of them individually. If you used a style to format the subtitles, however, you could simply edit the style to the desired formats. All 20 subtitles would change immediately to the new style formats.

Corel WordPerfect comes with a set of styles ready for you to use. The styles are really provided because they are used by certain Corel WordPerfect functions, such as outlining and table of contents. To apply a Corel WordPerfect style, pull down the Style list in the property bar and click on the style you want to apply.

Creating Styles by Example

If you decide that you want to use combinations of formats other than those provided in Corel WordPerfect's built-in styles, then create your own. You can create a style by selecting formats in a special dialog box, or by copying the formats from existing text. Copying the formats is called *style-by-example*.

The easiest way to create a style is by example, using QuickStyle. Here's how to use QuickStyle.

1. Format text using the options that you want to save in a style.

2. Place the insertion point in the text, pull down the Style list in the property bar, and click on QuickStyle to display this dialog box:

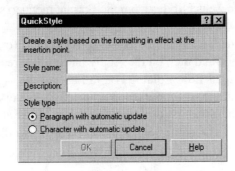

3. Type a name for the style in the Style Name text box, and enter a brief description of it in the Description box.

4. Select if you want the style to be a paragraph or character type. With a paragraph style, you can later apply it to the entire paragraph in which the insertion point is placed, without selecting the paragraph first. With a character style, you must select the text before applying the style, or apply the style and then type the text.

5. Click on OK. The name you gave the style will appear on the power bar.

6. To apply the same style to other text, pull down the Style list and click on the style name.

 NOTE: *The notation "with automatic update" in the QuickStyle dialog box means that Corel WordPerfect will change the style if you later change the format applied to text using the style.*

Defining Styles

Styles that you create are saved with the document. So whenever you open the document, the styles will be available in the Style list of the power bar. To make your styles available for all documents, you have two options:

- Add the styles to the default template, the file Corel WordPerfect uses for all new documents.

- Save the styles in a separate file, and then recall them when you need them.

In this chapter, we'll save the styles to a separate file. You'll learn how to modify the template later in this chapter.

To create a style, select Styles from the Format menu to see the Style List dialog box in Figure 7-7.

The box lists the built-in Corel WordPerfect styles. To apply a style from this list, click on the style and then on the Apply button. To create a new style, click on Create to see the Styles Editor dialog box in Figure 7-8.

In the Style Name box, type a name up to 20 characters. This is the name that will be shown in the Style list of the power bar, so make it something that clearly identifies the styles. The name "Style1," for example, would mean nothing to you

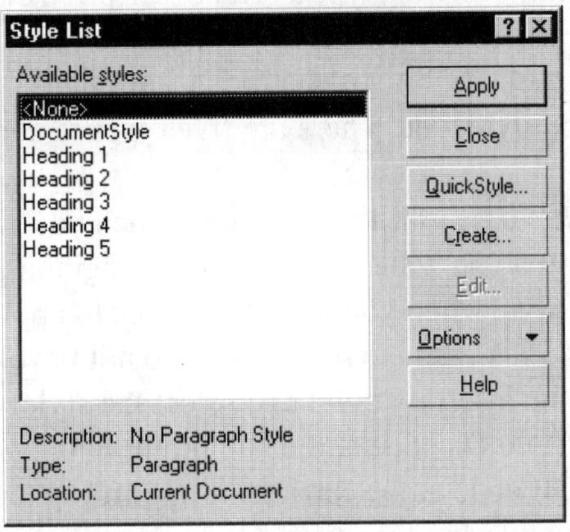

Style List
dialog box

FIGURE 7-7

several months from now, but "ReportTitle" clearly explains why you created the style.

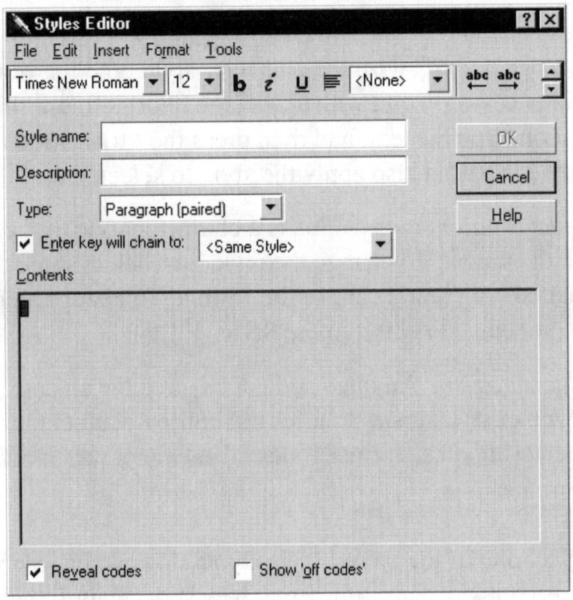

Styles
Editor
dialog box

FIGURE 7-8

In the Description text box, type a brief description of the style. You will see this description when you select a style in the Style List dialog box, so use it to further clarify the style's purpose.

Next, select the style type. There are five types to choose from:

- *Paragraph paired*—A style is paired when you can turn it on and off, when the area you want to format has a beginning and an end. Create a paragraph style when you want to be able to apply it to a section of text that ends with a carriage return. You do not have to select the text first, just place the insertion point and select the style. Corel WordPerfect will insert the Style On code at the beginning of the paragraph, and will insert the Style Off code at the carriage return. If you do not select text first, but choose the style and then type, Corel WordPerfect will turn off the style when you press ENTER.

- *Paragraph paired auto*—This is the same as a paragraph-paired style with one added attraction: you can edit the style directly in the document. When you want to change the style, simply select some text that is formatted by it and change the format. The style itself will change, as will other text formatted by it. With the paragraph-paired style, you have to edit it in the Styles Editor.

- *Character paired*—Use the character style type for words or phrases that do not necessarily end with a carriage return. To use this type of style, you turn it on, type the text, and then press the RIGHT ARROW key to turn off the style. You can also apply the style to selected text.

- *Character paired auto*—This is a character style that you can edit directly in the document. To change the style, just select some of the text formatted with it and change the format. To change a character-paired style, you have to edit it in the Styles Editor.

- *Document open*—An open style does not have an end. When you apply this type of style, it stays on for the entire document, or until you override it by entering other format codes. You cannot turn it off; simply change the formats.

If you select one of the paired styles, you also can choose what happens when you press the ENTER key. This is the Enter Key Will Chain To option. With paragraph styles, for example, select <Same Style> if you want to leave the style on when you press ENTER. This way, you can turn on a style and type one or more consecutive paragraphs in the same formats. The style is actually turned off when you press ENTER, but is reapplied to the next line automatically. To turn off the style, you have to use the Style list.

If you want to turn off the style when you press ENTER, select <None>. This way you can turn on the style for a title, for example, and have it automatically turn off when you press ENTER. In addition to <Same Style> and <None>, you will be able to choose any of your own custom styles in this list, once you create some. So you can have some other styles turned on when you press ENTER.

You can also select an action on the ENTER key with character styles. Remember, to turn off a character style, you press the RIGHT ARROW key. If the Enter Key Will Chain To option is checked, and the <Same Style> is used, then pressing ENTER when a character style is on will have no effect—it will not even move to the next line.

If you want to use the ENTER key to move the insertion point to the next line and repeat the same style, clear the Enter Key Will Chain To option. To turn the style off and move to the next line by pressing ENTER, leave Enter Key Will Chain To selected and choose <None>.

You enter the formats, and any text you want to insert, in the Contents box. Click in the Contents box, and then use the property bar or the menu bar in the Styles Editor to select format options. To enter a hard return code, so your style performs a carriage return, press SHIFT-ENTER. To enter a page break, press CTRL-ENTER. To enter a tab, press CTRL-TAB.

The two other options in this dialog box are Reveal Codes and Show 'Off Codes'. Deselecting Reveal Codes will only display text in the Contents box, not any codes. Use this option if the style contains text and you want to review it before accepting the style. By turning off the codes, you'll be better able to see and read the text.

Use the Show 'Off Codes' option to display off codes for corresponding on codes. Normally, only the on codes are shown, such as to turn on bold or underlining. When you turn off the style, the formats in it will also be turned off. But if you want to confirm it, select this option and then apply the same format to insert the off code.

As an example, let's create several styles. We will start with a memorandum heading, a style that will include text and formats:

1. Select Styles from the Format menu, and then click on Create to display the Styles Editor.

2. Type **Memorandum** in the Style Name text box, and then type **Starts a Legal Memo** in the Description box. This is going to be a document style because it sets the format for the entire document.

7

3. Pull down the Type list box, select Document (open), and then click in the Contents box.

4. We will start by selecting the legal-sized paper. Pull down the Format menu in the Styles Editor, point to Page, and click on Page Setup.

5. Click on the Size tab, choose Legal 8.5" x 14" in the Page Information list, and then click on OK. Corel WordPerfect adds the code to select that paper size in the Contents box.

6. Pull down the Font list in the Styles Editor property bar and choose the Arial font. You can also select Font from the Format menu, and use the Font dialog box.

7. Pull down the Size list in the property bar and choose 24 points.

8. Click on the Bold button in the property bar.

9. Click on the Justification button in the property bar, and click on Center in the list that appears.

10. Type **Memorandum**, the text you want to appear when you apply the style, and then press SHIFT-ENTER to enter a carriage return.

11. Using the property bar or Font dialog box, choose Times New Roman in 12 point, and deselect the Bold attribute.

12. Press SHIFT-ENTER two more times; then select Left from the Justification list in the property bar.

13. Select OK to accept the style and return to the Style List dialog box.

Now let's create two other paragraph styles. We'll use one to format headings, such as To, From, and Subject, and the other for a paragraph indentation format. Follow these steps:

1. Click on Create and type **MemoHeading** in the Style Name text box.

2. Type **Memorandum headings** in the Description text box.

3. Pull down the Style list and select Character (paired). This example uses a character style so it can be turned off to allow other text to be typed on the same line using a different font.

4. Pull down the Enter Key Will Chain To list box and select <None>.

5. Click in the Contents box.

6. Use the property bar or Font dialog box to select Arial, 14 point.

7. Select OK.

Now, define an indented paragraph style.

1. Select Create.

2. Type **DoubleIndent** in the Style Name box.

3. Type **Text indented on both sides** in the Description text box.

4. Pull down the Type list and select Paragraph (paired-auto).

5. Select <None> in the Enter Key Will Chain To list.

6. Click in the Contents box.

7. Select Paragraph from the Format menu in the Styles Editor property bar and click on Format.

8. Set the left and right adjustment settings to 0.5.

9. Select OK twice.

Saving Styles

If you now save the document, the style will be saved along with it. Because you want to use the styles with other documents, however, save the styles in a separate file that can be retrieved when needed.

Still in the Style List dialog box, pull down the Options list and select Save As. Type **MemoStyles** and then click on OK. Close the Style List dialog box and then the document.

Retrieving and Using Styles

When you want to create a memo using the styles, you have to retrieve the styles from the disk, as follows:

■ Pull down the Format menu and click on Styles.

■ Click on Options and choose Retrieve.

■ In the dialog box that appears, type **MemoStyles** and then click on OK. A message will appear asking if you want to overwrite any existing styles of those with the same name in the file you are retrieving.

■ Click on Yes.

Your custom styles are now listed in the dialog box, and they will be in the Style list of the power bar. We'll use the power bar, so close the dialog box.

1. Pull down the Style list in the power bar and click on Memorandum. Corel WordPerfect changes the paper size and displays the memorandum heading the screen. Now let's enter the headings, as follows.

2. Pull down the Style list and click on MemoHeading.

3. Type **TO:** and then press the RIGHT ARROW key to turn off the style.

4. Press TAB twice and type the recipient's name—pick someone you know.

5. Press ENTER.

Now in the same way, complete the headings as shown here:

Memorandum

TO: Joshua Schneider
FROM: Adam Chesin
SUBJECT: Budget

When you have finished, press ENTER twice. Now turn on the indented paragraph style. Pull down the Style list in the power bar and select DoubleIndent. Now type the following text and press ENTER. You will see the text that follows on the top of the next page.

We should get together to plan the budget for next year. Let me know what day is good for you, but we should meet no later than the 16ᵗʰ.

When you press ENTER, Corel WordPerfect turns off the style and returns to the default paragraph format.

You can also apply a style to existing text. To apply a paragraph style, place the insertion point anywhere in the paragraph, or select multiple paragraphs, and then choose the style from the power bar or Style List dialog box. To apply a character style, select the text first. For a document style, place the insertion point where you want the format to start.

If you created a paragraph style that does not turn off when you press ENTER, you have to turn off the style yourself. Display the Style List dialog box, and double-click on <None> in the list of styles.

Changing Styles

Styles are so powerful because they not only format text, but they also can change the format. For example, suppose we want to change the style of the memo headings. Since they are all formatted with the same style, we just need to edit the style.

7

1. Pull down the Format menu and click on Styles.

2. Click on the MemoHeading style in the list, and click on Edit to display the Styles Editor.

3. Click in the Contents box.

4. Click on the Bold button in the property bar to insert the bold code.

5. Select OK and then click on Close to return to the document.

All of the headings formatted with the style are now bold. Now let's see how the paired-auto style works.

1. Select the entire indented paragraph, and click on the Italic button in the toolbar. The Double-Indent style has now been changed.

2. To confirm this, move the insertion point after the paragraph, pull down the Style list, and click on the Double-Indent style.

3. Type some text. It will be indented and italic, conforming to the changed style. If you were to display the style in the Styles Editor, you would see the italic code in the Contents box.

Deleting a Style

To delete a style, use these steps:

1. Display the Style List dialog box, and click on the style name.

2. Pull down the Options menu and click on Delete. A dialog box will appear with the options Including Formatting Codes or Leave Formatting Codes in Document.

3. Select Leave Formatting Codes in Document to delete the style from the list and remove the codes that it has already applied to text. This deletes the code but does not change the format of any text in the document.

4. Select Including Formatting Codes to delete the style and remove its formats from the document.

Creating Templates

As you learned in Chapter 2, projects are documents that contain standard information and formats. Corel supplies a number of useful projects, but you may have your own special formats that you want to apply. Does your office use a standard format for faxes, memos, or letters? If so, you can create templates for those documents so you won't have to enter and format the standard text. *Templates* are similar to projects but they do not have PerfectExpert tasks linked to them. Like projects, however, templates can be interactive, prompting you for information to insert or taking it automatically from the Corel Office Address Book.

Why use a template, and not just a regular document that contains the "boilerplate" text? If you open a regular document and insert information into it, clicking the Save button will replace the original file. The document will now contain more than just boilerplate text, so the next person who uses it must delete the inserted information. If you use a template, the original file will remain on disk unchanged. In addition, you can use a template to build dialog boxes prompting for information, and even to insert items directly from the Address Book.

Let's create a new template now.

1. Select New from the File menu, and click on the Create New tab.

2. Pull down the Options list and select Create WP Template. Corel WordPerfect will open a template property bar. In this window, you enter any boilerplate text and formats that you want in every copy of the document.

 TIP: *If the formatting property bar no longer appears, right-click on the toolbar and select Font from the list. You can later turn off the extra toolbar the same way.*

3. Type and format the document shown in Figure 7-9. The empty spaces in the document will be filled in with template prompts that will be built on later.

4. When you've finished, click on the Save button in the toolbar to display the Save Template dialog box.

5. Type a brief description in the Description box.

6. Enter the name for the template, **Credit Notice**, in the Template Name box.

7. Click on Business Forms in the Template Group list. Using other techniques, you can create groups in which to store your templates.

8. Click on OK. Corel WordPerfect stores templates in a subfolder with the group name in the \COREL\SUITE8\TEMPLATE\CUSTOM WP TEMPLATES folder with the WPT extension.

9. Click on the Close button in the template property bar.

7

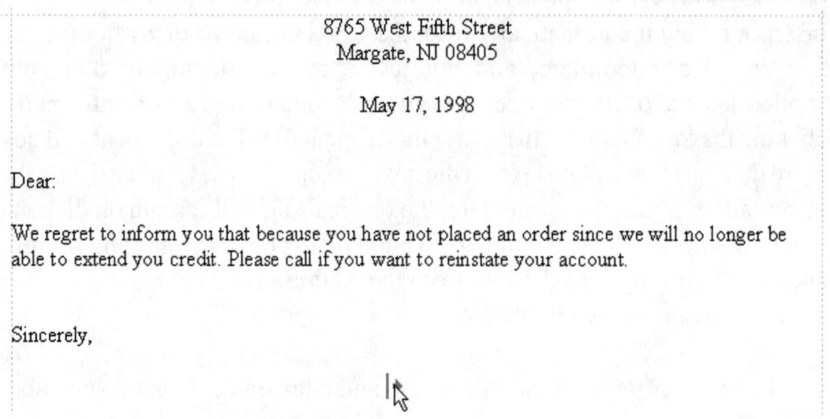

8765 West Fifth Street
Margate, NJ 08405

May 17, 1998

Dear:

We regret to inform you that because you have not placed an order since we will no longer be
able to extend you credit. Please call if you want to reinstate your account.

Sincerely,

Entering
information
into the
template

FIGURE 7-9

To use the template, select it just as you would one of Corel WordPerfect's. Select
New from the File menu, select the group you added the template to, and then
double-click on the template name.

Customizing Templates

The template feature bar gives you the tools you need to further customize your
templates.

Use the Insert File button, for example, to insert the contents of a document into
the template. This is useful if you've already created a document that contains the
boilerplate text and formats that you want the template to contain. Click on Insert
File and choose the document in the dialog box that appears. Once the document is
inserted, delete any text that you do not want in the generic template.

Building Prompts

The Build Prompts button lets you create a dialog box that prompts for information,
just like those provided in Corel WordPerfect's own templates. It may take a few
minutes to create the dialog box, but it helps to ensure that important information is
not overlooked when the template is used.

A template can actually use three types of information:

■   *Personal information* will be inserted automatically from the listing you
    designate in the Address Book. Once you select your personal listing,

Corel WordPerfect inserts it in templates without any further prompts. You can always change the information by editing it in the Address Book, or by selecting a new Address Book listing.

■ *Prompted information* must be entered into text boxes when you use the template. The Template Information dialog box will appear with prompts and text boxes for you to enter. Use these types of prompts for information that will change with each use of the template.

■ *Address information* is retrieved from another listing in the Address Book, such as the recipient of a fax or e-mail. When you use the template, you click on the Address Book icon and select a listing from the book. Corel WordPerfect will insert information from a listing into the appropriate prompts in the dialog box, and then into the document.

As an example, add the prompts to the Credit Notice template you just created, using the following steps:

1. If the template is not on your screen, select New from the File menu, choose the Business Forms group, click on your template, then choose Edit WP Template from the Options menu.

2. Click on the Build Prompts button in the feature bar to display the Prompt Builder dialog box shown here:

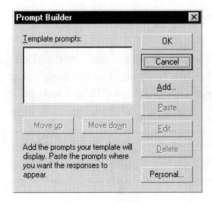

You want to enter codes that will insert the recipient's name and address from a list you select in the Address Book. Follow these steps:

1. Click on Add in the Prompt Builder dialog box to display the Add Template Prompt dialog box.

2. In the Prompt text box, type **Name of Recipient**, the prompt that you want to appear in the Template Information dialog box.

3. Pull down the Link to Address Book Field list. This will display a list of fields in the Address Book.

4. Click on Name, and then on OK. When you use the template, Corel WordPerfect will insert the name from a listing you select into this prompt in the dialog box, and then into the template.

5. Click on Add in the Prompt Builder.

6. Type **Address of Recipient**.

7. Pull down the Link to Address Book Field list.

8. Click on Address, and then on OK.

9. Now using the same techniques, add fields for the recipient's city, state, ZIP code, and first name.

Next, add a field to prompt for information that you need to enter into the document.

1. Click on the Add button in the Prompt Builder dialog box.

2. Type **Date of Last Order** and click on OK.

The prompts will appear in the dialog box. When you use the template, the prompts will be listed in the Template Information dialog box in the order shown in the list. Use the Move Up and Move Down buttons to reposition a prompt by selecting the prompt you want to move and then clicking on the appropriate button.

Finally, you have to add codes into the document showing where the prompted information will be inserted. Drag the Prompt Builder dialog box out of the way, so you can see the inside address section of the letter. You can move back and forth between the document and the dialog box to insert codes. Then follow these steps:

1. Place the insertion point in the second blank line under the date. If the insertion point is not at the left margin, pull down the Align Text button in the property bar and click on Left.

2. Click on Name of Recipient in the Prompt Builder box.

3. Click on the Paste button in the Prompt Builder dialog box. The prompt appears as "[Name of Recipient]" in the template.

4. Place the insertion point in the blank line under the prompt you just added, inserting a blank line as needed.

5. Click on Address of Recipient in the Prompt Builder dialog box, and then on Paste.

6. In the same way, add the prompts for the city, state, ZIP code, recipient's first name, and the date of last order so they appear as shown in Figure 7-10. The last step is to add your name from the Personal Information listing in the Address Book.

7. Move the insertion point four lines under "Sincerely" in the document.

8. Click on Personal in the Prompt Builder dialog box to see the Personal Fields box.

9. Click on Name in the list and then on the Paste button in the dialog box. The notation "<Name>" appears in your template.

10. Click on Close to return to the Prompt Builder dialog box and then click on OK.

7

8765 West Fifth Street
Margate, NJ 08405

May 17, 1998

[Name of Recipient]
[Address of Recipient]
[City of Recipient], [State of Recipient] [ZIP Code of Recipient]

Dear [Recipient's First Name]:

We regret to inform you that because you have not placed an order since [Date of Last Order], we will no longer be able to extend you credit. Please call if you want to reinstate your account.

Codes for
prompts in
the template   Sincerely,

◼ FIGURE 7-10

When you use the new template, Corel WordPerfect will display the dialog box shown in Figure 7-11.

Click on the Address Book icon next to Recipient Information, and then double-click on the listing for the recipient. The information from that listing will appear in the appropriate sections of the dialog box. Type the date of the last order in the corresponding text box, and then click on OK. Corel WordPerfect will insert the information from the dialog box and your name from your personal listing into the document.

NOTE: *For more advanced template designers, a template can also include custom styles, macros, abbreviations, toolbars, menu bars, and keyboards. You can design a special toolbar, for example, and have it opened when the template is being used.*

Editing the Default Template

You can change the settings used by the default template by changing styles. All of the default values are stored in styles in the default template. To change a default setting, you have to change the style in the template. You can do this from within any document, without opening the template itself.

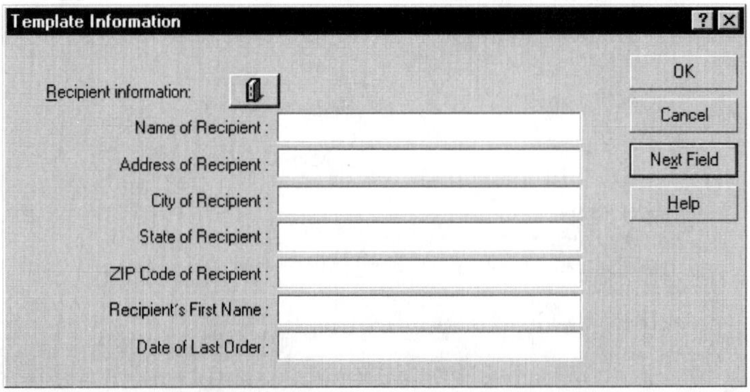

The
Template
Information
dialog box

Template Information

Recipient information:	OK
Name of Recipient :	Cancel
Address of Recipient :	Next Field
City of Recipient :	Help
State of Recipient :	
ZIP Code of Recipient :	
Recipient's First Name :	
Date of Last Order :	

FIGURE 7-11

Select Styles from the Format menu. Pull down the Options button, and select Setup to display the Style Setup dialog box shown in the next illustration.

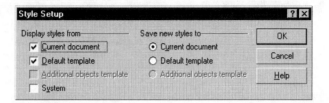

Click on the Default Template option button in the Save New Styles To section.

Corel WordPerfect only lists a set of basic styles in the Style List box. There are actually styles for every format that can be applied by built-in Corel WordPerfect features. To see these styles, click on System in the Display Styles From section. Then click on OK. If you chose to see the System Styles, they will be listed in the Style List box. To change a default setting, just edit the corresponding style. Edit the style named DocumentStyle, for example, to change the default font, paragraph, page size, and margin formats.

To return a style to its original format, select the style in the list, pull down the Options menu, and click on Reset.

7

Formatting Pages

8

Page formats affect the look of the entire page, or even the entire document. They include setting the margins, changing page size, dividing the page into sections, and even printing labels and envelopes. In this chapter, you'll learn how to apply these and other page formats to enhance your documents. Remember, you can also use the Corel PerfectExpert to apply formats of all types.

 IP: *You can access many formats from the Design Tools toolbar. Right-click on a toolbar, and then select Design Tools from the QuickMenu to display it.*

Entering Measurements

When you set margins, page sizes, indentations, and other settings in Corel WordPerfect, you can type a measurement directly in a text box. Corel WordPerfect is set to use a certain unit of measurement. This means that if you just type a number in a text box, Corel WordPerfect will assume it is that set unit. So if your system is set to use inches, when you type **2** and move to another text box, Corel WordPerfect will add the inch marks and display it as 2".

As you will learn in Chapter 10, however, the program can be set to use other units of measurement: millimeters, centimeters, points, and 1200ths of an inch. If your system is set for millimeters, for instance, and you do not type a unit following a number, Corel WordPerfect will assume it is in millimeters and add the characters "mm" after the number.

You can always designate the unit following the number, using " or "i" for inches, "c" for centimeters, "mm" for millimeters, "p" for points, and "w" for 1200ths of an inch. If you do, however, Corel WordPerfect will always convert the amount to whatever unit your system is set for. So if your system is set to accept inches, and you type **50mm**, Corel WordPerfect will convert it to 1.97".

You can also, by the way, enter a measurement as a decimal or a fraction. If you type **5 5/8** as a page size, for example, Corel WordPerfect will convert it to 5.63".

In this and other chapters in this book, measurements will be illustrated using inches expressed as decimal fractions. Just remember that you can use another unit of measurement instead.

Changing Margins

The top, bottom, left, and right margins determine how much text you can fit on a page. The left and right margins determine the length of the lines; the top and bottom margins determine the number of lines that fit on the page. All of the margins are set at one inch by default.

In most other word processing programs, the margins affect the entire page, if not the entire document. Corel WordPerfect is more flexible. When you change margins, Corel WordPerfect inserts a code at the beginning of the paragraph at the insertion point. The change affects only text starting at that location, up to the next margin code. This means that you can use the left margin to indent the entire page, or just individual or selected paragraphs. The margin command can serve as another way to indent text.

The advantage of using the margin command is that it is not canceled when you press ENTER, as are indentations. You can also see the spacing onscreen because the margin guidelines will show you the reset position, as shown in Figure 8-1. Indentations, on the other hand, only affect the current paragraph.

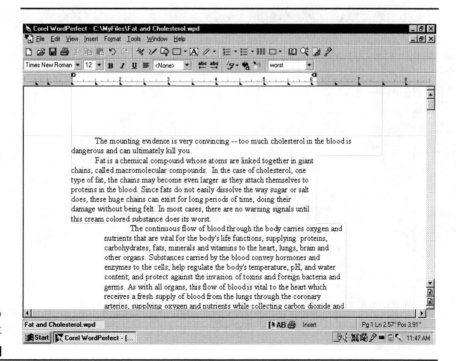

Using margins to indent text

FIGURE 8-1

The quickest way to change the page margins is to use the guidelines or the margin indicators in the ruler. To use the guidelines for the top and bottom margins, you must be in Page or Two-Page view; otherwise, those guidelines will not appear on the screen.

The margin guidelines are the dotted lines around the page. If the guidelines are not displayed, use these steps:

1. Select Guidelines from the View menu.

2. Check the Margins option in the dialog box that appears.

3. Click on OK.

When you point to a margin guideline, the mouse pointer will be shaped like a two-headed arrow. As you drag a guideline, Corel WordPerfect will display a QuickStatus box showing the margin position. Release the mouse when the margin is where you want it.

You can also set the margins using the ruler—drag the left or right margin indicators to the desired position:

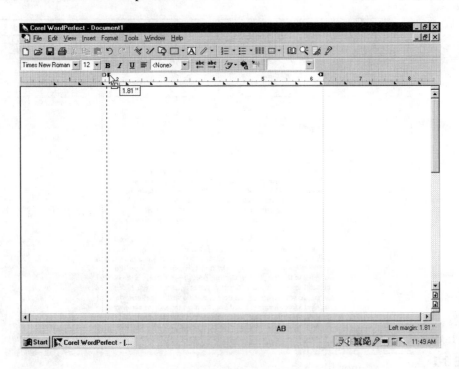

As you drag the indicator, a dotted line appears down the screen, in addition to the QuickStatus box. Use the QuickStatus box and markings on the ruler to position the margin where desired.

To enter a specific margin setting, use the Page Margins options of the Page Setup dialog box. Display the box using any of these techniques:

- Select Margins from the Format menu.

- Right-click on the top section of the ruler, and choose Margins from the QuickMenu.

- Select Page Setup from the File menu, and click on the Page Margins tab of the dialog box that appears.

Enter the measurements for the left, right, top, and bottom margins, and then click on OK.

Formatting Pages for Books

Pages destined to be bound—if only in a three-ring binder—present some additional formatting opportunities. In most cases, the binding will take up some of the space on each page. In a ring binder, for example, some space is taken up by the punched holes. This space is called the *binding width* or *printing offset.* You have to decide what side of the page the printing offset is located on, and the amount of the offset. How you lay out a page for binding depends on whether you are printing one side or both sides of the page, but it's all done using the Two-Sided Printing page of the Print dialog box, shown in Figure 8-2.

Binding Single-Sided Pages

To set the printing offset when you are binding one-sided pages, display the Two-Sided Printing page of the Print dialog box. Then follow these steps:

1. Make sure the Off option button is selected in the Two-Sided Printing section of the dialog box.

2. In the Shift Image for Binding section of the dialog box, choose the edge of the paper to which you want the extra space added: Left Edge, Right Edge, Top Edge, or Bottom Edge.

3. Enter the amount of the printing offset in the text box. If you are binding pages as a booklet, for example, choose the Left Edge. If you want to turn over the pages like a flip chart, choose the Top Edge.

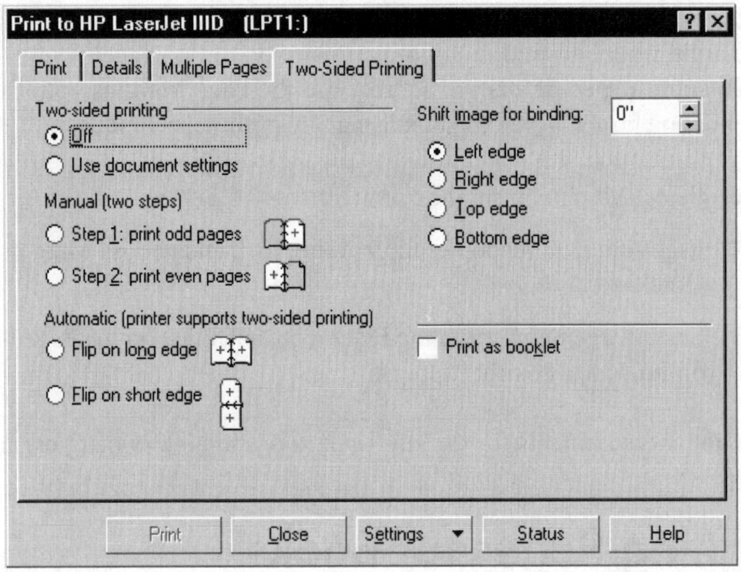

Two-Sided
Printing
dialog box

FIGURE 8-2

Using the Document Settings Code

When you print your document, the text will be shifted over to clear the offset amount. This shift, however, is performed by a command sent to your printer. It does not affect the format or spacing of your document. If your margins are not set just right, the text can shift too far over into the right margins, or even into your printer's unprintable areas. You may also not even print the ends of some lines.

Rather than worry about setting the margins correctly, let Corel WordPerfect take care of it for you using a Document Setting. A *Document Setting* is a format code inserted into the document that tells Corel WordPerfect to adjust the margins to accommodate a printing offset. Because it is a code, however, you must start by placing the insertion point at the start of the page where you want the format to take effect. To offset every page, for instance, place the insertion point at the start of the document. Then follow these steps:

1. Pull down the File menu, select Page Setup, and click on the Two-Sided Settings tab to display the dialog box shown in figure 8-3

2. Select either Flip on long edge or Flip on short edge, depending on how you plan to bind the document.

3. Select the margin for the offset, then enter the amount of the offset in the text box labeled "Margin to adjust for binding.".

4. Click on OK.

5. When you are ready to print the document, display the Two-Sided Printing page of the Print dialog box.

6. Click on the Use document settings option button.

7. Click on Print.

Because the code is inserted into the document, the printing offset will be reflected onscreen. The margins will still appear the same size as they are set, but the page size will actually appear reduced. The page size will be reduced by the amount of the printing offset.

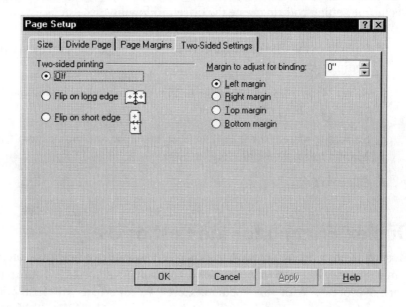

Two-Sided
Document
Settings
dialog box

FIGURE 8-3

8

TIP: *If you decide to turn off the printing offset, deselect the Use Two-Sided Document Settings checkbox.*

Duplex Printing

You can save a lot of money on paper, binding, and mailing costs by *duplex printing*—printing on both sides of the paper. The more expensive duplex printers have this capability built in by printing on both sides of the paper at the same time. If you have a duplex printer, you turn on this feature in two ways: using a printer command or using a document setting.

To enter a printing command, display the Two-Sided Printing page of the Print dialog box. In the Two-Sided Printing section of the dialog box, select how you plan to turn over the pages: either Flip on Long Edge like a book, or Flip on Short Edge like a flip chart.

When you select a two-sided printing option other than Off, the choices in the Shift Image for Binding section change to Inside Edge and Outside Edge. Click on the button that indicates the side you want the printing offset on, and then enter the amount of the printing offset.

If you are not sure that your margins will accommodate the offset, use a Document Setting code to create the offset, following these steps:

1. Pull down the File menu, select Page Setup, and click on the Two-Sided Settings tab.

2. Select either Flip on long edge or Flip on short edge, depending on how you plan to bind the document.

3. Select the margin for the offset, then enter the amount of the offset in the Margin to adjust for binding text box.

4. Click on OK.

Duplex Printing for the Rest of Us

Most of us probably do not have duplex printers; ours can only print on one side at a time. You can still print on both sides of the paper, but you have to use the two-step manual process. With this method, Corel WordPerfect will first print all the odd-numbered pages. You then reinsert the pages, and Corel WordPerfect prints the even-numbered pages on the other side of the sheets.

To use the two-step method, do the following:

1. Display the Two-Sided Printing page of the Print dialog box, and then click on the Step 1: Print odd pages button.

2. If you are binding the pages and want an offset, choose the edge of the paper that you will be binding on and enter the offset amount.

3. Click on Print. Corel WordPerfect will print just the odd-numbered pages.

Now comes the critical step. You have to reinsert the same pages so they will be printed on the blank side, and so the top of the pages are in the proper position. It may take you a few tries to get it just right.

4. Display the Two-Sided Printing page again, and click on the Step 2: Print even pages option.

5. Click on Print to complete the document.

When you use the two-step process, you cannot enter Document Setting codes.

Changing Page Size

Corel WordPerfect's default page size is 8 ½ x 11 inches. To use a different page size, such as legal paper or personal stationery, you have to display the Size tab of the Page Setup dialog box. Display the box by selecting Page Setup from the File menu, or choose Page from the Format menu and then Page Setup. You can also use any of the Margin commands, and then click on the Size tab. The page size options are shown in Figure 8-4. Pull down the Name list box to see the page sizes that Corel WordPerfect has set for your printer.

To see the orientation of a page size, click on the page size in the list, then see which orientation option button is selected. In *landscape* orientation, your lines print across the wider dimension of the page, which is useful for wide tables and graphics. In *portrait* orientation, your lines of text print across the narrow dimension of the page. Select the orientation desired.

Choosing a page size inserts a code at the beginning of the page at the insertion point. It affects every page from that point to the end of the document, or until another page size code appears. To use the same page size for an entire document, place the insertion point at the start of the document before selecting a page size.

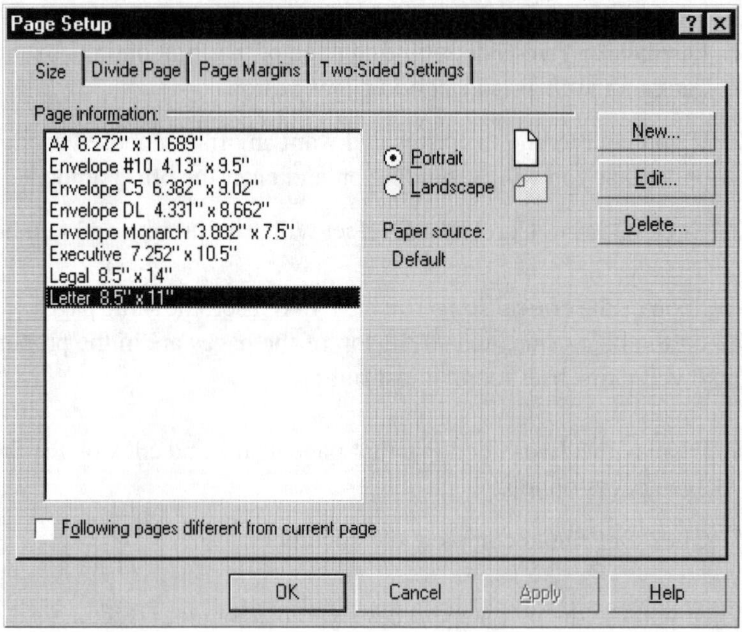

Page Setup   ? X

Size | Divide Page | Page Margins | Two-Sided Settings |

Page information:

A4 8.272" x 11.689"
Envelope #10 4.13" x 9.5"
Envelope C5 6.382" x 9.02"
Envelope DL 4.331" x 8.662"
Envelope Monarch 3.882" x 7.5"
Executive 7.252" x 10.5"
Legal 8.5" x 14"
Letter 8.5" x 11"

⊙ Portrait
○ Landscape

Paper source:
  Default

New...
Edit...
Delete...

☐ Following pages different from current page

OK   Cancel   Apply   Help

Setting a
page size

FIGURE 8-4

For example, follow these steps to change to landscape orientation on 8 ½ x
14-inch paper:

1. Place the insertion point at the start of the existing document, or start a
   new document.

2. Pull down the File menu and click on Page Setup.

3. Click on the Size tab.

4. Click on Legal 8.5" x 14" in the Page Information list.

5. Click on the Landscape option button.

6. Click on OK.

NOTE: *Changing the page size does not affect the margins. If you choose
a small-sized paper, make certain the default margins are still suitable.*

Custom Page Sizes

The available Corel WordPerfect page sizes should be appropriate for most situations. If you need to use a paper size that is not already defined, you can create your own. Get a sample of the paper, and carefully measure its length and width. Decide if you want to print in portrait or landscape orientation and then follow these steps:

1. Pull down the File menu and click on Page Setup.

2. Click on the Size tab.

3. Click on New.

4. In the Name text box, type a descriptive name for the paper. Include the word "landscape" if you plan to set it up for landscape orientation. This isn't necessary but it serves as a reminder to help you select the correct paper size later on.

5. Choose a type from the Type list. This also is not critical, but it will help you identify the paper later on.

6. Scroll the Size list and click on User Defined Size.

7. Enter the width of the page in the Width text box, and enter the height in the Height box.

8. To print in landscape orientation with a laser printer or inkjet printer, select Rotated in the Font section, and select Short Edge in the Paper Feed section. Otherwise, for portrait orientation, select Normal in the Font section and Short Edge in the Paper Feed section.

9. Pull down the Source list, and choose where you feed the paper. The options in the list are determined by your printer. With laser printers, for example, you can usually choose from one or more paper trays and manual feed. Select Manual Feed if you plan to insert the sheets yourself in the manual input tray.

10. Select OK to return to the Page Size dialog box.

Your custom page size should print correctly. However, in a few rare cases, the first line of text may not print in the expected location. Something about your printer or paper may cause the first line of text to print at some location other than the top margin, or the left edge of lines to not align with the left margin. If this occurs, you have to set the Vertical and Horizontal settings in the Printing Adjustment section of the New Page Size dialog box.

TIP: *If you just want to change the orientation of a page, display the Size tab of the Page Setup dialog box, and click on the desired orientation. To reset later pages to the default orientation, place the insertion point at the start of the first page you want to reset, and then select the orientation from the Page Setup dialog box.*

If you've already created the page size, click on the page size in the Page Size dialog box, and then click on the Edit button. The setting in the Vertical option determines the distance of the first line of text from the top edge of the page. You can choose to move the first line Up or Down, and you can designate the distance to move it. So if your text always prints 1/8 inch too high, choose Up and enter **.125**. The Horizontal setting adjusts the distance of the left margin from the left edge of the page. Choose Left or Right, and enter the measurement to move the text.

Subdividing the Page

There are occasions when you want to print small documents, such as tickets, announcements, or envelope stuffers. These documents are usually too small to feed through your printer. One solution is to print one on each regular-sized sheet, and then cut off and throw away the waste. A more economical choice is to print several of the items on one sheet of paper, and then cut them apart.

If the paper size you want is close to some even portion of a page, such as one-half, one-quarter, or one-sixth of a sheet, then you can subdivide the page. This creates more than one logical page on the physical sheet. Corel WordPerfect will treat each logical page as a separate sheet of paper for page numbering, headers and footers, and other page elements. When you press CTRL-ENTER with a subdivided page, for example, Corel WordPerfect inserts a page break. However, Corel WordPerfect will move the insertion point to the next logical page on the sheet and will only start a new sheet when all of the logical pages have been used on the physical page.

To subdivide a page, you specify the number of rows and columns you want the page divided into. You do not have to worry about specifying their exact width and height.

To subdivide a page, display the Divide Page tab of the Page Setup dialog box. Specify the number of columns and rows of logical pages, and then click on OK. Your screen will appear as in Figure 8-5, with the logical page size shown. When you press CTRL-ENTER to end one logical page and start the next one, Corel WordPerfect will display a new logical page on the screen, in the position it will print on the page. You can also press ALT-PGDN or ALT-PGUP to move to the next or previous logical page.

As with changing page size, subdividing the page does not automatically change the margins. If you create a small logical page, the default one-inch margins may be too large. If you are in Page view, you'll be able to see right away the actual area in which you can enter text on the page, and whether you have to change the margins.

Printing Booklets

One of the best examples of using a subdivided page is printing booklets. Picture a booklet as a document with two logical pages on each side of a sheet of paper, printed

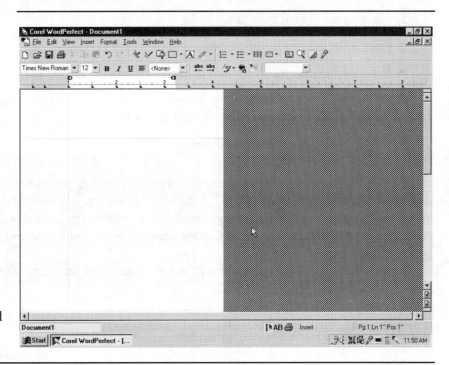

Subdivided
page

FIGURE 8-5

in landscape orientation. You print on both sides of the page, and then fold the sheet in half for four pages on each sheet. Creating a booklet requires a landscape orientation and a subdivided page.

It also requires one other very important element, the correct order of the pages. If you just typed the pages of a four-page booklet in the order 1-2-3-4, the pages would not be in the correct order when printed. Depending on how you folded the sheet, either page 2 or 4 would be on the cover, with pages 1 and 2, or 3 and 4 on the inside. Rather than try to arrange the pages in the correct order yourself, you can turn on Corel WordPerfect's booklet printing feature. Start by selecting a page size in landscape orientation and then subdividing the page into two columns.

1. If you already typed the text, move the insertion point to the start of the document.

2. Display the Size tab of the Page Setup dialog box.

3. Choose Letter in the name list.

4. Click on Landscape.

5. Click on the Divide Page tab.

6. Enter **2** for the number of columns, and then click on OK.

7. Set all of the margins to **0.5** inch to accommodate the smaller paper size.

8. Finally, turn on booklet printing. Display the Two-Sided Printing page of the Print dialog box, and click on Print as Booklet.

9. Click on Print to print the document.

Corel WordPerfect organizes the pages in the correct order, then prints the first sides of all of the pages. It then displays a message telling you to reinsert the paper to print on the other side. Insert the pages so the blank side will be printed on, in the correct position, and then click on OK in the message box. Fold the pages in half, and you have a booklet.

If you have a duplex printer, you can print both sides at the same time using the Document Settings option.

Title Pages

A title page usually contains some text that is centered both horizontally and vertically on the page. Following the title page is the first page of the document. You could create the title page manually by pressing ENTER until the text appears to be centered. However, all of these extra carriage returns could be a problem if you later insert or delete text. So rather than center the page manually, let Corel WordPerfect do it for you.

To center the text vertically on the page, use these steps:

1. Select Page from the Format menu, and click on Center to display the Center Page(s) dialog box.

2. Select Current Page to center only the page at the insertion point, or Current and Subsequent Pages to center all of the pages.

3. Click on OK.

To also center the text between the left and right margins, use the line center or justification center formats.

Enclosing the Page in a Border

In Chapter 6, you learned how to use the Border/Fill command to enclose text in a border and to add a shaded background. You can also enclose the entire page in a border, and even select from decorative borders of graphic and fancy lines.

To add a page border, place the insertion point in the page, select Page from the Format menu, and click Border/Fill to display the dialog box shown in Figure 8-6. There are two general types of borders, Fancy and Line. Fancy borders use graphic images and clip art, while Line borders use one or more straight lines of various thicknesses and shades.

If you select the Line type, you'll display the same options that were available for paragraph borders, but the border will surround the whole page. You can also choose to apply the border to just the current page, the default value.

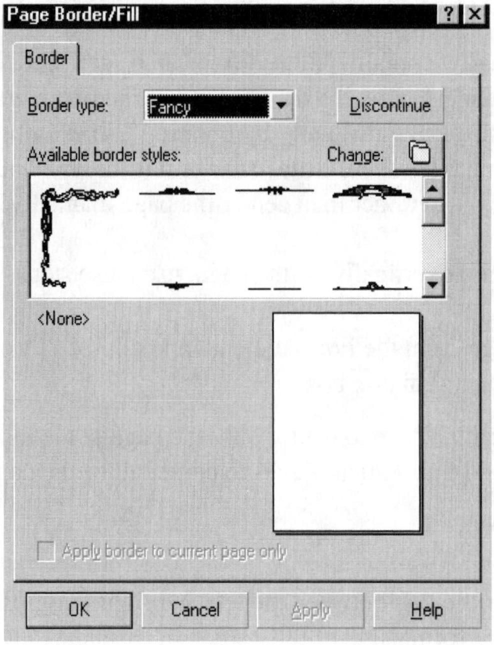

Page
Border
dialog box

FIGURE 8-6

TIP: *Deselect the Apply Border to Current Page Only checkbox to apply the border to all of the pages in the document.*

If you select the Fancy type, you can only choose one of the available styles; no other options are available. Some of the styles are quite decorative, and many are in color if you have a color printer. When you select a style, a sample of it appears in the preview area, and the name of the file storing the graphic is shown under the list box.

Decorating Pages with Watermarks

A *watermark* is a graphic image or text that appears in the background of the page. It prints in a light shade of gray, so you can see it and still read the text in the foreground. Watermarks are useful to display your company logo, or even an advertising or other message, such as the word "Draft" or "Confidential."

TIP: *Corel WordPerfect includes a macro named watermrk.wcm that helps you insert a graphic watermark.*

You can have up to two watermarks on one page. Corel WordPerfect will automatically insert the watermark on all subsequent pages, but you can discontinue it when you no longer want the watermark to appear. You can also change the watermark at any time, so every page could have two different watermarks.

 You can create a drawing in Corel Presentations, and open it as an image to use as a watermark in Corel WordPerfect.

Watermarks appear onscreen only in Page and Two-Page views, so change to one of these before starting these steps:

1. Choose Watermark from the Insert menu. (In Page view, you can also right-click in the margin area and select Watermark from the QuickMenu.) A dialog box appears where you can select either Watermark A or Watermark B, the two watermarks for the page. Choose either of these and then click on Create. Corel WordPerfect will change to a full-page display and show the special property bar, as in Figure 8-7.

2. If you want the watermark to be text, move the insertion point to where you want the text to appear. You can just click in the spot using the shadow cursor, or choose to center it in the page as you learned for creating a title page. If you do use the center page option in this view, only the watermark will be affected, not the regular text on the page.

 NOTE: *You'll learn how to add graphics to the watermark in Chapter 12.*

3. To use an existing document as the watermark, click on the Insert File button in the property bar, and choose the document file from the dialog box that appears.

4. Corel WordPerfect watermarks appear in a 25 percent shade, that is, 25 percent of the density of a solid color. To make the watermark either lighter or darker, click on the Watermark Shading button in the property bar, and then enter a percentage.

5. Corel WordPerfect will repeat the watermark on all subsequent pages. If you want a watermark to repeat on just odd or even pages, click on the Watermark Placement button on the property bar and choose Odd Pages, Even Pages, or Every Page from the box that appears.

6. When the watermark appears as you want it, click on Close in the feature bar. To add a second watermark to the same page, repeat the procedure but choose the other watermark option, either A or B.

To stop the watermark from appearing on a page, place the insertion point on the page, and choose Watermark from the Insert menu. Click on the watermark you want to stop, either A or B, and then click on Discontinue. To use a different watermark on the page, repeat this procedure. When you create a new watermark for a page, it replaces the one continued from a previous page.

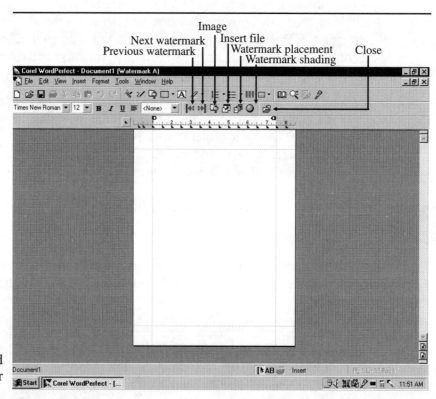

Watermark window and property bar

FIGURE 8-7

You can use the Next and Previous buttons on the watermark feature bar to display the watermarks on other pages.

 TIP: *Use the Edit button in the Watermark dialog box to change the watermark.*

Using Headers and Footers

Pages of a long document can easily get separated. They can get out of order or be misplaced, or one page may get stuck in the copying machine and never make it into the document at all. Headers and footers help to identify the pages of your document, as well as the document itself, and they can even create pleasing visual effects that grab and hold the reader's attention. A *header* is text or a graphic that prints at the top of every page. A *footer* is text or a graphic that prints at the bottom of every page. Two common uses of a header or footer are to number pages and to repeat the document's title on each page.

You create headers and footers in much the same way as a watermark. Each page can have up to two headers and two footers, and you can repeat them on every page, or just on odd or just on even pages. You can discontinue headers or footers when you want, or change headers or footers so each page can have different ones.

To create a header or footer, follow these instructions:

1. Place the insertion point on the first page you want to contain the header or footer.

2. Choose Header/Footer from the Insert menu. (In Page view, you can also right-click in the margin area and select Header/Footer from the QuickMenu.)

3. Select Header A or Header B, and then Footer A or Footer B, and click on Create to see the property bar shown here:

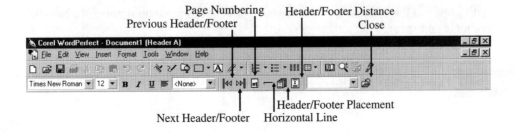

4. Enter the text of the header or footer, using the property bar or menus to format it.

5. Click on the Horizontal Line button to insert a horizontal line across the page.

6. Use the Header/Footer Placement button to select even pages, odd pages, or every page. If you are using two headers or two footers on the same page, however, coordinate them so they do not overlap.

7. By default, Corel WordPerfect leaves 0.17 inch, about one line, between the document text and the header and footer. To change the distance, click on the Header/Footer Distance button, and enter the measurement in the box that appears.

8. To number your pages in a header or footer, place the insertion point where you want the number to appear, pull down the Page Numbering button in the property bar, and click on Page Number. You can also select Total Pages to display the number of pages, such as "Page 1 of 5."

9. To align text on the right of the header, select Flush Right from the Format menu.

10. Click on the Close button in the property bar to return to the document.

 TIP: *Remember, you can use the Insert Date/Time command to display the date or time in the header, or Insert Other to include the filename.*

Page Numbers

You can also number pages without using a header or footer. The Page Numbers command actually gives you great flexibility in numbering, since you can choose the number style and position, and you can even number using chapters and volumes. You can number every page of your document consecutively, use sections to start with page 1 at the beginning of every chapter, or use Roman numerals for a table of contents and index.

 TIP: *If you use page numbers, headers, and footers at the same time, make sure the numbers do not overlap.*

Select Page from the Format menu, and then click on Numbering to see the dialog box shown in Figure 8-8.

Pull down the Position list box and select a position. The options are no page numbering, top left, top center, and top right; top outside alternating and top inside alternating; bottom left, bottom center, and bottom right; and bottom outside alternating and bottom inside alternating. Your choice will be reflected in the preview area.

 NOTE: *To insert the page number once at the location of the insertion point in the document, click the checkbox labeled "Insert page number format in text."*

Next, select a format. By default, an Arabic page number will appear by itself, but you can choose other options:

- Change to letters or Roman numerals

- Include the word "Page"

- Include the total number of pages, as in "Page 1 of 10"

The page number will appear in the default document font. To change the font, size, or character style, click on the Font button and make your selections from the dialog box that appears.

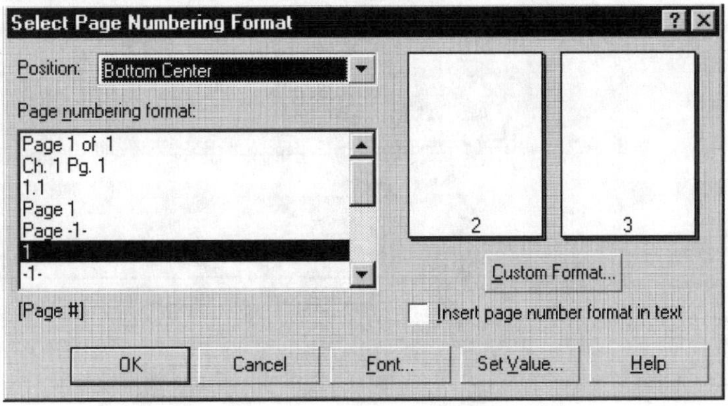

8

Inserting page numbers and selecting formats

Select Page Numbering Format

Position: Bottom Center

Page numbering format:

Page 1 of 1
Ch. 1 Pg. 1
1.1
Page 1
Page -1-
1
-1-

[Page #]

2   3

Custom Format...

☐ Insert page number format in text

| OK | Cancel | Font... | Set Value... | Help |

FIGURE 8-8

You can also change the page number, itself. For example, suppose you created a long report in a number of documents. You already printed the first document, with the pages numbered 1 through 10. Before printing the second document, you need to change the page number of the first page to 11, so its pages will be numbered consecutively from there.

To change the number, click on the Set Value button to see the dialog box shown in Figure 8-9. Enter the number you want for the page in the Set Page Number box, or optionally change the chapter, volume, or secondary page numbers. You always set the number using Arabic numbers, regardless of the number format. Enter **5**, for example, if you are using Roman numerals and want to number the page as V.

TIP: *To set a new page number without placing the number on the page, select No Page Numbering from the Position list.*

If you want to add your own text to a page number, then click on the Custom button in the Select Page Numbering Position dialog box. A dialog box will appear with a text box labeled "Edit custom format and text," with the code [Page #] that represents the number. Add your text, such as "Senate Report, Page [Page #]."

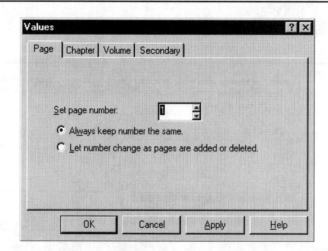

Setting the
page number

FIGURE 8-9

Suppressing Page Elements

Many documents do not include headers, footers, or page numbers on title pages or cover letters. You may also want to turn off one of these elements on a specific page of the document. If you choose the Discontinue option for a header, footer, or watermark, however, it turns the feature off for all subsequent pages as well.

To suppress one of the elements from appearing on a page, choose Page from the Format menu, and then click on Suppress to see the dialog box shown here. Select the checkboxes for the items that you do not want to appear on the current page, or click on All to suppress all of them. If your page numbering is included in a header or footer, you can suppress the header or footer but number the page anyway by checking the Print Page Number at Bottom Center on Current Page option.

Delaying Codes

Normally, the page formats take effect on the page where you insert them. Using the Delay Codes command, you can specify that they take effect on another page. As an example, suppose you plan to use letterhead paper for the first page and legal paper for the remaining pages. Rather than trying to remember to change page sizes when you start the second page, you can enter the legal size code at the beginning of the document but delay it one page.

Here's how you would format the pages that way:

1. Go to the start of a document that uses letter-sized paper.

2. Select Page from the Format menu and click on Delay Codes. A dialog box appears asking how many pages you want the codes to be delayed.

3. Click on OK to accept the default setting of one page. You'll see the Define Delay Codes window with a feature bar and reveal codes area, as shown in Figure 8-10. You use the buttons in the feature bar to select the codes you want to delay. Notice you can delay when an inserted image appears, and delay page size codes, headers and footers, and watermarks.

4. Click the Page Size button to display the Page Size tab of the Page Setup dialog box.

5. Pull down the Name list and select Legal.

6. Click on OK to close the dialog box. The Paper Sz/Typ codes appear in the reveal codes area.

7. Click on Close.

The second page of the document will now be formatted as legal size.

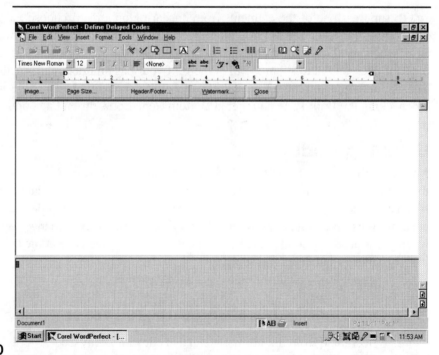

Delaying codes

FIGURE 8-10

IP: *Double-click on a code in the reveal codes area to display a dialog box for editing the code.*

Numbering Lines

Legal documents, such as contracts, pleadings, and depositions, often have line numbers down the left margin—so may printed copies of computer programs and macros. The numbers make it easy to reference a specific line in the document. If you did not have Corel WordPerfect, you could try to type the numbers yourself, but fortunately, Corel WordPerfect can number lines automatically for you.

When you want to number lines, use these steps:

1. Select Line from the Format menu and click on Numbering to see the dialog box in Figure 8-11.

2. Check the Turn Line Numbering On box to start line numbering.

3. Specify the numbering method or style, what number to begin counting from, the first line you want numbered, and the intervals of numbers. As you select options, the effects will be displayed in the preview area.

4. By default, the numbers appear 0.6 inch from the left edge of the paper. You can adjust this measurement or set a distance relative to the margin.

5. You can specify whether to restart numbering on every page, count blank lines, or insert numbers when using columns.

6. Click on the Font button to change the font, size, and style of the numbers.

7. Click on OK.

Making Text Fit

You can adjust the margins, fonts, and font size to fit text into fewer or more pages. If one or two lines of text spill over into the page, for example, you can try a slightly

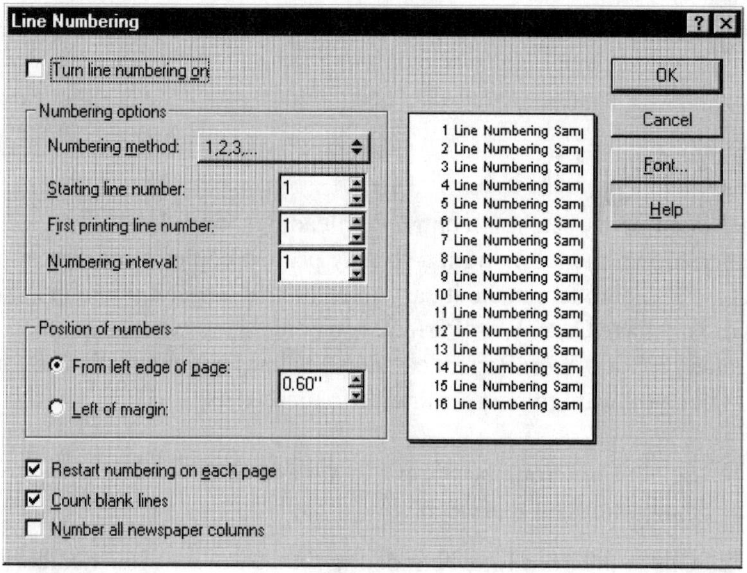

Turning on
line
numbering

FIGURE 8-11

smaller top or bottom margin for the entire document. You can also have Corel WordPerfect try to make the text fit for you. Here's how:

1. Click on the Make It Fit option from the Format menu to see the dialog box shown in Figure 8-12. You can only select the option when your document is more than one page long.

2. Specify the number of pages that you want the text to fit in.

3. Select the items that Corel WordPerfect can modify to adjust the text. By default, for example, Corel WordPerfect will only change the font size and line spacing. If you want Corel WordPerfect to adjust only the margins, deselect the Font Size and Line Spacing boxes, and select the margins that you want Corel WordPerfect to adjust.

4. Click on Make It Fit to adjust the text.

NOTE: *The number of pages you set must be within 50 percent of the document's current size.*

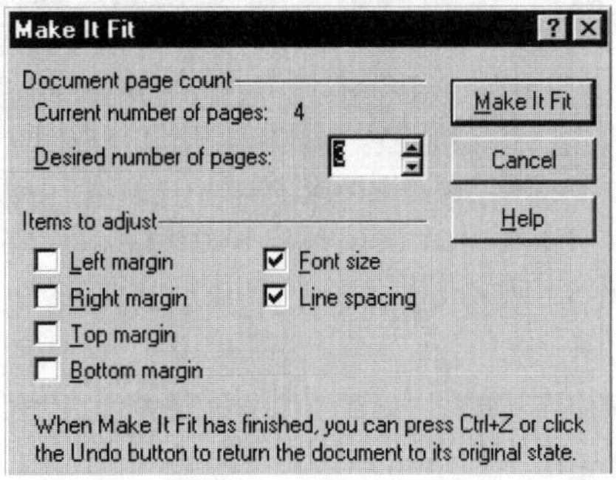

Make It Fit
dialog box

FIGURE 8-12

Hyperlinks

You learned in Chapter 7 to create hyperlinks for Web pages. You can use the same handy tools in any document to move quickly from one location to another. Start by creating a bookmark at the location where you want to jump. You can use the Bookmark option from the Tools menu, or select the text, click on the Hyperlink button in the Property bar and click on Insert Bookmark.

Once the bookmark is set, move to the location that you want to use as the link. Type, format, and select the text you want to use as the link, click on the Hyperlink button in the Property bar and choose Create Link to display the dialog box shown here:

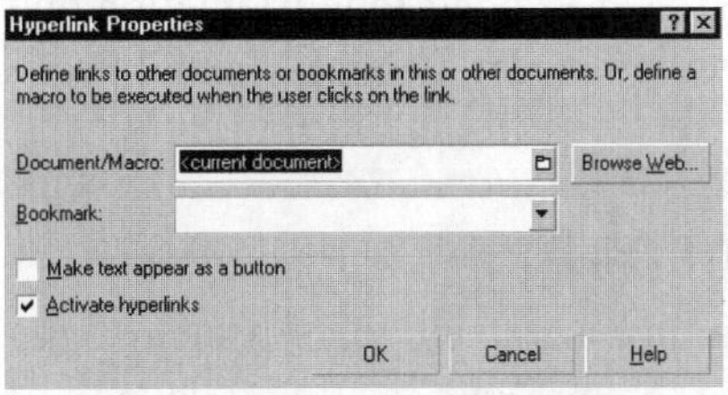

Select the bookmark in the current document that you want to jump to, or choose another document to open. You can also click on Browse Web to launch your Web browser and select a Web site to jump to.

Decide if you want the link to appear as text or a button. By default, the text will appear in blue or some other color, indicating it is a link. If you select the Make Text Appear as a Button checkbox, the text will appear on the face of a button. Click on the link to move to the bookmark, open the document, or jump to the Web site.

Formatting and Printing Envelopes

An envelope is just another page size, but formatting and printing envelopes can often be intimidating. Corel WordPerfect makes it easy, however, because it provides a built-in envelope feature that not only selects the correct page size, but can also insert the return address, mailing address, and POSTNET bar code for you automatically.

> **TIP:** *Some printers have an alternate input tray, or a switch or knob, that allows you to feed envelopes and other types of paper straight through the printer to avoid wrinkling. The glue on some envelopes may become sticky when fed through a laser printer—open the flap immediately after the envelope is printed.*

Envelope Page Size

To use the envelope feature, you need to have an envelope page size defined. Chances are there is one for your printer, but check ahead of time, anyway. Select Page Setup from the File menu, and click on the Size tab. Scroll the Name list and look for the item Envelope #10 4.13" x 9.5"—the standard business envelope for letter-sized paper.

If it is not there, create the page size as explained earlier in this chapter. Use a width of 4.13" and a height of 9.5", and then select the envelope type. If you have a laser or inkjet printer, select Rotated font orientation and Short Edge paper feed. Unless you have an envelope feeder, choose Manual Feed as the paper source.

Creating an Envelope

You can format and print just an envelope, or print an envelope for a letter or other document already on the screen. Here is all you have to do, for example, to create an envelope for a letter:

1. Select the recipient's address. If you just need to print a quick envelope by itself, start with a blank document screen.

2. Choose Envelope from the Format menu to display the Envelope dialog box, shown in Figure 8-13. The dialog box has two address sections, Return addresses and Mailing addresses. Each section has a place to enter

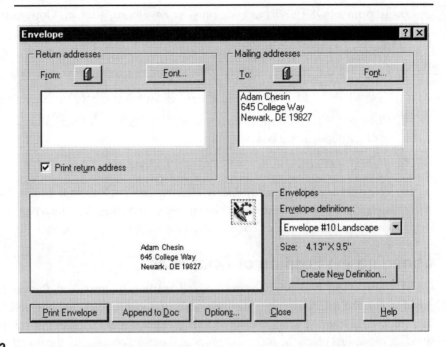

Envelope
dialog box

FIGURE 8-13

8

an address, a Font button to change the font and font size, and an Address Book icon to select an address listing.

3. If you selected the inside address of a letter, it will automatically appear in the Mailing addresses section. Otherwise, click in the section and type the address.

4. To include your return address on the envelope, enter it in the Return Addresses section, or click on the Address Book icon in that section and select your listing in the Corel Address Book.

TIP: *If you are using preprinted envelopes, and your name or address already appears in the Return Addresses section, deselect the Print Return Address checkbox.*

5. You may have more than one envelope page size defined for your printer, so pull down the Envelope Definitions list and check that the correct envelope size is being used.

6. To print a POSTNET bar code on your envelopes, click on Options in the Envelope dialog box to display the Envelope Options box shown in Figure 8-14.

7. Select the position for the bar code—Position bar code above address, or Position bar code below address—in the USPS Bar Code Options section.

8. Click on OK. You'll now see a text box labeled "POSTNET Bar Code" in the Envelope dialog box.

9. Enter the ZIP code in the POSTNET Bar Code box.

10. To print the envelope immediately, click on the Print Envelope button. To insert the envelope at the end of the current document, following a page break, click on Append to Doc. You can then print the letter, envelope, or both.

Changing the Position of Addresses

Corel WordPerfect will print the return and mailing addresses at the customary position for the size envelope you selected. You can adjust the position if it is incorrect, or if you just want to change it. If you already inserted the envelope into the document, just place the insertion point in the page containing the envelope and adjust the page margins. Either drag the margin guidelines, or use the Margins dialog

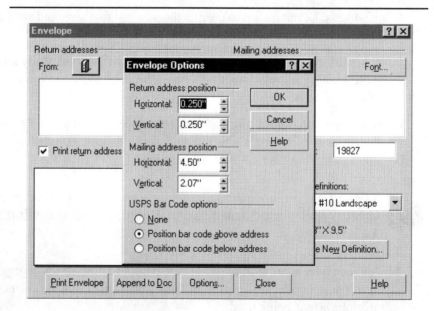

Envelope options to add bar code and change address position

FIGURE 8-14

box. If you included a return address, drag or set the corresponding margins. To use the dialog box, for example, change the position of the return address by clicking in it and then choosing Margins from the Format menu. To change the position of the mailing address, click in it before displaying the dialog box.

If you are just creating the envelope and the Envelope dialog box is still on the screen, change the position by clicking on Options and then adjusting the horizontal and vertical settings in the Mailing Address Position and Return Address Position sections. To move the mailing address further up on the envelope, for example, decrease the Vertical Position setting in the Mailing Address Position section. To move it more to the right, increase the Horizontal Position setting.

Formatting and Printing Labels

In many organizations, mailing addresses are printed almost exclusively on labels rather than directly on envelopes. In addition, labels can be used for any number of documents: name badges, diskette and tape identifiers, even business cards and postcards.

 NOTE: *In Chapter 11 you will learn how to create a data file for labels, and how to sort labels.*

 8

It is easy to format and print labels because Corel WordPerfect includes page definitions for the most popular sizes of labels made by the major label company, Avery. If you have labels from another manufacturer, you will probably find a compatible Avery number. You can also define your own label size when you cannot find a match.

TIP: *You should work with labels in Page view so you can see the arrangement of labels on the page.*

To format labels, use these steps:

1. Choose Labels from the Format menu to see the dialog box shown in Figure 8-15. Corel WordPerfect classifies labels as either Laser, which come on individual sheets of paper, or Tractor-fed, continuous pages for use with dot-matrix printers. The Labels list will show all of the

predefined labels, but you can click on either Laser or Tractor-fed to display just that category.

2. Scroll the Labels list and click on the label that matches yours. The specifications for the label will be shown in the Label Details section, and its layout will appear in the preview area. If none of the specifications match your labels, try another selection from the list.

3. When you find the correct label, click on Select.

NOTE: *All of the label definitions are in a file called WP_WP_EN.LAB. If your label vendor provides another file, click on the Change button and select the file in the dialog box that appears.*

If you are in Page view, you'll see one label on the screen. Most of the label definitions do not include margins, so you should set margins yourself to avoid printing in unprintable areas. Type the address or other information you want on the label, and then press CTRL-ENTER. Corel WordPerfect will display the next blank label in the same layout as on the page. Corel WordPerfect completes each row of labels before starting another row. In Draft view, labels always appear one below the other, separated with page break lines.

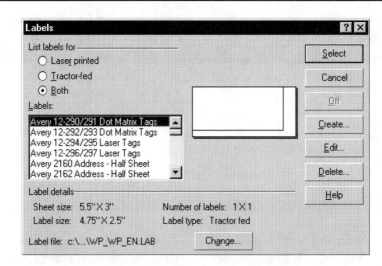

Selecting a predefined label format

FIGURE 8-15

If you want to stop using the label format in the document, select Labels from the Format menu, and then click on Off in the Labels dialog box. Corel WordPerfect will add enough blank labels to fill out the current page, and then start a new page. The page will be the same size as the label carrier sheet that you turned off. If you're using a laser label that is 8.5 x 11 inches, the page size will be 8.5 x 11 inches. If you are using what's referred to as a half-size label sheet, the page size will be 4.25 x 5 inches. Change the page size to the desired size.

Defining a Label

If you cannot find an Avery label definition that matches your label stock, you can easily create your own definition. It will then appear in the Labels list so you can select it when needed.

To create a label, follow these steps:

1. Select Labels from the Format menu to display the Labels dialog box. If there is an Avery label close in specifications to the label you are using, select it on the list. This will serve as the starting point for your own label, and you won't have to enter the elements matching the specifications. If you have a half-sheet laser label, for example, select another half-sheet label from the list. At least that way you won't have to enter the page sizes.

2. Click on the Create button to see the dialog box shown in Figure 8-16. Start by entering the Label Description. This will be the name that appears in the Labels list, so make sure it describes the label.

 TIP: *Labels are listed alphabetically, so to have a particular label appear at the top, start the description with a number.*

3. Make sure the size shown under Label Sheet Size is correct. If not, click on the Change button, which will be dimmed until you enter a description, to display the Edit Page Size dialog box.

4. Enter the sheet size and orientation, just as you did when creating a page size.

5. Click on OK.

6. Select the Label Type. This determines if the label will be listed with Laser labels, Tractor-fed labels, or both.

7. Finally, enter the measurements that describe the label. Remember, you can enter measurements in inches, points, millimeters, centimeters, or even 1200ths of an inch.

Corel WordPerfect changes the preview of the label as soon as you enter a measurement, assuming the default is inches. So if you type **5** in the width box, for example, the preview label will widen to show five inches. Once you enter "p" or "m," the size will adjust to the actual measurement, so don't panic if your 50 millimeter labels start to appear wider than the page.

Try to be as accurate as possible with the measurements—you might even find them on the label box.

In the Label Size section, enter the width and height of the labels themselves, not including any space between labels or any margins between the labels and the edge of the carrier sheet. In the Labels Per Page section, specify the number of labels in each column and in each row. The product of those two numbers should equal the total number of labels on the page.

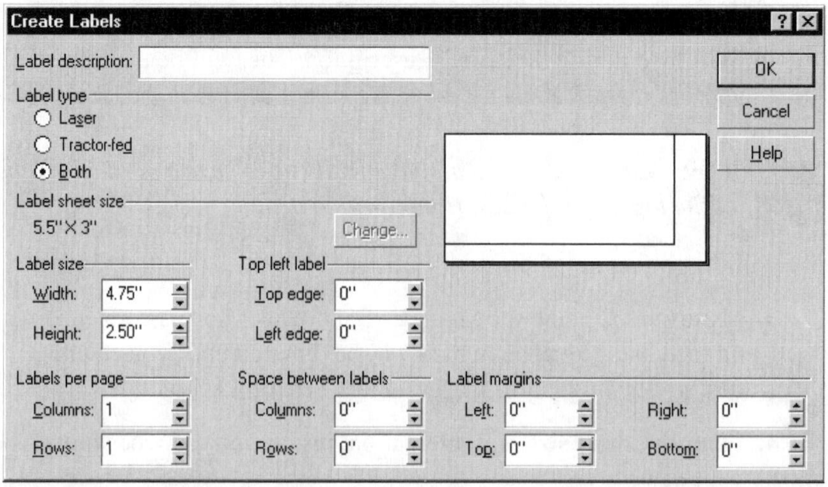

Creating a custom label size

FIGURE 8-16

The Top Left Label section determines the exact position of the first label on the page. This tells Corel WordPerfect where the first line of text can be and sets up the spacing for the remainder of the labels. If this measurement is off, then all of the labels will be off. In the Top Edge box, enter the distance from the top of the page to the top of the first label. In the Left Edge box, enter the distance from the left edge of the page to the left edge of the label.

In the Distance Between Labels section, enter any spacing between the rows and columns of labels. These are usually small measurements, so try to be precise.

The Label Margins section determines the margin areas within the label. Imagine it as the page margins for each individual label. The margins for most of Corel WordPerfect's defined labels are set at zero. If you set a margin when defining the label, however, you won't have to set the margins in the document after selecting the label.

When you've completed the specifications, click on OK. If your settings create an impossible layout, such as more labels than will fit on the page, a dialog box will appear telling you so. Click OK in the message box and correct the problem. Once your label definition is complete, it will appear in the Labels list for you to select.

NOTE: *You can define as many custom labels as you want, giving each its own name.*

8

Using Tables and Columns

9

Numbers and text sometimes look best when they are neatly arranged in columns. Numbers formatted into a table are easy to read and can show relationships and trends that cannot easily be expressed in text. Text formatted in columns makes newsletters look professional and can enhance almost any document.

Creating Tables

A table lets you enter text in neatly arranged rows and columns, just as you would in Corel Quattro Pro. By adding a table to your Corel WordPerfect document, you can display columns of numbers to maximize their impact. You can create a table by dragging the mouse or by selecting from a dialog box.

 If you've already created a table as a Corel Quattro Pro worksheet, don't duplicate your efforts. You can share the worksheet with a Corel WordPerfect document.

Building a Table

To create the table with the mouse, use the following steps:

1. Click and hold down the mouse button on the Tables button on the toolbar. A miniature grid will appear representing the rows and columns of a table.

2. Hold down the mouse button, and drag down and to the right. As you drag, you select squares in the grid; the number of rows and columns will be indicated at the top of the grid.

3. Drag the mouse until you select the number of rows and columns that you want in the table, and then release the mouse button.

Use this method to create a table with seven rows and five columns. Corel WordPerfect inserts a blank table with grid lines and displays a special Table property bar, as shown in Figure 9-1.

Corel
WordPerfect
table and
Table
property bar

FIGURE 9-1

 TIP: *You can add or delete rows and columns at any time.*

The table extends from the left to the right margin, with equal-sized columns. As with a spreadsheet program, each cell in the table is referenced by its row and column numbers; for example, the upper-left cell is A1. The ruler shows the width of the cells, and the status bar shows the cell in which the insertion point is placed.

The Table property bar contains the first standard six buttons, as well as these features:

- *Table Menu* provides a complete list of table options, some of which are not found in the property bar.

- *Vertical Alignment* lets you select the alignment of text in the cell in relation to the top and bottom lines. Use the Justification button as usual for left-to-right alignment.

- *Number Format* controls the way numbers appear.

- *Fill Style* lets you add a fill pattern to cells.

- *Foreground Color* selects the fill color or color for the pattern.

- *Outside Lines* lets you customize the lines around the table cells.

- *Rotate Cell* rotates the contents of the cell 90-degrees counterclockwise.

- *QuickJoin* displays a tool for joining several cells into one larger cell.

- *QuickSplit Row* displays a tool for splitting a cell into two rows.

- *QuickSplit Column* displays a tool for splitting a cell into two columns.

- *Insert Row* inserts a row at the current location.

- *Select Table* selects the entire table.

- *Select Row* selects the current row.

- *Select Column* selects the current column.

- *Formula Toolbar* displays an input bar and feature bar below the ruler. Use the input bar and feature bar to perform math on the cell contents.

- *QuickSum* computes and displays the total of the values in the cells above.

TIP: *The Table toolbar will only appear when the insertion point is located in the table.*

Creating Tables Using Other Methods

The largest table you can create with the mouse is 32 columns by 45 rows. To create a table with up to 64 columns and 32,767 rows, select Table from the Insert menu to display the dialog box you see here. Enter the number of columns and rows desired in the appropriate text boxes, and then click on OK.

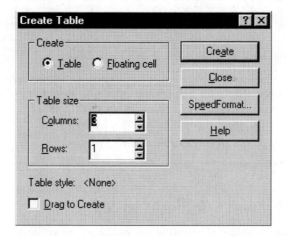

You can also insert a table using the drag-to-create feature. Click the mouse in any white space on the screen (where the shadow cursor appears), and then drag to form a box the width that you want the table. When you release the mouse, you'll see the options shown here. Click on Table to see the Create Table dialog box; then choose the number of columns and rows. The columns will be sized to fit within the box, but the height will automatically adjust to fit in the rows you selected.

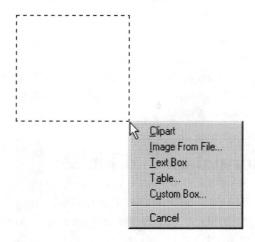

A table that you create using drag-to-create is treated as a graphic object. You can change its size and position by dragging, just as you can for other graphic objects. You'll learn more about graphic objects in Chapter 12.

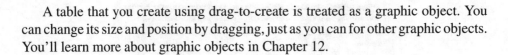

TIP: *Select the Drag to Create checkbox in the Create Table dialog box to use drag-to-create for all tables. With this option, you'll need to drag-to-create the table whenever you use the Create Table dialog box or the Table button in the toolbar. The Drag to Create function stays on as long as the checkbox is marked.*

Converting Between Tables and Text

If you've already typed information in columns separated by tabs, you can automatically convert the text into a table. For example, suppose you had typed the text shown here before reading this chapter.

Joan	President	$35,987
Jane	Vice President	$31,998
Paul	Secretary	$21,500
Ringo	Treasurer	$18,750

Since the information would look better as a table, select the text and then choose Table from the Insert menu to display a dialog box asking if you want to create a table from Tabular Columns or from Parallel Columns. Because the sample table uses tabs between information in each line, click on Tabular Columns and then on OK to convert the text into a table.

Entering Information into Tables

After you create the table, you are ready to enter text into it. To enter text, place the insertion point in a cell and type. You can place the insertion point by clicking in the cell, or by pressing TAB, SHIFT-TAB, or the arrow keys. If you type more text than can fit in a cell, Corel WordPerfect will automatically wrap the text and increase the row height. It will not widen the cell automatically.

CAUTION: *Do not press ENTER to move out of a cell. When you press ENTER, the height of the current cell will increase by one line. To delete the extra line, press BACKSPACE.*

Make sure the insertion point is in the first cell in the second row and type **Chesin**. By default, everything you type in a cell—text and numbers—is left-aligned. Press the DOWN ARROW to reach the next cell in the row, and then complete the table as shown here:

Chesin	67584	56544	345345	75467
Schneider	56390	67493	45612	78000
Wilson	43457	45774	46900	56890
Randolph	67512	56557	45760	54690
Total				
Average				

TIP: *Use the property bar, toolbar, and Format menu to format text in cells just as you format any text in the document.*

Selecting Cells

To format a cell, row, or column at a time, you do not necessarily have to select it first. But if you want to cut or copy an entire column or row, you must select it. To select a cell, point to its top border so the mouse appears as an up-pointing arrow, or point to the left border so the mouse appears as a left-pointing arrow.

- Click once to select the cell.
- Click twice to select the row (if you are pointing to the left) or the column (if you are pointing up).
- Click three times to select the entire table.

To select multiple cells, rows, or columns, select one first and then drag the mouse.

You can select a row, column, or the entire table using the buttons in the Table property bar.

When cells are selected, the property bar changes. The property bar displayed when you have a cell, row, or column selected includes the first standard six buttons as well as these:

9

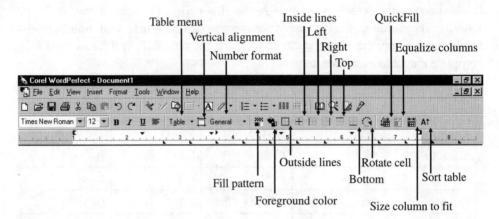

The property bar displayed when you select the entire table is shown here:

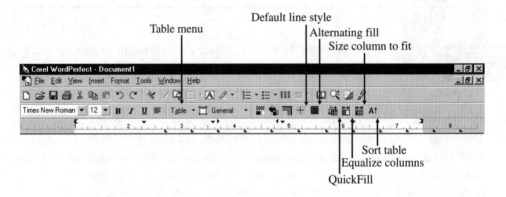

Working with Tables

Corel WordPerfect provides a number of special ways to work with tables in addition to the Table property bar. Most of these options are in the property bar, and more are also in the Table pull-down menu at the far left of the property bar. You'll also find most of the options in the QuickMenu that appears when you right-click in a table, as shown here:

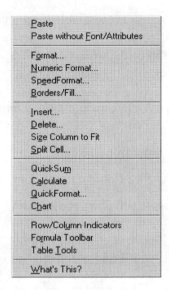

Finally, you can display the Table Tools shown here by choosing Table Tools from the QuickMenu.

9

All these methods offer access to most table functions. You can perform a given function using any of several techniques. For example, the Size Column to Fit option adjusts the width of a column to the widest entry. You can perform this function using any of these techniques:

- When cells are selected, click on the Size Column to Fit button in the property bar.

- Select Size Column to Fit from the Table menu.

- Right-click and select Size Column to Fit from the QuickMenu.

- Display the Table Tools, pull down the Adjust Columns list, and click on Size Column to Fit.

As you work with tables, you'll find which method you prefer.

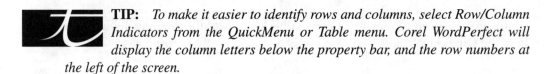

TIP: *To make it easier to identify rows and columns, select Row/Column Indicators from the QuickMenu or Table menu. Corel WordPerfect will display the column letters below the property bar, and the row numbers at the left of the screen.*

Saving Time with QuickFill

In many cases, a row or column of labels or values will be a *series,* such as the days of the week, months of the year, or four quarters. When you need to enter a series of incrementing values such as these, you only need to type the first element of the series yourself. The QuickFill command will do the rest. Here's how to use it:

1. Enter the first element of the series into its cell—type **Qtr 1** in cell B1.

2. Select the cell and drag to select the other cells in the row or column that you want to fill. In this case, drag over cells B1 to E1.

3. Click on the QuickFill button in the Table property bar, or select QuickFill from the Table menu or QuickMenu.

Corel WordPerfect will complete the series for you, inserting "Qtr 2," "Qtr 3," and "Qtr 4" in the other selected cells.

If Corel WordPerfect does not recognize the series, it will repeat the first value in the remaining cells. In this case, try entering the first two members of the series yourself, and then select both and drag across the row or down the column before using QuickFill. Corel WordPerfect will complete a series of Roman numerals if you start with "I," for example, but it will not enter consecutive Arabic numbers or letters based on one initial value. To number cells "1," "2," "3," "4," and so on, you must enter the first two values. To insert a series of years, enter the first two years and then use QuickFill.

Moving and Copying Cells

All of the same techniques that you know for moving and copying text can also be applied to tables. You can move cells using drag-and-drop or the Clipboard.

To move or copy just the contents of a cell but not the formats applied to it, click in the cell and drag so the text within it is selected. Do not click on the cell border.

When you move or copy cells, you insert the contents and formats of the cells into another location. If you move or copy an entire row or column, however, other rows or columns will shift over or down to make room. The row or column that you paste does not replace the one where you paste or drop it; so copying an entire row, for instance, actually inserts another row into the table.

To move a cell, row, or column by drag-and-drop, select what you want to move and drag it to the new location. To copy the selection rather than move it, hold down the CTRL key when you release the mouse button.

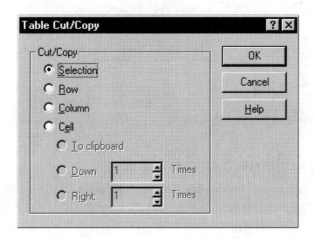

You can also move and copy cells, rows, and columns using the Clipboard with the Cut, Copy, and Paste commands. When you select cells and choose Cut or Copy, however, you'll see the dialog box shown here. Select to cut or copy just the selected cells (Selection), or the entire row or column of the selected cells. Click on OK, move the insertion point to where you want to insert the cells, and select Paste.

You can also use the Table Cut/Copy dialog box to copy a single selected cell into any number of consecutive cells in the row or column. Click on the Cell option in the Table Cut/Copy dialog box. The default option will be Clipboard, indicating that the cell will be placed into the Clipboard for pasting elsewhere. To copy the cell down to cells in the column, click on the Down option, and then enter the number of cells you want to paste it to in the Times box. To copy the cell across the row, click on the Right option and enter the number of cells.

Sorting Tables

If you do not like the order of information in your table, you can have Corel WordPerfect sort rows for you, rather than moving individual rows. You can perform a numeric or alphabetic sort in either ascending or descending order.

The sort is performed using the values in the current column. Select the rows that you want to sort, or select the entire column to sort the entire table. Then pull down the *Sort Table* list in the property bar to see the options shown here and make your choice.

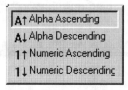

 NOTE: *The Sort Table option is only available in the property bar, and only when cells are selected.*

Changing Cell Width and Height

Corel WordPerfect gives you complete control over the size of rows, columns, and cells.

You can change the width of a column in several ways. If you point to a vertical grid line in the table, the pointer will appear with a two-headed arrow. Point to and drag a line between two cells to change the width of the cells on either side. As you drag, a QuickStatus box will appear showing the dimensions of the cells. If you drag the leftmost or rightmost grid line, only the cell next to it will be affected.

You can also adjust columns with the ruler using the markers in the Indentation and Margin area. The down-pointing triangles represent the lines between columns. Drag a triangle to change the width of the cells on both sides. Drag the left or right margin indicator to adjust the width of the end cells. When the insertion point is in a table, dragging the margin indicators does not change the page margins, just the column width.

You will also see left- and right-pointing triangles in the ruler. These represent the indentation of text within the column in which the insertion point is placed. Drag these markers to change the indentation of text within the cell.

Adjusting Column Width Automatically

Rather than dragging column indicators to change column width, you can have Corel WordPerfect automatically adjust the column for you. To adjust the column so it is as wide as the widest entry in it, right-click in any cell in the column and then choose Size Column to Fit in the QuickMenu. You can also choose Size Column to Fit from the Table menu in the property bar, or from the Adjust Columns list in the Table Tools.

To make a column just wide enough for a specific entry, first select the cell containing that entry and then use the Size Column to Fit command—using the button on the property bar, or selecting the command from the QuickMenu, Table menu, or Table Tools. If any cells contain wider entries, however, their text will be wrapped onto two or more lines, making their row higher.

TIP: *The Equalize Columns command makes selected columns the same size, equally dividing the existing space occupied by the columns. Choose the command from the property bar, Table menu, or QuickMenu when you select cells in the columns you want to equalize.*

Splitting and Joining Cells

You can also change the size and shape of cells by splitting and joining. *Splitting* divides a cell into two rows or columns. *Joining* combines selected cells into one large cell. You can split and join cells by using the mouse, or by selecting the cells first and choosing a command.

To join cells by using the mouse, click on the QuickJoin Cells button in the table property bar—the mouse pointer will appear as shown here.

45774
56557

Now select the cells that you want to combine. Corel WordPerfect leaves the tool on so you can join other cells. To turn off the function, click on the QuickJoin Cells button again.

You can also join cells by selecting them first, and then choosing Join Cells from the QuickMenu, or then choosing Join from the Table menu and clicking on Cell. Any contents in the cells will also be combined, with a tab separating information from side-by-side cells and a carriage return separating cells that were in the same column.

To split a cell into two rows, click on the QuickSplit Row button in the property bar. The mouse pointer will appear as shown here, and a horizontal line will appear in the cell you point to. Point to the cell you want to split into two rows and click. Click on the button again to turn it off.

45774
56557

To split a cell into two columns, click on the QuickSplit Column button in the property bar. The mouse pointer will appear as shown here, along with a QuickStatus box showing the size of the column. Click where you want the cell divided; then click on the button again to turn it off.

45774	46900
56557	45760
	0.9" 0.4"

TIP: *When using either the QuickSplit Row or QuickSplit Column tool, hold down the* ALT *key to switch to the other—from the QuickSplit Row to the QuickSplit column tool, for example. Hold down the* SHIFT *key to switch to the QuickJoin tool.*

To split cells into multiple rows or columns, use the Split Cells command. Right-click in the cell that you want to split, and then choose Split Cell from the QuickMenu to see this dialog box:

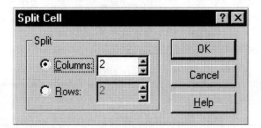

Choose if you want to split the cell into rows or columns, enter the number of cells you want to create, and then click on OK.

 NOTE: *The Join and Split commands are available in the Table Tools.*

Changing Grid Lines

The grid lines in a table help to separate cells, and they make it easier to keep track of rows and columns. To give your table a more polished look, you can customize grid lines, and even add color backgrounds and patterns to the cells. Of course, grid lines and background fills are for more than just good looks; they can call attention to parts of the table and make it easier to read.

You can add grid lines and fills using the property bar, QuickMenu, Table menu, or Table Tools. You can format a single cell without selecting it, or a cell or cells after you select them.

USING THE PROPERTIES DIALOG BOX To format the lines around a single cell, click in the cell; otherwise select the cells you want to format. To customize the lines or fill of the entire table, you can be anywhere in the table. Choose Borders/Fill from the QuickMenu or Table menu to see the dialog box shown in Figure 9-2.

9

Properties for Table Borders/Fill   ? ✕

Cell | Table

Cell lines

Left: ⬜   Default
Right: ⬜   Default
Top: ⬜   Default
Bottom: ⬜   Default
Inside: ⬜   Default
Outside: ⬜   Default
Color: 🖎

Cell fill

Fill: ✕   Default
Foreground: 🖎
Background: 🖎

Styles...

OK   Cancel   Apply   Help

Properties
for Table
Borders/Fill
dialog box

FIGURE 9-2

The options in the Cell tab let you select the type and color of lines around the cell, and its fill color and pattern. The lists in the Cell Lines section let you select from 32 types of lines for the left, right, top, and bottom of the cell, as shown here:

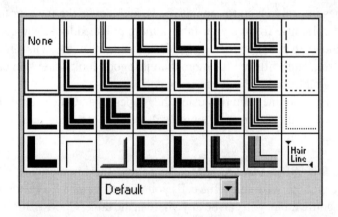

You can either click on one of the displayed options, or pull down the list and select one by name.

Choosing an option from the Outside list adds the selected pattern to all four lines. If you selected a block of cells, however, the Outside option only affects the border around the selected area, and you can choose an Inside line pattern to appear on the grid lines between the cells, without affecting the border.

Select the line color from the Color list. Use the Fill list to add a pattern or shading to the cell, from the options shown here. If you choose a fill pattern, you can also select foreground and background colors.

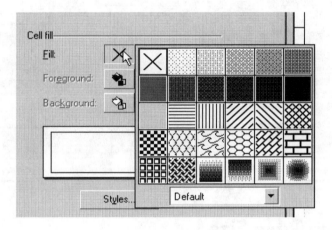

The Table page of the dialog box is shown in Figure 9-3. These options affect the grid lines on the outside border of the table, and the default line between cells. You can also add a fill pattern and alternate patterns in rows and columns.

USING THE PROPERTY BAR   You can also use buttons on the property bar to customize the borders and fill of selected cells.

If cells are not selected, use the Outside Lines, Cell Fill, and Foreground Color buttons. If cells are selected, pull down the Left Line, Right Line, Top Line, Bottom Line, Inside Lines, Outside Lines, Cell Fill, and Foreground Color lists, and choose the line and fill type desired.

If you selected the entire table, choose options from the Outside Line, Line Style, Cell Fill, Foreground Color, and Alternating Fill buttons.

TIP: *Border and fill options are available in the Table Tools.*

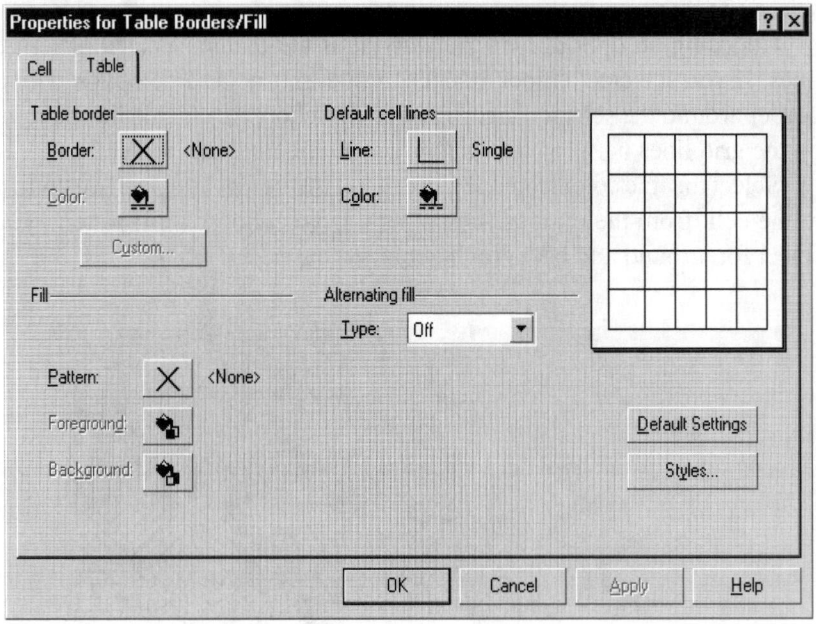

Customizing
all table
lines

FIGURE 9-3

Changing Table Size

You may create a table, only to realize later that you want to change the size. When this happens, you'll need to insert or delete rows or columns.

Inserting Rows and Columns

If you only need to insert an additional row at the end of the table, place the insertion point in the last cell of the last row and press TAB. Corel WordPerfect will insert a blank row and place the insertion point in the first cell of the new row.

To insert a new row above the current row, click on the Insert Row button in the toolbar. You can also insert a row using shortcut key combinations. Press ALT-INS to insert a row above the insertion point, or press ALT-SHIFT-INS to insert a row below the insertion point.

To insert several rows at one time or to insert new columns, use the Insert command. Start by placing the insertion point in the row or column that you want to insert a new row or column before or after. Then select Insert from the Table menu, or right-click on the cell and select Insert from the QuickMenu, to see the dialog box in Figure 9-4. Here's how to use the dialog box.

 TIP: *The Insert and Delete commands are available in the Table Tools.*

1. Click on either Columns or Rows to choose what you want to insert.

2. Enter the number of rows or columns desired.

3. Choose either Before or After the row or column.

4. If you are inserting columns, choose Keep Column Widths Same if you want to insert the columns in the same width as existing ones.

5. Click on OK.

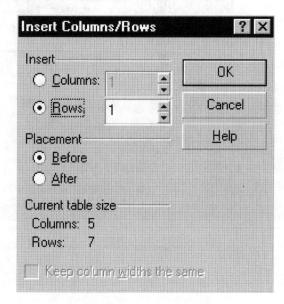

Inserting
columns
and rows

FIGURE 9-4

Deleting Rows, Columns, and Cells

It's as easy to delete rows, columns, and cells as it is to insert them. To delete the current row, press ALT-DEL. This deletes the row at the insertion point. To delete any number of rows or columns, place the insertion point in the first row or column you want to delete, and then choose Delete from the Table menu to see the dialog box in Figure 9-5. Delete rows or columns using these steps:

1. Click on either Columns or Rows to choose what you want to delete.

2. Enter the number of rows or columns you want to delete.

3. Choose if you want to delete Cell Contents or Formulas Only. Choosing Formulas Only will delete any formulas in the cell by leaving the results of the formulas as text.

4. Click on OK.

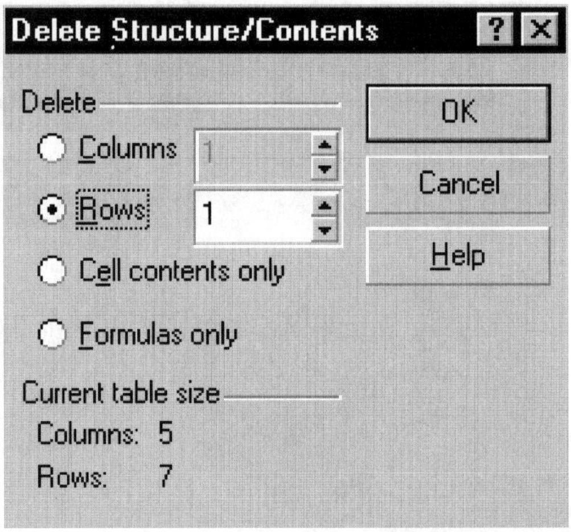

Deleting
columns
and rows

FIGURE 9-5

Splitting and Joining Tables

One other way to change table size is to split a table into two, or join two tables. You can only split and join tables at rows, not columns.

To split a table, start by placing the insertion point in the row that you want to start the new table, and then choose Split from the Table menu and click on Table.

To combine tables, click on the bottom row of the first table, choose Join from the Table menu, and then click on Tables. To join tables, they must have the same number of columns, and there must be no blank lines between the tables.

Deleting Tables

You can delete a table by selecting the entire thing and then pressing DEL. Corel WordPerfect will display the dialog box shown here. Make your choice from the dialog box and click on OK.

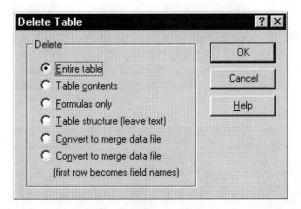

Selecting a Table Format

Rather than using a variety of means to format the parts of a table, you can choose a complete set of formats to apply to the entire table at one time by use of the SpeedFormat command. With the insertion point in any cell of the table, select SpeedFormat from the Table menu or the QuickMenu to see the dialog box in Figure 9-6.

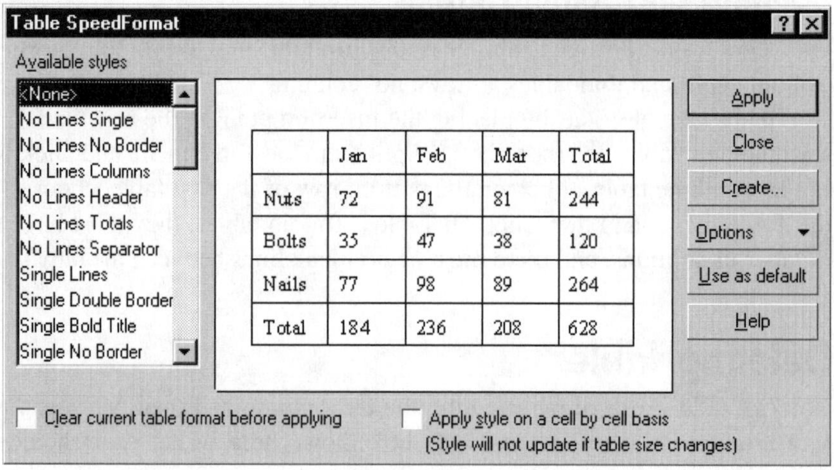

Selecting a
table format

FIGURE 9-6

The Available Styles list contains a series of complete table formats. Click on each format and see how it affects the sample table in the preview panel area. Choosing the Fancy Shading format, for instance, will change our sample table to this:

	Qtr1	Qtr2	Qtr3	Qtr4
Chesin	67584	56544	345345	75467
Schneider	56390	67493	45612	78000
Wilson	43457	45774	46900	56890
Randolph	67512	56557	45760	54690
Total				
Average				

Now take a look at some of the options in the dialog box:

■ The Apply Style on a Cell by Cell Basis checkbox will automatically apply the same formats to rows or columns that you later add to the table. Deselect this checkbox if you want to add unformatted rows or columns.

- The Clear Current Table Settings Before Applying checkbox will remove all of the table's original formats so none of them will be retained when you apply a selected style.

- The Initial Style button will apply the selected formats to all new tables that you create. Select the style, click on Initial Style, and then click on Yes in the message box that appears.

When you find a format that you want for your table, click on Apply.

Creating Your Own Styles

If you don't like any of the built-in table styles, you can create your own. This way you can quickly reapply the same formats to another table. First, use all of Corel WordPerfect's formatting features to format the table the way you want to. You'll learn more about formatting tables soon. Then follow these steps:

1. Use any of the techniques you learned previously to display the Table SpeedFormat dialog box.

2. Decide where you want to save your styles. Pull down the Options button menu, and click on Setup to see the Table Style Settings dialog box.

3. You can save your styles in the current document or in the default template. Click on your choice and then on OK.

4. Click on the Create button.

5. In the dialog box that appears, type a name for the style and then click on OK. Your style will now be listed in the Available Styles list and shown at the top of the list, along with the most recently used style.

You can also save your styles in a separate file on the disk, as follows:

1. Pull down the Options menu.

2. Click on Save.

3. Type a name for the file in the box that appears.

4. Click on OK.

9

When you want to apply a table style, you have to select the style from the Available Styles list. To display styles that you saved in a separate file, follow these steps:

1. Pull down the Options menu.

2. Select Retrieve.

3. Type the name of the file.

4. Click on OK.

To list styles in either the document or the default template, pull down the Options button menu, click on Setup, and make your choice from the dialog box.

You can also use the Options menu to delete or rename one of your custom styles. You cannot delete or rename Corel WordPerfect's built-in styles.

Applying Table Formats

You can always format the text in cells using the options in the property bar and format menus. Selecting text in a cell and clicking on the Bold button, for example, will format the text in boldface. To adjust the width of columns, you can always use the mouse to drag the column border or the column indicator in the ruler.

You have greater control over formats, however, if you use the Format command to display the dialog box shown in Figure 9-7. Display the dialog box using any of these techniques:

■ Select Format from the Table menu.

■ Right-click and select Format from the QuickMenu.

■ Click on Format in the Table Tools.

The pages in this dialog box let you format cells, rows, columns, or the entire table. The default page displayed will depend on what is selected in the table. If you select a row before displaying the dialog box, for example, the Row page will be open. Let's look at each of the pages and the options they offer.

Applying Cell Formats

These options affect the current cell or the group of selected cells.

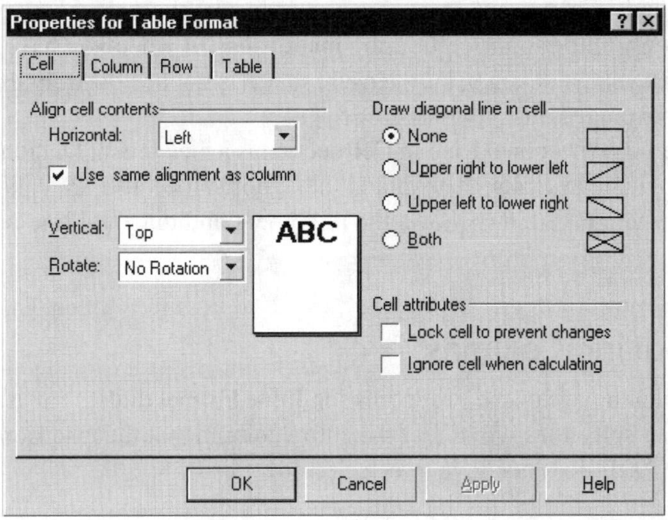

Properties for Table Format dialog box

FIGURE 9-7

Use the Horizontal list to align the text in the cell on the left, right, center, or on the decimal point, or use Full or All justification. When you choose an option, the check mark will be cleared from the Use Same Alignment as Column box. Select the box if you want the cell to use the default alignment, or the alignment that you've assigned to the entire column.

NOTE: *Selecting an alignment is the same as choosing an option from the Justification list in the power bar.*

The options in the Vertical and Rotate boxes control where the text appears vertically in the cell, and its rotation. You can select a vertical position of top, center, or bottom, and you can rotate the text in 90-degree increments—90, 180, and 270 degrees.

TIP: *Quickly rotate text in a cell in 90-degree increments by clicking on the Rotate Cell button in the Table property bar.*

In the Cell Attributes section, decide if you want to lock the cell so it cannot be edited and if you want to ignore the value in the cell when performing math operations. Ignoring the cell during math is useful when you have a numeric label, such as a year, and you want to ensure that it is not accidentally used to calculate a total or average value.

The Draw Diagonal Line in Cell section is a nice touch. Diagonal lines are often used to indicate cells that should be ignored because they have no value or significance. Figure 9-8 shows the alignment and diagonal line options applied to cells.

Formatting Columns

The Column page of the Properties for Table Format dialog box is shown in Figure 9-9. Your selections will affect the entire column that the insertion point is in—the column itself does not have to be selected.

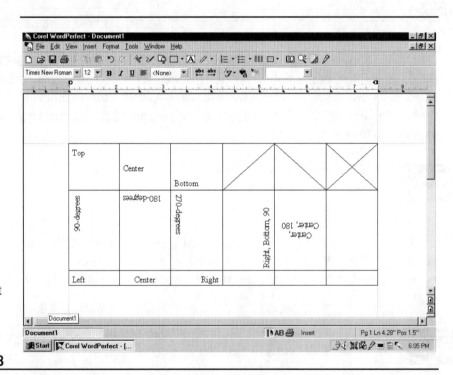

Alignment and diagonal options

FIGURE 9-8

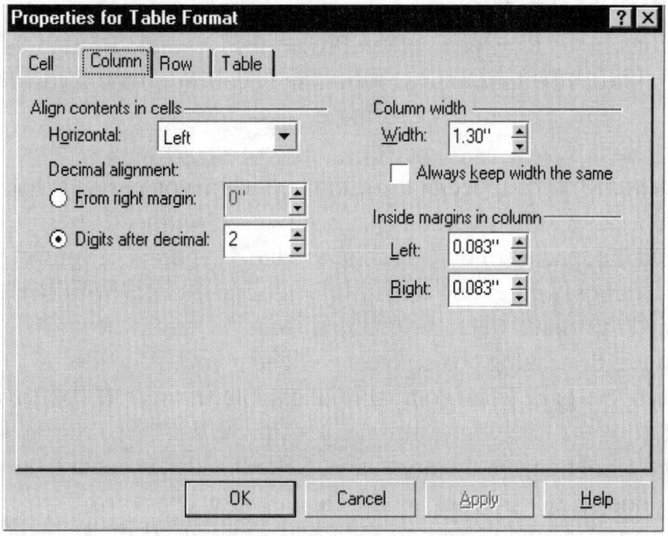

Properties for Table Format

Cell | Column | Row | Table

Align contents in cells
Horizontal: Left

Decimal alignment:
○ From right margin: 0"
● Digits after decimal: 2

Column width
Width: 1.30"

☐ Always keep width the same

Inside margins in column
Left: 0.083"
Right: 0.083"

OK | Cancel | Apply | Help

Column format options

FIGURE 9-9

Use the Horizontal section to assign an alignment to every cell in the column. It will not affect any cell that you've already applied an alignment to using the power bar or the Cell page of the dialog box. If you select Decimal Align justification, you should also select one of the options in the Decimal Alignment section. These determine the position of the decimal point in the cell, and thus where the numbers align. To position the decimal point a number of characters from the right, choose Digits after Decimal and enter a number in the corresponding box. To position the decimal point at set distances, choose Position From Right and enter a measurement in the text box.

The Inside Margins are the space Corel WordPerfect leaves on the right and left of text. The margins determine how much text fits in the cell before Corel WordPerfect wraps the text to the next line.

Use the Column Width box to set the width of the column to a specific measurement. Use this if you have trouble getting the width to an exact amount by dragging. If you select the Always Keep Width the Same box, Corel WordPerfect will not change the width of the column as you change the width of other columns in the table.

You can also apply justification formats using the power bar. Try that now. Select cells B1 through E1, pull down the Justification list in the power bar, and click on Center.

Formatting Rows

The options in the Row page of the Properties for Table Format dialog box, shown in Figure 9-10, affect the entire row. As with columns, you do not have to select the row first; simply click in any cell in the row.

By default, Corel WordPerfect is set to accept multiple lines in a cell—either lines that are word wrapped or those created when you press ENTER. If you carefully designed a table to fit a certain space, however, wrapped lines will widen the row height and the spacing of the table on the page. If you select Single Line in this dialog box, you can only enter one line of information—Corel WordPerfect will just stop accepting keystrokes when the cell is filled.

Also use this dialog box to create a header row. A header is a row or rows that repeat on every page when your table spans a page break. If you have a row of labels at the start of the table, for example, you might want it to repeat so the reader can identify the columns on the next page. Select the row, display the Row page of the Format dialog box, and click on the Header Row checkbox.

You can also allow a row to span a page break. If the row contains more than one line of text, this will let the row be divided between pages. Deselect this option

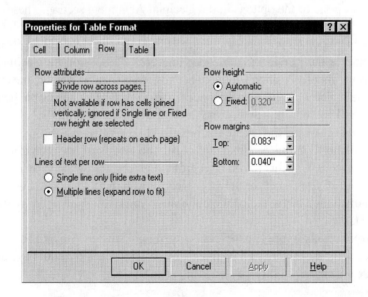

Row format
options

FIGURE 9-10

to keep the entire row on the same page. The dialog box also lets you set the row height and width to a specific measurement.

Formatting the Table

This last page of the Properties for Table Format dialog box applies formats to the entire table. Some of these options are the same as those you can set for columns, but they apply to all of the cells. For example, you can select a default justification, set the number of decimal digits and distance from the right cell border, and enter default column margins and width.

In addition, you can determine the position of the entire table between the margins, and you can change the table size by specifying the number of rows and columns.

You can also disable all of the cell locks so you can enter and edit information, and you can control whether you can insert rows.

Changing the Numeric Format

As you insert numbers and perform math operations, you may want to customize the way numbers appear. You can, for example, display values as currency, with dollar signs and with commas separating thousands, or you can control the number of decimal places that appear. To change the format of numbers of a single cell, pull down the Number Format list in the Table property bar, and choose an option from those shown next:

```
Mixed
General
Integer
Fixed
Percent
Currency
Accounting
Commas
Scientific
Date
Text
Other...
```

TIP: *The number formats are available in the Table Tools.*

For even more choices use the Properties for Table Numeric Format dialog box. The box will let you set the format for a group of selected cells, entire columns, or the entire table. Display the dialog box by choosing Numeric Format from the QuickMenu or Table menu, or by selecting Other from the Number Format button in the property bar. The dialog box is shown in Figure 9-11.

Choose if you want to apply the format to the selected cells, columns, or to the entire table, and then select one of the numeric formats. An example of this follows.

1. Select cells B2 through E7.

2. Right-click on the cells and choose Numeric Format from the QuickMenu.

3. Click on the Currency format, and then click on OK. All of the amounts will include dollar signs and two decimal places. The cells should still be selected, so align them on the decimal point.

4. Right-click on the cells, and select Format from the QuickMenu.

5. Pull down the Horizontal list and click on Decimal Align.

6. Click on OK.

If you want a special format, create your own. Click on the Custom button, and set the options in the Customize Number Type dialog box.

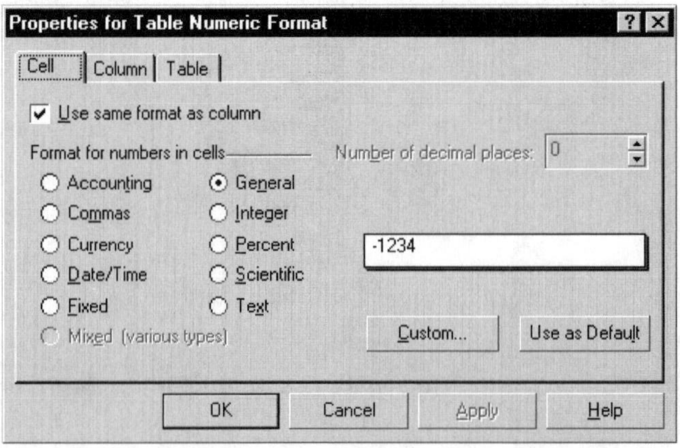

Changing
the numeric
format

FIGURE 9-11

TIP: *You can also assign the type as the default initial style for all tables.*

Performing Calculations in Tables

A Corel WordPerfect table has many of the same characteristics as a spreadsheet. Information is presented in rows and columns, and each cell is referenced by its row and column position. And as with a spreadsheet, you can perform calculations on the numbers in your table. For example, you can display the sum of values in a row or column, compute averages, and insert formulas that reference cells and other values.

The quickest calculation you can make is to total the values in rows or columns using the QuickSum feature. You place the insertion point in the empty cell below the ones you want to total, and then click on QuickSum in the property bar. (You can also select QuickSum from the Table menu or from the QuickMenu.) Do that now:

1. Place the insertion point in cell B6.

2. Click QuickSum in the property bar.

QuickSum will total the values of the numeric values above the cell, and display the results in the current cell. However, QuickSum totals numbers up to the first blank cell or cell that contains text. If you have a column label that is a year, such as 1997, Quick Sum may mistakenly include that in the total. If you have a column label such as that, or want to total numbers when there are blank cells in the column, select the cells you want to total first, including the blank cell where you want to insert the total—then use the QuickSum command.

You can also use QuickSum to total the values in a row. Click in the blank cell after the last number in the row and then select QuickSum. If you have values in both the row and column surrounding the cell, however, first select the cells containing the values you want to add.

Using the Formula Bar

QuickSum is useful, but it only totals. When you want to add, subtract, multiply, divide, and perform other types of math operations, you must enter a formula. With Corel WordPerfect, you enter formulas in a special formula bar. Display the bar, shown here, by clicking on the Formula Bar button in the Table property bar, or by selecting Formula Bar from the Table menu or the QuickMenu.

Here's how to use it. Click in the cell where you want to insert a formula, and then click in the formula bar. The cell's coordinates will appear in the text box on the left. Type the formula in the next text box, and then click on the check mark in the formula bar to accept the entry, or click on the "X" to cancel the formula. If a formula starts with a cell reference, begin it with a plus sign, as in *+B3-B4*.

You create a formula with a mathematical operation using the plus sign (+) to perform addition, the hyphen (-) for subtraction, the asterisk (*) for multiplication, and the forward slash (/) for division. Your formula can contain numbers and cell references. For example, to calculate a 6 percent sales tax on the value in cell A6, use the formula +A6*.06. When you accept the entry, Corel WordPerfect inserts a plus sign in front of the operation.

Keep in mind the order of precedence that computer programs give to operators. Corel WordPerfect, like other programs, does not necessarily perform the operations from left to right. It gives precedence to multiplication and division over addition and subtraction. If you enter **100+100+100/3**, Corel WordPerfect will calculate 233.3333 because it first divides 100 by 3 and then adds 100 twice. To perform the calculation correctly, use parentheses to force Corel WordPerfect to follow a different order, such as **(100+100+100)/3**.

Rather than typing the cell reference into the formula bar, you can insert it by clicking. When you are ready to add the reference to the formula, make sure the insertion point is in the formula bar, and then click on the cell that you want to reference. Drag over cells to insert a reference to their range.

The other options in the formula bar will help you work on tables and perform math:

- *QuickSum* performs the same function as clicking on QuickSum in the Table toolbar.

- *Functions* displays a dialog box of functions that perform operations.

- *Names* lets you name cells and select names to insert in formulas.

- *View Error* displays a description of an error in the cell.

- *Calculate* recalculates the values of formulas and functions.

- *QuickFill* completes a series of entries, just like the QuickFill button in the Table toolbar.

- *Copy Formula* lets you copy a formula from a cell down or across to the cells.

- *Row/Column Indicators* toggles the display of column letters and row numbers.

- *Close* closes the formula bar.

Using Copy Formula

The Copy Formula button lets you copy the contents of a cell down or across cells, in much the same way as copying cells. It displays the dialog box shown here.

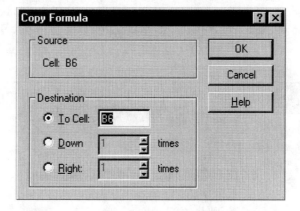

When you use the button to copy a formula, however, it is copied in a relative way. This means that the cell references in the formula are adjusted for the cell in which the formula appears. To see how this works, follow these steps:

1. Click in cell B6.

2. Click on the Copy Formula button to display the dialog box.

3. Click on Right.

4. Enter **3** in the Times box.

5. Click on OK.

Corel WordPerfect copies the formulas, but adjusts the cell references. Each copy of the formula computes the total of the cells above it in the column.

TIP: *You can also copy formulas using the QuickFill button. Select the formula and the cell you want to copy it to, and click on QuickFill.*

Working with Functions

The QuickSum button actually inserts a function into the cell. A *function* is a shortcut because it performs a math operation that may have taken an entire series of operations, or even a number of formulas. For example, the QuickSum command might insert a formula that looks like SUM(A1:A20). This tells Corel WordPerfect to total the values in the cells from A1 to A20 in a much faster way than the formula A1+A2+A3..., and so on.

Corel WordPerfect comes with over 100 functions that perform all types of operations. To see the functions, and to insert one into the formula bar, click on the Functions button in the formula bar to see the dialog box in Figure 9-12.

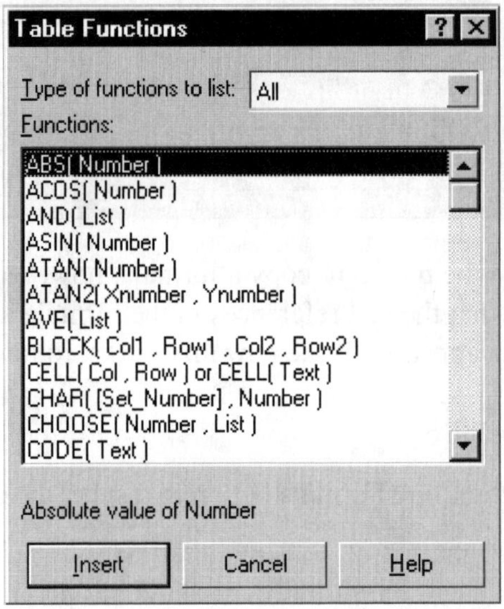

Corel
WordPerfect's
table
functions

FIGURE 9-12

By default, all of the functions will be available in the Functions list. You can also pull down the List Functions list and choose to see only functions in these categories:

- Mathematical

- Date

- Financial

- Logical

- Miscellaneous

- String

To insert a function into the formula bar, click on it in the Functions list and then click on the Insert button.

Most functions require one or more arguments. An *argument* is a value or cell reference that follows the name of the function in parentheses. For example, in the @SUM function, the argument is the range of cells that you want to total. This function needs just one argument, the range of cells that contains the values to average. Many other functions require several arguments, which are separated from each other by commas.

When you insert a function into the formula bar, you'll see its name and a list of its arguments. The first argument will be highlighted, so all you have to do is click on or drag over the range of cells that you want to insert into the argument. After you insert the reference, double-click on the next argument, if it has one, and then click on or drag over the cell references for it. Continue the process until all of the arguments are complete.

Let's use a function now to calculate the average for each quarter in the table:

1. Click in cell B7.

2. Click on the Functions button.

3. Click on AVE(List) and then on Insert. The function will appear in the formula bar with the word "List" selected.

4. Drag over cells B2 through B5, and then click on the check mark in the formula bar to insert the calculated average.

5. Drag over cells B7 through E7, and then click on the QuickFill button to copy the function.

Figure 9-13 shows the table.

If you are interested in learning how to use functions, read Chapter 18 in Part III, the Corel Quattro Pro section of this book. The principles that you'll learn about functions in that chapter apply to Corel WordPerfect as well. In fact, many of the functions are similar if not identical.

Creating Columns

Tables are fine for displaying numbers in columns, but you can format text in columns just as easily. Newsletters, reports, and other published documents look good in columns where text flows from one column to the next. Corel WordPerfect makes it easy to create columns. In fact, you can type your text first, and then apply the column formats to see how it appears, or you can turn on columns before you type.

Creating Newspaper Columns

Newspaper columns are just as you see in the newspaper—columns of text flow from one column right to the next on the page. When you fill the column on the far right of the page, the text moves to the left column on the next page. The text will adjust, moving from column to column, as you insert or delete text above it.

	Qtr1	Qtr2	Qtr3	Qtr4
Chesin	$67,584.00	$56,544.00	$345,345.00	$75,467.00
Schneider	$56,390.00	$67,493.00	$45,612.00	$78,000.00
Wilson	$43,457.00	$45,774.00	$46,900.00	$56,890.00
Randolph	$67,512.00	$56,557.00	$45,760.00	$54,690.00
Total	$234,944.00	$226,370.00	$483,620.00	$265,051.00
Average	$58,735.75	$56,592.00	$120,904.25	$66,261.75

The average added to row 7

FIGURE 9-13

When you create columns, you actually insert a column code into the document. Like a justification code, the column code affects all text from the paragraph in which the insertion point is placed to the end of the document, or until the next column code. This means that you can mix single-column and multiple-column text on the same page, and you can even mix the number of columns on the same page, such as some two-column and three-column text on the same page.

When you want to format text in columns, follow these steps:

1. Place the insertion point where you want the columns to begin.

2. Pull down the Columns button menu from the toolbar.

3. Select the number of columns desired, from 2 to 5.

Corel WordPerfect will display dotted boxes on the screen representing the width of the columns and the spacing between them, as in Figure 9-14. The word "Col" will appear in the status bar, followed by the number of the column in which the

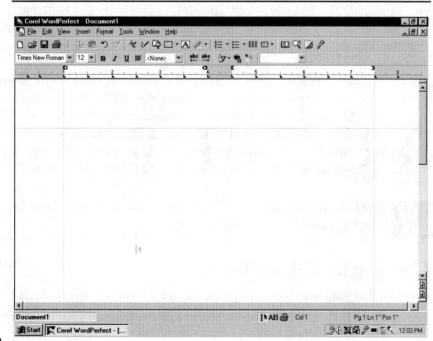

The width and spacing between columns shows on the screen

FIGURE 9-14

insertion point is placed. If you have the ruler displayed, it will indicate the width of each column, with the space between the columns.

TIP: *If you do not see the dotted lines, select Guidelines from the View menu, click on Column in the dialog box that appears, and then click on OK.*

If you selected columns in existing text, the text will appear in the column format. Otherwise, type your text starting in the leftmost column. As you type, the text will flow from column to column and from page to page, repeating the column format on each page.

If you want to end a column before the text flows, press CTRL-ENTER, or select Column Break from the Column list in the toolbar. What occurs when you press CTRL-ENTER depends on where the insertion point is placed, and how previous columns were ended. If you press CTRL-ENTER in a column that's not the rightmost one, Corel WordPerfect will end the current column and move the insertion point into the column to its right.

What about pressing CTRL-ENTER in the rightmost column? If your previous columns were ended by Corel WordPerfect flowing the text, then Corel WordPerfect will insert a page break and begin the left column on the next page. However, if you've ended all of the previous columns by pressing CTRL-ENTER, pressing CTRL-ENTER in the rightmost column ends it and starts a new column group, as shown in Figure 9-15. The group will have the same number of columns and will start under the longest column in the previous group.

You can now continue typing, or change the number of columns in the group by selecting another option in the Columns button of the toolbar. To type single-column text, for example, pull down the Columns button in the power bar and select Columns Off. You can also select Columns from the Format menu and click on Discontinue. To change the number of columns on the page, simply place the insertion point at the start of the group, and choose an option from the Columns button on the toolbar.

NOTE: *If you want the columns in a group to be the same length, see "Defining Columns" later in this chapter.*

Changing the Column Width

Columns that you create using the power bar are always the same width, a half-inch apart, and spaced to fill the page width. You may sometime want to design a

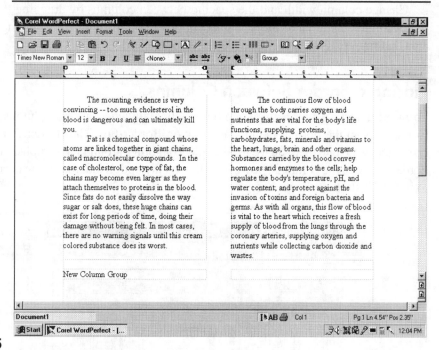

A new
column
group

FIGURE 9-15

newsletter or other document that has uneven columns. To change the column width, use either the column guidelines or the ruler.

The dotted lines on either side of a column are its guidelines. To change the width of a column, drag its guidelines. Dragging the leftmost guidelines on the page really changes the left margin, but the left column adjusts in width accordingly. Dragging the rightmost column guideline changes only the column width, not the right page margin.

When you drag any other column guidelines, you change the width of the column and of the spacing between the columns. As you drag a guideline, a QuickStatus box will appear showing the resulting column and spacing width.

If you want to maintain the same spacing between columns and just change the column width itself, point in the space between columns and drag. Only the space will move as you drag, changing the columns on both sides of it.

As an alternative to dragging the guidelines, you can change the column or spacing width using the ruler. The ruler will contain individual sections with left and right margin indicators that represent the left and right edges of the column. The section for the column that has the insertion point will also have left and right indentation indicators.

Change column width and the spacing between columns by dragging the right or left column margin indicators. Change only the column width by dragging a gray area that represents the space between two columns.

Placing a Border Between Columns

To insert a vertical line between columns, click anywhere in the columns, select Columns from the Format menu, and click on Border/Fill. The Border/Fill dialog box is the same one that you've used to place a border around paragraphs. To add a border between the columns, however, click on the option that the arrow is pointing to in the illustration shown here:

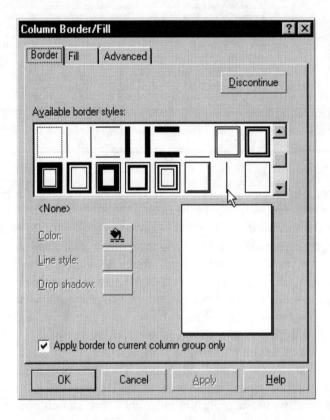

Defining Columns

If you want to create columns of specific sizes without dragging, or a column group in which all of the columns are the same length, then you have to define the columns. Select Format from the Column list in the toolbar, or select Columns from the Format menu to display the dialog box shown in Figure 9-16.

Enter the number of columns you want to create in the Number of Columns text box. When you move to another section of the dialog box, Corel WordPerfect will calculate the width of the columns and display their measurements in the Column Widths text boxes, along with 0.5 inch spacing between them. To customize the column widths or spacing, enter a measurement, or click the up or down arrows to change the widths. The preview graphic of the page will illustrate the resulting columns.

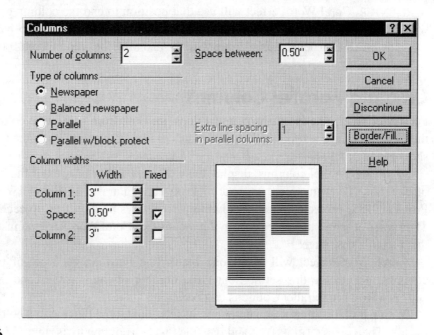

Defining
columns

FIGURE 9-16

As you increase or decrease the width of one column, Corel WordPerfect will automatically adjust the width of the other columns to fit the columns between the margins. If you want a column to remain exactly as you set it, regardless of how you change the other columns, select the column's Fixed checkbox.

You can also change the width of the spaces between columns. To set them all to the same width in one step, enter the width in the Spacing Between box.

Balancing Columns

If you want all of the columns in a group to be the same length, click on the Balanced Newspaper button in the Type of Columns section. As you type, Corel WordPerfect will shift text back and forth between the columns to keep them the same length.

You can also apply the Balanced Newspaper format to existing columns. Use this, for example, if you complete a document and the last column on the page is not full. However, if you ended a column other than the one on the right by pressing CTRL-ENTER, Corel WordPerfect will use that position to end the column group. It will divide all of the text above the position of the column break into balanced columns, and start a new column group with the text after the column break position.

Creating Parallel Columns

Parallel columns are ones in which text does not flow from column to column. In this case, you have text on the left that relates to text in the column on the right, as shown in Figure 9-17.

To create parallel columns, display the Columns dialog box, enter the number of columns you want to create, and click on either Parallel or Parallel W/Block Protect. Block-protected parallel columns will always be kept next to each other. They will not span a page break, even if it means that Corel WordPerfect must move them all to a new page.

Corel WordPerfect will insert one blank line between each set of parallel columns. To change this setting, enter the number of lines in the Line Spacing Between Rows in Parallel Columns text box.

With parallel columns, you enter text in sets. First, type the text in a column on the left. Then press CTRL-ENTER and type the text in a column to its right. When you press CTRL-ENTER in the rightmost column, Corel WordPerfect starts a new column group. It only inserts a page break when there is not enough room for another set of parallel columns on the page.

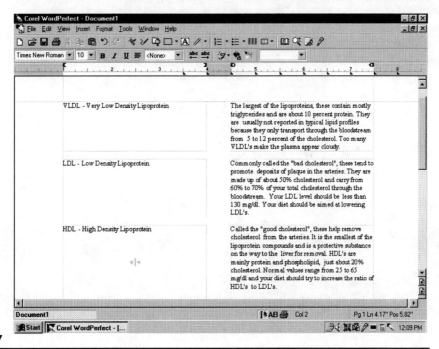

Parallel
columns

FIGURE 9-17

Customizing Corel WordPerfect

10

Y ou probably have personalized your desk and office to suit yourself. You've spread out your pictures and desk accessories, and arranged things for the way you like to work. Your office probably looks different from other offices, because we all have our own tastes and ways of working. You can customize Corel WordPerfect the same way, adjusting how things look and work to suit your own work habits.

You learned in earlier chapters how to change Corel WordPerfect's default document settings. These settings determine how your documents will appear if you don't bother changing any formats.

For example, in Chapter 7, you learned how to change the default template and system styles. In Chapter 6, you learned how to select a new initial font, and in Chapter 9, you found out how to select an initial format for tables.

In this chapter you'll learn how to customize the way Corel WordPerfect works.

Saving Printer Settings

Let's start with something that has everyday use: printer settings. When you display the Print dialog box to print a document, you have to select options, such as the number of copies, printer resolution, and so on. If you find yourself changing the same settings frequently, then consider saving the settings. If you want to use the settings with every new document—as the new default printer settings—then follow these steps:

1. Click on the Print button to display the Print dialog box.

2. Set the printer options the way you want them.

3. Click on the Settings button at the bottom of the Print dialog box, and select Save as Application Default from the list.

4. Click on OK in the message box that appears.

The printer settings in the dialog box will be used for every document because they are now Corel WordPerfect's default settings. If you only use the settings occasionally, you may not want to use them as the default. Instead, you can save the settings under a separate name, and then recall them when you need to. To save settings, adjust the Print dialog box options, click on Settings, and then on Named Settings. Corel WordPerfect will display the Named Settings dialog box. The box lists the categories of print settings that you can save. Enable the check boxes next to the categories that you want to save. You can also click on the plus sign next to a check box to display and select the specific settings in that category. When you've indicated which settings you want to save, type a name for the settings in the Name for Current Settings, and then click on Add.

The setting name that you entered will now be included in the Settings drop-down list. To later use the specifications, just click on the Settings button and click on the setting name.

NOTE: *You can also apply the settings by clicking on the setting name in the Named Settings dialog box and clicking on Retrieve.*

If you want to return to Corel WordPerfect's default printer settings, pull down the Settings list and click on Retrieve Application Default Settings.

Making changes to a saved setting is easy. Here's how:

1. Choose the options that you want to save in the Print dialog box.

2. Click on Settings and select Named Settings.

3. Pull down the Name for Current Settings list, click on the setting name that you want to change and then click Replace.

TIP: *To delete a setting, click on it in the list and then click on the Delete button.*

Changing Relative Font Ratios

The percentages that Corel WordPerfect uses to apply relative font sizes are stored as entries in the Windows 95 registry. You can't easily change these settings directly unless you know how to edit registry entries. Because changing the registry can lead to serious problems if you don't do it correctly, it's best not to mess around with it.

However, you can change the font size ratios by using a macro named SIZEATTR.WCM. You'll learn about macros later in this chapter, but if you want to customize the relative font sizes, follow these steps:

1. Select Macro from the Tools menu, and click on Play. Corel WordPerfect will display macro files—those with the WCM extension—in the \Corel\Office8\Macros\WPWin folder.

2. Scroll the list of files and click on SIZEATTR.WCM.

3. Click on Play to display the dialog box shown here:

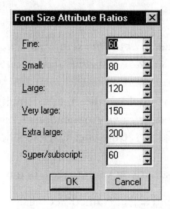

4. Set the ratios that you want to use and then click on OK.

Changing Corel WordPerfect Settings

All of the other default ways that Corel WordPerfect works are stored as settings. You edit the settings, for example, to change the default view and magnification, and even to add your own custom toolbars and menu bars. To set any of the settings, start by selecting Settings from the Tools menu to display the dialog box shown here:

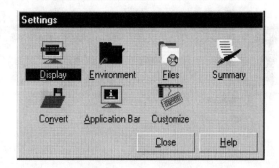

The options in the Settings box represent the categories of default settings. To change settings, double-click on the icon to display a dialog box, select your options, and then click on OK. Now let's look at the settings.

Setting Display Settings

The Display Settings dialog box, shown in Figure 10-1, controls the default appearance of the Corel WordPerfect document window. The box contains several pages, each dedicated to a classification of options.

Document Page

The Document page of the dialog box controls what Corel WordPerfect elements are displayed on the screen. In the Show section, you can choose to display text and dialog boxes using the Windows 95 color settings rather than Corel WordPerfect's, and you can choose to display or hide these elements:

- Table grid lines
- Tab bar icons
- Comments
- Graphics
- Hidden text

10

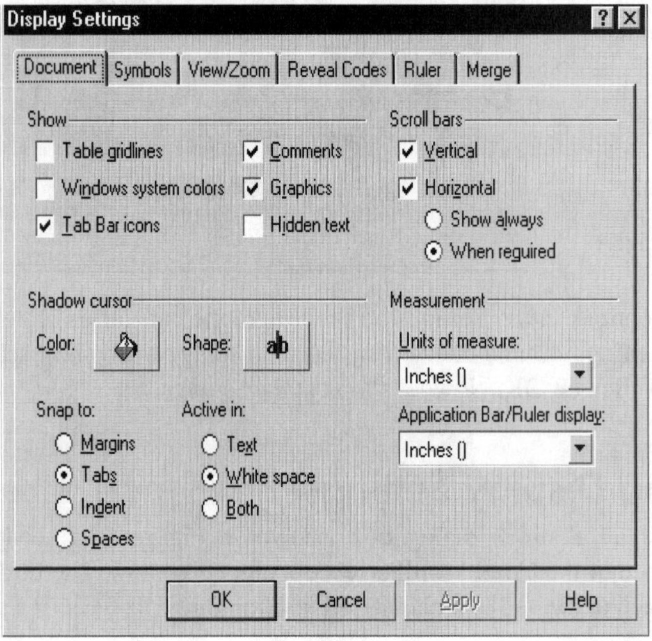

Display
settings

FIGURE 10-1

Use the options in the Shadow Cursor section to determine when and how the shadow cursor appears. By default, the shadow cursor appears only when you're pointing in a blank white space, but you can choose to have it appear only when you're in text or both. The Snap To options determine where the actual cursor appears when you click. If you select Margins, for example, you can only click to place the cursor at the left or right margin, or in the center of the page. You can also choose to have the cursor snap to tab stops (the default), indentation positions, or any character (spaces) position. Use the options in the Appearance section to select the color and shape of the shadow cursor.

In the Scroll Bars section you can deselect the Vertical or Horizontal checkboxes if you do not want the scroll bars to appear on the screen. You can also choose to have the horizontal scroll bar only appear when required—when there is text scrolled off the screen. If you choose this option, the scroll bar will appear automatically.

Use the Measurement section to set the units of measurement in dialog boxes and in the application bar and ruler. Use the Units of Measure list to determine the default unit accepted in dialog boxes, such as when changing margins and creating a page size. Your choices are inches (" or i), centimeters (c), millimeters (mm), points (*p*), and units of 1200ths of an inch (*w*), formerly known as "Corel WordPerfect units." Use the Application Bar display list, which offers the same options, to determine the way measurements are displayed on the ruler and in the position section of the application bar. In this case, for example, the ruler appears marked in points:

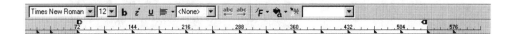

Symbols Page

When you click on the Show ¶ command in the View menu, Corel WordPerfect displays symbols for many characters and codes that normally do not appear, such as spaces, tabs, and carriage returns. You can choose which characters appear in this page of the dialog box. Deselect the checkbox for any items that you do not want to appear.

To turn on the display of codes from within this dialog box, click on the Show Symbols on New and Current Document checkbox. When you exit the Settings dialog boxes, the Show ¶ feature will be turned on, and it will be on for all new documents. You can turn off the feature in a specific document by selecting Show ¶ from the View menu, but the symbols will still appear for new documents. To turn off the feature, deselect the option in the Symbols page of the Display Settings dialog box.

View/Zoom Page

Corel WordPerfect starts by default in Page view and at 100% magnification. Many users, however, like to work in Draft view so they can see more lines on the screen; they change to Draft view every time they run Corel WordPerfect.

Use the View/Zoom page to change the default view and magnification. For example, selecting Draft view and Margin width as the default zoom minimizes the amount of your scrolling.

Reveal Codes Page

The options in this page of the dialog box, shown in Figure 10-2, let you change the appearance of the Reveal Codes window.

10

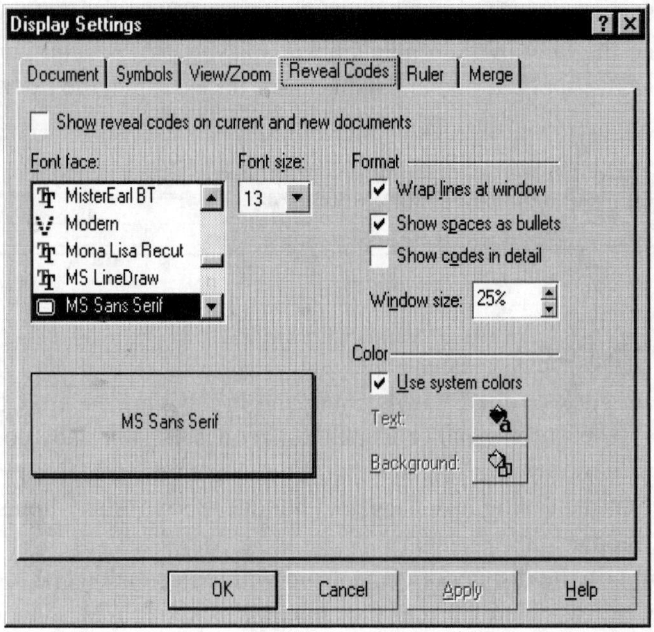

Reveal
Codes
settings

FIGURE 10-2

Click on the Show Reveal Codes on New and Current Document checkbox to
have the Reveal Codes window appear automatically. You can always turn off the
codes for individual documents by choosing Reveal Codes from the View menu.

Also select the font and size that you want the text to appear in the window—the
default is 13 point MS Sans Serif. Make the font smaller, for example, if you want
to see more lines of codes in the Reveal Codes window without taking up additional
space on the screen. The options in the Color section let you change the color of the
window. You can use the default Windows system colors, or you can choose your
own color for the text and background.

Your choices in the Options section determine the appearance of the text and the
default size of the window:

■   *Wrap Lines at Window* will divide codes between lines if they do not fit
    on the line. With this option deselected, the code may scroll off the right
    edge of the window.

- *Show Spaces as Bullets* uses bullet characters to represent when you pressed the SPACEBAR in a document. Deselect this option to show spaces as blank spaces.

- *Show Codes in Detail* displays the full details of all codes. With this option off, many codes are shown abbreviated, and only shown in detail when you place the insertion point immediately to the left of a code.

- *Window Size* determines the default size of the Reveal Codes window as a percentage of the document window area. The default is 25 percent.

Ruler Page

There are only two options in this page of the dialog box.

Tabs Snap to Ruler Bar Grid forces tabs that you set to appear at the nearest grid point on the ruler. When the unit of measurement is inches, for example, the ruler has grid points every 1/16 inch—at each of the tick marks along the ruler. In addition, there are also grid points in the middle between the tick marks. With this option turned off, you can set a tab between the grid lines, for example, at 1/32-inch intervals. With this option on, the tab stop will automatically appear at a grid point, so every tab is at some 1/16th-inch multiple along the ruler.

Show Ruler Bar Guides controls the display of the dotted line that appears down the screen as you move tabs and margin markers.

Merge Page

When you create a merge document, as you will learn in Chapter 11, special codes are inserted to indicate where you want information from the database to appear. In this page of the dialog box, you set how the codes will appear—as codes, as graphic markers, or not at all.

10

Environment Settings

The environment settings, shown in Figure 10-3, determine some basic ways that Corel WordPerfect performs.

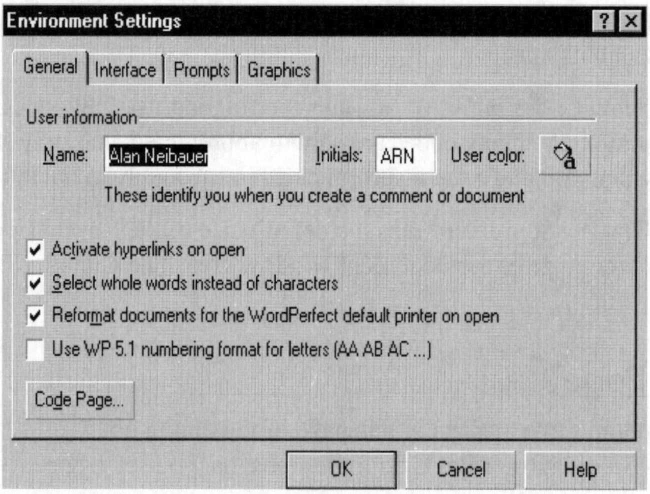

Environment
Settings
dialog box
FIGURE 10-3

The General Page

The User Information determines what appears on the summary page and in comments you create. Enter the name you want in the summary page, the initials you want to appear with comments, and the color you want to indicate your comments.

The Activate Hypertext Links on Open option determines if hypertext links are on or off. When this option is selected, clicking on a hypertext or Web link will move to the bookmark or Web page. If you are working in a document with Web page links and don't want to launch your browser accidentally, deselect this option.

The Select Whole Words Instead of Characters option controls how Corel WordPerfect selects words when you drag the mouse. With this option turned on, Corel WordPerfect will select the entire word when you drag over the space before or after it. Turn this option off if you want to select parts of a word, and the space before or after, without selecting the entire word.

Corel WordPerfect documents contain font and other codes that correspond to the features of your printer. If you open a document that was created for another printer, the codes will not match those of yours. To avoid any printing problems, Corel WordPerfect will reformat the document when you open it to match the printer currently being used. You'll know this is happening because you'll see a message on the screen reporting that the process is taking place. Here's the rub. If you save the document and later open it on the computer using the other printer, Corel WordPerfect will have to reformat it again. In some cases, the reformatting back and forth may change spacing or other formats, so you can turn off this feature by deselecting the Reformat Documents for the WordPerfect Default Printer on Open checkbox.

Interface Page

In the Menu section, choose what you want to appear in menus. You can turn off the display of recently used documents in the File menu, and choose to display the shortcut key combinations in menus or the QuickTips that appear when you point to a menu item, a toolbar button, or other button or screen object.

The Save Workspace section can save you a great deal of time. The *workspace* is the arrangement of your document windows on the screen. If you save the workspace, the next time you start Corel WordPerfect, you'll see the same documents, in the same window arrangement that was displayed when you last exited Corel WordPerfect. You can choose to always save the workspace when you exit Corel WordPerfect, to never save the workspace, or to display a prompt asking if you want to save the workspace when you exit. Prompt on Exit is a good compromise, since it will give you the choice. This way, you can determine if you want to return to the same window arrangement the next time you start.

The Language section determines the interface language—chances are you'll have only one choice.

Prompts Page

In the Beep On section you tell Corel WordPerfect when to beep at you—when an error occurs, when an automatic hyphenation is suggested, or when a find command cannot locate the text.

Use the Prompt section to control when Corel WordPerfect will prompt you to select a hyphenation point and how it operates when you delete codes and table formulas. Pull down the Hyphenation Prompt list, and choose if you want Corel WordPerfect to always or never prompt you to select a hyphenation point, or just to display a prompt when a suitable automatic hyphenation is not available. You can also choose if you want Corel WordPerfect to stop the insertion point when pressing BACKSPACE or DEL would erase a hidden code, or to display a message asking you to confirm if you are about to delete a formula in a table cell.

10

Graphics Page

When you want to use a graphic in a document, as you'll see in Chapter 12, you insert it and then you change its position and size to fit in your document. The Graphics page gives you the option of using the mouse to first drag a box where you want the graphic to appear and then selecting the graphic.

This page also lets you select between two equation editors, or choose to display a prompt asking which one you want to use each time you begin an equation.

Files Settings

The Files Settings dialog box, shown in Figure 10-4, determines where documents, templates, graphics, and other files used by Corel WordPerfect are stored on your disk. Each page of the dialog box sets the location of one type of file.

   TIP: *Click on View All for a summary of all file locations.*

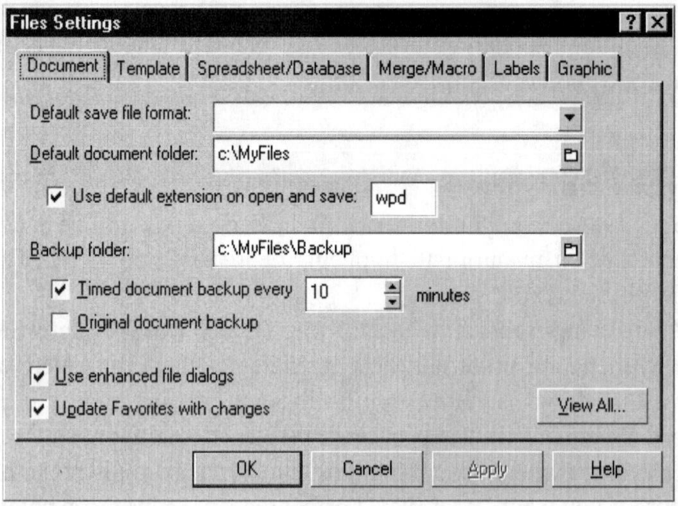

Files
Settings
dialog box

FIGURE 10-4

Use the options in the Document page of the dialog box, for example, to determine the directory and extension of your documents, and to automatically save documents. In the Default Document Folder text box, enter the folder where you want your documents to be saved. When you display the Open and Save dialog boxes, the files in that directory will automatically appear. You can also designate another default document extension, or choose not to use a default extension at all.

By default, Corel WordPerfect performs a timed backup of your document every ten minutes. As you work, Corel WordPerfect saves the document to a temporary file, so if your computer goes haywire and you have to reboot, you'll have the opportunity to open the temporary file to retrieve your work. This option is turned on when the Timed Document Backup Every checkbox is selected. The number of minutes between backups is specified in the corresponding text box. The backup files are stored in the location specified in the Backup Folder box. You can turn off this feature by deselecting the checkbox, or change the folder or number of minutes between backups.

You can also choose to create an Original Document Backup. With this option on, Corel WordPerfect saves a copy of the current version of the document with the same name but using the extension BK!. This file will not contain any of the editing or formatting that you performed since you last saved the document. If you change your mind about all of the last changes you made, open the BK! file.

The Update Favorites with Changes setting will change the shortcuts in the Favorites folder to the directories that you select in this dialog box.

Summary Settings

A summary sheet contains statistical information about your document and reference information about who created it, when it was modified, and what the document is all about, including a descriptive name. You can see the document's summary sheet by selecting Properties from the File menu.

In the Summary page, enter the information requested. You can also click on the Configure button to choose additional text boxes to add to the summary. The Options lists in the Summary page will let you print or delete the summary, save it as its own document, or extract information from the document into the Subject text box. If you select Extract, Corel WordPerfect looks for a line starting with the characters "RE:" and inserts any text following the characters into the Subject text box.

10

In the Summary Settings dialog box, you can set Corel WordPerfect to display the Summary page when you save and exit a document, so you can enter information into it. You can also choose these options:

- On open, use the descriptive name as the new filename

- When saving a new document, use the long filename as the descriptive name

In addition, you can enter a default descriptive type that will initially appear in all Summary pages, and enter subject search text other than "RE:". For example, if your office uses "Subject:", enter it in place of "RE:". Then when you click on Extract in the Options list of the Summary box, Corel WordPerfect will insert the text following "Subject:" in the Subject text box.

Convert Settings

When you open graphic files or documents created by other word processing programs, Corel WordPerfect converts them into a format that it understands. The Convert Settings option controls how this process is performed.

The Delimiters section of the dialog box controls how ASCII-delimited text files are converted. This is usually a file created by a database or spreadsheet program—each row of the spreadsheet or database record is a document line. You use this section of the dialog box to determine the character that separates database fields or spreadsheet cells, and the character or code that separates rows or records.

The Characters section designates any special characters that surround database fields or information from a spreadsheet cell. The default is the quotation mark. You can also designate characters that you want Corel WordPerfect to remove—strip—from the information when it is converted.

The Windows Metafile options control how graphic files are converted. The Metafile format (using the WMF extension) is a common format that Windows applications use for graphic objects. By default, Corel WordPerfect opens a metafile graphic and inserts it into the document but leaves it in its original format. You can also choose to convert the file into Corel WordPerfect's own WPG format, or to save the file in both formats. Choose the WPG option if you want to use the document with earlier versions of Corel WordPerfect.

The Options button in the Convert Settings dialog box lets you set other conversion settings. The options are as follows:

- *Code Pages* lets you select sets of characters that will be used to convert characters in a document. In most cases, for example, the letter "A" in the original document will be displayed as the letter "A" on the screen. Depending on the system and the font that you used to create the file, there may be some characters in the document that do not have equivalents in Corel WordPerfect. The Code Pages option lets you select character sets to use when converting documents.

- *Document* lets you select the language, units of measurement, underline style, margins, and page size for converted documents.

- *WP 4.2 Fonts* lets you designate the fonts that you used with documents created with Corel WordPerfect 4.2 for DOS so Windows fonts can be substituted for them.

- *DCA/DisplayWrite Fonts* lets you designate the fonts you used for DCA- and DisplayWrite-formatted documents.

Application Bar Settings

When you want to change the items that appear on the application bar, double-click on the Application Bar icon in the Settings dialog box to display the options shown in Figure 10-5. Click on the checkboxes for the items that you want to add or remove from the application bar, and select a font size—either small, normal, or large. You can also remove an item from the bar by dragging it off, and you can change an item's position by dragging it within the bar.

The default bar is a mix of icons and text. The Shadow Cursor, Caps Lock, and Printers items are icons; Insert and the position indicators are text. Double-click on an item in the bar to toggle it between text and an icon. Double-clicking on the position indicator, for example, displays an icon for the Go To dialog box.

TIP: *Click on Default to return to the default Corel WordPerfect application bar.*

Customization Settings

You customize toolbars, property bars, menus, and keyboard layouts using different tabs of the Customize dialog box. Access the dialog box from Settings, or by right-clicking on a toolbar or property bar and choosing Customize from the QuickMenu. The options are similar in each.

10

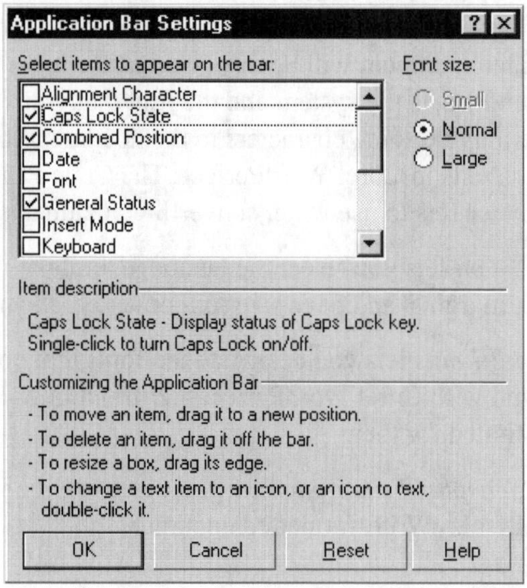

Application Bar Settings

Select items to appear on the bar:

- Alignment Character
- ☑ Caps Lock State
- ☑ Combined Position
- Date
- Font
- ☑ General Status
- Insert Mode
- Keyboard

Font size:
- ○ Small
- ● Normal
- ○ Large

Item description

Caps Lock State - Display status of Caps Lock key. Single-click to turn Caps Lock on/off.

Customizing the Application Bar

- To move an item, drag it to a new position.
- To delete an item, drag it off the bar.
- To resize a box, drag its edge.
- To change a text item to an icon, or an icon to text, double-click it.

[OK] [Cancel] [Reset] [Help]

Changing the items on the application bar

FIGURE 10-5

Toolbar Settings

The Toolbars page of the Customize dialog box, shown in Figure 10-6, lets you create and edit toolbars. Use this feature to add buttons for features that you use often, or to create new toolbars for custom combinations of tools. By adding frequently used functions to a toolbar, you can activate a function with a single click of the mouse. You can create various toolbars and recall them to the screen when needed.

TIP: *You can select tabs from the Customize dialog box to customize the other objects. You do not have to return to the Settings dialog box.*

To change the position of a toolbar, as well as the appearance of its tools, click on the toolbar in the list, and then click on Options to see the dialog box shown in Figure 10-7. Choose a Font Size to use for the style of text on the button face, and select if you want the tool to show the name of the command (Text), an icon representing the function (Picture), or both (Picture and Text). Use the Toolbar Location options to place the toolbar on the top, bottom, or sides of the screen, or to display it as a rectangular palette. You can also choose to include a scroll bar when

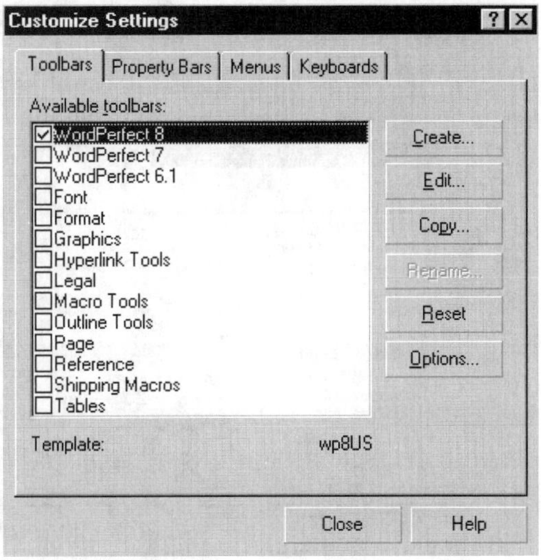

Customize Settings

Toolbars | Property Bars | Menus | Keyboards

Available toolbars:

☑ WordPerfect 8
☐ WordPerfect 7
☐ WordPerfect 6.1
☐ Font
☐ Format
☐ Graphics
☐ Hyperlink Tools
☐ Legal
☐ Macro Tools
☐ Outline Tools
☐ Page
☐ Reference
☐ Shipping Macros
☐ Tables

Create...
Edit...
Copy...
Rename...
Reset
Options...

Template: wp8US

Close | Help

Customize
dialog box
for toolbars

FIGURE 10-6

there are more buttons than fit across the screen, or to display the buttons in more than one line. Click on OK to return to the Toolbars page.

To add or delete a button from a toolbar, select it in the Available Toolbars list and click on Edit. The toolbar will appear onscreen along with the Toolbar Editor, shown in Figure 10-8. To create a new toolbar, click on Create, type the name for

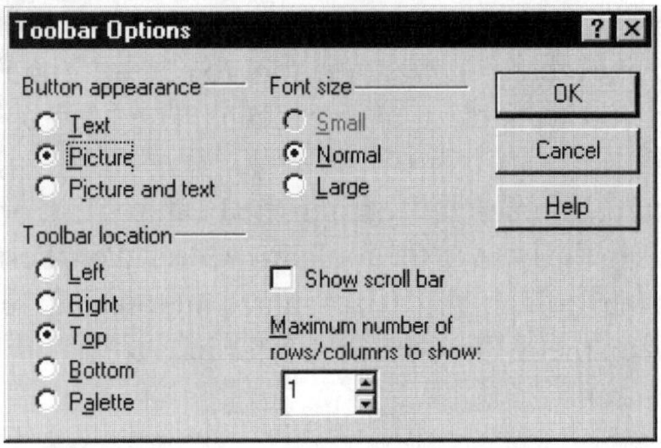

10

Toolbar Options

Button appearance
○ Text
◉ Picture
○ Picture and text

Font size
○ Small
◉ Normal
○ Large

OK
Cancel
Help

Toolbar location
○ Left
○ Right
◉ Top
○ Bottom
○ Palette

☐ Show scroll bar

Maximum number of
rows/columns to show:

1

Changing
the position
and
appearance
of the
toolbar

FIGURE 10-7

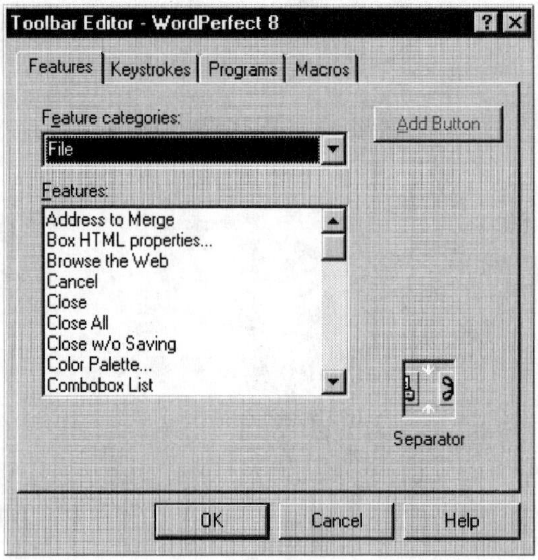

Creating a
new toolbar

FIGURE 10-8

the bar in the box that appears, and click on OK. The Toolbar Editor will appear with a blank toolbar on the screen.

TIP: *You can also edit the current toolbar by right-clicking on it and choosing Edit from the QuickMenu.*

The first step is to select the type of item you want to add as a tool. A *feature* is a command that you can perform by selecting an item from a pull-down menu. You select the feature category that corresponds to the menu bar commands and then choose the specific Corel WordPerfect feature. The Keystrokes page lets you enter a series of keystrokes that you want the tool to repeat. The Programs page lets you select a program you want the tool to execute. The Macros page lets you assign a macro to the tool.

To add a feature, double-click on it in the Features list, or click on it and then on Add Button, or drag the item to the toolbar—Corel WordPerfect will insert a button for the feature in the toolbar. You can organize buttons into related groups by adding extra space between them. Drag the Separator icon to the bar where you want to add space between buttons.

To remove a tool from the toolbar and change its position, use the Toolbar Editor. Remove a tool by dragging it off the bar; change its position by dragging it to another location on the bar. When you're satisfied with the toolbar, click on OK.

You can always edit it by selecting it in the Available Toolbars list and clicking on Edit. You can also use the Customize dialog box to delete, rename, and copy a toolbar.

EDITING TOOLBAR BUTTONS   To customize the toolbar even more, you can change the icon on a tool or the text that appears on it, and edit the text of the QuickTip that appears when you point to the button. To do this, however, you must be in the Toolbar Editor. In the Toolbars page of the Customize dialog box, click on the toolbar that contains the tool you want to change, and then click on the Edit button. Next, point to the tool that you want to change in the toolbar, right-click the mouse, and select Customize from the menu that appears. Corel WordPerfect will display the Customize Button dialog box, shown here:

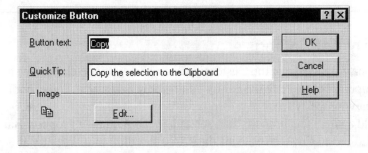

Enter any text that you want to appear on the tool in the Button Text box, and enter the text for the tool's QuickTip. To change the icon on the tool, click on the Edit button to see the Image Editor shown in Figure 10-8. In the box that displays the enlarged icon, click with the left or right mouse button to add one pixel of color. Choose the color by clicking the left or right mouse button on the color in the Colors section. In the Drawing mode section, select Single Pixel or Fill Whole Area to select the action of the click. Single Pixel inserts one pixel; Fill Whole Area inserts the color in all consecutive cells the color of where you click. You can also draw in the small graphic of the button in the lower-right corner. Select Undo to cancel your last change, or click on Clear to erase the entire icon to start from a blank button.

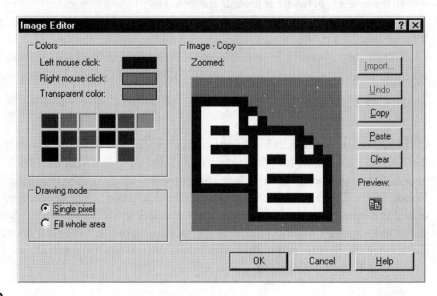

Editing the
button icon

FIGURE 10-9

Property Bar Settings

The Property Bars page of the Customize dialog box lets you change the appearance
of the property bar and edit the bar by adding new items to it. You cannot, however,
create a new property bar.

To add an item to a property bar, select it in the Available Property Bars list, and
click on Edit to display the Toolbar Editor. Use the editor the same way as you learned
previously for customizing toolbars, but drag items to the property bar instead.

   TIP: *You can also edit the current property bar by right-clicking on it and
choosing Edit from the QuickMenu.*

Menu Bar Settings

Just as you can edit and create toolbars, you can also edit and create menu bars and
pull-down menus. Double-click on the Customize icon in the Settings dialog box,
then click on the Menus tab to see the options shown here.

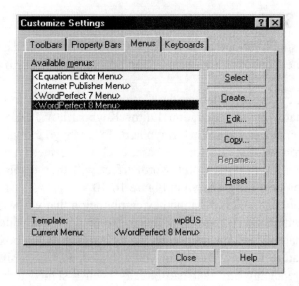

You can display any of the four built-in menu bars, or create your own. You cannot edit one of the built-in bars, but you can create new menu bars by adding menus and items to an existing one. Start by clicking on the built-in bar that you want to use for the base, and then click on the Create button. Type a name for the bar in the box that appears, and then click on OK.

You'll see the Menu Editor, which is exactly like the Toolbar Editor but with icons labeled "Menu" and "Separator." To add features to the menu that you can perform with a single click, double-click on the Menu icon. To create a new menu, drag the Menu icon to the menu bar. The item labeled "Menu" will appear; double-click on it to display a dialog box where you give it a name and a description that appears when you point to it. Use an ampersand to designate the underlined selection letter; for example, "&Special" becomes "Special."

To add an item to a menu, drag the item to the menu you want to insert it in, continue pulling down the menu, and place the item in the desired position. You can also double-click on the program feature to place it in the menu bar, and drag it to the menu. To delete an item, or a menu, drag it off the menu bar.

Drag the Separator icon to add a separator line between items in the menu.

Keyboard Settings

If you prefer using keyboard combinations to perform commands, you are in luck. You can use the Keyboard Shortcuts dialog box to create your own shortcut key combinations.

Click on the Keyboards tab on the Customize dialog box to see a list of four built-in keyboard layouts: Equation Editor Keyboard, WPDOS 6.1 Keyboard, WPWin 7 Keyboard, and WPWin 8 Keyboard. To create your own keyboard, select the one that you want to use for the base, click on Create, type a name for the keyboard, and click on OK. Corel WordPerfect will then display the Keyboard Shortcuts dialog box that is shown in Figure 10-10.

In the list on the left, click on the key combination that you wish to assign to a feature, key combination, program, or macro. To assign the new item to it, select it in the appropriate page in the section on the right of the dialog box, and then click on Assign Feature to Key. The item you selected will be assigned to the key combination, replacing any that had already been assigned to it. For each key combination in the list, you can also deselect the Shortcut Key Appears on Menu checkbox so the key combination will not appear on the related pull-down menu.

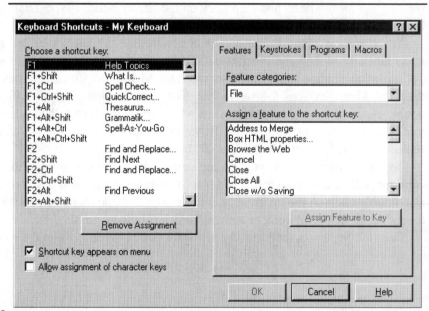

The
Keyboard
Shortcuts
dialog box

FIGURE 10-10

If you click on Allow Assignment of Character Keys, the list on the left will change to contain all of the regular character keystrokes. You can then assign a feature or other keystroke to it.

TIP: *To remove a shortcut key function from a key combination, click on it in the list and click on the Remove Assignment button.*

Creating Macros

One other way to customize Corel WordPerfect is to add you own commands through macros. A *macro* is a series of keystroke, menu, property bar, and toolbar selections that you can store on your disk or in a template. You can then repeat all of the keystrokes and commands by just "playing" the macro at some other time. You can use a macro to insert formatted text, to apply a set of commonly used formats, or to perform any action that you can save time by repeating.

The easiest way to create a macro is to record it. You just enter the keystrokes, or perform any other function, and Corel WordPerfect records them.

TIP: *You can also create a macro using the PerfectScript accessory from the taskbar.*

You can record macros in two locations: as a file on your disk or in a template. Storing the macro on the disk means that you can later access it no matter what document or template you are using. You can also copy the macro onto a floppy disk and use it on another computer that's running Corel WordPerfect for Windows. If you store the macro in a template, you still may have two choices. If you are using a template other than the default, you can choose to store the macro with either the default template or the one being used with the document. Saving the macro in the default template will make it available with every document using that template.

To record a macro, pull down the Tools menu and select either Macro or Template Macro, depending on where you want to save it.

Storing Macros on the Disk

To save the macro on the disk, point to Macro and then click on Record in the menu that appears. A dialog box will appear where you select the folder in which to store the macro and enter the macro name. By default, macros are stored in the

10

\Corel\Office8\Macros\WPWin folder and use the WCM extension. It's best to use the default folder so you'll be able to access your macros easily in the default location. Type a name for the macro and then click on Record.

Saving Macros in a Template

To save your macro in a template, pull down the Tools menu, point to Template Macro, and then click on Record. In the dialog box that appears, type a name for the macro.

Your macro will only be available to documents using the template where it is stored. If you started the document using the default template, then the macro will be available to all new documents that use the default template. If you started the document with another template, the macro will be saved there. To store the macro in the default template, click on Location to see this dialog box:

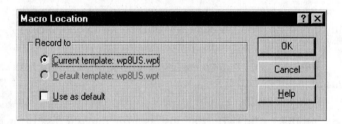

Choose the template where you want to store the macro. To use your choice as the default for all template macros, click on the Use As Default checkbox. Click on OK to return to the Record Template Macro dialog box. Now click on Record to start recording your macro.

Recording Macros

Once you select Record, Corel WordPerfect will display the macro bar shown here and will start recording your keystrokes.

When you are recording a macro, you can only use the mouse to select menu, toolbar, property bar, and dialog box options. You cannot use it to select text and to position the insertion point—use keystrokes for that. Perform all of the functions that you want to record, and then click on the Stop button in the macro bar.

Playing Macros

To play a macro, pull down the Tools menu and select either Macro or Template Macro, depending on where the macro is stored. Then click on Play.

If the macro is stored on the disk, the Play Macro dialog box appears listing macros in the default directory. Double-click on the macro name, or type the name and click on Play.

If the macro is stored in a template, the Play Template Macro dialog box appears. Double-click on the macro name, or select it and click on Play. If the macro isn't listed, click on Location and then choose the template where the macro is stored. Click on OK and then select it in the Play box.

Assigning Macros to Menus, Toolbars, or the Property Bar

Earlier in this chapter, you learned how to customize Corel WordPerfect by adding items to the menu bar, toolbar, or property bar. In each case, the Toolbar Editor dialog box used to add items also contained a page called "Macros" (see Figure 10-8 earlier in this chapter).

To add a macro to the bar, select either Add Template Macro or Add Macro, depending on where the macro is stored. Double-click on the macro to insert it into the menu, toolbar, or property bar.

Editing Macros

If you make a mistake when recording a macro, you can record it again. You can also edit the macro to change or add commands. Editing and writing macros requires knowledge of the command language and an understanding of the principles of computer programming. (For more information about the macro command language refer to the Corel WordPerfect Help system.)

To edit a macro, pull down the Tools menu and select either Macro or Template, depending on where the macro is stored, and then click on Edit. In the dialog box that appears, double-click on the macro you want to edit, or select it and then click

10

on Edit. The macro commands will appear in a separate window, numbered, along with the macro bar, as shown in Figure 10-11.

All of the commands are listed in Corel WordPerfect's macro language. This is an extensive programming language that can be used to write complete applications built around Corel WordPerfect for Windows.

The first line of the macro identifies the program and default language that it uses. The remainder of the macro performs the reported instructions. For example, the Type command inserts text into the document using the syntax Type(Text: "*insert this text*"). Pressing ENTER when recording the macro inserts the HardReturn( ) command.

If you want to change the text that a macro generates, just edit any of the text within the quotation marks in the Type command. To insert new text, you have to insert a new Type command, following the proper syntax. If you want the macro to perform a carriage return, type the HardReturn( ) command; pressing ENTER in the macro itself will not perform a carriage return when you play the macro. Remember that when you play the macro, Corel WordPerfect will follow the macro commands

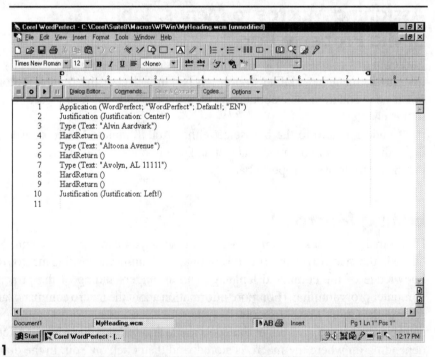

Editing a macro

FIGURE 10-11

exactly. So if you enter commands in the wrong order, or don't use the proper syntax for a command, your macro will not operate correctly.

Rather than type commands into the macro, it is more efficient to add them by recording. Place the insertion point in the macro where you want the new commands to appear, and then click on the Record button in the macro bar. Corel WordPerfect will open a new blank window with another macro bar. Type the text or perform the functions that you want to add to the macro, and then click on the Stop button. Corel WordPerfect will switch back to the macro window, with your newly recorded commands inserted. Click on the Save & Compile button in the macro bar, and then close the window.

The Command Inserter

Corel WordPerfect's macro language is a sophisticated programming language with hundreds of commands. You can learn about the commands using the online help system and the Reference Center that comes with the Corel WordPerfect Suite CD. You can quickly insert macro commands by clicking on the Commands button in the macro bar to display the dialog box shown in Figure 10-12.

In the Command Type box, select the type of command you want to insert. By default, the box will list all PerfectScript commands. To record a Corel WordPerfect function, pull down the list and select WordPerfect. Then select the command in the Commands list box. If you select a command that includes parameters, the parameters will appear in the Parameters list box. Select the parameter you want to

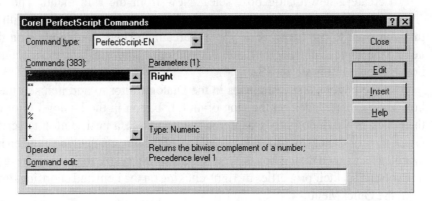

Selecting
a macro
command

FIGURE 10-12

set. If the parameter has optional items, an additional list box will appear labeled Enumerators, and you can select a value from the list. In the Command Edit text box, you can edit the macro command. When you are ready to insert the command, select Insert.

Other Macro Features

You might find the other options in the macro bar useful. Both of these are for advanced macro writers. The Codes button displays a list of merge codes.

The Options button lets you change how the macro is saved. If you are editing a template macro and now want to save it on the disk, for example, click on Options and select Save as Macro. You can also choose Save as Template Macro to store a disk macro on the template. The other options let you remove the macro bar and close the macro.

The Dialog Editor

The Dialog Editor displays a dialog box for creating dialog boxes for your macros. While creating a dialog box is easy using the editor, taking advantage of the box in your macro requires extensive knowledge of the Corel WordPerfect macro language. You can get additional information on the macro language using the Corel WordPerfect Help menu and on the Corel Web site.

The general procedure, however, is to click on Dialog Editor to see the dialog box shown here. The box will list all of the dialog boxes that have been created and stored for use with the current macro.

To create a new dialog box, select New from the File menu. The notation "NewDialog" will appear highlighted in the list. Replace "NewDialog" with a name that you want to use for the box you are creating. Then, double-click on the icon next to the name to display the Corel PerfectScript Dialog Editor and a blank dialog box as shown in Figure 10-13.

Use the buttons and commands in the Dialog Editor to add items to the dialog box. For example, click on the icon of an OK button in the Dialog Editor toolbar, then click in the dialog box where you want to place a push button to serve as an OK, Close, or Cancel button. You can add all of the objects that you've seen in Corel WordPerfect's own dialog boxes. You can move and resize the objects by dragging, and you can set their properties by right-clicking on the item and choosing Properties from the QuickMenu.

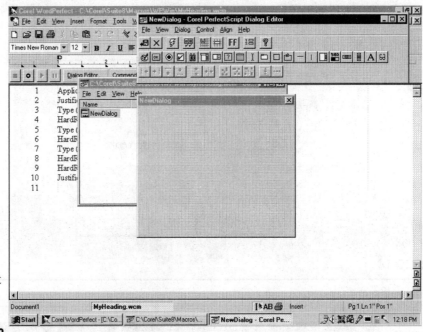

Corel
PerfectScript
Dialog
Editor

FIGURE 10-13

 To see how the dialog box will actually appear in your macro, click on the Test the Dialog button in the Dialog Editor toolbar, as shown in the margin. Figure 10-14, for example, shows a custom dialog box with option buttons, a text box, push buttons, and a list box. To return to editing, press ESC or click on a push button that you've added.

When you've finished, select Save from the Dialog Editor File menu, and then choose Close from the File menu to return to the list of dialog boxes. Finally, select Close from the File menu to return to the macro.

When you want to use the dialog box in your macro, insert the DialogShow command using the syntax DialogShow("*macroname*","WordPerfect"). The macro name is case sensitive, so you must enter the macro name exactly as you created it. The macro in Figure 10-15, for instance, uses the dialog box shown in Figure 10-14. The dialog box was named MyDialog in place of NewDialog, and that name was used in the macro. Note that you use the name assigned the box in the Dialog Editor, not the title displayed on the box itself.

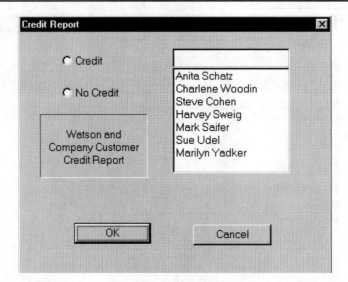

Custom
dialog box

FIGURE 10-14

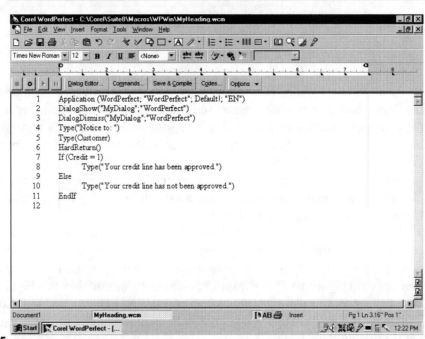

Macro
using
custom
dialog box

FIGURE 10-15

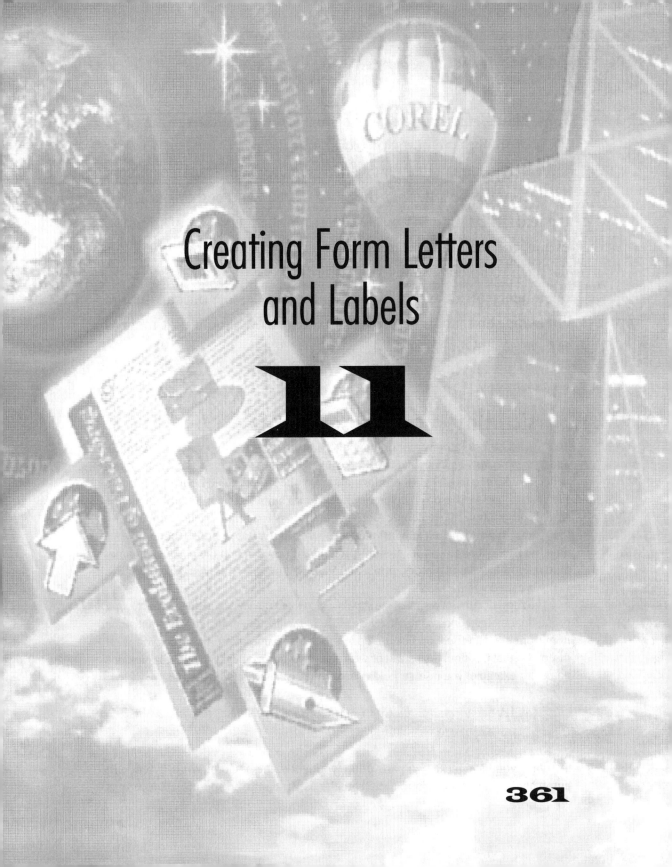

Creating Form Letters and Labels

11

lthough form letters may have a bad reputation, they are one of the best features of Corel WordPerfect. A *form letter* is merely a document that you want to send to more than one person. Each copy of the letter has the same format, and perhaps much of the text, in common. You just need to change some of the text, even if it's only the address and salutation, to customize the letter for each recipient. With Corel WordPerfect you can create form documents of all types—not just form letters. You can merge envelopes and labels, and even create any document that merges information from a database.

Understanding Form Documents

To create a form letter or other document, you actually need two things: a *data file* and a *form document*. The data file is like an electronic index card file. Every card, called a *record*, contains all the information you need about each object your data file is all about—a person or inventory item, for example. If your data file contains stored information about people—clients, members, patients, friends, enemies— then it may have their first and last names, address, city, state, and ZIP code. If your data file is about an inventory item or products, it may contain the product's name, amount you have in inventory, price, and vendor who sells it to you. Each of these items is called a *field*.

The form document contains the standard text that you want to include in each copy of the final merged documents. In every place in the document where you want some item from the data file, you insert a code giving the name of the field that you want inserted at that position. So instead of writing a letter and actually typing the recipient's name, for example, you insert a field code for the last name and first name.

 TIP: *You can use the Corel Address Book as the data file, just as it is.*

Once you have these two parts done, you merge them. Corel WordPerfect will automatically insert the information from the data file into the appropriate locations in the letter. For example, Corel WordPerfect inserts the information from the first record in the data file into the appropriate locations in the first copy of the document. It then inserts the information from the second record in the data file into the second copy of the document, repeating the process until all of the records have been used.

You can create the data file and document in any order. For example, you can write the form document and then complete the data file. Before merging the two parts, however, you have to tell Corel WordPerfect what data file to use for the merge operation. You can also create the data file first and then complete the document. This way, you can link the data file with the form document from the start. In fact, once you create the data file, you can use it any time for form documents—letters, envelopes, labels, or any other documents that include the merge codes associated with the data file.

Creating a Data File

With Corel WordPerfect, the data file can take either of two forms. It can appear as a table, with each row in the table a record with the fields in the columns, or as a merge file, with records and fields separated by special codes. Either way, the data file works the same way. Because of the number of steps involved in creating a data file, it would be useful to go through the process together this first time. If you want to use your Address Book as the data file, skip ahead to the section "Associating a Data File."

 You can use a Corel Quattro Pro worksheet or a Paradox database as your data file.

1. Pull down the Tools menu and select Merge to display the dialog box shown in Figure 11-1. The dialog box gives you four choices. Selecting Create Data will help you create a data file by prompting for field names, and even displaying a handy form for entering information. Selecting Create Document lets you create the form document. Choosing Perform Merge lets you combine the data file and the form document. You can also select to edit the records in the Corel Address Book to use as the data file.

2. Click on Create Data.

3. If the current document is not blank, you will now be asked if you want to use the file in the currently active window or create a new document

Merge
dialog box

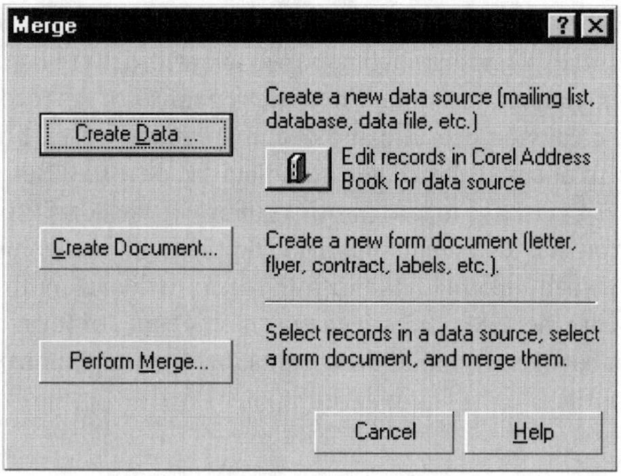

FIGURE 11-1

window. Click on New Document Window and then click on OK. You should only use the current window if it is empty, or if it contains a table that you want to use for the data file.

4. Corel WordPerfect displays the Create Data File dialog box. You use this dialog box to enter the names of the fields.

5. Click on Format Records in a Table. This will create a data file in a table format, so you can later work with it using all of Corel WordPerfect's table commands.

6. In the Name a Field box, type **Last Name** and then press ENTER. Corel WordPerfect adds the field name to the list.

7. Type **First Name** and then press ENTER to insert the next field.

8. Now in the same way, add the fields Address1, Address2, City, State, Zip, Greeting, Last Order Date, Amount Due, and Credit.

9. Select OK to display the Quick Data Entry dialog box shown in Figure 11-2. The Quick Data Entry box makes it easy to enter information into the data file, as well as to edit and find records. The insertion point will be in the text box for the first field.

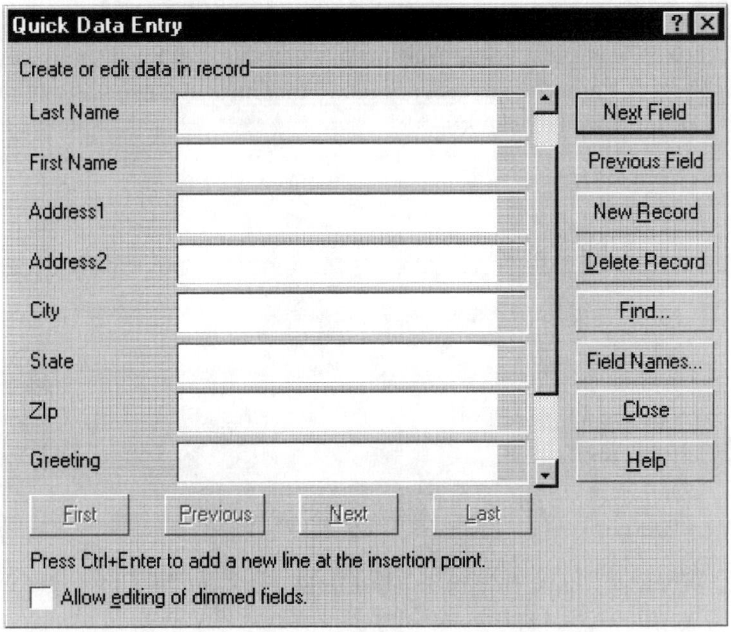

Quick Data Entry ? ✕

Create or edit data in record

Last Name		Next Field
First Name		Previous Field
Address1		New Record
Address2		Delete Record
City		Find...
State		Field Names...
ZIp		Close
Greeting		Help

First   Previous   Next   Last

Press Ctrl+Enter to add a new line at the insertion point.

☐ Allow editing of dimmed fields.

Quick
Data Entry
dialog box

FIGURE 11-2

---

10. Type **Chesin**, and then press ENTER. Corel WordPerfect moves the insertion point to the next field. Now fill in the rest of the fields as shown here, pressing ENTER after each. To enter text that appears on two lines within a field, press CTRL-ENTER.

Chesin
Adam
877 West Avenue
Suite 302
Camden
NJ
08765
Adam
11/1/98
500
1000

11

11. When you press ENTER after typing the entry for the Amount Due field, Corel WordPerfect adds the record to the data file, clears all of the text boxes, and places the insertion point in the first text box to start a new record. Enter the next record using this information, noting that the field Address2 is left blank:

> Schneider
> Josh
> 767 Fifth Avenue
>
> New York
> NY
> 20918
> Mr. Schneider
> 10/11/98
> 467
> 1000

12. When you have entered the last field, click on the Close button. Corel WordPerfect displays a dialog box asking if you want to save the database.

13. Click on Yes.

14. Type **Clients** and then click on Save. Corel WordPerfect saves merge data files with the DAT extension.

Leave the data file onscreen for now.

The Data File Window

The data file will appear onscreen as a table, with the field names in the first row, the Table Property bar, and the Merge feature bar, as in Figure 11-3. The Row and Column buttons let you insert or delete rows and columns. You use the Merge Codes button to display special codes that perform operations with the merge file.

The Merge button will display a dialog box where you can merge the data file with the form document. Click on Go To Form to display the open form document, if any, that is associated with the data file. The options let you sort and print the database, and control how the codes appear onscreen.

Use the Quick Entry button to return to the Quick Data Entry dialog box for inserting and editing records. The box will appear showing the information from the

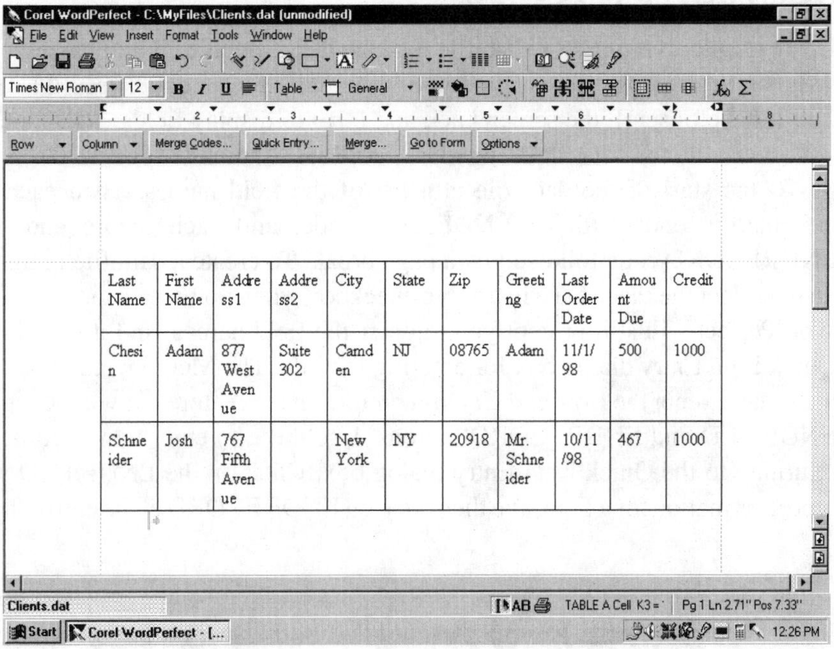

Data file in Merge window

FIGURE 11-3

record in which the insertion point is placed. Here's how to use the Quick Data Entry dialog box:

- Edit the information for that record, or click on the New Record button to enter a new record.

- To display a record in the box, click on the buttons along the bottom of the box—First, Previous, Next, and Last.

- To search for a specific record, click on Find to display the Find Text dialog box, type the information you are looking for, and then click on Find Next. Corel WordPerfect will display the first record containing that information. Continue clicking on Find Next to locate additional records with that information.

- To add or edit the field names, click on the Field Names button.

11

Using Merge Files

Using a table to organize a data file has one disadvantage. If you have more fields than can be displayed across the screen, you can't see an entire record at one time. You'll have to scroll the screen back and forth to display fields. As an alternative, you can create the data file using merge codes, as shown in Figure 11-4.

At the start of the data file is a list of the field names. Then each field of information ends with an ENDFIELD code, and each record ends with an ENDRECORD code followed by a page break. To create a data file in this format, do not select the Place Data in a Table checkbox when you create the data file. Corel WordPerfect will still prompt you to enter the field names, and it will display the Quick Data Entry dialog box for entering records. The Merge window will also be the same, except the Row and Column buttons in the feature bar will be replaced by ENDFIELD and ENDRECORD buttons. Use these to enter new records without returning to the Quick Data Entry dialog box. Click on the ENDFIELD after you type information for a field, and then click on ENDRECORD at the end of the record.

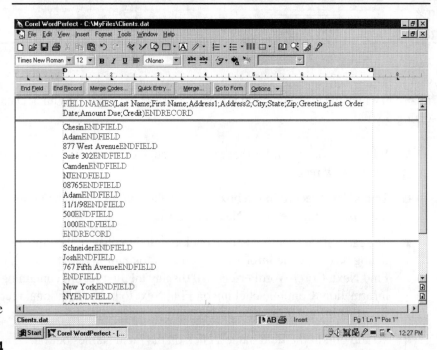

Data file using merge codes

FIGURE 11-4

Using Field Numbers Instead of Names

You can create a database where each field is associated with a field number rather than a field name. In our sample database, for example, field 1 is the last name, field 2 is the first name, and so on.

If you do not want to use names, select OK in the Create Data File dialog box without entering any field names. A dialog box will appear asking for the number of fields in each record. Enter the number of fields, and then select OK. The Quick Data Entry dialog box appears with each text box numbered.

Writing the Form Letter

You write, format, and edit a form document using the same techniques you use in any Corel WordPerfect document. However, when you come to a place where you want to insert information from the data file, you enter a field code.

You can use the fields in any order—they do not have to be in the order they are in the data file—and you can use a field as many times as you want to repeat the information in the same document.

Associating a Data File

To access the field names when writing the form document, however, you need to associate the data file with the form document. By creating the association, you can later merge the documents without selecting the data filename. Corel WordPerfect keeps track of the association, so it knows what data file to use during the merge process.

You do not have to associate a form document with a data file when you create it, because you can always associate it later. You can even change the data file associated with a form document—as long as the data file contains the same field names.

You can start a form letter directly from the new data file, or at any time after. Now that the data file is on the screen, here's how:

1. Click on Go To Form in the Merge feature bar. A dialog box will appear reporting that the file is not associated with a form letter.

2. Click on Create to start a new form letter. (Use the Select button to associate the data file with an existing form letter.)

If you closed the data file after you created it, you can start a form letter and associate it with the data file. To do so, select Merge from the Tools menu and click on Create Document. A dialog box appears where you select the data file that you want to associate with the form document. Select the data file from the box, changing folders and drives if necessary. To associate the form document with the Corel Address Book, click on the Associate an Address Book option button, and then select either My Addresses, Frequent Contacts, or another Address Book. If you want to create the association later, click on No Association.

Corel WordPerfect displays a blank document with a Merge toolbar, as shown here:

| ? | Insert Field... | Date | Merge Codes... | Keyboard... | Merge... | Go to Data | Options ▼ |

Here are the functions of the feature bar buttons:

- *Insert Field* displays a dialog box of fields in the associated data file or Address Book. Double-click on the field that represents the information you want to insert in the document at the location of the insertion point.

- *Date* inserts the date code.

- *Merge Codes* displays a list of merge codes that you can use in your form document. Use these merge codes to create more sophisticated merge operations.

- *Keyboard* inserts a code that will allow you to type information into the form document as it is merged.

- *Merge* displays the Merge dialog box to begin the merge operation.

- *Go To Data* displays the associated data file or Address Book so you can add or edit information. To return to the document from the data file, click on the Go To Form button.

- *Options* lets you determine how the merge codes appear onscreen.

Inserting Fields and Text

Now that the letter is associated with the data file, you can access its fields. Follow these steps to create the form document.

1. Click on the Insert Field button to display the Insert Field Name or Number dialog box shown here:

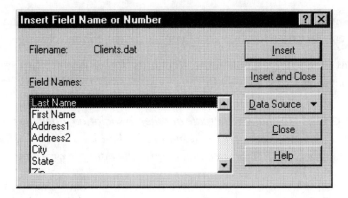

2. Double-click on the First Name field. Corel WordPerfect displays the code FIELD(First Name) in the document, indicating that the contents of that field will be placed into the form letter when it is merged. You'll notice that the dialog box stays on the screen so you can enter other field codes.

3. Press the SPACEBAR to insert a space after the code, and then double-click on the Last Name field. Press ENTER to move to the next line in the document.

4. Double-click on the Address1 field and then press ENTER.

5. Double-click on Address2 and press ENTER to move to the next line. You want to place the next three fields on the same line—City, State, and Zip.

6. Double-click on City.

7. Type a comma, press the SPACEBAR, and insert the State field.

8. Press the SPACEBAR twice, insert the Zip field, and then press ENTER. So far the address looks like this:

> FIELD(First Name) FIELD(Last Name)
> FIELD(Address1)
> FIELD(Address2)
> FIELD(City), FIELD(State) FIELD(Zip)

9. Now press ENTER again, type **Dear**, and then press the SPACEBAR.

10. Insert the Greeting field, type a colon, and press ENTER twice.

11

11. Complete the form letter as shown in Figure 11-5, entering the fields in the appropriate locations, and your own name in the closing.

12. Save the letter with the name **Accounts**. Corel WordPerfect saves form documents with the FRM extension.

NOTE: *To change or create another association, open the form document and click on the Insert Field button. In the Insert Field or Number dialog box, click on Data Source and choose the data file or Address Book.*

Merging Form Documents

With the form document and data file complete, you can merge them at any time. If you start from a blank screen, start a merge by selecting Merge from the Tools menu

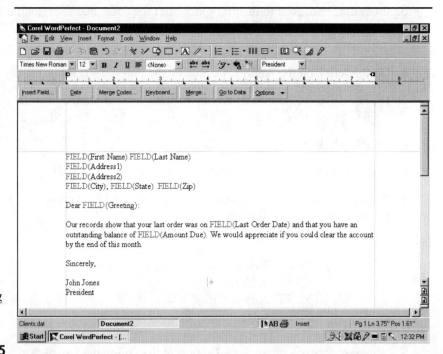

Completing the form letter

FIGURE 11-5

and clicking on Perform Merge. You then have to enter the name of the form document and select its associated data file or Address Book.

It is easier if you open the form letter first. Whenever you open the form document, it will automatically appear with the Merge toolbar, and it will be linked with the associated data file. Once you open the form letter, merge it using these steps:

1. Click on the Merge button in the toolbar to display the Perform Merge dialog box shown in Figure 11-6. Because the document is associated with the data file, the options in the dialog box list the associated data filename.

2. Select where you want to output the letters. The Output setting determines where the merge is performed. When set at New Document, Corel WordPerfect performs the merge, creating one large document containing all of the form letters. Each of the letters will be separated by a page break. You can now edit the documents, print them, or save them together as a new document.

3. To print the form documents as they are merged, select Printer in the Output list. Other Output options let you insert the merged documents into the current document, save them directly to a file on the disk, or e-mail the merged documents.

4. Click on OK to start the merge.

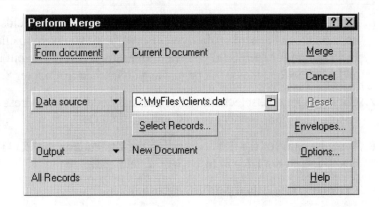

Perform
Merge
dialog box

FIGURE 11-6

Printing Envelopes for Form Letters

When you are merging form letters, you might want to merge their envelopes at the same time. You could use the Envelopes option in the Format menu. This way, each envelope appears after its corresponding letters. If you don't have an envelope feeder, however, you'd have to stand or sit by the printer inserting an envelope into the manual tray after each letter prints.

A better method is to use the Envelopes command from the Perform Merge dialog box. Using this procedure, the envelopes are inserted in a group after all of the letters. This also has the advantage that you can store the arrangement of field codes for various envelopes, and then simply retrieve the arrangement that you want to use for the set of envelopes. Use these steps to create envelopes:

1. Open the form document that contains the letter or other mailing.

2. Click on the Merge button in the feature bar to display the Perform Merge dialog box.

3. Click on the Envelopes button to display the Envelope window shown in Figure 11-7.

4. Click in the Mailing Addresses section, and design the layout of the fields for the mailing address, just as you did when creating the inside address for the form document. Click on the Field button to display a list of the fields in the associated data file.

5. Double-click on a field to insert it into the mailing address.

6. Repeat steps 4 and 5 to complete the layout. Because the Fields list does not remain on the screen after you insert a field, you have to click on the Field button for each field you want to insert. When the layout is done, add a bar code to the envelope just as you learned in Chapter 8.

7. Click on Options, select either Position bar code above address or Position bar code below address, and click on OK.

8. Type the name of the field containing the ZIP code in the POSTNET text box—you do not have to insert it as a field code.

9. Click on OK and then perform the merge.

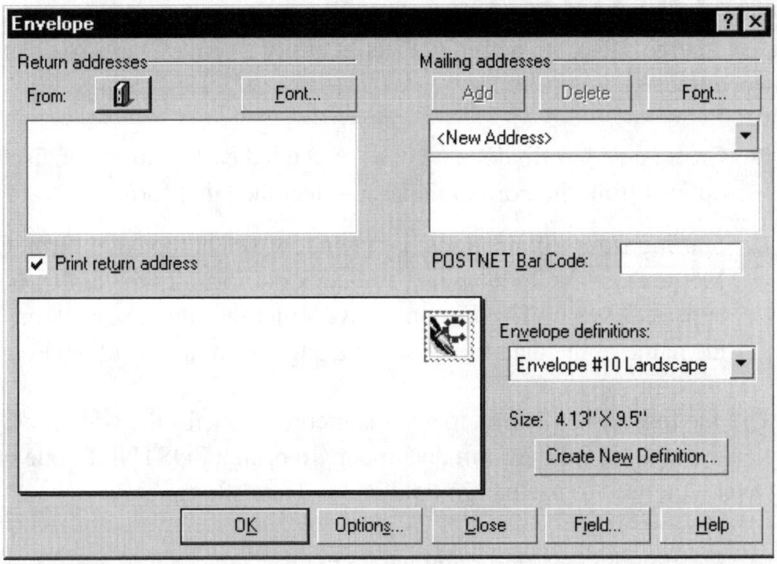

Envelope dialog box for merging with a data file

FIGURE 11-7

Building Address Formats

Because the Fields box does not remain on the screen, it can be time-consuming to design the envelope layout. Rather than re-create it for each form letter, you can save the layout of the fields and recall it later.

The Envelope dialog box that appears when you open it from the Perform Merge dialog box contains a mailing address list, as well as the Add and Delete buttons. You use the Add button to save the configuration of the merge fields, and you can later call up that configuration by selecting it in the address list.

After you create the address format, make sure that New Address appears in the list box, and then click on the Add button. You can store any number of configurations the same way. To select one, pull down the address list. Corel WordPerfect will list the first line of each of the stored addresses. Click on the address format that you want to use, scrolling the list if necessary.

Merging to Labels

You can merge data onto mailing labels as easily as envelopes. You can get started in two ways:

■ Create a new form document, as explained earlier, and then use Labels options from the Format menu to select the label form.

■ Starting from a blank document window, select the label form. Choose Merge from the Tools menu, and click on Form. In the dialog box that appears, click on Use File In Active Window, and then click on OK. Enter the name of the data file or select a page from the Corel Address Book.

Use the Insert Field button to add the merge codes for the addresses, just as you created the address for the form document. To print a POSTNET code on the label, however, you need to use merge field codes. Here's how:

1. Position the insertion point where the bar code should appear.

2. Click on the Merge Codes button in the feature bar to see the dialog box shown here:

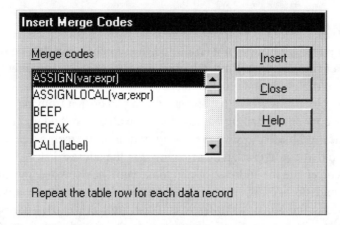

3. Scroll the list and click on the POSTNET(string).

4. Click on Insert and then on Close to close the dialog box. Corel WordPerfect will display the code POSTNET( ), with the insertion point between the parentheses.

5. Click on the Insert Field button, double-click on the field representing the ZIP code, and then close the dialog box.

The final code will appear as POSTNET(FIELD(ZipCode)).

When you merge this form document, the labels will be filled in with the information from the data file. Perform the merge to a new document, and then insert the label stock into the printer and print the labels.

Merging Lists

When you create letters or envelopes, each record is separated by a page break. Labels print on special label paper. There may be times when you want to use the merge feature to create a list, such as an inventory of your clients or club members. In these cases, you want the records to appear after each other, not on separate pages.

To do this, start by creating a form document, arranging the field codes as you want the list to appear. To create a columnar list, for example, you might arrange the codes like this:

FIELD(First Name) FIELD(Last Name) FIELD(Amount Due)

Before merging the document, however, you have to tell Corel WordPerfect not to insert a page break after each record. To do so, click Merge in the Merge feature bar, and then click on Options to see the dialog box shown in Figure 11-8.

The choices in this dialog box let you print more than one copy of each merge document, and control how blank fields are handled. By default, for example, Corel WordPerfect will not print a blank line in an address, if there is no information in one of the fields, such as Address2. If you want, you can pull down the If Field Is Empty in Data Source option and choose to leave the blank line in place. You can also use this dialog box to control how merge codes appear during interactive merges.

11

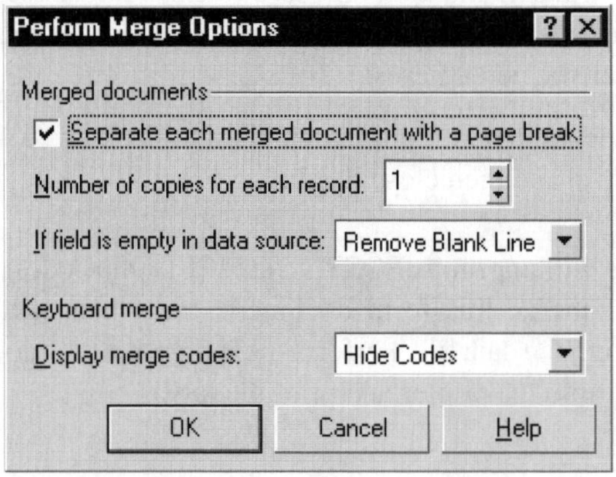

Perform
Merge
Options
dialog box

FIGURE 11-8

To create a list, however, deselect the Separate Each Merged Document with a Page Break checkbox, and then click on OK. Now when you perform the merge, the records will appear neatly arranged in rows.

Selecting Merge Records

Sometimes you do not want to merge all of the records in a data file with a form document, just selected ones. You might want to send a mailing, for example, to clients who owe you money or who are located in a certain community. Rather than merge all of the records and throw away the letters you do not want, you can select records before performing the merge.

To select records, use this procedure:

1. Open the form document.

2. Click on the Merge button in the feature bar, and then click on the Select Records button in the Perform Merge dialog box. Corel WordPerfect will display the Select Records dialog box shown in Figure 11-9.

3. Select records using either the Specify Conditions or Mark Records option.

   ■ *Specify Conditions* lets you enter search criteria based on the content of the fields. Use this option if you have a large data file and want to select records that have a field value in common. You should also use this option if you want to merge a specific range of records, such as the first ten or the last five.

■ *Mark Records* lets you click on the records that you want to merge. Use this option if your database is relatively small, or if you want to select records that may not have a common field value.

Let's look at both methods in more detail.

Specifying Conditions

When you want to merge a selected range of records, or records based on a field value—such as all clients in California—use the Specify Conditions options.

To merge a range of records, enter the beginning record number in the From box and the ending record number in the End box. The record number corresponds to the table row of the record in the data file.

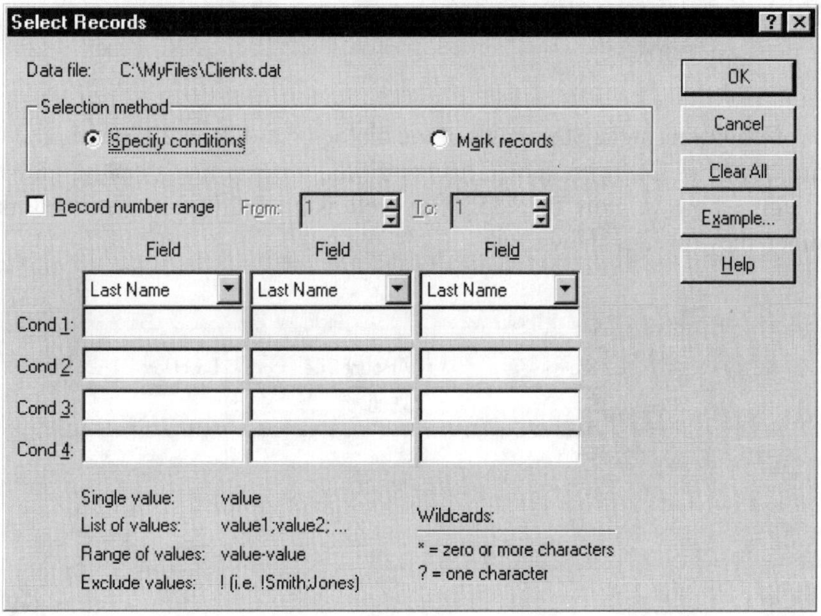

Selecting records

FIGURE 11-9

If you want to limit the records to those meeting a certain condition, create a filter. A *filter* tells Corel WordPerfect to use only the records that meet certain conditions for the merge operation, ignoring those that do not meet the conditions. The records not used during the merge remain in the data file—they are just ignored, not deleted.

You can select records based on up to three fields. Starting with the column on the left, pull down the list and choose a field that you want to use for a condition.

You can specify up to four selection criteria, each on one to three fields. In the first row, enter the values or conditions that a record has to meet. For example, to merge the records of clients who are in New Jersey, select State for the first field and enter **NJ** in the column under State. To further specify which clients are selected, use up to two additional fields. When you have more than one condition in a row, Corel WordPerfect treats them as AND conditions. This means that the record must meet all of the specifications to be selected. For example, to merge with records for New Jersey clients who owe over $500, add the Amount Due field to the second column, and type **>500** as the condition under it. The condition will appear as shown here.

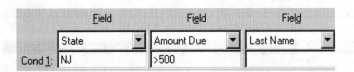

Conditions in the other rows of the dialog box—Cond 2, Cond 3, and Cond 4— are treated as OR operations. This condition, for example, displays all New Jersey clients who owe more than $500, as well as all California clients no matter how much they owe, as shown here.

	Field	Field	Field
	State ▼	Amount Due ▼	Last Name ▼
Cond 1:	NJ	>500	
Cond 2:	CA		

When you want to select records based on a specific value, just type the value in the condition box. You can also use > and < operators to meet conditions above and below value.

If you have a list of possible matching values, enter them in the same condition, separated by semicolons, rather than on separate rows in the dialog box. For instance, enter **PA;NJ** under the State field to match clients in either Pennsylvania or New Jersey. You can also choose records in a range of values using a hyphen, as in 200-1000 for clients with a value from 200 to 1000 in the field. To exclude a specific value, precede it with an exclamation point. For example, to list clients in every state but California, enter **!CA** in the State field.

Finally, you can use the * and ? wildcard characters to represent, respectively, any number of characters, and a single character. Entering **N*** in the Last Name field, for example, will select all clients whose last names begin with the letter "N." Entering **8450?** under the Zip Code field will select clients whose ZIP codes start with the numbers "8450."

Marking Records

To pick the records you want to use, click on the Mark Records option. The dialog box will change as shown in Figure 11-10, listing all of the records in the data file with checkboxes. Then follow these steps:

1. In the Display Records boxes, enter the starting and ending numbers of the records you want to pick from. To select from all of the records, leave the boxes with their default values.

2. In the First Field to Display list, select the field that you want to use to select records. For example, if you want to pick records based on the state of residence, pull down the list and click on the State field.

3. Click on the Update Record List. Corel WordPerfect will display the records in the Record List.

4. Click on the checkboxes for the records that you want to merge.

5. Click on OK when you have finished, and perform the merge.

11

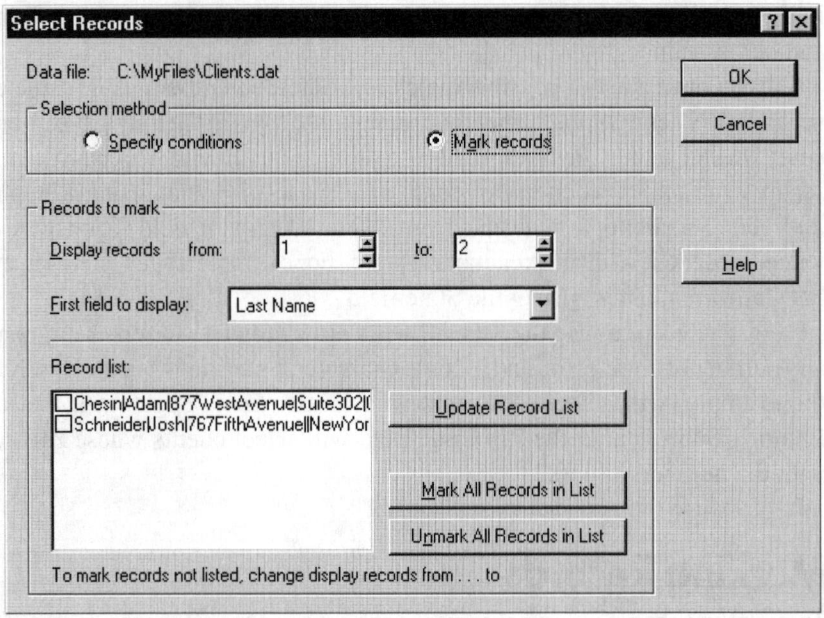

Select Records

Data file: C:\MyFiles\Clients.dat

Selection method

○ Specify conditions ● Mark records

Records to mark

Display records from: 1 to: 2

First field to display: Last Name

Record list:

☐ Chesin|Adam|877WestAvenue|Suite302|(
☐ Schneider|Josh|767FifthAvenue||NewYor

Update Record List

Mark All Records in List

Unmark All Records in List

To mark records not listed, change display records from . . . to

OK

Cancel

Help

Marking
records to
select

FIGURE 11-10

Customizing a Merge with Fields

The Merge Codes and Keyboard buttons in the Merge feature bar give you great flexibility in controlling the merge process. You can use the merge codes, for example, to automate operations in much the same way that you can use macros. In fact, you can even run a macro directly from a merge file.

As an example of using merge codes, the next section will illustrate several useful codes, starting with an interactive merge that lets you enter information into the merged document.

Interactive Merges

In most cases, your data file should have all of the variable information that you need to personalize the form document. But suppose it doesn't? Suppose you want to enter a personal salutation for a letter using a client's first name or nickname. To enter information into the form letter when it is being merged, you need to use the Keyboard code.

Place the insertion point in the form letter where you want to enter the information, and then click on the Keyboard button in the Merge feature bar. In the dialog box that appears, type a prompt that will appear asking for the information you want to enter, and then click on OK.

When you merge the documents, Corel WordPerfect will pause and display the prompt and a special feature bar as shown in Figure 11-11. The bar contains these buttons:

- *Continue* inserts the text you enter into the document and continues the merge.

- *Skip Record* continues the merge without inserting any information in the current documents.

- *Quit* continues the merge but ignores all remaining merge codes.

- *Stop* ends the merge at the current document.

Dialog box and feature bar for keyboard merge

FIGURE 11-11

Type the text that you want to insert into the document, and then click on Continue in the feature bar. Corel WordPerfect will pause at the same location for every letter.

Performing Calculations

In addition to typing information as the merge progresses, you can also perform calculations. For example, suppose you want to send a letter telling clients how much money remains in their credit line. You have the fields Credit and Amount Due, so you must subtract them to calculate the difference. To perform this function, you need two commands: Assign and Variable. To insert a merge command into the document, use the Merge Commands button in the Merge feature bar to display the Insert Merge Code dialog box, and double-click on the command you want to enter. In some cases, a dialog box will appear where you can enter a parameter for the command.

The Assign command uses the syntax **Assign(variable; value or expression)**. Double-click on the command in the Insert Merge Code box to see this dialog box.

```
┌─────────────────────────────────────────────────────┐
│ Insert Merge Code                                    │
│                                                      │
│   FORMAT: ASSIGN(var;expr)           ┌──────────┐    │
│   Variable:                          │    OK    │    │
│                                      └──────────┘    │
│   ┌──────────────────────────────┐   ┌──────────┐    │
│   │                              │   │  Cancel  │    │
│   └──────────────────────────────┘   └──────────┘    │
│   Expression:                        ┌──────────┐    │
│   ┌──────────────────────────────┐   │   Help   │    │
│   │                              │   └──────────┘    │
│   └──────────────────────────────┘                  │
└─────────────────────────────────────────────────────┘
```

Type **Net** in the Variable text box, and then click on OK. Because the expression will use field codes, you have to enter them in using the Insert Field button. The Assign(net;) code will appear in the document. Move the insertion point to the left of the closing parentheses, and then click on Insert Field. Double-click on the Credit field, press the hyphen, and then double-click on the Amount Due field. The final command will appear as Assign(net; Field(Credit)_Field(Amount Due)).

Now when you want to insert the amount in the merged document, use the Variable command. Display the Insert Merge Code box, and double-click on the Variable code near the bottom of the list. Type **Net** in the dialog box that appears, and click on OK. The code will appear as Variable(Net).

There are two drawbacks to this method. First, merge commands will only work with integers—whole numbers. That's why whole numbers were used in the sample data file. Second, if you place the Assign command in a line by itself in the form document, it will generate an extra carriage return, resulting in a blank line. Corel WordPerfect will perform the calculation to compute the amount, but it will insert the carriage return that ends the line. To avoid this problem, write the line like this, with the closing parenthesis on the next line:

Assign(net; Field(Credit)_Field(Amount Due))Comment(
)

Start the document on the same line as the closing parenthesis. The Comment command tells Corel WordPerfect to ignore any text or codes that follow it, so it ignores the carriage return.

Sorting Database Records

Your form document will be merged with the data file in the same order as the records appear in the file. In some instances, however, you may want to merge the file in some other order, such as by ZIP code to take advantage of bulk mail.

To sort a database, click on Sort in the Options menu of the Merge feature bar, or select Sort from the Tools menu. This will display the dialog box shown in Figure 11-12. The box offers a number of predefined sorts, such as the first cell in a table or the first characters in a merge file. It also lets you designate the input file (the data

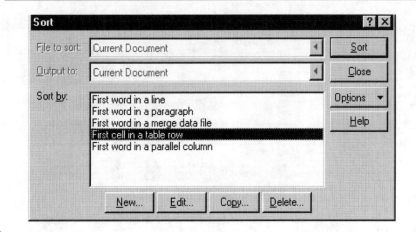

Predefined sort options

FIGURE 11-12

that you are sorting) and the output file where you want to place the document. Leaving both set at Current Document will actually change the order of the records in the table.

To create your own sort to use any other merge field, click on New to display the dialog box shown in Figure 11-13. Type a name for the sort in the Sort Description text box.

You use this dialog box to sort records in a data file, as well as lines, paragraphs, parallel columns, and table rows in a document. Our data file appears in the form of a table, so we want to select the Table Row option in the Sort By section. You would use the Merge Record option button if your data file used merge codes.

Corel WordPerfect will sort the information based on one to nine key fields. A *key* represents a field to sort on, or a word or line within the field. Each key can be sorted in either alphanumeric or numeric order, depending on its contents.

To sort the table by the Amount Due field, pull down the Type list and select Numeric. Then choose if you want to sort your records in ascending or descending order. Enter **10** in the Column text box because the Amount Due field is in the tenth column. Leave the Line and Word options set at 1.

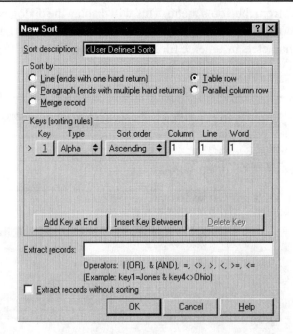

Defining
a sort

FIGURE 11-13

You can also enter a criteria to select records, so the function sorts and selects at the same time. If you click on the Extract Records Without Sorting checkbox, Corel WordPerfect selects records that meet the condition without sorting them.

To add another key to the sort, click on the Add Key at End button, and then enter its specifications. The new key is added after the existing ones. Since the sort is performed in key order—giving precedence to key one, then key two, and so on—you can also click on Insert Key Between to add a new key before the current one.

When you have finished defining the keys, click on OK. Your sort will now be listed in the Sort dialog box. Double-click on it to perform the sort.

11

Working with Graphics

12

A ll of the formatting techniques that you've learned so far go a long way toward making a professional-looking document. But sometimes nothing does it better than graphics. Corel WordPerfect has a full range of graphics features that let you add clipart, charts, special text effects, horizontal and vertical lines, custom drawings, and even scientific equations to your document.

Picture Basics

Inserting a picture into your document is one of the easiest ways to add pizzazz to a document. In Chapter 2, you learned how to add a graphic from the Scrapbook. Click on the ClipArt button in the toolbar to display the Scrapbook, select the graphic, then drag and drop it into the document. You can also insert other graphic files just as easily, by following these steps:

1. Place the insertion point where you want the graphic to appear.

2. Pull down the Insert menu, point to Graphics, and click on From File to display the Insert Image dialog box. This box lists graphic files in the Corel\Suite8\Graphics\ClipArt folder. To access images in other folders, use the Look In list and the directory/file listing. Click on the Up One Level button, for example, to select folders containing backgrounds, borders, pictures, and textures.

3. To see what a graphic looks like before inserting it, click on the Toggle Preview On/Off button in the dialog box's toolbar.

 NOTE: *Some of the graphics are words or phrases, such as "Secret," "Confidential," and "Do Not Duplicate." Others are dividers that you can use between paragraphs, or at the top or bottom of the page.*

4. Double-click on the name of the file you want to insert, or click on it and then on the Insert button.

The graphic will appear in the document with the upper-left corner at the position of the insertion point, along with the Graphic property bar, as shown in Figure 12-1.

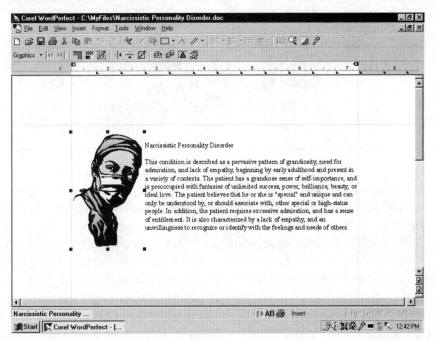

Graphic
inserted into
a document

FIGURE 12-1

The image will be surrounded by small black boxes, called *handles,* showing that it
is selected. To deselect the graphic, click elsewhere on the page.

 *If you have a graphics-intensive layout, you can create the graphics in Corel
Presentations and then import your text from Corel WordPerfect.*

Corel WordPerfect Suite comes with more than 10,000 graphic files, many of
which are not copied onto your computer but kept on the CD. Table 12-1 summarizes
the locations of the files. Substitute the letter of your hard disk where you installed
the Suite and the letter of your CD drive.

Using Drag to Create

You can always change the size and position of a graphic after you insert it. As an
alternative, you can start by drawing a box the size and in the position you want the

Directory	Description
C:\Corel\Suite8\Graphics	backgrounds, borders, pictures, textures, and general clipart
CD:\Corel\Suite8\Graphics	backgrounds, borders, pictures, textures, and general clipart
CD:\Photos	photographs

Where to Find Graphics

TABLE 12-1

graphic and then inserting the image into the box. This is a good technique if you've already typed and formatted your document and you know exactly where you want the image to appear.

To do this, point at some white space on the screen to see the shadow cursor, then drag the mouse. When you release the mouse, choose ClipArt or Image from File from the shortcut menu, then select the graphic.

TIP: *You can change Corel WordPerfect's setting to let you drag-to-create all new graphic boxes. See Chapter 10 for more information on using the Graphics Environment settings.*

Linking Graphic Files

Adding graphics to your documents increases their impact, but it also enlarges them. Graphics can take up a lot of disk space, and when you insert a graphic into a document, you are actually inserting the entire graphic file.

Inserting a graphic has one other drawback. Suppose you used a drawing program to create your company logo and then inserted the logo into your letterhead and other documents. If you later changed the logo with the drawing program, you'd have to reinsert the new logo into all of the documents.

You can solve both the space problem and the new-logo problem by selecting the Image on Disk checkbox when you select the graphic in the Insert Image dialog box. This creates a link to the graphic on the disk, displaying it onscreen but not inserting the entire file into the document. If you later edit the drawing and save it to a file with the same name, the edited version will be retrieved automatically when you open the document in Corel WordPerfect.

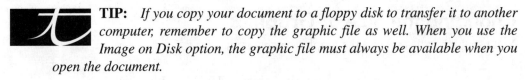

TIP: *If you copy your document to a floppy disk to transfer it to another computer, remember to copy the graphic file as well. When you use the Image on Disk option, the graphic file must always be available when you open the document.*

Using Graphics in Headers, Footers, and Watermarks

You can insert a graphic directly into the document. But if you want the graphic to appear on every page, you can insert it into a header, footer, or watermark.

Small graphics and decorative dividers are useful in headers and footers. Create or edit the header or footer, as explained in Chapter 8, and then insert the graphic into the header or footer area.

Some graphics are especially effective when used in a watermark. Displaying "DO NOT COPY" in large letters across a page, for example, certainly gets your point across. It cannot be cut out or ignored, and makes it perfectly clear that copies are not endorsed.

To insert a graphic in a watermark, create or edit the watermark as you learned in Chapter 8, then use the Clipart button on the toolbar to select and insert the graphic. You can insert several graphics as watermarks to create a special effect. In this chapter you will learn how to edit the graphic in the watermark window.

Changing the Position of Graphics

Once you insert a graphic, you can move it to any other position on the page—even to areas below the last text on the page. Use these steps.

1. If the graphic is not selected—that is, the handles do not appear around it—click on it.

2. Point inside the graphic, not on any of the handles, so the pointer appears as a four-headed arrow.

3. Drag the mouse.

4. As you drag, an outline of the graphic box moves with the pointer. When the box is where you want to place the graphic, release the mouse button.

Changing the Size of Graphics

You use the handles around the graphic to change its size.

- Drag a corner handle to change its height and width at the same time.

- Drag the center handle on the top or bottom to change its height.

- Drag the center handle on the left or right to change its width.

TIP: *You will learn later how to adjust the settings for a graphic to determine if dragging a corner handle maintains the current height-width ratio.*

Customizing the Graphic Box

Corel WordPerfect gives you a variety of ways to customize graphic images. First, understand that when you insert a graphic, you are really inserting two elements into the document—a graphic box and the graphic inside the box. By selecting ClipArt from the Graphics option in the Insert menu, you are telling Corel WordPerfect to insert a box using the Image Box style. You are then telling Corel WordPerfect what graphic to place inside the box. We'll look at the issue of box styles later; for now, let's consider ways to edit the box, as well as the image inside the box.

When you edit the graphic box, you are changing the container in which the graphic is placed. Dragging the box, or changing its size, for example, does not affect the image itself. These are the other ways you can edit the box:

- Add or change the border line around the box.

- Insert a fill color or pattern.

- Set the way text wraps around the box and the contour of the graphic.

- Set the position of the box in the document.

- Edit the box style.

- Add a caption.

- Modify the position of the contents within the box.

- Change the box size.

Corel WordPerfect provides a number of special ways to work with a graphic. The property bar that appears when you select a graphic includes these tools:

- *Graphics Menu* provides a complete list of graphic options, some of which are not found in the property bar.

- *Previous Box* selects the graphic box preceding the current one.

- *Next Box* selects the next graphic box in the document.

- *Border Style* determines the type of border line around the graphic.

- *Box Fill* determines the fill pattern and color within the box.

- *Caption* inserts a caption and numbers the graphic.

- *Flip Left/Right* flips a graphic from side to side.

- *Flip Top/Bottom* flips a graphic from top to bottom.

- *Image Tools* displays tools for changing the appearance of the graphic.

- *Object Forward One* moves the selected graphic in front of another that may be blocking it.

- *Object Back One* moves the graphic behind another.

- *Wrap* determines how text flows around the graphic.

- *Hyperlink* converts the graphic into a link.

Many of these same options, and more, are also available in the Graphics pull-down menu at the far left of the property bar, as shown here:

12

And you can choose them from the QuickMenu, as seen here:

Since many graphic functions are in all of these items, you can perform them using various techniques. For example, to determine the type of line around the graphic, you need to display the border options. You can display these options using any of these techniques:

- Click on the Border Style list in the property bar.

- Select Border/Fill from the Graphics pull-down menu on the property bar.

- Right-click and select Border/Fill from the QuickMenu.

As you work with graphics, you'll find which method you prefer.

Changing the Borders and Fill

Each of Corel WordPerfect's graphic box styles includes a default border and fill style. Image boxes have no border and no fill. Adding a border to the image is similar to adding borders around paragraphs and pages, except the Fancy borders are not available.

To add a border, pull down the Border Style list in the property bar and select the border you want. To add a fill pattern, pull down the Fill list and make a selection.

In addition, you can select from the Border/Fill dialog box. Display the box by choosing Border/Fill from the Graphics pull-down menu or QuickMenu. Corel WordPerfect will display the familiar Border/Fill dialog box with the Border, Fill, and Advanced pages. Select options from the box, just as you learned for adding borders around paragraphs.

When you select a fill pattern, you can also select foreground and background colors. Picture a pattern of vertical lines. The foreground color determines the color of the lines; the background color fills in between the lines.

Wrapping Text Around Graphics

Wrap refers to the way text flows around a graphic. The default setting for an image box is called *Square Both Sides.* This means that text will appear on all sides of the image—if there is room for it between the margins—up to the rectangular shape of the image box.

You can select other wrap methods from either the Wrap list in the property bar or from the dialog box that appears when you choose Wrap from the QuickMenu. Figure 12-2 shows the dialog box (the Wrap list offers the same options displayed differently).

Choose In Front of Text if you want the graphic to be superimposed over the text, so the text behind it does not appear. Choose Behind Text if you want the graphic to appear in the background, or to create special effects by combining text and graphics. Choose Neither Side if you want the graphic to appear with no text on its left or right. Select Square and then a Wrap option to let text wrap but stop the text

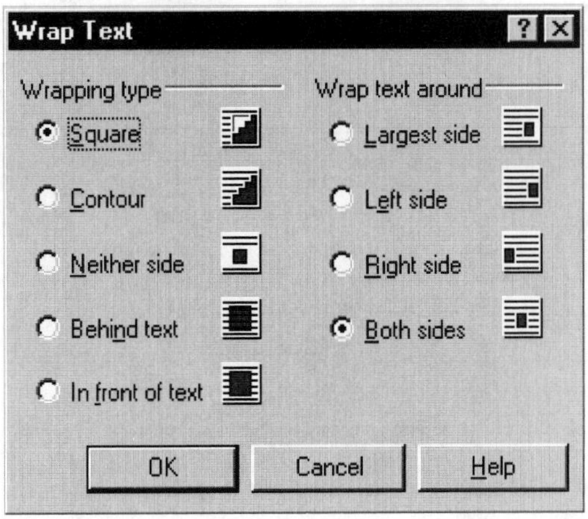

Wrap
options in
the Wrap
Text dialog
box

FIGURE 12-2

12

at the box borders. Select Contour and then a wrap option to allow you to wrap text but only up to the contour of the graphic.

Setting the Graphic Position

When you insert a graphic, Corel WordPerfect *anchors* it to the page. This means that the graphic is inserted in a specific location on the page, and inserting or deleting text above it will not change the position.

You can also anchor a picture to a paragraph or character. A *paragraph anchor* means that the box will move up or down with the paragraph as you insert or delete text above it. A *character anchor* means that the box is treated just like any other character in the line, and it will move with the line as you insert or delete text before it. Use a paragraph or character anchor when the text refers to the graphic and you want the graphic to be on the same page as its reference. Use a *page anchor* when you want the graphic to remain in the same position on the page regardless of the text.

To change the type of anchor, select Position from the QuickMenu or from the Graphics pull-down menu to see the dialog box shown in Figure 12-3. Pull down the Attach Box To list and select Page, Paragraph, or Character. You can also select a horizontal and vertical position relative to the page margins, to the edges of the

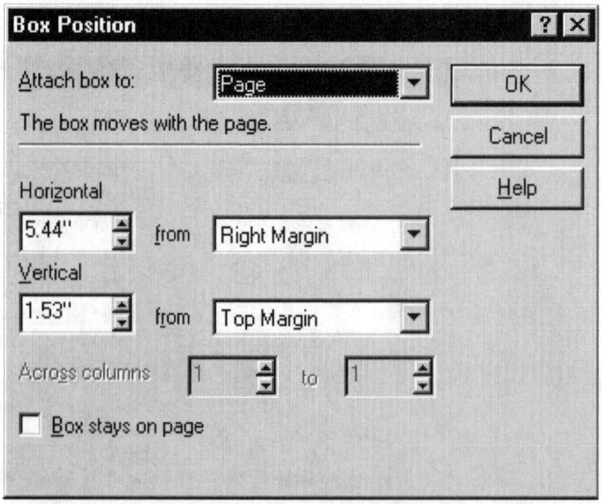

Position
options for
graphics

FIGURE 12-3

pages, or to the center of the page. If the graphic is within columns, you can also choose the relative position between columns. When you are working with a three-column newsletter, for example, you can choose to center the box across the first two columns. Select Column in the Vertical position list, and then enter **1** and **2** in the column text boxes.

TIP: *To keep the box on the page, however, you must select Page in the Attach Box To list, and select the Box Stays on Page checkbox.*

When you select a paragraph or character anchor, the image is anchored at its current location. If you later drag the image to another location, the anchor changes as well. Corel WordPerfect displays a paragraph anchor graphically as you drag, as shown here:

The Push-pin icon shows the paragraph to which the graphic will be linked. Release the mouse when the icon is at the desired paragraph.

Inserting a Caption

You can also add a caption that numbers the graphic and includes a descriptive word or phrase, just like the captions used with the figures in this book. Numbering graphics makes it easy to refer to them in the text. To add a caption to a graphic, follow these steps:

12

1. Click on the Caption tool in the property bar. Corel WordPerfect will insert the word "Figure," along with a figure number. Each image that you insert is associated with a number, even if you do not add a caption. The first image box in the document is Figure 1, the second is Figure 2, and so on, based on their positions in the document.

2. Corel WordPerfect leaves the insertion point to the right of the label, so you can type the descriptive text, as shown here.

Figure 1

3. When you have finished, click elsewhere on the page.

The position of the caption and its label (such as "Figure") are determined by the graphic box style. The default style for image boxes places the caption on the left below the graphic, outside the box, and using the label "Figure."

To change the position and orientation of the caption or its text, select Caption from the QuickMenu on the Graphics pull-down menu.

 TIP: *To edit the text of the caption, click on the Edit button in the dialog box.*

The Caption Position option determines the position of the caption in relation to the graphic box. You can select the side of the box and whether the caption is inside or outside of it. Pull down the Position list to choose if the caption is at the top, center, or bottom of the selected side. You can also enter a specific location using an absolute measurement, or a percentage offset, such as 25 percent from the left edge.

Use the Rotate Caption option to rotate the text. If you position the caption on the left border, for example, you might want to rotate it 90 degrees so the characters print in landscape orientation up the edge, as shown here:

The Auto Width option in the Caption Width section lets Corel WordPerfect wrap the caption as necessary based on the amount of text, the size of the box, and the caption's position. Sometimes, however, this may result in too much blank space around the caption, taking up needless room on the page. As an alternative you can designate a fixed width in inches, but no wider than the box if the caption is on the bottom, or no taller if it is on the side. You can also set the width as a percentage of the box size, between 1 and 100 percent.

The Caption Numbering and Styles options let you change the counter used to number the graphic.

Setting Content Options

The graphic box style also affects the position of the graphic within the box and the type of contents in the box. When you select ClipArt from the Graphics option in the Insert menu, Corel WordPerfect assumes you want to insert a graphic image and creates a box the default size for the graphic image. The Content option in the QuickMenu and Graphics pull-down menu gives you some control over these default settings. Click on Content to see the Box Content dialog box.

Keep in mind that the graphic and the box in which the graphic appears are two separate objects. This dialog box is designed to let you change what is in the box and its position.

The name of the graphic file you inserted appears in the Filename text box. If you want to replace the graphic with another, enter the new name in the box or use

12

the List button to select the file. The Content list lets you choose the type of content. It is set at Image or Image on Disk, based on how you inserted the graphic. You can also select Empty, Text, or Equation from the Content list. Selecting any of these, however, will delete the graphic from the box because it will no longer be considered an image box. You use the Content list mainly when you are creating a custom box style and you need to specify the type of contents that it will hold, or to switch to an Image on Disk.

If you inserted a graphic in a format other than Corel WordPerfect's own WPG format, the Image on Disk option in the Content list has a nice side effect. Remember, Image on Disk creates a link to the graphic file. If you select Image on Disk after inserting a graphic, a dialog box appears asking where you want to save the graphic. You can then choose to save the graphic as a WPG file, converting it to Corel WordPerfect's own format.

The Content Position options in the dialog box determine the position of the image within the graphic box. They do not affect the position of the box on the page. The default settings center the image horizontally and vertically, but you can change the vertical position to the left or right, and the horizontal position to the top or bottom.

You won't see the effect of your changes immediately because, by default, the box size is the same as the graphic. This is because the Preserve Image Width/Height Ratio checkbox may not be selected. As you change the size of the graphic box by dragging a handle, the graphic changes as well. If you check this box, however, Corel WordPerfect will always maintain the original proportions of the image inside the box. If you enlarge the box in a different proportion, the box will become larger than the graphic, and you can then adjust the position of the graphic within the larger box.

You can select options from the Rotates Text Counterclockwise section only when you are using a text box.

Setting the Box Size

Trying to adjust a graphic to an exact size by dragging can be difficult, especially if you do not have a steady hand. To use measurements to change the graphic box size, select Size from the QuickMenu or Graphics pull-down menu to open the Box Size dialog box.

Use the Set options in the Width and Height sections to enter a specific size. Use the Full options in the Width section to automatically extend the box fully between the margins or the full width of the columns. Choose Full in the Height section to extend the box to the top and bottom margins and to anchor the graphic to the page.

Choose Maintain Proportions in either section to automatically adjust the width or height when you change the other size to maintain the picture's original proportions.

Changing the Image Settings

So far, all of the editing techniques have modified the box in which the graphic is placed. You can also edit the graphic itself. Editing the graphic changes the appearance of the image without affecting the box in which it is placed.

There are actually two ways that you can edit the graphic: you can edit its appearance without changing the actual design, or you can modify the design—the shape and elements that make up the graphic.

For example, the options to flip the graphic left/right and top/bottom are on the property bar. Flipping left/right (horizontally) is useful for some graphics that appear to be pointing in a certain direction. Flipping top/bottom (vertically) is useful for designs that do not contain text or other recognizable people, places, or things. For instance, if you use a divider graphic along the top of the page, insert the same graphic along the bottom, and then flip the graphic horizontally, the graphics appear to be framing the page. Use the same technique with graphics down the left and right edges of the page, but flip one horizontally.

To customize the graphic's appearance even further, click on the Image Tools button in the property bar or QuickMenu to display the palette of tools shown in Figure 12-4. Now take a quick look at each of these tools. How well you use them will depend on your own design and artistic abilities.

Rotating Graphics

The Rotate tool lets you rotate the image within the box without rotating the box itself. Here's how it works:

1. Click on Rotate to display four corner handles around the graphic.

2. Drag one of the handles to rotate the image.

3. Click on the Rotate tool when you've finished.

You can also drag the handle in the center of the graphic to change the focus point of the rotation.

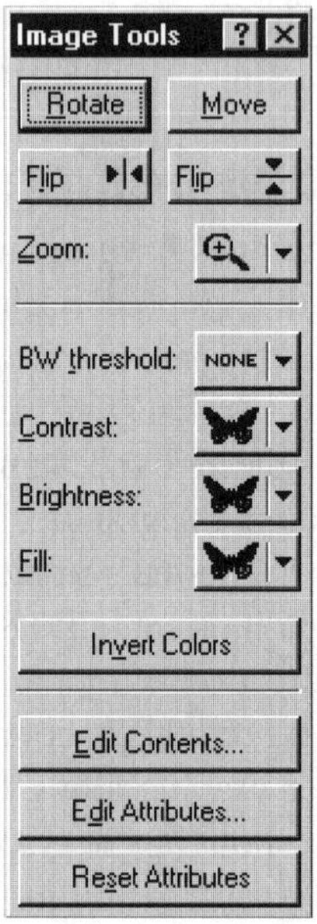

Image tools

FIGURE 12-4

Because you are only rotating the image within the box, some of it may now extend beyond the borders of the box and will no longer appear. Don't worry if part of the image seems to be missing, as shown here. The complete image is still in the document, so it will be diplayed if you rotate the image back or enlarge the box size. For more precise control over rotation, use the Image Settings options that will be discussed later in this chapter.

Figure 1 Doctor

Moving the Image

The Move tool lets you change the position of the image within the box. Follow these steps:

1. Click on the Move tool.

2. Point to the graphic and drag the image.

You can drag the image so some parts of it scroll out of the box, but again, the parts that scroll are not lost—you can later move the image so they appear again.

Mirror Imaging

These Flip buttons let you flip the image horizontally or vertically, just like the Flip buttons in the property bar.

Enlarging the Image

By default, the image box is the same size as the graphic. Changing the size of the box also changes the size of the image within it. You use the Zoom tool to change the size of just the image within the box. Clicking on the Zoom tool displays these three options.

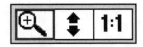

Use the Magnifier icon when you want to enlarge a selected portion of the graphic so it fills the image box. Follow these steps:

1. Click on the Magnifier icon—the pointer will appear as a magnifying lens and a crosshair.

2. Drag the mouse to select a rectangular portion of the graphic.

3. When you release the mouse, that portion is enlarged to fill the image box.

12

Use the up and down arrows to enlarge or reduce the entire image. Here's how:

1. Click on the Arrows icon in the Zoom list. Corel WordPerfect will display a vertical scroll bar next to the graphic.

2. Scroll the bar up to reduce the size of the graphic.

3. Scroll the bar down to enlarge the graphic.

To return the graphic to its original size, click on the 1:1 icon.

 TIP: *Click on Reset Attributes to return the image to its original state.*

Changing the Black-and-White Threshold

You can convert a color graphic or one that contains shades of gray to black and white. This is useful if you want to create some special effect, if you want to print in black and white on a color printer, or if your monochrome printer does not output gray shades correctly. When you do convert a color to black and white, the color threshold determines which shades of gray are converted to white and which to black. The lower the threshold, the darker the image, since more of the gray shades will be over the threshold and will be converted to black.

If you click on the B/W Threshold button, you'll see a palette representing different threshold levels. Click on the one that you want to use to convert the graphic to black and white.

Changing the Contrast

Contrast is the range of shades between light and dark areas of a color image. To change the contrast, click on the Contrast button and then select a setting from the palette that appears.

Setting the Brightness

Brightness determines the overall saturation of colors in a graphic or the brightness of a black-and-white image. To change the brightness, click on the Brightness button and then select a setting from the palette that appears.

Choosing a Fill Style

The Fill tool controls the transparency of the image. By default, the images are set at the normal fill. This means that areas of the graphic appear in the color or gray shade in which the graphic was designed. The Fill tool offers these options:

The option on the left is the default normal style.

The middle option removes the fill displaying the graphic as an outline, so the paper's color or any background text can be seen.

The option on the right inserts an opaque white as the fill pattern.

 NOTE: *Fill patterns will affect graphics with the WPG extension, but not BMP graphic files.*

Inverting Colors

When you *invert* an image, you change it to its complementary colors. With a noncolor image this will have the effect of displaying it as a photographic negative. To invert the color, click on the Invert Colors button.

Specifying Attributes

Many of the image settings interact with each other, so changing one will have an effect that will require you to change another. You may also want to set the brightness, size, or other attribute to a specific setting. To enter settings and to change all of the attributes from one location, click on the Edit Attributes button to see the dialog box in Figure 12-5.

12

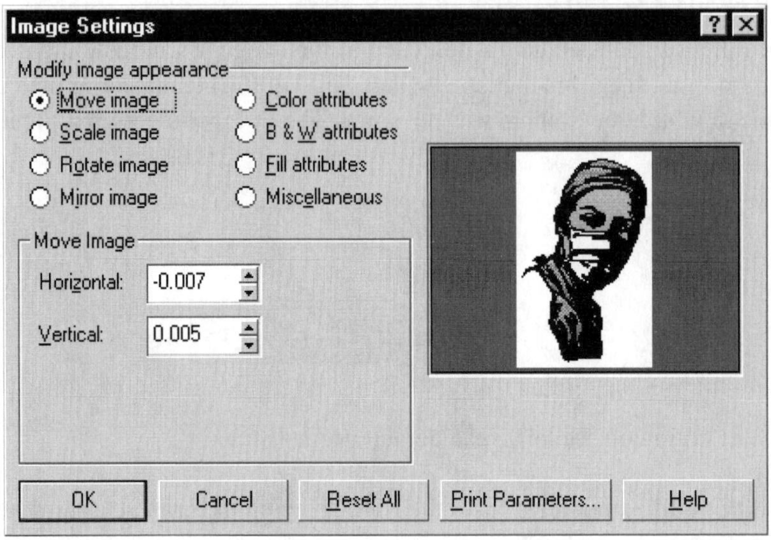

Changing
the image
settings

FIGURE 12-5

When you click on the attribute you want to change in the top section of the dialog box, the settings that you can make or choose from will be shown in the bottom of the box. Select each of the categories that you want to adjust in turn, and then make your choices. The preview of the graphic will show how your choices will affect the picture.

The Print Parameters button displays a dialog box where you can adjust how graphics are printed. The options available in the dialog box will depend on your printer, but you may be able to set a dithering method and source, and a halftone option.

Dithering is the process of mixing printed dots to simulate colors or shades of gray. You can choose a method to determine how the dot pattern is created, and choose the source—whether dithering is created by your printer or by Corel WordPerfect. The Halftone options determine the number of lines of dots per inch and their angle.

Resetting the Attributes

Corel WordPerfect always stores the original settings of the graphic with the document. If you want to restore the graphic to these settings, click on the Reset Attributes button. You can also select Reset All in the Image Settings dialog box.

Editing the Graphic

Changing the image settings affects the way the graphic appears without actually changing the graphic design. To change the graphic itself, you need a set of drawing tools. Corel WordPerfect provides these tools in a special window that accesses the drawing features of Corel Presentations, the graphic presentation segment of the Corel WordPerfect Suite.

To display the graphic in that window, double-click on it or select Edit Contents from the Image Tools box. Figure 12-6 shows one of Corel WordPerfect's graphics in the Corel Presentations window.

Use the tools to draw objects over the graphic and to edit the lines and objects that make up the graphic itself.

Creating Text Boxes

In Chapter 6 you learned how to insert a border around text. The border isn't a graphic box because you cannot drag it within the document or use any of the image

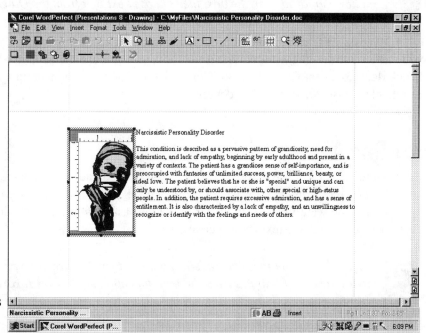

Editing a graphic using Corel Presentations tools

FIGURE 12-6

tools, such as rotating the text, to customize it. You can, however, create a graphic text box.

TIP: *To create a text box with existing text, select the text and then click on the Text Box tool or select Text Box from the Insert menu.*

To create a text box, click on the Text Box tool in the toolbar, or select Text Box from the Insert menu. Corel WordPerfect will insert a graphic box into the document 3.25 inches wide and one line high, with thin outside borders, and with the insertion point within the box. The borders are the default styles for a text box. Type and format the text you want in the box, and then click outside of it when you have finished:

> The physical and psychological training has practically eliminated minor health problems such as colds.

TIP: *To insert a text box of some other size, use drag-to-create. Drag the shadow cursor to form the box, then choose Text Box from the QuickMenu.*

You can drag a text box within the document, and you can change its size. Though you cannot use the image tools with a text box, you can use the property bar and QuickMenu to customize it. Use the Contents box, for example, to rotate the text counterclockwise 90, 180, or 270 degrees.

Using TextArt

Corel WordPerfect's TextArt application lets you create headlines, banners, logos, and other graphics from text. Instead of using plain text in a text box, you can select a shape that you want the text to appear in, choose a fill pattern and shadow, and even rotate or stretch the text for a special effect.

TIP: *If you want to create an effect with text you've already typed, select the text, choose Graphics from the Insert menu, and click on TextArt.*

To create an effect with text, follow these steps:

1. Choose Graphics from the Insert menu, and click on TextArt to display the window shown in Figure 12-7.

2. In the Type Here window, type the text that you want to use for the logo, headline, or other effect.

3. Click on one of the options shown in the Shapes box to choose the shape for the text, or click on More to see all of the available patterns.

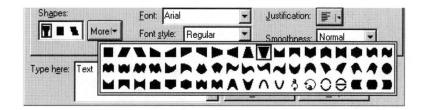

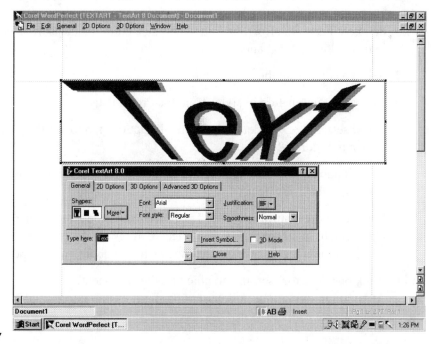

TextArt window

FIGURE 12-7

12

4. Use the Font, Font Style, Justification, and Smoothness buttons to create the effect that you want. For example, since diagonal lines can sometimes have a jagged or stepped look, select Normal, High, or Very High from the Smoothness list.

5. Use the Insert Characters button to add a special character from the font that is not available on the keyboard. The characters available are determined by the current font.

6. Click on 3D Mode to create text art with a more realistic 3-D look.

7. If you are creating a 2-D image, click on the 2D Options tab to see the page shown in Figure 12-8.

8. Use the Pattern button to choose a pattern and color for the fill.

9. Use the Shadow button to choose a shadow position and color.

10. Use the Outline button to choose a line thickness and color to surround the characters.

11. To rotate the text, click on the Rotation button to display four handles. Drag one of the corner handles to rotate the text as desired, and then click on Rotation again. To use measurements to rotate the text, double-click on the Rotation button and then enter the measurement in the dialog box that appears.

12. Select a color from the Text Color list.

13. Choose a combination of styles from the Preset list.

14. If you selected 3D mode, click on the 3D Options tab to see the page shown in Figure 12-9.

15. Select options from the Lighting 1, Lighting 2, Bevel, and other lists to customize the 3-D effect.

16. For even more control over 3-D TextArt, click on the Advanced 3D Options tab. In this page, you can select textures for the front, back, and bevels of the image, as well as set the resolution quality in dots per inch.

17. Click on Close to insert the graphic into the document.

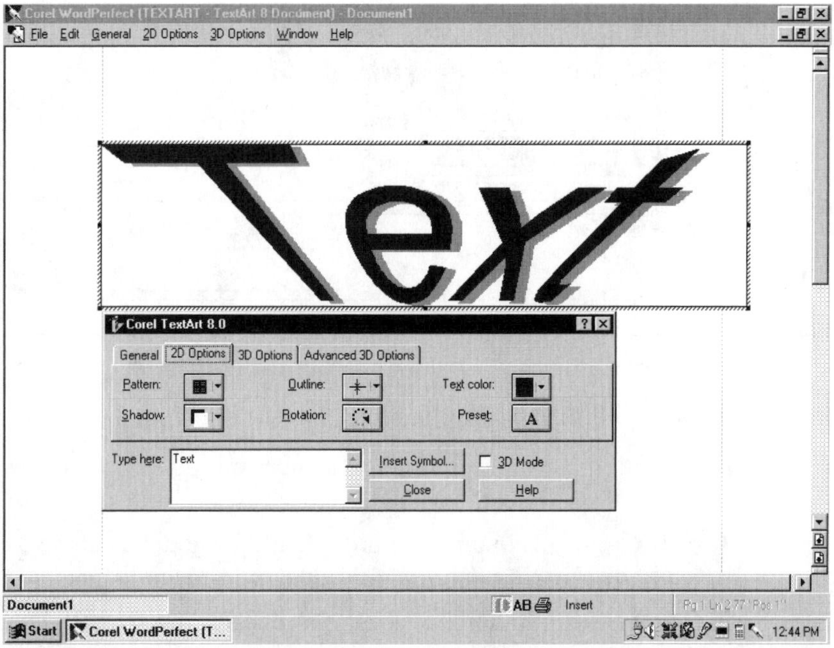

TextArt 2D
Options
page

FIGURE 12-8

You can change the size and position of the box, and add borders and fill, just as you learned how to do for graphics. To edit or change the format of the text, double-click on the box to redisplay it in the TextArt window.

You can also use TextArt in Corel Quattro Pro and Corel Presentations.

Graphic Box Styles

Graphic box styles have been mentioned a number of times in this chapter. When you select Text Box from the Insert menu, or ClipArt from the Insert Graphics menu, you are actually selecting a box style. The style tells Corel WordPerfect the contents you want to place in the box, its default border and fill styles, and the caption position and label. There are really 14 different box styles, as shown in Table 12-2.

To change the style applied to an existing box, follow these steps:

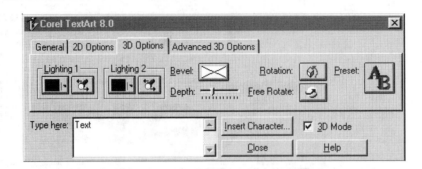

TextArt 3D
Options
page

FIGURE 12-9

Style	Description
Image	No borders, page anchor, top-right corner at the insertion point, 1.5 inches wide, auto height
Text Box	Thin outside border lines, paragraph anchor, at the right border, 3.25 inches wide, auto height
Equation	No borders, paragraph anchor, full size between the margins, auto height
Figure Box	Thin outside border lines, paragraph anchor, at the right border, 3.25 inches wide, auto height
Table	Top and bottom thick border, paragraph anchor, at the right border, 3.25 inches wide, auto height
User	No borders, paragraph anchor, at the right border, 3.25 inches wide, auto height
Button	Borders and fill to appear as a button, character anchor, at the position of the insertion point on the baseline, 1 inch wide, auto height
Watermark	No borders, page anchor, full-page size
Inline Equation	No borders, character anchor, at the position of the insertion point on the baseline, auto width, auto height
OLE 2.0	No borders, page anchor, top-right corner at the insertion point, 1.5 inches wide, auto height
Inline Text	No borders, character anchor, at the position of the insertion point on the baseline, auto width, auto height

Box Styles

TABLE 12-2

Style	Description
Draw Object	No borders, page anchor, top-right corner at the insertion point, auto width, auto height
Draw Text	No borders, page anchor, top-right corner at the insertion point, 1.5 inches wide, auto height

Box Styles
(*continued*)

▮ TABLE 12-2

1. Right-click on the box, and choose Style from the QuickMenu.

2. Select the style you want to apply from the Box Styles list.

These styles can hold three types of information—a graphic image, text, or an equation—and each box style can store any of the types. For example, you can insert text in a Figure box or a piece of clipart in a Text box. So if you want to insert a graphic in a box with thin borders all around, you can use a Text box style. The styles help you organize and coordinate your graphics. Choosing ClipArt, Text, or Equation gives you a place to start. But you can create any type of box using the Custom Box option, by following these steps:

1. Drag to create the box, and choose Custom Box from the QuickMenu. You can also select Graphics from the Insert menu and click on Custom Box.

2. From the Custom Box dialog box that appears, choose the style of box that you want.

3. Click on OK.

Use the Contents dialog box to determine what goes in the box—an image, image on disk, text, or equation.

You can also create a custom box type:

1. Display the Custom Box dialog box.

2. Click on Styles and then on Create.

3. In the dialog box that appears, enter a name for the type.

12

4. Specify the borders, fill, contents, and other specifics.

5. Click on OK, and then close the Box Style dialog box.

Your new type will appear on the Custom Box list.

Graphic Styles

In addition to boxes, Corel WordPerfect includes graphic styles for borders, lines, and fill patterns. You can edit these styles or create your own to apply custom styles to these graphic elements.

Select Graphics Styles from the Format menu to see this dialog box:

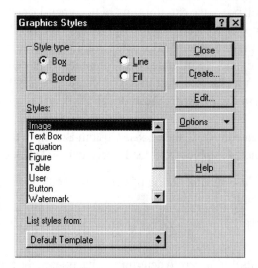

Choose the type of style you want to edit; the current styles in the Styles list will be displayed. Then click on Create to design your own style, or choose a style from the list and click on Edit to customize it. The dialog box that appears depends on the style type you selected. If you choose to create a fill style, for example, you'll see options for choosing the pattern, foreground, and background colors. If you choose to create a Gradient fill in the dialog box, you'll see the options in Figure 12-10.

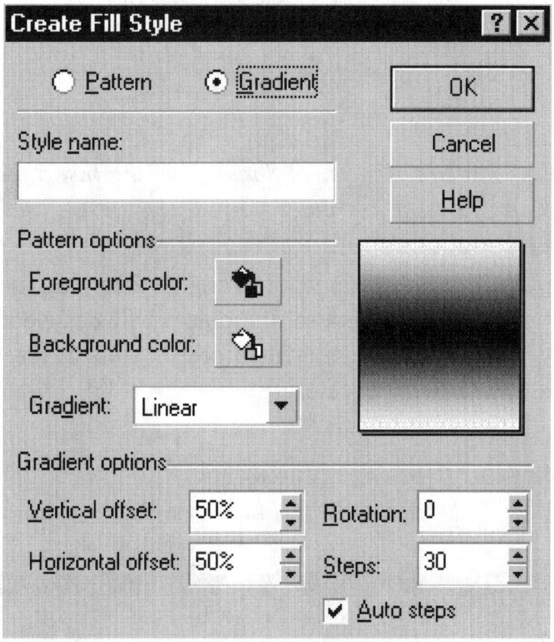

Creating a gradient fill style

FIGURE 12-10

Enter a name for your style, select options from the box until the sample appears the way you want it, and then click on OK.

Drawing Custom Graphics

You can access the Corel Presentations drawing tools at any time to create your own graphics. Click on the Draw Picture button in the toolbar to display the Corel Presentations window with a blank graphic box. Use the drawing tools and menu options to create your drawing. For example, select Organization Chart from the Insert menu to add an organization chart to your document. When you're done with the drawing, click outside the box to return to Corel WordPerfect. Edit the drawing just as you learned in this chapter.

If you just want to draw geometric shapes and freehand sketches, click on the Draw Object button on the toolbar to see the options shown next:

12

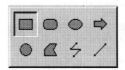

 NOTE: *You can also select Shape from the Insert menu, and choose the shape that you want to create.*

Choose the type of object you want to create, then drag the mouse to form the object. When you release the mouse, the object will be selected and you'll see a special property bar. If you create a filled object, such as a rectangle or oval, the property bar will contain these features:

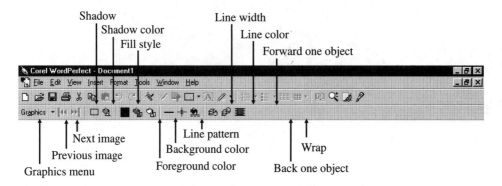

If you draw a line, the property bar will contain Arrow Start and Arrow End lists to add an arrowhead to the line.

Use the tools on the property bar to customize the object.

Drawing Lines

If you just want to add a small unobtrusive graphic element to a page, consider using a horizontal or vertical line. The easiest way to draw a horizontal line is using the QuickLines feature:

1. Start a new line by typing four hyphens or four equal signs.

2. Press ENTER.

Corel WordPerfect will replace the characters with a solid single or double line across the page.

You can also draw a horizontal line by selecting Horizontal Line from the Insert Shape menu. To draw a vertical line down the entire page at the horizontal position of the insertion point, select Vertical Line from the Insert Shape menu. To draw any type of line, select Draw Line from the Insert Shape menu, then drag-to-create the line.

NOTE: *The Horizontal Line and Vertical Line options create a predefined line to use mostly as a rule, not a customizable graphic line.*

Because the lines are graphic elements, you can change their sizes and positions just as you can for graphic boxes:

1. Click on the line with the left mouse button to select it, displaying the handles.

2. To move the line, point to the line so the mouse is shaped like a four-headed arrow, and then drag the mouse.

3. To change the size of the line, point to a handle so the mouse is a two-headed arrow. Drag the center handle on top or bottom to change the height of the line, and drag a handle on a corner to change both the width and height at the same time. If the line is thick enough, drag the center handle on the left or right to change the width of the graphic.

4. To add an arrowhead to the line, select an option from the Arrow Start and Arrow End lists in the property bar.

Creating Custom Lines

You can create a custom-sized and -formatted line by choosing Custom Line from the Insert Shape menu to display the Create Graphics Line dialog box. Choose to create either a horizontal or vertical line, and then use the Line Style list to choose the line's shape and thickness or to insert multiple lines.

NOTE: *The Line Style lists shows right-angled sample lines, although only a straight line will be inserted. To draw a right angle, you have to coordinate the position of separate vertical and horizontal lines.*

12

You can then use the remaining options in the box to customize the line:

■ Choose from a palette of 256 colors in the Line Color list.

■ Choose a line thickness. The list has eight options ranging from 0.01 to 0.12 inch, and you can enter a custom thickness.

■ Set Space Above Line and Space Below Line to determine the distance of the line from the text above and below it.

■ Enter the Length of the line.

■ Set the line's Horizontal Position in relation to the left and right margins.

■ Set the line's Vertical Position in relation to the top margin. The default Baseline positions the line on the same baseline as the text.

Corel WordPerfect also lets you create your own line style:

1. Click on Line Styles in the dialog box, then click on Create to open the dialog box in Figure 12-11. (Click on Edit to edit an existing line style.)

2. Give your style a name, so you can later choose it from the Line Style list.

3. Select a color, pattern, and thickness.

4. To create a multiple-line style, select a distance between lines in the Spacing Below Line list, and then click on Add. Select options for the new line, and then add and format any others.

5. Once you have multiple lines, you have to choose which one you want to edit or change. The current line will be indicated by an arrow pointing to it in the preview area. Click on the line you want to edit, or click on the up or down arrow button to select the line.

6. When you've finished, click on OK and then Close.

To use your style, display the Create Graphics Line dialog box. Your style will be listed at the bottom of the Line Style list.

Inserting Charts

Numbers can be very boring and difficult to read in a document even when displayed in a table. When you want to show a trend or make a quick point, nothing is better than a chart. Corel WordPerfect lets you create charts directly from the document window—you don't have to start Corel Quattro Pro or Corel Presentations.

If you already typed the information into a table, you are halfway there.

1. Select the cells that you want to chart.

2. Select Graphics from the Insert menu and click on Chart.

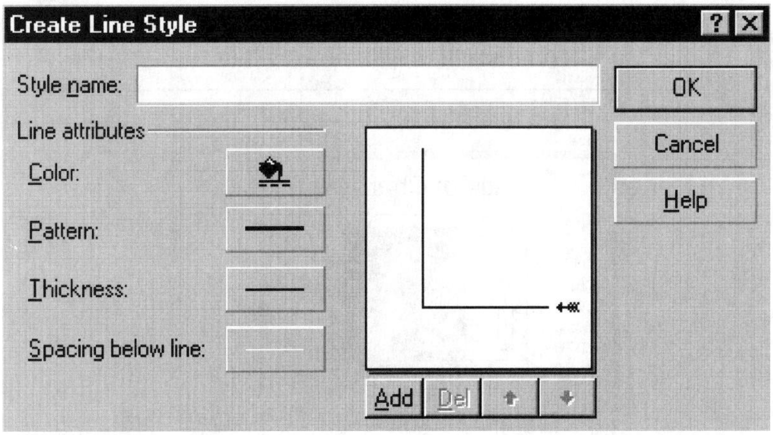

Creating a
custom line
style

FIGURE 12-11

Corel WordPerfect starts Corel Presentations and begins its chart function, displaying your table data and a default bar chart, as shown in Figure 12-12.

Charting works about the same in Corel WordPerfect, Corel Quattro Pro, and Corel Presentations. You can move charts, and the information you need to create them, between applications.

If you did not already create a Corel WordPerfect table, then don't bother. You can enter the information as you create the chart, by following these steps:

1. Select Graphics from the Insert menu, and click on Chart to see a sample chart and table of information, as shown in Figure 12-13. Notice that the X-axis labels are listed in the row marked "Labels" and the name for each series in the column marked "Legend." The color next to each legend entry shows the color that the chart bar or line will appear in. The Range Highlighter box lets you customize the colors in the table—just move the box out of the way, or close it if desired.

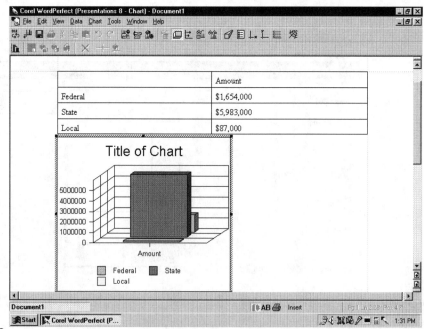

Chart with data from a Corel WordPerfect table

FIGURE 12-12

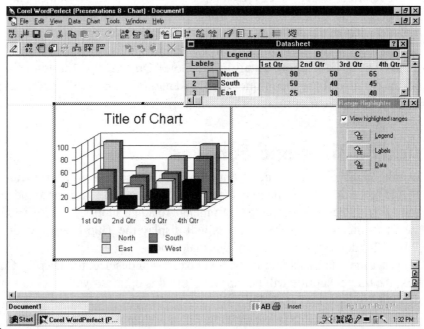

Default
chart and
data when a
table is not
selected

FIGURE 12-13

2. To enter your own information into the chart, delete the sample data by
clicking on the empty box above the word "Labels" to select all of the
data and then pressing DEL.

3. In the box that appears, click on Both to delete both the data and formats
from the chart. Click on OK.

4. Type the information that you want to chart.

Corel Presentations will create the chart as you enter the information. If it
doesn't, click on the Redraw button in the toolbar.

TIP: *Using the default chart and entering your own data will enable you*
to quickly update the chart when you change the information.

12

To return to Corel WordPerfect, click outside of the chart. You can now change the size, position, borders, and fill using the property bar, QuickMenu, or Edit Box tools. To change the design of the chart, double-click on it.

There are a lot of options to choose from to customize the chart. We'll be looking at these in more detail in the Corel Quattro Pro section of this book because many of the techniques are the same. For now, we'll summarize some of the most typical options.

Adding Titles and Subtitles

Even though you may be describing the chart in the text of your document, you should add a title or subtitle to make its purpose immediately clear to the reader. To add a title, select Title from the Chart menu. To add a subtitle, choose Subtitle from the Chart menu. Corel Presentations will display the Title Properties dialog box. Table 12-3 describes the pages of this dialog box.

Enter the title or subtitle in the text box. If you deselect the Display Chart Title box, the title or subtitle will not appear—use this option if you want to remove the title but leave the text available.

Customizing the Chart

By default, Corel Presentations creates a bar chart. You can change the type of the chart in two ways, by using the Gallery and Layout/Type options from the Chart menu.

Page	Description
Title Font	Select the font, size, and color of the text.
Text Fill	Select a fill style, pattern, foreground and background colors, and fill method.
Text Outline	Choose the width and line style of the text.
Box Type	Choose the type of the box surrounding the text.
Box Fill	Select a fill style, pattern, foreground and background colors, and fill method for the box.
Position	Position the text on the left, center, or right of the chart.

Setting
Options
for Text

TABLE 12-3

The Gallery lists 12 general categories of charts that you can create. When you select a category, two or more different styles of the type will appear in preview boxes. Click on the style that you want to use and then click on OK.

For more control over the chart type, use these steps:

1. Select Layout/Type from the Chart menu to display the dialog box in Figure 12-14.

2. Choose a category from the Chart Type list. As with the Gallery, two or more styles of the type will appear in the preview area.

3. Click on the style you want.

4. Select or deselect the 3D checkbox to select either a 3-D or 2-D chart.

5. Click on Horizontal for a horizontal chart; clear the box for a vertical chart.

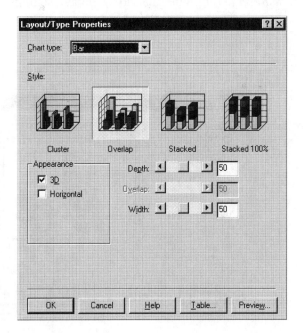

Selecting
a chart
category,
type, and
other
options

12

FIGURE 12-14

The other options that appear in this dialog box will depend on the type of chart you select. Choose from the options and click on Preview to minimize the dialog box so you can see how the chart will appear. In the box that does appear, click on OK if you want to accept the chart as it appears. Click on Back to reopen the dialog box, or on Cancel to return the chart to its previous settings.

If you do create a 3-D chart, you can further customize it by selecting Perspective from the Chart menu to see the dialog box shown in Figure 12-15.

- Use the *Horizontal* text box or the horizontal scroll bar to rotate the chart around its base. The settings range from 0 to look directly at the chart from its side, to 100 to view the chart from the front.

- Use the *Vertical* setting or the vertical scroll bar to rotate the chart from top to bottom. The settings range from 0 to view the chart from the top, to 100 to view it from "ground level."

- Select the *Right Angle Axes* checkbox to make the X axis and Y axis perpendicular to each other.

- Select *Wire Frame View* to display the chart as an outline.

- Click on *Reset* to return the chart to the default settings.

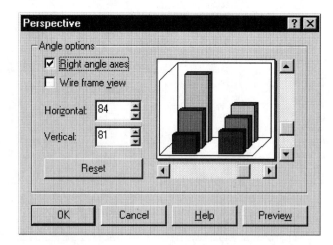

Changing
the 3-D
perspective

FIGURE 12-15

You can change the settings for any part of the chart by double-clicking on the part. This opens a dialog box of options for just that part. For example, double-click on the Y-axis lines to see the Primary Y Axis Properties dialog box. In this box you can change the spacing, appearance, and position of axis labels, as well as the scale of the measurements along the axis. Double-click on a series bar to change its shape, color, and spacing. Double-click on a grid line to change its shape and color, and to set the spacing between lines. Double-click on a title or subtitle to change its color, font, size, fill, or the border surrounding it.

Using the Equation Editors

Mathematical and scientific equations require special characters and formats. You can access special characters using the Insert Characters command, and you can create subscripts and superscripts using the Font dialog box and the Advance command from the Typesetting menu. But even with these features, creating complex equations could be difficult.

Corel WordPerfect doesn't want anything to be difficult for you, so they've given you the Equation Editor. This is a special set of tools for formatting equations of all types. Through these tools you have easy access to special characters and formats that would be difficult to access any other way.

NOTE: *The Equation Editor formats equations for you—it does not do the math. That you have to do yourself.*

Selecting an Equation Editor

Corel WordPerfect doesn't just offer one Equation Editor—it offers you two. The WordPerfect 5.1 to 7 Equation Editor is the same one used in previous versions of WordPerfect. The WordPerfect 8 Equation Editor is new.

To select the Equation Editor you want to use, follow these steps:

1. Select Settings from the Tools menu.

2. Double-click on Environment.

3. Click on the Graphics tab to see the dialog box in Figure 12-16.

4. In the Default Equation Editor section, click on the option button for the editor you want to use. To select an editor each time you want to create

12

an equation, click on the checkbox below the Default Equation Editor section.

5. Click on OK, and then close the Settings dialog box.

To start the Equation Editor, choose Equation from the Insert menu. If you chose to indicate the editor each time, a box will appear listing the two editors. Make your choice, then click on OK.

Using the WordPerfect 8 Equation Editor

If you select this option, you'll see the window shown in Figure 12-17. You interact with the Equation Editor using the menus and the toolbar, creating the equation in the entry window. The small dotted rectangle in the entry window is called a *slot*. You enter all text and symbols in slots, which expand to fit what you enter.

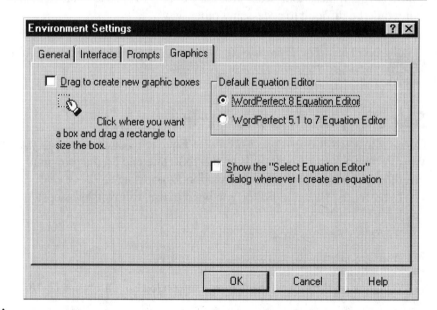

Selecting an Equation Editor

FIGURE 12-16

Equation menu bar
Toolbar

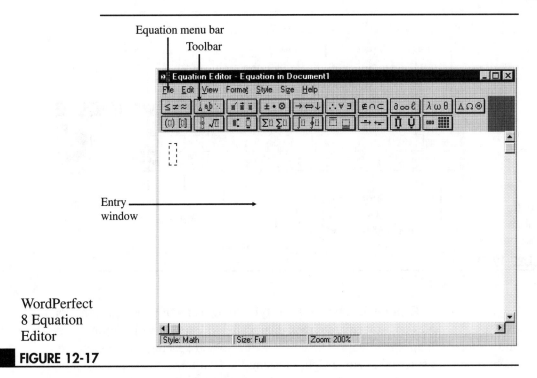

Entry
window

WordPerfect
8 Equation
Editor

FIGURE 12-17

Type letters, numbers, and most punctuation marks from the keyboard. You select other special characters and equation graphics and formats from the toolbar. Clicking on a toolbar button displays a list of options—click on the option you want to insert into the equation. Figure 12-18 shows the functions of the toolbar buttons.

The buttons on the top of the toolbar insert symbols. Clicking one inserts the symbol into the active slot in the equation. The buttons on the bottom of the toolbar insert templates. A template is one or more slots, often combined with an equation character, such as a radical or fraction line. You can nest as many templates as you want, such as adding a superscript template to the numerator of a division operation, or to the slot under a radical.

The nested slots represent various levels in the equation. The Equation Editor will display an insertion point where the next character typed or inserted will appear. You'll also see a horizontal line under the section of the equation at that level.

12

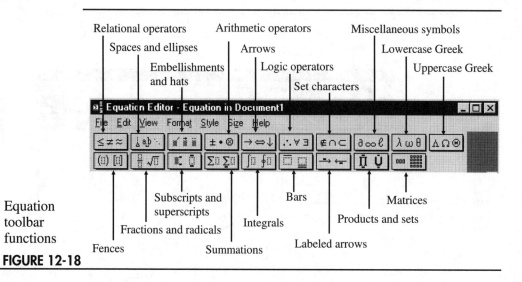

Relational operators

Spaces and ellipses

Embellishments
and hats

Arithmetic operators

Arrows

Logic operators

Set characters

Miscellaneous symbols

Lowercase Greek

Uppercase Greek

Equation
toolbar
functions

Subscripts and
superscripts

Fractions and radicals

Fences

Integrals

Summations

Bars

Products and sets

Labeled arrows

Matrices

FIGURE 12-18

The Equation Editor will apply built-in styles to the parts of your equation. For example, variables and lowercase Greek characters will appear in italic; matrices and vectors will appear in bold. The editor will also add spacing where required, such as on both sides of an equal sign. Pressing the SPACEBAR while in the editor, however, has no effect except when you apply the text style. To add spaces yourself between characters when using other styles, you have to select a space character from the toolbar.

Let's go step by step through the process of creating a simple equation shown here. We'll also look at the concept of equation levels.

$$X = \frac{\sqrt{Y}}{2_{-z}}$$

1. Type **X=**. The Equation Editor inserts a space between the X and the equal sign. It displays the X in italic, the default format for variables.

2. Click on the Fraction and Radical button in the toolbar to see following options.

3. Click on the fraction template on the left side of the first row. (Don't count the icons from the button as a row.) You'll see this template with two slots. The insertion point is in the top slot, so you are ready to insert the radical:

$$X = \frac{[\;]}{[\;]}$$

4. Click on the Fraction and Radicals button again, and click on the template on the left side of the fourth row. The radical appears with a slot underneath.

5. Type **Y** in the slot.

$$X = \frac{\sqrt{Y|}}{[\;]}$$

Now look carefully at the template, shown enlarged here. The insertion point is immediately following the letter Y, and below the radical. The underline appears just under the letter Y, showing that the next character you type or insert will also be under the radical.

6. Press the RIGHT ARROW key. The insertion point now becomes the full height of the radical, and the underline is the full length of the radical. This means that the next character will not be under the radical, but will be above the division.

12

7. Press the RIGHT ARROW key again. Now the insertion point is the full size of the fraction, showing that the next character will be to the right of the fraction.

8. Press SHIFT-TAB or click in the slot under the fraction.

9. Type **2**. Next enter a subscript template.

10. Click on the Subscripts and Superscripts button to see these options:

11. Click on the middle option in the top row. A slot appears in the subscript position.

12. Type **-Z**.

13. Select Exit and Return to Document from the File menu.

The Equation Editor closes, and the equation appears in the document in a graphics box. Click outside of the box to display the equation. You can now change the position and size of the box, or its border or fill, as you would any graphic. To edit the equation itself, double-click on it to open the Equation Editor.

Equation Editor Options

When you are creating or editing an equation, you can use some special techniques, options, and styles.

For example, to make a small change to the position of a character or symbol, select it, hold down the CTRL key, and press the arrow key for the direction you want to move. This is called *nudging*.

You can also change the style that the editor applied to a character. Pull down the Style menu, and choose the style that you want to apply to the next or the selected character. For example, if you don't want a variable to be italic, select the Text style. You can also change the size by selecting an option from the Size menu. To redefine the styles, select Define from the Style menu to see the dialog box in Figure 12-19. For the style you want to change, select a font and the bold or italic operator.

 TIP: *The Greek and Symbol styles must use a font that contains Greek and symbol characters.*

Using the WordPerfect 5.1 to 7 Equation Editor

If you select this option, you'll see the window shown in Figure 12-20. You interact with the Equation Editor using the menus and the toolbar. The functions of the toolbar are shown in Table 12-4.

You use three panes to create and display your equations. The Editing pane is the large empty box near the top of the window, just below the Equation Editor toolbar. You use this part of the window to type the text and numbers you want in the equation, and to insert formatting commands and codes for special characters. Everything in this pane will appear as plain, unformatted text.

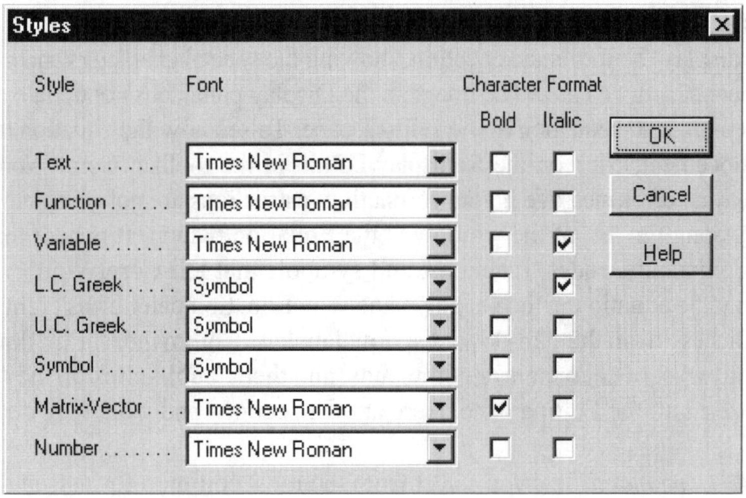

Changing the styles of the Equation Editor

Style	Font	Bold	Italic
Text	Times New Roman	☐	☐
Function	Times New Roman	☐	☐
Variable	Times New Roman	☐	☑
L.C. Greek	Symbol	☐	☑
U.C. Greek	Symbol	☐	☐
Symbol	Symbol	☐	☐
Matrix-Vector	Times New Roman	☑	☐
Number	Times New Roman	☐	☐

FIGURE 12-19

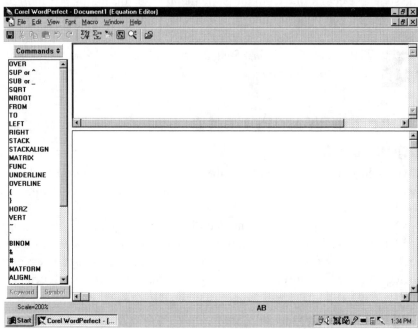

WordPerfect
5.1 to 7
Equation
Editor

FIGURE 12-20

Below the Editing pane is the Display pane. This is where Corel WordPerfect will display the formatted equation, showing the special characters and symbols in the proper spacing and size. The image in the Display pane does not update automatically as you enter the equation in the Editing pane. To see how the equation will appear in the document, click on the Redisplay button in the toolbar. Corel WordPerfect will display an error message if your formatting instructions are not complete.

Along the left of the window is the Equation palette. It is here that you select the commands, codes, functions, and symbols that tell Corel WordPerfect how to format the equation in the Display pane. The Equation palette has eight sections that you access from the pull-down list now labeled "Commands." Pull down the list to display a set of characters or commands, and then double-click on the one you want to insert into the Editing pane. Here are the sections and what they do:

■ *Commands* lets you select from the most common formats and symbols.

■ *Large* displays popular mathematics symbols.

■ *Symbols* includes many miscellaneous symbols.

- *Greek* offers Greek characters.

- *Arrows* lists various arrows, triangles, squares, and circles.

- *Sets* includes relational operators and set symbols.

- *Other* includes diacritical marks and ellipses.

- *Function* includes symbols for mathematical functions.

Some of your choices can be inserted into the Editing pane as keywords or symbols—they always appear as formatted symbols in the Display pane. To choose

Button	Function
Save As	Saves the equation in a separate file from the document
Cut	Places the selected portion of the equation into the Clipboard
Copy	Copies the selected portion of the equation into the Clipboard
Paste	Inserts the contents of the Clipboard at the position of the insertion point in the Editing pane
Undo	Cancels changes
Redo	Cancels an undo
Close	Closes the Equation Editor
Insert Equation File	Recalls an equation from disk into the Equation Editor window
Redisplay	Updates the Display pane
Zoom Display	Displays the Zoom dialog box to select a display magnification
Equation Font	Displays a font dialog box for changing the font and point size of the displayed characters
Corel WordPerfect Characters	Displays the Corel WordPerfect Characters dialog box for inserting special characters

Equation
Toolbar

TABLE 12-4

12

how you want Corel WordPerfect to insert items, click on either the Keyword or Symbol button under the Equation palette. You can usually also type the commands yourself, such as typing **sub** to create a subscript. You can also enter *variables*—characters or words that represent unknown values.

Here's a simple illustration using the Equation Editor:

1. In the Editing pane, type **X~=~** and then click on Redisplay. The tilde character (~) tells Corel WordPerfect to insert a space (you can use the grave accent [`] to insert a quarter space), so the equation will appear as shown here:

$$X =$$

2. If the Commands palette is not shown, switch to that set.

3. Double-click on SQRT, the square root command.

4. Type **Y OVER 2 SUB {–Z}**. This means to place the letter *Y* on a line over 2, and add a subscript –Z to the 2.

5. Click on Redisplay to see the completed equation, as shown here:

$$X = \frac{\sqrt{Y}}{2_{-Z}}$$

6. Click on the Close button in the toolbar and return to the document, inserting the equation into a graphic box using the equation box style.

7. You can now change the size and position of the box, add a caption, or customize the border and fill. Double-click on the equation if you want to edit it in the Equation Editor.

Sharing Information

13

Corel WordPerfect lets you share information between it and other parts of the Corel WordPerfect Suite, and even with other Windows applications. Sharing information lets you create compound documents without having to retype information. A *compound document* is one that includes information from more than one application. For example, suppose you created a spreadsheet in Corel Quattro Pro, an organization chart in Corel Presentations, and a drawing in Windows Paint. You can add all of these items to your Corel WordPerfect document to create a professional-looking document. For instance, you don't need to retype the spreadsheet into a Corel WordPerfect table—you can just cut and paste it into Corel WordPerfect, or even open it directly in a document as a table.

Sharing information will also let you send a Corel WordPerfect form document, or name and address information in a Corel Quattro Pro or other spreadsheet, to a mailing list that you've created in Paradox. In fact, you can even link the database or spreadsheet with Corel WordPerfect so your document always has the most up-to-date information.

In Chapter 21 you will learn how to use cells from a Corel Quattro Pro spreadsheet in a Corel WordPerfect document. In this chapter, you will learn how to use Corel WordPerfect information with other applications, and how to import and link database and spreadsheet information. You will also learn how to open documents into Corel WordPerfect that have been created with other programs, and how to save your Corel WordPerfect documents in other formats.

Saving Files

While it is difficult to imagine why, not everyone uses Corel WordPerfect as their word processing program. If you have to share your files with these unfortunates, you can make it easier on them by saving your files in a format their program understands.

You should first save your document normally, in Corel WordPerfect's own format. Then follow these steps:

1. Select Save As from the File menu.

2. Pull down the File Type list. You'll see a list of formats that Corel WordPerfect can save your documents in.

3. Scroll the list and click on the format that you want to use.

4. Enter a filename, and then click on Save.

In addition to all previous Corel WordPerfect formats, you can select from the formats shown in Table 13-1. Notice that you can also save your document in a spreadsheet format, such as Corel Quattro Pro, Excel, and Lotus 1-2-3. When you choose Corel Quattro Pro, however, only tables in your document will be saved. Each table will become another page in the Corel Quattro Pro workbook, labeled Table A, Table B, and so on.

Application	Version
AmiPro	1.2 to 3.0
ANSI Windows	Text, generic word processing, and delimited text
ASCII DOS	Text, generic word processing, and delimited text
EDGAR	
Excel	3.0 to 4.0
HTML	
Lotus 1-2-3	1.0 to 4.0 for Windows, 3.0 and 3.1 for DOS
MS Word for Windows	1 to 7
Corel Quattro Pro for Windows	1.0, 5.0, and 6.0
RTF	
Spreadsheet DIF	

File Formats

TABLE 13-1

13

The next time you save the document, Corel WordPerfect will display a Save Format dialog box asking you to confirm the format. You can choose to save it in Corel WordPerfect format or in the original type, or click on Other to display the Save As dialog box.

 You can save your Corel WordPerfect documents, Corel Quattro Pro worksheets, and Corel Presentations slide shows as Envoy documents. See Chapter 24 for more information.

Opening Documents

In Corel WordPerfect, one of the quickest ways to use a file that you created with another program is simply to open it. You can open documents created in all of the formats that you can save them in, as well as these additional ones:

- Borland Sprint
- IA5
- QuickFinder Log
- Corel WordPerfect for the Macintosh
- WP Works

While the Open dialog box has a File Type list, it only contains the All Files (*.*) option, the text file format, and the default formats used by Corel WordPerfect. You don't see the other formats because in most cases you don't have to select a format when you open a file. Corel WordPerfect will automatically determine the type of file and do what it must to open it and display it on the screen. If it can't determine the file type, one of two boxes will appear. If you try to open a binary file, such as one with a COM, EXE, or DLL extension, the message "Unknown File Format" will appear. Click on OK to remove the message.

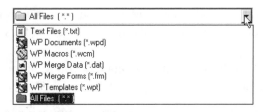

If you try to open a text file, the Convert File Format dialog box will appear. You can then scroll through the Convert File Format From list and select the format.

ASCII and ANSI text files, by the way, can be opened using two methods. These text files have a carriage return and line feed code at the end of each line. These are the codes, abbreviated CR/LF, that tell the computer to move the insertion point to the start of the next line. You can choose to open the document normally, which converts each CR/LF code to a hard carriage return, HRt; or you can select to convert each CR/LF to a soft carriage return, the SRt code. Selecting the SRt option will let you format the document as a series of paragraphs, but you will lose the original line breaks.

When you open a spreadsheet or database file, Corel WordPerfect will display a special dialog box. Refer to "Using Databases and Spreadsheets," later in this chapter.

Sharing Problem Documents

You may have a document in a format that Corel WordPerfect cannot open, or you may be using a program whose format Corel WordPerfect cannot save in. All is not lost. Try to find an intermediate format that both programs can accept. Most programs, for example, have the option to save in ASCII text format. While you will lose your formatting by saving as ASCII text, at least you won't have to retype everything.

Sharing Information Through the Clipboard

If you do not want to use an entire document file from or in another application, you can cut/copy and paste information from one program to the other.

For example, suppose you want to copy some information from a Microsoft Word for Windows document to Corel WordPerfect. Follow these steps:

1. Open Corel WordPerfect and the document you want to insert the information into.

2. Open Word for Windows and the document containing the information.

3. Cut or copy the information in the Word for Windows document.

4. Switch to Corel WordPerfect.

5. Click on the Paste button in the toolbar, or select Paste from the Edit menu.

You can also paste information from a DOS application. When you run a DOS program in Windows, it will appear in a DOS window with this toolbar:

To copy information from the DOS-application window, follow these steps:

1. Click on the Mark button in the DOS window toolbar.

2. Drag the mouse over the text you want to copy.

3. Click on the Copy button on the DOS window toolbar.

4. Switch to Corel WordPerfect and place the insertion point where you want to insert the text.

5. Click on the Paste button in the Corel WordPerfect toolbar.

You can also use the Clipboard to copy information within the DOS application itself. Mark and copy the text in the DOS window, place the cursor where you want the text to appear, and then click on the Paste button in the DOS window toolbar.

Creating Organization Charts

You can easily create organization charts in Corel Presentations, but you do have to enter the information and create the structure showing the chain of command. A quicker way to create an organization chart in Corel Presentations is to type the chain of command as a Corel WordPerfect outline.

1. Start Corel WordPerfect.

2. Select Outline/Bullets & Numbering from the Insert menu.

3. Click on the Numbers tab, if it is not displayed.

4. Click on the first option in the second row—the Paragraph Numbers only (no styles) format, and then click on OK.

5. Enter the name of the top executive as paragraph number 1, and the immediate subordinate as paragraphs 2, 3, and so on.

6. Enter other levels as indented paragraphs, using TAB to move down a level and SHIFT-TAB to move up.

```
------------------------------------
1.John Smith
2.William Watson
        a.Kate Jackson
        b.F. F. Majors
3.Steve Austin
4.William Kildair
        a.Ben Casey
        b.Horace Rumpole
```

7. Save the document.

8. Open or switch to Corel Presentations.

9. Display the slide where you want to add the organization chart.

10. Select Organization Chart from the Insert menu, drag to draw the chart, select a chart type from the box that appears, and click on OK.

11. Choose Import Outline from the Chart menu.

12. Select the file containing the organization, and then click on Insert.

Corel Presentations will form the organization chart using the text and structure of the outline, as shown in Figure 13-1.

 You can also save an organization chart as a Corel WordPerfect outline. See Chapter 22.

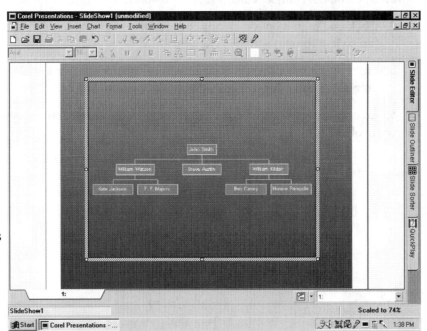

Corel Presentations organization chart using a Corel WordPerfect outline

FIGURE 13-1

Embedding and Linking Information

Windows lets you insert information from other applications using two general techniques, *embedding* and *linking*.

When you embed information into an application, such as Corel WordPerfect, you are actually placing a complete copy of it in the document. You won't be able to edit or format the information using Corel WordPerfect commands because it is treated as one solid object. If you double-click on the object, however, Corel WordPerfect will perform these steps:

1. Start the application that you used to create the object.

2. Transfer a copy of the information from Corel WordPerfect to the application so you can edit the object in that application.

When you edit and close the application, the edited version will appear in Corel WordPerfect. However, there is no actual connection between the object's file on the disk and the copy of the object in the document. If you edit the object separately by opening it directly into the application, the copy of it in Corel WordPerfect will not be affected.

When you insert information using a link, however, there is a connection. When you double-click on the object in Corel WordPerfect, it will do this:

1. Start the application.

2. Open the original file on the disk in which the object is stored.

When you save the edited copy of the object, it will be updated in Corel WordPerfect as well. But because there is a link, you can also open the object directly with the application to edit it. The updated version will automatically appear in Corel WordPerfect.

There are several ways that you can embed and link information. One method is to use the Paste Special dialog box from the Corel WordPerfect Edit menu. You'll learn how to do that when we discuss using a Corel Quattro Pro spreadsheet in Corel WordPerfect in Chapter 20.

You can also embed and link information using the Object command from the Insert menu. To create and insert an embedded object, select Object from the Insert menu and click on Create New to see the options in Figure 13-2. The Object Type

13

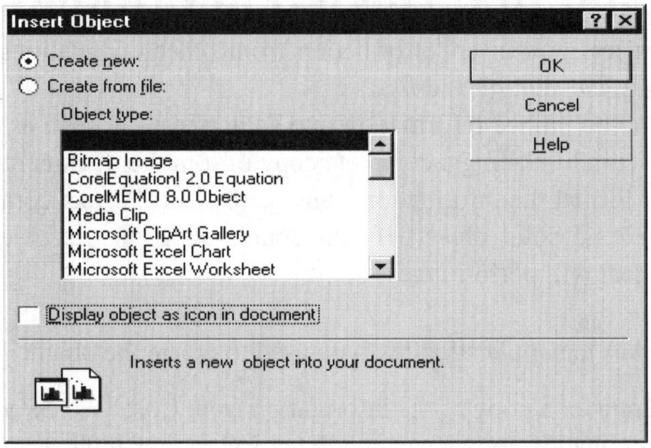

Insert Object   `? X`

◉ Create new:
○ Create from file:

Object type:

Bitmap Image
CorelEquation! 2.0 Equation
CorelMEMO 8.0 Object
Media Clip
Microsoft ClipArt Gallery
Microsoft Excel Chart
Microsoft Excel Worksheet

`OK`
`Cancel`
`Help`

☐ Display object as icon in document

Inserts a new object into your document.

Embedding
a new object

FIGURE 13-2

list contains all of the applications that are registered in Windows as usable as the source of an embedded object.

Select the application that you want to create the object, and then click on OK. Windows will start that application so that you can create the object.

If you already created the object, such as a drawing in Paint, click on the Create From File option in the Insert Object dialog box. Enter the path and name of the file, or use the Browse button to select it. To embed the object into the document, click on OK. To link the object, click on the Link checkbox and then on OK.

Multimedia Documents

By adding sound and video to a document, you can create an onscreen presentation, a document that comes alive to the reader. While sound and video clips can create very large document files, they can be effective. We'll look at some of the techniques that you can use.

Inserting a Sound Clip

You can insert or record a sound clip for either special effects or just as an annotation that can be played back at some later time. Corel WordPerfect can use sound files in either the WAV or MIDI format, and you can even record WAV sound directly into the document.

To insert an existing sound file, follow these steps:

1. Select Sound from the Insert menu to see the Sound Clips dialog box.

2. Click on Insert to see the Insert Sound Clip into Document dialog box.

3. Enter a name that you want to identify with the clip, and then enter the path and name of the file, or use the Browse button to locate it. Once you choose a file, you can then select Link To File on Disk to create a link to the original file, or Store in Document to place a copy of the sound in the document.

4. Click on OK. Corel WordPerfect will insert a Sound Clip icon in the left margin.

5. To play the sound, click on the icon.

You can also record and save a new sound file. In the Sound Clips dialog box, click on Record to display the Windows Sound Recorder dialog box:

Click on the Record button, and then speak or sing into the microphone or play the sound you want to record. Choose Save from the File menu, and then Exit the Sound Recorder. Finally, insert the sound file as you just learned.

To play or delete any sound clip in the document, or edit its description, select Sound from the Insert menu to display the Sound Clips dialog box. Figure 13-3 shows the dialog box with several inserted files. To play a sound, click on its name in the list box and then click on the Play button. There are also buttons to stop,

13

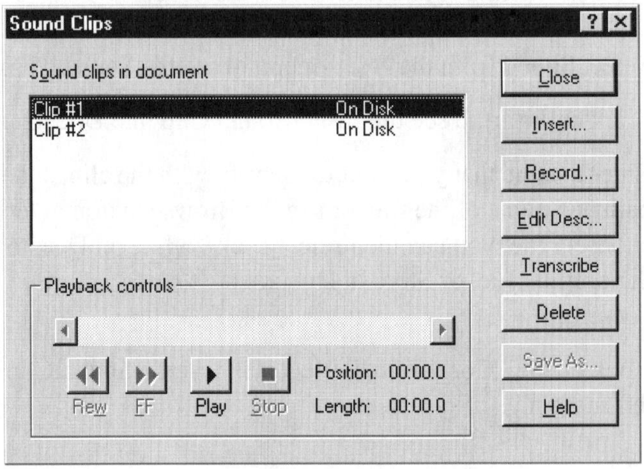

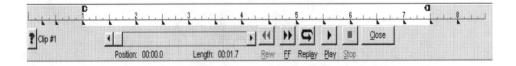

Select and
play sound
clips

FIGURE 13-3

rewind, and fast-forward the clip. The Length indicator shows how long the clip is;
the Position indicator shows how far into the clip is the sound you are hearing.

If you want to access these same features later without redisplaying the dialog
box, click on the Transcribe button. The dialog box will close, and you'll see a feature
bar (shown in the following illustration) under the ruler. Click on the Sound Clip
icon to hear the sound, and then use the feature bar buttons to replay, rewind, or fast
forward it. Click on Close to remove the feature bar.

Other Multimedia Files

To insert a sound, video, or other multimedia object into the document, select Object
from the Insert menu, and then double-click on the Media Clip option. Corel
WordPerfect will display the options shown in Figure 13-4. Click on Insert Clip to
see the options shown here.

Click on Video for Windows to insert a video clip, Sound or MIDI Sequencer to insert a sound clip, or CD Audio to insert a track from an audio CD in your CD drive. Depending on what you inserted, you'll see either an icon representing the object, or a window displaying the object, such as an video clip. Double-click on the icon or window, or click on the play button to display it.

Using Databases and Spreadsheets

So far you've learned several ways to insert spreadsheet information into a document—you can cut and paste it through the Clipboard, or you can embed or link it using the Object command from the Insert menu.

 In Chapter 21 you will learn even more about using Corel Quattro Pro information in a Corel WordPerfect document.

You can also use information from a spreadsheet or database by importing it, or by creating a link through a process known as *Dynamic Data Exchange (DDE)*. When you import the information, you are placing a copy of it into the Corel WordPerfect document. When you create a DDE link, the information appears in your document, and you can format and edit it, but it is also linked with the original file on the disk. Changing the file will change the information in Corel

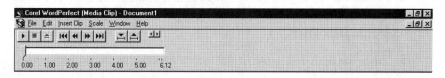

Media Clip
feature bar

█ FIGURE 13-4

13

WordPerfect as well. This differs from the link you learned about previously, which is called an *OLE link*. With an OLE link you cannot edit or format the information in Corel WordPerfect.

Using the import or DDE link technique, you have the choice of how you want to insert the spreadsheet or database information—as a Corel WordPerfect table, into tabular columns, or as a Corel WordPerfect merge file with merge codes. Inserting the information into either a table or merge file will let you then use the information as a data file for a merge operation. So, for example, you can send form letters to clients listed in a Paradox database or a Corel Quattro Pro worksheet.

 TIP: *Import or link a spreadsheet or database to use it as a data file for a merge.*

Follow these steps to import or link a spreadsheet or database file.

1. Select Spreadsheet/Database from the Insert menu.

2. Click on Import to import the information, or click on Create Link to link it. Corel WordPerfect will display either the Import or Create Data Link dialog box. Figure 13-5 shows the Create Data Link dialog box. The Import box is identical except for the name in the title bar, and the text box label Link As is replaced by Import As.

 NOTE: *Corel WordPerfect will display this same dialog box when you use the Open command to open a spreadsheet or database file.*

3. Pull down the Data Type list and choose Spreadsheet, if you want to use a spreadsheet file, or one of these database options: Clipper, dBase, FoxPro, Paradox, ODBC, ODBC (SQL), ASCII Delimited Text, and ANSI Delimited Text.

4. Pull down the Import As or Link As list, and choose how you want to insert the information: Table, Text (as tabular column), or as a Merge Data File.

5. Enter the path and name of the spreadsheet or database file in the Filename text box, or use the Browse icon to search for the file on your disk.

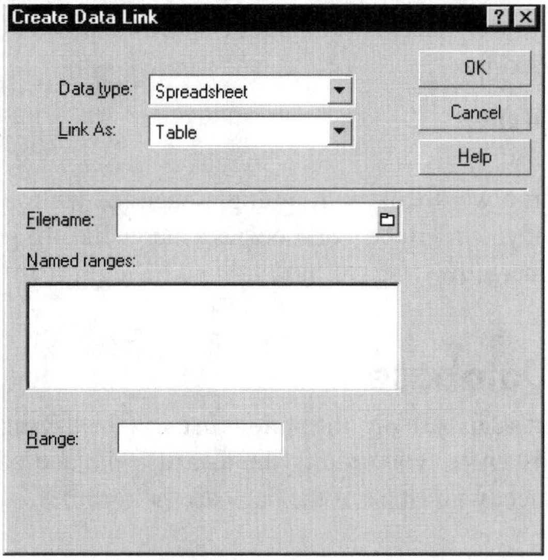

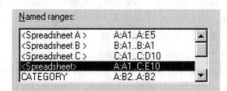

Create
Data Link
dialog box

FIGURE 13-5

The procedure now differs if you are inserting spreadsheet or database information.

Using a Spreadsheet

If you are inserting information from a spreadsheet file, follow these steps:

1. Click in the Named Ranges box. Corel WordPerfect will display all of the named worksheet ranges, as well as the notation <spreadsheet> that represents the entire worksheet. The Range box will show the range of cells that contain data. If you named a spreadsheet that has information on more than one worksheet page in the file, you'll see a notation for each page:

2. Click on the page you want to insert, or select <spreadsheet> to insert the entire worksheet file, or enter a specific range of cells in the Range text box.

3. Click on OK.

If you insert a workbook with multiple pages as tables, each will appear in a separate table. If you insert the workbook as a merge file, the pages will be combined into one large merge file.

Using a Database

When you insert a database file, the options in the Named Ranges list will be replaced by the Fields list. After you specify the database file and click in the Fields box, Corel WordPerfect will list all of the database field names:

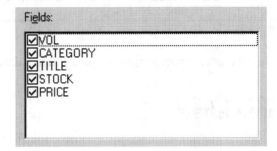

Deselect the checkboxes for the fields that you do not want to insert, and select Use Field Names as Headings to place the field names as the row in the table. Click on OK to insert the information.

Updating Links

When you import the information, it appears just like any other Corel WordPerfect text. When you link it, however, Corel WordPerfect will indicate that it is indeed linked. This is an important reminder that you should update the information to retrieve the most current version of the data.

When you insert the information as a merge file, you'll see the Start Link icon and the End Link icon at the beginning and end of the merge information. When you insert the information in a table or as tabular columns, Corel WordPerfect will display a link icon following the information:

VOL	CATEGORY	TITLE	STOCK	PRICE
E11	Entertainment	Great Classical Compose	122.	23.
H32	History	Austrian Arms and Armor	450.	35.95
T24	Travel	Great European Cathedra	3.	110.09
T35	Travel	Tibetan Adventures	4.	36.

   To see the name of the file being linked, and the type of file, click on one of the icons. If you do not want the icons displayed, select Spreadsheet/Database from the Insert menu, click on Options, and deselect the Show Icons checkbox.

   When you want to ensure that the document contains the most up-to-date information, select Spreadsheet/Database from the Insert menu, and click on Update. A dialog box will appear asking you to confirm that you want to update all of the linked objects in the document—select Yes or No. If you edited or formatted the information in Corel WordPerfect, however, your changes will be replaced by the data and formats in the linked file, just as if you were linking the information for the first time. To have all of your linked files update automatically when you open the document, select Spreadsheet/Database from the Insert menu, click on Options, and select the Update on Retrieve checkbox.

NOTE: *To change the name of the file being linked and its format, select Edit Link from the Spreadsheet/Database submenu.*

13

PART
III

Corel Quattro Pro

Introducing Corel Quattro Pro

14

Corel Quattro Pro lets you work with information in table format—neatly arranged rows and columns of numbers or text. Formatting capabilities let you design professional-looking tables—combining grid lines, colors, shadings, and special effects for maximum impact. Because the table is computerized, however, you can also perform mathematical and even complex statistical analysis quickly and easily. Don't let the words "mathematical" and "statistical" scare you off. You don't have to know anything about statistics or even much about mathematics to take advantage of the powers of Corel Quattro Pro.

How difficult is using Corel Quattro Pro? Not difficult at all. In most cases, all you need are one or more basic formulas that perform math using values in the table. You have to know when to add, subtract, multiply, and divide—not do the math yourself. Corel Quattro Pro does the actual math for you. In fact, in many cases, you can just click on a button, or select options from a list, and Corel Quattro Pro builds the formula for you.

What's It Used For?

Since you can easily create a table in Corel WordPerfect, you may be wondering why you need a separate program such as Corel Quattro Pro. Corel WordPerfect gives you just some basic capabilities to perform math and organize information in table format. Corel Quattro Pro specializes in it, as you'll see.

Financial Records

Use Corel Quattro Pro to create financial records and documents of all types. Produce budgets, reports, income statements, balance sheets, sales forecasts, projections, and most of the records that you need to maintain your business, household, or organization. Corel Quattro Pro makes it easy to create professional-looking printouts that will impress your stockholders, bankers, and accountant—perhaps even the IRS.

But Corel Quattro Pro is for more than good looks. It can help ensure that your numbers are accurate, even if you have to make last-minute changes. Suppose that after creating the quarterly budget, you realize that you've entered the wrong numbers in certain areas. If you created the budget on paper, you'd have to change the numbers and then recalculate and change all of the gross and net profit figures. Not so with Corel Quattro Pro. Just change the figures that you have to, and Corel Quattro Pro will use the simple formulas that you've entered to make the recalculations for you.

Business Forms

Use Corel Quattro Pro to create business forms of all types, such as invoices, statements, schedules, planners, and professional time and billing logs. Forms are often difficult to create in word processing programs but a snap in Corel Quattro Pro.

And don't imagine that we are talking about only blank forms. By adding simple formulas, ones that Corel Quattro Pro can even create for you, you can complete the forms on the screen. For example, how about a sales tool for computing loan or lease information that automatically calculates the customer's maximum purchase amount, total interest, and other statistics to help close that deal, as shown in Figure 14-1? All you have to do is fill in a few items and then fax, e-mail, or print and mail it to your customer.

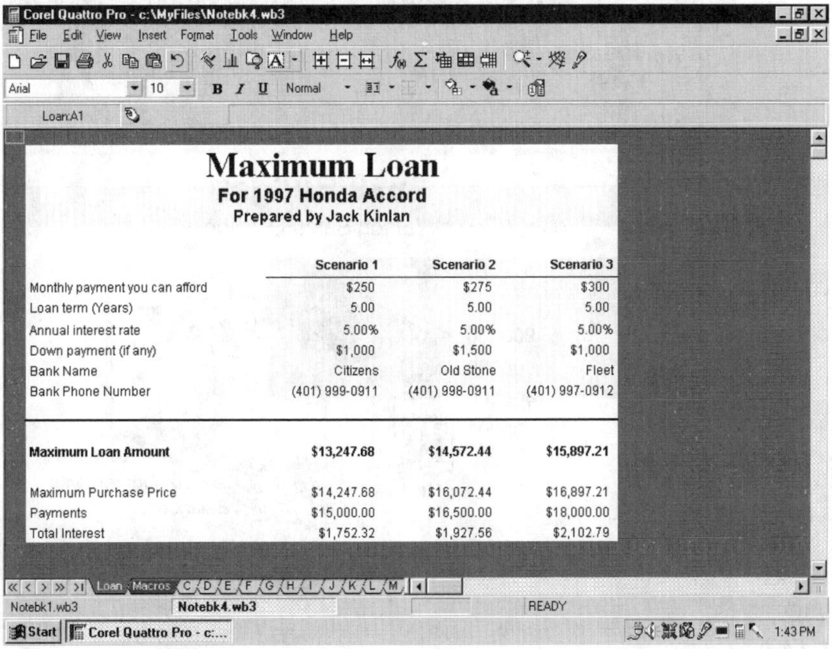
Corel Quattro Pro - c:\MyFiles\Notebk4.wb3
File Edit View Insert Format Tools Window Help
Arial
10
Normal
Loan:A1
Maximum Loan
For 1997 Honda Accord
Prepared by Jack Kinlan
Scenario 1
Scenario 2
Scenario 3
Monthly payment you can afford $250 $275 $300
Loan term (Years) 5.00 5.00 5.00
Annual interest rate 5.00% 5.00% 5.00%
Down payment (if any) $1,000 $1,500 $1,000
Bank Name Citizens Old Stone Fleet
Bank Phone Number (401) 999-0911 (401) 998-0911 (401) 997-0912
Maximum Loan Amount $13,247.68 $14,572.44 $15,897.21
Maximum Purchase Price $14,247.68 $16,072.44 $16,897.21
Payments $15,000.00 $16,500.00 $18,000.00
Total Interest $1,752.32 $1,927.56 $2,102.79
Loan Macros C D E F G H I J K L M
Notebk1.wb3
Notebk4.wb3
READY
Start
Corel Quattro Pro - c:...
1:43 PM

Using Corel Quattro Pro to create business forms of all types

FIGURE 14-1

Charts and Maps

Use Corel Quattro Pro to create eye-catching charts and maps directly from information that you've already entered. There is no need to retype the numbers. Just tell Corel Quattro Pro which part of your table contains the numbers you want to chart and where the chart should appear, and the program does the rest. If you want, you can choose the chart type and customize its design; otherwise, just sit back and let Corel Quattro Pro do the work. The chart in Figure 14-2, for instance, was created from a quarterly budget table with a few clicks of the mouse.

When your worksheet contains geographic information, such as sales per state or country, then create a map. You'll see at a glance where your strong sales areas are and where you need to concentrate your efforts. You can even overlay maps with major highways, major cities, and capitals.

For even greater impact, you can combine charts and graphs into slide Corel Presentations. Hook up your PC—even a laptop—to a projector, and you have a complete onscreen presentation for board or sales meetings.

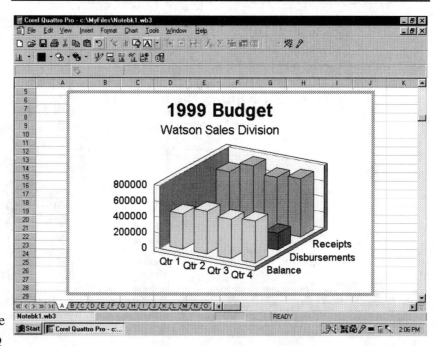

Creating graphs and charts with a few clicks of the mouse

FIGURE 14-2

Integrate IT! *You can share all of your worksheets, graphs, and maps with Corel WordPerfect to create compound documents.*

Databases

Use Corel Quattro Pro to create databases for recording, finding, and analyzing information. Keep records of clients, employees, products, members, or any other item that you need to track and report.

A database is like an electronic version of an index card file or folders in your filing cabinet. With Corel Quattro Pro, you create the database in table format. Each row of the table represents another item in the database, as shown in Figure 14-3. You can print reports, locate specific information when you want it, perform statistical analysis on your information, and even print graphs.

Integrate IT! *You can use your Corel Quattro Pro database to create form letters in Corel WordPerfect, or transfer it to a database program such as Paradox or Microsoft Access. You can also move data in the other direction, importing information from a database program into Corel Quattro Pro to analyze or chart it.*

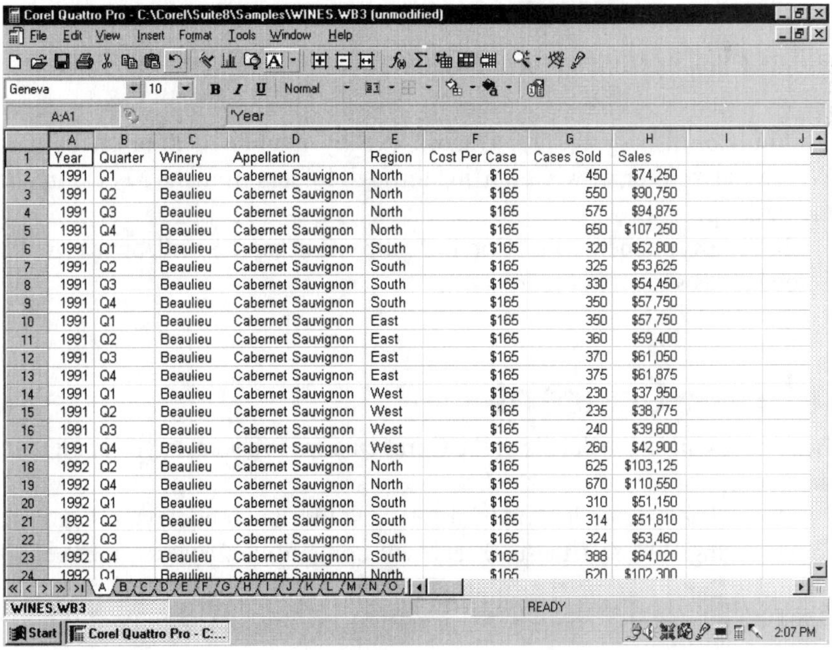

Using Quattro Pro to record and analyze data

FIGURE 14-3

Solving Problems

The real jewel in the crown of Corel Quattro Pro, however, is its ability to solve what's known as "What If?" problems. What if costs increase by 5 percent? What if employees are given a raise? What if sales go down? What if inventory is increased?

Since Corel Quattro Pro can automatically recalculate the values in an entire table when you change even a single number, you can see the effects of that change in every place that it affects. Just change a value or two and then analyze the results.

Corel Quattro Pro even has special features for those tougher problems. You can have it solve a problem by automatically changing values itself—for example, to find the optimum combination of factors that give you the results you want. A feature called Scenario Manager even saves different combinations of results so you can switch back and forth between them as you attempt to make a decision.

Starting Corel Quattro Pro

Starting Corel Quattro Pro is as easy as pointing and clicking:

1. Click on the Start button in the Windows 95 taskbar.

2. Point to Corel WordPerfect Suite 8.

3. Click on Corel Quattro Pro 8.

You can also start Corel Quattro Pro by double-clicking on its name in the Windows Explorer, or while surfing through folders from the My Computer icon on the desktop.

In a few moments the Corel Quattro Pro screen will appear with a blank notebook, as shown in Figure 14-4.

Notebook Concept

Before looking at the details of the Corel Quattro Pro screen, you should understand the concept of the notebook.

A *notebook* is a collection of sheets, just like a notebook you'd carry to class or to a meeting. Most of these sheets will contain *worksheets*—numbers, text, and formulas that make up the forms, financial reports, or databases that you create. Worksheets can also contain charts and graphs that illustrate the values elsewhere

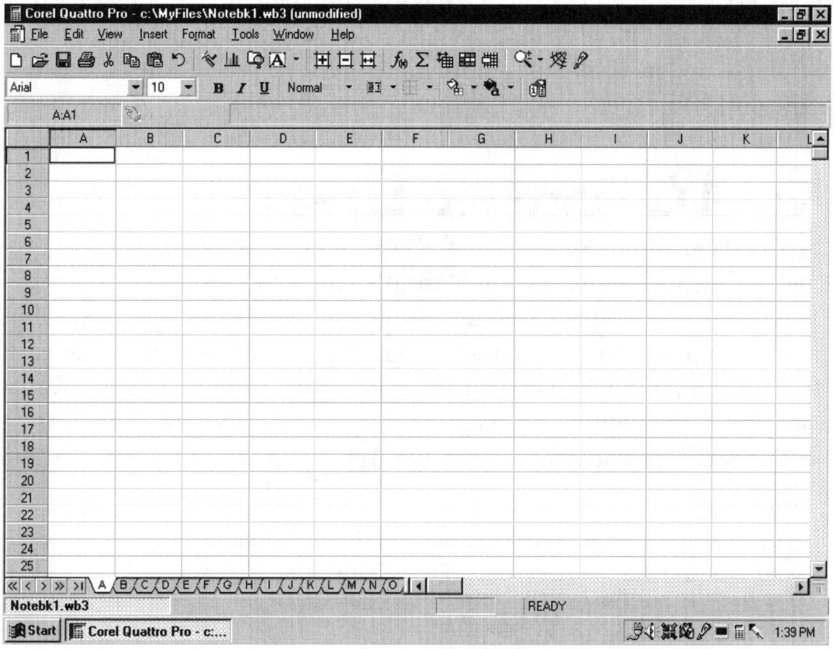

The Corel
Quattro Pro
screen

FIGURE 14-4

on the sheet. At the very end of the notebook is a special sheet called the *objects sheet.* This sheet stores copies of all of the charts and graphs in the notebook, as well as slide shows and maps. There are 256 sheets plus the objects sheet.

What's the benefit of a notebook? With a notebook, you don't need a separate file for every worksheet you want to create. Your budget, for example, may include several related worksheets. Rather than store each one separately on your disk, you can create them on different sheets in the same notebook. When you save the notebook, Corel Quattro Pro saves all of its worksheets, charts, and slide shows in one file on your disk. Then you can simply open one file to access all of the worksheets. If you need to transport the worksheet from the office to home, just copy the one file to a floppy disk or to a Windows 95 briefcase to synchronize the notebook between your home and office.

In addition, all of the sheets in a notebook can share common information. A worksheet can refer to values in another worksheet, so changing a number on one sheet might have an impact on other sheets, even on the entire notebook.

While it is best to use a notebook to store related worksheets, there are other possibilities. You can enter totally unrelated worksheets in the same notebook. In

14

fact, you can have more than one report, form, database, or other item on a sheet. If you think of the worksheet as a very large piece of paper, you can imagine dividing it up into sections to store more than one table. Corel Quattro Pro won't know the difference.

The Corel Quattro Pro Screen

The Corel Quattro Pro screen, shown labeled in Figure 14-5, is full of useful items, most of which are standard Corel WordPerfect Suite features.

At the very top of the screen are the title bar, the menu bar, the Notebook toolbar, and the property bar. As expected, pointing to a button or bar area displays a QuickTip, so you can be sure you are choosing the correct command for the job you want to perform. Figure 14-6 shows the buttons in the Notebook toolbar, and Figure 14-7 shows the parts of the property bar. You'll learn more about these buttons later.

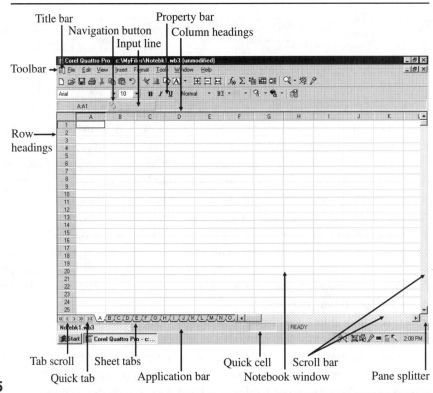

Parts of the Corel Quattro Pro screen

FIGURE 14-5

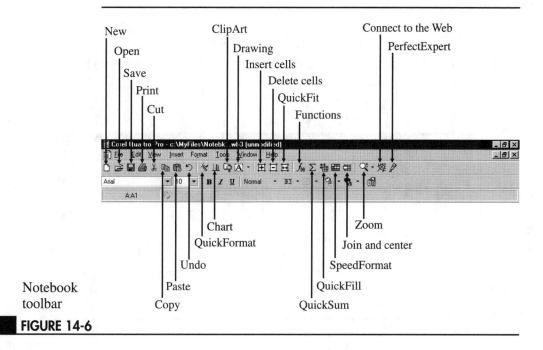

New
Open
Save
Print
Cut
ClipArt
Drawing
Insert cells
Delete cells
QuickFit
Functions
Connect to the Web
PerfectExpert

Chart
QuickFormat
Undo
Paste
Copy
Zoom
Join and center
SpeedFormat
QuickFill
QuickSum

Notebook
toolbar

FIGURE 14-6

Below the property bar is the input line. Here is where you can edit the information that you add to the spreadsheet. On the left side of the input line is the Active Cell Address box that shows your location in the worksheet. Next to that is the Navigation button, which will list block names that you can give to sections of the worksheet.

Below the input line is the Notebook window, where the sheets of the notebook will appear. If necessary, you can open more than one notebook at a time, as you'll learn in Chapter 17.

The first notebook you open during a Corel Quattro Pro session is called NOTEBK1.WB3; the second, NOTEBK2.WB3; and so on. Of course, you can give the notebook a name of your choice when you save it.

A *worksheet* is a series of numbered rows and lettered columns. The blocks containing the column letters are called *column headers,* the row numbers are called *row headers.* The intersection of a row and a column is called a *cell.* For example, the cell in the top left corner is called cell A1 because it is in column A and row 1—the column letter always precedes the row number. The cell to its right is cell B1, and the cell below A1 is A2.

14

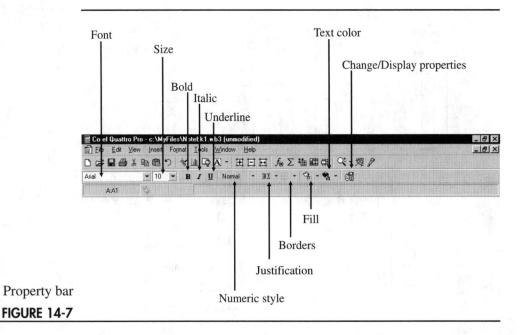

Property bar

FIGURE 14-7

Even though you can't see much of the worksheet on the screen, worksheets are very large. There are 256 columns, numbered A through Z, then AA through AZ, BA through BZ, and so on up to column IV. There are 8,192 rows. So each worksheet has a total of 2,097,152 cells, and the entire notebook—all 256 sheets—has 536,870,912 cells!

The cell selected at the current time is called the *active* cell. This is the cell that will be affected by what you type or by the commands that you select. You can always tell the active cell because:

■ It is surrounded by the *selector*, a dark rectangle.

■ You'll see its *cell reference*—the row and column number it represents, as well as its sheet in the notebook—on the left side of the input line.

■ Its row and column headers will appear to be pressed down.

Below the Notebook window is the application bar. This is where Corel Quattro Pro displays the names of open notebooks, the current program mode, and certain indicators, such as when CAPS LOCK and NUM LOCK are turned on. The word

"READY" on the right of the line means that you are in Ready mode—Corel Quattro Pro is prepared to accept your commands. Most menu, toolbar, and property bar commands cannot be selected unless you are in Ready mode. There are more then two dozen status and mode indicators, including these that you'll see most often:

Mode	Meaning
Edit	You are changing the contents of the cell.
Label	You are entering text.
Value	You are entering a numeric value, a date or time, or a formula that results in a value.
Point	You are pointing to cells with the mouse to insert their addresses into a formula.

In addition to the mode, the application bar/status line will also contain these items:

QuickCell	You can insert a cell into this section of the application bar, and watch it recalculate as you work in the notebook. This saves you the trouble of scrolling back to the cell itself to see its contents.
Calculator icon	An icon of a calculator will flash in the application bar when Quattro Pro recalculates the notebook.
Calc-As-You-Go	Quattro Pro displays the sum, average, count, maximum, and minimum values of the selected range of cells.
Function help	When you are entering a function, the function syntax appears on the right of the application bar.

The *sheet tabs* let you change sheets of the notebook. The 256 notebook sheets are numbered like columns from A to IV, followed by the objects sheet. Just click on the tab for the worksheet that you want to display. After completing a table on the first sheet, for example, click on the next sheet tab—B—to start another worksheet. If necessary, you can delete sheets and change their order.

14

NOTE: *Use the tab number when you want to reference a cell on another sheet. For example, F:A1 represents cell A1 on sheet F of the notebook. The syntax is always* Sheet:Coordinates.

The *tab scroll* lets you scroll through the sheets. This is useful when you're not sure which sheet you want to view, and it works like a scroll bar. Click on > to move to the next sheet, or < to move to the previous. Click on >> to scroll a new set of sheets forward, and << to move a set of sheets backward.

Use the *QuickTab* to quickly move from the sheet you are looking at to the end of the notebook, and vice versa. Click on the speed tab to see the objects sheet; click on it again to move back to the previous sheet you were viewing.

TIP: *You can also move back and forth between the objects sheet and a worksheet by choosing Objects from the View menu to see the objects sheet, or by choosing Draft or Sheet from the View menu to return to the worksheet.*

The scroll bars, standard Windows controls, move you around the worksheet. Use the vertical scroll bar to move up and down, the horizontal scroll bar to move side to side. Remember, the Notebook window is a virtual window of the worksheet. While you see only a few rows and columns, the Corel Quattro Pro worksheet is really very large, so use the scroll bars to display other sections of the sheet.

As you drag the scroll box within the bar, Corel Quattro Pro will display a row or column indicator. When you drag the horizontal scroll box, it will show the letter of the column that will be at the far left when you release the mouse. When you drag the vertical scroll box, it will show the number of the row that will be at the top of the screen.

At the lower-right corner of the worksheet—right where the scroll bars meet—is the *pane splitter.* This lets you divide the worksheet into two or more separate panes, or sections. You can view different parts of the worksheet in each sheet, or even different tables or charts that share the same sheet.

Changing Toolbars

Like other Corel WordPerfect suite applications, Corel Quattro Pro includes a number of toolbars that you can use to perform common functions. To choose one, right-click on the displayed toolbar to see a QuickMenu of other available toolbars. The toolbars already displayed will be indicated with a check mark. Check or uncheck the bars to determine which are displayed.

You can also select toolbars by choosing Toolbars from the View menu to see the dialog box shown in Figure 14-8. Click on the checkboxes for the toolbars that you want to display—they will appear onscreen immediately—and then click on Close.

Moving Around the Worksheet

To create a worksheet, you'll have to move from cell to cell to enter or edit information or to see the results of your actions. Using the mouse, click in the cell that you want to enter information into, edit, or format. Use the scroll bars if necessary to bring the cell into view.

Using the keyboard, move around the worksheet using the keystrokes shown in Table 14-1. Pressing ENTER does not move the insertion point from cell to cell, as you will soon learn.

To move to a specific cell, pull down the Edit menu and select Go To to see the dialog box shown in Figure 14-9. Type the cell reference, including the sheet letter if it is not on the current sheet, and click on OK.

Selecting Cells

To perform an action on a cell, you must select it. To select a single cell, just click on it. This makes it the active cell and selects it at the same time. When you make a cell active, whatever is in the cell will also appear in the input line.

Selecting
the toolbars
to display

FIGURE 14-8

14

Keystroke	Direction
LEFT ARROW	One cell left
RIGHT ARROW	One cell right
UP ARROW	One row up
DOWN ARROW	One row down
CTRL-PGDN	Next sheet
CTRL-PGUP	Previous sheet
PGUP	One screen up
PGDN	One screen down
HOME	To cell A1
CTRL-HOME	Cell A1 of the first sheet
END-HOME	To the lower-right nonblank corner
END-CTRL-HOME	To the last nonblank cell in the notebook
END-ARROW	To the next nonblank cell in the direction of the arrow
TAB	One cell right
SHIFT-TAB	One cell left
CTRL-LEFT ARROW	One screen left
CTRL-RIGHT ARROW	One screen right

Keystrokes
for Moving
in a
Worksheet

TABLE 14-1

There are many actions that you'll want to perform on more than one cell. Groups of selected cells are called *blocks*. To select a block of cells, point to a cell in one corner of the block, hold down the mouse button, and drag to the opposite corner. As you drag the mouse, the cells in the block will become highlighted, with a black background. The first cell you selected, however, will just be surrounded by a border, called the *selector,* letting you know that it was the starting point of the block.

NOTE: *If the mouse pointer changes to a hand, and the selected cell becomes bordered with yellow, then you've held down the mouse button too long before dragging. This means Corel Quattro Pro has shifted into Drag-and-Drop mode for moving cells. Just release the mouse button and start over. See Chapter 16 for more details on drag-and-drop.*

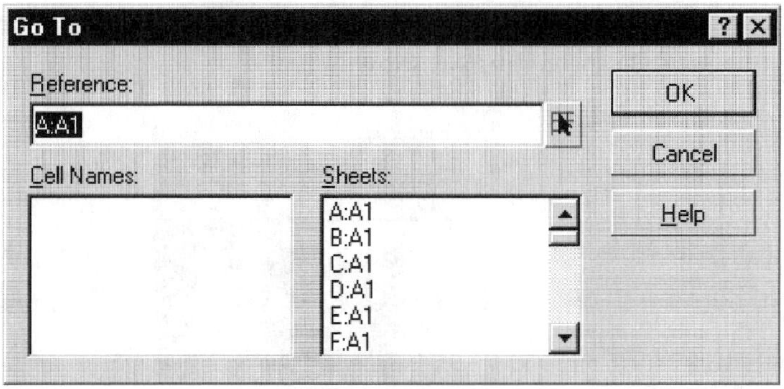

Using the
Go To
command
to move to a
specific cell

FIGURE 14-9

To select an entire row, point to its row header so the mouse pointer appears as a right-pointing arrow and then click. To select an entire column, point to the column header so the mouse pointer appears as a down-pointing arrow and then click. Drag over row headers with the right-pointing arrow, or over column headers with the down pointing arrow, to select adjacent rows or columns.

Notice that there is an empty shaded cell in the very upper-leftmost corner of the worksheet. This is the Select All button—click on it to select the entire sheet.

Using basic Windows techniques, you can also select cells, rows, and columns that are not adjacent to each other. Hold down the CTRL key and click on the cells, rows, or columns that you want to select. With the CTRL key pressed, Corel Quattro Pro will not deselect sections already highlighted when you click elsewhere.

Many Corel Quattro Pro functions refer to a block even though they also act upon a single selected cell. So throughout this part of the book, we'll use the term "block" to refer to any number of selected cells, rows, and columns. When an instruction says to select a block, it means select any number of cells that you want to work with, even if it's only a single cell.

Designating Block References

You reference a single cell by its row and column coordinates. To refer to a block, you designate the starting and ending cell references of the group. If the cells are all in one row or column, just use the two end cells in the format A1..A8. In this example, the block A1..A8 includes eight cells—A1, A2, A3, A4, A5, A6, A7, and A8.

14

If the cells are in more than one row or column, reference any two cells in opposite corners. For example, the reference A1..B5 includes the ten cells A1 through A5, and B1 through B5 as shown here:

	A	B
1		
2		
3		
4		
5		

When you type a block reference, you can type a single period between the cells. Corel Quattro Pro will insert the second period when you accept the entry. In addition, you can use any opposite cells. Traditionally, block references use the cell in the upper-left and lower-right corners, or the first and last cells if they are all in a row or column. You can actually enter the cells in any order, such as the lower-left and upper-right corners of a block, as in A5.C1. When you accept the entry, Corel Quattro Pro will rewrite the reference in the traditional way for you.

A block reference can also include noncontiguous cells, that is, cells that are not next to each other. Reference single cells by separating them with commas, as in A2,B4,C10. Include both types of references using the format A1.A10,C3,D5. This refers to the cells in the range A1 through A10, as well as cells C3 and D5.

Pointing to Cells in Dialog Boxes

Many dialog boxes perform a function on a block of cells. In some cases you can select the block of cells before opening the dialog box, and the block reference will appear automatically. If the block is incorrect, or you did not select it beforehand, you can change the reference by typing the block coordinates.

In most cases there will also be a Point Mode button, as shown here:

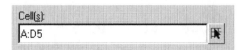

You use Point mode to temporarily leave the dialog box to select the block of cells, rather than type in their references. Here's how:

1. Click in the text box where you want to insert a range of cells.

2. Click on the Point Mode button. Corel Quattro Pro will reduce the dialog box to two lines—the title bar and a line showing the range the box will act upon—and move it up so you can see the worksheet cells.

3. Drag over the cells that you want to reference, or click on a single cell to reference it. To point to a block on another sheet, click on the sheet tab and then drag over the cells. As you select the cell, the block reference will appear in the range indicator.

4. When the range is correct, release the mouse button, and then click on the Maximize button in the dialog box's title bar to redisplay it.

If the cells you want to reference are not contiguous, enter a comma after clicking or dragging on one cell or block, and then click or drag on the next cell or block. The reference cells will be separated by commas in the dialog box.

 TIP: *If you can see the start of the block in the background of the dialog box, just point to it and hold down the mouse button. Corel Quattro Pro will automatically minimize the dialog box and then redisplay it when you release the mouse button.*

Selecting 3-D Blocks

A 3-D block is a block of cells selected on more than one consecutive notebook sheet. For example, suppose you have the budgets for the last four years on separate sheets of the notebook, one year per sheet occupying the same area on each sheet. You can apply the same formats to every sheet at one time by selecting them as one block—a 3-D block.

To select a 3-D block, start by selecting the cell or cells on the first sheet you want to include. Then hold down the SHIFT key while you click on the tab for the last sheet you want to include. Corel Quattro Pro will display a black line under the tabs indicating that the 3-D block extends across those sheets. While the line appears under the tabs, perform the function that you want to apply to the selected group.

 NOTE: *You cannot use this type of 3-D block to enter text into all of the cells, although you can use it with QuickFill. See Chapter 15 for more information.*

The 3-D block is temporary; it remains in force only until you click on another cell. You can create a more permanent 3-D block by using a group, as you'll learn in Chapter 17.

Object Inspector

Everything in Corel Quattro Pro is called an *object*. To change an object's properties (one or more of its characteristics), point to it, click the right mouse button, and choose the Properties option at the bottom of the QuickMenu. You'll see a dialog box with several sheets, each representing a classification of properties that you can change.

Click on the tab for the properties you want to set, and make your selections. Corel Quattro Pro will change the color of the tab title to remind you that you've already used that tab. When you close the dialog box, your selections will be applied.

- To set the properties for a cell or selected group of cells, click on the Change/Display Properties button on the property bar, or right-click on the block and choose Cell Properties from the QuickMenu.

- To set the properties of the entire sheet, just right-click on the sheet tab and select Sheet Properties from the QuickMenu.

- To set properties for the entire notebook, restore the notebook so it appears in its own window, then right-click on the title bar and choose Active Notebook Properties from the QuickMenu.

- To customize Corel Quattro Pro itself, right-click on the Corel Quattro Pro title bar and choose Application Properties from the QuickMenu, or choose Settings from the Tools menu.

You'll learn about properties later, in Chapter 16.

Changing the View

When you start Corel Quattro Pro, it displays the notebook in Draft view and at 100% magnification. Draft view means that you won't see the sheet margins on screen and the worksheet will not be divided into sheets—it appears as one large sheet. The default magnification means that text and graphics appear the same size onscreen as they will be when printed.

To see how the worksheet will be paginated, select Page from the View menu. In Page view, the worksheet will be divided into sheets, just as it will be when printed, and you'll see margin guidelines, sheet break lines, headers, and footers. You can even change the margins by dragging the guidelines, and insert headers and footers by right-clicking in the top or bottom margin area. Return to Draft view by selecting Draft from the View menu.

If your worksheet is large, then you may spend a lot of time scrolling to see certain sections. One way to avoid scrolling is to reduce the displayed magnification. You'll be able to see more cells on the screen, although they will be smaller and may be difficult to read. You can also enlarge the magnification to make cells appear larger—although you will see fewer of them.

To quickly change magnification, pull down the Zoom list in the property bar and select the magnification desired. You can also choose to zoom the selected cells so they fill the screen, and to display a dialog box for using a custom magnification.

The setting applies only to the current sheet, not to other sheets in the notebook. For example, Figure 14-10 shows a worksheet in Page view and at 50% magnification. The dashed lines are the margin guidelines, and the solid line represents a sheet break.

Worksheet in Page view at 50% magnification

FIGURE 14-10

14

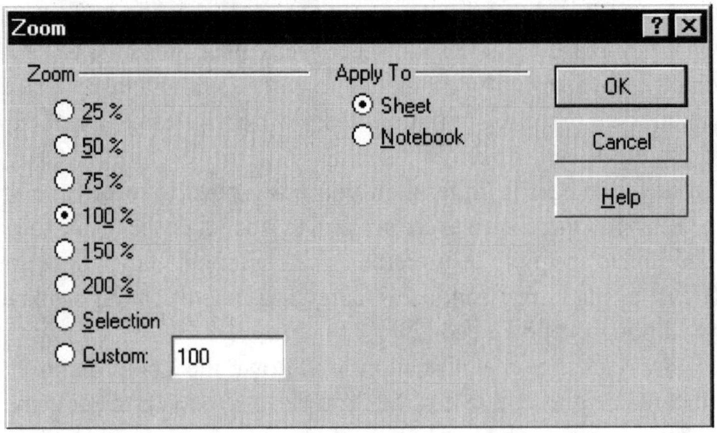

Using
Zoom to
enlarge or
reduce the
display

FIGURE 14-11

You have more control over changing magnification using the Zoom dialog box. Select Other from the Zoom list, or select Zoom from the View menu to see the dialog box shown in Figure 14-11. Click on the desired magnification, or click on Custom and enter another setting. Click on Notebook to set the view for every sheet in the notebook.

Getting Help

The help system in Corel Quattro Pro works just about the same as it does in Corel WordPerfect. The Help Topics dialog box contains the Contents, Index, and Find tabs. You can also use Ask the PerfectExpert to answer your questions and Corel Web Site to go directly to Corel over the Internet or CompuServe.

Creating a Worksheet

15

Creating a worksheet is easy if you follow a few basic steps. Most worksheets contain titles, labels, and values. The *titles,* normally at the top of the worksheet page, explain the purpose of the worksheet, just like a title on a report. *Labels* are text that explains what the numbers in the other cells represent. These are usually column and row headings, but text can appear anywhere in a worksheet. *Values* are numbers, formulas, or functions that display information or calculate results.

Basic Principles

To enter information into a cell, make the cell active by clicking on it or moving to it using the keyboard, and then type. When you start typing, the insertion point will appear in the cell, whatever you type will appear in the input line, and you'll see four additional boxes, as shown here:

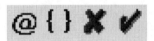

Clicking on the box with the @ symbol will list Corel Quattro Pro's built-in functions; clicking on the box with the braces will list macros.

The box with the X is called the Cancel box. Click on this box, or press the ESC key if you want to start again. The box with the check mark is called the Enter box. Click on this box or press the ENTER key to accept your entry and enter it into the cell. You can also accept your entry and move to another cell at the same time by pressing an arrow key, TAB, or SHIFT-TAB. Pressing ENTER accepts the entry but does not move to another cell.

Before you cancel or accept the entry, you can edit it by pressing the BACKSPACE or DEL key, or by moving the insertion point with the arrow keys. Edit the contents as you would if you were using a word processing program.

NOTE: *When you're entering information into a cell, the property bar will change to include text-formatting buttons. You'll learn more about this property bar in Chapter 16.*

The basic procedure for entering information into a cell is as follows:

1. Click in the cell to make it active.

2. Type the information you want in the cell.

3. Click on the Enter box—the box with the check mark—or press ENTER.

When you are entering or editing information in a cell, the property bar will be dimmed and most of the toolbar and menu commands will be inactive. The word "Ready" in the status line will be replaced by the word "Label," "Value," or "Edit," depending on the kind of information you are typing or if you are editing the contents of the cell. To use the features of the menu, tool, and property bars again, you must accept or cancel the entry to return to Ready mode.

Entering Text

Corel Quattro Pro treats text differently from numbers and distinguishes the two by the first character that you type. This difference is important because Corel Quattro Pro can perform math operations only on numbers, and it aligns text and numbers differently in the cells.

NOTE: *Corel Quattro Pro includes QuickCorrect, so common mistakes will be corrected automatically.*

If you start a cell entry with a letter, Corel Quattro Pro assumes you are typing text and displays the word "Label" on the right end of the status line. When you click on the Enter box or press ENTER, the text starts on the left side of the cell, the default format for text.

To fill a cell with repeating characters, start with the backslash. Typing *, for example, will fill the cell with asterisks; entering \12 will repeat the characters "12" across the cell.

NOTE: *You will learn how to format the text in a cell in Chapter 16.*

Using QuickType

Sometimes you want to repeat a label in a column, or use a similar word or phrase. For example, you may have a worksheet that includes the text "Total Income," and later want to enter the label "Total Expenses." Fortunately, Corel Quattro Pro uses a feature called QuickType.

Rental	
Sales	
Leases	
Total Income	
Salaries	
Utilities	
Rental	
Total Income	

When you type a label, Corel Quattro Pro looks through the column for other labels beginning with the same characters and displays the closest match, as shown here, where Corel Quattro Pro has supplied the "otal Income" after "T" is typed. To accept the entry, press ENTER. To reject the QuickType suggestion, just keep typing—Corel Quattro Pro will continue to look for matching entries using the additional characters that you type. To edit the suggested entry, press the left arrow or right arrow keys, edit the entry, and then press ENTER.

Aligning Text in Cells

You can change the alignment of information in a cell by using the property bar or by starting your entry with a special formatting character.

The Justification list is quick and convenient, but because it is not in the property bar while you are entering data in a cell, you need to select the alignment before you start typing or after you accept the entry. To choose or change alignment, follow these steps:

1. Click in the cell that you want to format.

2. Pull down the Alignment list of the property bar to see these options:

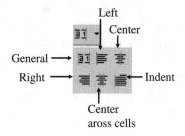

3. Select the alignment desired.

NOTE: *You'll learn about the Join and Center option later.*

You can also change alignment using a special formatting character as the first character of the entry. To center a label in the cell, start it with the caret (^) symbol, as in ^Net. When you accept the entry, the caret in the cell will disappear, and Corel Quattro Pro will center the text. To align text on the right of the cell, start with a quotation mark (").

If you actually want to start the label with a caret or quotation mark, as in "Swifty" Lazar, enter it as "Swifty" Lazar. Corel Quattro Pro uses the apostrophe to align the entry on the left, inserting the opening quotation mark rather than using it as an alignment command.

The apostrophe is also useful when you want to insert labels that contain all numeric characters, such as year labels. It tells Corel Quattro Pro that you are entering a label (for example, the year 1998), to align it on the left, and not to use it in a formula if you accidentally include it as a reference.

You do not have to use the apostrophe, however, when entering social security and phone numbers. If you just type a phone number, such as 555-1234, Corel Quattro Pro will display the word "Value" in the status line, as it does when you enter numbers, but it will display the entry exactly as you enter it. It will not subtract 1234 from 555, as it would if this were a math operation.

Remember that the apostrophe, quotation mark, and caret characters will not appear in the cell unless you are editing it, but they will appear on the input line when the cell is active. This is an important concept to understand. What you see in the cell is the result of what is in the input line. The input line shows the actual contents stored in the worksheet. If the worksheet contains ^Title, the cell displays the word "Title" centered. This concept is even more important when you are working with formulas and functions.

Centering Across Cells

A title often looks better centered across the page, and it is no different with Corel Quattro Pro. Rather than trying to center a title by placing it in a column, use the Join and Center feature. This automatically centers text across the group of cells that you select.

Start by entering the text in the leftmost cell of the block. For example, if you want to center a title across the page, use the following steps:

1. Enter the title in cell A1.

2. Drag it from cell A1 to the end of the page. Using the default column width and orientation, cell H1 will be last on the page.

3. Click on the Join and Center Cells button on the toolbar. You can also pull down the Alignment button on the property bar and select the Center Across Cells option. The selected cells will be joined into one cell, and the text centered:

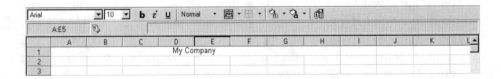

 TIP: *It is best to wait until you have finished adjusting the width of columns before centering text across a block. If you center first and then change column width, the text may no longer appear centered.*

Wide Text Entries

If you type more characters than will fit in the cell, Corel Quattro Pro will run them into adjacent blank cells. If an adjacent cell has an entry of its own, however, Corel Quattro Pro will display only as many characters as will fit. Don't worry; the full entry is actually stored in the worksheet, and it will appear in the input line when the cell is active. Again, the input line shows the real contents of the worksheet; the cell shows only what can be displayed.

 TIP: *To display the full entry, you have to widen the cell or reduce the font size.*

Entering Numbers

To enter a number into a cell, start the entry with a number, a plus sign, or a minus sign. Corel Quattro Pro displays the word "Value" on the status line to indicate it recognizes your entry as numeric. When you accept the entry, Corel Quattro Pro will align it on the right side of the cell. You can later change its alignment using the property bar.

 TIP: *You can use a dollar sign for currency, and commas to separate thousands when typing numbers.*

By default, numbers appear without *trailing zeros,* zeros that come at the end of a number following the decimal point. If you enter **12.10**, for example, Corel Quattro Pro will display 12.1. If you enter **12.00**, Corel Quattro Pro will display 12.

If you type more characters than will fit in the cell, Corel Quattro Pro will display the number in exponential format. It does not run long numbers into adjacent cells as it does text. To display the number, you have to widen the column width, reduce the font being used, or change its format.

Editing Cell Contents

Once you accept an entry, typing something else in the same cell erases its current contents. This is convenient if you enter the wrong number, for example, and want to quickly correct your mistake. Just move back to the same cell and type the new entry. This is not convenient, however, if you don't want to erase the entire entry—but only want to edit a long line of text or a complex formula.

You can edit the contents of a cell either in the input line or in the cell itself. To edit in the input line, make the cell active and then click on the input line. The insertion point will appear where you click. To edit in the cell, double-click on it or make it active and then press F2.

In either case, the word "Edit" appears in the status line, and you may now delete and insert text and numbers, just as you would in a word processing program. Once in Edit mode, you can switch between the input line and the cell by clicking where you want to work.

In Edit mode, use the LEFT ARROW and RIGHT ARROW to move the insertion point in the cell. Press TAB to move to the end of the entry, SHIFT-TAB to move to the start of the entry. Press F2 to exit Edit mode, or to accept or cancel your entry as usual. If you change your mind about editing the entry, just press ESC or click on the Cancel box to retain the cell's original contents.

Entering Formulas

The real power of a worksheet comes from its ability to recalculate values as you change the contents of cells. This is achieved by using formulas whenever possible. A *formula* is a mathematical operation that uses any combination of cell references and actual values. You can use a formula to simply perform math, such as entering **+106/3** to display the result of the calculation, but the most important use of formulas is to reference other cells.

TIP: *With Corel Quattro Pro's new Fit-As-You-Go feature, if the formula results are too large to fit in the cell, the column width will automatically adjust to display the full value.*

You should start every formula with a plus or equal sign, especially if it begins with a cell reference or could be mistaken for a date. This tells Corel Quattro Pro that you want it to calculate and display results. Corel Quattro Pro will change the starting equal sign to a plus sign when you accept the entry.

For example, if you enter **40 * .33**, Corel Quattro Pro will perform the math and display the result—you do not need to start it with a plus or equal sign. If you type

15

5+C3, it will add 5 to the value in cell C3. If you type **12/3** (to mean 12 divided by 3), however, Corel Quattro Pro will assume you're entering December 3. Similarly, if you enter **B5+4**, it will simply display your entry as a label—you must type it as **+B5+4**.

TIP: *It is a common beginner's mistake to forget the plus sign. If you type a formula and the formula rather than the result appears in the cell, you forgot the plus sign.*

When you want to refer to the value in some other cell, just enter its cell reference. For example, the formula to subtract whatever is in cell A1 from what is in cell A2 is +A2-A1. When you enter the formula, Corel Quattro Pro will calculate the math and display the result in the cell. If you later change the value in either cell A1 or A2, Corel Quattro Pro will recalculate the value and display the new result. Corel Quattro Pro does not perform the calculation until you accept the change in the cell.

Even though you see the *results* of the formula in the cell, the worksheet actually contains the formula. When you make the cell active, you'll see the results of the calculation in the cell but the formula itself in the input line.

As a rule of thumb, use cell references wherever you can in a worksheet—wherever you are performing math using the contents of other cells. For example, suppose you have the worksheet shown in Figure 15-1. The gross pay could have been calculated using the values themselves, as in +40*15.65. But if you have to change either the pay rate or the number of hours worked, you'd need to reenter the value itself and retype the formula with the new value. If you'd used the cell references, +D5*D4, you'd only need to change the value; Corel Quattro Pro would recalculate the formula for you.

TIP: *If you need to use the same value in more than one cell, enter it once and reference its cell number elsewhere, as in +B2.*

You can also reference a cell on another page of the worksheet using the format *Tab:ColumnRow,* as illustrated by the cell reference on the left of the input line. For example, B:A1 refers to cell A1 on page B of the notebook. To refer to a cell in another notebook, use the syntax *[Notebook_name]Cell.*

You can add your Corel Quattro Pro worksheet to a Corel WordPerfect document with a link. Using a link ensures that the Corel WordPerfect document is updated whenever the Corel Quattro Pro worksheet is recalculated.

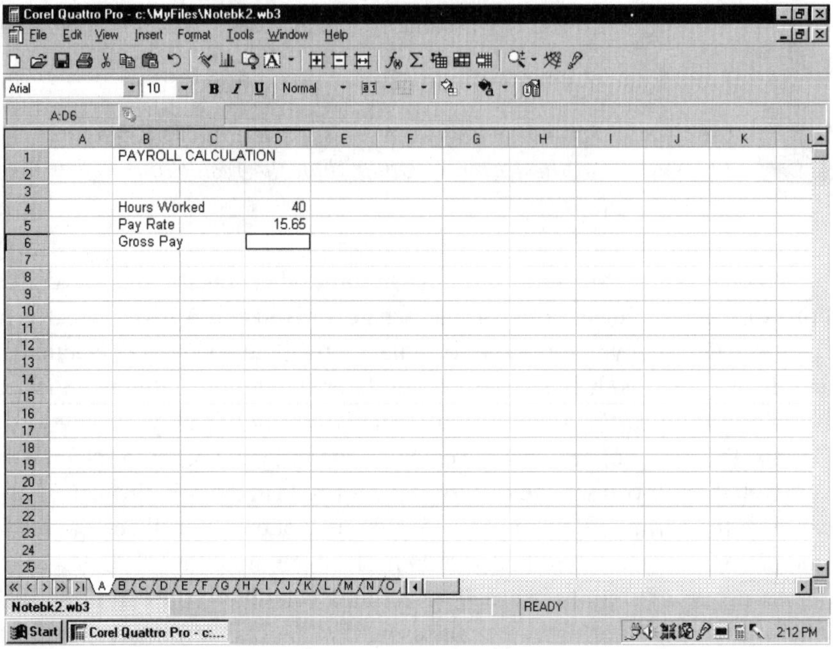

Worksheet
for
calculating
gross pay

FIGURE 15-1

Precedence of Operators

When typing formulas, remember "My Dear Aunt Sally," a memory helper for Multiplication-Division-Addition-Subtraction. Corel Quattro Pro, and almost every similar program, does not perform math in the exact order of operators from left to right. Instead, it scans the entire formula, giving precedence to certain operators over others. "My Dear Aunt Sally" means that multiplication and division are performed first (whatever order they are in) and then addition and subtraction.

The most common example of this is computing an average. If you enter the formula **+100+100+100/3** (using the values or their cell references), Corel Quattro Pro will display the result as 233.3333. It first divides 100 by 3 and then adds 100 twice.

To perform the calculation correctly, use parentheses to force Corel Quattro Pro to follow a different order, such as **(100+100+100)/3**. Notice that you can start a formula with an opening parenthesis without using a plus sign. Corel Quattro Pro assumes that entries starting with the "(" character are values.

Table 15-1 lists the operators by their order of precedence.

15

Operator	Function
^	Power of
-, +	Used to denote negative or positive
*, /	Multiplication and division
+, -	Addition and subtraction
>=	Greater than or equal to
<=	Less than or equal to
<, >	Less than, greater than
=, <>	Equal, not equal
#NOT#	Logical NOT operation
#AND#, #OR#	Logical AND, logical OR operations
&	String concatenation

Operators
by Their
Order of
Precedence

▌ TABLE 15-1

Automatic Parentheses Matching

 TIP: *Save time by not typing the parenthesis that comes at the very end of a formula. When you accept the entry, Corel Quattro Pro will add it for you.*

You can use more than one level of parentheses, if needed, with complex formulas. You must, however, have a closing parenthesis for every opening parenthesis. To help you out, Corel Quattro Pro has a parenthesis-matching feature. As you enter a formula, parentheses will appear in black when they are unmatched. When you type a closing parenthesis, the pair will change color.

Before accepting complex formulas, scan for black, unmatched parentheses. If you find any, check your formula carefully. You either need to add or to delete a parenthesis to have matching pairs while still performing the math in the order desired.

Pointing to Reference Cells

Making sure you have the correct cell reference is important, so rather than type the entry into a formula, you can point to it. This places the reference to the cell in the input line. To point to a cell, just click in it. To point to a block, drag over the cells.

For example, create the simple worksheet shown in Figure 15-1. To calculate the employee's gross pay, you need to multiply the number of hours in cell D4 times the pay rate in cell D5. You could do this by typing the formula +D4*D5. Instead of typing the cell references, however, point to them using these steps:

1. Click in cell D6 to make it active.

2. Press the + key to enter Value mode.

3. Click in cell D4. Corel Quattro Pro inserts the cell reference into the active cell so it appears as +D4.

4. Press the * key to enter the multiplication operator.

5. Click in cell D5 to enter its reference into the formula.

6. Press ENTER to accept the entry.

You can also use this technique to reference a cell or block of cells in another page of the notebook. When you want to point to the cell, click on the tab of the page where it is located, and then select the block. As soon as you enter the next operator, or accept or cancel the entry, Corel Quattro Pro will switch back to the original page.

 NOTE: *To point to noncontiguous blocks, separate each with a comma in the input line.*

Editing Formulas

You edit formulas the same way you'd edit any cell—double-click on the cell, and either select it and press F2, or select it and click in the input line.

When you edit a formula that contains cell references, however, each referenced cell will be enclosed in a blue frame. The frame shows you the values that are represented by the formulas.

To change a reference, either edit the cell address as you would any other text, or use Point mode:

1. Select the address of the cell in the formula.

2. Click on the cell you want to use as its replacement.

15

Corel Quattro Pro will insert the address of the cell in place of the selected address in the formula.

Formatting Numbers

The default format displays numbers without trailing zeros. You can easily change the format of numbers by pulling down the Number Format list in the property bar to see the options shown here:

Select from the style list either before you start typing in the cell or after you've accepted the entry. Once you start typing, the list is not displayed in the property bar. The date and heading styles are not used for numbers, but here's how the number 1234.50 will appear in each of the numeric styles:

	A	B	C
1			
2	Normal		1234.5
3	Comma		1,234.50
4	Comma0		1,235
5	Currency		$1,234.50
6	Currency0		$1,235
7	Fixed		1234.50
8	Percent		123450.00%
9	Total		1234.5

The Total style does not change how the numbers appear, but inserts a double line on the top of the cell. Choose a number format first, and then click on the Total style to add a line to it.

Both Comma0 and Currency0 display no decimal places. The Fixed style uses a set number of decimals that you can designate using the Block Properties.

If adding the dollar sign, commas, or decimal places of a style causes the cell contents to be wider than the column, the Fit-As-You-Go feature automatically widens the column for you.

Entering Dates

In addition to text and values, a cell can contain a date or a time. Dates and times are treated as values because Corel Quattro Pro can perform calculations on them, such as figuring the number of days between two dates. To be used in calculations, the date or time must be entered in one of the formats that Corel Quattro Pro recognizes.

Enter the date in any of these formats:

DD-MMM-YY	11-Nov-97
DD-MMM	11-Nov
MMM-YY	Nov-97
MM/DD/YY	11/16/97
MM/DD	11/16

The last two formats are accepted as the default Long International and Short International date formats of Corel Quattro Pro. You can change these settings to accept other formats by changing the Application Properties.

If you do not enter the year, as in 11/16, Corel Quattro Pro assumes the current year and adds it to the date using all four digits. If you enter two digits for the year, however, it tries to anticipate the turn of the century. For example, if the year 2000 has not yet arrived, Corel Quattro Pro will assume years that you enter from 51 to 99 are in the 1900s—changing 11/16/65 to 11/16/1965, for example. If you enter the years 00 to 50, it assumes you want the next century, changing 11/16/45 to 11/16/2045.

Enter times in either of these formats:

HH:MM:SS AM/PM	04:12:30 AM
HH:MM AM/PM	04:30 AM

You can also select a Long International and Short International time format using the Application Properties. If you do not enter PM, or enter time in 24-hour format, Corel Quattro Pro assumes times are AM.

When you accept a date or time entry, Corel Quattro Pro displays the date or time in the cell but shows a serial number that represents the date or time in the input line. The serial numbers for dates range from -109,571 for January 1, 1600, to 474,816 for December 31, 3199. December 30, 1899, is represented by serial number 0. The serial number for a time is a decimal between 0.000 for the stroke of midnight and 0.99999 for one second before midnight the next day.

Corel Quattro Pro uses the serial numbers to perform math operations. To calculate the number of days between two dates, for example, just subtract the cell reference of the first date from the last date, such as +B6-B3. The number that appears is the difference between their serial numbers.

 TIP: *You can use Block Properties to force a cell to only accept date formats.*

Totaling Numbers Using QuickSum

 One of the most typical uses for a formula is to total a series of numbers in a column or row. This is such a common task that Corel Quattro Pro gives it its own button on the toolbar, the QuickSum button.

If the values in a column are contiguous—that is, there are no blank cells among them—click in the blank cell below the last value and then on the QuickSum button. If the values are in a row with no blank cells between them, click in the blank cell to the right of the last value and then on QuickSum. Corel Quattro Pro will calculate and display the total of the cells above (or to the left) of the active cell.

When the cells are not contiguous, select the cells first, including the blank cell below or to the right of the series, and then click on QuickSum. The total will appear in the blank cell. To create the total, Corel Quattro Pro uses the built-in function @SUM that you'll see in the input line. The function uses a range reference, citing the first and last cells in the group to be added, such as @SUM(A1..A12).

 NOTE: *All functions begin with the @ symbol.*

Always check the range reference, especially when you did not select the cells first, to confirm that the correct cells have been included. If the range is incorrect, edit it or point to the range using these steps:

1. Make the cell containing the function active.

2. Click in the input line.

3. Drag over the range reference in the input line that you want to replace. You do not have to delete the range, as long as you leave it selected.

4. Drag over the range in the worksheet.

5. Accept the entry.

You can calculate totals for several rows and columns of numbers at one time. The selection in Figure 15-2, for instance, will calculate totals for the rows and for the columns, as well as a grand total in cell F12.

Using Calc-As-You-Go

If you are interested in the total, average, or other statistic about a range of cells, but don't necessarily want to add it to the worksheet, then use Calc-As-You-Go.

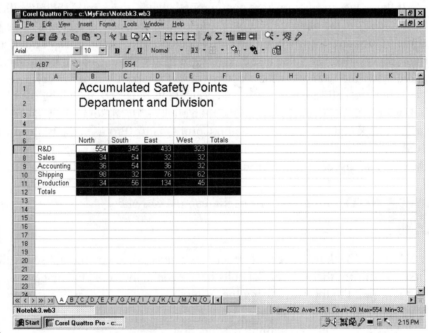

Selecting cells to total rows and columns and create a grand total in one step

FIGURE 15-2

When you select a range of cells and release the mouse button, Coral Quattro Pro will display information on the right of the application bar, as shown here:

In addition to the total (Sum) and average (Ave) of the cells, Count displays the number of cells containing numeric values, Max shows the largest value in the range, and Min shows the smallest. Calc-As-You-Go ignores blank cells and cells with labels. If you want a blank cell included in the statistics, enter a zero in it.

Using QuickCell

Once you start referencing cells in formulas, you may want to see the effects of your work on a specific cell. For example, suppose you have a worksheet that calculates an estimate for a proposal. As you add or change values in the worksheet, you want to see how the total estimate is affected.

This is not a problem if the cell is displayed onscreen; but with larger worksheets, the cell might be scrolled out of view. Rather than scroll back and forth between the cell and the area where you are working, insert the cell into the QuickCell box, the second box in the application bar. Now, as you work, you'll see the contents of that cell displayed in the status line, even if the cell itself does not appear onscreen:

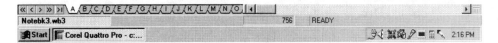

To add the cell to the status line, use either of these techniques:

- Click on the cell, right-click on the status line, and choose Display Current Cell in QuickCell from the QuickMenu.

- Drag the cell to the QuickCell box using drag-and-drop, as you'll learn in Chapter 16.

To remove the cell from the QuickCell, right-click on the status line and choose Clear QuickCell from the QuickMenu.

Entering Data with QuickFill

In many instances, row and column labels are a series of sequential entries, such as the months of the year or incrementing numbers. These types of entries are so common that Corel Quattro Pro gives you QuickFill, a way of entering a sequence without typing the entire series yourself. This works as follows:

1. Enter the first one or two values of the series. These are called the *seed values.*

2. Select the seed values and the remaining cells in the row, column, or block that you want to fill with the remaining sequence.

3. Click on the QuickFill button, and Corel Quattro Pro will complete the range for you.

  NOTE: *You can also right-click and select QuickFill from the QuickMenu.*

Let's try it:

1. Type **Jan** in cell A1.

2. Click on the Enter button.

3. Drag over cells A1 to L1 and then click on QuickFill. Corel Quattro Pro automatically completes the series, inserting the month labels "Feb" to "Dec."

Table 15-2 shows the single seed values that Corel Quattro Pro recognizes.

When the values you want are not consecutive, enter the first two or three of the series. For example, to number rows with even numbers, enter **2** in one row and enter **4** in the next row. QuickFill will complete the sequence of even numbers in the selected cells.

Seed Values	Sequence
1st	2nd, 3rd, 4th, 5th…
Qtr 1	Qtr 2, Qtr 3, Qtr 4, Qtr 1…
1st Quarter	2nd Quarter, 3rd Quarter…
Jan	Feb, Mar…
January	February, March…
Mon	Tue, Wed, Thu…
Monday	Tuesday, Wednesday…
Week 1	Week 2, Week 3…
Jan 97	Feb 97, Mar 97, Apr 97…
100 Days	101 Days, 102 Days, 103 Days…
1,3,5	7, 9, 11, 13…
11/16/97	11/17/97, 11/18/97…

Seed
Values for
QuickFill

TABLE 15-2

When QuickFill does not complete the series, or when you don't want to drag across a large number of cells, use the Fill option in the Edit menu. Here's how:

1. Click in the cells that you want to fill.

2. Pull down the Edit menu, point to Fill, and click on Fill Series. The dialog box shown in Figure 15-3 appears.

3. The reference for the current active cell or selected range of cells will be in the Cells box. If the range is incorrect, enter a new range, or use Point mode to select it, and click on the Maximize button in the Data Fill title bar.

4. Once the range is set to the cells you want to fill, enter the starting value that you want to place in the first cell. The starting value can be a number, a date, or a time.

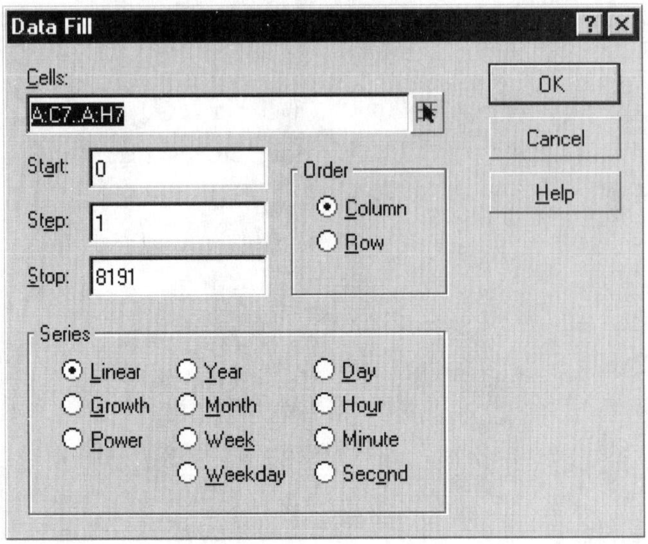

Data Fill
dialog box

FIGURE 15-3

5. Enter a step value that you want to increment the series by. A step value of 2, for example, would display every other number, date, or time, depending on the series.

6. Enter a stop value. Corel Quattro Pro will stop the series when it reaches the last cell in the range or the stop value, whichever is reached first. If you enter a date as the start value, enter a stop value of at least 50,000. Remember that Corel Quattro Pro converts dates to serial numbers, so you need an ending serial number certain to be larger than the last date in the series.

7. Choose if you want them to be filled by column or by row. Filling by column, for example, will add the series down the cells, filling out the first column and then continuing in the column to the right until the range is filled. Using row fill will complete the series in the cells across the first row, then the second row, and so forth.

8. Choose the type of series that you want to complete. If the values are numbers, Linear increases it by the step value, Growth multiplies the step value by the previous value, and Power uses the step value as an exponent.

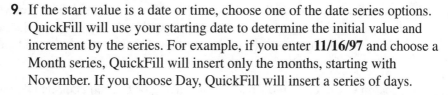

9. If the start value is a date or time, choose one of the date series options. QuickFill will use your starting date to determine the initial value and increment by the series. For example, if you enter **11/16/97** and choose a Month series, QuickFill will insert only the months, starting with November. If you choose Day, QuickFill will insert a series of days.

10. Click on OK.

If none of the series options suits your needs, you can create and save your own custom QuickFill lists. A *list* is a series of values that you can have QuickFill insert for you. For example, suppose your company uses two-letter state abbreviations for column headings. You can create a QuickFill list to access the abbreviations when you need them. To create a list, use these steps:

1. Click on any empty cell.

2. Click on the QuickFill button. You can also right-click on the cell and choose QuickFill from the QuickMenu, or choose Define QuickFill from the Edit Fill menu. The box that appears lists the built-in series that Corel Quattro Pro uses for QuickFill.

3. Click on the Create button to display the dialog box shown in Figure 15-4.

4. Type a series name that you will later use to select the series for a QuickFill operation.

5. In the Series Type section, choose List. Choosing Formula lets you enter formulas as the series elements. Choosing the Repeating option will cause the list to start over again each time every element has been inserted once.

6. In the Series Elements text box, type the first item in the series and then click on Add.

7. Insert the other items in the list the same way. Each item will be added to the bottom of the list. If you want to insert an item elsewhere in the list, click on the list where you want to add it, type the new item, and then click on Insert. Use the Delete button to remove an item from the list, and use Modify to change an element.

8. If you've already typed the values in a worksheet, you do not have to type them again. Click on Extract. In the dialog box that appears, enter or point to the range that contains the value. If you want the extracted range to

replace the values in the list, click on Override Existing Values. When you click on OK, the items from the worksheet will be inserted into the list. Extract is useful because you can enter the values in a worksheet and then sort them before adding them to the list.

9. Click on OK to close the Create Series dialog box. Then click on OK to close the QuickFill dialog box.

Now when you want to use your list for a QuickFill operation, use these steps:

1. Select the cells you want to fill.

2. Choose QuickFill from the QuickMenu, or choose Define Fill Series from the Data menu.

3. Pull down the Series list, and click on the name of your custom list.

4. Click on OK.

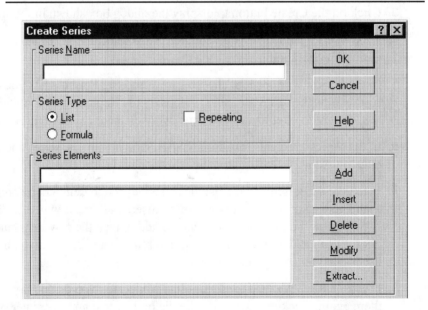

Dialog box for creating your own QuickFill series

FIGURE 15-4

Inserting a Comment

When you want to make a note to yourself or another user, you can add a comment directly to a cell. The comment will appear onscreen as a QuickTip when you point to the cell, so it is useful to explain the type of information that should be inserted, or how a formula was calculated. Here's how:

1. Click on the cell that you want to add a comment to.

2. Select Comment from the Insert menu, or right-click and choose Insert Comment from the QuickMenu menu. You will see a balloon pointing to the cell.

3. Type the text of the comment.

4. Click outside of the balloon.

Corel Quattro Pro displays a small triangle in the top-right corner of the cell indicating that it contains a comment. When you point to the cell, the comment appears as a QuickTip.

To edit the comment, right-click on the cell and choose Edit Comment from the QuickMenu, or choose Comment from the Insert menu. To delete a comment, right-click on the cell and choose Delete Comment from the QuickMenu.

Changing Column Width

If your entry is too wide for the cell, widen the column so you can see the full text or number. You can also reduce column width to display more columns on the screen and on the printed page. Reducing column width is useful for columns that have short entries—just a character or two—where space is being wasted.

To quickly change the width of a column so it is as wide as the widest entry, click on the column letter to select the entire column, and then click on the QuickFit button in the toolbar. You can also double-click on the right boundary of the column header. Corel Quattro Pro will widen or reduce the column as necessary.

If you want to make the column as wide as a specific entry, click on the cell and then on QuickFit. Corel Quattro Pro will adjust the column around the entry in the cell, so longer entries elsewhere in the column will not show entirely.

You can also change the width of a column by dragging. Point to the line to the right of the column letter—the line between the column and the column to its right. The mouse pointer will change to a double-headed arrow. Hold down the left mouse button, and drag the pointer until the column is the size you want.

To resize several columns to the same width, select the columns by dragging over their column letters, and then change the size of any one of the selected columns. When you release the mouse, all of the selected columns will be the same size as the changed column.

 NOTE: *Column width and row height also can be set by use of properties, as explained in Chapter 16.*

Changing Row Height

You can also adjust the height of rows by dragging. Point to the line under the row letter so the mouse pointer appears as a two-headed arrow and then drag. Resize several rows by selecting them first.

Printing Worksheets

You'll probably want a hard copy of your worksheet for reference or distribution. To print the worksheet, just click on the Print button on the toolbar. Corel Quattro Pro will print your worksheet, using all of the default print settings.

For more control over the printing process, use this technique:

1. Select Print from the File menu to see the dialog box shown in Figure 15-5.

2. Make sure that the Current Sheet button is selected.

3. Click on the Print button. This will print the entire contents of the worksheet.

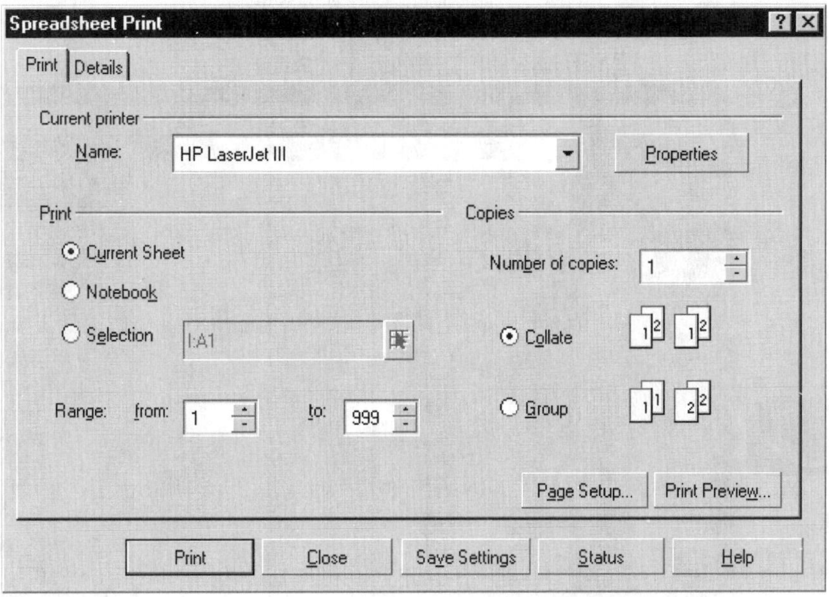

Print
dialog box

FIGURE 15-5

Previewing Before Printing

You can always tell which cells will print by looking at the Block text box in the Spreadsheet Print dialog box. If you want to see how the block will print, select Print Preview from the File menu, or click on the Print Preview button if you've already opened the Spreadsheet Print dialog box, to see a screen, as in Figure 15-6. Corel Quattro Pro reduces the image so you can see an entire printed page at one time.

To enlarge the image so it is easier to read, move the mouse pointer over the representation of the page so it appears like a magnifying lens. Now each time you click the left mouse button, the magnification will be doubled—from 100% to 200%, then to 400%, up to 1600%.

Each time you click the right mouse button, the image will be reduced to the previous magnification back down to 100%.

Use the Print Preview toolbar to adjust the image and select options, as shown in Figure 15-6. When you are satisfied with the print preview, click on the Print button to print the worksheet as it is displayed, or close the Print Preview window to change the print range or to return to the worksheet.

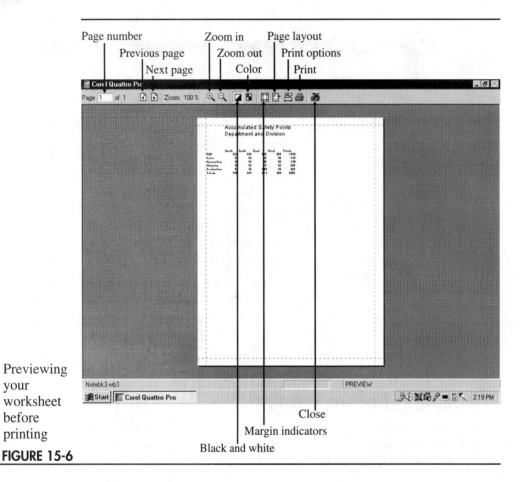

Page number

Previous page

Next page

Zoom in

Zoom out

Color

Page layout

Print options

Print

Previewing your worksheet before printing

Close

Margin indicators

Black and white

FIGURE 15-6

Saving Your Worksheet

Soon after you begin entering information into your worksheet, you should save the worksheet on your disk. You wouldn't want to lose any of your work if your computer suddenly were to act up. When you are ready to save your worksheet, follow these steps:

1. Click on the Save button. If this is the first time you've saved the notebook, you'll see the Save File dialog box.

2. Type a document name in the Name text box.

3. Click on Save. Corel Quattro Pro saves documents with the WB3 extension.

TIP: *You can use Version Control to save versions of the worksheet, just as you learned how to do for Corel WordPerfect documents.*

Once you save a notebook the first time, you'll need to save it again if you make changes to it. When you click on Save, Corel Quattro Pro saves it immediately under the same name without displaying a dialog box. If you want to save the edited copy under a new name, select Save As from the File menu and then save the file as if it were being saved for the first time.

Closing Notebooks

To close the notebook, click on the notebook's Close button, or select Close from the File menu. If you did not save the notebook since you last changed it, a dialog box will appear giving you the chance to do so. Closing the notebook does not exit Corel Quattro Pro, so you can start a new notebook or open one on your disk.

Opening a Notebook

There are several ways that you can open an existing notebook. To quickly open one of the last notebooks you worked with, use either of these methods:

■ Pull down the File menu, and click on the notebook's name in the list.

■ Select New from the File menu, click on the Work On tab, then double-click on the file you want to open.

To open a notebook not listed on the File menu or in the New dialog box, use these steps:

1. Click on the Open button or choose Open from the File menu to display the Open File dialog box.

2. Select the file, changing folders or drives if necessary. If worksheets are not listed, pull down the File Type list and choose QPW v7/v8 ("*.WB3").

3. Click on Open.

File Formats

Corel Quattro Pro lets you save worksheets in formats other than its own, and it allows you to open files created by other spreadsheet and database programs. This means that you can share files with others who do not have Corel Quattro Pro, and that you can use other programs to analyze and work with your Corel Quattro Pro information.

Use the Open command to retrieve data from a Paradox database to analyze it using Corel Quattro Pro or to open an HTML document created with Corel WordPerfect's Internet Publisher.

To open a file in some other format, pull down the File Type list in the Open dialog box, and choose the type of file you wish to open. Then locate and select the file using the File Name, Folders, and Drives boxes. To save a file in another format, pull down the Save As Type list in the Save As dialog box, and click on the file type. Corel Quattro Pro can open and save files in these formats:

Corel Quattro Pro for Windows and DOS	Text
Microsoft Excel	DIF
Lotus 1-2-3	SYLK
Paradox	HTML (Web documents)
dBASE	

Starting a New Notebook

To start a new notebook, click on the New button to display a new blank notebook onscreen.

You can also use the New command from the File menu to start a new notebook or to load a completely formatted notebook already designed for a specific purpose, such as tracking accounts receivable, computing your net worth, or printing a purchase order. Follow these steps:

1. Select New from the File menu. You'll see the dialog box shown in Figure 15-7.

2. To start a new blank notebook, select [Quattro Pro Notebook] on the Create New page and then click on OK.

3. To load a formatted notebook, select one of the projects from the Create New page and then click on OK.

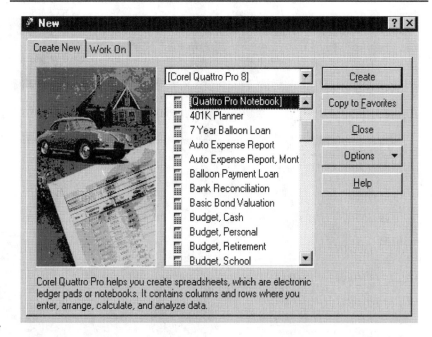

Using a template to create a professional worksheet

FIGURE 15-7

When the project opens, add the information required and then save and print it. The Personal Budget project is shown in Figure 15-8, along with the Perfect Expert box.

While each Project is different, there are certain common elements in the Perfect Expert box.

- There are cells designed for data entry, where you need to enter your own information without replacing built-in formulas and functions. If these cells are not highlighted, making them easy to identify, click on the Turn Highlight On/Off button.

- Click on the Insert Sample Data button to fill the data entry cells with sample information so you can see how the template is used.

- When you are ready to enter your own information, click on the Remove Sample Data button.

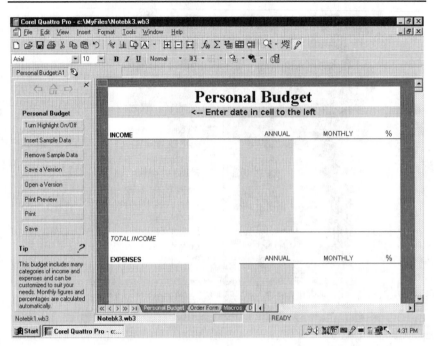

Personal
Budget
project

FIGURE 15-8

Using Budget Expert

An *Expert* is a series of dialog boxes that leads you step-by-step through a complete task. The Budget Expert will help you create a formatted budget document—all you have to enter are the numbers. To start the Expert, follow these steps:

1. Pull down the Tools menu, point to Numeric Tools, and click on Budget. Now select options in a series of dialog boxes, clicking on the button labeled "Next Step" after you've completed each dialog box. In the first box, select the type of budget you want to create. Your choices are

   ■ Home—Actual

   ■ Home—Actual vs Plan

   ■ Business—Actual

   ■ Business—Actual vs Plan

■ Business Income Statement

2. Select the type of budget you want to create and then click on Next. The second box lists several sample sources of funds. You can delete sources that are not appropriate and add your own.

3. To add a source, type it in the New Item text box and then click on Add.

4. To delete a source, click on it in the list and then click on Delete.

5. When you are satisfied with the list, click on Next. The next dialog box lists sample items where your money goes. Add or delete items and then click on Next.

6. You now need to select the period for the budget, the starting date, and the duration. Click on the desired period: Monthly, Quarterly, or Yearly.

7. Select a starting date. The options that appear depend on the period. If you selected Monthly, you can choose a starting month and year. If you selected Quarterly, you can choose a starting quarter and year. If you selected Yearly, you can select only a starting year.

8. Select the duration of the budget: the number of months, quarters, or years.

9. Click on Next.

10. Select summation options: Quarter-to-date or Year-to-date.

11. Click on Next.

12. In the next dialog box, enter a worksheet title and subtitle. Then click on Next.

13. Choose whether to insert the budget in a new notebook or the current one. Then click on Next.

14. Depending on the selected period, you can now choose to change pages each month, quarter, or year. You can also choose to display the worksheet in color or in monochrome for output to a laser printer.

15. Click on Finish and Corel Quattro Pro does the rest.

 NOTE: *In Chapter 19, you'll learn how to use other Experts to save time.*

Editing and Formatting Worksheets

16

It is as easy to edit your worksheet—even make major changes to it—as it is to create it. You can insert and delete information, change its appearance and format, and move and copy information until the worksheet is perfect.

Erasing Information from Cells

Sometimes you'll want to erase all of the information from a cell rather than just edit it. You have two choices: clearing and deleting. Although these have similar effects, they are in some ways quite different. *Clearing* removes the contents from a cell, row, or column, but leaves the cells in the worksheet. *Deleting* actually removes the cells from the worksheet, moving any remaining cells up or over to take the deleted cells' place. If you clear row 5, for example, the row itself remains empty in the worksheet. If you delete row 5, then row 6 moves up to take its place, and it becomes the new row 5.

Clearing Cells

Choose clearing when you do not want to change the position of other information in the worksheet. You can clear everything from a cell, just the characters, or just the format. Here's how:

1. Select the block you want to clear.

2. Pull down the Edit menu, point to Clear, and select one of these options:

    ■ *Cells* clears all characters and formats from a cell, returning all of the default properties.

    ■ *Values* clears just the displayed contents, leaving formats such as alignment and shading. If you later enter information in the cell, it will automatically take on the formats stored there.

    ■ *Formats* leaves the contents in the cell but returns the cell to the default formats.

    ■ *Comments* clears just the comment from the cell.

NOTE: *Pressing DEL also clears the contents.*

3. To erase the contents of the entire sheet, click on the Select All button (or choose Select All from the Edit menu) and then press DEL.

Deleting Blocks

When you delete a block, you are actually removing it from the worksheet. If you delete rows or columns, the remaining ones are renumbered. If you just delete a block of cells, other cells in the row or column shift into their position.

To delete a block, select it and then use any of these techniques:

- Click the Delete button in the toolbar.
- Choose Delete from the Edit menu.
- Right-click on the selection, and choose Delete Cells from the QuickMenu.

To delete entire rows or columns, select the ones you want to remove by clicking on their headers. When you choose Delete, Corel Quattro Pro will remove them immediately. When you delete a cell or block of cells, Corel Quattro Pro will first display the dialog box shown in Figure 16-1, which asks how much you want to delete. When this box is displayed, use these steps to ensure that the correct cells are deleted:

1. If the block reference is incorrect, enter or point to the proper reference.
2. Select the Dimension that you want to delete: Columns, Rows, or Sheets.
3. Select a Span option: Entire or Partial.
4. Click on OK.

When Entire is selected in Span, Corel Quattro Pro will delete the entire column, row, or sheet (based on the Dimension setting) in which the selected cells are located. So, if you select cell C5 and choose Entire and Rows, all of row 5 will be deleted, not just the single cell.

Selecting
what you
want to
delete

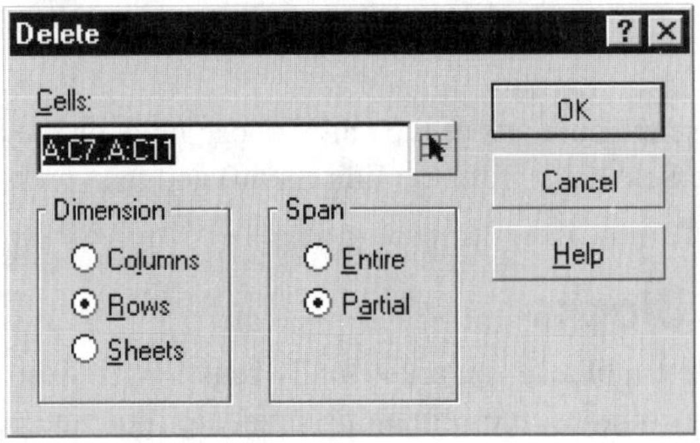

FIGURE 16-1

To remove just the selected cells, not their entire row or column, click on Partial. Your choice in the Dimension section determines what cells take the place of the deleted ones. If you choose Rows, for example, the cells below the deleted cells will move up. If you select Columns, the cells to the right of the deleted cells will move over. Perhaps the best way to visualize this is to look at Figure 16-2. On the left of the figure is the original block of cells showing the ones to be deleted. In the center is the same block of cells after Columns was chosen in the Delete dialog box. On the right is the same block after Rows was chosen.

REMEMBER: *When you select Partial, only the cells selected will be deleted. Existing cells will move up or over, and they will no longer appear in the same row or column as they were originally. If the contents relate to a label, then the label may no longer be in the same row or column. Thus, make certain that is the effect you want to achieve.*

NOTE: *To delete the entire sheet, right-click on it and choose Delete Sheet from the QuickMenu.*

Inserting Blocks

No matter how well you plan, you may have to insert cells into the worksheet. When you insert cells, existing ones shift down or to the right to make room. You insert using either the Insert button in the toolbar or the Insert Cells option from the QuickMenu.

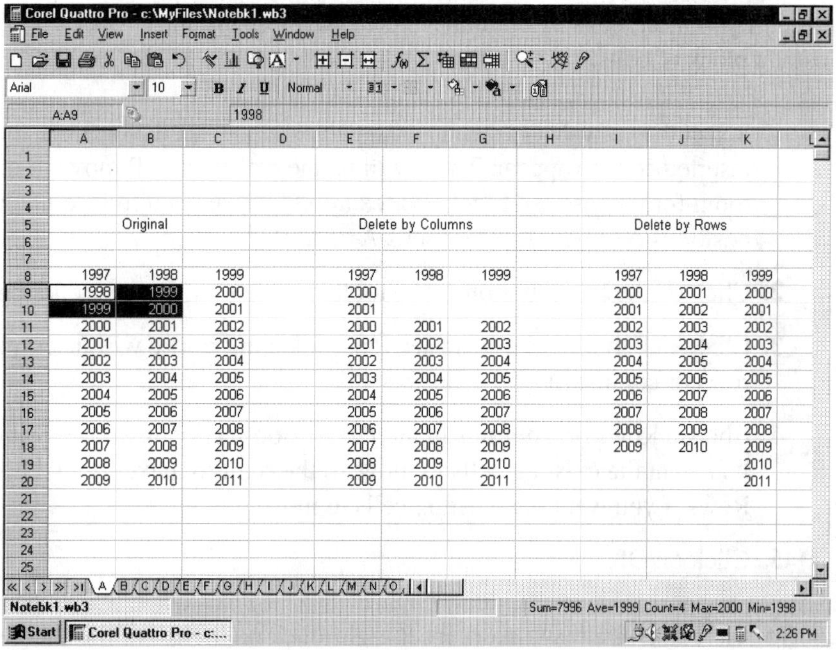

The different effects of deleting by rows and by columns

FIGURE 16-2

To insert an entire row, use these steps:

1. Click on the number of the row that you want to shift down. For example, to insert a new row number 5, click on the row 5 header.

2. Click on the Insert button in the toolbar. A new row will be inserted, causing the remaining ones to be renumbered.

3. To insert an entire column, click on the letter of the column that you want to shift to the right and then click on the Insert button.

4. To insert several rows or columns at one time, select the desired number of rows or columns before clicking on Insert. To insert two rows, for instance, drag to select two entire rows. To insert four columns, drag to select four columns.

You can also insert a cell or block of cells into the worksheet, rather than entire rows or columns. As with deleting, you can choose to perform the operation by row or by column. If you insert cells by row, then cells below will move down to make room. If you insert cells by column, cells to the right will move over. Here's how to insert a block of cells:

1. Select the cells that currently occupy the space where you want the inserted cells to appear. These will be the cells that will move to make room for the inserted block. For example, if you want to insert cells in positions A1 and B1, select cells A1 and B1.

2. Click on the Insert button in the toolbar to display the Insert dialog box.

3. Click on Partial in the Span section. (Selecting Entire will insert entire rows or columns.)

4. Choose Rows or Columns in the Dimension section. Choose Columns if you want the existing cells to move to the right to make room; choose Rows if you want the existing cells to move down.

5. Click on OK.

To insert an entire blank worksheet, right-click on the tab of the sheet you want to follow the new one, and then choose Insert Sheet from the QuickMenu. Corel Quattro Pro will insert a new sheet, adjusting the tab letters as needed.

 TIP: *Change the name on the sheet tab by double-clicking on the tab, or by right-clicking on it and choosing Edit Sheet Name from the QuickMenu. Type the name you want and then press ENTER.*

Moving and Copying Information

The capability to move and copy information from one location to another is as useful in Corel Quattro Pro as it is in Corel WordPerfect. You may need to move information when you've entered it in the wrong location, or when you want to copy it to avoid having to reenter it elsewhere. Copying information is especially useful when you need similar formulas in several locations, even when the cell references are not exactly the same.

Before moving or copying information, however, you need to decide how you are going to do it, because Corel Quattro Pro gives you three choices: drag-and-drop, the Clipboard, and the Copy Cells command.

Using Drag-and-Drop

Drag-and-drop works about the same as in all Corel Suite applications. You can drag and drop a single cell or a block of selected cells, as long as they are contiguous—that is, the cells must be next to each other and selected as one group. The advantage of drag-and-drop over other methods is that you can see where you are placing the information. Here is how it works:

1. Start by selecting the block of cells that you want to move.

2. Point to an edge of the selected block until the pointer appears like a four-headed arrow.

3. Press and hold down the mouse button so the selection is surrounded by a colored outline.

4. Drag the mouse; a colored outline will move along with it.

5. When the outline is in the desired location, release the mouse button. Corel Quattro Pro moves both the contents and format of the cell, so the original cell will be returned to its default format.

To move or copy cells to another open notebook, drag the cells to the notebook name on the application bar. Corel Quattro Pro will display the notebook so you can drop the cells in the appropriate location. Remember, to copy the cells, hold down the CTRL key when you release the mouse button.

 NOTE: *Depending on the speed of your system, it may take a little time for the colored outline to appear as you drag.*

To copy a block using drag-and-drop, hold down the CTRL key when you drag and drop. Technically, you have to hold down the CTRL key only when you release the mouse button, not the entire time. Just make sure that the plus sign appears before you release the button. If it does not, move the mouse slightly but make sure the colored outline remains where you want it.

To drag and drop an entire sheet, drag the sheet tab. As you drag, an outline of the tab with a plus sign in it will move with the mouse. Release the mouse when the tab is where you want the sheet. Hold down the CTRL key to copy the sheet rather than move it.

 NOTE: *If you did not rename the sheet, Corel Quattro Pro places the moved sheet in alphabetical order; it does not move the original sheet letter to the new position.*

You can also move a worksheet with the Move Sheets option from the Edit menu. In the dialog box that appears, enter the number of the sheet you want to move and the number of the sheet you want to move it ahead of and then click on OK.

Using the Clipboard

Moving and copying blocks with the Clipboard are standard Windows techniques—use any of these options:

- Cut, Copy, and Paste buttons in the toolbar

- Cut, Copy, and Paste options from the Edit menu

- Cut, Copy, and Paste from the QuickMenu

- CTRL-X (Cut), CTRL-C (Copy), and CTRL-V (Paste) key combinations

The Clipboard gives you several advantages over drag-and-drop. Once the information is in the Clipboard, for example, you can paste it as many times as you want. You can paste the same information in several locations after cutting or copying it just once. With drag-and-drop, you'd have to select the information each time.

You can also select and then cut or copy noncontiguous cells. Hold down the CTRL key while you select the cells, and paste them in a new location. Drag-and-drop won't allow that. Use the following steps for this operation:

1. Select the block you want to move.

2. Choose Cut using any of the methods just described.

3. Click where you want to place the block. If you are moving a block of cells, click where you want the upper-left corner of the block to begin.

4. Choose Paste.

Copy information the same way but using the Copy command instead of Cut.

Using Paste Special

When you copy using drag-and-drop or the Clipboard, Corel Quattro Pro copies everything in the block, including the contents and formats, called *properties*. You have more control over what gets pasted using the Paste Special command. When you are ready to paste your copied cells, use the following steps:

1. Select Paste Special from the Edit menu to see the dialog box shown in Figure 16-3.

2. In the Paste section, select what types of cells in the Clipboard you want to paste.

3. Deselect the appropriate checkboxes if you do not want to paste formulas, labels, or numbers. Deselect the Properties box if you do not want to include the formats with the pasted cells. Select Cell Comments if you want to include comments that are attached to the cells.

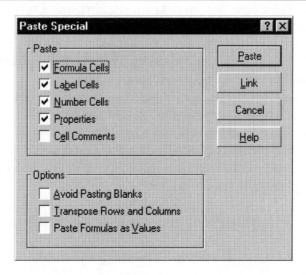

Paste
Special
dialog box

FIGURE 16-3

The following settings in the Options section determine how objects are pasted:

■ *Avoid Pasting Blanks* will not overwrite the existing contents of a cell by pasting a blank cell into it.

■ *Transpose Rows and Columns* rearranges the pasted cells, placing copied rows into columns and columns into rows.

■ *Paste Formulas as Values* pastes the *results* of formulas, not the formulas themselves.

When you've selected your options from the box, click on Paste. You can also click on Link, which inserts a reference to the original cells; so if you change a value in the original cells, it will change in the linked position as well.

Using the Copy Cells Command

The Copy Cells command from the Edit menu is yet another way to copy cells. However, this command lets you use block names, and you can control what properties of a block are copied.

 NOTE: *You'll learn about naming blocks in Chapter 17.*

Select the block that you want to copy, and choose Copy Cells from the Edit menu to see the dialog box shown in Figure 16-4. If the reference in the From box is incorrect, enter it manually or use Point mode to select the block.

In the To box, enter or point to the location where you want to copy the block. You only need to select the upper-left corner.

The Model Copy option lets you select what elements of the block you want to copy. When the option is not selected, Corel Quattro Pro copies everything—contents, formats, formulas, properties, objects, and the row and column sizes. If you want to copy only certain elements, click on the Model Copy option, then remove the checks from the elements you do not want to move. For example, deselecting Formula Cells will not copy any cells that contain formulas.

 NOTE: *When Model Copy is turned on, absolute references are also adjusted.*

Copy Cells   ? ✕

From: A:E9..E13   ▶   OK

To: A:E9..E13   ▶   Cancel

☐ Model Copy   Help

☑ Formula Cells
☑ Label Cells
☑ Number Cells
☑ Properties
☑ Objects
☑ Row/Column Sizes
☐ Cell Comments

Copy Cells
dialog box

◼ FIGURE 16-4

Moving and Copying Formulas

You can use any of the techniques described to move formulas from one cell to another. When you move a cell containing a formula, the same formula is placed in the pasted cell. When you copy a formula, however, it is copied using a relative reference. This means that the cell references in the formula are adjusted to use corresponding cells in the new location.

As an example, look at the worksheet in Figure 16-5. This worksheet needs a number of formulas. The income and expenses in each column must be totaled, and then expenses must be subtracted from income to calculate the net profit in the quarter columns. Because of the way Corel Quattro Pro copies formulas, you only need to enter them once—in the first column—and then copy them across the rows.

Create the worksheet that you see in the figure, using the following steps. (Use QuickFill to repeat the Rent and Insurance figures across the row in the Expenses section.)

1. In cell B7, click on the QuickSum button to add the total. Notice that the input line shows *@SUM*(B5..B6).

2. Click on cell B7 and drag over to select up to cell E7.

3. Point to the selection, press the right mouse button, and click on QuickFill from the QuickMenu. (You could also click on the QuickFill button in the toolbar.) Corel Quattro Pro copies the formula across the selected cells.

4. Click on cell C7 and look at the formula in the input line: *@SUM*(C5..C6). Corel Quattro Pro did not copy the exact formula, which totals values in column B, but adjusted it to total the values in the cells above it in column C. The formulas in the remaining cells have been adjusted as well.

In a sense, Corel Quattro Pro sees the formula in cell B7 as saying, "Total the values in the two cells above." So when it copies the formula, the cell references automatically change to reflect the two cells above the formula (each formula really says the same thing). Continue this process.

5. Enter the total in cell B15 and copy it across the row to cell E15.

6. In cell B17, enter the formula **+B7-B15** to compute net income.

7. Copy the formula across the row to cell E17.

You've completed the worksheet with 12 formulas by entering only three.

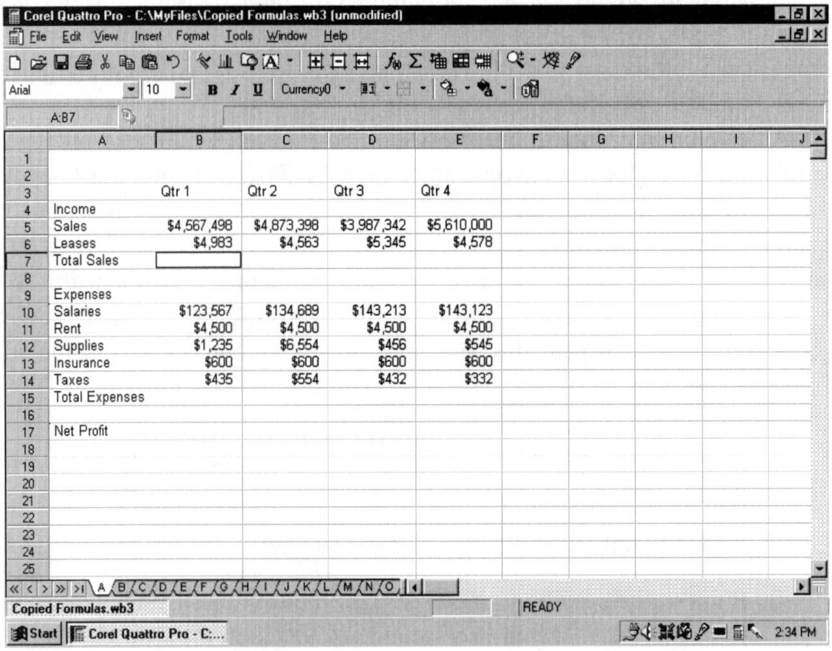

Corel Quattro Pro - C:\MyFiles\Copied Formulas.wb3 (unmodified)				
File Edit View Insert Format Tools Window Help				
A:B7				
	A	B	C	D	E
1					
2					
3		Qtr 1	Qtr 2	Qtr 3	Qtr 4
4	Income				
5	Sales	$4,567,498	$4,873,398	$3,987,342	$5,610,000
6	Leases	$4,983	$4,563	$5,345	$4,578
7	Total Sales				
8					
9	Expenses				
10	Salaries	$123,567	$134,689	$143,213	$143,123
11	Rent	$4,500	$4,500	$4,500	$4,500
12	Supplies	$1,235	$6,554	$456	$545
13	Insurance	$600	$600	$600	$600
14	Taxes	$435	$554	$432	$332
15	Total Expenses				
16					
17	Net Profit				

Copied Formulas.wb3   READY

Worksheet to use with copied formulas

FIGURE 16-5

Cell Reference Checker

As you just learned, relative references make it easy to complete a worksheet, but they can create problems. For example, you could copy a formula to a location where the relative reference has no meaning, such as copying a Sum formula to a location where there are no values to total.

Fortunately, Corel Quattro Pro can help with the *Cell Reference Checker*. When you copy a formula, Corel Quattro Pro checks to determine if the newly referenced cells contain the appropriate types of values. If they do not, it indicates the range of cells affected and displays the Cell Reference Checker dialog box with a brief description of the problem, as shown here:

Qtr 1	Qtr 2	Qtr 3	Qtr 4	
$4,567,498	$4,873,398	$3,987,342	$5,610,000	
$4,983	$4,563	$5,345	$4,578	
$4,572,481	$4,877,961	$3,992,687	$5,614,578	
$123,567	$134,689	$143,213	$143,123	
$4,500	$4,500	$4,500	$4,500	
$1,235	$6,554	$456	$545	
$600				
$435				
$130,337				
$4,442,144				
$0				

Cell Reference Checker [?] [X]

Fix It   Undo Fix   Close

This formula is using an empty cell.   Help

Details >>

If you click on the Fix It button, the program displays the correction it will make by showing the cells that will be referenced in the formula. In this example, the Cell Reference Checker is indicating that it will use the same cells referenced in the original formula:

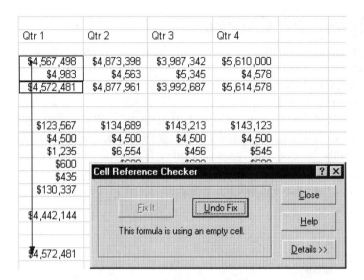

You can also click on Details to see the original formula and the formula that will be inserted by the Cell Reference Checker. Click on Close if you agree with the correction; click on Undo Fix if you don't.

Copying Values of Formulas

In most cases, you enter formulas in such a way that they will recalculate if referenced cells change. Sometimes, however, you may want to copy the results of formulas to other cells without changing the values in the new location. You can paste formulas as values using the Paste Special dialog box, or by following these steps:

1. Select the block that contains the formulas.

2. Select Convert to Values from the Edit menu. A dialog box will appear with two boxes, From and To.

3. In the To box, enter or point to the destination where you want to copy the values.

4. Click on OK.

CAUTION: *By default, the From and To boxes will contain the coordinates of the selected block. If you leave the To block unchanged, the formulas will be replaced by their values.*

Absolute References

In most cases, you want Corel Quattro Pro to adjust cell references when you copy a formula, but not always. There are times when you'll want to copy a cell reference exactly as it appears. This is called an *absolute reference.*

For example, look at the worksheet in Figure 16-6. The worksheet will calculate costs based on the labor charges in cell B3. In several cells, we need a formula that multiplies the hours in row 7 times the labor cost to calculate the labor charges. We can do this easily by entering a formula such as **+B7*B3** in cell B8. But if we copy

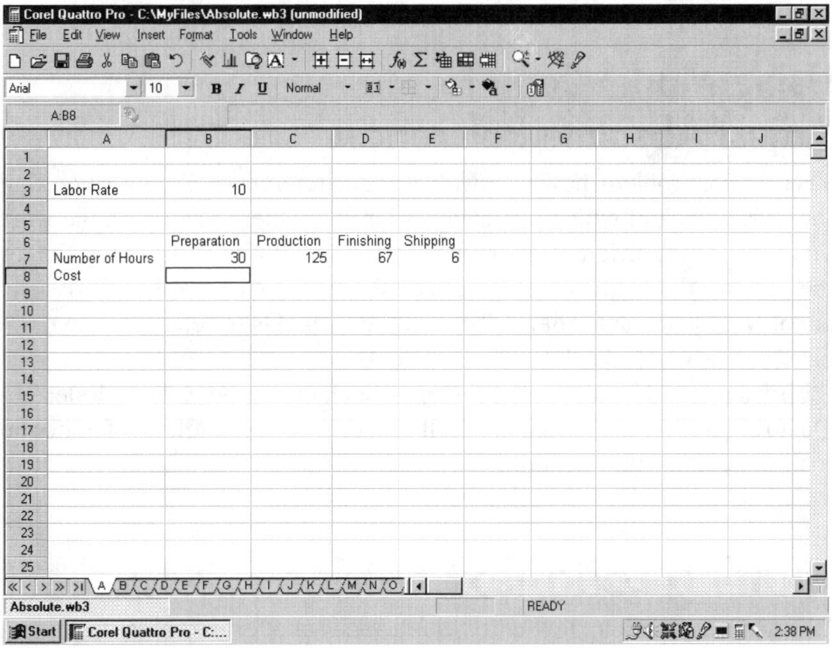

Copying
formulas
without a
relative
reference

FIGURE 16-6

the formula across the row, Corel Quattro Pro will use a *relative* reference. Only the original formula will reference cell B3. Here's why. The formula in B8 means "multiply the value one cell above times the value in the cell five rows up." This same relationship will be applied where the formula is copied. So when it is copied to cell C8, for example, it will be copied as +C7*C3—multiplying the labor amount (one cell up) times the value in cell C3—which is wrong.

When you want a reference to a cell to remain constant no matter where it is copied, use an absolute reference. To create an absolute reference, place a dollar sign ($) in front of each part of the reference that you want to remain constant. In this case, enter the formula as **+B7*B3**. This tells Corel Quattro Pro not to change the reference to column B and row 3.

Create the worksheet and enter the absolute reference now, and then use QuickFill to copy the formula across the row. The reference to cell B7 will be adjusted because it is not absolute, but the reference to cell B3 will remain constant.

Depending on your worksheet, the $ symbol is not always needed before both parts of the reference. For example, $C5 tells Corel Quattro Pro to always reference a cell in column C, but to change the row number relative to the location.

Using Model Copy to Adjust Absolute References

There is one problem, however, with absolute references. Suppose you want to copy the entire block of cells illustrated earlier to another location on the worksheet so you can use two different labor charges. If you copy cells A3 to E8, the formulas in the new location will still reference cell B3, because of the absolute reference. This is not what you want. You really want the formulas to reference the new location, but again using an absolute reference to it.

To perform this copy, use the Copy Block option but select Model Copy. Corel Quattro Pro will copy the block of cells, modifying the absolute reference but leaving it absolute to its new location.

Formatting Long Text Entries

When you type a long text entry, characters run over into blank cells on the right. When there aren't enough blank cells to display the entire entry, some of it won't show onscreen or print with the worksheet. The Reformat command divides a long entry into more than one row, as in the following steps:

16

1. Select the cell that contains the long entry—only that cell, not the ones that it spreads into.

2. Choose Text Reformat from the Format menu. A dialog box will appear asking for the block where you want to place the text.

3. Enter the block, or use Point mode to select it.

4. Click on OK.

The block must start with the active cell at the upper-left corner, and it must be large enough to hold all of the text. Pick sufficient cells, in as many rows and columns as needed. For instance, suppose you have a note that spans three columns. Your block can be three or four rows and one column wide, or two rows and two columns wide. Both blocks would be sufficient to hold the text.

Keep in mind, however, that Corel Quattro Pro reserves a little space before the first character in a cell and after the last. Some long entries may require a slightly larger block than you imagine. An entry that completely fills three columns, for example, would require a block four cells high.

NOTE: *Using Cell Properties, you can also wrap a long entry so it fits entirely within a cell.*

Transposing Columns and Rows

Once you set up your worksheet, you may find it more convenient if your rows and columns were switched, or *transposed*. For instance, you may find that you have more columns than rows, and that the worksheet would look better if the row labels were used for the columns instead. That way, perhaps, you could fit the entire worksheet on one page, rather than have some columns print on a second sheet.

Before transposing rows and columns, however, find an empty place in the notebook large enough to store the transposed block (a block that contained information would be overwritten with the transposed cells). Remember that the rows and columns will be reversed, so make sure there are enough empty rows to store the original columns and enough empty columns to store the original rows.

You can transpose a copied block using the Paste Special dialog box, or by following these steps:

1. Select the block that you want to transpose.

2. Pull down the Tools menu.

3. Point to Numeric Tools, and click on Transpose. A dialog box will appear with two boxes, From and To.

4. In the To box, enter or point to the destination where you want to copy the values.

5. Click on OK.

CAUTION: *Cell references are not adjusted when you transpose cells, so avoid transposing cells with formulas or functions.*

Formatting Your Worksheet

Not only must your worksheet be accurate, but it should look good. It should be easy and pleasant to read—formatted to enhance the material, not distract from it. By formatting a worksheet, you can change the typeface and size of characters, add lines and shading to cells, and change the way and position that text appears in the cell.

You can format cells before or after you enter contents into them. You can also format text as you enter or edit it. In fact, you can even apply formats to cells and later add information to them. Your entries will automatically assume the applied formats. One word of caution: formatting blank cells that you never use, such as entire rows or columns, will needlessly increase the size of your files.

There are two ways to format cells—using the property bar or setting Cell Properties. Setting Cell Properties may take a little longer than the other method, but it gives you the most options and enables you to set multiple formats at one time.

Remember, you must be in Ready mode to apply most formats to blocks. Except for character formats, you cannot format while you are entering or editing information in a cell.

TIP: *Character formats, such as typeface and size, bold and italic, can now be applied to individual characters in a cell.*

Formatting with the Property Bar

The property bar contains a number of buttons for formatting cells. The buttons shown will depend on the mode—whether you are in Ready mode, or are entering or editing information in the cell.

When you are in Ready mode, the buttons affect all of the text in the cell or block of selected cells. If you click on the Bold button, for example, all of the text will become bold. When you make a cell active, by the way, the buttons will appear pressed down to indicate the formats that have been applied to the entire cell.

When you're entering information into a cell or editing a cell, the property bar will change as shown next. You can use the buttons to format specific characters, just as you can format text in Corel WordPerfect.

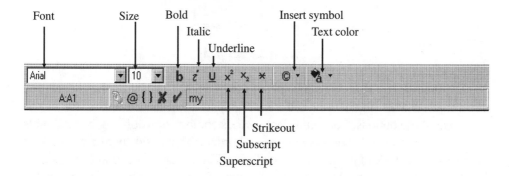

Changing the Font and Text Size

To change the font or size of characters, make your selection from the Font and Size lists in the property bar.

If you are in Ready mode, your choices will be applied to the entire cell. If you are entering or editing the information in a cell, your choices will be applied to new characters that you type or to characters that you've selected.

Changing the Text Style and Color

Click on the Bold, Italic, or Underline buttons to format text. To change the text color, pull down the Text Color list and make your choice from the pallet that appears. Again, if you are entering or editing information in a cell, your choices will be applied to new characters that you type or to characters that you've selected.

When entering or editing text, you can also select to make characters subscript, superscript, or strikeout.

NOTE: *Use the Style list to select a style. A style is one or more formats that are applied at one time. The two built-in text styles are Heading 1 and Heading 2. Heading 1 is 18-point Arial bold; Heading 2 is 12-point Arial bold. You can create your own styles and add them to the list.*

Changing Cell Grid Lines and Fill Color

In Ready mode, you can also use the property bar to specify the type of lines around the cell or block of selected cells.

The icon on the Border button shows the lines that will be applied when you click on the button. To choose a different line, pull down the list next to the button to display these options. You can select various combinations of single and double lines, as well as outside borders and inside borders. The outside border choice adds the line to the outside of a selected range of cells. The inside border choice adds lines inside the selected range. Your choice will be applied to the cell, and placed on the face of the button as the new default.

To add a fill pattern to a cell or selected block of cells, pull down the Fill Color list and make your choice from the palette that appears. You can also choose two colors and a specific blend of them, ranging between a solid color fill of each. To select a blend of colors, choose More from the palette. In the dialog box that appears, select the two colors and the blend. Your choice will be applied to the cells and placed on the button as the new default.

Inserting Special Characters

When you are entering or editing information in a cell, you can insert special symbols and other characters. Start by placing the insertion point where you want the character to appear; then use the Font list to choose the font that contains the character.

Most fonts, for example, contain accented characters and some other symbols. To select from graphic icons, however, choose the Wingdings font, or use the Symbol font to insert a Greek character or mathematical symbol.

Next, pull down the Insert Symbol list in the property bar to display the available characters in the font. The Wingdings symbols are shown here:

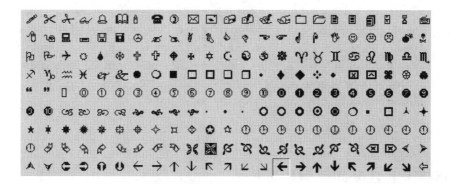

The character that you select will be inserted into the cell and on the face of the button as the new default. If you insert a character from a special font, you'll have to change back to the original font to continue entering text and numbers.

SpeedFormats

As you will soon learn, you can apply a number of different formats to an entry, such as the font and size, grid lines, and cell shading. Assigning each of the formats individually yourself develops your creativity but can be time-consuming. The SpeedFormat command lets you completely format an entire block of cells, even the entire worksheet, by choosing from a list of designs. You can even create and save your own custom SpeedFormat so you can apply it again later with a few clicks of the mouse. Here's how:

1. Select the block that you want to format.

2. Click on the SpeedFormat button in the toolbar to display the dialog box shown in Figure 16-7. The Formats list box on the left contains the names of all of Corel Quattro Pro's built-in designs. When you click on a design in the list, a sample worksheet using that style appears in the Example box.

3. Choose what aspects of the design will be applied to the cells. In the Include section, deselect the items that you do not want applied. For example, to accept all of the formats except the shading, click on the Shading option to deselect its checkbox.

4. The items on the right of the Include section determine if special styles are applied to those parts of the worksheet. Deselect any element that you do not want formatted. If you deselect Column Heading, for example, the column headings will not be formatted differently from the body of the cells. As you choose options in the Include section, the example will illustrate the results.

5. Click on OK to apply the format to the selected cells.

Creating Custom Formats

If you've designed a worksheet, you can add the design to the SpeedFormat list. The next time you want to apply that combination of formats, you can select it from the list just as easily as you can select those built-in by Corel Quattro Pro. Use the following steps:

1. Start by selecting the block of cells that contain the design.

2. Click on the SpeedFormat button and then on Add.

3. In the dialog box that appears, type a name for the format and then confirm—or reenter or point to—the block of cells.

4. Click on OK. Your new format will be added to the list.

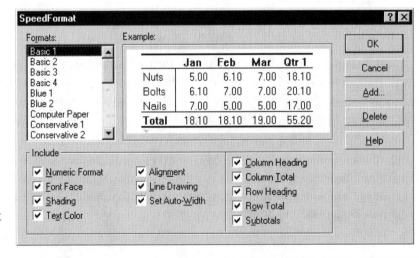

Applying an entire design to the worksheet with SpeedFormat

FIGURE 16-7

Formatting with Properties

Every format and style that you can apply is a property. Instead of using a variety of bars and menus to apply formats one at a time, you can select multiple formats in the Active Cells dialog box. You can also set the properties for a sheet or for the entire notebook, and even to customize Corel Quattro Pro itself.

Active Cell Properties for Cells

The Active Cells dialog box, shown in Figure 16-8, is used for formatting cells, rows, and columns. To display the box, click on the Change/Display Properties button in the property bar (in Ready mode), or right-click on the selected block and choose Cell Properties from the QuickMenu. The coordinates of the block that will be affected will be shown on the title bar. If that is not the block you want to format, close the dialog box and start over by selecting the desired block. You cannot change the reference while the dialog box is open.

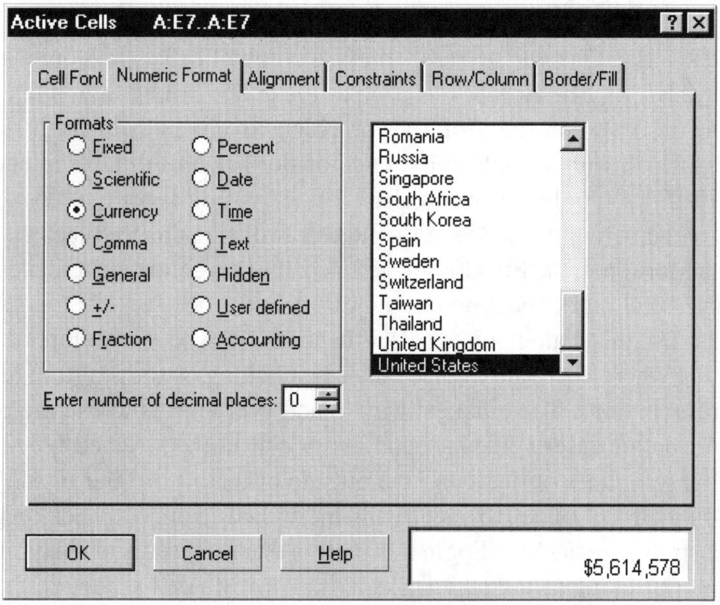

Using Cell
Properties
to format
cells

FIGURE 16-8

When you select an option from a page in the dialog boxes, its title on the tab will change color. This is Corel Quattro Pro's way of reminding you which pages you've already used.

Let's take a look at the properties that you can set.

NUMERIC FORMAT   As you can see in Figure 16-8, the Numeric Format tab gives you more choices than the Style list in the property bar. When you choose some items in the list, additional choices will appear to the right. For example, clicking on Currency will give you the option to select the number of decimal places and the country, so Corel Quattro Pro can use the correct currency format.

The Hidden format will prevent the contents from appearing in the cell, onscreen, and when printed. Values in the cell will still be used in formulas that reference it, and you can still edit the cell to change its contents. The information in the cell will reappear when you are in Edit mode, but disappear again when you accept the entry.

CELL FONT   Use the Cell Font tab to select the typeface, size, style, and color of the characters. The styles are Bold, Italic, Underline, and Strikeout. Use Strikeout to indicate information that you want to delete.

You can also select an accounting underline style that uses a single or double underline. With an accounting style, the underline extends the full width of the cell, not just under the characters within the cell.

BORDER/FILL   One way to really make a block of cells stand out is to add custom borders and fill. The Border/Fill page of the dialog box is shown in Figure 16-9.

The fill is a color, shade of gray, or a blend of colors that fills the selected block. To fill a block with a single color, click on the Border/Fill tab and choose the color from the Fill Color list. You can also choose two colors for the block and a specific blend of them, ranging between a solid color fill of each. To select a blend of colors, choose More from the Fill Color list. Select the two colors and the blend. For shades of gray, select black and white as the two colors.

Also use this dialog box to select the location, type, and colors of lines. Start by choosing where you want to place lines by clicking on the diagram of a block or on the preset buttons. The quickest way to add grid lines is to use the preset buttons. The All button inserts lines around every cell in the selected block. The Outline button inserts lines only around the outside of the block. The Inside button inserts lines only on the inside. To specify the individual segments, click on the location in the illustration in the Line Segments section that represents where you want to place the lines. Clicking on a line will place small arrows on its sides that indicate where

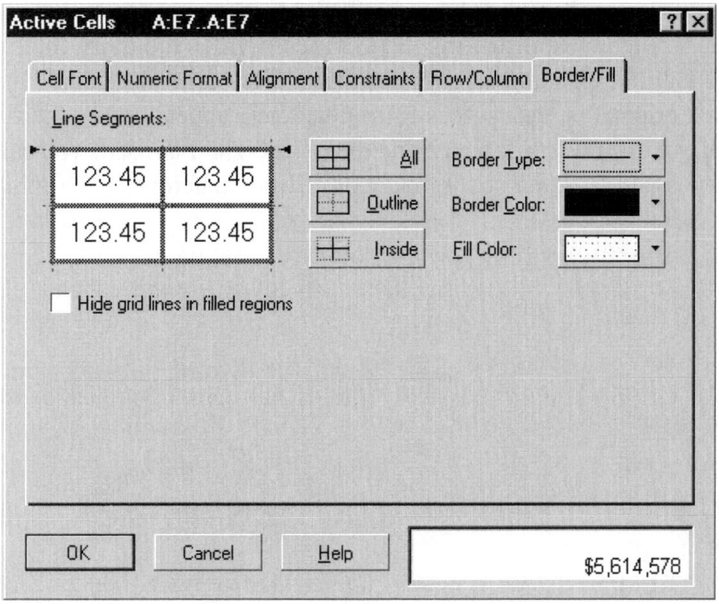

Choosing a
fill pattern
and lines

FIGURE 16-9

the line will be placed. Clicking at the intersection of two lines will add the line to both of them. For example, if you click on the lower-right corner of the drawing, Corel Quattro Pro will insert a line on the bottom and right of the block.

Next, choose the border type and color. Choose No Line in the Border Type list to remove lines from the cell; choose No Change to cancel your selections.

You can choose a color and line type for each individual line if you want. To give the block a shadow box look, for example, add a thin line to the top and left side and add a thick line to the bottom and right.

ALIGNMENT The alignment section on the property bar gives you choices for horizontal alignment—the position of text in relation to the right and left sides of the cell. Using the Alignment page in the Cell Properties dialog box, you can also choose vertical alignment and orientation, and choose to wrap a wide text entry so it fits within the cell borders.

The default vertical alignment is bottom. If you increase the row height or use a smaller font, you'll see that the characters appear nearer the bottom of the cell. Vertical Alignment lets you place the text in the center or near the top of the cell.

Long text entries run over into blank cells on the right. The Wrap Text option increases the row height and divides the long entry so it fits entirely within the cell. This differs from Reformatting Text, which divides the entry into more than one cell. The Join Cells option combines the selected cells into one.

Text orientation determines if the characters appear across the cell (the default setting), or up and down, increasing the row height if needed. You can also select to rotate text a specific number of degrees, as shown here:

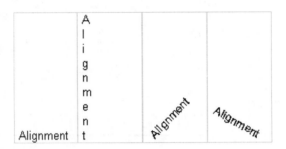

ROW/COLUMN   These properties let you set the row height and column width to an exact measurement in points, inches, or centimeters. It is more exact than dragging the row with the mouse, but you may have to experiment to get the height correct for your text.

You can also choose to temporarily hide rows or columns that you do not want to appear onscreen or to print with the worksheet. This feature is useful when you've added some information for limited distribution, or notes and messages to yourself. This format is similar to the hidden numeric format, except that it affects entire rows and columns, not individual cells or blocks of cells. When hidden, values in the cells will still be used to calculate formulas, but you cannot edit the contents until you reveal them.

To hide a row or column, click in any cell within it and then display the Row/Column page of the Active Cells dialog box. Select Hide in the Row Options or Column Options section, depending on what you want to hide. When you close the dialog box, the rows or columns will no longer appear, but the remaining rows and columns will retain their original numbers and letters. If you hide row 5, for example, your visible rows will be numbered 1, 2, 3, 4, 6, 7, 8, and so on.

You can reveal hidden rows and columns with the mouse or using Cell Properties. Using the mouse, point just to the right of the border before the column you want to see. To reveal hidden column C, for example, point just to the right of column B's right border. The mouse pointer will appear as if you are changing the width of the column, but when you drag, the hidden column will appear. Use the same technique to reveal rows—just point below the border line before the row you want to see.

With the mouse you can reveal only one row or column at a time, and you have to resize the row or column as needed. To reveal more than one row or column, and to have it appear in its original width, use the Active Cells dialog box. Select a block that contains the hidden area. To redisplay row 5, for instance, select cells in rows 4 and 6. Display the Row/Column page, then click on Reveal in the Row Options or Column Options section.

CONSTRAINTS   The Constraints tab lets you protect a cell from being changed and allows you to specify the type of entry that will be accepted.

By default, all cells are set to be protected. To implement the protection, you need to turn it on using the Sheet Properties that you'll learn about later. In the Constraints tab, however, you designate if you want the cells to be protected or not when page protection is turned on.

You can also specify if you will allow any type of information to be inserted into the cell, or if you just want labels or dates. If you select labels, whatever you type in the cell will be treated as text. Numbers, formulas, dates, and functions will appear just as you type them, aligned on the left, and treated as text. If you select Dates Only, Corel Quattro Pro will display an error message if you do not enter a valid date into the cell.

Sheet Properties

The Sheet Properties control the overall look of the sheet, rather than selected cells. To display the Sheet Properties dialog box, shown in Figure 16-10, right-click on the sheet tab and select Sheet Properties from the QuickMenu. Here's a recap of the Sheet Properties:

- *Display*—Display or hide zeros when entered or when they are the result of a calculation; display or hide row and column borders; display or hide the nonprintable grid lines without affecting borders you added yourself.

- *Zoom Factor*—Select a default magnification for the entire sheet, without affecting other sheets.

- *Name*—This is one of the most useful of the properties. Rather than stick with tabs A, B, C, and so on, you can name them for the type of worksheet that appears on the sheet—such as "Budget" or "Amortization."

■ *Protection*—Turn on cell and object locking. Only cells with the Cell Property set for locking in the Constraints tab will be affected. By default, all of the cells are set for protection, so if you turn this on, you will not be able to enter or edit information until you turn it off again.

■ *Conditional Color*—Choose to automatically color the contents of a cell based on its value or error condition. The options are shown in Figure 16-11. Enter a minimum and maximum value, and what color will appear when an entry is below the minimum, within the range, above the maximum, or when an error occurs. Click on each option you want and choose a color. To turn on the coloring, you must click on the Enable box. This is useful for displaying negative numbers in a special color.

■ *Default Width*—Set the width of every column in characters, inches, or centimeters.

■ *Tab Color*—Select the color for the sheet tab. To choose a color, deselect the Use System Color option in the dialog box, and then pick a color from the list.

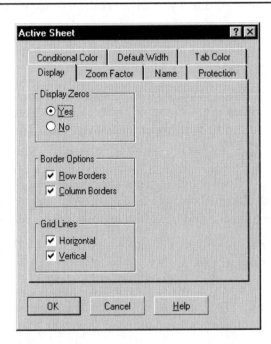

Using Sheet Properties to format the entire worksheet

FIGURE 16-10

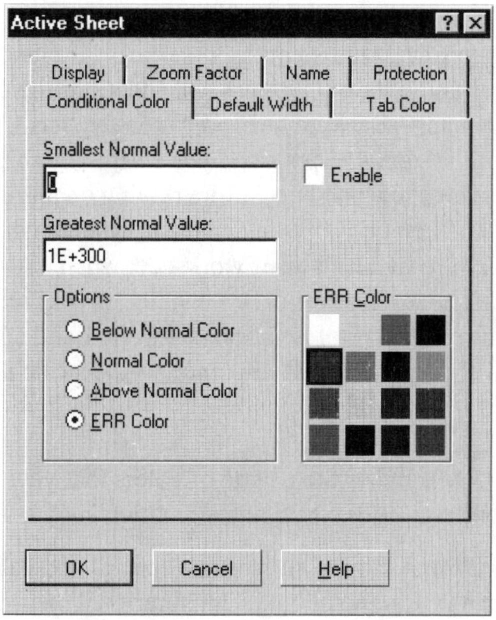

Using
Conditional
Color to
color cells
based on
their
contents

FIGURE 16-11

Notebook Properties

The Notebook Properties affect every sheet in the notebook. To set these properties, however, you must right-click on the Notebook title bar, which does not appear when the Notebook window is maximized. If necessary, click on the restore button on the right of the menu bar, and then right-click on the Notebook title bar and select Active Notebook Properties from the QuickMenu.

Here are the Notebook Properties:

- *Display*—Chooses whether to display the scroll bars and sheet tabs, and whether to display or hide objects or just to show their outline.

- *Zoom Factor*—Selects the default magnification for every sheet.

- *Recalc Settings*—Determines how and when Corel Quattro Pro will recalculate your worksheet. The Mode section has three options. Background recalculates as you work, Automatic waits until you stop working, and Manual lets you recalculate by pressing F9. You can also select a calculation order. Natural first calculates formulas that are referenced by other formulas; Column-wise calculates all formulas in column A, then column B, and so on; Row-wise calculates all formulas in row 1, then row 2, and so on.

If you have a lot of formulas and functions in your worksheet—and a slow computer—Background and Automatic recalculation may slow down your system's response. If you select Manual, however, remember to recalculate the worksheet before relying on any of its numbers.

The # of Iterations option determines the number of times Corel Quattro Pro recalculates your worksheet when circular references are used. A circular reference occurs when formulas refer to each other. You can choose a number of iterations between 1 and 255. The Audit Error option will display the cell reference where a calculation problem first started.

- *Palette*—Determines the palette of colors that you can select from when setting other properties that relate to color, such as text color.

- *Macro Library*—Stores macros in a special file, called the macro library, rather than in your notebook. The library will be available for every notebook. Select Yes and Corel Quattro Pro will automatically search the macro library when a macro you are running is not in the active notebook.

- *Password Level*—Uses a password to protect a notebook. Refer to "Protecting Your Worksheet" later in this chapter.

- *System*—Converts a notebook into a system notebook—a special notebook that you can hide but keep open even when all other notebooks are closed. The system notebook becomes a convenient location to store macros and other objects that you want available at all times. To convert a notebook into a system notebook, choose Yes for this property and then hide the notebook with the Window Hide command.

- *Summary*—Stores a title, subject, the author's name, keywords, and comments about the notebook for later reference.

- *Statistics*—Displays the notebook's name and path, when it was created and last saved, who saved it, and the revision number.

Application Properties

When you want to customize the way Corel Quattro Pro works, set Application Properties. Right-click on the Corel Quattro Pro title bar and choose Application Properties from the QuickMenu, or pull down the Tools menu and choose Settings. Here's a review:

- *Display*—Displays the toolbar, property bar, application bar, input line, scroll indicators, and QuickTips, and chooses the syntax of 3-D block references. The syntax choices are A..B:A1..B2 or A:A1..B:B2. You can also set the default view to Draft or Page, choose to use letters or numbers on the sheet tabs, and set the default number of sheets in new workbooks.

- *International*—Selects the format of currency, punctuation, dates, times, country, and if negative values are displayed with a minus sign or in parentheses.

- *Macro*—Chooses what elements of the screen appear while a macro runs. By default, all menus, dialog boxes, and other elements used to record the macro are suppressed so they do not appear as the macro performs its steps. You can choose to suppress just panels (menus and dialog boxes) or windows. Suppressing everything allows macros to run faster and without distracting elements appearing onscreen. You also use this tab to choose what element of the screen is made active when you press the slash key (/), and what macro runs automatically when you start Corel Quattro Pro.

- *File Options*—Selects the default directory and file extension used for the Save and Open dialog boxes, and a worksheet that will open each time you open Corel Quattro Pro. You can also choose to automatically save your work at a specified interval, to display the complete path with the filename in the title bar, and to list templates that you can choose from when you select New from the File menu.

- *General*—Customizes some ways that Corel Quattro Pro operates. You can turn off the Undo feature, use the key combinations from Corel Quattro Pro for DOS, and move the cell selector down when you press ENTER. The Compatible Formula Entry option lets you start formulas without first entering the plus sign. If you choose this option, however, entering a phone number or social security number will be seen as a formula. The number 555-1234, for example, will appear as -679. You can also turn off Fit-As-You-Go, Calc-As-You-Go, QuickType, and the Cell Reference Checker. The Cell Drag And Drop Delay Time option sets the interval at which drag-and-drop mode is activated when pointing at cells with the mouse.

Protecting Your Worksheet

The Password level setting in the Active Notebook Properties dialog box lets you determine the extent to which your notebook is protected. When you choose a setting other than None, you will be prompted to enter and then to confirm the password when you exit the dialog box.

- *None*—Requires no password

- *Low*—Requires a password to edit and view formulas. With the password, only asterisks appear in the input line

- *Medium*—Automatically hides the notebook once it is saved and closed

- *High*—Requires a password to open the notebook and to perform any actions on the notebook

 TIP: *To quickly save and protect a notebook, select the Password Protect checkbox in the Save File dialog box. When you click on Save, a box will appear for you to enter the password. This applies High-level security to the notebook.*

Opening Password-Protected Notebooks

When you open a notebook protected at the High level, a dialog box will appear asking for the password. A notebook protected at the Low and Medium settings, however, must be opened with a special command line from the Run menu. Click on Start, click on Run, and then enter the command line in this format:

C:\COREL\OFFICE8\PROGRAMS\QPW
C:\COREL\OFFICE8\PROGRAMS*FILENAME*.WK3 /S*PASSWORD*

Substitute the path where Corel Quattro Pro and your notebooks are stored. Be sure to enter the /S command at the end of the line, followed by your password. If your password is Aardvark, for example, type **/SAardvark**.

If the Medium-level protected notebook doesn't appear after you open it with the password, pull down the Window menu, click on Show, and then double-click on the notebook's name in the dialog box that appears. The Hide and Show commands in the Windows menu let you temporarily hide your notebook from prying eyes.

Formatting with Style

The SpeedFormat dialog box is handy when you want to create a style for an entire spreadsheet. Often, however, you want a style for a section or element of a worksheet, such as a heading, grand total, or note. A style is merely a collection of properties saved under one name. You can apply all of the properties in the collection by selecting the style name.

Corel Quattro Pro already comes with the Heading 1 and Heading 2 styles. You can modify these styles and create your own so they are available in the Style list of the property bar.

The easiest way to create a style is to first apply all of the formats to a cell and use the cell as a pattern. The following steps show this process:

1. Click in the cell and then choose Styles from the Format menu to see the dialog box shown in Figure 16-12.

2. Type a name for the style, and then click on the Merge button.

3. In the dialog box that appears, click on Cell and then point to or type the cell reference.

4. Click on OK.

The formats applied to the cell will be used to create the new style.

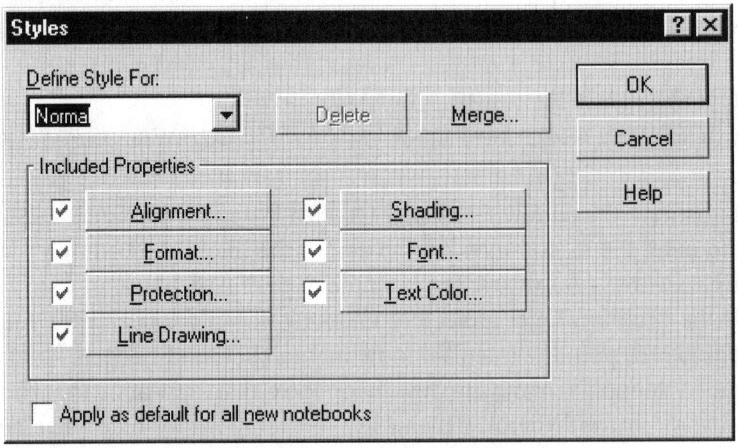

Creating
your own
styles

FIGURE 16-12

To create a style from scratch, type a name for it in the Styles dialog box, and then select options from the dialog boxes that appear when you click on the Alignment, Format, Protection, Line Drawing, Shading, Font, or Text Color button. To apply the selected options, make sure the checkbox next to the button is selected. You can also choose to use the style as the default for all new notebooks.

You can delete any style except the Normal style. You can also copy styles to other notebooks. To delete a style, select Styles from the Format menu, click on the style name in the list, and then click on Delete.

To apply your style, pull down the Style list on the property bar and click on the style name.

Creating Numeric Formats

Corel Quattro Pro offers a variety of numeric formats, but you still might have your special requirements. You can create your own custom formats for numbers, dates, and times, so they can be easily selected from the list. To create a format, follow these steps.

1. Select the cells that you want to format.

2. Right-click on the cells, and choose Cell Properties from the QuickMenu.

3. Click on the Numeric Format tab, if necessary.

4. Click on the User Defined option button. A list box appears labeled "Formats Defined."

5. Delete the text in the box, or choose one of the formats in the list to use as a basis for your own.

6. Enter a format using the codes shown in Table 16-1. Start a numeric format with an "n" or "N," and start a date or time format with a "t" or "T."

7. Click on OK.

Your custom format will be added to the Formats Defined list and will be available for all notebooks. To apply a custom format, display the Cell Properties dialog box, click on User Defined in the Numeric Format tab, and then choose the format from the Formats Defined list.

Symbol	Action
N or n	Designates a number format
T or t	Designates a date or time format
0	Placeholder for any digit (displays a 0 if empty)
9	Displays a digit in that location
%	Displays the number as a percentage
,	Uses a thousands separator
.	Decimal point separator
;	Delineates different formats for positive and negative values, as in positive_format;negative_format
E- or e-	Uses scientific notation, with minus sign before negative exponents
E+ or e+	Uses scientific notation, with minus or plus sign
d or D	Shows the day of the month in one- or two-digit number
dd or DD	Shows the day of the month in two digits, as in 05
wday, Wday, WDAY	Shows the day of the week as a three-character abbreviation all lowercase, initial capitalized, or all uppercase

Characters Used to Create Your Own Numeric Format

TABLE 16-1

Symbol	Action
weekday, Weekday, WEEKDAY	Shows the complete day of the week all lowercase, initial capitalized, or all uppercase
m, M, or Mo	Shows the month in one or two digits (1-12)
mm, MM, or Mmo	Shows the month in two digits
mon, Mon, MON	Shows the month as a three-character abbreviation, all lowercase, initial capitalized, or all uppercase
month, Month, MONTH	Shows the complete name of the month all lowercase, initial capitalized, or all uppercase
yy or YY	Shows the year in two digits
yyyy or YYYY	Shows the year in four digits
h or H	Shows the hour in one or two digits using 24-hour format. Follow by ampm or AMPM for 12-hour format
hh or HH	Shows the hour in two digits; include ampm or AMPM for 12-hour format
Mi	Shows the minutes in one or two digits
Mmi	Shows the minutes in two digits
s or S	Shows the seconds in one or two digits
ss or SS	Shows the minutes in two digits
AMPM	Uses 12-hour format displaying either AM or PM
*	When the entry is shorter than the column width, fills the remainder of the cell to the right of the last character with asterisks
"	Displays the characters enclosed in single quotation marks; use when you want to display a character that is also used as a format code (quotation marks are not needed for characters not used as codes)
\	Performs the same function as quotation marks but only for the single character following the backslash

Characters Used to Create Your Own Numeric Format (*continued*)

TABLE 16-1

Working with Blocks, Windows, and Notebooks

17

ometimes you need to make sweeping changes to a worksheet or take actions that affect entire groups of cells, multiple worksheets, or the whole notebook. With Corel Quattro Pro you don't have to repeat your work on individual cells or sheets. In this chapter, you will learn how to use names to quickly refer to sections of your worksheet, set up your sheets for printing, create groups of sheets, and use other timesaving techniques.

Cell Names

Point mode makes referring to cells and ranges of cells easier than typing coordinates, but it can be inconvenient when you need to scroll to a distant area of the worksheet or refer to the same cell or range frequently. You can try to remember the references of cells that you use often, but who can keep all of those numbers in their head?

The solution to this common problem is using *cell names*—giving an easy-to-remember name to a cell or group of cells. When you need to refer to the cells in a formula or dialog box, just use the name. You can even display a list of your cell names to make them easier to recall.

Not only are names easier to remember than coordinates, they make more sense. After creating a large worksheet, you may forget what the formula +G4-H5 means, but not the formula +Gross-Expenses. The names show you what your formula represents and make it easier to track down worksheet errors. Corel Quattro Pro won't necessarily know, for example, if you enter the wrong coordinates in a formula, but it will warn you if you use a name that hasn't been defined.

To name a group of cells, follow these steps:

1. Select the group of cells you want to name. Remember, you can also name a single selected cell.

2. Choose Name from the Insert menu, and click on Cells to see the Cell Names dialog box listing any existing cell names.

3. In the Name text box, type a name for the cell or group of cells that is not already assigned.

4. Click on Add, and then close the dialog box.

A cell name can be up to 63 characters long, including numbers, letters, spaces, and most punctuation marks. You can't use the operator characters (+, _, *, /, ^, =, <, >, #, or &) because they are reserved for formulas; you also cannot use the dollar sign and the opening and closing parentheses. Don't use all numbers or names that are cell coordinates, such as A1. Cell names are not case sensitive, but they always appear uppercase in the input line.

You can have as many cell names as you need in a worksheet, and their ranges can overlap. The same cells can be in more than one name. In fact, the same set of cells can have more than one name.

 NOTE: *When you click in a cell that has its own name, the name will appear in place of the coordinates in the input line.*

Using Cell Names

When you want to use a cell name in a formula or dialog box, just enter its name where you would otherwise type coordinates or use Point mode.

To see a list of cell names when you are in the input line, press the F3 key or click on the Navigate button in the input line. This procedure only works, however, when you are ready to enter a cell coordinate, such as after a plus sign, an operator, or an opening parenthesis. Otherwise, the Navigate button will be dimmed, and pressing F3 selects the File menu command. If you are in a dialog box, press F3 to see the cell name list when you are in a text box that accepts cell coordinates. Click on the cell name in the list to insert it into the formula or dialog box.

 NOTE: *When you are not entering or editing information into a cell, use the Navigate button to quickly select a cell or group of cells. Click on the button and then on the name representing the cells you want to select.*

Changing a Cell Name

To rename a cell, you must first delete the name and then start over by redefining the same cell. Delete a name by selecting it in the Cell Names dialog box and clicking on Delete. (Click on Delete All to remove all of the names from the worksheet.)

Deleting a cell name will not affect formulas. Corel Quattro Pro will automatically replace the names with their references wherever the name appears in a formula. However, it will not automatically replace the coordinates when you give a name to a referenced cell or group of cells.

It is easier to change the reference that a name represents. Display the Cell Names dialog box and click on the name you want to reassign. Enter the cell coordinates and then click on Add. The name now refers to the new cell.

Creating Cell Names from Labels

It is common to have a number of cells that correspond to a series of labels, as shown in Figure 17-1. You can automatically assign the labels as the names for their corresponding values. In the example, each label in column B would become the name for the value to its right in column C.

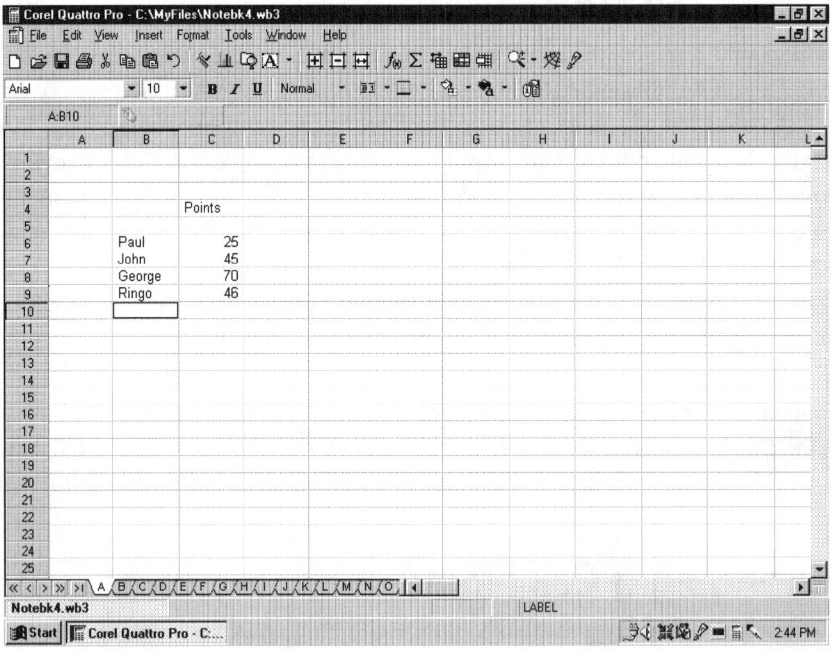

Assigning labels as cell names

FIGURE 17-1

Here's how to use labels as cell names.

1. Select the labels that you want to use as the cell names. They must be labels, not values.

2. Point to Name in the Insert menu and click on Cells.

3. Click the Labels button to display the dialog box shown here:

17

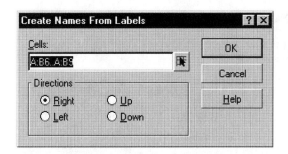

4. Select the position of the cells you want to name in relation to the labels. In the example, you'd select Right.

5. Click OK. Each of the labels will now be listed as cell names.

6. Close the Cell Names dialog box.

If you later change the text of a label, the cell name does not change automatically. You must still use the old label as the name. To change the name, you must delete it and assign a new one.

If error messages appear when you use one of the names, check the label carefully for extra spaces before or after your label text. For instance, you may accidentally enter a blank space after a label when you're typing it in the cell. You may not notice the space in the cell, but Corel Quattro Pro will include the space in the cell name. If you later leave out the space when typing the cell name, Corel Quattro Pro will display a message indicating that the cell name does not exist.

Using Labels for Multiple Cell Names

The Labels button can be used only when naming single cells immediately next to the label. You can also assign label names to a range of cells, or to combine a row and column label into one cell name. Follow these steps:

1. Select the labels that you want to use as the cell names. They must be labels, not values.

2. Point to Name in the Insert menu and click on Cells.

3. Click on the Generate button to see these options:

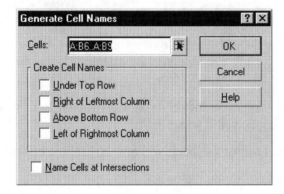

4. Enter or use Point mode to indicate the range of cells, including the labels and the values.

5. Select the locations that represent the position of the values in relation to the labels.

6. Click on OK, and then close the Cell Names dialog box.

The most important step in this procedure is selecting the correct location options. For example, to use a label as the name for a group of cells in the row to its right, click on Right of Leftmost Column. To use a column header as a label for cells below it, click on Under Top Row.

You can select more than one option to use a label for a group of cells that spans rows or columns. To use a label for values next to it and in the following row, for example, choose both Under Top Row and Right of Leftmost Column.

You can also combine a row and column heading together to reference a single cell. For example, suppose you have a value in the row labeled Wages and in the column labeled Qtr 1. Select the range, choose both Under Top Row and Right of Leftmost Column, and click on Name Cells at Intersections. The value at the intersection of those labels will now be named Qtr1_Wages.

Displaying a Cell Name Table

The Navigate button and F3 key make it easy to list your cell names. As a more visual reminder, you can display a table directly on your worksheet listing the cell names and their coordinates. To do so, follow these steps:

1. Display the Cell Names dialog box, and click on the Output button.

2. Select the top-left cell where you want the name table to appear on your worksheet. Corel Quattro Pro will overwrite existing information when it displays the table, so make sure there are enough blank cells below and in the column to the right to display all of the names and their references.

3. Click on OK, and then close the dialog box to display the table. The cell names will be in the first column sorted alphabetically.

If you add, rename, or delete cell names, Corel Quattro Pro will not update the table automatically. Create the table again in the same location to replace it.

Page Setup

The default print settings are fine if you're printing a draft copy of a small worksheet. When you're printing a worksheet for distribution, however, you may want to adjust the page size and margins, or add other elements such as headers and footers. A *header* is text that prints on the top of each page; a *footer* prints on the bottom of each page. You can enter your own text into the header and footer, and choose built-in elements such as the date, page number, or filename.

You can adjust the margins, and add headers and footers, directly in the worksheet in Page view. Those, and other page options, are also accessible in the Page Setup dialog box.

Using Page View

To display your worksheet in Page view, select Page from the View menu. In Page view, you'll see the margin guidelines as well as elements such as headers and footers.

To change the margins, point to a guideline so the mouse appears as a two-directional arrow, and drag.

 NOTE: *You can also set margins by dragging margin lines in Print Preview mode.*

To enter a header directly into the worksheet, right-click in any margin area—the area outside of the guidelines. To see the options shown here, select Create Header from the QuickMenu.

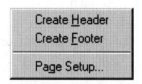

Corel Quattro Pro will display a header area between the margin and the worksheet, indicated by another guideline. To enter the header, double-click in the header area to place the insertion point there, and type your header.

 NOTE: *Use the same technique to create a footer, but choose Create Footer from the QuickMenu.*

You can also use the special codes shown in Table 17-1. For example, enter Page #p of #P to display Page 1 of 4, or File #f printed on #d for the notebook name and date it was printed. You can use any combination of the codes in the header, footer, or both.

The vertical bar (usually entered with the SHIFT and backslash keys) works like a tab. Enter one to center text, two to align text on the right. To center the notebook name and its full path, for instance, enter |#F.

 TIP: *To remove a header or footer, right-click in the margin area and select Remove Header or Remove Footer.*

Code	Function
|	Centers or right-aligns text
#d	Inserts the current date in the Short International format as set in the Application Properties
#D	Inserts the current date in the Long International format as set in the Application Properties
#ds	Inserts the current date in the Windows Short Date format
#Ds	Inserts the current date in the Windows Long Date format
#t	Inserts the current time in the Short International format as set in the Application Properties
#T	Inserts the current time in the Long International format as set in the Application Properties
#ts	Inserts the current time in the Windows Short Time format
#Ts	Inserts the current time in the Windows Long Time format
#p	Inserts the page number
#p+n	Inserts the current page number plus the number n
#P	Inserts the number of pages being printed
#P+n	Inserts the number of pages plus the number n
#f	Inserts the name of the notebook
#F	Inserts the name and path of the notebook
#n	Prints the remainder of the header or footer on a second line

Codes for Creating Headers and Footers

■ TABLE 17-1

Using the Page Setup Dialog Box

You can set even more page options using the Spreadsheet Page Setup dialog box shown in Figure 17-2. To display the box, select Page Setup from the File menu, or right-click in the margin area and choose Page Setup from the QuickMenu.

In the Paper Type page, select the paper size and orientation. Your choices depend on the printer you have installed in Windows 95. Use landscape orientation when you want to print more columns on a page.

To add a header or footer, click on the Header/Footer tab. Click on the Create checkbox in the Header or Footer section, and then enter the text that you want to appear on your printout. Use the Font button to change the font and size of the text, and use the codes shown in Table 17-1 to enter page numbers and other elements. Use the Header and Footer height settings to control the distance between the header and the first row, and between the footer and the last row. The exact position of the first row, then, is the sum of the top margin and header settings.

Setting Margins

The margin settings contribute to determining the number of rows and columns that fit on the page. Click on Print Margins in the Spreadsheet Page Setup dialog box, and then enter the top, bottom, left, and right margins. As you highlight a measurement, a line darkens in the drawing at the lower-right corner of the dialog box, and an arrow points to the line, showing you the margin you are setting.

The top margin determines the distance between the top of the paper and the headers; the bottom margin determines the distance between the bottom of the page and the footer. Enter your settings in the same unit that is displayed, inches or centimeters.

Many laser printers cannot print very close to the edge of the page and need at least a quarter-inch margin. If you get a printer error, or some text does not print properly, widen the margins.

When your worksheet is more than one page long, Corel Quattro Pro inserts soft page breaks to divide it into pages. If you are using continuous paper or want to fill

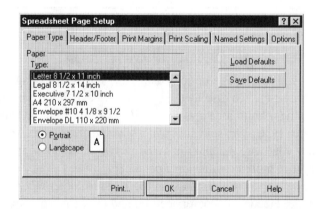

Spreadsheet
Page Setup
dialog box

FIGURE 17-2

up as much of the page as possible and let your printer change pages, deselect Break Pages in the Margins tab. This will also turn off all headers and footers.

PRINTING LARGE WORKSHEETS   Corel Quattro Pro prints a large worksheet by printing as many columns as can fit on the first page, and all of the rows in those columns on consecutive pages. It then goes back to the first row and begins printing the next series of columns.

If you want your pages divided differently, add hard page breaks where you want one page to end and another to begin. To insert a hard page break, click in the row where you want the break to occur, and then choose Page Break from the Insert menu.

In Page view, you can also change page breaks relative to rows and columns by dragging the page break lines. These are the solid slides that represent the ends of the pages. Drag a horizontal page break line, for example, to adjust the number of rows on the page. Drag a vertical page break line to adjust the number of columns.

Changing the Print Scale

By adjusting the font size, margins, column width, and row height, you can determine how much of a worksheet prints on a page. You can also reduce or enlarge the entire printout without changing any other formats. Reducing the print size fits more cells on each page but makes it more difficult to read. If you've already adjusted margins and other settings and still need to fit an extra row or column on the page, try reducing the scale slightly.

To change the scale, use the Print Scaling option in the Page Setup dialog box. In the Print To box, enter a setting less than 100 to reduce the printout, more than 100 to enlarge it. You can enter a setting between 1 and 1,000. To scale the worksheet to fit on a specific number of pages, click the Print To Desired Width option button, and then enter the number of pages wide and high. Corel Quattro Pro will automatically reduce the scale to print the worksheet on the designated number of pages.

Scaling affects the size of all characters and graphics, as well as the header and footer margin settings. Other page margins will not be affected.

Page Setup Options

The Options tab of the dialog box lets you further customize your printout.

Headings are rows or columns that will print on every page. If you have a long worksheet, labels in the top row will not print on the top of every page, so readers may have difficulty relating information in the columns. To repeat a row on each page, enter the coordinates of at least one cell in the row in the Top Heading box. To print several rows as a heading, select cells in all of the rows. To repeat a column, enter cells in the columns you want to repeat in the Left Heading box. When you specify the print range, do not include the heading rows or columns. If you do, they will print twice.

The choices in the Print Options group determine what elements of the worksheet appear on paper.

- *Cell Formulas* prints the actual formulas in the cells, not their calculated results. This is handy for a backup copy of your worksheet; however, headings, grid lines, and row and column borders will not print at the same time, and groups of cells will not be centered.

- *Gridlines* prints the normally nonprinted grid lines. Don't use this option if you've already added your own grid lines using line drawing.

- *Row/Column Borders* prints the row letters and column numbers. This is a good choice if you're printing a reference or backup copy.

- *Center Cells* centers your printout between the left and right margins. Normally, the first column prints at the left margin.

If your print range includes two or more noncontiguous groups of cells, you can determine how they are spaced on the page. The Lines setting in Print Between Selections determines the number of blank lines to place between groups. The Lines setting in the Print Between 3D Sheets group determines the number of lines to print between groups on each page. To start each group of cells on a new page, click on Page Advance.

Saving and Restoring Print Settings

If you change your mind about Sheet Options or Page Setup settings, you can quickly return to Corel Quattro Pro's default values by selecting the Load Defaults button in either dialog box.

Your sheet and page setup settings only affect the current worksheet. If you want to use the same settings with every notebook, make them the new default values. To do so, click on the Save Defaults button in either dialog box. Keep in mind that your own settings will now be used when you click on the Load Defaults button.

To return to Corel Quattro Pro's original settings, use the Windows 95 Notepad accessory to delete the Print Settings section in the file QPW.INI in Windows.

Saving Named Group Settings

If you use a variety of setups, you can save each as a group and then load the group by name when you need to. The group includes the settings in the Print, Print Options, and Page Setup dialog boxes. Save your settings under a name using these steps:

1. Display the Page Setup dialog box.

2. Click on Named Settings.

3. In the New Set text box, type a group name and then click on Add. Click on Update if you want to change an existing group.

4. Click on OK.

5. Save the notebook. Unlike default settings, which are globally available to all notebooks, named groups are stored with the notebook itself.

When you want to use a group, click on the Named Settings tab, select the group you want to use, and then click on Use.

Preventing Titles from Scrolling

As you scroll around a worksheet, the row and column labels will scroll out of view. So if you scroll down the page, for example, you will no longer see the labels that identify the purpose of each column. Likewise, as you scroll to the right, you will no longer see the labels that identify the rows. By locking titles into place, you prevent rows or columns from scrolling out of view, making it easier to enter information into large worksheets.

To lock titles from scrolling, use these steps:

1. Select the uppermost cell that you do not want to be locked. For example, to lock row 1 and column A, click in cell B2. To lock just rows 1 and 2, but no columns, click in cell A3.

2. Pull down the View menu and click on Locked Titles. (Click on the same option again later to unlock the titles.)

A blue line will appear indicating the locked rows and columns.

Locking titles prevents them from scrolling, but it does not affect your printout. The locked titles will not print on every page even though they always appear onscreen. To repeat the titles on each page, set the Top Heading and Left Heading sheet options.

Creating Groups

In Chapter 14 you learned how to select a 3-D group of cells by clicking on the page tabs while holding down the SHIFT key. These groups are temporary because they only remain in effect until you take some action on the group, such as applying a format or using QuickFill. If you want to use a group periodically, or add or delete information to multiple pages at one time, then name the group of pages and turn on Group mode.

For example, suppose you want to enter the same label in a cell in the first ten pages of the notebook. Or perhaps you want to use Point mode to quickly select the same group of cells on several pages. Rather than repeat your actions on each page every time, you create a group so Corel Quattro Pro will duplicate your actions on every page for you.

You create a group by selecting the pages that you want to include, and then giving the group a name. Here's how:

1. Click on the first tab of the sheets that you want to group.

2. Hold down the SHIFT key and click on the last tab of the sheets you want to include in the group.

3. Pull down the Insert menu, point to Name, and click on Group of Sheets to display the Define/Modify Group dialog box shown in Figure 17-3.

4. Type a name for the group using the same rules as cell names.

5. Confirm that the correct pages are shown in the First Sheet and Last Sheet boxes—correct them if necessary.

6. Click on OK to close the dialog box.

When you want to perform an action on a 3-D block of cells in the group, you must first turn on Group mode. Pull down the View menu and click on Group mode, or press ALT-F5. Corel Quattro Pro will display a blue line below the tabs in all of your group to indicate that Group mode is turned on.

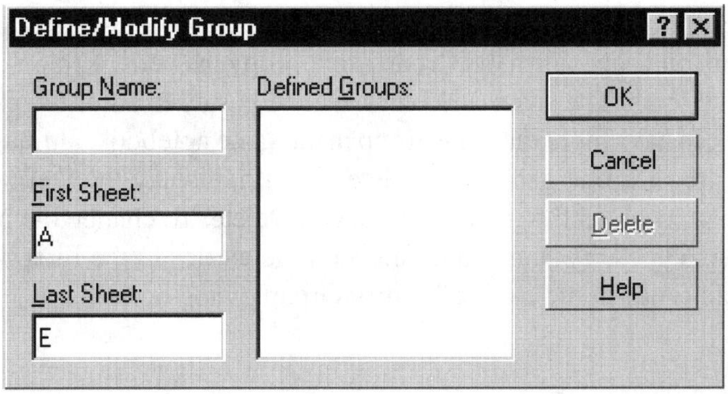

Creating a
group name

FIGURE 17-3

Now, formatting and other changes to one cell or group of cells on a sheet in a group (except entering and deleting) are duplicated on every sheet in that group. When you no longer want to act on the 3-D block, turn off Group mode—deselect Group mode on the View menu or press ALT-F5 again. The line under the tabs will disappear, showing that the group function is turned off.

To avoid unwanted effects, text that you type directly in a cell when Group mode is turned on will not be duplicated across the pages. When you want to enter text on every page, turn on Group mode, type the text on any of the pages in the group, hold down the CTRL key, and press ENTER. This is called "drilling down." You must press ENTER; clicking the Enter box in the input line will not drill down the text.

NOTE: *Use the Clear command or CTRL-DEL to delete information from every page.*

When Group mode is turned on, most actions affect every sheet of the group. You have to be careful not to accidentally change something on one page that will affect others. For example, if you select a group of cells and choose Clear or Delete from the Edit menu, all of the cells on every page of the group will be cleared. The Delete command from the Edit or QuickMenu works the same way. To erase information from just one page, use the DEL key or turn off Group mode first.

The same warning applies to pointing to cells for formulas, functions, and in dialog boxes. With Group mode turned on, you'll get a 3-D reference, using the syntax *group-name:range*. So if you point to a range on one sheet to average a row of cells, you will actually calculate the average of the cells from all of the pages in the group. Before pointing to cells, turn Group mode off.

If you want to copy information from one page to all of the pages, you'll also need to turn off Group mode; otherwise, you'll copy a 3-D group rather than just cells from one page. Turn off Group mode, copy the cells, turn on Group mode, and then paste them. The same 2-D block will be pasted to all of the pages.

You can have more than one group in the same notebook, although a sheet cannot be in more than one group. To delete a group, display the Define/Modify Group dialog box, click on the group and then on Delete. To change the pages included in the group, choose its name, and then edit the entries in the First Sheet and/or Last Sheet edit fields in the Define/Modify Group dialog box.

Splitting Windows into Panes

When you need to refer to a section on a large worksheet, you can always scroll or use the Go To command. But then you'd have to scroll back to your original location to continue working. Instead of scrolling back and forth, you can divide your screen into two *panes*, either vertically or horizontally, and view two parts of the same worksheet at the same time. You create panes using the pane splitter at the lower-right corner of the window, where the horizontal and vertical scroll bars meet, or by using the Split Window command from the View menu.

To split the screen into two horizontal panes, point to the top portion of the pane splitter so the arrows point left and right. To split into two vertical panes, point to the lower portion so the arrows point up and down. Now drag the mouse into the window. As you drag, a line appears showing the position of the pane. Release the mouse when the line is where you want the panes to appear. As shown in Figure 17-4, both panes have page tabs, tab scrolls, and scroll bars to move about the notebook. The pane splitter will appear where the two panes meet.

Changes you make in one pane will be duplicated on the other. By default, the two panes are synchronized. This means that scrolling one pane in the direction of the split will scroll the other as well. For example, scrolling horizontal panes in a horizontal direction and vertical panes in a vertical direction will be synchronized.

If you unsynchronize the panes, you can scroll them independently to reveal different parts of the same worksheet. To unsynchronize panes, choose Split Window from the View menu, and deselect Synchronized. Click on the same option if you later want to synchronize the panes again.

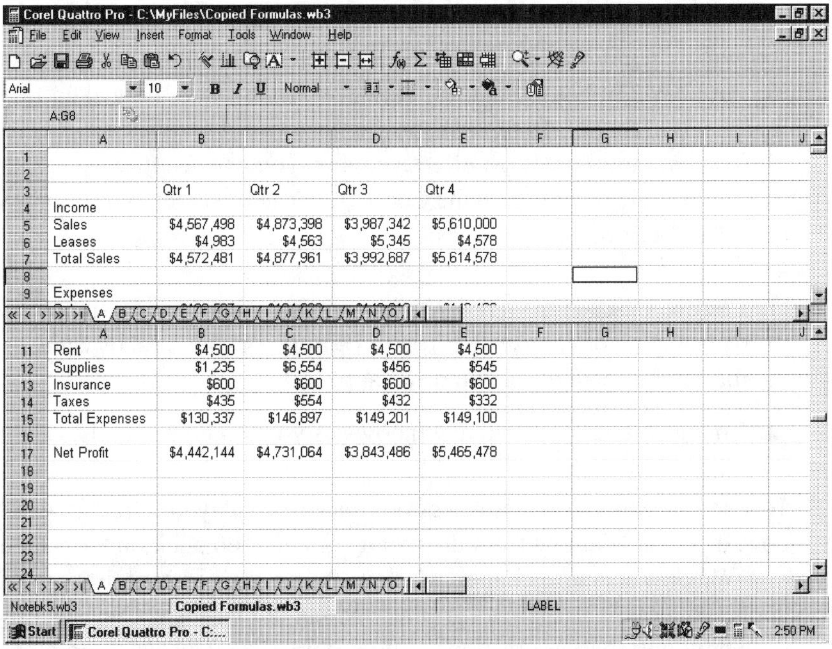

17

Worksheet divided into panes

FIGURE 17-4

To move from one pane to another, click in the pane with the mouse or press the F6 key to move from pane to pane.

To change the size of the panes, drag the pane splitter. Dragging it all the way off the window will remove a pane, displaying one view of the worksheet.

Duplicating Windows

You use panes to look at different parts of the same worksheet, but both panes will be in the same magnification, and you cannot drag-and-drop cells from one pane to the other. When you want to use different magnifications and drag-and-drop between sections of the worksheet, create a second view window for the same worksheet.

Choose New View from the Window menu. Another window appears, displaying the same worksheet. In the title bar, the name of the notebook will be followed by a colon and the window number. Changes that you make to cell contents and format will be duplicated in both windows. However, changes to the locked titles, panes, or magnification are not. To remove the duplicate window, click on its Close button.

Multiple windows are most effective when you can see them at the same time. Arranging multiple windows on the Corel Quattro Pro screen is a straight Windows 95 technique, performed as follows:

1. Choose Cascade from the Window menu to display the windows overlapped; or choose Tile Top to Bottom, or Tile Side by Side, to divide the screen so all of the windows appear.

2. Change the size and move windows as you would normally.

To select a window when more than one is displayed, click anywhere in the window, or select Window from the menu bar and then click on the window name. Use the Window menu to change windows when they are not arranged onscreen, when one window is in the background and cannot be seen. Copy and move cells between windows the same as you would within a window, using drag-and-drop or cut-and-copy.

All of these techniques apply as well to windows from more than one notebook. To work with several notebooks at one time, open each of them and then arrange the screens as desired, cascading or tiling them with the Window menu.

Working with Functions and Formulas

18

You use formulas and functions to take advantage of the recalculation and "What If?" capabilities of Corel Quattro Pro. In fact, you should use formulas whenever possible, especially when you need to perform a mathematical operation on the values in other cells. To begin with, formulas help ensure that your results are accurate. As long as you use the proper formula, Corel Quattro Pro will calculate the correct result. In addition, formulas can save you a great deal of time. The few extra seconds or minutes it takes to enter a formula can save you countless hours manually recalculating and checking your work.

In Chapter 15, you learned how to enter formulas, and you saw how the @SUM function could quickly total a row or column of numbers. In this chapter, you will learn how to enter formulas that perform all types of operations.

Functions

A *function* is a built-in shortcut that you can use to do in one quick statement what might take a very complex single formula or even a series of formulas to accomplish. For example, suppose your budget worksheet includes a series of daily expenditures. To calculate the average of the expenditures, you could count how many items you have listed (let's suppose 30), and enter a formula such as +(A1+A2+A3+A4+A5 ..., and so on)/30. That's quite a lot of typing. If you now insert another item into the worksheet, you'll have to edit the formula, adding the other cell and increasing the count to 31.

The alternative is to use the built-in function for calculating an average, @AVG. If you want to average the values in cells A1 through A30, all you have to enter is @AVG(A1.A30). The function returns—calculates and displays—the average of the values specified in that range. If you later add a row of information within the range, Corel Quattro Pro will automatically adjust the range reference to include the additional values.

A function can also perform a calculation that you would not otherwise know how to do using a formula alone. As an example, suppose you're looking for a home and want to calculate your monthly mortgage payments. Unless you are an accountant, you probably won't even know where to begin to write a formula to perform the calculation. Fortunately, Corel Quattro Pro has a built-in function for this called @PAYMT. Entering the function @PAYMT(.07/12, 25*12, 56000), for instance, would return the monthly mortgage payment for a loan of $56,000 for 25 years, at 7 percent annual interest. Just substitute your own values, or cell references to the values, in place of the numbers.

NOTE: *The result of the PAYMT function, by the way, will appear as a negative number. For a positive result, precede the principal amount with a minus sign, as in -56000.*

You don't have to know how the function works, just its syntax—its name and how to enter the information that it needs to calculate its results.

The Structure of Functions

Functions use the general syntax of @NAME(Arguments). The @ symbol tells Corel Quattro Pro that a function, not a label, follows. The function name can be entered in either uppercase or lowercase, with no spaces between it and the @ sign. The arguments, in parentheses, are the values, cell references, or special instructions that the function needs to do its work. You can have spaces around arguments, but Corel Quattro Pro will remove them when you accept the entry.

There are some functions that have no arguments. The function @TODAY, for example, displays the current date's serial number, and the function @MEMAVAIL displays the amount of conventional memory available. Just type the function into the cell, without any parentheses. When you accept the entry, the result appears in the cell.

In the function @AVG(A1..A30), the argument is the cell range A1..A30. This function needs just one argument: the range of cells that contains the values to average. Many other functions require several arguments, separated from each other by commas. The mortgage payment function, for example, requires three: the rate per period, the number of payments, and the principal amount, in that order. If you insert them in any other order, you'll get incorrect results.

There are some functions that have optional arguments. These are arguments that you can enter if you need to use them. The mortgage payment function, for example, has two optional arguments. The first represents any future value of the investment; the second indicates if you pay at the beginning or end of the period. The function @PAYMT(.07/12, 25*12, 56000, -20000, 1) uses the optional arguments to calculate the payment on a mortgage that includes a balloon payment of $20,000, with payments at the end of the month.

NOTE: *The help system and online manual will show you the syntax of functions and how to use optional arguments.*

When you leave out the optional arguments, Corel Quattro Pro assumes a default value for them. The defaults for the @PAYMT function, for instance, assume no future value and payments at the beginning of the month. If you use an optional argument, however, you must use all the information that comes before it. You could not, for instance, use the second optional argument without including the first.

You use functions by themselves in the input line or in combination with formulas and other functions. Using a function as an argument for another function is called *nesting*. Here are some examples.

+B3+@AVG(A1.A10)	Here a formula includes a function, adding the value in one cell to the average of a block of cells. Since the formula does not begin with the function, it must start with the + sign.
@PPAYMT(B1/12, 1, B2*12, B3)	Arguments can be formulas when their values are calculated. This function returns the amount of the first payment on a loan that goes to pay off principal. It contains formulas to calculate monthly interest from the annual rate in cell B1, and the number of monthly payments from the number of years in cell B2. The loan amount is in cell B3.
@TODAY - @Date(A1)	A formula can include several functions. In this example, two functions are used to determine the number of days between the date in cell A1 and the current date.
@INT(@Avg(A1.A10))	A function can even be used as the argument to another function. Here, the @INT function returns the integer (whole number) portion of the calculated average.

Entering Functions

You type a function directly into the cell or input line as you would any other formula. If you are just using a function, start with the @ symbol; there is no need to enter the + sign. Corel Quattro Pro recognizes the @ sign as a value entry.

Once you start to enter the name of the function, QuickType will display the first function name starting with those letters, along with the opening parentheses for the arguments. For example, if you type @**p**, QuickType displays @pbday(. If the suggested function is incorrect, continue typing. If you then press the letter *a*, QuickType will change @pbday(to @paymt(. When the function is correct, press the RIGHT ARROW key to begin entering the arguments.

Corel Quattro Pro will also display a Function Hint in the application bar at the bottom of the window: the function name and the name and order of the arguments. The argument names will be abbreviated with <> symbols around optional arguments, as in @paymt(rate, nper, pv, <fv>,<type>). This will help you enter the required and optional arguments in the correct order.

As you type in the function, the argument that you should enter at the position of the insertion point will appear uppercase in the application bar. So, for example, after you type the opening parentheses for the @PAYMT function, the application bar will display @paymt(RATE, nper, pv, <fv>,<type>), reminding you to enter the value, cell reference, or formula for the mortgage rate. Once you enter the comma following the rate, the application bar will appear as @paymt(rate, NPER, pv, <fv>,<type>), telling you to enter the number of periods. As you move the insertion point within the function, Corel Quattro Pro will uppercase the current argument.

 NOTE: *The parentheses-matching function will help ensure that you match opening and closing parentheses properly. Parentheses will appear in black when unmatched.*

Selecting Functions

If you can't remember or don't know the function name, use the Function dialog box. If you are not yet in the input line, press ALT-F3, or right-click in the cell and choose Insert Function from the QuickMenu. If you are entering or editing in the cell already, click on the Function button in the input line. You'll see the dialog box shown in Figure 18-1.

 NOTE: *You can move into the input line and display the list at one time by pressing ALT-F3.*

Displaying the function list to select a function

FIGURE 18-1

The list on the left of the dialog box shows the categories of functions; the list on the right shows the functions within the selected category. Choose the ALL category to display every function in alphabetic order, or choose Recently Used to see the functions that you've recently entered. Select the category of the function you want, and then double-click on the function, scrolling the list as needed, to insert it into the input line. Corel Quattro Pro will insert the @ symbol, the function name, and the opening parentheses. The function categories are

Database
Date

Engineering - Bessel
Engineering - Boolean
Engineering - Complex Numbers
Engineering - Miscellaneous
Engineering - Number Conversion

Financial - Annuity
Financial - Bill
Financial - Bond
Financial - Cash Flow
Financial - CD
Financial - Depreciation
Financial - Stock
Logical
Mathematical
Miscellaneous - Attribute
Miscellaneous - Cell and Table
Miscellaneous - Status
Miscellaneous - Table Lookup
Statistical - Descriptive
Statistical - Inferential
String

NOTE: *The Engineering Bessel functions are only available if you peform a custom installation.*

Getting Help with Functions

Once you type or insert the name of the function, you can press the F1 key to get help on the function, or you can look it up in the help system. In the Help Contents page, double-click on @Function Reference. You can then choose to select or list functions alphabetically or by category.

To find a function by its category, double-click on the category name and then work your way through the Help windows to get more information on the specific functions. In some cases, the category will be further subdivided. Clicking on Function Index lists all of the functions in alphabetic order.

The help system will show you the syntax of each function, what the arguments represent, and even samples of their use, as in Figure 18-2.

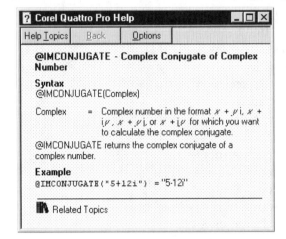

Using
Help for
complete
information
on functions

FIGURE 18-2

Formula Composer

Perhaps the best way to enter functions and complex formulas is to use Formula Composer. This is a special dialog box that helps you check your syntax and pinpoint errors in your logic, and that prompts you for arguments. You can use the Formula Composer to create a formula or function, or to troubleshoot one that you've already entered.

Click in the cell where you want to enter or edit a formula, and then click on the Formula Composer button to see the dialog box.

The box is shown labeled with a function already selected in Figure 18-3. The toolbar buttons, except the standard Cut, Copy, Paste, and Undo buttons, are shown in Table 18-1.

You enter or edit a formula in the Expression text box. To enter a function, either type it in or click on the Function button and make your choice from the dialog box that appears. As you work on the formula, the results are calculated and displayed in the Cell Value box so you can watch the effect of your formulas to see where a mistake takes place. The Cell Value will appear as ERR (error) until you enter a complete function or formula, without any missing or incorrect arguments and with the correct syntax.

The @Function pane explains the function being used, while the Argument pane lists each of the arguments for you to enter. The Outline pane displays a breakdown of the formula in sections, showing the value of cell references and calculations.

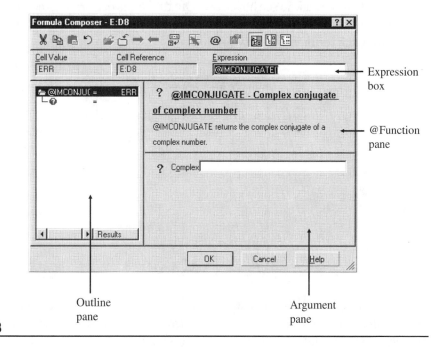

Formula
Composer

FIGURE 18-3

Outline
pane

Argument
pane

Expression
box

@Function
pane

Button	Function
Expand the formula	Expands the outline one level
Collapse the formula	Collapses the expression one level
Follow the formula	Displays the referenced cell
Return from the formula	Moves back to the selected cell
Convert to Value	Converts an expression into a value
Point	Switches to Point Mode
Function	Displays the function dialog box
Insert a cell name	Displays block names
Standard view	Displays all panes
Argument view	Displays just the Outline and Argument panes
Outline view	Displays just the Outline pane

Formula
Composer
Toolbar
Buttons

TABLE 18-1

18

Use the Outline pane to see how Corel Quattro Pro is performing the calculation. For example, here is what appears in the pane if you incorrectly tried to average values using the formula +100+100+100/3:

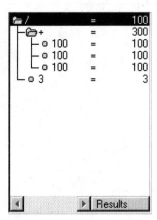

The result of the division is shown as 33.333333 and the values under it, 100 and 3, indicate how the operation was performed. You would know right away that you don't want to divide 100 by 33, so you would know that the structure of the formula is incorrect. Here is the outline when the formula uses parentheses:

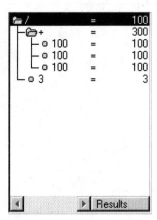

Now you can see that the values are grouped correctly.

You can double-click on the folder icons or the Collapse and Expand buttons to expand or collapse parts of the outline to concentrate on certain sections of the formula, just as you can expand and collapse an outline. Folder icons to the left of the outline indicate whether expressions have been expanded or collapsed. A small yellow circle means that that part of the expression cannot be expanded. A red question mark indicates that the expression is incorrect. When you select a section of the formula in the Outline pane, it also appears in the Expression box.

Sometimes, just seeing the cell references in the Outline pane is not enough. Because the value of a cell will depend on the cells that it references, you often have to trace through the worksheet to find the source of a problem.

You can trace a cell's references directly from Formula Composer, using the following steps:

1. Click on the cell reference in the Outline pane.

2. Click on the Follow button in the Formula Composer toolbar.

3. Look at the dialog box's title bar. The title bar will indicate the cells being referenced.

For example, if cell C6 refers to cell B4, clicking on the Follow button will display A:C6 -> A:B4 in the title bar, and show cell B4 selected in the background. If cell B4 refers to cell A1, then clicking on Follow again will display A:C6 -> A:B4 -> A1 in the title bar and select cell A1. Clicking on Back moves back to the original cell.

Perhaps the best way to visualize Formula Composer is to actually use it, so let's calculate a mortgage payment. We'll be entering values directly in the function, although you can enter or point to cell references just as well.

1. Click on cell B5, and click on the Formula Composer button.

2. Click on the Function button to display the Functions dialog box.

3. Choose the Financial - Annuity category.

4. Scroll the list and double-click on PAYMT. The Formula Composer dialog box will appear as in Figure 18-4. Each of the required and optional arguments are listed in the Argument pane.

5. Click on the Monthly Payment option button. This lets you enter annual interest and number of years rather than worry about calculating monthly interest and the number of monthly payments. It also adds the necessary operators into the Expression box, so it appears as @PAYMT(/12,*12,).

6. Click in the Rate (Yearly) argument and type **.06**. Corel Quattro Pro will add the value to the appropriate location in the Expression box; you do not have to worry about positioning the insertion point.

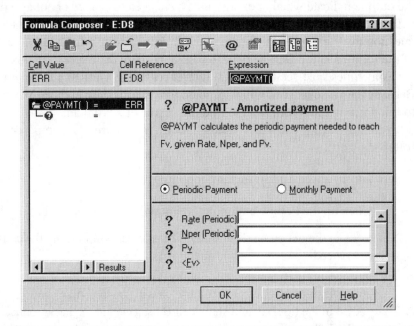

Formula
Composer
with
PAYMT
function

FIGURE 18-4

 TIP: *For help with a specific argument, click on the Help button before its name. Take a moment to notice the other sections of the dialog box. The Cell Value shows ERR because the function is not yet complete. The Outline pane indicates that section of the function and the values.*

7. Click in the Nper argument box and type **30**.

8. Click in the Pv argument box and type **_50000**. The Cell Value now indicates a valid result, and the breakdown is shown in the outline.

9. Click on OK to display the results in the cell.

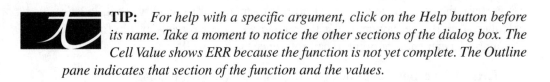 **NOTE:** *Right-click on a section of the Outline pane to display a useful QuickMenu.*

If you need to edit a function or formula, select its cell and click on the Formula Composer button.

Function Reference

Corel Quattro Pro includes hundreds of functions, ranging from the simple to the sublime. Some functions, such as @SUM and @AVG, are used quite often because they perform commonly used mathematical operations. Other functions are designed for very special needs. After all, how many of us will need to use the @IMAGINARY function to determine the imaginary coefficient of a complex number, or the @SPLINE function to find a polynomial fitted piecewise to pass through a given set of points?

If you need to perform an operation, and want to see if there is a built-in function that can help you, use the Function dialog box or scan through the categories in the help system. As a quick reference, however, you'll find a list of key functions here, grouped by category, along with their arguments.

18

Database Functions

You use database functions to help analyze information. You will learn about databases in Chapter 20. All of the functions use the same three arguments: Block, Column, and Criteria. *Block* is the range of cells that contains the database. *Column* is where the data is located that you want to analyze. *Criteria* are cells that indicate conditions that values have to meet to be included in the process. For example, the @DAVG function computes the average of the values in the designated column, using cells meeting the criteria.

Here are the database functions:

@DAVG(Block,Column,Criteria)	Calculates the average of the values
@DCOUNT(Block,Column,Criteria)	Calculates the number of values
@DGET(Block,Column,Criteria)	Returns a value or label from a field
@DMAX(Block,Column,Criteria)	Calculates the maximum value in the column
@DMIN(Block,Column,Criteria)	Calculates the minimum value in the column

@DPRODUCT(Block,Column,Criteria)	Multiplies the values in a field from all records in the database
@DPURECOUNT(Block,Column,Criteria)	Calculates the amount of all number field entries
@DSTD(Block,Column,Criteria)	Calculates the population standard deviation of the values
@DSTDS(Block,Column,Criteria)	Calculates the sample standard deviation of the values
@DSUM(Block,Column,Criteria)	Calculates the sum of the values
@DVAR(Block,Column,Criteria)	Calculates the population variance of the values
@DVARS(Block,Column,Criteria)	Calculates the sample variance of the values

Date Functions

These functions calculate dates, times, and days, or convert location coordinates. The date and time functions can be used in processing accounts. If you enter dates and times in an accepted format, Corel Quattro Pro can use these functions to perform math operations. For example, the function @TODAY-A4 determines how many days have passed since the date in cell A4.

To calculate the difference between two dates, just subtract them, as in +A4-A1, where both references are to cells containing dates. Dates are always converted to a series number, so subtracting them results in the number of days between them.

You can also move in the other direction, from a date serial to a formatted date. For example, suppose you want to schedule an appointment 30 days from today. Use the function @ACDAYS(@Today, 30) to insert the date of the appointment in the active cell. To count just business days, use the formula @ABDAYS(@TODAY, 30). Both of these functions, however, will display the serial number of the date. To see the date itself, use the Block Properties to change the Numeric Format to Date.

Common arguments used in these functions include a date, time, number of days, years, months, hours, and minutes. Some optional arguments include the following:

- *Holidays* indicates whether a range of dates contains dates that are holidays. Use 0 to indicate no holidays, or enter the date of a holiday in the group.

- *Saturday* signifies if you want to include Saturday as a business day (1) or not (0).

- *Sunday* indicates if you want Sunday to be counted as a business day (1) or not (0).

Here are some useful date and time functions:

@ABDAYS(Date,Days,<Holidays>, <Saturday>,<Sunday>)	Calculates the date in a specific number of business days
@ACDAYS(Date,Days, <Calendar>,<EndMnth>)	Calculates the date in a specific number of calendar days
@AMNTHS(Date,Months,<EndMnth>)	The date in a specific number of months
@BDAYS(StartDate,EndDate, <Holidays>,<Saturday>,<Sunday>)	Calculates the number of business days between two dates
@BUSDAY(Date,<Direction>, <Holidays>,<Saturday>,<Sunday>)	Calculates the closest business date
@CDAYS(StartDate,EndDate, <Calendar>,<February>)	Calculates the number of calendar days between StartDate and EndDate, including EndDate
@DATE(Yr,Mo,Day)	Calculates the serial number for a date
@DATEDIF(StartDate,EndDate, Format)	Calculates the number of years, months, or days between two dates
@DAY(DateTimeNumber)	Calculates the day of the month
@EMNTH(Date)	Calculates the last day of the month

@FBDAY(Date,<Holidays>, <Saturday>,<Sunday>)	Calculates the first business day in the month
@LBDAY(Date,<Holidays>, <Saturday>,<Sunday>)	Calculates the date of the last business day of the month
@MDAYS(Month,Year)	Calculates the number of days in the month
@NBDAY(Date,<Holidays>, <Saturday>,<Sunday>)	Calculates the first business day after a date
@TODAY	Calculates the serial number of the current date

Engineering Functions

These functions perform calculations used in engineering applications. They are divided into five categories.

Bessel functions calculate values that satisfy the Bessel equation or the modified Bessel equation, used in physics and engineering applications. Here are the Bessel functions:

@BESSELI(x,n)	Performs the modified Bessel function *In(x)*
@BESSELJ(x,n)	Performs the Bessel function *Jn(x)*
@BESSELK(x,n)	Performs the modified Bessel function *Kn(x)*
@BESSELY(x,n)	Performs the Bessel function *Yn(x)*

Boolean functions deal with logic and bitwise operations. They are useful if you are working with binary or hexadecimal numbers. Some of the useful functions are listed here:

@ADDB(Binary1,<Binary2>,<BitIn>,<Bits>)	Adds two binary numbers
@ADDBO(Binary1,Binary2,<BitIn>,<Bits>)	Returns the overflow bit of a binary sum
@ADDH(Hex1,<Hex2>,<BitIn>,<Bits>)	Adds two hexadecimal numbers
@ADDHO(Hex1,Hex2,<BitIn>,<Bits>)	Returns the overflow bit of a hexadecimal sum
@INVB(Binary,<Bits>)	Returns the inverse of a binary number

@INVH(Hex,<Bits>)	Returns the inverse of a hexadecimal number
@ORB(Binary1,<Binary2>,<Bits>)	Returns the OR results of two binary numbers
@ORH(Hex1,<Hex2>,<Bits>)	Returns the OR results of two hexadecimal numbers
@SUBB(Binary1,Binary2,<BitIn>,<Bits>)	Returns the difference between two binary numbers
@SUBBO(Binary1,Binary2,<BitIn>,<Bits>)	Returns the overflow bit of difference between two binary numbers

Complex number functions convert or modify a complex number. A complex number is one whose square is a negative real number. Some complex number functions are as follows:

@IMCOS(Complex)	Returns the cosine of a complex number
@IMDIV(Complex1,Complex2)	Returns the result of dividing one complex number by another complex number
@IMLN(Complex)	Returns the natural logarithm of a complex number
@IMLOG10(Complex)	Returns the base 10 logarithm of a complex number
@IMLOG2(Complex)	Returns the base 2 logarithm of a complex number
@IMPOWER(Complex,Power)	Returns a complex number raised to a power
@IMSQRT(Complex)	Returns the square root of a complex number

Miscellaneous functions serve assorted engineering needs, such as data conversion and returning error codes. Here is a sample:

@CONVERT(*X*,FromUnit,ToUnit)	Returns the value *X* in FromUnit units, converted to a value in ToUnit units
@GAMMA(*X*)	Calculates the gamma function of the value *X*
@SPLINE(Known*X*'s, Known*Y*'s, OutputBlock)	Returns a polynomial fitted piecewise to pass through a given set of points

Number conversion functions convert a value from one number system to another. These can be useful if you are working with a programming language or application that uses ASCII codes, binary, hexadecimal, or octal numbers.

Some conversion functions include the following:

@ASCTOHEX(ASCII,<Places>)	Returns the hexadecimal equivalent of an ASCII value
@BINTOHEX(Binary)	Returns the hexadecimal equivalent of a binary number
@BINTONUM(Binary)	Returns the decimal equivalent of a binary number
@BINTOOCT(Binary)	Returns the octal value equivalent of a binary number
@HEXTOASC(Hex)	Returns the ASCII character of a hexadecimal number
@HEXTOBIN(Hex)	Returns the binary equivalent of a hexadecimal number
@NUMTOBIN(Decimal)	Returns the binary equivalent of a decimal number
@OCTTOBIN(Oct)	Returns the binary equivalent of an octal number
@OCTTOHEX(Oct)	Returns the hexadecimal string equivalent of an octal number
@OCTTONUM(Oct)	Returns the decimal equivalent of an octal number

Financial Functions

These functions perform financial calculations and operations. They are divided into several categories based on their use, and most have a number of arguments.

Annuity functions deal with periodic payments and investments. Arguments typically include interest rates, the number of payment periods, loan amounts, and payment amounts. The functions return one value when given the others.

Some of the less obvious arguments include

- *n*—The number of payments made

- *Part*—Part of a period passed

- *Residual*—Remaining loan balance at the end of loan term

- *ResOff*—The number of periods after the last periodic payment that residual is to be paid

- *Adv*—The number of advance payments

- *Odd*—The number of periods between start of the loan and the first payment

- *Simp*—Compound (0) or Simple (1) interest

Here's a sample of the annuity functions:

@AMAINT(Principal,Int,Term,*n*, <Part>,<Residual >,<ResOff>, <Adv>,<Odd>,<Simp>)	Calculates the accumulated interest paid on a loan after *n* payments
@AMPMTI(Principal,Int,Term,*n*, <Residual>,<ResOff>,<Adv>, <Odd>,<Simp>)	Calculates the interest portion of a loan payment
@AMRPRN(Principal,Int,Term,*n*, <Part >,<Residual>,<ResOff>, <Adv >,<Odd>,<Simp>)	Calculates the balance remaining after so many loan payments
@CUMPRINC(Rate,Nper,Pv, StartPeriod,EndPeriod,Type)	Calculates the cumulative principal paid on a loan between two periods
@FVAL(Rate,Nper,Pmt,<Pv>, <Type>)	Calculates the future value of an annuity

@MTGACC(Int,TtlPer,Principal, Residual,ExtraPrin,<Fper>,<Lper>, <Rper>,<Option>)	Calculates the interest saved, and the new loan term and payoff date, after paying extra monthly principal
@PPAYMT(Rate,Per,Nper,Pv,<Fv>, <Type>)	Calculates the portion of a loan payment that goes to principal

Bill functions calculate values for Treasury Bill investments. The arguments typically include the settlement and maturity date of the issue and the investment amount. Other arguments include

- *Price*—The price per 100 face value

- *Redemption*—The redemption value per 100 face value

- *Calendar*—A number that represents the type of calendar: 0 = 30/360, 1 = actual/actual, 2 = actual/360, and 3 = actual/365

Here are the functions in this category:

@DISC(Settle,Maturity,Price, <Redemption>,<Calendar>)	Returns the discount rate based on the discount price
@INTRATE(Settle,Maturity, Investment,Redemption, <Calendar>)	Returns the simple annualized yield
@PRICEDISC(Settle,Maturity, Discount,<Redemption>, <Calendar>)	Returns the price of a discounted security
@RECEIVED(Settle,Maturity, Investment,Discount,<Calendar>)	Calculates the redemption value of a discounted security
@TBILLEQ(Settle,Maturity, Discount)	Returns the bond equivalent yield for a Treasury bill
@TBILLPRICE(Settle,Maturity, Discount)	Calculates the price-per-100 face value of a Treasury bill
@TBILLYIELD(Settle,Maturity, Price)	Calculates the yield of a Treasury bill
@YIELDDISC(Settle,Maturity, Price, <Redemption>,<Calendar>)	Returns the annualized yield for a discounted security

Bond functions deal with corporate and municipal bond investments. The arguments also include the settlement and maturity date, as well as coupon dates and frequency of payments.

The functions include the following:

@ACCRINT(Settle,Maturity,Coupon, <Issue>,<FirstCpn>,<Par >,<Freq>, <Calendar>)	Calculates the accrued interest on a bond
@COUPDAYBS(Settle,Maturity, <Freq>,<Calendar>)	Returns the number of days from the start of a coupon period to the settlement date
@COUPDAYSNC(Settle,Maturity, <Freq >,<Calendar>)	Returns the number of days between the date of settlement and the next coupon date
@PRICE(Settle,Maturity,Coupon, Yield,<Redemption>,<Freq>, <Calendar>)	Calculates the price-per-100 face value of a security that pays periodic interest
@YIELD(Settle,Maturity,Issue, Coupon,Price,<Calendar>)	Returns the yield on a security

Cash-flow functions perform analysis on income and expenditure data. Here are some cash-flow functions:

@FUTV(Intrate,Flows,<<Odd |Periods>>,<Simp>,<Pathdep>, <Filter>,<Start>,<End>)	Returns the future value of a cash flow
@IRR(Guess,Block)	Returns the internal rate of return
@NETPV(Discrate,Flows,<Initial>, <<Odd |Periods>>,<Simp>,<Pathdep>, <Filter>,<Start>,<End>)	Returns the net present value of a cash flow

CD functions perform calculations relating to certificates of deposit. These functions are as follows:

@ACCRINTM(Issue,Settle,Coupon, <Par>,<Calendar>)	Returns the accrued interest for a security that pays interest at maturity

@PRICEMAT(Settle,Maturity, Issue,Coupon,Yield,<Calendar>)	Calculates the price-per-100 face value of a security that pays interest at maturity
@YIELDMAT(Settle,Maturity, Issue,Coupon,Price,<Calendar>)	Returns the annual yield of a security that pays interest at maturity

Depreciation functions calculate depreciation of assets over time using a specific method. Arguments include the cost of the item, its salvage value, and its life. They may also include the current period held, or a starting and ending period. The depreciation functions are as follows:

@DB(Cost,Salvage,Life,Period, <Month>)	Returns the depreciation of an asset using the fixed-declining balance method
@DDB(Cost,Salvage,Life,Period)	Returns depreciation using the double-declining method
@SLN(Cost,Salvage,Life)	Returns depreciation using the straight-line method
@SYD(Cost,Salvage,Life,Period)	Calculates the sum-of-the-years'-digits' depreciation allowance
@VDB(Cost,Salvage,Life, StartPeriod,EndPeriod,<Factor>, <Switch>)	Returns depreciation allowance using the variable rate method

Stock functions calculate common values when dealing with stocks. The stock functions are as follows:

@DOLLARDE(FracDollar,Denom)	Converts a fractional price into dollars
@DOLLARFR(DecDollar,Denom)	Converts a dollar price into a fractional price
@FEETBL(Tu,Ppu,<StdTbl |Val>, <<MinTbl |Val>>,<<MaxTbl |Val>>,<RndPlcs>)	Returns the fee for a stock transaction, using values established in a fee table
@STKOPT(OptCode,OptPrem, UndStkVal,Date,Load,CmdString)	Calculates the time value and earnings value of a stock option

18

Logical Functions

These functions deal with logical expressions. They return a true or false value based on a range of cells, filename, or value. These functions are normally used to test the value or contents of a block of cells, to determine a course of action.

The most important of the functions is @IF. This function tests the results of an expression, inserting one value into the active cell if the expression is true, another if false. The syntax is @IF(Condition, TrueExpression, FalseExpression).

For example, suppose cell D3 contains the number of days a client's bill has been outstanding. This could have been calculated with an expression such as @TODAY-A4, where A4 is the date the bill should have been paid. To determine an entry based on the number of days, use a function such as @IF(D3>30,"Deadbeat","Valued Customer"). The function says "If the value in cell D3 is greater than 30, then insert the label 'Deadbeat' into the active cell; otherwise insert the label 'Valued Customer.'"

The condition can be any logical expression that returns a true or false value. It can be a formula or one of the other logical functions. One very typical use of the function is to avoid error messages generated when you attempt to divide a value by 0, an improper mathematical operation. Suppose you need to perform the formula +A1/A2. To avoid generating the error, use a function such as @IF(A2=0,"NA", +A1/A2). If cell A2 has a value of 0, the formula will display the characters "NA". Otherwise, it will perform and display the calculation.

Here are some other useful logical functions:

@FILEEXISTS(FileName)	The function is true if the file exists; false if not.
@ISBLANK(Cell)	The function is true if the cell is blank.
@ISBLOCK(Block)	This function returns true if the block is a defined name or a valid block address.
@ISNUMBER(X0)	This function returns true if the argument is a numeric value; otherwise, it returns false.

Mathematical Functions

Mathematical functions calculate numeric values. Many of these functions use one or two arguments representing a value or cell reference. Some common mathematical functions, such as Average and Sum, are classified as Statistical functions and will be discussed later.

There are quite a few mathematical functions, including these:

@ABS(*X*)	Returns the absolute value of *X*
@COS(*X*)	Returns the cosine of angle *X*
@DEGREES(*X*)	Returns the number of degrees in *X* radians
@EVEN(*X*)	Returns the closest even value of *X*, rounded away from zero
@GCD(*X,Y*)	Returns the greatest common divisor of *X* and *Y*
@LCM(*X,Y*)	Returns the least common multiple of *X* and *Y*
@LOG(*X*)	Returns the Log base 10 of *X*
@MOD(*X,Y*)	Returns the remainder of the division *X/Y*
@ODD(*X*)	Returns the closest odd value of *X*, rounded away from zero
@PI	Returns the value of pi
@RAND	Returns a random number between 0 and 1
@RANDBETWEEN(*N,M*)	Returns a random number between *N* and *M*
@ROMAN(Number,<Form>)	Returns the Arabic numeral corresponding to the Roman numeral in the argument
@ROUND(*X*,Num)	Rounds the value *X* to the number of digits specified with Num (up to 15)
@SQRT(*X*)	Returns the square root of *X*

Miscellaneous Functions

These are functions that do not fall into other categories, but are quite useful. They are divided into four categories.

Attribute functions return a specific attribute or property of a cell, or of the top-left cell in a block. The Block argument is the cell or block of cells for which you want to find an attribute. The Attribute argument determines what attribute is returned. The function @CELL("type",A1), for example, will return a code representing the type of entry, either *v* (value), *l* (label), or *b* (blank). The Attribute arguments are

- *"address"*—Cell coordinates

- *"row"*—Row number

- *"col"*—Column notebook pages A through IV

- *"sheet"*—Sheet number

- *"NotebookName"*—Notebook name

- *"NotebookPath"*—Path where the notebook is referenced

- *"TwoDAddress"*—2-D address

- *"ThreeDAddress"*—3-D address

- *"FullAddress"*—Complete address, including notebook name

- *"contents"*—Contents of the cell

- *"type"*—Type of the contents: *b* (blank), *v* (value), or *l* (label)

- *"prefix"*—The alignment character: ' (left), ^ (centered), " (right), or \ (repeating)

- *"protect"*—The protected status: 0 (not protected) or 1 (protected)

- *"width"*—Column width

- *"rwidth"*—Block width

- *"format"*—Format

Here's a recap of the attribute functions:

@CELL(Attribute,Block)	Returns the requested attribute of the cell block
@CELLINDEX(Attribute,Block, Column,Row,<Page>)	Returns the attribute of the cell in the position offset from the block
@CELLPOINTER(Attribute)	Returns the requested attribute of the active cell

Cell and Table functions supply information about a cell or block, such as its block name or the number of rows and columns it contains. The functions include these:

@@(Cell)	Returns the contents of the cell—both @ signs are required
@BLOCKNAME(Block)	Returns the name assigned to the cell or block
@CHOOSE(Number,List)	Returns the value in a cell in a list of cells
@COLS(Block)	Returns the number of columns in a block
@COLUMN(<Block>)	Returns the column number for a cell or block
@COUNTBLANK(Block)	Returns the number of blank cells in a block
@FIRSTBLANKPAGE(Block)	Returns the letter of the first unnamed blank page in a notebook
@ROW(<Block>)	Returns the row number for a cell or block
@ROWS(Block)	Returns the number of rows in a block

Status functions return a setting for a command, property, or other element of the Corel Quattro Pro environment. They include the following:

@AREAS(Block)	Returns the number of areas in a block
@COMMAND(Command Equivalent)	Returns the current setting of command equivalent
@MEMAVAIL	Returns the amount of available conventional memory
@MEMEMSAVAIL	Returns the amount of available expanded (EMS) memory
@PROPERTY	Returns the current setting of Property for the requested Object
@VERSION	Returns the version number of Corel Quattro Pro

Table Lookup functions search for a value in a block of cells. These are typically used with lookup tables. For example, you can create a table of shipping charges based on the number of items and the designation zone, as shown in Figure 18-5. Use the function @Index(A7..E12,G3,G2) to find the shipping charge for a specific shipment and insert the charge into an invoice.

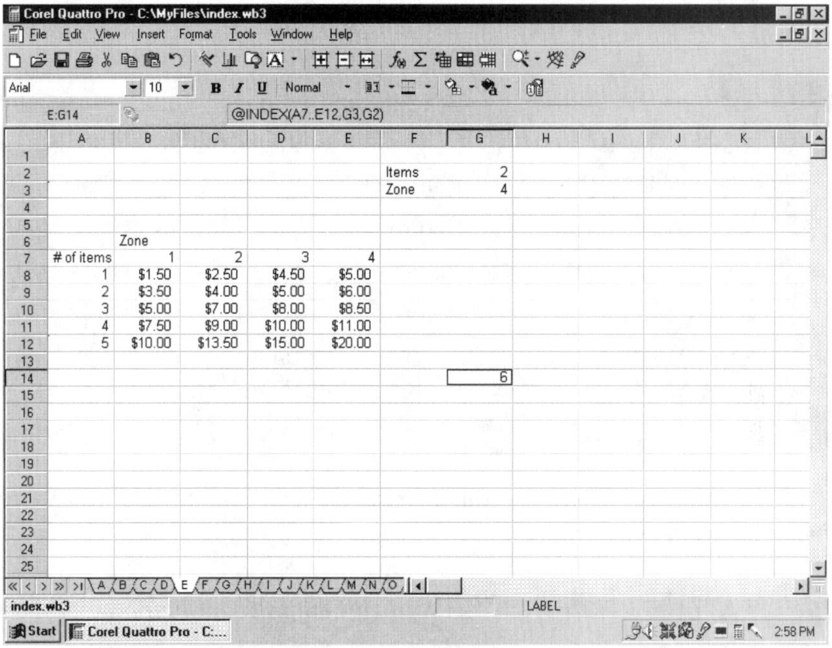

Using a
table to
retrieve
information

FIGURE 18-5

Here is a sampling of the functions:

@HLOOKUP(X, Block, Row)	Returns the value of the cell in Row number of rows beneath X in a block
@INDEX(Block, Column, Row)	Returns the value in the column and row of the specified block
@LOOKUP(Value, LookupVector, ResultVector)	Returns a value in a specified row or column
@VLOOKUP(X, Block, Column)	Returns the value of the cell in Column number of columns to the right of X in a block

Statistical Functions

Statistical functions perform mathematical and analysis operations on a list or group of values. They are divided into two types—Descriptive and Inferential.

Descriptive functions return a value to describe or summarize a group of values. Typical descriptive functions include the following:

@AVG(List)	Returns the average of a block or list of cells
@COUNT(List)	Counts the number of nonblank cells in a block
@GEOMEAN(List)	Returns the geometric mean of values in a block
@MAX(List)	Returns the largest value in the block
@MEDIAN(List)	Returns the median of values in the block
@MIN(List)	Returns the smallest value in the block
@STD(List)	Returns the population standard deviation of all nonblank values in the block
@SUM(List)	Returns the sum of the values in the block

Inferential functions help you draw conclusions about a group of values. These functions include the following:

@AVEDEV(List)	Calculates the average deviation of the items in a block from their mean
@NORMSDIST(X)	Calculates the standard cumulative normal distribution function
@SUMSQ(List)	Calculates the sum of the squares of the numbers in a block
@ZTEST(Array,X,<S>)	Calculates the two-tailed probability value of a z-test

String Functions

These functions perform tasks on strings of characters or text. Arguments include one or more strings, and the function returns either a string or a numerical value. For example, suppose you have an e-mail address in cell D19 and you want to find the domain—the characters following the @ sign. Use this function:

@RIGHT(D19,@LENGTH(D19)-@FIND("@",D19,1)-1)

The function @FIND("@",D19,1) locates the position of the @ character from the left of the string, starting with position 0. The function @LENGTH(D19) returns the number of characters in the string. The formula @LENGTH(D19)-@FIND("@",D19,1)-1) determines the number of characters following the @ sign, and the @RIGHT function displays them in the cell.

Here are some string functions:

@CHAR(Code)	Returns the ANSI character that corresponds to the decimal code
@CLEAN(String)	Returns the string with all nonprintable ASCII codes removed
@CODE(String)	Returns the ANSI code of the first character in the string
@CONCATENATE(List)	Combines all of the strings in the list into one large string
@FIND(SubString,String, StartNumber)	Returns the position of a substring in a given string, starting from a specified position
@LEFT(String,Num)	Returns a given number of characters from the beginning of the string
@LENGTH(String)	Returns the number of characters, including spaces, in a string
@LOWER(String)	Converts a string to all lowercase letters
@MID(String,StartNumber,Num)	Returns a number of characters from the string, starting with the character in the specified position
@RIGHT(String,Num)	Returns a number of characters from the end of the string
@STRING(X,Num)	Converts a numeric value into a string
@TRIM(String)	Removes all leading, trailing, and multiple spaces from a string
@UPPER(String)	Converts a string to all uppercase (capital letters)
@VALUE(String)	Returns the numeric value of a string; results in ERR if the string cannot be converted to a number

Charts, Maps, and Graphics

19

When you want your data to have maximum impact, try presenting the information as a graph or map, or emphasizing points with another graphic. You can insert ClipArt and TextArt into a Corel Quattro Pro worksheet just as you can with a Corel WordPerfect document. Charts and maps, however, are ideally suited to Corel Quattro Pro because they can visually convey trends and patterns in numeric data. The techniques for charts and maps are similar—if not almost identical—so once you learn how to create one, you can easily create the other. There are some important differences, so read over each section in this chapter carefully. You can also combine charts, maps, and slides that contain text into an onscreen slide show for an impressive presentation.

 Add TextArt to a worksheet by choosing Graphic from the Insert menu and clicking on TextArt. Use the TextArt window just as you learned to do in Chapter 12.

Creating Charts

Before creating a graph for the first time, you should understand a few things that go into one. A graph must have at least one data series. A data series is a set of numbers representing the values of something you are measuring or reporting. For example, the graph shown in Figure 19-1 has two series, both of which show dollar amounts in each of four quarters. The first series, represented by the lighter color bars, shows revenue in the four quarters. The second series, in the darker bars, shows expenses. The chart also contains X- and Y-axis labels. The X-axis labels explain what each set of numbers represents, in this case the four quarters of the year. The Y-axis label shows the values being represented.

 NOTE: *When you have more than one series, you can have a legend that explains what each series represents.*

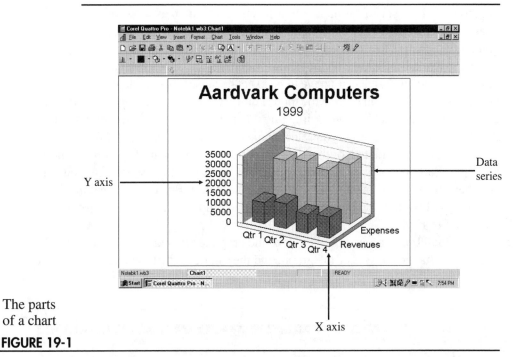

The parts
of a chart

FIGURE 19-1

You can create a graph either as a floating object or in a separate window. A floating object appears on the worksheet page, so you can print it on the same sheet as the data that it represents and change its position on the page. When you create a chart in its own windows, you must print it separately from the worksheet.

 You can insert charts and maps that you create with Corel Quattro Pro into your Corel WordPerfect documents.

Floating Objects

You can create a floating chart in two ways—using the QuickChart button in the toolbar or the Chart Expert. The Expert lets you choose the chart type and other options as you create the chart. You don't get those options with the QuickChart tool, although you can edit any chart to change its properties after you create it.

To create a chart, select the block that contains the information you want to chart—including the row and column labels. The column labels will become the X-axis labels, while the row labels will identify each series in the legend. If you use numbers, such as years, for the column labels, enter them as text starting with the apostrophe character. Then click on the QuickChart button in the toolbar. The mouse pointer will change to a crosshair with a miniature chart.

In the worksheet, drag a rectangle the size you want the chart to appear into the position you want it. It doesn't have to be exact because you can change its size and position later. When you release the mouse button, the chart will appear. (If you just click on the worksheet instead of dragging the mouse, Corel Quattro Pro will create the chart in a default size.) If you selected only one series, Corel Quattro Pro would create a pie chart. With two or more series, it creates a bar chart. Figure 19-2 shows a sample chart and the data that was used to create it. Enter the worksheet yourself, and then create a chart next to it as shown in the figure. Be sure to select the range of cells A4..D7, click on the QuickChart button, and then drag the mouse around blocks E1 to K24.

The small boxes around the border of the graph are called *handles*. You use the handles to change the size of the graph, and they indicate that the chart is selected.

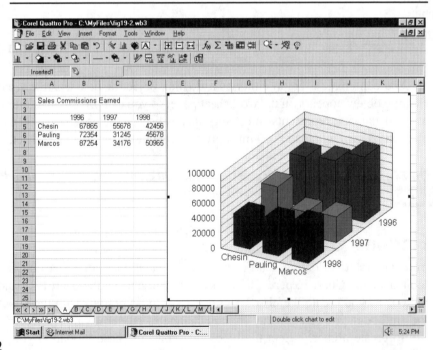

Sample
chart and
worksheet

FIGURE 19-2

If you click outside of the chart area, the handles will disappear and the chart will no longer be selected. To change the chart's size or position, or other properties, click on the border around the chart to select it first.

NOTE: *Click on the border around the chart to display the handles. You can also click on the chart itself to edit it, as you will soon learn. However, clicking on the chart will not display the handles for changing the chart's size or position.*

The chart is linked to the worksheet cells that you selected to create it. So if you change any of the data used to create the graph, Corel Quattro Pro will adjust the chart automatically. One advantage of the floating chart is that you can place the chart and the worksheet side by side on the screen to instantly see the effects of changing values on the chart.

19

TIP: *To delete a floating chart, select it and then press DEL.*

Using Chart Expert

You can also create a chart using the Chart Expert. It takes a few extra steps, but you get to select chart options in the process. You can also choose to create a floating chart or to place the chart in its own window. Here's how to use Chart Expert:

1. Select the range of cells that you want to chart.

2. Pull down the Insert menu and click on Chart. The first Chart Expert box appears, showing the coordinates of the selected block.

3. If you did not select the range first, or if it is incorrect, enter the range or use Point mode. The box has two other options:

   ■ *Swap rows/columns* plots columns as the series and places the X-axis series labels in the legend.

   ■ *Reverse series* plots last series first. Use this option if you are creating a 3-D chart, for example, and the first series would have larger bars that obscure the others. Reversing the plot would place the smaller bars in the foreground.

4. Click on Next to see the second Expert dialog box. In this box, you choose the general type of chart. The options are Bar, Rotate Bar, Pie, Line or Area, Specialty, and Experts Choice.

5. Select the general category of chart you want to create.

6. Click on Next to display a dialog box showing several specific types of charts in the category you selected, as shown in Figure 19-3. If you selected a bar chart as the general category, for instance, the dialog box includes several different types of bar charts.

7. Click on the type of chart you want and then click on Next.

8. Choose an overall color scheme and click on Next.

9. Enter a chart title and subtitle and labels for the X axis and Y axis. You can also choose if you want to place the chart on the current sheet (floating) or in its own chart sheet.

10. Click on Finish. If you choose to place it on the notebook sheet, drag the mouse to indicate the position and size. When you release the mouse button, the chart will appear.

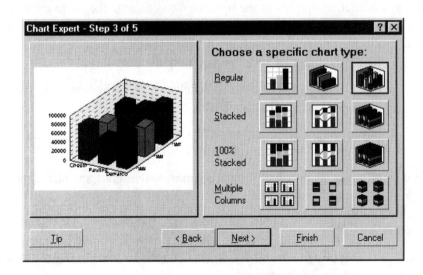

Selecting a chart type in the Chart Expert dialog box

FIGURE 19-3

Changing Graph Size

You can easily change the size and position of a chart, using the same techniques as editing a graphic in Corel WordPerfect. To change the size of a floating chart, point to one of the graph handles and drag.

- Drag a handle on the top or bottom border to change the height.

- Drag a handle on the right or left to change the width.

- Drag a handle on a corner to change the height and width at the same time.

To move a graph, use the following steps:

1. Place the mouse pointer inside the graph and hold down the mouse button so the pointer appears as a hand.

2. Drag the mouse to change the location. The screen will scroll as you drag the mouse, and an outline of the graph will move with the pointer.

3. Position the outline where you want the graph to appear and release the mouse button.

Creating a Chart in a Window

When you create a chart in its own window, the chart is not on the worksheet page and Corel Quattro Pro determines its size. This is a good choice if you don't want the chart and worksheet to appear together, and you don't want to use worksheet space for the chart.

To create a chart in a window, use Chart Expert or the New Chart Window command from the QuickMenu. With Chart Expert, just select the Chart Window option in the last Chart Expert dialog box.

To use the New Chart command, select the cells that you want to chart, right-click on the cells and choose New Chart Window from the QuickMenu to see the dialog box in Figure 19-4. The pages in the dialog box give you the same options as Chart Expert. Use the following steps:

1. In the Series page, designate the blocks to use for the X axis, legend, and data series. Corel Quattro Pro will try to identify the blocks from the type of data in them.

19

2. In the Type page, select the general and specific chart type.

3. In the Titles page, enter the title and subtitle, and axis labels.

4. In the Name page, give the chart a name.

When you close the dialog box, the completed chart will appear in its own window and with its own Chart menu, toolbar, and property bar as shown in Figure 19-5.

As with a floating chart, the chart in the window is also linked to the worksheet data, and it will change if you edit the values in the associated cells. To see both the chart and worksheet onscreen at the same time, however, you must tile the windows and adjust their sizes.

The Chart window appears in the foreground, with the worksheet behind. Both windows, however, are listed on the application bar. When you want to return to the worksheet, just click on its name in the application bar. You can also pull down the Window menu and click on the worksheet name in the list of windows. To redisplay the chart, select its name from the application bar or from the Window menu.

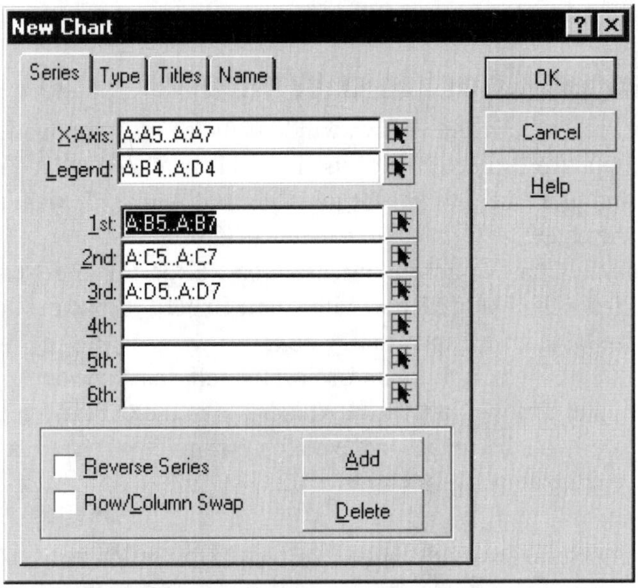

New Chart
dialog box

FIGURE 19-4

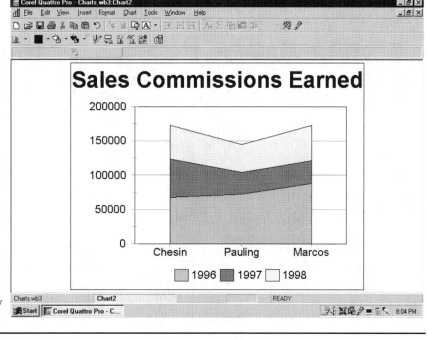

Chart in its
own window

FIGURE 19-5

If you close the Chart window by clicking on its Close button, you can open it
again only from the Objects page. Icons for every chart and map—floating or in
their own windows—are placed on the Objects page that you'll learn about later.

Editing Charts

You can modify a chart at any time, changing its type, titles, appearance, and other
properties. If you created a chart in its own window, all of the menu and toolbar tools
for editing will appear when its window is active.

One way to change some properties of a floating chart, however, is to point to
its border (so the mouse pointer appears as a four-pointer arrow) and click, and then
use the property bar and QuickMenu. The buttons in the property bar that appear
when a chart is selected are shown here:

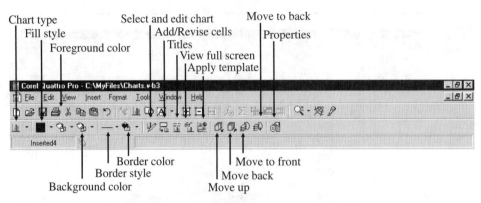

Figure 19-6 shows the QuickMenu that appears when you right-click on the chart. Using the property bar and QuickMenu, you can change the type, series, and titles. Choose View to display the chart full screen—click the mouse when you have finished.

To access a full range of editing tools to customize a floating chart, you need to display the Chart menu as well. You can do this two ways with a floating chart. If you click on the chart, inside of the border around it, you can edit it in place. This means that the Chart menu and property bar will appear onscreen, but also that you can see the chart along with the worksheet. You can also edit the chart in place by

QuickMenu
for editing
a chart

FIGURE 19-6

selecting Edit from the chart's QuickMenu. When you edit in place, however, the Border Style and Border Color buttons are not on the property bar.

To edit the chart in a separate window, even though it was created as a floating chart, right-click on the chart and choose Open from the QuickMenu. As an alternative, click on the Select and Edit Chart button in the property bar to see a list of charts in the workbook. Select the chart you want to open and then click on OK. When you close the separate Chart window, however, you will still see the chart on the worksheet page.

 TIP: *The Edit and Open options will only appear in the QuickMenu when the chart is not already in the Edit mode. If you are already editing the chart, click outside of it and then right-click on the chart to show the QuickMenu.*

Use the Chart menu bar and the property bar to edit the chart and add other elements to it. The Chart menu offers these features:

- *View* lets you change the aspect ratio the chart is shown in. Options include Floating Chart, Screen Slide, 35mm Slide, Print Preview, and Full Extent. Experiment with the options to find the most pleasing appearance onscreen and when printed.

- *Insert* lets you add other elements to the chart, such as clipart from your disk, a drawing object from the Shape submenu, or another object from other Windows applications. You can also choose Link to Cells to add a live picture of the charted cells right in the chart box. That way, you'll see your worksheet data when you print the chart.

- *Format* arranges the relationship of the graphics to the page and to other graphics, with options Align, Position, Space, Group, Ungroup, and Object Order.

- *Chart* lets you change the appearance and type of the chart. Options are Gallery, Type/Layout, Series, Titles, Legend, Axis, Perspective (for 3-D charts), Background, and Export to File.

- *Tools* lets you insert, edit, and delete charts; run Spell Check and display QuickCorrect options; create, edit, and play slide shows; and change Corel Quattro Pro settings.

Let's take a look at some of the ways you can customize a chart.

Changing the Chart Type

After you create your chart, you may find that the type you selected does not adequately portray what you want to get across. You may also want to experiment by selecting other chart types and subtypes until you find the most effective design. To change the chart type, whether you are editing a floating chart or a chart in a window, pull down the Chart Type list in the property bar to see the options shown here. Click on the chart type that you want to apply.

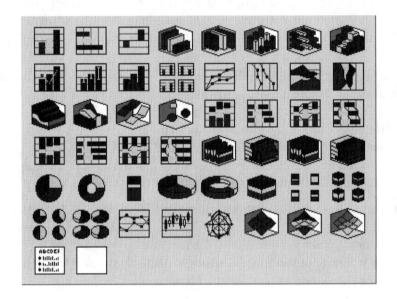

For even more choices, click on the Apply Template button in the property bar to open the Chart Gallery, shown in Figure 19-7. From this dialog box, select the general and then specific type of chart. The Gallery dialog box also offers a Color Scheme list and an Advisor button. Pull down the Color Scheme list to select from background colors and patterns.

Click on Advisor to let Corel Quattro Pro help you choose the best type for your data, as shown in Figure 19-8. Start by specifying qualifications called *constraints*. Use the sliders in the Constraints section to indicate your preferences between

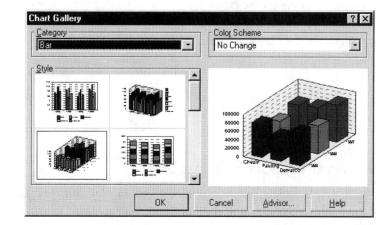

Chart
Gallery
dialog box

FIGURE 19-7

stressing individual or cumulative results, showing differences or trends, or using a
simple or fancy layout. Also, set the number of series and data points. When you
click on Advise, Corel Quattro Pro will suggest the chart style for you. To change
the chart to that style, click on Apply.

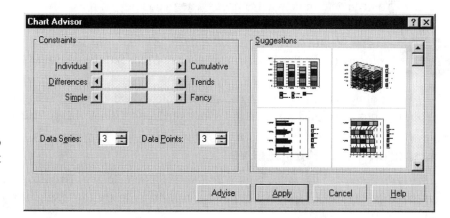

Using
the Chart
Advisor to
help select
the best
chart for
your data

FIGURE 19-8

If you are working on the chart in a window, you can also use these steps:

1. Pull down the Chart menu.

2. Click on Gallery or on Type/Layout.

3. Choose the category and style from the dialog box that appears.

4. Click on OK.

Changing the Chart Background

By default, charts appear in a box with a single border and clear background. To select other settings, select from the Fill Style, Foreground Color, and Background Color lists in the property bar.

If you are editing the chart in a window, you can also select Background from the Chart menu to see a dialog box with two pages:

■ *Fill settings* determine the fill style, pattern color, and background color of the chart. You can select from three style types—patterns, washes (gradients), and bitmaps (a selected clipart graphic).

■ *Chart button* lets you use the chart as a live button during a slide show. You can determine what happens when you click on the chart.

 TIP: *When you are editing the selected chart, you set the box type and color using the Border Style and Border Color buttons in the property bar.*

Select options from the two pages, and then close the dialog box. You can always reopen the box and change your settings if the overall effect is not what you had in mind.

Changing 3-D Perspective

Charts rendered in 3-D can be quite effective and eye-catching. To customize their appearance, choose Perspective from the Chart menu to see the dialog box shown in Figure 19-9.

In the 3-D View page, adjust the rotation and elevation. Changing rotation would change the perspective as if you were walking around the chart on a plane even with the X axis. It would be like walking around a house. If you rotate in one direction, you'd be looking at the chart more from the right; in the other direction, from the left.

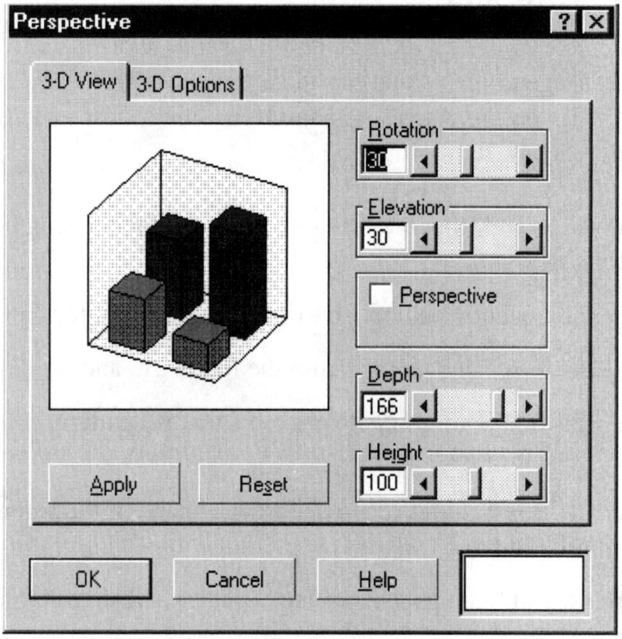

Setting
options for
3-D charts

FIGURE 19-9

Elevation is the view from top to bottom, as if you could float above the chart at various angles. Elevate in one direction to look "down" at the top of the chart; the other direction to look up at it.

The depth setting affects the distance from the front of the chart to its back wall, the rectangle behind the charted data. Height is the size of the chart from the bottom to the top—the distance from the X axis to the top of the chart.

TIP: *Click on the Perspective checkbox to maintain the current ratio as you change settings.*

The 3-D Options page determines if the left and back walls and the base appear. You can also choose between thick or default walls.

Inserting a Legend

When you create a 2-D chart with at least two series, Corel Quattro Pro will normally also include a legend. If not, you can add a legend yourself. You may have to do this, for example, if you add a series to an existing chart, or if you delete the legend by mistake. Here's how to insert a legend:

1. Select Legend from the Chart menu to display a dialog box with five tabs.

2. Use the Legend Position tab to choose a position for the legend.

3. Use the Text Font tab to choose the font, size, and style of the text.

4. Use the Text Settings tab to choose a text fill pattern, color, and background color.

5. Use the Box Settings tab to choose the shape of the legend box and the background color.

6. Use the Fill Settings tab to select a pattern, wash, or bitmap.

7. Click on OK.

You can later move the legend and change its properties.

NOTE: *You can only add a legend to charts that do not already have labels identifying the series.*

Changing the Charted Cells

If you realize that you created the chart with the wrong cells, you can change the cells without having to delete the chart and start over. Click on the Add/Revise Cells button in the property bar. In the dialog box that appears, you can enter or point to the cells to use for the X axis, legend, and up to six series. You can also choose to reverse the series, and to swap rows and columns.

Choosing Overall Chart Settings

Every element of the chart, including the chart itself, is associated with a series of properties. While you are editing a floating chart, you can change the properties by clicking on the Properties button in the property bar. The dialog box that appears has five tabs:

- *Source Chart* lets you select the chart you want to edit.

- *Border Color* sets the color of the border around the chart.

- *Box Type* lets you select none, thin, medium, or thick border lines; add a drop shadow; or make the chart transparent so you can see the worksheet in its background.

- *Protection* allows you to unlock the chart so it can be edited when the sheet is protected.

- *Object Name* specifies the name of the chart for use in macros.

Editing Chart Sections

In addition to editing the overall chart, you can customize each of its individual elements, such as an axis, series bar, or section of the pie. You can only edit individual sections when editing the chart in a window—either an in-place window or a separate chart window. If the Chart menu bar is on the screen, you can select and edit individual chart sections.

The trick is to first select only that portion of the chart. You'll know the part is selected when the handles appear just around it—not around the entire chart or some other section. Once you select a section, choose options from the menu bar, the property bar, or from the QuickMenu that appears when you right-click on the section. Before choosing options, however, make certain that only the desired portion is selected—sometimes it takes a few tries.

The options that appear on the property bar and in the QuickMenu depend on the object you selected. Regardless of the object, however, every property bar contains a Properties button, so you can click on this button to display settings for the selected object.

Properties for wall and background areas, for example, are usually limited to the fill color and pattern, and the shape and size of the border line. The properties for series and axis are more extensive.

Customizing a Series

Setting the properties for a data series controls how the bar, line, area, pie slice, or data points appear on the chart. To change a series, right-click on any of the bars or lines that represent one of its values, or click on it and choose options from the property bar. Changing the color of one bar in the series, for example, will affect all of the bars in the series.

The exact options that you can set depend on the type of chart, and whether it is 2-D or 3-D. With 2-D bar charts, for instance, you can change the width of the bars, the spacing between them, and the extent that they overlap. In some cases, you can also change the type of just the selected series, so you can show one series with bars and another with lines, for example. For pie charts, you can explode a section and choose the distance it appears from the center. Properties for 3-D bar charts also let you change the shape of the bars, called *risers*, as shown here:

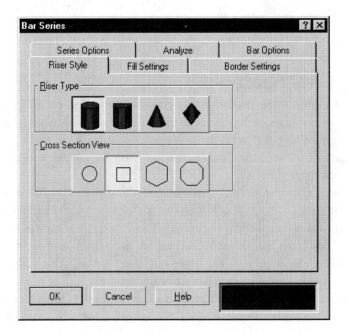

 TIP: *When you print a chart on a noncolor printer, Corel Quattro Pro colors will be converted to shades of gray. To control how the chart prints, set the series properties to use patterns of black and white instead.*

Axis Settings

Select and customize the properties for the Y axis to change the scale, tick marks, and appearance of the line.

The *scale* determines the values that appear along the axis. When Corel Quattro Pro creates a chart, it automatically assigns values to the axis. The uppermost value, at the very top of the Y-axis line, corresponds to the largest value being plotted. The bottom of the scale will usually be set at the lowest number, with negative values below the zero line. You may want the scale to rise above the highest value.

For example, suppose you are charting student grades and want the scale to reach 100, even though no student had a perfect score. To change the scale, click on the Y axis so only it is selected, and then click on the Properties button in the property bar (or right-click on it and select Y-Axis Properties from the QuickMenu). Corel Quattro Pro will open the dialog box shown in Figure 19-10. In the Scale tab, enter the highest and lowest values that you want to appear on the axis, and the steps in between. The No. of Minors represents grid lines between the numbered points.

If your values are in the thousands, click on Show Units. This abbreviates large values and displays their units, such as thousands, next to the axis.

Printing Charts

When you print your worksheet, Corel Quattro Pro will also print any floating charts or maps on the page or in the print block.

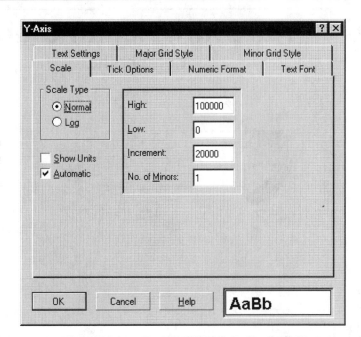

Customizing
the Y axis

FIGURE 19-10

TIP: *Before printing a chart, select the most pleasing aspect ratio of the chart by using the View menu.*

If you have a chart selected, or a Chart window is active, Corel Quattro Pro will print only the chart itself.

NOTE: *These same techniques apply also to printing maps.*

Creating Maps

When your data is organized by geographic areas, such as states or countries, you can chart it on a map. The map will use colors and patterns to represent the values, and this is quite useful in revealing trends and patterns. The map in Figure 19-11, for example, shows membership by state in the United States. By studying the map, you can see where the sales need improvement.

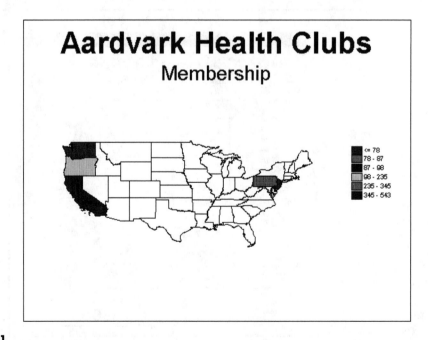

Corel
Quattro Pro
map

FIGURE 19-11

TIP: *To use mapping, you must perform a custom installation of the Corel WordPerfect Suite.*

Before creating a map, make sure that your worksheet is set up using state or country names as the row labels. You can use the state name or the standard postal abbreviations for states. Then follow these steps:

1. Select the cells that contain the data.

2. Choose Graphics from the Insert menu and click on Map to see the first Map Expert box, shown in Figure 19-12.

3. Select a map to use. Corel Quattro Pro will suggest a map based on your data and illustrate it on the pane on the left.

4. Click on Next.

5. Accept or enter the cells representing the region names, and color and pattern ranges. You can chart two different sets of data on a map, using colors for one set and patterns for the other. The color and pattern ranges would correspond to two series on a chart.

6. Click on Next.

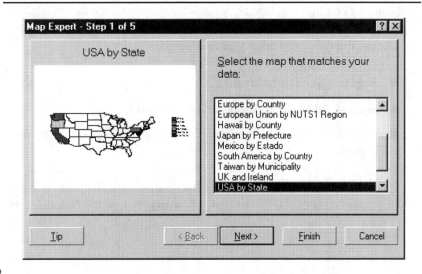

Map Expert
dialog box

FIGURE 19-12

CAUTION: *Corel Quattro Pro will warn you if you've entered a region that it does not understand and let you choose a new label. The warning will appear, for example, if you used England as a label. In this case, scroll the list of choices, choose Britain, and then click on Replace.*

7. Choose a color scheme and click on Next.

8. Choose an optional overlap map or have Corel Quattro Pro mark the locations with pin numbers or labels.

9. Click on Next.

10. Enter a title and subtitle, choose to insert a legend, and choose if you want to place the map in the notebook as a floating object or in a separate window.

11. Click on Finish and then drag to draw the map areas.

Map Overlays

An *overlay* is an additional map that appears superimposed over the map that you've charted. You can overlay a world map on the United States or Europe, for example, to get a broader view. You can also overlay U.S. highways on maps of the United States, and add major cities or state capitals.

To add an overlay, right-click on the map and choose Data from the QuickMenu. In the dialog box that appears, click on Add Overlay to see the dialog box shown in Figure 19-13.

Choose the type of overlay you want to add:

■ *Region*—Select another map.

■ *Static*—Add U.S. highways or a World Grid.

■ *Pin*—Add names or coordinates of major cities or state or national capitals.

Click on OK to return to the Map Data dialog box. To later delete an overlay, select it in the list in the Map Data dialog box and click on the Delete Overlay button.

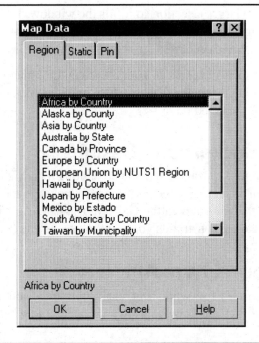

Adding
overlays
to enhance
a map

FIGURE 19-13

Zooming Maps

Corel Quattro Pro inserts an overlay map in a position in relation to its actual coordinates on the globe. If you overlay a map that does not share a common area with the charted map—for example, overlaying Japan on Europe—you may not see it onscreen. To display the overlay, you have to Zoom Out the display to see a larger section of our planet.

While you are editing the map in place or in a window, right-click on the map and select Zoom Out from the QuickMenu, reducing the magnification until you can see the overlay.

Other Zoom options available in the QuickMenu, and from the Zoom command in the Edit menu, are

■ *Zoom to Normal* returns the map to its default size.

- *Zoom In* enlarges a section so it fills the window. The mouse pointer changes to a magnifying glass, and then you drag over the section of the map you want to enlarge.

- *Center* displays the area of your choice in the center of the window. The mouse pointer changes to a crosshair, and you click on the location you want to be centered.

Selecting Background Designs

The property bar that appears when you are editing a map is the same as when you are working with a chart. Use the property bar to change the fill styles and colors, or choose from the templates in the Gallery. You can also click on Advisor in the Gallery to indicate the constraints you want to use, as you learned for charts.

Creating Your Own Art

You can really customize a worksheet, chart, or map by adding text boxes, arrows, and other objects that you draw, as shown in Figure 19-14.

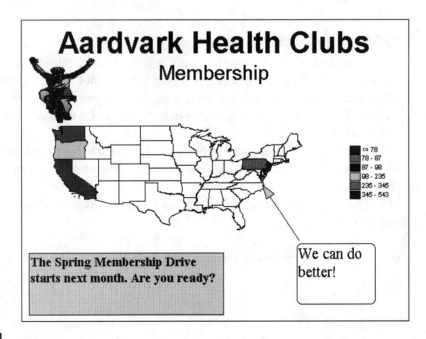

Customizing a chart or map

FIGURE 19-14

To draw basic shapes or a text box, pull down the Shapes list in the toolbar, or select Shape from the Insert menu and choose the shape you want to draw. When you select the shape, you'll see a property bar with buttons for changing the fill style and the foreground and background colors, setting the border style and color, and displaying the objects properties.

Add a piece of clipart using the ClipArt button in the toolbar, or by selecting Graphic from the Insert menu and clicking on ClipArt. You can also select Graphic from the Insert menu and click on Draw Picture to access the Corel Presentations drawing tools.

For more drawing options, display the Chart and Drawing Tools toolbar and take the following steps:

1. Right-click on the toolbar to display the QuickMenu.

2. Click on Chart and Drawing Tools.

The toolbar is divided into three lines, with these features, from left to right across each line of the toolbar:

First Line of Toolbar:

New Chart	Starts Chart Expert
Floating Chart	Lets you drag to insert a chart from selected cells
Insert Object	Adds a clipart or graphic image from your disk

Second Line of Toolbar:

Selection Tool	Selects objects after performing some other function
Text Box	Inserts a box where you enter text
Line Tool	Draws lines; hold down the SHIFT key for a straight horizontal or vertical line

19

Arrow Tool	Draws arrows
Rectangle Tool	Draws a rectangle; hold down the SHIFT key for a square
Rounded Rectangle Tool	Creates rectangles and squares with rounded corners
Oval Tool	Draws ovals and circles (with the SHIFT key)
Segmented Line Tool	Draws a series of connected lines
Filled Segmented Line Tool	Draws a series of connected lines, and fills in the resulting shape
Freehand Tool	Doodles
Filled Freehand Tool	Fills in doodles
Third Line of Toolbar:	
Move Up	Moves the selected object in front of an overlapping object
Move Back	Moves the selected object behind an overlapping object
Move to Front	Moves the selected object to the top of all objects
Move to Bottom	Moves the selected object to the back of all objects
Add Live Picture	Inserts a copy of the referenced cells to the chart or map
Select Template	Lets you select a template

To draw an object, click on the button and drag the mouse where you want the object to appear. After creating a text box, type the text that you want in it. Use the Properties option from the QuickMenu or the Properties button in the property bar to change fill patterns and line colors and other characteristics.

Grouping Objects

Each object that you draw is independent of the others. You can select and move it, or change its properties, without affecting the other objects on the page. Sometimes you want to apply the same formats to several objects at the same time, or combine objects to treat them as one unit for moving or copying. This is called *grouping*.

When you draw objects on a chart or map, you can group them by following these steps:

1. Click on the first object to select it.

2. Hold down the SHIFT key and click on the others.

3. Right-click on the objects and select Group from the QuickMenu. You can also pull down the Format menu and click on Group. There will now be one set of handles around the entire group rather than around the individual objects. When you now select a format, it will be applied to the entire group.

NOTE: *You cannot group objects drawn directly on the notebook window, but only when on a chart or map.*

To ungroup the objects so you can work with them individually, right-click on the group and choose Ungroup from the QuickMenu.

NOTE: *The QuickMenu that appears when you right-click on a drawing object on a chart or map also includes options for setting the object's order, position, alignment, and spacing.*

Working with Layers

Each new object you draw appears overlaid on top of existing ones, so one object may obscure, or partially obscure, another. You can rearrange the relative position of objects if you picture the screen as consisting of many layers of clear plastic, and you can change the layer that an object is on.

To change the layer of an object, click on it and then choose one of these buttons from the Chart and Drawing Tools toolbar:

- Move Up
- Move Back
- Move to Front
- Move to Bottom

You can also change the object's order by right-clicking on it, pointing to Object Order in the QuickMenu (or choosing Object Order from the Format menu). Your choices are as follows:

- *Bring Forward* moves the object one layer closer to the top layer.

- *Send Backward* moves the object one layer closer to the bottom layer.

- *Bring to Front* moves the object to the foreground, the top layer.

- *Send to Back* moves the object to the background, the bottom layer.

Bullet Charts

You can combine your charts and maps into a slide show for a formal presentation. However, you will also probably want to have one or more title slides, or slides that contain explanatory text. You can use title slides directly from your worksheet using the QuickChart button or New Chart options in the QuickMenu. Corel Quattro Pro calls them *bullet charts* because they can contain a title and subtitles, as well as up to two levels of bulleted items. By adding drawing objects and gallery background, you can enhance bullet charts so they match the design of your charts and maps.

 TIP: *To create a totally custom slide from a blank background, see the "Creating a Slide Show" section later in this chapter.*

You create a bullet chart just as you do a graphic chart: as a floating chart using the QuickChart button, or in its own window using the New Chart command from the QuickMenu. You can also create one or more bullet charts in one step using the Slide Show Expert.

Before creating the chart, however, you must prepare the worksheet. Follow these steps. Just remember that you do not have to type the bullet character yourself because Corel Quattro Pro will insert it for you in the bullet chart.

1. Type the title of the chart in any cell.

2. Optionally enter a subtitle in the cell directly below the title.

3. Enter the first major bulleted item in the cell under and to the right of the title or subtitle. If you enter a title in cell A1 with no subtitle, for example, enter the first major bulleted item in cell B2. If you want any minor bulleted items under it, enter them in the cells under and to the right.

4. Add any additional major and minor bulleted items. Make sure that the major items are in the column to the right of the title and subtitles. The minor items must be in the column to the right of the major items.

To create a floating bullet chart, use the following steps:

1. Select the block of items.

2. Click on the QuickChart button.

3. Click or drag in the notebook to create the chart.

NOTE: *To create multiple slides at one time, see the "Slide Show Expert" section later in this chapter.*

To create the chart in a window, use the following steps:

1. Select the block of items.

2. Right-click on the block and choose New Chart from the QuickMenu.

3. Click in the Name tab of the dialog box and enter a chart name.

4. Click on OK.

Figure 19-15 shows a floating bullet chart along with the worksheet cells used to create it.

Formatting Bullet Charts

You can customize a bullet chart, just as you can a chart or map, by adding clipart and your own drawings, and by choosing options from the property bar. Double-click on the chart to edit it in place, or right-click on it and select Open to display it in a separate window.

If you select the Apply Template button on the property bar, you'll see an abbreviated version of the Chart Gallery that lets you select an overall design that you want to apply to the background of the slide. You can also click on Advisor to see the dialog box in Figure 19-16. Use the dialog box to set constraints, choose an overall background, and specify the media you plan to use and the room you plan to show the chart in.

19

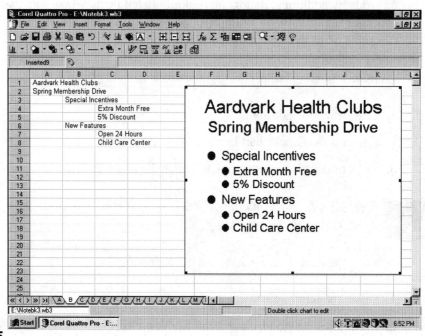

Worksheet
cells and
bullet chart

FIGURE 19-15

NOTE: *You can also select the media type from the View menu and the Background from the Format menu.*

To format the text of the chart, double-click on it and then click on the section of the chart you want to format. Use the lists and buttons in the property bar to choose the font, size, and color of the text; to format in bold, italic, underline, or strikeout; to change the bullet style and color; or to display the Properties dialog box. You can also right-click on a chart element and choose the Properties command from the QuickMenu.

Setting the properties of one item affects all of the other items at that level. If you change the font of a major bulleted item, for example, all of the other major bulleted items in that chart will change as well.

To change the text on the chart, edit the corresponding cells in the notebook.

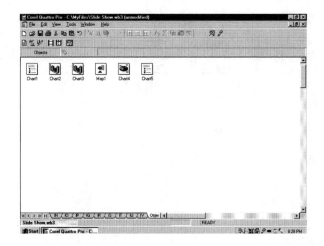

Template
Advisor for
bullet charts

FIGURE 19-16

19

The Objects Page

The Objects page at the end of the notebook will display an icon for every chart, map, and slide show that you create. To display the page, select Objects from the View menu, or click on the QuickTab navigation button. Figure 19-17, for example, shows the Objects page with several charts and maps. You use the Objects page to organize your charts and maps in slide shows.

When you display the Objects page, the property bar will contain these features:

- *New Chart*—Lets you create a new chart without returning to the worksheet

- *Display Full Screen*—Shows the selected object full-screen

- *Edit Chart*—Opens the selected chart in a window ready for editing

- *Create Slide Show*—Creates a slide show

- *Play Slide Show*—Lets you run a slide show

- *Create Dialog Box*—Creates a dialog box

Objects page

FIGURE 19-17

To edit an object, double-click on its icon. Corel Quattro Pro will open it in a separate window, even though you might have created it as a floating chart or map. Double-click on a slide show icon to display it in the Light Table, which you will soon learn about.

Slide Shows

A slide show is exactly what it says—a group of charts and maps displayed in a series full screen. With Corel Quattro Pro, you can even add special transition effects that appear when one slide ends and the other begins. You don't have all of the options that are available in a program such as Corel Presentations, but you can still create some rather sophisticated and effective presentations.

Creating a Slide Show

To create a slide show, go to the Objects page and select the icons of the charts and maps that you want to include. Use these steps:

1. On the Objects page, click on the icon of an item you want to include in the slide show.

2. Hold down the SHIFT key and click on the others. Don't worry if you miss some; you can always add slides later on.

3. Click on the Create Slide Show button in the property bar, or choose New Slide Show from the Tools menu.

4. In the dialog box that appears, enter a name for the show and then click on OK. The selected items will appear in the Light Table view, shown in Figure 19-18.

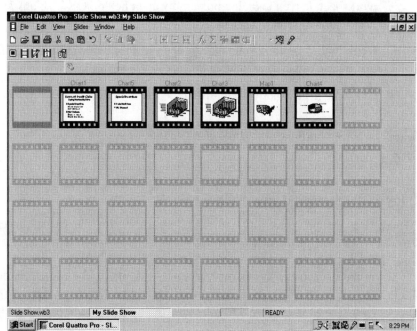

Slides in the Light Table view

FIGURE 19-18

To add additional slides in the Light Table view, use the following steps:

1. Pull down the Slides menu.

2. Point to New Slide.

3. Click on From Existing Slide. A list of the items in the Objects page will appear.

4. Double-click on the item you want to add to the show.

To add a blank slide that you edit as you want, use these steps:

1. Click on the Create a Slide button in the Light Table property bar to display the New Chart dialog box. You can also pull down the Slide menu, point to New Slide, and click on From New Chart.

2. Instead of entering cell ranges to create a chart from the contents of a worksheet, leave the dialog box empty and click on OK. A blank slide will be added to the Light Table.

3. Double-click on the blank slide to open it in an edit window, and then add text boxes, clipart, or drawing objects.

4. Close the Edit window to return to the Light Table.

 TIP: *To change the order of slides in the show, click on a slide and drag it to its new location.*

Customizing Slide Shows

You can set the properties for individual slides, or for the entire presentation. Properties include items such as the transition from one slide to the next, and how long slides remain on the screen.

To set the default properties for the entire slide show, right-click on the Light Table, but not on a slide, and select the Light Table Properties option from the QuickMenu. The Default Effect pages of the dialog box that appears are shown in Figure 19-19.

Choose the transition effect and its speed, and the amount of time you want each slide to appear. You can always change slides with the mouse or keyboard regardless of the timing.

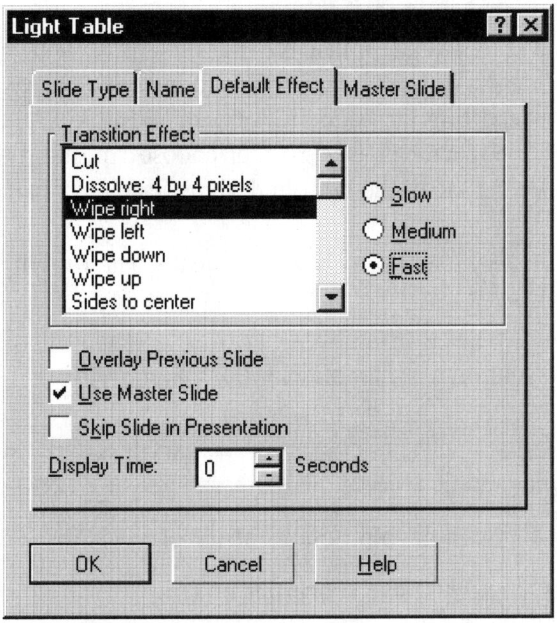

Setting the
defaults for
the entire
slide show

FIGURE 19-19

Select the Use Master Slide property when you want all the slides to have the same general color scheme and background. Use the Overlay Previous Slide and Skip Slide in Presentation options only when changing the properties of a particular slide.

The Slide Type page of the dialog box lets you choose the size of the slide in the Light Table—options are Small, Medium, Large, and Name Only. The Master Slide page lets you choose one of your own slides as the master.

Changing Slide Properties

You can change the properties of individual slides. Click on the slide and then on the Properties button in the property bar, or right-click on the slide and choose Slide Properties from the QuickMenu.

The dialog box that appears has two pages: Slide Effect and Slide Comment. The Slide Effect page is just like the Default Effect page for setting the overall effects. Use it to select a transition, speed, and delay time, and to overlap the previous slide, use the master, or skip the slide.

Using a Master Slide

A master slide serves as a template for the background and color scheme for every slide in the slide show. Use a master slide to include your company name or logo, or some other repeating message on every slide. In the Light Table, the first slide position is reserved for the master. You can choose a master slide that you've created for that purpose, or one of the built-in designs from the Chart Gallery.

 TIP: *Slides will only use the master when their properties are set to Use Master.*

To design your own master slide, follow these steps:

1. First create it as a bullet chart or from a blank slide, adding any standard text and graphic objects.

2. In the Light Table, right-click outside of any slide.

3. Select the Light Table Properties option.

4. Choose the slide from the Master Slide page of the Properties dialog box. When you close the dialog box, your slide will appear in the first position in the Light Table, and will be applied as a background to all of the others.

You can also create the master slide directly in the Light Table by selecting New Master Slide from the Slides menu. Corel Quattro Pro will display a bullet chart in an Edit window showing generic formats for the title, subtitles, and bulleted items. The text shown in the chart will not appear onscreen; it just illustrates formats. Add graphics, drawing objects, and text using the Text Box tool, and then close the window.

For the greatest impact, select one of the professionally designed templates in the Master Slide Gallery. You cannot choose from the gallery, however, until you have a master slide in the show. Start by creating your own master slide with any text that you want to appear, or use the New Master Slide command to create a blank master slide. Next, pull down the Slides menu and click on Master Slide Gallery. Select one of the templates, using the Advisor if desired, and then click on OK. The template will be applied to every slide whose property is set to use the master, as shown in Figure 19-20.

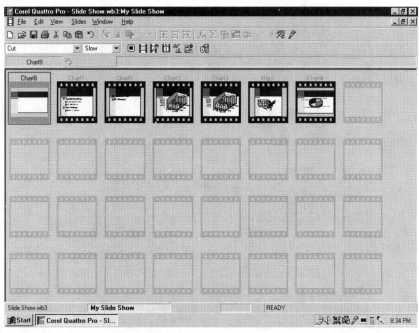

A
background
applied to
all slides

FIGURE 19-20

Showing Slide Shows

When you are ready to show your slide, display the Objects page, click on the Slide Show icon, and then click on the Play Slide Show button in the property bar. (You can also run the slide from the Light Table in the same way.) If you assigned times to your slides, Corel Quattro Pro will display each for the time selected. To change slides yourself, even when you did assign times, use these techniques:

- Click the left mouse button to show the next slide.

- Click the right mouse button to show the previous slide.

- Press any key to show the next slide.

- Press BACKSPACE to show the previous slide.

- Press ESC to stop the slide show.

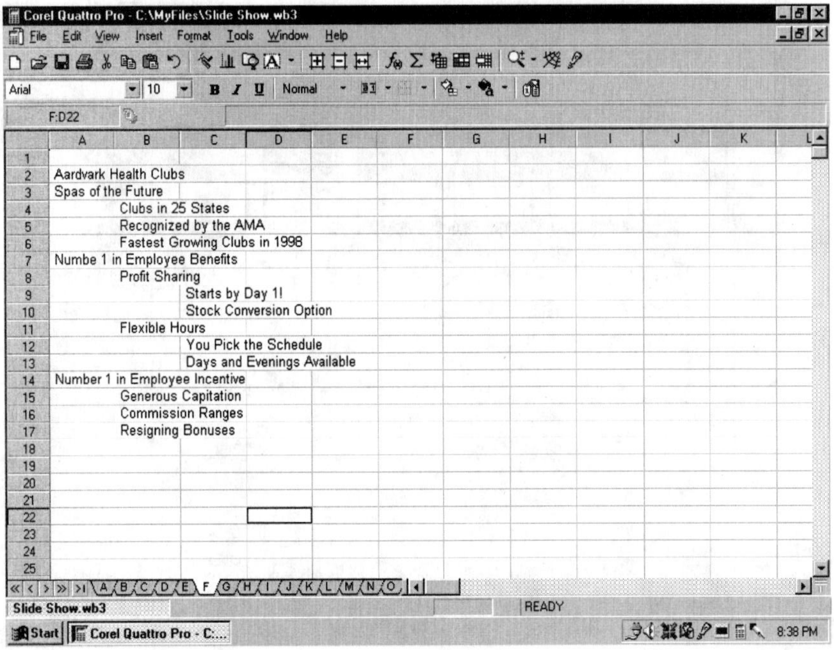

Worksheet
for three
slides in
Slide Show
Expert

FIGURE 19-21

Slide Show Expert

You can create any number of bullet charts and create a slide show of all of them at one time using the Slide Show Expert from a worksheet window. You can then add other charts and maps to the show later on. Here's how to create a slide show using the Slide Show Expert:

1. To prepare the worksheet, type the text for each of the slides consecutively, with no blank lines between them. Make sure that all of the titles are in the same column. Figure 19-21, for example, shows a worksheet that will become three slides. Slide Show Expert can create only bullet slides.

2. Select the entire block of cells that you want to use for slides.

3. Pull down the Tools menu, point to Slide Show, and click on New. The first Expert box will display the block coordinates and the number of slides that will be created.

4. If the coordinates are incorrect, enter or point to them and then click on Next. The second Expert box shows all of the background templates available in the Chart Gallery.

5. Choose the template you want to use as the master slide, or click on User Defined and select one of your own. You can also choose to use no master slide.

6. Click on Next.

7. Enter a name for your slide show and select either Random Transitions or a choice from the list.

8. Click on Finish. Corel Quattro Pro creates the slides and displays them in Light Table view.

19

Analyzing Data

20

While charts and maps can help you see trends, sometimes you have to analyze data the old-fashioned way. You have to draw conclusions by examining the values in cells and performing statistical operations on them. By analyzing your data, you can make wiser business decisions, and prepare plans and projections. There are hundreds of ways to analyze information and perform statistical analysis with Corel Quattro Pro. You can work with information as a database, sort rows to group records, and apply some rather sophisticated analytical techniques. This chapter will survey some of the techniques that you can use.

Working with Databases

A *database* is a place where you store information, an electronic version of a box of 3 x 5 index cards, or even a filing cabinet full of folders and papers. In Corel Quattro Pro you store a database as a series of rows and columns. Each row holds a record, which is a collection of information about one object in the database, such as a client, inventory item, or sales record.

 You can use Corel Quattro Pro to analyze information in databases you've already created with other programs. See "Analyzing External Data" later in this chapter.

The columns represent the *fields,* each piece of information that makes up a record. The fields for a client record, for example, can include first and last names, address, and phone number. The fields for an inventory record might include the item name and stock number, quantity on hand, and price. Each column is another field, and all of the columns in a row represent the complete record for that item.

Corel Quattro Pro has one other element in a database, the *criteria table.* This enables you to find information quickly based on its content, and to create a subset of your database so you see only the information that you are interested in.

You can import or link the database into Corel WordPerfect for use as a data file for merging.

Creating a Database

Your first task is to enter the information into the table. A database must be one contiguous block and fit on one page. It can be no more than 8,191 rows and up to 256 columns. It must have labels in the first row that represent the names of the fields, and each label must be unique. Field names can contain up to 16 characters. They can have spaces between words, but not before or after.

 TIP: *If you are entering ZIP codes into a database, enter them as text using the apostrophe. Otherwise, leading zeros will not appear with ZIP codes that have them.*

20

Next, assign a block name to the entire database. This isn't mandatory, but it will save time when you need to refer to the database in dialog boxes and functions. Use these steps to assign a block name to the database:

1. Select the database, including the column headings.

2. Pull down the Insert menu, point to Name, and click on Cell Names.

3. Type **Database** as the name, so it will be easy to remember.

4. Click on Add and then Close. Whenever you need to insert the database block, just use the name "database."

If you later insert additional rows within the database, Corel Quattro Pro will automatically adjust the block definition. However, if you add information to the blank row following the database, you have to reassign the block name to include the new row as well. It doesn't matter where you add new rows because you can sort them at another time. You'll learn how later.

Next, make each of the column labels a field name. Again, this isn't necessary, but it will make it easier to enter criteria to locate specific records. Select the entire database block, pull down the Tools menu, point to Data Tools, and click on Notebook Query to see the Notebook Data Query dialog box. Click on the Field Names button and then on Close. This assigns a block name to each of the labels.

Searching for Information Using Criteria Tables

Corel Quattro Pro lets you search for information in the database using a method called *query by example*. This means that you type the information you are looking for, as well as any logical conditions, and Corel Quattro Pro searches the database for you.

You have to start by creating a criteria table—a worksheet of at least two rows. Create the table anywhere in the notebook, even on the same page as the database if there is room for it on the page. The first row of the criteria table must contain the names of the fields that you want to search in the database. As a shortcut, copy the field names from the first row of the database and paste them into the first row of the criteria table. This ensures that the field names in the criteria table exactly match those in the database.

 TIP: *Copy the field names to a row directly below the database. This way, you can take advantage of QuickType to insert values from the rows above.*

You use the other rows in the criteria table to enter the information that you want to search for. For example, Figure 20-1 shows a criteria table to find a record in a database that has the name "Adam" in the First Name column, and "Chesin" in the Last Name column. Searching for values in more than one column of a row is treated as an *And* operation. This means that a record must match all of the information in the criteria table row. So, for example, the same search will not locate the record for Adam Smith because only the First Name field would match.

To create an *Or* operation, enter search information in more than one row. The following criteria table will locate records for Adam Chesin, as well as records for everyone with the last name of Smith, matching one row or the other in the criteria table:

	Last Name	First Name	Company	Address	City	State	Zip Code	Phone Number	Credit	
12										
13	Chesin	Adam								
14	Smith									

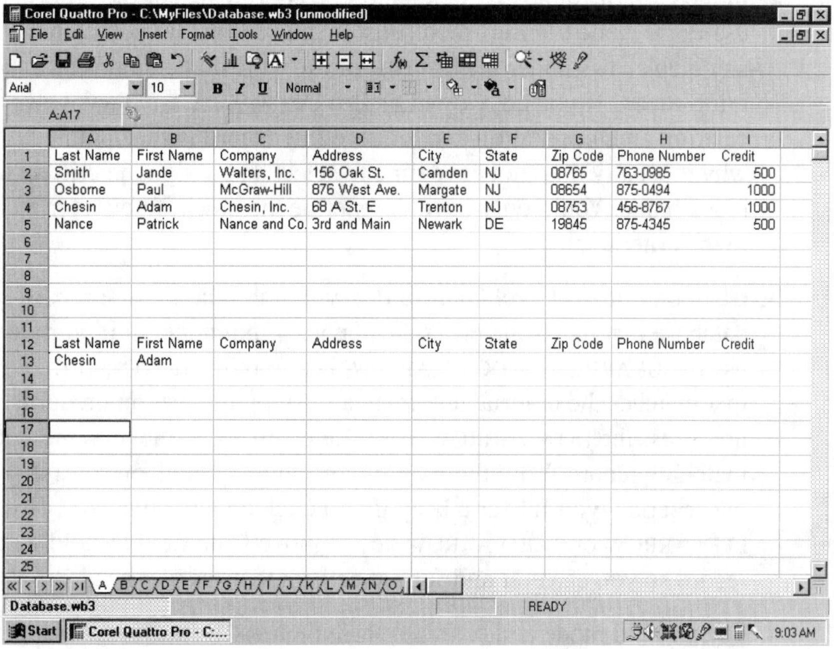

	A	B	C	D	E	F	G	H	I
1	Last Name	First Name	Company	Address	City	State	Zip Code	Phone Number	Credit
2	Smith	Jande	Walters, Inc.	156 Oak St.	Camden	NJ	08765	763-0985	500
3	Osborne	Paul	McGraw-Hill	876 West Ave.	Margate	NJ	08654	875-0494	1000
4	Chesin	Adam	Chesin, Inc.	68 A St. E	Trenton	NJ	08753	456-8767	1000
5	Nance	Patrick	Nance and Co.	3rd and Main	Newark	DE	19845	875-4345	500
6									
7									
8									
9									
10									
11									
12	Last Name	First Name	Company	Address	City	State	Zip Code	Phone Number	Credit
13	Chesin	Adam							
14									
15									
16									
17									

Using a criteria table to locate a name

FIGURE 20-1

Searching for Information

Once you define the database and labels, and create a criteria table, you're ready to search. Here's how:

1. Pull down the Tools menu, point to Data Tools, and click on Notebook Query to display the Notebook Data Query dialog box. You'll notice that the coordinates you used to define the field names are still shown in the Database Block text box. Corel Quattro Pro maintains the last settings you used in this box as default values for the notebook. If you wish, you can replace the coordinates with the name "Database," but the results will not change. If you ever want to clear the defaults, click on Reset and then Close.

2. In the Criteria Table text box, enter the coordinates of the criteria table, or use Point mode to insert them. Just make certain that you do not include any blank rows under the last row of the table that contains search information. If you do, Corel Quattro Pro will use the blank rows to perform an Or operation and locate every record in the database. That's why it usually does not save time to select and assign the criteria table a block name. You'd only have to redefine the block if you later add rows to the criteria table.

3. Click on Locate. Corel Quattro Pro will highlight the first record in the database that meets the criteria and enter Find mode. In Find mode you use the UP ARROW or DOWN ARROW key to move from record to record that matches the criteria, automatically skipping over any records that do not. Press the DOWN ARROW once, for example, to move to the second matching record. With the mouse, you can only click on rows that meet the criteria—you'll hear a beep if you click on any other row. Use the LEFT ARROW or RIGHT ARROW key to move from field to field within a record so you can edit and format cell contents as you need.

4. To exit Find mode and return to the Notebook Data Query dialog box, press ESC or ENTER.

 TIP: *Press F7 to repeat the last Data Query operation.*

Deleting Records

The Delete button in the Notebook Data Query dialog box clears the contents of records that meet the criteria. You will be asked to confirm the deletion, and you can immediately undo it with the Undo button.

As a safeguard, however, perform a Locate first to confirm the records that will be deleted, using these steps:

1. Click on Locate.

2. Press the DOWN ARROW to scroll through the database looking at the selected records.

3. The DOWN ARROW key should select only records that you want to delete. If that's the case, open the Notebook Data Query dialog box again, and then delete the records.

If pressing DOWN ARROW locates a record that you do not want to delete, then try refining the search criteria.

Using Criteria to Pinpoint Information

Searching for specific values is useful, but it has limitations. If you misspell a person's name in the criteria table, for example, it will not be located in the database. By using *wildcards* and *logical operations* in the criteria table, however, you can design searches that pinpoint the exact information you are looking for.

Using Wildcards

Wildcards are special characters that represent one or more characters in text that you are searching for:

?	Represents a single character
*	Represents any number of characters
~	Excludes text from the search, locating records that do not match the value

If you want to find all persons whose last name begins with the letter "N," for example, type **N*** in the Last Name column of the criteria row. This tells Corel Quattro Pro to locate records that start with the letter "N" and have any number of characters following it in that field.

The phrase **c*r** would locate all words that start with "c" and end with "r"—no matter how many characters are between them. On the other hand, entering **c?r** would only locate labels that have one letter between them—"car" but not "caviar."

To locate all clients except those in California, enter **~CA** in the State field. The tilde character must be the first character of the search text.

Logical Conditions

To locate records that fall within a certain range, enter a logical condition in the form of a formula as the search criteria. The condition +Amount Due > 400, for instance, would locate records with a value greater than 400 in the Amount Due field. You can use any of the usual operators:

=	Equal to
<>	Not equal to
>=	Greater than or equal to
>	Greater than
<=	Less than or equal to
<	Less than

 TIP: *If you did not assign the column labels as field names, use the cell reference of the column label instead.*

You can enter a logical statement in any cell of the criteria table. It does not have to be in the column that it represents. The Amount Due condition, for instance, can be in any column and still locate the proper records.

When you type the formula in the criteria table, however, Corel Quattro Pro will evaluate it and display its results rather than the formula itself. So all you'll see in the cell is a 1 (for true) or 0 (for false). To make criteria tables easier to work with, format the cells by setting their Numeric Format to Text in the Active Cells dialog box. This way you'll see the formulas in the table, as under the Credit label in the criteria table shown here:

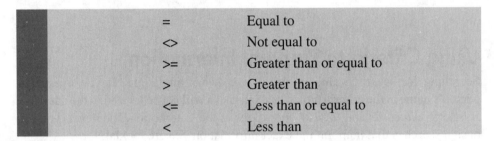

12	Last Name	First Name	Company	Address	City	State	Zip Code	Phone Number	Credit
13						NJ			+Credit>500

Output Blocks

The problem with locating records is that you have to scroll down the database with the DOWN ARROW key to see which records have been located. If you have a large database, you won't get an overall view of the selected records because they are spread out over the entire table.

As an alternative, you can copy all of the located records to an output table. This is a separate table that will contain just the located records. You can then view the selected records as a set, without being distracted by the other rows in the database.

To create an output table, follow these steps:

1. Copy the field names to the location where you want the table to appear. If you leave out any fields, they will not be copied along with the record. So, if you only want to see selected fields in the output table, copy only those field names.

2. Pull down the Tools menu, point to Data tools and click on Notebook Data Query to display the Notebook Data Query dialog box.

3. Enter the coordinates of the row of field names for the output table in the Output Table text box, or use Point mode or an assigned block name.

4. Click on Extract to copy all of the matching records to the output table, or click on Extract Unique to remove any duplicate records when the output table is created.

When you designate the output table coordinates, only include the cells containing labels. If you select blank rows under the cells, Corel Quattro Pro will only copy as many records as there are selected rows.

 When you want to merge a form document with selected records from a Corel Quattro Pro database, extract them to a separate block. Then import the block into Corel WordPerfect.

Using Database Functions

As you learned in Chapter 18, database functions help you locate and analyze information in a database. All database functions have the same three arguments: Block, Column, and Criteria.

■ *Block* is the range of cells that contains the database. Use the block name or coordinates.

■ *Column* is where the data is located that you want to analyze, counting from 0. The first column is 0, the second is 1, and so on.

■ *Criteria* is the coordinates of the criteria table. If you use the @DAVG function, for instance, only the values in rows meeting the criteria will be averaged. To include all of the rows, create a criteria table using the field names and one blank row under them.

 NOTE: *You can still use standard functions to calculate sums, averages, and other operations on rows and columns.*

Using QuickFilters to Find and Sort Information

You learned how to use a criteria table to locate specific information, and how to separate it into an output table. Creating and using a criteria table, however, takes quite a few steps. When you want to find specific information, or sort the records in your database, use a QuickFilter instead. If you have a database of student information, for instance, you can use a QuickFilter to list only students with failing grades, or those in the top 10 percent of the class.

To use QuickFilter, click anywhere in the database, pull down the Tools menu, and click on QuickFilter. Corel Quattro Pro will add drop-down arrows to each of the field names:

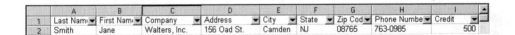

	A	B	C	D	E	F	G	H	I	
1	Last Nam▼	First Nam▼	Company ▼	Address ▼	City ▼	State ▼	Zip Cod▼	Phone Numbe▼	Credit ▼	
2	Smith	Jane	Walters, Inc.	156 Oad St.	Camden	NJ	08765	763-0985	500	

Clicking on the drop-down arrow displays a menu of options and a list of the values in the column:

To display records that match a value, just click on the value in the list. Using our illustration, for example, you could display only records in Delaware by selecting DE in the pull-down list. When you select a value from the list, the arrow on the list button changes color to remind you that the display is being filtered.

 TIP: *Remove all QuickFilters, displaying all records in their original order, by selecting QuickFilter from the Tools menu.*

Select values from other lists to perform an And operation, further limiting the records displayed. Use two lists, for example, to select records meeting two criteria, three lists for records meeting three criteria, and so on.

To remove the filter from a column, pull down the list and choose [Show All]. This removes the filter from the selected column, but not from others. To display all of the records in your database, you must choose [Show All] from every filtered column.

Use the [Sort A-Z] and [Sort Z-A] options in the list to quickly sort the rows of the database. You can sort on more than one field by selecting sort options in multiple lists. Select [Blanks] to display records with no value in the column, or [Non Blanks] to display records with information.

The [Top 10] and [Custom] options give you greater control over selecting records, helping you to analyze the information as well as to limit the records displayed. The [Top 10] option actually lets you select any number of records at the top or bottom in terms of value or percentage, such as the items with the top 5 amounts, the top 20 percent, or the two lowest. Selecting Top 10 displays this dialog box:

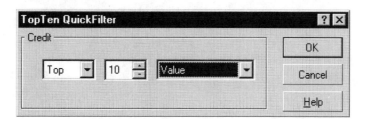

 NOTE: *You can only use the Top 10 option with a column containing numeric values.*

From the first list, select if you want to find records in the top or bottom. Use the second list to specify the number of values you want to locate, such as the top

10 or bottom 5. From the last list select if you want to locate items by their value or percentage.

The Custom options let you select records on up to three criteria. You can choose an operator and value for each criteria, and select to perform an And or Or operation.

Using the Data Sort Feature

When you sort records using a QuickFilter, the sort is always performed from left to right across the database. The leftmost sorted column is sorted first, followed by those to its right. Use the Sort command from the Tools menu to sort the database in any order.

To sort a table, select the block that you want to sort. If you are sorting a database or other worksheet that has column labels, it doesn't matter whether you include the row of labels—you can later choose not to include that row with the sort. If you do include the row in the sort, however, the labels will be sorted along with the other information and may end up in some row other than the first.

Next, pull down the Tools menu, and click on Sort to see the dialog box shown in Figure 20-2. The block that you selected will appear in the Cells text box. If it doesn't, enter or point to the coordinates.

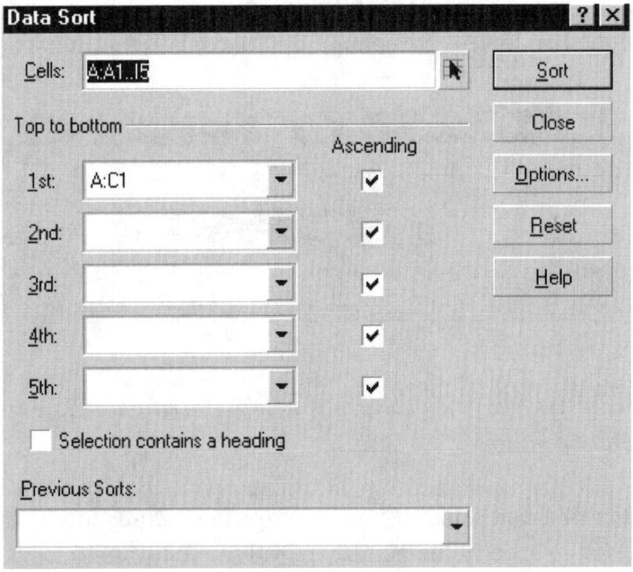

Data Sort
dialog box

FIGURE 20-2

You now must specify up to five keys in the Left to Right section. A key is a column that you want to sort by. If you want the records for clients in their name order, for example, enter **Last Name** as the first key, and **First Name** as the second key. If you are sorting a database, enter the field names; otherwise, enter or point to any cell in the column. Corel Quattro Pro will sort all of the records by the first key, then by the second, and so on.

By default, records are sorted in ascending order. Uncheck the Ascending checkbox to sort in descending order.

Next, click on the Options button to see the dialog box shown here. Choose Top to Bottom to sort the rows in the database, or choose Left to Right to sort the columns. Check Sort Blank Cells First to place blank cells at the start regardless of the sort order.

Also by default, numbers are placed before labels, so a cell containing "1" will appear before a cell containing "A." To change the order, click on the Sort Numbers Last checkbox.

The Selection Contains a Heading box determines how Corel Quattro Pro handles the column labels. Chances are this will be set correctly for you. If you selected the label row, for example, the box will be checked so the labels will not be sorted. If you did not select the row, the box will most likely be cleared. Just to be safe, confirm that the option is set the correct way. Click on OK to accept your settings, and then click on Sort to sort the database.

You can always revert to the previous order by using the Undo command. If you want to be able to revert to the rows' original order, then include an extra column in the table. Number the rows consecutively using AutoFill, or use some other identifying number in consecutive order, such as a client or stock number. You can then quickly return to the original order by sorting on that field.

 CAUTION: *Avoid sorting cells that contain relative references to outside the block. The references will be changed. Use absolute references before sorting.*

Creating a Cross Tabulation

A *cross tabulation* (cross tab, for short) analyzes information based on two or more variables. For example, the worksheet shown here compares the sales from four regions in two different years. The information for the cross tab was taken from a database. The values across the top of the cross tab were extracted from the Years column, and the values down the left of the cross tab from the Regions column. The information analyzed according to the variables Years and Region was summarized by another column in the table—the Sales column.

A	B	C
	1991	1992
	Sales	Sales
East	$1,048,040.00	$1,318,657.00
North	$1,297,444.00	$1,102,320.00
South	$912,869.00	$680,163.00
West	$724,832.00	$863,299.00

Corel Quattro Pro helps you create cross tabs using up to three different variables for the columns, three for the rows, and two to be summarized. Here's how:

1. Click in any cell in the database.

2. Pull down the Tools menu, point to Data Tools, and click on Cross Tabs. Corel Quattro Pro will select the database and display the dialog box shown in Figure 20-3.

The Fields list shows the column headings of the table. The buttons next to the list represent the elements of the cross tab—the three columns, three rows, and two data fields—with the color indicating the specific area. Use the first two buttons for the first row and column, the next two buttons for a second row and column, and

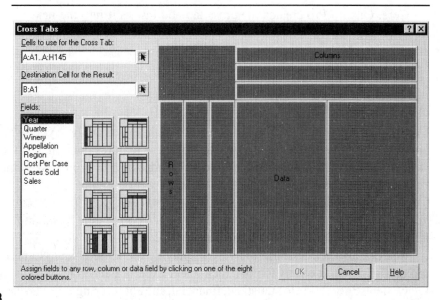

Creating a
cross tab

FIGURE 20-3

the third set for the third row and column. You do not have to have an equal number
of rows and columns. You can, for example, use two fields for columns with only
one for rows.

1. Click on the field that you want to use for a row, then click on the first
   row button—the button on the top left.

2. Click on the field you want to use for a column, then click on the first
   column button—the button on the top right.

3. Click on the field you want to summarize, then click on the first data
   button—the button on the bottom left.

4. Add any additional row, column, or data fields. To remove a field from
   the table, click on the button you assigned to it.

5. Click on OK.

Corel Quattro Pro creates the cross tab and inserts it into the next worksheet. You can now add more informative labels, and format the cross tab for printing or onscreen display.

Analyzing Data

Corel Quattro Pro offers a number of features to help you analyze your worksheet and solve real-life problems. While many of these features perform sophisticated statistical analysis, others are easy to use and can help you make important business decisions.

Access these features from the Numeric Tools and Data Tools options of the Tools menu. Choosing Analysis from the Numeric Tools option, for example, begins an Expert that includes the tools listed next.

You can also access these tools by displaying the Experts and Numeric Tools toolbar—right-click on any toolbar, then select Experts and Numeric Tools from the QuickMenu. In addition to statistical, financial, and engineering Experts, the toolbar includes buttons for creating a new chart and map, and to create a slide show from a series of bullet charts.

In this chapter, we'll explain several especially useful features that do not require an MBA or Ph.D.

- Advanced Regression
- One-Way ANOVA
- Correlation
- Descriptive Statistics
- Fourier Transformation
- Histogram
- Moving Average
- Rank and Percentile
- t-Test

- Amortization Schedule
- Two-Way ANOVA
- Covariance
- Exponential Smoothing
- f-Test
- Mortgage Refinancing
- Random Number
- Sampling
- z-Test

Using Solve For

In most cases, you use a formula or function to calculate and display results from the values you already know. Sometimes you have to work in reverse. You know the result you would like to achieve, but not the combination of arguments that will get those results. The mortgage payment function is a good example. If you know the loan rate, number of periods, and amount of principal, then you can calculate the amount of your monthly mortgage payment.

But suppose you already know how much you can afford to spend each month, and you'd like to determine how much of a dream home those monthly payments can obtain. You now have to work backward, a perfect use for the Solve For feature.

To use Solve For, you need a formula that contains a reference to the unknown value. In the @PAYMT function, you would reference a cell that will contain the principal amount. Solve For automatically changes the value in the referenced cell until the results of a formula reach a value that you specify.

Suppose you know the rate for a 25-year mortgage is 6 percent. You want to find out how much you can borrow to maintain a maximum monthly payment of $1,000. Enter the function @**PAYMT(.06/12,25*12,_A1)**, where A1 is a blank cell.

Pull down the Tools menu, point to Numeric Tools, and click on Solve For to see the dialog box shown here:

20

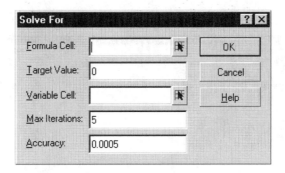

1. In the Formula Cell box, enter or point to the coordinates of the formula you want to solve, the @PAYMT function.

2. In the Target Value box, enter **1000**, the result that you want to achieve.

3. In the Variable Cell box, enter the cell that Corel Quattro Pro can vary to achieve the results, cell **A1**.

4. Adjust the other options as desired. The Max Iterations option determines how many times Solve For will run through its steps to solve the problem. Accuracy determines how close the result has to be to the target value.

5. Click on OK.

Solve For will perform its calculations and display the result in cell A1.

Optimizer

Solve For is limited because it can only adjust one variable cell. When you have more variables to consider, or have constraints placed on their values, use Optimizer. The worksheet shown in Figure 20-4 is a good example. It is our friend the @PAYMT function, but with three cells that can vary: mortgage rate, number of years, and amount of principal. Use Optimizer to find a combination of values that results in a target payment.

In real life, however, we'd have to place some constraints on the values that Corel Quattro Pro can use. We know that a realistic mortgage rate might be between 6 and 8 percent, and that we need a loan for at least 20 years to minimize our payments. We're also going to add another constraint: our monthly mortgage payment cannot be more than 1/24th of our salary. That is, we don't want to spend more than half of our monthly income on the mortgage. When we tell Corel Quattro

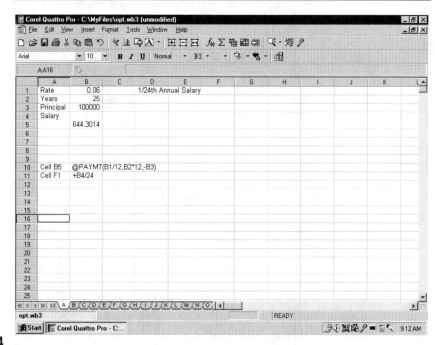

Worksheet
to solve a
formula
based on
three
variables

FIGURE 20-4

Pro our constraints, we cannot include a formula, but we can reference a formula in a cell. So create the worksheet shown in the figure, using these steps:

1. In cell B5, enter the function **@PAYMT(B1/12,B2*12,-B3)**.

2. In cell F1, enter the formula **+B4/24** that you'll use to limit the mortgage payment based on salary.

3. Type your annual salary in cell B4.

4. Pull down the Tools menu, point to Numeric Tools, and click on Optimizer to display the Optimizer dialog box shown in Figure 20-5.

5. In the Solution Cell box, enter the coordinates of the formula that will be calculating the result, cell **B5**.

6. Click on the Max button if it is not selected already, so Corel Quattro Pro calculates the maximum payment that you can afford. If you wanted to find a specific value, click on Target Value and enter the amount.

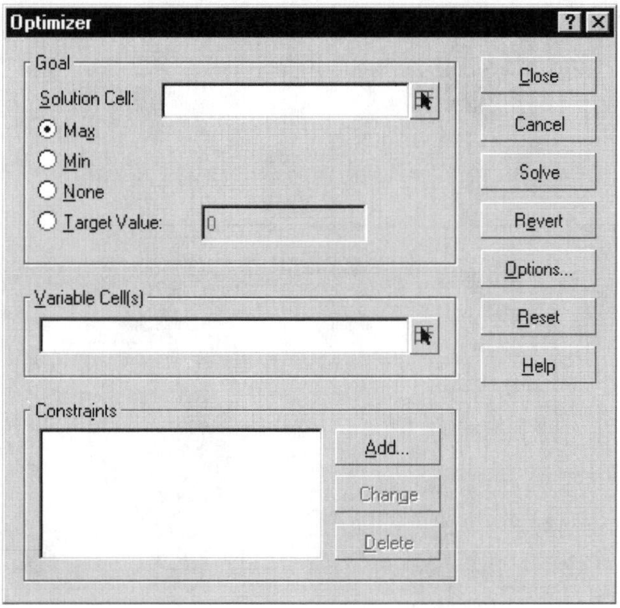

20

Optimizer
dialog box

FIGURE 20-5

7. Next, specify the variable cells, the ones that Corel Quattro Pro can change. In this case, enter cells **B1..B3**.

We now have to enter the constraints. Each constraint will be a logical expression referencing a changing cell and the limitations that we want Optimizer to consider. Click on Add to see the dialog box in Figure 20-6.

The first constraint is that the rate must be 8 percent or less. Enter **B1** in the Cell column, leave the operator set at <=, and enter **.08** in the Constant box. The expression B1<=.08 means that the values entered in the cell by Optimizer must be less than or equal to 8 percent. Click on Add Another Constraint.

The second constraint is that the rate must be 6 percent or greater. Enter **B1** in the Cell column, click on >=, and enter **.06** in the Constant box. With these two constraints, Corel Quattro Pro will only test rates between 6 and 8 percent. Click on Add Another Constraint.

Now complete the remainder of the constraints, clicking on OK after you complete the last:

Constraint	Cell	Operator	Constant
Number of years less than 30	B2	<=	30
Number of years greater than 19	B2	>=	19
Mortgage payments no more than 1/24 of your salary	B5	<=	F1

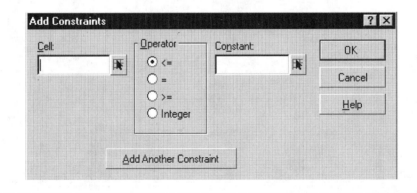

Adding a
constraint to
Optimizer

FIGURE 20-6

When you have finished entering the last constraint, click on Close. The constraints will appear in your Optimizer dialog box, as shown next. If they do not, select the constraint that is incorrect and click on Change. Use Delete to remove a constraint. Now click on Solve. Corel Quattro Pro will calculate the maximum value for cell B5 using the constraints specified. If you do not want to change the worksheet to these values, select Undo, or display the Optimizer dialog box and click on Revert.

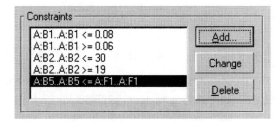

Optimizer Options

You can customize Optimizer for your specific problem by clicking on Options in the Optimizer dialog box to see the options shown in Figure 20-7. Most of these options perform rather sophisticated operations, and they require an equally sophisticated understanding of data analysis. We'll look at options that are more frequently used.

REPORTING   The Optimizer solves your problem, but it does not automatically show you how it arrived at its conclusion. The Reporting option lets you create two types of detailed reports explaining how Optimizer works:

- The *Answer Report* lists the coordinates of the solution and variable cells, along with the starting and final values that Optimizer calculated. It also lists the variable gradient, increment, and decrement values.

- The *Detail Report* lists values from the solution and variable cells at each iteration, so you can see how they changed during the process.

To create one or both of the reports, click on Reporting. In the dialog box that appears, enter or point to the range of cells where you want to place one or both of the reports. You can designate an entire block, or just the upper-left corner.

Because the report overwrites any existing contents, make sure there are enough blank cells. The Answer Report needs six columns and at least ten more rows than

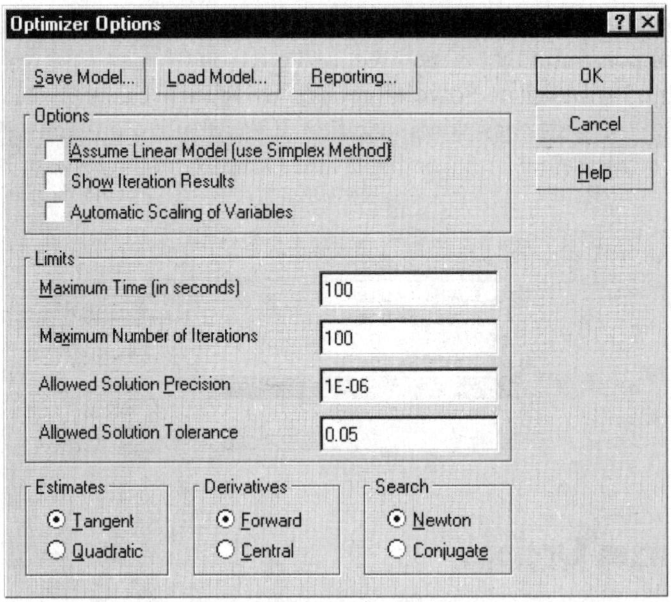

Optimizer
options

FIGURE 20-7

the total number of solution cells and constraints. The Detail Report uses as many rows as iterations, plus three headings.

When you solve the problem, the reports will appear in the designated blocks.

SAVING OPTIMIZER SETTINGS When you save your worksheet, Corel Quattro Pro saves the Optimizer settings along with it. If you use Optimizer to solve several problems, you should save each set so you can quickly retrieve it. You save the set in a blank area of the worksheet.

Once you have the settings the way you want them, click on Options in the Optimizer dialog box, and then click on Save Model. In the dialog box that appears, enter or point to a location in the worksheet at least three columns wide and six rows deep, and then click on OK. Saved settings appear like this:

Solution Cell		
+B5	Maximize	0
Variable Cells		
@COUNT(B1..B3)		
Constraints		
@COUNT(B1..B1)	<=	0.08
@COUNT(B1..B1)	>=	0.06
@COUNT(B2..B2)	<=	30
@COUNT(B2..B2)	>=	19
@COUNT(B5..B5)	<=	+F1..F1

When you want to use the settings, choose Load Model from the Optimizer Options dialog box, and enter the top-left cell where you saved the settings.

Saving Scenarios

Using formulas and functions makes it easy to solve "What If " problems. Each time you change a value, you can see the results throughout the worksheet. But once you change them again, the previous results are gone. Certainly you can use Undo to revert to the last values. But what if you want to see the results of values that you entered before that, or even on another day?

A *scenario* is a set of values that you've used to generate results—a snapshot of the worksheet with one set of values. By saving a scenario, you can quickly return to it when you want to see its effects. By saving a number of scenarios, you can quickly compare results to help make informed decisions.

For example, suppose you create a presentation for an important client. The worksheet contains a series of cost projections based on varying expenses. You can use scenarios to switch between the sets of data, so the client gets a feel for the pros and cons of each plan.

Start by deciding on three things:

■   The range of cells that you want to include in the scenario

■   The cells that will change in value for each scenario, called the changing cells

■   The formulas that reference the changing cells, called the result cells

Using Scenario Expert

The fastest way to create a series of scenarios is to use the Scenario Expert. Start by preparing the worksheet so it contains the first set of the values and results that you want to save. This is called the *base scenario*. Then pull down the Tools menu, point to Scenario, and click on New. A series of dialog boxes will appear for you to select options.

In the first dialog box, enter or point to the changing cells, the cells whose values will change with each scenario.

The second dialog box contains text boxes for each of the changing cells, showing the base settings currently in the worksheet (Figure 20-8). To create another scenario, change the values in the text boxes, type a name for the scenario, and then click on Add Scenario. Repeat this for each set of values and then click on Next.

The next Expert dialog box lists all of the scenarios. To see the values in the worksheet, click on a scenario name and then on Show Scenario. If you want to remove one of the scenarios, click on it and then on Delete.

In the last Expert dialog box, you can create an optional report or just exit. If you create a report, Corel Quattro Pro will create a Scenarios page after the worksheet. Display the page to see the changing and result cells and their values in each scenario.

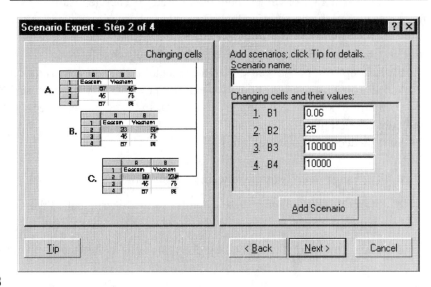

Using base settings and adding scenarios in Scenario Expert

FIGURE 20-8

Scenario Manager

Scenario Expert saves the scenarios in the Scenario Manager, a dialog box where you select which scenarios to display, and where you can add, delete, and modify scenarios.

Pull down the Tools menu, point to Scenario, and click on Edit to display the dialog box shown in Figure 20-9. You will see a list of scenarios that you created with the Expert—the base and other scenarios. To see a scenario, just click on it in the list. The values from the scenario will be applied to the worksheet.

 NOTE: *Use the Highlight button to select a color for the formulas and to select changing cells for each scenario.*

To add a new scenario, exit Scenario Manager and edit the values in the changing cells. Then display Scenario Manager and click on Capture. Type a name for the scenario and then click on Close. A scenario can also include a change in a result cell formula.

20

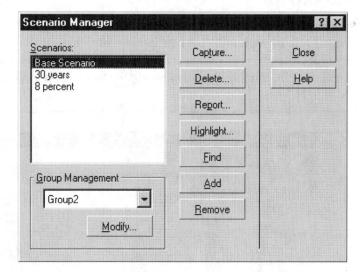

Scenario
Manager

FIGURE 20-9

Creating Scenarios Manually

It is just as easy to create scenarios without using the Expert. Prepare the worksheet with the base values and then display Scenario Manager. By default, the scenario will include the entire page of the worksheet, keeping track of cells with changing values and formulas that reference them. If you want to track just a specific block of the page, or the entire notebook, then click on the Modify button. In the dialog box that appears, enter or point to the range of cells, or click on Notebook or Page to change the capture area. Then close the dialog box to return to Scenario Manager.

Now click on Capture and enter a name for the base scenario—the default is Base—and then click on OK and close Scenario Manager.

You can now edit the changing cells and capture each of the scenarios. When you capture the first scenario after the base, Corel Quattro Pro will automatically identify the changing and the result cells and show them highlighted. The changing cells will be those that have different values than in the base. The result cells are formulas that reference the changing cells. If the cells are not identified correctly, click on the Find button in Scenario Manager. If this still doesn't identify the cells, do it manually—select the cells and then click on Add.

Scenario Groups

You can have more than one group of scenarios in a notebook. Each set can track a different set of cells or page, and each can have its own base. To create a new group, prepare the worksheet the way you want the base scenario to appear. Open Scenario Manager and click on Modify to display the dialog box shown in Figure 20-10.

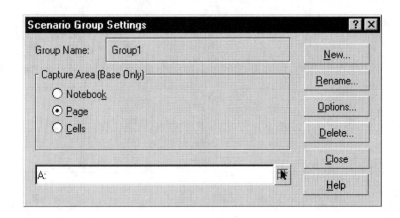

Adding a group

FIGURE 20-10

Click on New and enter a name for the group. Use the Rename button to change the name of an existing group. Close the dialog box.

Use the Group Management list at the bottom of Scenario Manager to change groups. First, display the page of the worksheet that contains the captured cells, and then open Scenario Manager and choose the group that you want to display. The scenarios in the group will be listed.

Deleting Scenarios

You can delete individual scenarios or entire groups. To delete a scenario, select it in the Scenario Manager list and click on Delete. If you delete the base scenario, Corel Quattro Pro will also delete all of the other scenarios that are based on it.

To delete a group, select it in the Group Management list, click on Modify, and then click on Delete.

Creating What-If Tables

One problem with Scenario Manager is that you must choose a scenario each time you want to see the results of changing cells. Wouldn't it be easier if you could just create a table showing the various values in the changing cells and each effect on the result cell? You can do this by creating a What-If table.

There are two types of What-If tables. A one-variable table displays the results of changing one cell on one or two formulas. A two-variable table shows the results of changing two variables on a single formula. As an example, look at Figure 20-11. Both of the tables use the @FVAL function to determine how much an annual investment is worth after a number of years. On the left is a one-variable table that compares the results of saving different annual amounts. The amounts are shown in column B, and the total savings after ten years for each amount is shown in column C. The table on the right compares different amounts and interest rates. The formulas for a one-variable table must reference only one cell, while two-variable formulas reference only two cells.

You can create What-If tables manually or by using the What-If Expert. Let's use the What-If Expert to create the one-variable table shown in the figure.

1. Enter **200** in cell A1, and the formula **@FVAL(6%,10,-A1)** in cell A2.

2. Pull down the Tools menu, point to Numeric Tools, and click on What-If.

3. In the dialog box that appears, click on Expert.

4. In the first Expert, leave the option set at Vary One Cell Against One or More Formulas, and then click on Next.

5. Now you specify the cell containing the formulas. Enter or point to cell A2, and then click on Next.

6. You can now designate a second formula to track. This example only uses one, so click on Next.

7. In this box, you designate the input cell that is referenced in the formula, and a name for it that will appear on the table. Enter **A1** as the input cell, type **Annual Investment** as the name, and then click on Next. The input cell must contain a value.

8. This box lets you select the values that will be used in the input cell. As you can see in Figure 20-12, Corel Quattro Pro suggested some values for you. For this example, increase the savings.

9. Click on Calculate Different Values. Text boxes will appear so you can enter the starting and stopping values, as well as the steps between.

10. Enter **1000** as the Start value, **100** as the Step value, **2000** as the Stop value, and then click on Next.

11. In the last box, enter or point to the block where you want the table to appear, and then click on Make Table.

NOTE: *The two-variable Expert is the same, except you designate two input cells.*

To create a What-If table manually, you have to start the table by entering the column of values that you want to substitute in a formula. In the cell above and to the right of the first substitute value, enter the formula that you want to calculate, including a reference to a blank input cell. Pull down the Tools menu, point to Numeric Tools, and click on What-If to see the dialog box shown in Figure 20-13. In the What-If Table box, enter or point to the block of cells that contains the substitution values and formula. In the Input Cell box, enter the cell referenced in the formula. Click on Generate to create the table.

To create a two-variable table using the What-If Expert, you need a second changing cell. In Figure 20-11, for example, A1 is the first changing cell, and A2 is

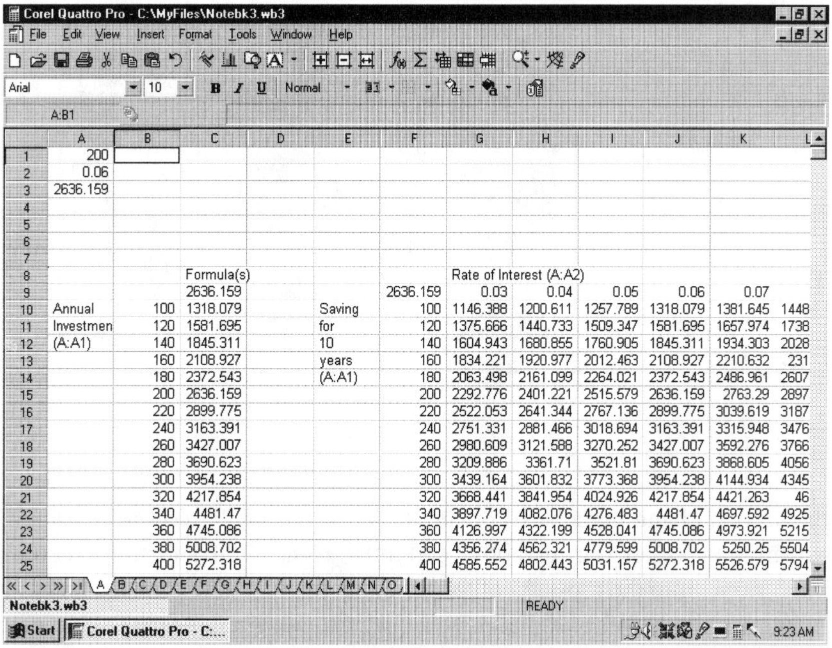

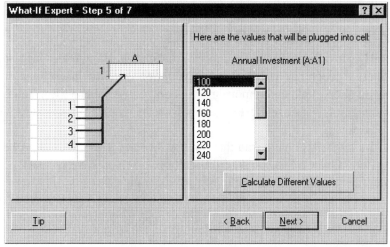

	A	B	C	D	E	F	G	H	I	J	K	L
1	200											
2	0.06											
3	2636.159											
4												
5												
6												
7												
8			Formula(s)				Rate of Interest (A:A2)					
9			2636.159			2636.159	0.03	0.04	0.05	0.06	0.07	
10	Annual	100	1318.079		Saving	100	1146.388	1200.611	1257.789	1318.079	1381.645	1448
11	Investmen	120	1581.695		for	120	1375.666	1440.733	1509.347	1581.695	1657.974	1738
12	(A:A1)	140	1845.311		10	140	1604.943	1680.855	1760.905	1845.311	1934.303	2028
13		160	2108.927		years	160	1834.221	1920.977	2012.463	2108.927	2210.632	231
14		180	2372.543		(A:A1)	180	2063.498	2161.099	2264.021	2372.543	2486.961	2607
15		200	2636.159			200	2292.776	2401.221	2515.579	2636.159	2763.29	2897
16		220	2899.775			220	2522.053	2641.344	2767.136	2899.775	3039.619	3187
17		240	3163.391			240	2751.331	2881.466	3018.694	3163.391	3315.948	3476
18		260	3427.007			260	2980.609	3121.588	3270.252	3427.007	3592.276	3766
19		280	3690.623			280	3209.886	3361.71	3521.81	3690.623	3868.605	4056
20		300	3954.238			300	3439.164	3601.832	3773.368	3954.238	4144.934	4345
21		320	4217.854			320	3668.441	3841.954	4024.926	4217.854	4421.263	46
22		340	4481.47			340	3897.719	4082.076	4276.483	4481.47	4697.592	4925
23		360	4745.086			360	4126.997	4322.199	4528.041	4745.086	4973.921	5215
24		380	5008.702			380	4356.274	4562.321	4779.599	5008.702	5250.25	5504
25		400	5272.318			400	4585.552	4802.443	5031.157	5272.318	5526.579	5794

What-If tables

FIGURE 20-11

Corel Quattro Pro's suggested values based on the content of the changing cells

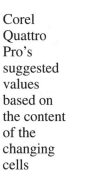

FIGURE 20-12

What-If
dialog box

the second changing cell. To create the table manually, you need to add a row of substitution values starting above and to the right of the substitution column. Enter the formula into the top-left cell of the table, making sure that it refers to two blank input cells. In the What-If dialog box, click on Two Free Variables. Indicate the Data Table and the Column Input and Row Input cells, and then click on Generate.

If you later change a formula used for the table, click on Generate to recalculate the results.

Analyzing External Data

Corel Quattro Pro includes a number of tools for working with data that was created with other programs. The External Data option from the Insert menu, for example, lets you query, link, and import information from database files. You can also take advantage of Database Desktop, an advanced feature for working with external databases.

You might also have data that you've saved as a text file. Importing a text file into Corel Quattro Pro could be difficult because you have to specify how the text in the file should be divided into rows and columns.

QuickColumns is a fast solution to importing text files. Pull down the Tools menu, point to Data Tools, and click on QuickColumns to see the Expert dialog box shown here:

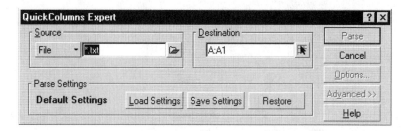

 NOTE: *Dividing text into usable sections, such as worksheet columns, is called* parsing.

Click on the browse button next to the text box, and select the file containing the data you want to import. Specify the range to place the data in the Destination box. QuickColumns will try to divide the data based on its spacing or the use of delimiting characters, but to check the spacing, click on the Advanced button to see the additional information illustrated in Figure 20-14.

The preview pane shows how the text will be divided into columns and the numeric format applied to each column. Column width is indicated in character positions along the ruler in the preview pane, with column boundaries marked by a triangle.

- To change the format or alignment, click on the column header in the preview pane, choose options from the Alignment and Type lists, and in the Format section, select the number of decimal places.

- To change the width of columns, drag the column boundary in the preview pane.

- To select how each row is treated, pull down the list at the start of the row, and choose Parse, Skip, or Label.

- For even more control over the parsing process, click on the Options button to see these choices:

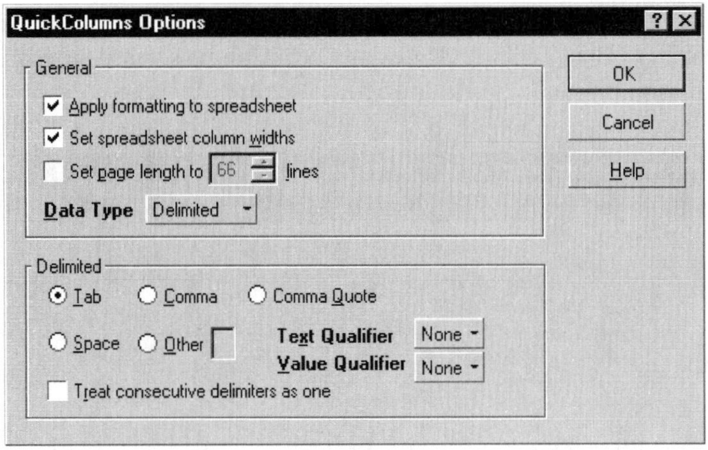

In the General section, choose whether to apply the formats and column widths from the preview pane, set the page length, and specify the type of data—delimited or fixed width.

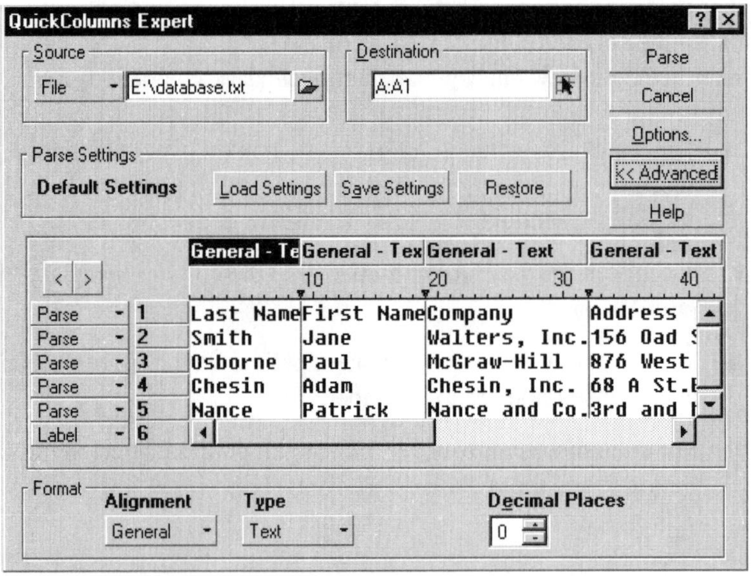

Advanced
parsing
options for
importing
a text file

FIGURE 20-14

In the Delimited section, specify the characters used to separate data into columns, and which may surround text and numbers. Click on OK when you're done.

Finally, click on the Parse button to import the data.

TIP: *Use the Parse Settings options to save and load the specifications that you establish for the data file.*

20

Streamlining Your Work

21

Y ou have a wide range of tools and Experts to make your work easier with Corel Quattro Pro. But there is still more. By recording macros, you can quickly repeat a series of keystrokes and menu selections whenever you need to. You can build libraries of macros to carry out common tasks, and you can write macros that perform sophisticated functions. By linking macros with the keyboard, you run them without using a menu or dialog box, and you can even create a button to run a macro with a single click.

Another way to increase your productivity is to share your Corel Quattro Pro worksheets, charts, and maps with Corel WordPerfect and Corel Presentations. Use the formatting capabilities of these programs to display or publish your data and graphics with maximum impact.

Macros

A macro serves the same function in Corel Quattro Pro as it does in Corel WordPerfect and any computer application. It lets you save a series of keystrokes and commands, and then replay the entire series at any time. Recording a macro in Corel Quattro Pro, however, is a little different than in Corel WordPerfect because of the nature of the program.

 Use PerfectScript from the Corel WordPerfect Accessories menu to create a macro so you can run it from the taskbar.

You can record and play two types of macros in Corel Quattro Pro. PerfectScript macros are compatible with the macro language used by other Corel Office applications and by the PerfectScript accessory. The macros are stored on your disk as individual files, and you can edit them using an editor of your choice, even Corel WordPerfect. Corel Quattro Pro macros are compatible with previous versions of Quattro Pro for Windows. They are stored directly in a worksheet, and you can edit them as you would any labels in the worksheet. These are the easiest macros to create and troubleshoot because it's all done in one application. You can even take advantage of macros that you or others have written for previous versions of Quattro Pro.

Recording a Macro

You don't have to do any preparation before recording a PerfectScript macro because it is stored on your disk. But before creating a Corel Quattro Pro macro, locate a blank area in the worksheet to store the macro. It should be one column wide, with at least as many blank cells as steps that you want to record. To play it safe, make sure that the remainder of the column is empty, and that you won't need any of those cells for the task you'll be recording. You might consider recording all of the macros you want to use for the notebook on sheet IV, which you probably won't be using for anything else, and which you can reach with the QuickTab button. Using one column for each macro allows you to record 256 macros before you have to worry about space.

To record a macro, follow these steps:

1. Pull down the Tools menu, point to Macro, and click on Record to display the dialog box in Figure 21-1. Your first choice it to select to record either a Corel Quattro Pro or PerfectScript macro. If you choose a PerfectScript macro, the box will change so you can indicate the macro name and location where you want to save it.

2. To record a Corel Quattro Pro macro, designate in the Location text box where in your notebook you want the macro recorded. Enter the coordinates or use Point mode to indicate the first empty cell that you've identified for the macro location. If you gave a block name to the cell, select the name from the Block name list. Only designate a single cell. If you designate a block of cells, Corel Quattro Pro will only record commands until the block is filled. By specifying a single cell, it will continue recording commands until the column ends or you stop recording the macro.

3. Click on OK to close the dialog box. Corel Quattro Pro displays an icon of a recording tape in the status bar as a reminder that you are recording a macro.

4. Perform the tasks that you want to record in the macro. You'll even see the commands appear if the macro block is onscreen.

5. When you have finished recording the macro, pull down the Tools menu, point to Macro, and click on Record again.

6. Give your macro a name so you can replay it easily. Click in the first cell in which the macro is stored, pull down the Insert menu, point to Name and click on Cells, and then give that cell a name.

To play a macro, just follow these steps:

1. Select Macro from the Tools menu, and click on Play.

2. In the dialog box that appears, double-click on the macro name.

If you need to stop a macro while it is running, press CTRL-break and then click on OK in the message box that appears. Corel Quattro Pro will sound a beep and display an error message if it cannot follow the macro instruction. You usually will get errors not with recorded macros, but from ones that you edit or write.

NOTE: *You can play a macro even if you did not give it a name. In the Location text box of the Play Macro dialog box, simply enter the coordinates of the first instruction in the macro and then click on OK.*

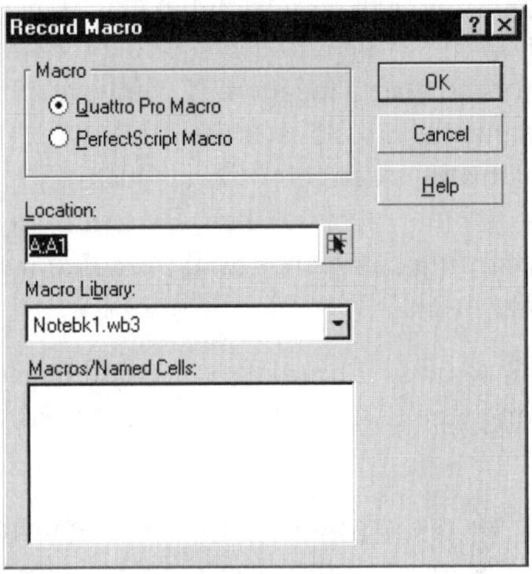

Selecting
the type of
macro you
want to
record

FIGURE 21-1

Relative and Absolute Addresses

By default, macros are recorded using *absolute addresses*. This means that if you click on cell A:A1 when recording the macro, the macro will always select cell A:A1 when you run it. There's nothing wrong with that if that's what you want. But suppose you want to record a macro that will insert a series of labels at a different location each time you play the macro?

To accomplish that, you must change to *relative addresses*. Here's how:

1. Pull down the Tools menu, point to Macro, and click on Options to see this dialog box.

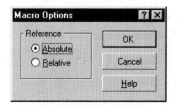

2. Click on Relative and then on OK.

Now each cell selection command you record will select a cell relative to whatever is the active cell at that time. So suppose you start recording when you're in cell A1, and your first action is to click in cell B2. When you run the macro, it will start by selecting the cell one column over and one row down from the current active cell.

This all means that you have to plan your macro well, and think about what you want it to do and where. Consider starting by selecting the cell you will first want to use when you record the macro. Then as your first recorded step, click on that same cell, even though it is already active. This ensures that your macro will start at some known location.

If you are using an absolute address, the macro will start in that cell no matter what cell is active when you begin. If you use relative addresses, the macro will always begin in whatever cell is active at the time—just select it before running the macro.

 NOTE: *If you select a cell at the start of the macro but perform any action on it except selecting another cell, the command to select the first cell will not be recorded in the macro.*

Let's record a small macro so you get the feel for it. The macro will enter a series of row and column labels starting in the cell next to the active cell, and insert a row of formulas. Follow these steps:

1. Click in A1.

2. Select Options from the Tools Macro menu, click on Relative, and then on OK.

3. Pull down the Tools menu, point to Macro, and then click on Record to display the Record Macro dialog box.

4. In the Location box, enter **B:A1** to save the macro in the first column of worksheet B. (You can also point to the cell by clicking on the sheet B tab and then on cell A1.)

5. Click on OK. You can now record the macro.

6. Click in cell B1, type **Qtr 1**, and press ENTER.

7. Drag over cells B1 to E1, and then click on the QuickFill button to complete the series.

8. Click in Cell A2, and type **Income**.

9. Click in Cell A3, and type **Expenses**.

10. Click in cell B4, type **+B2-B3**, and press ENTER.

11. Drag over cells B4 to E4, and click on QuickFill to copy the formulas.

12. To stop recording, pull down the Tools menu, point to Macro, and click on Record.

 NOTE: *The Absolute and Relative macro record options do not affect the way Corel Quattro Pro copies formulas.*

Naming Your Macro

To name the macro, you assign a block name to the first cell of the macro instructions. Let's name the macro we just recorded.

1. Go to sheet B to see the instructions of the macro, as shown in Figure 21-2. The instructions of the macro are listed in the block you selected in the Corel Quattro Pro macro language.

2. Click on cell A1.

3. Pull down the Insert menu, point to Name, and click on Cells.

4. Type **Budget** as the block name.

5. Click on Add.

6. Click on Close.

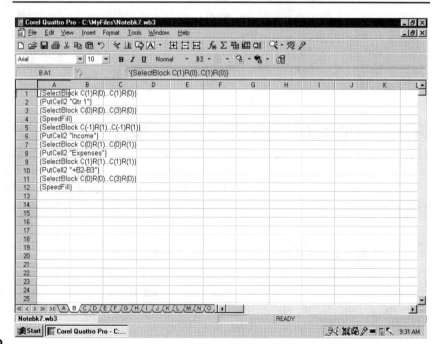

Recorded
macro
instructions

FIGURE 21-2

Running Your Macro

Now run the macro. Click on any cell in worksheet A, pull down the Tools menu, and click on Play. Double-click on Budget in the macro list. The labels and formulas will be inserted starting in the cell next to the active cell on the sheet.

Creating a Macro Library

A *macro library* is a notebook in which you can store macros. You open the notebook and leave it in the background as you work with other notebooks. When you play a macro, Corel Quattro Pro will first search for it in the current notebook. If it is not there, it will look for the macro in the macro library. You can also tell Corel Quattro Pro to find it there when you play the macro to save time.

To create a macro library, record the macros in a worksheet. Right-click on the notebook's title bar (you have to restore the notebook to a window first), and choose Active Notebook Properties from the QuickMenu. Click on the Macro Library tab, and then click on Yes. Close the Properties dialog box and save the notebook.

When you want to access the macros in the library, open the notebook. It must be open to access its macros. If you want Corel Quattro Pro to run the macro without first searching through the active notebook, pull down the Tools menu, point to Macro, and click on Play. Pull down the Macro Library List dialog box, and click on the library name. You'll see a list of the macros and cell names. Double-click on the macro you want to run.

Assigning a Macro to a Keystroke

If you have a macro that you run often, assign it to a CTRL-SHIFT key combination. That way, you can run it by pressing the combination without having to display the Macro dialog box. When you name the macro, name it with a backslash (\ ) followed by one letter (a to z), such as \c. Then to run the macro, press CTRL-SHIFT and the letter.

Assigning a Macro to a Button

One problem with using a keystroke to run a macro is that you have to remember the keystroke. As an alternative, you can assign the macro to a button on the worksheet. Just click on the button to play the macro.

First, create the button.

1. Display the worksheet where you want the button to appear.

2. Select QuickButton from the Insert menu.

3. Either click where you want a default-sized button to appear, or drag to create a button any size. When you release the mouse, the button appears selected with handles.

You can always change the size of the button later by dragging the handles. To move a button, use drag-and-drop.

 TIP: *To place a graphic image on the face of the button, copy it to the Clipboard, select the button, and click on Paste.*

If you click elsewhere in the worksheet, the handles will disappear. Until you assign a process to the button, you can click on it with the left mouse button to select it so the handles appear. Once you assign a process to the button, right-click on it to select it. If you click the left mouse button, Corel Quattro Pro performs whatever function the button has been assigned.

Once you create the button, you must associate the macro with it, using these steps.

1. Right-click on the button and choose Button Properties from the QuickMenu to see the dialog box shown in Figure 21-3.

2. In the Enter Macro text box, type the command {**Branch macroname**}, substituting the name of your macro for macroname. You must enclose the command in braces.

3. Click on the Label Text page of the Properties dialog box and enter what you want to appear on the button's face.

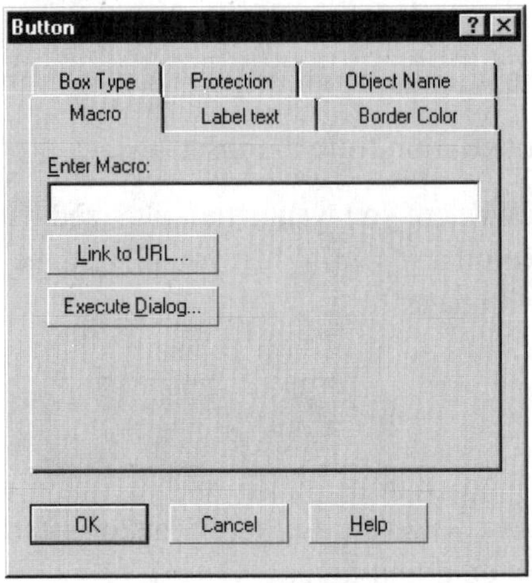

Button
Properties

FIGURE 21-3

You can also link the button to an URL address on the Web. Select Link to URL, and enter the URL address. To browse the Web to select a site, click on the Web Browse button in the toolbar.

The other button properties let you change the border color and button box style, protect the button from change, and give it an object name so you can refer to the button itself in macros.

Running Macros Automatically

Sometimes you want to run a macro every time you start Corel Quattro Pro, or when you open or close a specific notebook. You may want to open your Macro Library file, for example, or insert a standard heading on the initial worksheet. You can designate both an *autoload file* and a *startup macro*. An autoload file will be opened whenever you start Corel Quattro Pro. A startup macro will be played when you start Corel Quattro Pro.

You create both features in the Application Properties dialog box. Right-click on the Corel Quattro Pro title bar and select Application Properties from the QuickMenu. Click on the Macro tab, and enter the macro's cell name in the Startup Macro text box. Also use this dialog box to determine what elements are suppressed as the macro runs.

You may also have a macro that you want to run whenever you open or close a specific notebook. Perhaps you want to display a certain area of the worksheet when you open the notebook, or want to print the worksheet when you close the notebook. These are called startup macros and exit macros.

To create a notebook startup macro, just give it the name _NBSTARTMACRO. Name an exit macro _NBEXITMACRO. When Corel Quattro Pro starts, it will look for a macro named _NBSTARTMACRO. If it finds it in the worksheet, it plays the macro. When you exit Corel Quattro Pro, it runs the macro called _NBEXITMACRO.

The Macro Language

Macros follow their own rules of syntax. Each macro command may be followed by one or more arguments, and the entire instruction is enclosed in braces. For example, the command {ESC} has no arguments because it simply equals the task of pressing the ESC key. The command to select a cell, SelectBlock, has one argument: the coordinates to select. A relative address is shown as {SelectBlock C(1)R(0)..C(1)R(0)}. This means to select a block starting one column to the right of the current cell in the same row. The 0 in the cell reference means to use the current row. Movement to the right and down is shown in positive numbers, movement to the left and up in negative numbers. An absolute address would appear as {SelectBlock A:D6..D6}. The command to select an entire row uses only the sheet and row number, as in {SelectBlock A:1} to select row 1 on sheet A. The command {SelectBlock C:H} would select the entire column H on sheet C.

Multiple arguments must be separated by commas, as in the command {BlockInsert.Rows A:1,Entire}. The first argument (A:1) specifies where to insert the row; the second argument indicates an entire, not a partial, row. Notice that the command name itself includes a period. The BlockInsert command is used generically to insert many different objects. The syntax is {BlockInsert.Object block, entire|partial}, using commands such as BlockInsert.Columns and BlockInsert.Pages.

Macro commands do not simply mimic keystrokes. If you use the arrow keys to select a cell, for example, you won't see instructions for each arrow that you press. Corel Quattro Pro records the results of your keystrokes, not individual actions. If you press the UP ARROW and RIGHT ARROW keys to select cell B3 using absolute addressing, the command will simply appear as {SelectBlock A:B3..B3}.

Dialog Boxes Commands

It is likely that you'll be recording macros that select options from dialog boxes, such as opening or printing a file. The command to open a file is simply {FileOpen filename}, as in {FileOpen C:\Corel\Office7\Corel Quattro8\Notebk1.wb3}.

When a dialog box contains multiple options, there is usually a different command for each option, often starting with the name of the dialog box. All Print macros, for example, begin with the word "Print," followed by a period and then the command that it performs. Use {Print.DoPrint}, for example, to print the current worksheet using all of the default values.

Other commands are used to set the print options before actually printing. This macro, for example, prints three copies of a block:

```
{Print.Block "A:A1..H4"}
{Print.Copies "3"}
{Print.DoPrint}
```

The first command sets the print block. The name shows that it involves the Print function and the Block option. The second command designates three copies using the Print function and the Copies option. The final command initiates printing.

Writing Macros

Macro instructions are stored as text in the worksheet, so you can edit a macro by changing, deleting, or inserting commands just as you edit worksheet labels. You can also copy instructions from one macro to another, even if they are on different sheets or in different notebooks.

One way to insert additional commands into a macro is to record them as a new macro in another location in the worksheet, and then cut and paste them where you want them inserted. Do not try to record additional instructions directly into the macro—new instructions could overwrite existing ones—unless you record them in the first blank cell after the macro's last command.

You can also edit and write macros by typing the macro commands yourself. In order to write macro commands, however, you need to know the Corel Quattro Pro macro language, and a little about the way computer programs work.

To write a macro, just start in any blank cell in an area of a worksheet that you won't need for anything else. Type the commands, making sure to enclose them in braces. At the end of the macro, make sure there is a blank cell, or enter the command {Quit} or {Return}. If there is anything else immediately after the macro, Corel Quattro Pro will try to run it as a macro command and will generate an error.

When you've finished, give a cell name to the first instruction, and then save the worksheet.

If you need help writing the command or using its arguments, refer to the help system. You'll find detailed examples on each macro command, as shown in Figure 21-4. Click on Help Topics in the Help menu, and then double-click on the Macro Command Reference option. You can choose macros by category, or see an alphabetical listing.

You can test a macro quickly by clicking on the first cell, selecting Macro from the Tools menu, clicking on Play, and then on OK. The coordinates of the active cell will be in the Location text box of the Play Macro dialog box.

Copying Commands

If you are not certain of a command's syntax, you can paste the command in the macro rather than writing it. To paste a command, press SHIFT-F3 to see a dialog box listing the categories of macro commands.

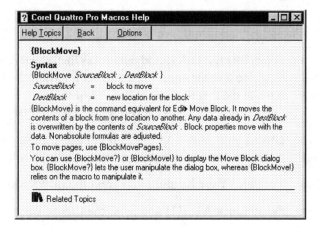

Using the help system for detailed information on macro commands

FIGURE 21-4

The categories are as follows:

- Keyboard
- Screen
- Interactive
- Program flow
- Cell
- File
- / commands

- Command Equivalents
- OLE and DDE
- UI Building
- Object
- Analysis tools
- Miscellaneous

Select the category of the command you want to use, and then click on OK. If you see a further listing of categories, choose one from the list, and click on OK again. You'll see a list of commands in the category. Click on the command you want to insert and then on OK. The command will appear in the cell and input line.

 TIP: *Click on Cancel to move back to the previous dialog box list.*

Use the following steps to write a macro that inserts your name on the top of the current worksheet.

1. Click on sheet tab C and then in cell A1.

2. Type **{SelectBlock A1..A1}** and then press the DOWN ARROW to select cell A2. Notice that the sheet name has been left off the range reference in order to make the macro move to cell A1 of the current sheet. In a sense, this command is absolute to the cell reference but relative to the sheet.

3. Type **{BlockInsert.Rows A1..A1,Entire}** and then press the DOWN ARROW. This command inserts a row into the rows of the worksheet.

4. Type **{PutCell "Your Name"}** and press the DOWN ARROW key.

5. Type **{SelectBlock A1..H1}** and press the DOWN ARROW key.

6. Type **{SetProperty "Alignment.Horizontal",Center across block}**. This command centers the label in the active cell across the selected block.

7. Type **{Quit}** and then press ENTER. The completed macro is shown in Figure 21-5.

8. Select cell A1, the first cell of the macro.

9. Pull down the Insert menu, point to Name, and click on Cells.

10. Type **\n** as the cell name, and then click on Add, and then on Close.

To run the macro, just press CTRL-SHIFT-N. Try it now. Click on sheet tab D and type something in cell A1. Press CTRL-SHIFT-N to run the macro. You can also select Macro from the Tools menu, click on Play, and then double-click on the macro name.

TIP: *To quickly go to your macro, click on the Navigate button in the input line and click on the macro name.*

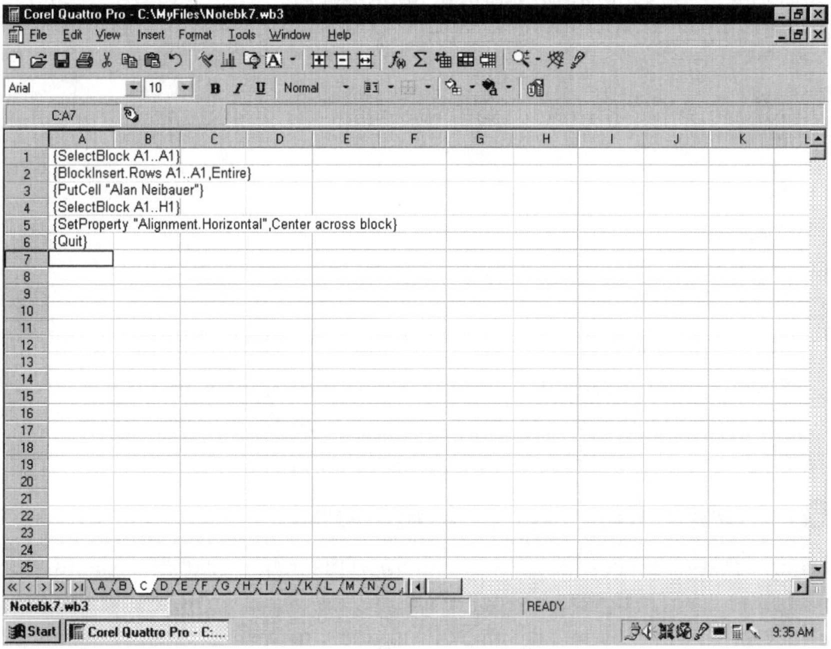

21

	A	B	C	D	E	F	G	H	I	J	K	L
1	{SelectBlock A1..A1}											
2	{BlockInsert.Rows A1..A1,Entire}											
3	{PutCell "Alan Neibauer"}											
4	{SelectBlock A1..H1}											
5	{SetProperty "Alignment.Horizontal",Center across block}											
6	{Quit}											
7												

Completed macro

FIGURE 21-5

Fundamental Macro Commands

There are hundreds of macros. As with functions, many of them are for rather sophisticated purposes. In this chapter, however, we will review a basic set of commands that also illustrate some principles of programming.

Entering Information into Cells

There are several commands for inserting information into cells. The simplest is PutCellL, which uses the syntax {PutCell*Data*,[*Date*(0|1)]}. To insert a numeric value in a cell, enter the value as the argument, as in {PutCell764.76}. Enclose labels, formulas, functions, and dates in quotation marks.

The optional argument is only needed when you insert a date. Use 1 to store the value as a date, or 0 to insert it as a label. The command {PutCell"11/16/45",1}, for example, inserts the date into the active cell as a date.

You can also use a related command, {PutCell2*Data*}, which has only one argument. You must start all numeric values with a plus sign, as in {PutCell2+345}, and dates are always inserted as dates, not labels.

To enter the same information in multiple cells, use the PutBlock and PutBlock2 commands, using the syntax

```
{PutCellData,[Block],[Date(0|1)]}
```

and

```
{PutCell2Data,[Block]}
```

If you do not specify the optional block, the contents are inserted into the active cell or selected block. Designate noncontiguous blocks in parentheses.

Controlling the Flow of Commands

Macros that you record are always *linear*. This means that all of the instructions are performed, and in the exact order in which they appear in the macro. When you write a macro, however, you can control the order in which commands are performed, repeating or skipping over them as you want.

These types of macros, more than any others, require a basic understanding of program logic, the type of logic applied to programming languages such as C or Basic. If you are familiar with a programming language, you will find the concepts discussed in this chapter familiar. If you are new to programming, you will get a good starting lesson.

USING SUBROUTINES   A *subroutine* is a series of macro instructions that you can perform when needed. For example, suppose you need to perform a series of tasks several times in the same macro. Rather than repeat the same lines each time, write them once in a separate location on the worksheet and give it its own name.

Now whenever you need to perform those tasks, you call the routine by enclosing the name in braces, as in {Do_This_Routine}. The macro performs the commands in the subroutine until it reaches a blank cell, a value, or the command {Return}, after which it goes back and follows the instructions where it left off in the original macro.

By creating a library of subroutines, you can write complex macros more easily and quickly. In fact, some macros may contain little more than subroutine calls to other macros.

MOVING TO OTHER INSTRUCTIONS   One other way to perform another macro, or set of commands in the running macro itself, is to use the Branch command. Unlike a subroutine, however, the Branch command does not return to the original location when the command ends.

You use the Branch command to leave one macro and perform another, or to move to another location in the same macro that you've given a cell name. The syntax is {Branch macro}. The command is most commonly used in conjunction with the IF command.

MAKING DECISIONS   One advantage of writing a macro is that you can have it make decisions for you—for example, skipping over some instructions that you may not want it to perform, or moving to other instructions only under certain conditions.

For example, suppose you only want to print your worksheet if the value in a cell reaches a certain level. Use the IF command to test the value in the cell and print the worksheet based on that value. The syntax is {If *Condition*}{DoWhenTrue} {DoWhenFalse}. *Condition* is a logical expression. Look at this example:

```
{If due>500}{Branch Overdue_Notice}
{Branch GoodClient}
```

When the value in the cell named "due" is over 500, the macro branches to the macro named "Overdue_Notice" and performs its instructions. When the amount is not over 500, the macro branches to the GoodClient subroutine.

In a strict sense, the If macro command does not work like an If..Else statement in most programming languages. In these languages, the command specified in the (DoWhenFalse) part of the IF statement is only performed when the condition is false. With Corel Quattro Pro, if you do not use the BRANCH or QUIT command, the macro will perform both statements when the condition is true. Look at this example:

```
{If due>500}{PutCell "Deadbeat"}
{PutCell "Good Client"}
```

If the condition is true, Corel Quattro Pro will perform the command and insert "Deadbeat" into the cell. However, it will then continue with the macro, immediately placing "Good Client" in the same cell. It will not skip over the command just because the condition is true.

If this is the last command in the macro, you can always write it like this:

```
{If due>500}{Putcell "Deadbeat"}{Quit}
{PutCell "Good Client"}
```

Then the macro will not run the last statement when the condition is true.

Keep in mind that you can use multiple Branch statements to perform multiple tests. For example, suppose you are checking student grades to determine what values to enter in a cell. Use a macro such as this:

```
{If grade>=90}{Branch a_student}
{If grade>=80}{Branch b_student}
{If grade>=70}{Branch c_student}
{Branch Failing}
```

The macro now tests for three conditions, and if none of them are true, it performs the macro named Failing.

Even though you are branching elsewhere to the macro, or to another macro, you can still return to the statement following the false statement. Give a cell name to the command after the false statement, and then branch back to that when you are ready. For example, look at this logic:

```
{If grade>=90}{Branch a_student}
{If grade>=80}{Branch b_student}
{If grade>=70}{Branch c_student}
{PutCell2 "You are failing, sorry"}
{Putcell "The End"}
```

Now assume that you've assigned the cell name Continue to the cell with the command {Putcell "The End"}. When a student has a grade of 90 or more, the macro branches to this macro named a_student:

```
{SelectBlock A1}
{PutCell2 "You are very smart. You got an A."}
{SelectBlock A2}
{Branch Continue}
```

The last command branches back to the original macro, and continues after the final test of the If command.

REPEATING COMMANDS   In addition to making decisions with the IF command, let's say you want a macro to repeat a series of instructions with the For macro. The syntax is

```
{For CounterLoc,Start#,Stop#,Step#,StartLoc}
```

Here's the purpose of each argument:

- *CounterLoc* is a cell that Corel Quattro Pro will use to keep track of the number of repetitions. The value in the cell will change with each repetition of the loop, so Corel Quattro Pro will know when the maximum value has been reached.

- *Start#* is the initial value that Corel Quattro Pro places in the CounterLoc cell.

- *Stop#* sets the maximum value of CounterLoc. When the number in CounterLoc exceeds this value, the repetition ends.

- *Step#* determines how Corel Quattro Pro increments the value in CounterLoc. When set at 1, for example, the value in CounterLoc is incremented by 1 with each repetition.

For example, the following command runs the subroutine Repeat_This ten times:

```
{For A1,1,10,1,Repeat_This}
```

It places the value 1 in cell A1, and then performs the subroutine starting at the cell named Repeat_This. It then increments the value in cell A1 by 1—the Step value—and runs the macro again. It repeats this process until the value in cell A1 is greater than 10.

INTERACTIVE MACROS   Although Corel Quattro Pro has hundreds of macro commands, sometimes you just don't know exactly what you want the macro to do. You might want to insert different text each time the macro runs, or set a dialog box in some specific way. In these instances you want an interactive macro—one that pauses to give you a chance to enter text or select options from a dialog box.

When you want a macro to open a dialog box and then pause so you can select options from the box, use a command in the form {DialogBox}. The command {Print}, for example, displays the dialog box on the screen. Once you choose an option from the box and select Print or Close, the macro continues at the next instruction.

To pause a macro so you can enter text, use the GetLabel command with this syntax:

```
{GetLabel Prompt,Location}
```

The Prompt argument is a string up to 70 characters long that will appear telling you what type of information to enter. It can be text, such as "Enter your telephone number," or a reference to a cell containing the text you want to appear as the prompt.

To reference a cell, enter it as a formula, such as +D3. The Location argument is the cell where the information should be placed.

When Corel Quattro Pro encounters the GetLabel command, it pauses the macro and displays your prompt in the Enter a Label dialog box. Type the text you want to enter, up to 160 characters, and then click on OK or press ENTER.

For example, the following command displays a message on the screen and accepts an entry into cell A1:

```
{GetLabel "Enter your name", +A1}
```

The GetNumber command works the same way, but accepts a numeric value. The syntax is { GetNumber *Prompt,Location*}. You can enter a number or a formula that returns a numeric value.

Sharing Corel Quattro Pro Information

Corel Quattro Pro has a wide range of formatting capabilities, and you can enter text into cells, but it is far from a word processing program. When you need more than a few lines of explanatory text with your worksheet, consider sharing it with Corel WordPerfect.

Share a worksheet with Corel WordPerfect so you do not have to retype the information into a Corel WordPerfect table.

The quickest way to use a worksheet with Corel WordPerfect is to cut and paste. Select the range of cells in Corel Quattro Pro, switch to your Corel WordPerfect document, and then click on Paste. The worksheet will be inserted into the document as a Corel WordPerfect table. You can now use Corel WordPerfect's table commands to format the information and work with rows and columns.

When selecting cells in Corel Quattro Pro, keep in mind the page margins and width of your document. In Corel Quattro Pro, worksheets wider than a page will just run over into additional columns. If you paste a wide table into Corel WordPerfect, however, the columns will scroll off the edge of the page, as shown in Figure 21-6. Before printing the document, reduce the column size or font so the worksheet fits on the page. The information is there; it just doesn't fit on the page.

21

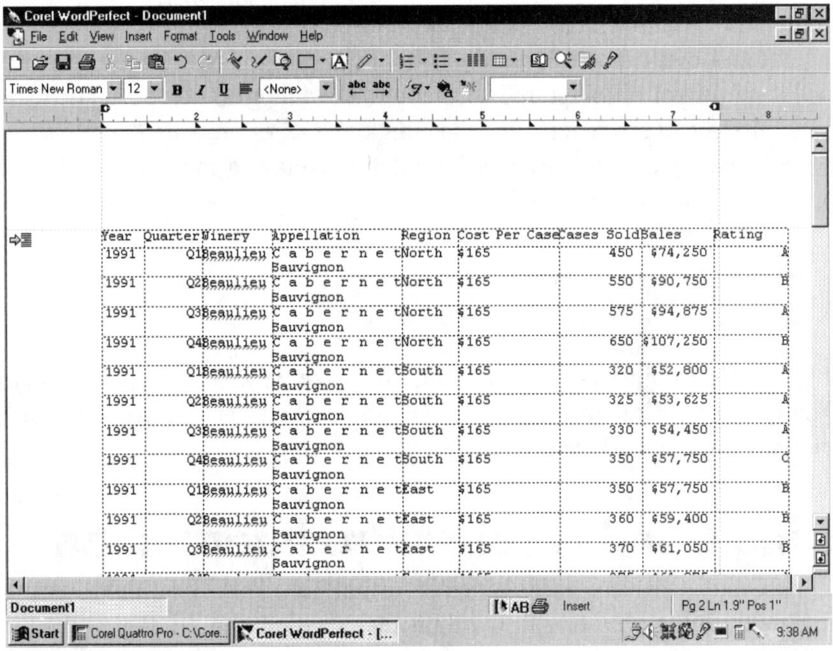

Figure showing Corel WordPerfect window with a pasted worksheet table containing wine sales data (Year, Quarter, Winery, Appellation, Region, Cost Per Case, Cases Sold, Sales, Rating columns).

Wide worksheets scrolling off the screen when pasted into Corel WordPerfect

FIGURE 21-6

Using Paste Special

For more choices in sharing a worksheet, select Paste Special from the Edit menu. You'll have several options, shown in Figure 21-7, including buttons to Paste and Paste Link. Let's look at the Paste options first.

You have a number of ways to paste the table:

- Corel Quattro Pro 8 Notebook inserts the worksheet as one object that you cannot edit in Corel WordPerfect.

- Rich Text Format inserts the worksheet as a Corel WordPerfect table, but using the text formats that it has in Corel Quattro Pro.

- WB1 also inserts the worksheet as a Corel WordPerfect table, but with the same grid lines and text formats as in Corel Quattro Pro.

- Unformatted text simply inserts the text from the worksheet, with cell contents separated by tabs.

- The Picture and Device Independent Bitmap options insert the cells as a graphic object. Double-click on the object to edit the graphic in Corel Presentations.

   TIP: *Pasting a Corel Quattro Pro chart or map always inserts it as an object. Double-click on the object to edit it in Corel Quattro Pro.*

If you select to paste the worksheet as a Corel Quattro Pro 8 Notebook, the cells will be inserted as one object, surrounded by handles:

Year	Quarter	Winery	Appellation	Region	Cost Per Case
1991	Q1	Beaulieu	Cabernet Sauvignon	North	$165
1991	Q2	Beaulieu	Cabernet Sauvignon	North	$165
1991	Q3	Beaulieu	Cabernet Sauvignon	North	$165
1991	Q4	Beaulieu	Cabernet Sauvignon	North	$165
1991	Q1	Beaulieu	Cabernet Sauvignon	South	$165
1991	Q2	Beaulieu	Cabernet Sauvignon	South	$165
1991	Q3	Beaulieu	Cabernet Sauvignon	South	$165
1991	Q4	Beaulieu	Cabernet Sauvignon	South	$165
1991	Q1	Beaulieu	Cabernet Sauvignon	East	$165
1991	Q2	Beaulieu	Cabernet Sauvignon	East	$165
1991	Q3	Beaulieu	Cabernet Sauvignon	East	$165
1991	Q4	Beaulieu	Cabernet Sauvignon	East	$165
1991	Q1	Beaulieu	Cabernet Sauvignon	West	$165
1991	Q2	Beaulieu	Cabernet Sauvignon	West	$165

This is an *embedded object*. This means that along with the object, Windows 95 also stores the name of the program used to create it—Corel Quattro Pro. You can't edit or format the information as an object in Corel WordPerfect, but if you

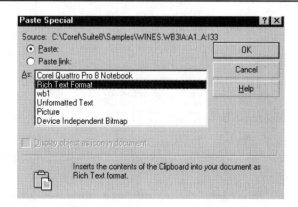

Paste
Special
dialog box

FIGURE 21-7

double-click on Object, Windows 95 opens Corel Quattro Pro and transmits the data from the object to it.

Corel Quattro Pro is opened, however, for in-place editing. You'll see a miniature version of the Corel Quattro Pro worksheet right on the Corel WordPerfect window. However, Corel WordPerfect's menus and toolbars are replaced by those of Corel Quattro Pro, as shown in Figure 21-8. This way, you can edit the worksheet data while seeing the document in which it will be printed. If you pull down a menu item, you'll see the Corel Quattro Pro menu options, not Corel WordPerfect's. Nevertheless, the worksheet window appears within the Corel WordPerfect document window.

Keep in mind that there is no link between the object in Corel WordPerfect and the actual Corel Quattro Pro file from which the data was copied. What's in Corel WordPerfect is a copy of the data linked to Corel Quattro Pro as its program of origination. If you change the information in the original disk file, the data in Corel WordPerfect will not change.

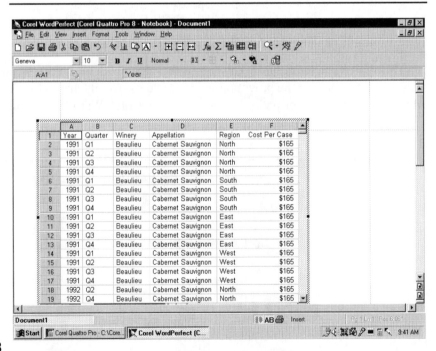

Editing an
embedded
object in
place

FIGURE 21-8

If you click on the Paste Link option in the Paste Special dialog box, you have one option—Quattro Pro 8 Notebook. Pasting the worksheet in this way inserts it as an object with an OLE (Object Linking and Embedding) link. Now there is a link between the object in Corel WordPerfect and the Corel Quattro Pro file from which it was obtained. If you change the information in the file, it will change in Corel WordPerfect as well.

When you double-click on the object, Windows 95 opens Corel Quattro Pro and the associated file, not in place but in a Corel Quattro Pro window. When you edit and save the worksheet, the changes are also shown in the Corel WordPerfect document.

NOTE: *If you want to copy the Corel WordPerfect document to another computer, however, you must also copy the original source file.*

PART IV

Corel Presentations

Using Corel Presentations

22

Corel Presentations 8 is a remarkable program that lets you create anything from a simple cover page for a report to a complete multimedia slide presentation. What makes it even more remarkable is that it's easy—you don't need a background in art or design, and you don't have to spend hours in front of your computer screen to create special effects.

Certainly the program gets its name because you can use it to create a presentation. You can design a series of slides to show on a monitor, to display on a large screen using a projector, or to convert to actual 33mm photographic slides or overhead transparencies. If you design the presentation for computer display, you can also add sound effects and create special effects with the transition from one slide to the next.

But you can use Presentations even when your goals are not that grand. You can create one or more slides to use for report covers, handouts for meetings, even for organization or data charts.

Corel Presentations Basics

Before starting Presentations, let's review some basic concepts that will help you along the way. Corel Presentations lets you create one or more slides. They are called *slides* even if you do not plan to convert them to photographic slides or show them on the screen. So if you use Presentations to design a report cover, for example, you are still creating a "slide."

 NOTE: *You can also create just a drawing and save it as a WPG graphic file. In fact, if your presentation consists of just one page, it will be saved as a drawing by default.*

Every slide consists of three separate layers. The bottom layer is appropriately called the *background*. The background contains designs and colors that make up the general appearance of the slide. Imagine going to the store and purchasing colored paper to draw on—the color on the paper is the background. With Corel Presentations, you can select from a list of professionally designed background designs, modify them, or create your own.

 NOTE: *You can also create pictures that are not slides and that do not have layers.*

Over the background is the *layout layer.* This determines the general position and type of contents for each slide. The contents are represented by placeholders, boxes that appear onscreen suggesting the type of items that should be on the slide. If you do not add any text to a placeholder, it will not appear onscreen when you show the presentation, and it will not print with the slide. Presentations comes with templates for seven general layouts, listed in Table 22-1.

 NOTE: *You can change the position and size of the placeholders, delete them, or add your own elements to a slide.*

The top layer is called the *slide layer.* This is where you enter the text, drawings, clipart, or other items that you want to appear on the slide.

With Corel Presentations you can work on your slides in three views:

- *Slide Editor* lets you create or edit the slide contents or background, one slide at a time.

- *Slide Outliner* displays the organization of a presentation as a text outline, using titles, subtitles, and bullet lists as the outline levels.

- *Slide Sorter* displays thumbnails of the slides for changing their order.

One of the first choices you should make when creating a presentation is the master category. The master determines the overall look of the slides, offering options best suited for the type of presentation intended, such as using 35mm slides, a formal business presentation, or displaying in color or in printed copies. The category determines basic design elements, such as the color choices and aspect ratio, for the type of media. You would use Color, for example, if you plan to display

Slide Template	Placeholders
Title	Title, subtitle
Bulleted List	Title, subtitle, bullet list
Text	Title, subtitle, text box
Organization Chart	Title, subtitle, organization chart box
Data Chart	Title, subtitle, chart box
Combination	Title, subtitle, bullet list, and chart box
Blank	No placeholders

Default Slide Layouts

TABLE 22-1

the presentation on a color monitor, or if you have a color printer. You might also select Color if you have a black-and-white printer but are using a background design that will translate well into shades of gray. Select the Printout category for simple backgrounds that will print well on a monochrome printer, or choose 35mm if you plan to convert the slides to photographic slides.

Starting a Presentation

You can start a new presentation using a template and then just fill in the information that you want to get across. Or you can design your presentation from scratch, but selecting from professional-looking backgrounds.

Follow these steps to create a presentation.

1. Click on Start in the taskbar, point to Corel WordPerfect Suite 8, and click on Corel Presentations 8. You'll see the New dialog box. You can choose to open a presentation template to use as the basis for your own work, or to open one of your existing presentations using the Work On tab.

2. Click on [Presentations Slide Show] in the Create New page and then on Create. The Startup Master Gallery window appears, as shown in Figure 22-1.

Your first choice should be to select a master slide background to set the overall look of the presentation. You can change the master background at any time, and you can choose a different background for individual slides.

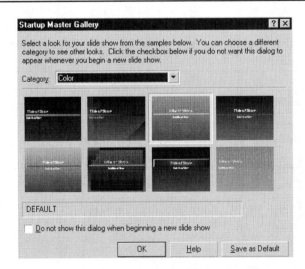

Startup
Master
Gallery

FIGURE 22-1

1. Pull down the Category list to see the categories available. When you select a category, several sample backgrounds will appear.

2. Look at all of the background designs, scrolling the list if necessary.

3. Click on the design you want, and then click on OK to apply the choice to your presentation.

 TIP: *For even more background choices, use the Background Gallery option. You'll learn about this option later.*

The Presentations window appears with a blank title slide, as shown in Figure 22-2.

The Corel Presentations Window

Look at the Corel Presentations window shown in Figure 22-2. Under the menu bar are the toolbar and a property bar. In addition to the first nine standard toolbar buttons, the toolbar contains the buttons shown here:

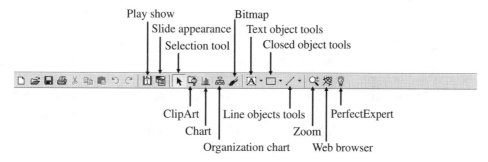

The default property bar contains these items:

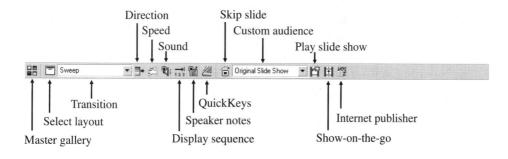

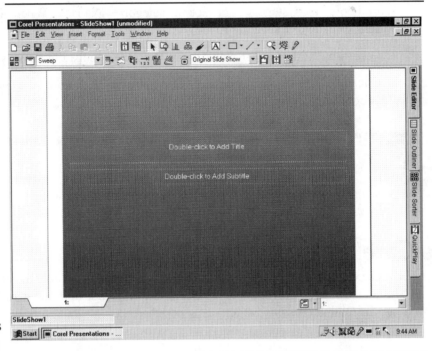

Corel
Presentations

FIGURE 22-2

Along the right of the screen are tabs for changing the view and for running the show. At the bottom of the screen is the application bar.

Corel Presentations starts with a blank title slide. Below the slide is a tab. A tab will appear for each slide you add so you can change slides quickly. To the right of the tab is the New Slides list and then the Slide List. You use the New Slides list to add a slide to the presentation, and the Slides List to change slides, as well as see the slide title.

Corel Presentations generally offers many of the same features as Corel WordPerfect and other applications. So, if you are familiar with one application, you'll feel at home here. In addition to the obvious common buttons in the toolbar and power bar, here are just some of the common features:

- Select Date from the Insert menu to insert the date as text or a code, or to select or create a date format.

- When you are editing a placeholder that contains text, choose to use Spell Check, Thesaurus, Grammatik, or QuickCorrect from the Tools menu.

- Use the Tools menu to access QuickCorrect and QuickLink.

- Select Settings from the Tools menu to customize the way Corel Presentations works. The Settings box offers these options: Display, Environment, Files, and Customize to change toolbars, property bars, tool palettes, keyboards, and menus.

- Use the File menu to access file management options.

- Play and record macros using the Tools menu.

Working with Placeholders

Now look at the template. The Title template contains just two placeholders, one for the title and one for the subtitle.

 You can use the Clipboard to paste text from other applications into slides.

To use a placeholder, double-click on it to insert contents into it. For example, double-click on the Title placeholder to enter and format text into the title.

Every placeholder is similar to a graphic box in Corel WordPerfect. Click on the placeholder to display handles around it, and then perform any of these functions:

- Drag the box to change its position.

- Drag a handle to change its size.

- Press DEL to delete the box.

- Cut, copy, and paste the box.

While a placeholder will not appear with the slide if you do not use it, you may want to delete unused placeholders from the slide. This will make it easier to select other objects that you add, without accidentally selecting the empty placeholder. To delete the placeholder, click on it and press DEL. If you later want to restore the original placeholders, select Slide Re-Apply Layout from the Format menu. However, this procedure will also return anything you've moved or resized to their default settings, so use this option with caution.

 TIP: *To change the layout of a slide, pull down the Layout List in the power bar and click on the layout you want to apply to the slide.*

Now let's create our first slide.

1. Double-click on the title placeholder. The box will be surrounded by heavy lines and the insertion point will appear in the middle, the default justification for titles and subtitles.

2. Type the text of the title: **Educational Technology**. Do not press ENTER, unless you want to add a second line to the title.

3. Double-click on the Subtitle placeholder.

4. Type **Planning for the Future** as the subtitle text.

 NOTE: *The font, size, and justification of the text will depend on the Master Gallery you selected.*

Formatting Text

To edit the text, double-click on the placeholder; then add, delete, or change the text as needed. When you are entering or editing text, the property bar will include these items:

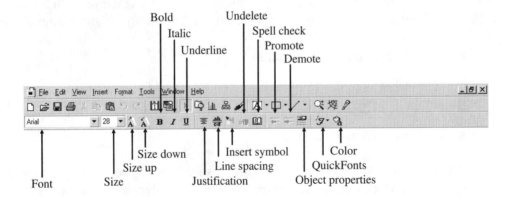

For other formatting options, select from the Format menu or the QuickMenu that appears when you right-click on the text. You can select line, paragraph, and justification formats similar to those for text in Corel WordPerfect.

To change the appearance of text, select Font from the Format menu or QuickMenu to see the Font Properties dialog box. Use the Font, Fill Attributes, and Outline pages in this dialog box to change the style, color, and size of text; add a fill pattern or color; and select the type and color of the outline around the characters.

Adding Graphics to Slides

The placeholders represent the items that Corel Presentations suggests should be included. You can use the drawing tools to add other elements, and you can add graphics from your disk. Inserting graphics into a slide is similar to adding a graphic to a Corel WordPerfect document.

In Chapter 23, you'll learn how to work with graphics of all types. In this chapter, however, we'll introduce the concept of adding clipart.

Just as in Corel WordPerfect, you can add graphics from the Corel Scrapbook or from a file on disk. To use an image from the Scrapbook, pull down the Insert menu, point to Graphics, and click on ClipArt to see the Scrapbook. Scroll the Scrapbook, or click on the CD ClipArt tab to select an image from the CD. Drag the image onto the slide, then close the Scrapbook window.

To insert another type of graphic, pull down the Insert menu, point to Graphics, and click on From File to see the Insert File dialog box. Go to the folder containing the graphic, then double-click on the image you want to insert, or click on it and then on the Insert button.

The graphic will appear in the slide surrounded by eight handles. Change the position and size of the graphic by dragging it or its handles. When you drag a handle to change its size, an outline of the graphic appears so you can see the resulting size. You can also drag a handle all of the way to the other side to flip the image vertically or horizontally. Later you'll learn other ways to edit and change graphics.

Here are the graphics folders on your hard disk in the COREL\ SUITE8\GRAPHICS folder and what they contain:

- *ClipArt* contains WPG graphics for general purposes.

- *Backgrounds* contains WPG graphics that you can use for the background of bullet charts or an entire slide. Most have a border line and one or two images around the border, with a large empty area inside.

- *Borders* contains WPG graphics that can be used for slide borders.

- *Pictures* contains bitmap graphics of various subjects, divided into these categories: business, commodities, finance, food products, government, and nature.

- *Textures* contains bitmap graphics of background designs in these categories: fabrics, food, nature, objects, oil, organic, paper, stone, and wood.

Adding a Slide

You are now ready to add another slide by selecting its template from the Add Slides list. Next, enter a *bulleted list slide.* A bullet slide is just like a bullet list in Corel WordPerfect, with major bullet items and minor ones indented to their right.

When you add a slide, Corel Presentations inserts it following the current slide. So if you are working on the last slide of the presentation, the new slide will be inserted at the end. To insert a slide elsewhere, click on the tab of the slide that you want to precede the new slide, and then add the slide. You can add a slide in any of Corel Presentations' views. You can also change the order of slides in Outliner and Slide Sorter views.

 You can create a bullet chart directly from a Corel WordPerfect outline.

1. Click on the down arrow next to the Add Slides button to see the types of slides you can add. If you click on the button itself, Corel Presentations will add the type of slide indicated on the button.

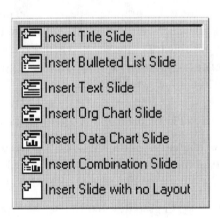

2. Select Insert Bulleted List Slide. Corel Presentations displays the new slide with the Bullet Chart layout, including a title, subtitle, and bullet chart placeholder.

3. Double-click on the Title placeholder, and type **Benefits of Technology**.

4. Double-click on the Subtitle placeholder, and type **Academic Achievement**.

5. Double-click on the bullet list placeholder. The first bullet appears at the left margin of the box, followed by the insertion point.

6. Type **Improved Test Scores,** and then press ENTER to insert the next bullet.

7. Press TAB to indent the insertion point and to insert a second-level bullet.

8. Type **National achievement tests, such as SAT,** and then press ENTER. The program will insert another bullet at the same level. You use TAB to enter entries at subordinate levels and SHIFT-TAB to move back to a higher level.

9. Complete the bullet chart shown in Figure 22-3.

If you need to edit a bullet chart, double-click on it. You can also click on it and choose Edit Text from the Edit menu or QuickMenu. To add a new bullet item at the end of the chart, place the insertion point at the end of the last line and press ENTER. Use TAB or SHIFT-TAB to change the position of the item.

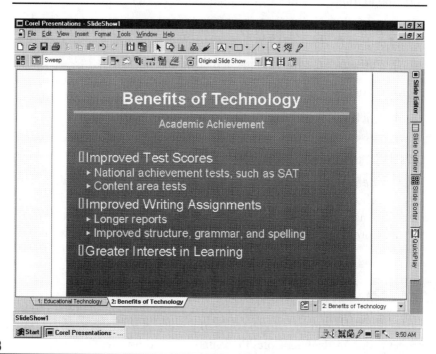

Completed
bullet chart

FIGURE 22-3

To insert an item within the chart, place the insertion point at the start of a line, following the bullet, and press ENTER. Use this technique, for example, to insert a new item at the top of the list.

You can add a bullet chart to a slide even if it does not have a bullet chart placeholder. Suppose, for example, that you created a title slide and then decide that you want it to have a bullet list. Follow these steps.

1. Pull down the Insert menu and click on Bulleted List or pull down the Text Object Tools button in the toolbar and click on the Bulleted List icon.

2. Drag to create a rectangle the size you want the chart, or just click to create one that fills the slide.

The Bulleted List placeholder will appear when you release the mouse.

Importing a Corel WordPerfect Outline

If you've already typed an outline in Corel WordPerfect using the Paragraph Numbers feature, you can import it into a bullet chart. The bullet levels will correspond to the document's indentation levels. Here's how.

1. Create a bulleted list chart, and then double-click on the chart placeholder.

2. Pull down the Insert menu and click on File.

3. Select the file that you want to use for the chart.

4. Click on Insert.

Creating a Text Slide

A *text slide* is similar to a bullet slide in that it has three placeholders. The Bulleted List placeholder, however, is replaced with a text box. Double-click on the box to place the insertion point there, and then type and format the text. When you press ENTER, Corel Presentations inserts a carriage return to start a new line.

Creating an Organization Chart

An *organization chart* shows the chain of command within an organization. Creating one manually means drawing boxes and lines, and trying to keep everything in the proper order. Instead, let Corel Presentations do it for you.

1. Pull down the Add Slides list.

2. Select Insert Org Chart Slide. Corel Presentations displays the new slide with three placeholders: title, subtitle, and the organization chart.

3. Add the title and subtitle, and then double-click on the Organization Chart placeholder to display a default chart as shown in Figure 22-4.

4. Double-click the Name placeholder in the top box.

5. Type the name of the person for that top position.

6. Press TAB to move to the Title placeholder.

7. Type the title.

8. Continue entering names and titles in the same way.

9. Delete the boxes you don't need by clicking on a box and pressing the DEL key.

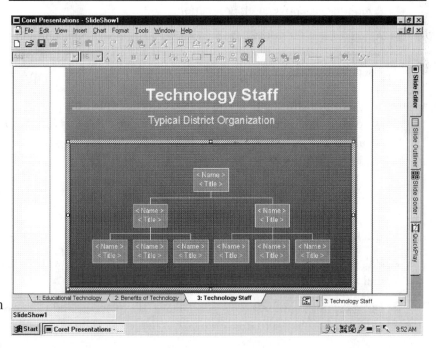

Organization
chart

FIGURE 22-4

The default organization chart includes a basic set of positions. You can add other positions as required by your organization's structure. Here are the positions that you can insert:

■ A *staff* position comes directly off of another position, as the assistant position in the following example. The position is not on the chain of command.

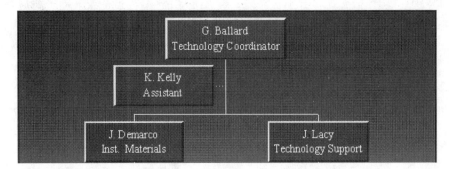

■ A *subordinate* is under another position in the chain of command.

■ A *manager* is above another position.

■ A *coworker* is a position of equal authority, neither under nor below the next box in the chain of command. The only limitation is that you cannot insert a coworker position in the box at the top.

TIP: *To change the structure of the chart, click on a box and select Branch Structure from the Format menu. Choose a design in the dialog box that appears, and then click on Close. You can use the same dialog box to change the branch's orientation.*

To add a position, use these steps:

1. Click the box that you want to add the position to.

2. Pull down the Insert menu, and click on the position you want to add. The dialog box that appears will depend on the position.

3. Enter the number of positions you want to add. When you add a coworker, you can also choose to insert the box to the left or right of the current box.

4. Click OK.

5. Double-click the Name and Title placeholders, and type the names and titles.

TIP: *Use the buttons in the property bar that appears when you are editing an organization to insert any number of subordinates and to customize the appearance of the chart.*

Inserting Organization Charts

You can add an organization chart to any slide, even one that does not have a placeholder for it.

1. Pull down the Insert menu and click on Organization Chart.

2. Drag to create a rectangle the size you want the chart to be, or just click to create one that fills the slide. A box appears showing formats of organization charts, as in Figure 22-5.

3. Click on the type of chart you want to insert.

4. Click on OK.

You can use a Corel WordPerfect outline to add titles and positions to an organization chart. Refer to Chapter 13.

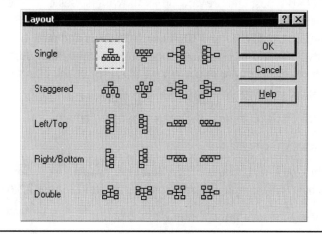

Selecting
the type of
chart to
insert

FIGURE 22-5

Creating Data Charts

A *data chart* is a chart or graph, exactly like the charts and graphs you can add to Corel WordPerfect and Corel Quattro Pro. In fact, you use almost the same techniques for working with charts—changing their type, customizing chart elements, adding legends, and so on.

 Use the Clipboard to insert Corel Presentations charts into Corel WordPerfect or Corel Quattro Pro.

To create a data chart, either select the Insert Data Chart Slide from the Add Slide list, or choose Chart from the Insert menu to place a placeholder for it on another slide. To use the template, follow these steps:

1. Pull down the Add Slide list.

2. Select Insert Data Chart Slide. Corel Presentations displays the new slide with the data chart slide template. It has three placeholders: title, subtitle, and data chart.

 NOTE: *A Combination template has four placeholders: title, subtitle, bullet chart on the left, and data chart on the right.*

3. Add the title and subtitle, and then double-click on the Data Chart placeholder to see the Data Chart Gallery. The gallery includes a list box of chart types, and preview areas showing styles of the selected type. There are two checkboxes: Use Sample Data and 3-D. Select the Use Sample Data when you want a default chart and datasheet to appear. This may be useful when you are not sure about the chart design, because you can change the data in the sample chart to see the effect on the chart itself. Use the 3-D box to determine if the chart is 2- or 3-D.

4. Click on the category of chart you want to create.

5. Click on the style of the chart.

6. Click on OK. If you used the default setting to use sample data, you'll see a chart with sample information, as shown in Figure 22-6.

7. Enter your own information into the chart.

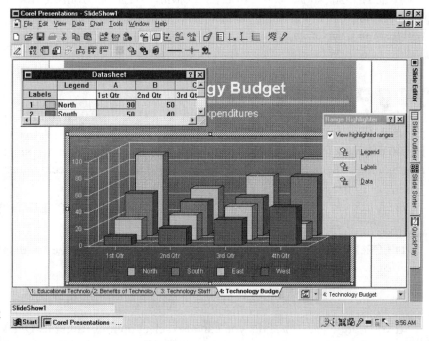

Default
sample chart

FIGURE 22-6

8. Select options from the menu bar or toolbar, and then click outside of
the chart area.

TIP: *Refer to Chapters 12 and 19 for more information on charts.*

To add a chart to a slide that does not have a chart placeholder, choose Chart
from the Insert menu, and then click on the slide or drag to create a rectangle that
will be the chart area.

Inserting Blank Slides

As you've seen, you can insert bullet, data, and organization charts into a slide even
when it does not have placeholders for the objects. So if you want, you can start with
a blank slide and then add all of your own elements.

To add a blank slide, choose Insert Slide with No Layout from the Add Slide list. You can then add charts using the Insert menu, and text and other elements as you will learn in Chapter 23.

Playing a Slide Show

To display a slide show of your work, with each slide displayed full screen, select the slide that you want to start with, and then click the QuickPlay tab to the right of the slide or click on the Play Slide Show button in the toolbar. The first slide in your presentation will appear. To move from slide to slide, use these techniques:

- Click the left mouse button or press the SPACEBAR to display the next slide.

- Click the right mouse button or press the RIGHT ARROW key to display the previous side.

- Press ESC to stop the slide show.

If you right-click on a slide, you can also select options from this QuickMenu:

Previous Slide	Page Up
Next Slide	Page Down
First Slide	
Last Slide	
Backtrack	Backspace
Goto Slide...	Ctrl+G
Next Transition	Space
Stop Sound	End
Replay Sound	Home
Increase Volume	+
Decrease Volume	-
Erase Highlighter	Ctrl+E
Stop Slide Show	Esc

To control how the slides appear, select Play Slide Show from the View menu to see these options:

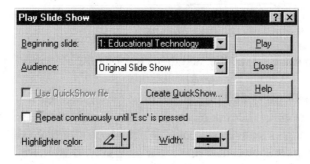

The Beginning Slide box will be set at the number of the current slide. Use the Beginning Slide box to change the starting slide number, or type the number of the slide in the text box, and then click on Play. You'll learn all about playing slide shows in Chapter 24.

Saving a Slide Show

Before doing too much work on your slides, you should save them to your disk. Corel Presentations uses the same file management dialog boxes as other Corel WordPerfect Suite applications. To save your slides, use these steps:

1. Click on the Save button in the toolbar, or pull down the File menu and select Save.

2. In the Name box, type a name for your presentation.

3. Click on OK. Corel Presentations saves your work with the default extension SHW.

You can also save an individual object, such as an organization or data chart. It will be saved as a WPG graphic image that you can then import into other Corel WordPerfect Suite applications. Here's how:

1. Click on the object to select it.

2. Pull down the File menu and select Save As.

3. If Selected Items is not already selected in the dialog box that appears, click on it.

22

4. Click on OK to display the Save As dialog box. The options in the box will be set to save the object as a WPG file.

5. Type a name for the file, and then click on OK.

On the Details page of the dialog box, the Adjust Image to Print Black and White option will print color slides in black and white. Deselect this option if you have a color printer and you want color copies. When you print a color slide on a noncolor printer, the colors will be converted to shades of gray. If your printer can reproduce the shades so they appear clear and the text and graphics are readable, then you may want to deselect this option as well. Leave this option selected, however, if you want to speed the printing process, if your printer does not handle shades well, or if you want to copy the pages on a copy machine that does not adequately reproduce shares or colors.

The Print background option determines if the slide background prints. Again, print the background only when your printer is color-capable, or can adequately print shades of gray.

There are also options to print the slide title and the slide number along with the slide.

Printing a Presentation

You need to print copies of your slides if you created them to be included in a report or as handouts. To print your slides, click on the Print button in the toolbar, or select Print from the File menu, to see the dialog box with all of your printing options. To print the entire presentation, just click on the Print button.

The dialog box offers a number of options that should be familiar to you from working with other Corel WordPerfect Suite applications, such as the number of copies and collating choices, and the Details and Two-Sided Printing pages of the dialog box. There are some new options that are only in Corel Presentations.

Click on Print Preview on the Print page of the dialog box to see how the slides will appear on paper. Click on Close in the Print Preview toolbar to return to the Print dialog box.

You use the Print option buttons in the dialog box to determine what gets printed. When set at the default Full Document, all of the slides will be printed. You can also choose from these options:

- Current view
- Selected objects

- Slides

- Handouts

- Speaker notes

- Audience notes

On the Details page of the dialog box, the Adjust Image to Print Black and White option will print color slides in black and white. Deselect this option if you have a color printer and you want color copies. When you print a color slide on a noncolor printer, the colors will be converted to shades of gray. If your printer can reproduce the shades so they appear clear and the text and graphics are readable, then you may want to deselect this option as well. Leave this option selected, however, if you want to speed the printing process, if your printer does not handle shades well, or if you want to copy the pages on a copy machine that does not adequately reproduce shades or colors.

The Print background option determines if the slide background prints. Again, print the background only when your printer is color-capable, or can adequately print shades of gray.

There are also options to print the slide title and the slide number along with the slide.

Printing Notes and Handouts

In addition to printing the slides themselves, you can print handouts, speaker notes, and audience notes.

Handouts have several slides on each page, as shown in the Print Preview in Figure 22-7. The audience can refer to them during your presentation, and take them home as a reference. To print handouts, follow these steps:

1. Click on the Print button in the toolbar, or select Print from the File menu.

2. Click on the Handouts option button.

3. In the Number of Slides per Page box, specify the number of slides you want printed on each page.

4. Click on Print.

22

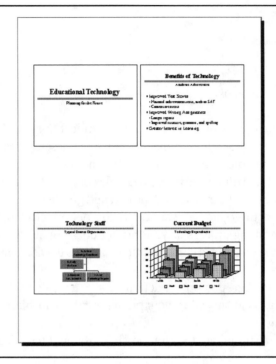

Handouts,
with four
slides on
each page

FIGURE 22-7

n   **NOTE:**   *The Audience Notes option is similar to handouts, but it prints a series of lines below each slide so the audience can take notes as you talk.*

Speaker Notes

It would be nice if you could memorize an entire presentation, but it's all too easy to lose track. To help you, you can print speaker notes. These are thumbnail sketches of each slide along with your own script, reminders, or notes. Before printing speaker notes, however, you must create them.

Use these steps to add speaker notes to your slides.

1. Click on the Speaker Notes button on the property bar to see the Speaker Notes dialog box.

2. Pull down the Slides list at the bottom of the dialog box, and select the number and title of the slide you want to add a note to.

3. In the large text box, type the note that you want to appear with the slide.

4. Repeat steps 2 and 3 for all of the slides.

5. Close the dialog box.

When you are ready to print the notes, follow these steps:

1. Click on the Print button in the toolbar, or select Print from the File menu.

2. Click on the Speaker Notes option button.

3. Specify the number of slides you want printed on each page.

4. Click on Print.

Using the Slide Sorter

So far, we've been working with slides in the Slide Editor, which lets you create and edit individual slides. For a general overview of your slides, change to the Slide Sorter view. To do so, use either of these techniques:

- Click on the Slide Sorter tab on the right of the slide.

- Pull down the View menu and click on Slide Sorter.

The Slide Sorter window, shown in Figure 22-8, displays thumbnail sketches of your slides. To change the order of a slide, just drag it to a new position. As you drag, a vertical bar will appear indicating the new position. Release the mouse when the position is correct. To move several slides at the same time, select them all. To choose slides that are not consecutive, hold down the CTRL key and click on each slide. To select consecutive slides, click on the first in the series, and then hold down the SHIFT key and click on the last in the series.

Below each slide thumbnail is the type of transition and its direction, as well as an icon representing the type of slide. If the slide is set to be displayed with a mouse click or keypress, you'll see a mouse icon. A clock will appear if the slide is set to change automatically.

To add a slide, select a template from the Add Slide list. The slide will be inserted after the currently selected slide.

TIP: *Use the buttons next to the Add Slide list to change the magnification of the display.*

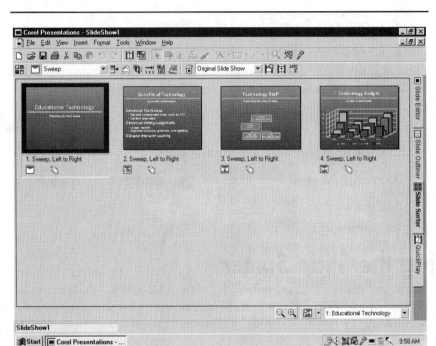

Slide Sorter

FIGURE 22-8

Using the Outliner

While the Slide Sorter is useful for viewing your slides graphically, you cannot read much of the information on the slides. When you want to look at the contents of the presentation, change to the Outliner. The Outliner displays the titles, subtitles, and other text from each slide in outline format. This makes it easy to see the structure of your presentation without being distracted by graphics and backgrounds.

You can also use the Outliner to add slides to the presentation, even to create an entire presentation of bullet lists, text, and titles (but not graphics or charts) by typing an outline. The outline will be converted into a series of slides when you change views. To change the order of slides, drag the slide icon up or down. As you drag, a red line will appear where the slide will be inserted—release the mouse when the line is in the correct position.

To change to the Slide Outliner view, either click on the Slide Outliner tab, or pull down the View menu and click on Slide Outliner.

A typical Outliner window is shown in Figure 22-9. Each slide in the chart will be marked by the Slide icon. The name of the text placeholders will be shown on the left, with the text in the placeholders on the right.

To add a slide to the presentation in Outliner view, use these steps.

1. Place the insertion point at the end of the slide above where you want the new slide to appear.

2. Press CTRL-ENTER.

3. Pull down the Add Slide list and choose the type of slide you want to add.

4. Type the title for the slide and press ENTER.

5. Type an optional subtitle.

6. Press ENTER and add other text that you want on the slide.

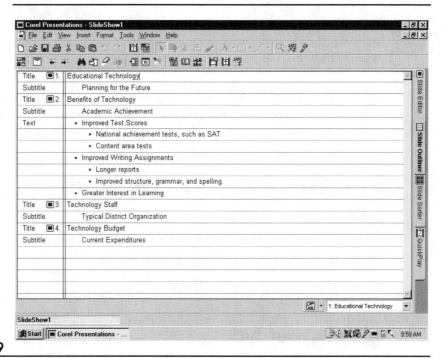

Outliner

FIGURE 22-9

Use a Corel WordPerfect outline to create a slide presentation. Pull down the File menu and click on Insert, select the file that you want to use for the chart, and click on Insert.

Editing Slides

You have complete control over the appearance and format of your slides. In addition to the toolbar and power bar formatting options, you can edit and format slides by setting properties and by changing the master background.

Changing the Master Background

After you create your slide show, it is not too late to select a different master background. Just click on the Master Gallery button in the property bar, or select Master Gallery from the Format menu, and select another master. Your selection will be applied to all of the slides in the presentation.

 TIP: *You can select from additional backgrounds to apply as the master using the Slide Appearance command. See the section "Changing a Slide's Background," later in this chapter.*

You can also add your own elements to the master background so it is used for all of the slides in the current presentation. For example, suppose you want your company logo to appear on every slide. Choose a master that you like and that has room for the logo. Then follow these steps.

1. Pull down the Edit menu and click on Background Layer.

2. A slide will appear with only the background.

3. Insert your logo using the ClipArt option from the toolbar, or add any other elements that you want in every slide.

4. Select Slide Layer from the Edit menu.

Changing Layout Type

You can also quickly change the slide's type, from a title slide to a bulleted list, for example. Select the slide in any view, and then pull down the Select Layout list in the property bar to see these options. Click on the type of slide.

Changing a Slide's Background

While the master background will be used as the default for all slides, you can apply a different background to an individual slide or a group of selected slides. You can select the slide or slides that you want to format first either before or after displaying the dialog box. Here's how:

1. In Slide Editor, click on the tab for the slide that you want to change. In Slide Sorter, click on the slide, or hold down the CTRL key and click on each of the slides you want to format. Use the typical Windows method to select a group of slides by clicking on the first slide, and then holding down the SHIFT key and clicking on the last slide.

2. Click on the Slide Appearance button in the toolbar, or choose Background Gallery from the Format menu, to see the Slide Properties dialog box shown in Figure 22-10. The background category is set at <Within slide show>, so you'll see thumbnail sketches of the current backgrounds being used in the presentation.

 NOTE: *You'll learn about the other options in this dialog box in Chapter 24.*

3. Look at the slide number in the slide list at the bottom of the dialog box. If the slide is not the one you want to format, choose the slide from the list. The list will be dimmed if you selected multiple slides from Slide Sorter view.

4. To change the slide's template, click on one of the samples in the Layout section.

22

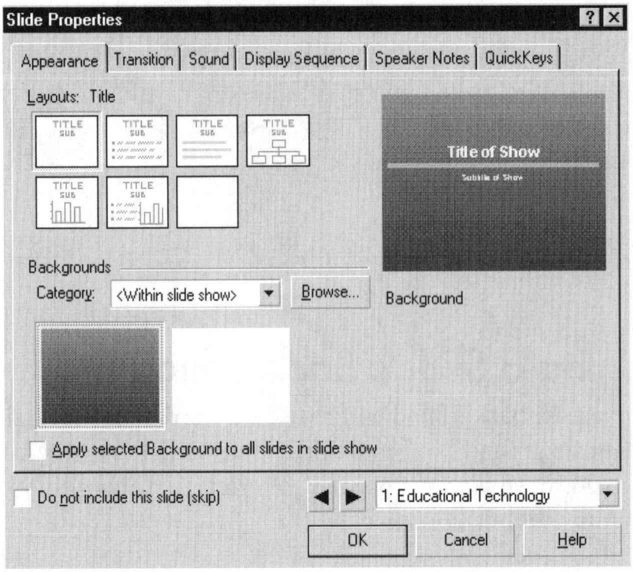

Changing
the slide's
appearance

FIGURE 22-10

---

5. To change a background, pull down the Category list and select from the choices. There will be more than were available in the Master Gallery. Thumbnail sketches of the category will appear in the dialog box.

6. Click on the background that you want to apply.

7. To use the background as the master for the entire presentation, click on Apply Selected Background to All Slides in Slide Show.

8. Click on OK.

Customizing Template Layouts

You know that each template has two or more placeholders in specific positions on the slide. The text in the title and subtitle placeholders uses a default format, font, and font size. While you can change the position of a placeholder and format the text within it, you can also change the default values for all slides using the template. This presents a consistent look throughout your presentation, so you don't have to worry about making the same changes to each slide individually.

1. Display a slide using the template that you want to change. For example, if you want to change the position of the subtitle in a bulleted list slide, display any slide using the Bulleted List template.

2. Select Layout Layer from the Edit menu. A slide will appear showing the placeholders.

3. Change the size or position, or format the font in the placeholder.

4. Select Slide Layer from the Edit menu.

Your changes will automatically be applied to all existing and new slides that use the template.

Changing Object Properties

In addition to changing the individual formats to text, you can customize all of the properties applied to slide objects, such as titles, subtitles, and charts.

Click to select the object, and then click on the Object Properties button in the property bar. The icon on the button, and the name of the button in the QuickTip, depend on the object. When you select a subtitle, for example, the icon will appear to point to a subtitle in the button, and the QuickTip is Subtitle Properties. The options that appear also depend on the object. Figure 22-11, for example, shows the properties for a title.

Use the pages of the dialog box to customize the objects. If you click on Apply to All, the formats will be applied to every slide using the current layout. So if you change the title properties when viewing a bulleted list slide, all bulleted list slides will be affected. Click on OK to apply the changes just to the current slide.

Customizing Bullet Charts

Bulleted lists contain several elements that you can modify—the appearance and spacing of the text and the bullets, and the box around the chart. While you can format selected text using the toolbar and power bar, it is best to be consistent. By setting Bulleted List Properties, you ensure that the style of the levels is consistent throughout the entire presentation.

To set properties, click on any bulleted list or placeholder and then on the Object Properties button in the property bar.

Use the Fonts page to format the text at each level. Select the level you want to change, and then choose options from the Font Face, Font Style, and Size lists.

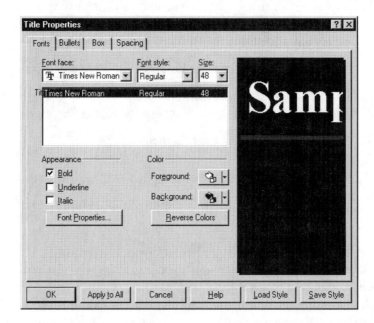

Changing
object
properties

FIGURE 22-11

Choose an appearance, foreground and background colors; select to reverse the colors; or click on Font Properties to see the options in Figure 22-12 for customizing the fill style and outline.

Changing Bullet Style and Justification

Use the Bullets tab in the dialog box, shown in Figure 22-13, to customize the type of bullet used for each level. The Bullet Set list contains several choices that apply styles to every bullet level. To change the style of individual levels, use these steps:

1. Click on the level that you want to change.

2. Pull down the Justification list (it says Auto) and select a justification—
   Left, Center, Right, or Auto.

3. Pull down the Bullet list, and choose the character to use for the bullet. To
   choose a special character from the Corel WordPerfect Characters box,
   select Other from the Bullet list. In the Characters dialog box, choose the

character set and the character, and then click on the Insert and Close button. This box works just as it does in Corel WordPerfect.

4. Choose a relative size for the bullet. By default, the bullets are the same size as the text. You can choose a relative size from 50 to 150 percent of the text size.

5. Select a color for the bullet.

6. Repeat the steps for each level bullet you want to customize.

7. Click on Apply or Apply to All.

To remove a bullet from a level, click on the level and choose None from the Bullet list.

 TIP: *Use the Save Style and Load Style buttons to save your custom bullet formats. You are actually creating a style as you do in Corel WordPerfect.*

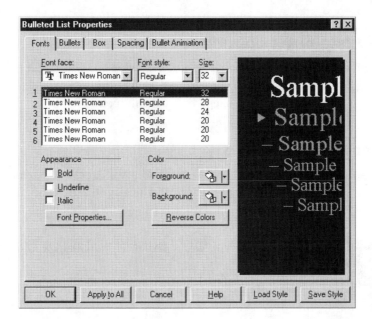

Changing font properties for bulleted lists

FIGURE 22-12

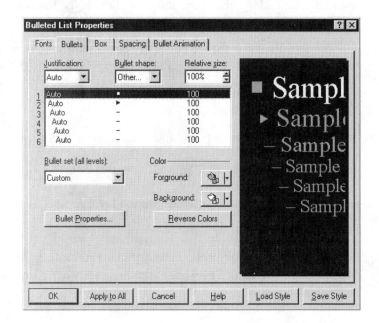

Customizing
bullet styles

FIGURE 22-13

Adjusting Bullet Spacing

The options on the Bullet Spacing page of the dialog box control the spacing between items. You can set the spacing between main and subordinate items, between consecutive subordinate items, and between all lines.

Setting Box Attributes

The Box page of the dialog box lets you add a box around the bullet chart, with a custom shape, color, pattern, or color fill. Click on the Box tab, and then choose options from the dialog box.

NOTE: *You'll learn about the Bullet Animation page of the dialog box in Chapter 24.*

Using the Page Setup Dialog Box

The Page Setup dialog box provides a number of other ways to customize your slides. Many of these options are similar to those found in Corel WordPerfect. Use the pages of the dialog box to select these options:

Page Size	Select the page size and orientation.
Page Color	Select a color and background other than that of the master. You can also choose to use a picture, texture, pattern, or gradient fill. If you choose a picture, you can select the way it is repeated on the slide.
Margins	Set the left, right, top, and bottom margins.
Save Options	Select the size of graphics and the amount of white space around them.

Creating a Presentation with Projects

So far, we've been concentrating on the format of slides, letting you decide on the contents. While you want your slides to look good, the most important part of your presentation are the messages within them.

If you need help organizing your thoughts, start a presentation using a project. The project will create an outline for you, showing the type of information that should be included in 11 common types of presentations. Here's how to use it:

1. Start Corel Presentations, click on the New button in the toolbar, or close your open presentation.

2. In the dialog box that appears, click on the Create New tab.

3. Instead of selecting [Presentation Slide Show], double-click on one of the projects that you want to use. The Slide Editor appears showing the first of the slides, along with the Corel PerfectExpert panel of options.

4. Click on the Slide Outliner tab.

5. Replace the text in the outline with your own.

6. Edit and format the presentation as desired, adding your own slides where needed.

Working with Corel Presentations Graphics

23

In Chapter 22, you learned how to insert clipart and other graphic images into a presentation. Part of the power of Corel Presentations, however, is that you can customize graphics, and even create your own drawings. In this chapter, you will learn how to work with and customize two types of graphics: vector and bitmap.

Working with Vector Graphics

Clipart and WPG images are vector graphics. This means that they are made up of a series of individual lines and curves. Putting three lines together, for example, creates a triangle—four lines, a rectangle. You can make changes to the entire graphic, such as altering its size or rotating it, and you can edit the individual lines and curves within it.

There are two ways to work with a graphic. You can click or right-click on the graphic to select it and to apply certain formats, such as changing its size and rotation. You can also double-click on it or select Edit Group from the QuickMenu to access the individual segments that comprise the graphic. If you want to rotate the entire graphic, for example, you right-click on it and choose Rotate from the QuickMenu. If you want to rotate one of the objects within the graphic, you have to double-click on the graphic to enter the Edit mode, and then right-click on the segment you want to rotate.

Vector images have a transparent background. This means that you'll be able to see the background of the slide under portions of the graphic that do not have any fill or color themselves. To select a graphic, click on a filled portion of it or a line, not on the background of the slide that shows through. If you want to display the QuickMenu, right-click on a filled portion.

 NOTE: *If the entire graphic is not selected when you click on it, choose the Selection tool in the toolbar, drag around the entire graphic, then right-click and select Group from the QuickMenu.*

When you select the graphic, Corel Presentations will display this property bar:

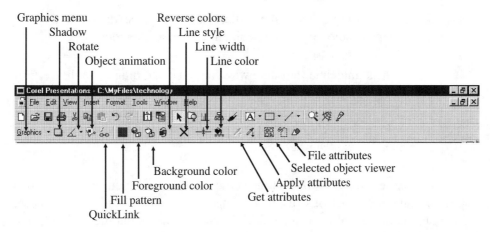

Setting View Options

Before learning how to work with graphics, however, consider four options on the View menu that can be very useful: Auto Select, Ruler, Crosshair, and Grid/Guides/Snap.

The *Auto Select* option in the View menu is selected by default. This means that after you create an object, it will appear selected with handles so you can immediately work with it. If you turn off this option, you have to select the object after you create it.

By selecting *Ruler* from the View menu, you will display a horizontal ruler along the top of the window and a vertical ruler down the left side. Use the rulers to position objects in precise locations. You can also use the rulers to position guidelines. A *guideline* is a horizontal line across the screen or a vertical line down the screen that you can place at a position along the ruler. Set and use the guidelines for aligning objects. To create a guideline, use these steps:

1. Select the Ruler option from the View menu to display the rules.

2. To create a horizontal guideline, click anywhere in the horizontal ruler, and then drag the mouse down into the window.

3. As you drag, a horizontal line appears across the screen at the mouse pointer.

23

4. Using the measurements on the vertical ruler as a guide, drag until the line is in the position you want it, and then release the mouse.

Create a vertical guideline the same way, but click and drag from the vertical ruler. Change the guide position by dragging it.

 TIP: *Hold down the SHIFT key as you drag to move in straight half-inch increments along the ruler.*

You can create as many horizontal and vertical guidelines as you need. To remove a specific guideline, point to it so the mouse appears with a two-headed arrow. Then, either drag the line off of the screen, or right-click on it and choose Delete Guide from the QuickMenu.

 TIP: *If the Delete Guide option does not appear in the QuickMenu, right-click on a section of the guide not over a placeholder.*

If you select *Crosshair* from the View menu, horizontal and vertical lines will appear with the intersection following the movement of the mouse pointer. As you drag the mouse, the crosshairs move with it. The crosshairs are useful for judging the position of objects in relation to others on the screen, and in relation to guidelines.

A grid is a pattern of evenly spaced dots superimposed on the screen. By displaying the grid, you can use the pattern to align objects. The *Grid/Guides/Snap* option has six choices:

- *Display Grid* displays the grid pattern. Click on the option to turn the grid off.

- *Snap to Grid* forces all objects that you move or draw to align on a grid line.

- *Display Guides* centers a horizontal and vertical guideline on the screen.

- *Snap to Guides* forces all objects that you move or draw to align on a guideline.

- *Clear Guides* removes the guidelines from the screen.

- *Grid/Guides/Snap Options* lets you change the spacing of the grid pattern and guidelines.

Changing the Graphic's Size and Position

You already know how to use the mouse to change the size and position of the image by dragging. You can also change its size and position using dialog boxes. The boxes let you change the size by entering a specific ratio, such as 50 percent, and by aligning the box with a side or the exact center.

To change the size, use these steps:

1. Click on the graphic to select it and display the handles.

2. Point to a handle so the mouse pointer appears as a two-headed arrow, and then right-click to see the Size dialog box.

3. In the Multiplier box, enter the amount to reduce or enlarge the box. For example, enter **1.2** to enlarge it 20 percent, or **0.8** to reduce it 20 percent.

4. Select the Around Center option to change the size of the box while leaving its center position in the same location. Without this checked, the upper-right corner of the graphic is the anchor position.

5. Select Size a Copy of the Object(s) when you want to create a copy of the graphic in the new size, leaving the original as it is.

6. Click on OK.

To adjust the position of the graphic, right-click on the graphic and point to Align in the QuickMenu, or select Align from the Graphics menu in the property bar. Your choices are

- *Left* moves the graphic to the left of the slide in its current vertical position.

- *Right* moves the graphic to the right of the slide in its current vertical position.

- *Top* moves the graphic to the top of the slide in its current horizontal position.

- *Bottom* moves the graphic to the bottom of the slide in its current horizontal position.

- *Center Left/Right* centers the graphic between the left and right.

■ *Center Top/Bottom* centers the graphic between the top and bottom.

■ *Center Both* places the slide in the exact center of the slide.

Rotating a Graphic

Another way to customize a graphic is to rotate it. Sometimes you can rotate a graphic that doesn't seem to fit, so that it no longer interferes with text. But most often, you rotate a graphic to add a special effect, or to have it appear as if it is pointing in another direction. With Corel Presentations, you can both rotate a graphic and skew it. *Skewing* changes just one axis of the image, while keeping the other stationary. Let's see how this works.

1. Right-click on Graphic and select Rotate from the QuickMenu, or select Rotate from the Graphics menu. The graphic will be surrounded by eight special handles that control rotation, and a center point:

2. Drag a handle in the corner to rotate the entire image.

3. Drag one of the center handles on the top, bottom, left, or right to skew the graphic. When you drag, only that side of the image moves with the mouse:

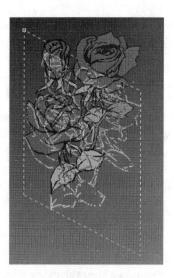

4. Drag the center point to change the pivot point of the rotation.

5. Click the mouse when you have finished.

You can also rotate the object using the Rotate button in the property bar. Each time you click the button, the graphic rotates in the amount shown by the icon on the face of the button. If the icon appears as 45 degrees, the object rotates 45 degrees counterclockwise. Pull down the list next to the button to see these options:

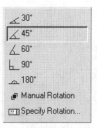

Selecting one of the degree options rotates the object that amount and inserts your selection on the face of the button as the new default. You can also select to manually rotate the graphic using handles, or to display a dialog box to enter a specific rotation amount.

TIP: *To flip the image, pull down the Graphics menu on the property bar, point to Flip, and select either Left/Right or Top/Bottom.*

Changing the Object's Appearance

In addition to rotating the graphic, you can use the property bar and Graphics menu to change the appearance in other ways. The Shadow button in the property bar, for example, lets you add a shadow to the graphic itself. Use the Fill Pattern, Foreground Color, and Background Color options to customize its appearance. You won't be able to add a pattern, by the way, until you select either a foreground or background color.

Use the Line Style, Line Width, and Line Color buttons to change the lines that create the vectors, or to remove the lines altogether.

Use the Selected Object Viewer to display the graphic in a separate window, so you can visualize how it appears without the other slide information.

Figure 23-1, for example, shows a graphic with a shadow and fill pattern, with the Selected Object Viewer displayed.

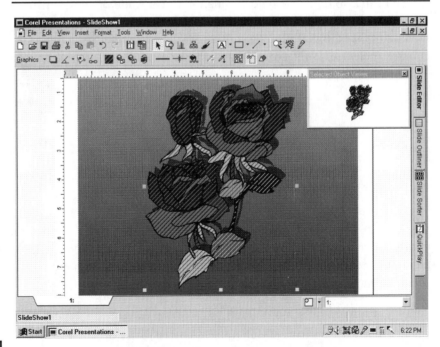

Vector graphic with shadow and pattern

FIGURE 23-1

To create even more visual effects, select Image Settings from the Graphics menu in the property bar. You can then choose to display the image in these effects:

- Silhouette

- Black and White

- Gray Scale

- Invert

- Outline

You can also select Object Properties from the QuickMenu to see the dialog box shown in Figure 23-2. Use the Fill, Line, and Shadow pages of the dialog box to change the appearance of the graphic. You'll learn about the QuickLink and Object Animation pages in the next chapter.

Editing Graphic Objects

While a vector graphic is composed of individual lines, groups of lines are collected into objects, such as a rectangle or other shape. You can customize the objects themselves, as well as the entire drawing. For example, the graphic shown on the next page contains a bird that is made up of several different objects. By selecting just the

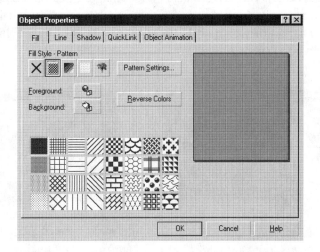

Setting
the object
properties

FIGURE 23-2

object that is the beak of the bird, you can change its fill pattern or color without affecting the rest of the graphic.

You can edit an object in two ways: by using Edit mode, or by separating the picture into a series of separate objects. Edit mode also lets you change the individual lines that make up each object, so let's look at it first.

 TIP: *Use the Selected Object Viewer to help edit vector graphics. Sometimes it is difficult to see which object is selected onscreen. Displaying the viewer shows exactly which object is selected.*

To enter Edit mode, either double-click on the image, or right-click on it and select Edit Group from the QuickMenu. You'll know you are in Edit mode when the graphic is surrounded by a thick line with *white* handles. You can now select and edit the individual objects that make up the image. Click on the part of the graphic that you want to edit, to display handles around that part. You can then move, resize, or delete that part of the artwork. For example, here is the graphic with one of its objects moved to another position:

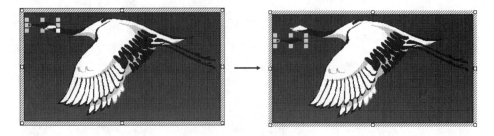

The choices in the QuickMenu, Graphics menu, and property bar affect just the selected objects. For example, choose Rotate from the QuickMenu to see rotation handles appear around only the selected object, or choose an Align option to change its position.

To change the object's appearance, for example, use these steps:

1. Click on the object so handles appear on it.

2. To change its color, use the fill pattern, foreground, and background buttons in the property bar. If the graphic property bar doesn't appear, click on the graphic again.

3. To change the color of the line around it, click on the Line Colors tool and choose a color from the palette.

4. To change its pattern, click on the Fill Attributes button and select an option.

5. To change the width and style of line around it, click on the Line Attributes button and select an option.

To make even more changes, use the Object Properties dialog box. Select the object that you want to edit, right-click, and then choose Object Properties from the QuickMenu.

 NOTE: *The Graphics menu offers a number of choices for further customizing a graphic element. Refer to "Customizing Objects" later in this chapter to learn more.*

In Edit mode, you can also select the Get Attributes button on the property bar. This button works like the QuickFormat button in Corel WordPerfect, in that it copies the formats applied to the selected object. When you click on the button, you'll see this box:

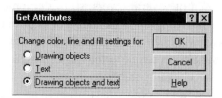

You can choose to copy the attributes of drawing objects, text, or both. To apply those same formats to another object, click on the object and then on the Apply Attributes button.

Separating Graphic Segments

While you can edit the individual parts of the graphic in Edit mode, the entire graphic is still treated as one object outside of that mode. As long as you do not double-click on it and select a specific object segment, for example, you can rotate and drag the entire graphic as one unit.

If you wish, however, you can separate the graphic into its objects so each one is a separate entity on the slide. Follow these steps:

1. Make sure you are not in Edit mode—click outside of the graphic so it is not selected.

2. Right-click on the graphic, and choose Separate Objects from the QuickMenu.

3. Click away from the object to deselect it.

4. You can now select the individual objects to change size, position, color, or rotation. As far as Corel Presentations is concerned, each object is a separate graphic.

If you later want to work with the entire graphic again as a unit, you have to regroup it. Here's how:

1. Select all of the individual objects. Either drag the mouse to draw a selection box around them, or hold down the CTRL key and click on them.

2. Right-click on the selected objects, and choose Group from the QuickMenu.

Working with Layers

Just as a slide is composed of several layers, so is a graphic. Two or more objects can overlap, with one in the foreground partially (or totally) obscuring the others in the background. You can also change the position of an object in relation to others, moving an object from the foreground to the background, even moving in several steps through multiple overlapping objects.

To change the position of one object in relation to another, use these steps:

1. Double-click on the graphic to enter Edit mode.

2. Right-click on the object.

3. Click on Back in the QuickMenu to move the object to the background, or click on Front to move it to the foreground.

 TIP: *You can use the Back and Front commands to layer separated graphic objects as well.*

Moving Segment Points

You already know that each object in a vector graphic consists of a series of lines. The intersection of two lines is called a *point*. If you drag the point, then you change the size and position of the lines on either side.

1. In Edit mode, right-click on the object and select Edit Points from the QuickMenu. The points that make up the object will appear as shown here.

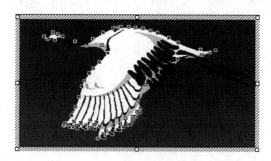

2. Drag one of the points to a new position; when you point to a point, the mouse will appear as a crosshair. To create the effect you want, you may have to drag a series of points.

If you right-click on a point, a QuickMenu will appear with these options:

- *Delete* deletes the selected point.
- *Add* inserts a new point after the selected one.
- *Split* divides the object at the selected point.
- *Open* removes the line between the points, removing its color.
- *To Curve* creates a Bézier curve at the selected point.

23

Creating Your Own Drawing

You can create your own vector artwork as stand-alone graphics, or to supplement a bulleted list, clipart graphic, data chart, or organization chart.

Each object that you draw is treated independently, and you can apply all of the same techniques to it as you learned previously—choosing colors and patterns, setting object properties, rotating objects, and editing points. If you create a picture by drawing and positioning several objects, however, you may want to combine them so you can move and resize them as one unit. You can also add an object to a graphic and combine them. To combine graphic objects, select them using the CTRL key, right-click on them, and choose Group from the QuickMenu.

Using the Toolbar

The toolbar offers a number of tools to add some of your own custom artwork to a slide. You can use the tools to draw objects directly on the slide, such as adding a text box or an arrow pointing to another object.

The Select Tool

You use the Select tool to return to Select mode after drawing an object. Select mode means that clicking on an object selects it. This cancels the function of the previously used tool.

Text Object Tools

Use the Text Object tools to insert text into the drawing. There are four tools, as shown here:

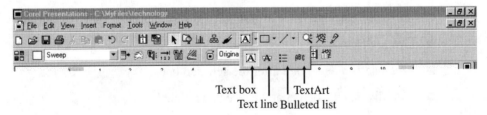

Use the Text Box tool to enter multiple lines of text, and use the Text Line tool to enter just a single line. Use the Bulleted list tool to insert a list of bulleted lines, and use the TextArt tool to create special effects.

For example, to add lines of text to the drawing, use these steps:

1. Pull down the Text Objects list, click on the Text Box tool, and then drag in the window to create a box the width you want the text. When you release the mouse, a box appears with the insertion point inside.

2. Type the text. When the insertion point reaches the right side of the box, it will wrap to the next line.

3. Click outside of the box when you have finished.

NOTE: *If you use the Text Line tool, just click where you want the line of text to begin, and then type.*

You can edit the text and the box just as you can the graphic box:

■ Drag the box to change its position.

■ Drag a corner handle to change its size.

■ Drag a side handle to add space between the text and the right side of the box.

■ Rotate the text in the box by choosing Rotate from the QuickMenu.

■ Change the position using the Align option in the QuickMenu.

■ Change the size ratio by right-clicking on the handle.

There are two property bars when you're working with text objects—the bar that appears when you are typing or editing text, and the bar that appears when you select the text object box itself. When you select the text box, the property bar contains these features, many of which you are already familiar with:

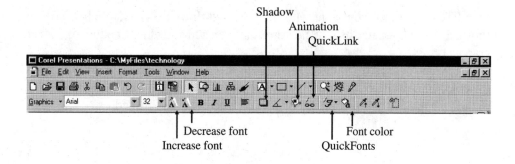

For example, to create special effects, click on the Shadow button on the property bar. Select a preset shadow, or click on More to see the Object Properties dialog box. In addition to the type of shadow, you can choose these options:

- Click on Use Transparent Shadow to lighten or darken the color.

- Select the color of the shadow from the Color list.

- Set the position of the shadow by setting the amount in the X Offset and Y Offset text boxes, or by dragging the scroll bars in the preview area.

When you are typing or editing text, the property bar does not contain the Graphics menu or the last eight buttons on the right as shown previously. In their place, you'll see buttons to set the line spacing, insert a symbol, restore deleted text, check spelling, select QuickFonts, and change the text color.

Drawing Closed Objects

The Closed Objects tool lets you create rectangles, circles, arrows, and other objects. Click on the tool to select from the following options:

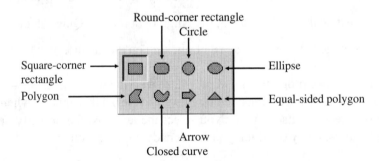

Click on the tool you want, and then drag to draw the object. When you've finished, you can change its size, position, or color, add a shadow, or edit it like other graphic boxes.

If you select the Arrow tool from the Closed Object Tool menu, drag away from the object you want to point to. After you release the mouse, move it to the left or right to create a curved arrow, and then click when you've finished:

 TIP: *If you create an object without a full pattern, you must select it by clicking on a border line. If you have trouble moving an unfilled object, drag it by the small white handle near the upper-left handle.*

Drawing Lines

The Line Object tool offers these choices:

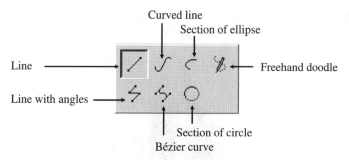

Select the object you want to create, and then drag to draw it. Simple.

Customizing Objects

The Graphics menu on the property bar and the Tools menu give you a number of ways to customize your object even further. Experiment with the options by selecting one or more objects and seeing the effects that each option applies.

For example, the Space Evenly option on the Graphics menu spreads out selected objects so they are spaced evenly between the left and right, or top and bottom of the slide.

In the Tools menu, take advantage of these features:

- *Trace Text* converts each character in selected text into a vector drawing.

23

- *Trace Bitmap* converts a bitmap drawing to a vector image.

- *Convert to Bitmap* converts the selected vector image to a bitmap.

- *Resample Bitmap* optimizes the display of a bitmap onscreen by adjusting the resolution after you resize it.

- *Blend* creates a blended object.

- *Quick3D* creates 3-D characters from a selected text box.

- *QuickWrap* forms selected text into a shape, similar to TextArt.

- *Contour Text* forms text around a graphic object.

Most of these options are rather intuitive and easy to use. If an option in the menu is dimmed, then you have not selected any objects. You'll know how these options work when you first try them. However, contoured text and blending may need some explanation.

While the QuickWrap command forms the text into a preset format, the Contour Text option forms it around any shape you can create with drawing tools, as shown here. Here is how to use it:

1. Drag the text so it is next to the object.

2. Select both the object and the text.

3. Choose Contour Text from the Tools menu to see the Contour Text dialog box.

4. Pull down the Position list, and choose where you want the text to appear around the graphic.

5. The Display Text Only option will make the object transparent. Leave this selected if you just used the object to create the shape for the text, and

you really do not want it shown. Deselect the checkbox if you want both the object and the text to appear.

6. Click on OK.

The Blend command will create a series of smaller objects. Select two or more objects, and then choose Blend from the Graphics menu. In the dialog box that appears, select the number of objects to create, and then click on OK. You can then delete duplicates that you do not want. The following illustration shows two examples of blending. On the left is the arrow and text object immediately after they were blended. On the right, the duplicate copies of the text were deleted.

Saving Your Drawing

Your drawing will be saved along with the slide presentation. You can also save the drawing as a separate graphic file for use later in a presentation or with any other document. Select the drawing object you want to save, and then click on the Save button. Choose Selected Items from the box that appears, and then click on OK.

By default, the For Type box will be set at WPG 7, so you can save the drawing as a Corel WordPerfect graphic file. You can also select from other graphic formats, such as PCX, JPEG, and GIF. For example, if you want to share the drawing with a friend who has a Macintosh computer, select MacPaint. Enter a filename and then click on OK.

23

Creating a Presentation Drawing

You can also create a new vector drawing outside of a slide presentation, in a separate drawing window. To create a new drawing, select the [Presentations Drawing] when starting Corel Presentations or after selecting New from the File menu. The Drawing window will appear as in Figure 23-3.

You have most of the same drawing options from the toolbar and the Graphics property bar, but with a few extra features:

Select all   Ruler
           Grid

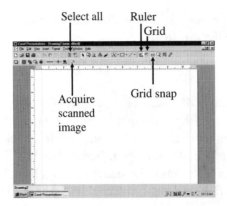

Acquire
scanned
image

Grid snap

In fact, when you draw and select an object, the Graphic property bar will be the same as you used from within a slide. When you click on Save, however, Corel Presentations won't give you a choice, it will automatically assume you want to save the drawing.

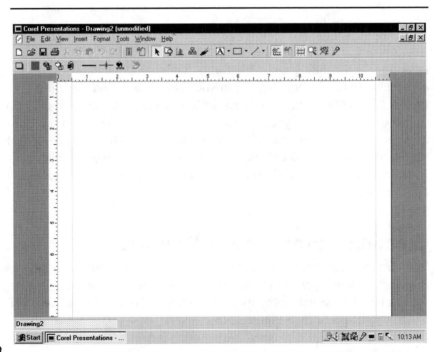

Drawing
window

FIGURE 23-3

Creating Bitmaps

Corel Presentations also lets you create a bitmap graphic. Unlike a vector drawing that consists of lines, a *bitmap graphic* is a series of individual pixels, or picture elements. When you create a bitmap image, you can add, delete, and modify each of the individual pixels.

To start a bitmap image, use these steps:

1. Click on the Bitmap tool in the toolbar, or pull down the Insert menu and click on Bitmap.

2. Click in the window to create a full-page bitmap area, or drag to create a bitmap of a selected size. Corel Presentations will display the Bitmap Editor window with its own toolbars (see Figure 23-4).

You can now create the bitmap drawing as you will learn next in the section "Using the Bitmap Editor." When you have finished, pull down the File menu or right-click to display the QuickMenu, and select Close Bitmap Editor, or click on the Close Bitmap button on the toolbar.

The bitmap will appear in the slide in a graphic box, just like vector images, so you can use the handles and other tools to change the size and position of the graphic, or to rotate or skew it. If you want to edit the graphic itself, however, double-click on it to display the Bitmap Editor.

 TIP: *Double-click on an inserted bitmap, such as those found in the Graphics\Pictures folder, to edit it in the Bitmap Editor.*

Using the Bitmap Editor

The Bitmap Editor has the tools you need to create and edit bitmap images. In addition to the toolbar and property bar, you can select tools from the menus. You will learn how to use these tools throughout this chapter.

 TIP: *If you do not like working with pixels, create the drawing as a vector graphic and then convert it to a bitmap drawing.*

Before you start drawing the picture, you can change the size of the drawing area by dragging one of the handles. After you start drawing, however, dragging the

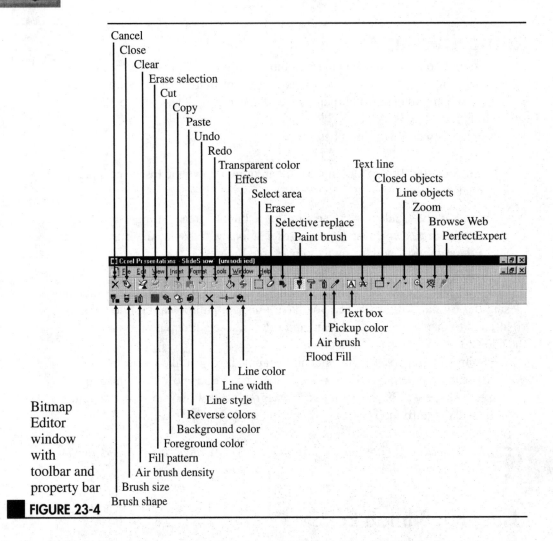

Cancel
Close
Clear
Erase selection
Cut
Copy
Paste
Undo
Redo
Transparent color
Effects
Select area
Eraser
Selective replace
Paint brush
Text line
Closed objects
Line objects
Zoom
Browse Web
PerfectExpert

Text box
Pickup color
Air brush
Flood Fill

Line color
Line width
Line style
Reverse colors
Background color
Foreground color
Fill pattern
Air brush density
Brush size
Brush shape

Bitmap
Editor
window
with
toolbar and
property bar

FIGURE 23-4

handles to make the box smaller crops the area—cutting out the part of the drawing no longer in the box. As long as you do not leave the Bitmap Editor, you can restore the deleted area by making the box larger. If you close and then return to the editor, however, the cropped area will be deleted.

Many of the tools in the Bitmap Editor are the same that are available for vector graphics. The toolbar has the closed object and text object tools; the property bar has the fill, foreground color, background color, reverse colors, line style, line width, and line color tools.

The Select Area tool is similar to that found in the Vector Editor, but you have to draw a selection box around the items you want to select.

Here's a review of the different tools.

Using the Eraser

There are a number of eraser tools to delete or change pixels. Make sure you select the correct tool for the function you want to perform:

The Eraser tool deletes (erases) pixels. When you select the tool, the mouse changes to a small square. Drag the mouse over the area that you want to erase.

The Selective Replace tool erases just the foreground color, replacing the pixels with the background color.

The Erase Selection tool deletes the currently selected area of the drawing.

The Clear tool deletes the entire drawing.

TIP: *Click on the Clear button on the toolbar to erase the entire contents of the image. Click on the Erase button to delete the selected object.*

Using the Painting Tools

There are several tools in the toolbar that let you draw by adding pixels to the drawing. Before using the tools, however, select the foreground and background colors, and a fill pattern from the property bar. Then select a tool and be creative.

- Use the *Paint Brush tool* to draw pixels by dragging the mouse.

- Use the *Flood Fill tool* to fill in an area. The tool looks like a paint roller with a small triangle of paint. Place the tip of the triangle in the area that you want to fill in, and then click. The tool adds the color to all of the consecutive pixels in that area that have the same color.

■ The *Air Brush tool* acts just like a can of spray paint. Hold down the mouse button and drag the can to spray the pixels onto the drawing. Drag the tool slowly for denser painting.

■ Use the *Pickup Color tool* to change the foreground color. Point it to the color that you want to use for the new foreground and then click.

You can change the size and shape of the Brush and Spray tools using either the property bar or a dialog box. By default, the brush shape is square, 11 pixels wide. The air brush has a density of 15 pixels. Change the size and shape, for example, if you don't like how your artwork appears. To do this with the power bar, follow these steps:

1. Pull down the Brush Shape list in the property bar, and choose a shape for the brush. The options are Circle, Square, Diamond, Horizontal Line, Vertical Line, Forward Slash, and Backward Slash.

2. Pull down the Brush Width list and select a width.

3. Pull down the Air Brush Density list, and choose the density of the spray.

You can also change all three settings from a dialog box using these steps:

1. Click on More in the Brush Width or Air Brush Density lists, or select Brush from the Format menu to see the Brush Attributes dialog box.

2. Pull down the Shape list and choose a new shape.

3. Set the brush width in pixels.

4. Set the density of the air brush.

5. Click on OK.

Editing Pixels

Because a bitmap is pixel oriented, Corel Presentations gives you a way to work on each individual pixel. This means you can edit the graphic at its smallest level, each dot that makes up a line or other shape.

You work with pixels in a special Zoom mode with three panes, as shown in Figure 23-5. In the upper left of the window is a pane containing a picture of the entire bitmap drawing area. The small rectangle within the pane represents the area

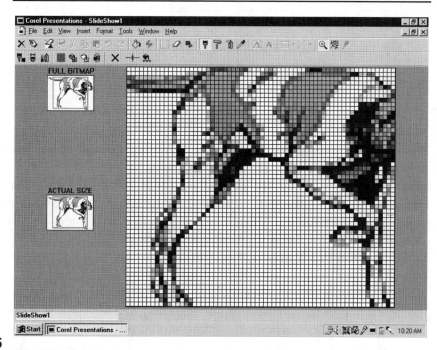

Zoom
display
of bitmap

FIGURE 23-5

that is enlarged on the right so you can see and work with the individual pixels. The pane in the lower left shows that area full size. That pane also has a rectangle indicating the enlarged area.

You can display the Zoom panes using any of these techniques:

- Click on the Zoom button in the toolbar.

- Select Zoom from the View menu.

- Right-click and select Zoom from the QuickMenu.

Here is how to work with pixels.

1. Enter Zoom mode using either of the techniques described.

2. To change the area of the drawing that is enlarged, drag one of the rectangles in the two smaller panes. Drag the rectangle to the area of the picture that you want to edit, and then release the mouse.

3. Select the pattern and foreground and background colors that you want to apply.

4. Click the mouse or drag it to change the color of the pixels.

5. When you have finished, select Zoom again.

Creating Special Effects with Bitmaps

You can apply a special effect to the entire bitmap drawing to create some unusual and appealing designs. The effects apply a pattern, adjust the colors, or modify the appearance of pixels. When you are satisfied with the content of your drawing, save it *before* applying an effect. You may not be able to restore your original design after choosing several effects. If you save the design first, you can always insert the original bitmap into a slide and double-click on it to edit it.

When you are ready to add a special effect, use these steps:

1. If you want to apply the effect to a specific area, choose the Select tool and then drag on the drawing. You can drag over an area that you want to apply the effect to, or drag over an area that you want to protect from the effect.

2. Click on the Effects button on the toolbar, or select Special Effects from the Tools menu or QuickMenu to see the dialog box shown in Figure 23-6.

3. Scroll the Effects list and choose the effect that you want.

4. If you selected an area prior to displaying the dialog box, select an option in the Apply Effect To area—the Full Image, Inside Area, or Outside Area.

5. Some effects will offer additional choices in the Options section. Set or select options as desired.

6. Click on the Apply button to see the effect of your choice in the After preview area. Compare it with the Before preview. If you change your mind, click on Reset, or click on Cancel.

7. When you are satisfied with your choice, click on OK.

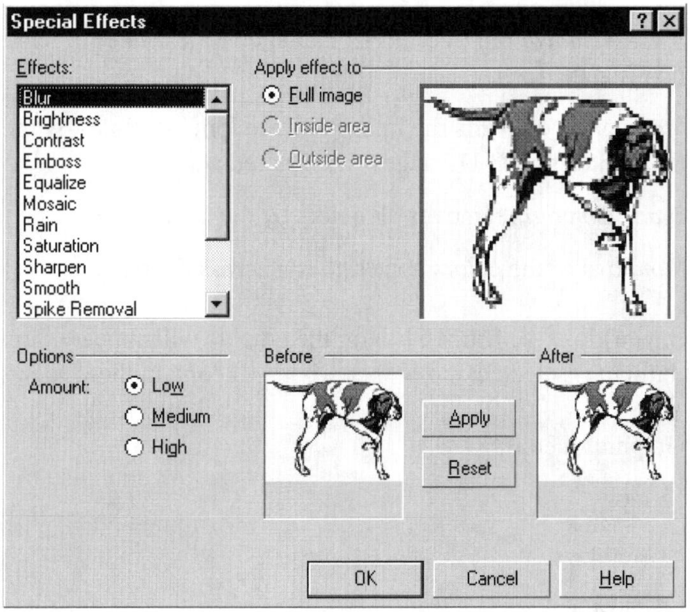

Special
Effects
dialog box

FIGURE 23-6

Here is a list of the effects:

- *Blur* blurs the borders between color and objects.

- *Brightness* darkens or lightens the drawing.

- *Contrast* changes the contrast between colors.

- *Emboss* adds a 3-D effect to pixels.

- *Equalize* evens the contrast between objects.

- *Mosaic* creates a pattern of squares of different colors, like mosaic tiles.

- *Rain* makes colors appear to be running down the page.

- *Saturation* makes colors more or less vivid.

- *Sharpen* sharpens the borders between colors and objects.

23

- *Smooth* smoothes the borders between colors and objects.

- *Spike Removal* removes horizontal and vertical lines in patterns, leaving pixels at the intersection.

- *Stereogram* converts the image to a random black-and-white stereogram that can display 3-D images when stared at.

- *Trace Contours* removes all colors by the contour lines.

- *Wind* makes the colors appear to run across the page.

When you close the Bitmap Editor, the graphic will appear selected in the slide. When a bitmap is selected, the property bar will contain these features:

- Graphics menu
- Shadow
- Rotation
- QuickLink
- Object Animation
- Resample Bitmap
- Trace
- Edit

Creating Slide Shows

24

One of the most effective ways to display Corel Presentations slides is as a slide show. By use of a large monitor or a video projection system, your slides become an instant multimedia presentation. You can add special effects, such as animation and transitions between slides, sound, and music. You can even link a slide to the Internet to jump to a Web page.

By publishing your entire presentation to the Internet, you make it accessible to the world. Web surfers can download your presentation to their own computer with a click of the mouse, and they can use a page frame to select slides from a table of contents.

In this chapter, you will learn how to create a slide show, adding effects and features that create professional presentations.

Slide Transitions

When you display a slide show, you click the mouse or press the spacebar to move from slide to slide. The next slide immediately replaces the previous one, just as if you had changed slides in a slide projector. By adding a transition, you create a special effect that takes place as one slide replaces the other.

You've probably seen a television show or movie in which one scene slowly fades out as the next fades in. A *fade* is just one of over 50 transitions that you can select for your slides. Other transitions make it appear as if a slide flies in from the side or appears slowly from a mosaic or other pattern. Because most transitions let you select what direction the slide appears from, there are more than 150 different combinations. Just don't overdo it. Adding too many transition effects can make the presentation difficult on the eye and can distract from the content of your slides.

You can add a transition using either the property bar or a dialog box. The property bar includes lists for the transition, direction, and speed:

To add a transition effect, use these steps.

1. In Slide Editor view display the slide you want to add the transition to. In Slide Sorter view, click on the slide, or select several slides to apply the same transition to them.

2. Pull down the Transition list in the property bar. When you point to one of the transitions, an actual moving sample of it will appear next to the list.

3. Click on the transition you want to apply.

4. Pull down the Direction list in the property bar. The options will depend on the transition; in some cases the list may be empty. For example, if you select the Sweep transition, your choices are Top to Bottom, Bottom to Top, Left to Right, and Right to Left. Other transitions include these sets of choices:

   ■ Clockwise or Counter Clockwise

   ■ Right & Down, Left & Down, Left & Up, or Right & Up

   ■ Horizontal or Vertical

5. Choose a direction.

6. Pull down the Speed list in the property bar.

7. Select Fast, Medium, or Slow.

You can also apply a transition using the Slide Properties dialog box, from any view. Click on the Slide Appearance button in the toolbar, and then click on the Transition tab to see the dialog box shown in Figure 24-1. Use the Slide List at the bottom of the dialog box to select the slide you want to format. Remember, the list will be dimmed if you selected a group of slides in Slide Sorter view. Then, choose the transition from the Effect list, and a direction and speed. Repeat these steps for each slide you want to add a transition to.

To use a transition for every slide in the show, click on the Apply to All Slides in Slide Show checkbox.

 TIP: *Click on the Do Not Include the Slide (Skip) checkbox when you do not want to show the current slide during playback.*

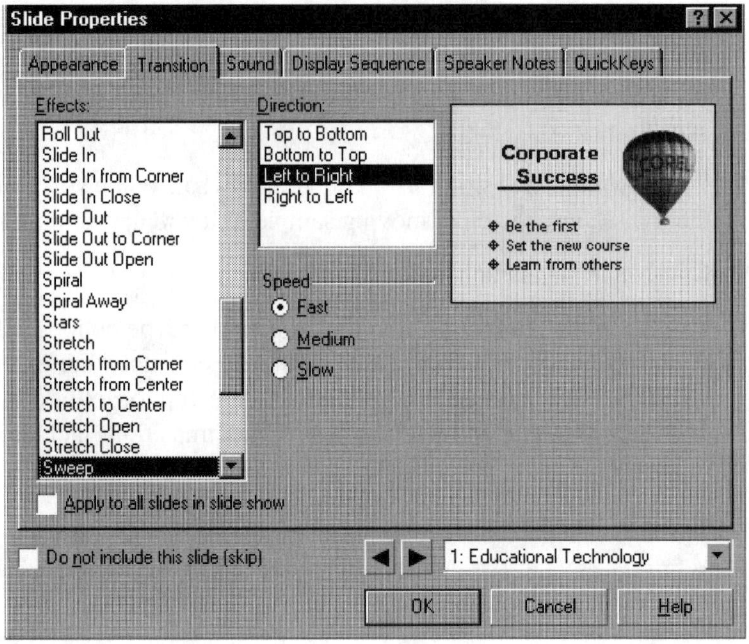

Slide Properties

Appearance | Transition | Sound | Display Sequence | Speaker Notes | QuickKeys

Effects:

Roll Out
Slide In
Slide In from Corner
Slide In Close
Slide Out
Slide Out to Corner
Slide Out Open
Spiral
Spiral Away
Stars
Stretch
Stretch from Corner
Stretch from Center
Stretch to Center
Stretch Open
Stretch Close
Sweep

Direction:

Top to Bottom
Bottom to Top
Left to Right
Right to Left

Corporate Success

◆ Be the first
◆ Set the new course
◆ Learn from others

Speed

◉ Fast
○ Medium
○ Slow

☐ Apply to all slides in slide show

☐ Do not include this slide (skip)

◀ ▶ 1: Educational Technology ▾

OK | Cancel | Help

Transition options

FIGURE 24-1

When you view your slide show in Slide Sorter view, the type of transition and its direction will be listed under the slide's thumbnail. In both Slide Editor and Slide Sorter views, the transition, direction, and speed will be indicated in the property bar. The name of the transition appears in the Transition box, and icons representing the direction and speed appear on the face of the Direction and Speed buttons.

 TIP: *Choose None in the Transition list to remove the effect from a slide.*

Advancing Slides

The default setting leaves a slide on the screen until you advance it manually by clicking the mouse or by pressing the spacebar. Rather than manually advancing slides, however, you can set a time delay—how many seconds each slide appears. By using a time delay, you can leave your slide show playing as you do other things.

You set advance options in the Display Sequence page of the Slide Properties dialog box, shown in Figure 24-2. Open the dialog box by clicking on the Display Sequence button in the property bar, or by clicking on the Display Sequence tab whenever the Slide Properties box is onscreen. Use the Slide List to select the slide you want to format, and then click on the After a Delay Of option button in the Display Next Slide section. Enter the number of seconds, or use the up and down arrows to increment or decrement the time. Use the Apply to All Slides in Slide Show checkbox to apply the delay to every slide, or repeat the procedure for other slides using the Slide List.

Animating Bullets

A slide transition determines how a slide appears on the screen. You can also create some special effects to determine how a bullet chart appears. There are two types

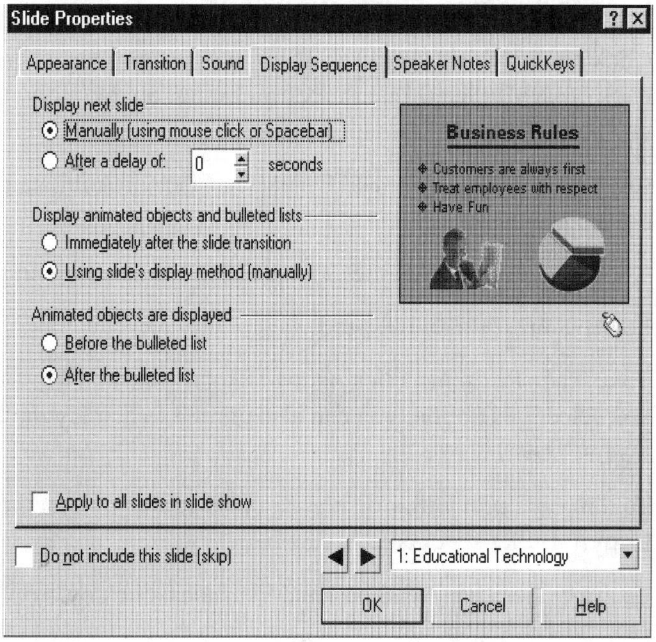

Display
Sequence
options

FIGURE 24-2

of effects that you can apply to bullet charts: *animate in place* and *animate across the screen.* When you animate in place, the options are the same as for transitions, except the bulleted items appear using the effect from within the slide. When you select to animate across the screen, the bullets appear from outside of the viewing area, flying into the screen.

After the title and subtitle appear, the bullet chart list is added to the display using the selected effect. By using one transition for the slide itself, and another for the bullet chart list, you can add a lot of movement to the slide display.

You can also choose to cascade the individual items in the bullet chart. With a cascade, each item appears by itself, rather than the entire list at one time. This is quite effective when you want to explain or describe each item separately. In fact, you can even have the program dim the bulleted items already shown to highlight just the current point.

You apply all of these techniques using the Bulleted List Properties dialog box, shown in Figure 24-3. Here's how to use it:

1. Display the slide in Slide Editor view.

2. Click on the bulleted list to select it.

3. Click on the Object Animation button on the property bar. You can also click on the Bulleted List Properties button on the property bar and then click on the Bullet Animation tab.

4. Click on either the Animate Objects in Place or Animate Objects Across Screen option button.

5. Choose an option from the Effects list to see a sample in the preview pane.

6. Select a direction and a speed.

7. To cascade the items, click on the Display One at a Time checkbox. If you select this option, you can also choose to display the bullets in reverse order.

8. To dim each previously displayed bullet item, click on the Highlight Current Bullet checkbox.

9. To apply the effect to all bulleted list slides, click on Apply to All; otherwise click on OK.

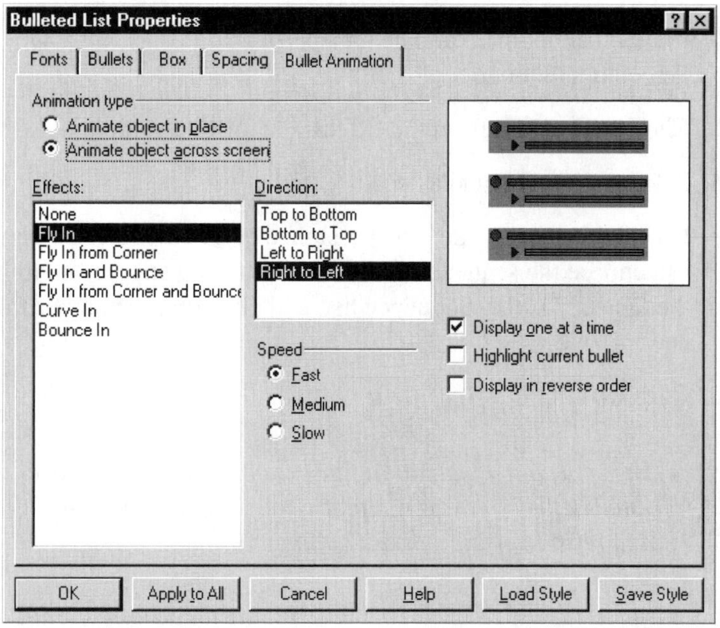

Animating
bullets

FIGURE 24-3

When you are using manual advance, click the mouse when you are ready for the bulleted list to appear. If you are using a time delay, however, Corel Presentations will begin the transition automatically before the next slide is displayed.

Animating Objects

You can also add an animation to one or more graphic objects in the slide, such as clipart, and even to text boxes. With animation, graphics bounce onto the screen or fade into view. You can select an animation for every object, so when combined with the slide transition and cascading bullets, the entire presentation can appear animated.

Follow these steps to animate a graphic object:

1. Display the slide in Slide Editor view.

2. Click on the object that you want to animate.

3. Select the Object Animation button in the property bar.

4. Click on either the Animate Objects in Place or Animate Objects Across Screen option button.

5. Choose an option from the Effects list to see a sample in the preview pane.

6. Select a direction and a speed.

7. If you already have an effect assigned to an object on the screen, you can choose the sequence that the current slide appears in. Pull down the Object Display Sequence list, and click on the number for the current object.

8. Click on OK.

TIP: *You cannot animate a title or subtitle in a slide placeholder. To create the same effect, however, replace the placeholder with a graphic text box and apply a transition or animation to it.*

Animating Text

When you apply an animation to a text box, all of the text in the box enters the screen at one time. You can also animate each character individually as a special effect. Use these steps:

1. Select the text object.

2. Choose Macro from the Tools menu and click on Play.

3. Double-click on the macro Textanim.

4. In the dialog box that appears, select an effect and a speed, then click on OK.

Advancing Animated Objects

Using the default settings, you have to click the mouse to begin each object transition or animation. If you want the items to appear automatically, choose options for the slide in the Display Sequence page of the Slide Properties dialog box, which you saw previously in this chapter.

You can, for example, have all of the objects appear automatically in sequence, or only after you click to display the first one. Here are the options you can select from:

- *Immediately after Slide Transition* starts to display the first object as soon as the slide appears—you do not have to click the mouse.

- *Using the Slide's Display Method (Manually)* shows the objects using whatever method you chose for the slide—either manually or delayed.

- *Before the Bulleted List* displays the objects before any bulleted list on the slide.

- *After the Bulleted List* displays the objects after the bulleted list.

Enhancing Slides with Sounds

Recorded music, sound effects, and narration make a slide show more entertaining and effective, adding another dimension to a purely visual presentation. You can insert a sound clip, a track from an audio CD, and your own narration into a slide.

There are two ways to insert sounds into a slide. You can add the sound as an object that plays automatically when the slide appears, or as a QuickLink that you have to click on or press a keystroke to play. You can insert three types of sound objects on a slide: Wave, MIDI, and tracks from an audio CD. You can add as many sounds as you want associated with QuickLinks, and, if your system supports it, up to three sound objects that play simultaneously.

NOTE: *Corel WordPerfect Suite comes with a selection of sound files that you can insert. They are in the Wave and MIDI formats in the Sounds subdirectory. Most of the filenames are self-explanatory.*

To insert an existing sound clip or CD track, follow these steps:

1. Click on the Sound button in the property bar, or click on the Sound tab when the Slide Properties dialog box is onscreen, to see the dialog box in Figure 24-4.

2. Use the Slide List to select the slide you want to add the sound to, or click on the Apply to All Slides in Slide Show checkbox.

3. Click on the Browse button next to the Wave or MIDI boxes, and select the sound file you want to play. Click on the CD icon to display the dialog box shown here, and select the track you want to play.

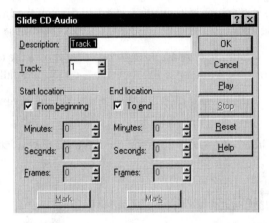

4. Repeat the steps, if desired, to add one or more of the other types of sound files to the slide.

5. For each type of sound you add, you'll see a slider and additional options, as shown here. Adjust the volume, and choose to save the sound with the presentation, or to loop the sound to play repeatedly. Saving the sound with the slide, which is not available for a CD track, will ensure that the sound is available whenever you play the slide show.

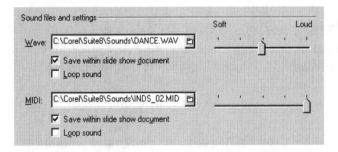

6. Click on Play to hear how the file sounds.

7. Repeat the procedure to add sounds to other slides.

8. Click on OK.

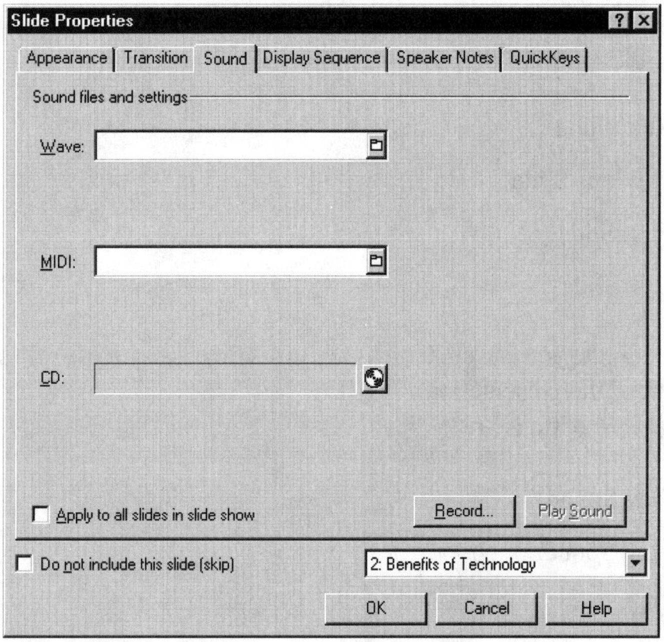

Slide Properties

Appearance | Transition | Sound | Display Sequence | Speaker Notes | QuickKeys

Sound files and settings

Wave:

MIDI:

CD:

☐ Apply to all slides in slide show   Record...   Play Sound

☐ Do not include this slide (skip)   2: Benefits of Technology

OK   Cancel   Help

Slide
Properties
dialog box
for sounds

FIGURE 24-4

The sounds will play when the slide appears.

You can record your own narration or sounds, and add them to the slide. Click on Record from the Sound dialog box to display the Sound Recorder application. Record and save the file, and then add it to the slide as just described.

Creating QuickLinks

A QuickLink is an object on the slide that you click on to perform an action. Use a QuickLink to play a sound file, launch your Web browser and jump to a Web site, open another application, or move to another slide in the show.

For example, suppose you have one or more slides in the show that you might not want to display, depending on the audience. You can add a QuickLink to the slide before these. When you choose not to display the slides, just click on the link to skip over them.

You can add a QuickLink to any graphic object in the slide layer. When you point to a link, the mouse appears as a hand—just click to perform the action. There are two general categories of functions a link can perform, a Go To event or an Action. A *Go To event* lets you display a slide. It can be linked to a specific slide number or to any of these options:

- Next Slide

- Previous Slide

- First Slide

- Last Slide

For example, you can click on a QuickLink to display a specific slide or to return to the start of the presentation.

The *Action* options are

- Play Sound

- Stop Sound

- Quit Show

- Launch Program

- Internet Browser

Integrate IT! You can use a QuickLink to launch another Corel WordPerfect Suite application.

To add a QuickLink, follow these steps:

1. Display the slide in Slide Editor view.

2. Click on the object that you want to use for the link.

3. Click on the QuickLink button in the toolbar to see the dialog box in Figure 24-5.

4. Select either the Go To or Action option button, and then choose the specific event or action.

5. If you choose to play a sound, click on the Sound button to display the Sound dialog box, and then select any combination of Wave, MIDI, or CD tracks just as you previously learned. If you choose to launch a program, select the program file. For the Internet Browser action, enter the URL of the Web site.

6. In the QuickLink Name text box, type a name for the link.

7. If you do not want the object to appear onscreen during the presentation or when printed, select the Invisible While Playing or Printing Slides checkbox. Use this when you want to perform an action but not take up screen space with the link. To find the link when showing the slides, move the mouse until the pointer changes to a hand.

8. Click on OK.

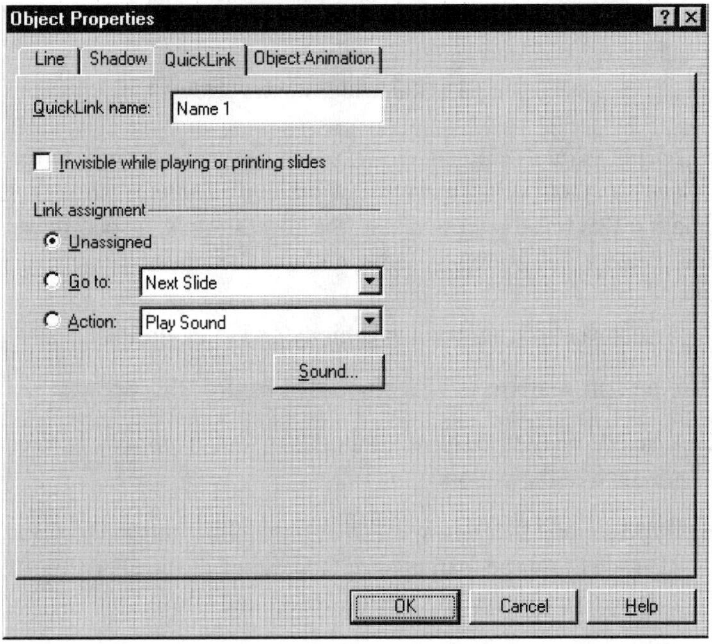

Creating a
QuickLink

FIGURE 24-5

24

Editing and Viewing Links

After you create QuickLinks, you can edit or delete them, or just display a list of the links in your presentation. Pull down the Tools menu and click on QuickLink List to see the QuickLink List dialog box. Use the arrow keys to display the slide that has the link you are interested in. To change a link, or to delete it, click on the link name and then on Edit to display the QuickLink dialog box. To delete a link, click on the Unassigned option button. To change the link, just choose other options from the box, and then click on OK.

Creating 3-D Buttons

One very effective way to use a QuickLink is to associate it with a 3-D button, as shown here.

By adding several buttons to a slide, you can give yourself, or the viewer, a menu of choices. In fact, you can create a table of contents slide at the start of the presentation that lets the viewer start the slide show at a specific section.

You create a 3-D button by using a Corel Presentations macro. Here's how:

1. Select Macro from the Tools menu and click on Play.

2. Click on Textbttn.wcm in the list of macros that appears.

3. Click on Play to display a dialog box that prompts you to enter the text for the face of the button.

4. Type the text that you want to appear in the button. To insert a special character into the text, press CTRL-W, select the character from the box that appears, and then click on Insert and Close.

5. Click on OK to display the 3-D button.

6. The button will appear selected, with handles. Use the handles to change the button's size, or drag the button to another location on the slide.

7. To edit the text on the button, double-click on it to place the insertion point in the text.

8. Assign a QuickLink to the button. Right-click on the button, choose QuickLink from the QuickMenu, and then assign the function to the link.

Using QuickKeys

While a QuickLink is associated with an object, a QuickKey is associated with the slide or even the entire slide show. You can assign a QuickKey, for example, to play a sound or to move to another slide at any time during the presentation. As with QuickLinks, you can assign a QuickKey to a Go To or an Action event. Here's how:

1. Open the slide show.

2. Click on the Slide Appearance button on the toolbar, and then click on the QuickKeys tab of the Slide Properties dialog box. You can also pull down the Format menu, point to Slide Properties, and click on QuickKeys. You'll see the dialog box shown in Figure 24-6.

3. Select the keystroke that you want to press from the Keystrokes list. The list contains the characters A to Z, followed by the 12 function keys. Below those are several system-assigned keystrokes, such as Escape to end the slide show, and Home for the first slide.

4. Select either Go To or Action, and then choose the function that you want the link to perform. You cannot change the function of a system-assigned keystroke.

5. Click on OK.

NOTE: *To remove a QuickKey, choose the keystroke in the QuickKey dialog box, and then click on the Unassigned option button.*

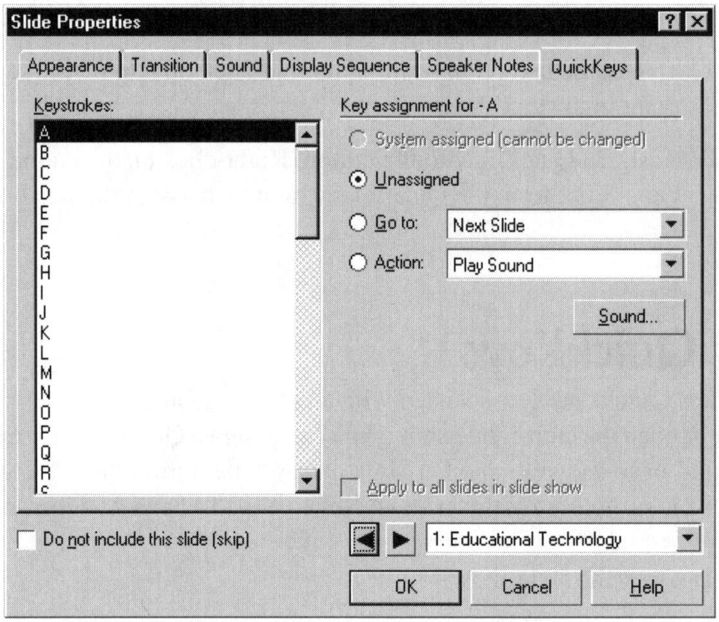

Creating a
QuickKey

FIGURE 24-6

Playing a Slide Show

You can run your slide show in two ways—from within Corel Presentations or directly from the Windows desktop.

- Run the slide show from Corel Presentations when you are still working on it and may want to make changes as you go along.

- Run the show from Windows on machines that do not have Corel Presentations installed, or when you want a stand-alone application.

Keep in mind that the quality of your presentation will depend to some extent on your hardware. Watching a slide show on a small laptop monitor or a low-resolution desktop monitor is not the best way to view your work. For greater impact, hook up your computer to a large-screen television or, better yet, to a projection device for even a larger screen.

In addition to the transition, animation, and sound effects that you've added to the slides, you can use the mouse as a pointing and highlighting tool. By dragging the mouse, you can draw directly on the screen, emphasizing major points.

Playing a Show from Corel Presentations

To play the show from within Corel Presentations, open the presentation and then click on the QuickPlay tab, or on the Play Show button on the toolbar. There will be some delay between slides as Corel Presentations displays them, but you can also select to create a QuickShow file. This is a separate disk file containing the slides. It runs a little faster than otherwise, but it can take up large amounts of disk space. If you edit the slides, you also have to generate a new QuickShow file to reflect the changes.

1. Start Corel Presentations and open the slide show that you want to play.

2. Pull down the View menu and select Play Slide Show to see the dialog box in Figure 24-7.

3. The presentation will be set to start with whatever slide is selected in the current view. To start with some other slide, enter the slide number in the Beginning Slide text box.

4. Choose a color and width of the highlighter. Choose a color that can be seen over the slide background, and a width that will support the type of highlighting you want to do. Use a smaller width, for example, if you want to write on the screen without taking up a great deal of space. Use a larger width to highlight an area with a line or circle.

5. To save a QuickShow version of the presentation, click on the Create QuickShow button.

6. To run the show continuously, click on the Repeat Continuously Until 'Esc' Is Pressed checkbox.

7. To use the QuickShow file, click on Use QuickShow.

8. Click on Play.

24

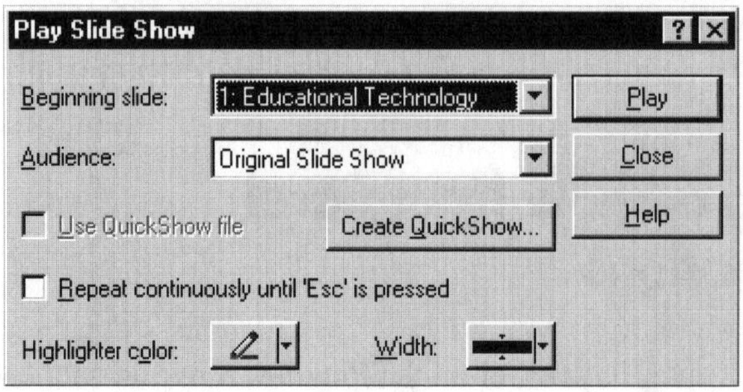

Playing a
slide show

■ **FIGURE 24-7**

9. If you are using manual advance, click on the left mouse button or press the spacebar to move from slide to slide, to display animated bullets and objects, or to click on QuickLinks.

10. Drag the mouse to draw in the screen with the highlighter. Your highlighting will disappear when you change slides.

11. Press ESC if you want to end the presentation before the last slide.

 NOTE: *If you edit the slides, you have to re-create the QuickShow file.*

Running the Show from Windows

Once you perfect your slide show, why go through the trouble of starting Corel Presentations just to show it? By creating a Show on the Go, or run-time, version of the show, you can display it on a computer that doesn't have the Corel Presentations program. This is ideal if you are on the road.

Save your slides as a Corel WordPerfect document—select Send To from the File menu, and click on Corel WordPerfect.

The run-time version will consist of a special version of your presentation and other files that will be required to run it. Those files depend on the configuration option you select. For example, you can choose to create a run-time version that only works with Windows 95 and Windows NT, or that works on Windows 3.1 and Windows 95. You can also choose to create a run-time version that can run with any

Windows display, or with one having the same resolution and color options as on your machine.

To create a run-time version of your presentation, follow these steps:

1. Open the presentation that you want to play.

2. Pull down the File menu and click on Show on the Go. A dialog box appears reporting the name of the file and the type of show that will be created.

3. Click on Change. A dialog box appears where you select the drive to place the show and the option to e-mail the show. The run-time version requires a number of files. If you plan to transport the show to another computer, select the floppy disk drive or other removable drive, so you don't have to copy the files yourself.

4. Select the drive, and then click on Next. A dialog box appears where you select to create a run-time version for either Windows 95 and Windows NT, or for Windows 3.1 and Windows 95. If you select the Windows 3.1 option, you won't be able to use QuickLinks and animations other than cascading bullets.

5. Select an option and then click on Next. A dialog box appears where you select to run the show on any Windows display, or only on a display matching the current setup. If you choose Any Windows Display, you can show the slides on a display at 640 x 480 resolution with 256 colors.

6. Make a choice from the box, and click on Finish to see the first Show on the Go dialog box.

7. Click on Create.

Publishing Your Show on the Web

Corel WordPerfect's Internet Publisher lets you create one or more linked Web pages. It's a great time-saver over learning and writing HTML documents, but it pales when compared with the Web capabilities of Corel Presentations.

In fact, with Corel Presentations, you can create several types of slide shows depending on the options you select. Start by selecting Internet Publisher from the File menu to see the dialog box shown in Figure 24-8. If you select Publish to Corel Barista, the dialog box will appear with options, as explained in Chapter 2.

24

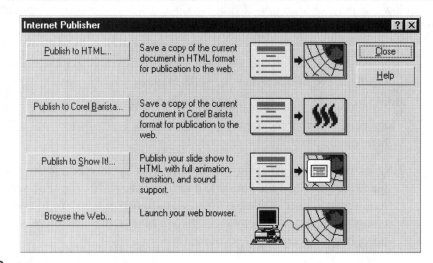

Internet
Publisher

FIGURE 24-8

Publishing to HTML

When you select to Publish to HTML, you can design more advanced Web page layouts. For example, you can

- Create a separate table of contents slide with hyperlinks.

- Create a page frame table of contents with hyperlinks, using either text or thumbnails of each slide.

- Add a Go To Slide Bar so the viewer can change slides.

- Insert a Download button for users to download the entire slide show.

- Include page numbers.

- Display your speaker's notes.

There are four default Web page organizations that you can create, shown in Table 24-1.

NOTE: *If the presentation does not appear correctly when you launch the Web browser, refer to "Corel Show It!" later in this chapter.*

Page Arrangement	Description
Frame-Enhanced Pages	Creates a Web page with two frames. The frame on the left contains a table of contents listing links to your slide and a link to Corel Corporation. The frame on the right contains your slides—each slide on another page. There will be arrows under the slide to move to the next and previous pages.
Multiple Pages	Creates one Web page for each slide. You can create a separate slide with a table of contents using the slide titles as links.
Single Page	Creates one long Web page containing all of the slides. You can include page numbers, but not a table of contents.
Thumbnail Page	Creates one Web page containing thumbnail sketches of the slides.

Web Page Organization

■ **TABLE 24-1**

Here are some of the other options available:

- *Slide Numbers* displays "Slide X of Y" at the top of each slide.

- *Slide Titles* inserts the title above each slide.

- *Speaker Notes* displays speaker notes under each slide.

- *Go to Slide Bar* inserts a bar under each slide for changing slides.

- *Table of Contents* creates a separate slide with text or graphic links to each slide.

- *AutoRunning Slide Show* starts the show automatically.

To publish your presentation to the Web, just follow these steps:

1. Open the presentation that you want to publish.

24

2. Pull down the File menu and click on Internet Publisher.

3. Click on Publish to HTML to see the dialog box in Figure 24-9. The dialog box includes a list of page arrangements. (The options are shown in Table 24-1.)

4. Click on the Use an Existing Layout option button, and then on the arrangement that you want. Click on View Layout Info to see details about the layout.

5. Click on Next.

6. In the box that appears, enter a show title and designate the location to save the show. You can also click on the Advanced option to see these choices:

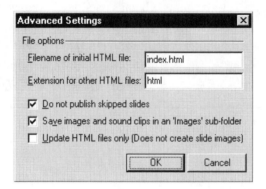

7. Click on Next. The dialog box that appears shows the four basic layouts. You can change your mind at this point and click on one of the other layouts. If you selected anything other than a thumbnail layout, you can also choose the type of border around the slide.

8. Click on Next.

9. You can now choose options for the show. The options for a frame-enhanced page and multiple pages are shown in Figure 24-10. If you select a single page, the options are limited to slide title, slide number, speaker notes, and navigation button. For a thumbnail layout, you can only pick the size of the thumbnail.

10. Select options from the dialog box, and then click on Next. You can now enter footer information, including your home page address, e-mail address, and other information. You can also include the show for downloading, display the date when updated, and show Corel Presentations copyright information.

11. Click on Next. You can now select the display size, slide size, and graphic format.

12. Select options from the box and click on Next.

13. Choose to use the browser's colors or custom colors, then click on Finish.

You'll see an animation appear as your slides are converted into graphics. Then a dialog box appears asking if you want to launch your Web browser to view the presentations. Click on Launch Web Browser with Slide Show to see the show, or click on OK to return to Corel Presentations.

Figure 24-11 shows a Corel Presentations slide show on a frame-based Web page.

Options for page arrangement when publishing to the Internet

FIGURE 24-9

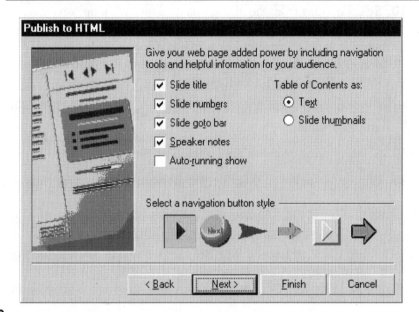

HTML
options

FIGURE 24-10

If you select the Include Slide Show File for Downloading option, there will be a link for downloading on the slide. When clicked, the slide show is downloaded to the viewer's computer, the viewer's copy of Corel Presentations is launched, and the slide show is started.

Corel Show It!

If you click on the Publish to Show It! option in Internet Publisher, Corel will display a series of dialog boxes for you to select options for the Web pages. When you complete selection options, it converts each of the slides to Web pages, then displays a dialog box asking if you want to launch your Web browser to view the presentation. Click on Launch Web Browser with Slide Show to see the show, or click on OK to return to Corel Presentations.

The charm of publishing your presentation to the Web is that it can be viewed over the Internet with all of the graphics and animations with which you can display it on your own computer. For example, the user can click the mouse to move from

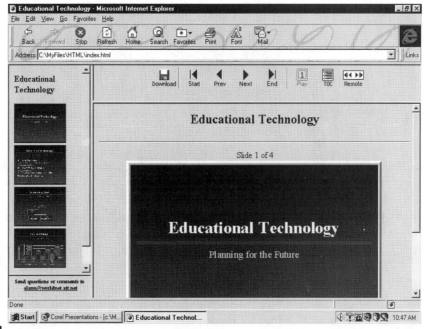

Published
Web page

FIGURE 24-11

slide to slide, or to display individual animated objects. This is achieved because the published presentation includes a Corel Presentation Player Control. To use the control, however, you need to install the Corel Show It! plug-in to your browser.

   If you have not yet installed the plug-in, you'll have the opportunity each time you select the Launch Web Browser with Slide Show option after publishing a presentation. Click on the link labeled Get the Corel Presentations Show It! Plug In to connect to the appropriate site and download the Show It! plug-in to your system. If you're using a dial-up connection and you are not yet online, the Connect To box will appear. Click on Connect to dial up your Internet service provider, and download and install the plug-in.

TIP: *If the plug-in is not automatically installed, click on the Download link at the bottom of the browser window to download the program SETUPEX, and then run the program to install the plug-in.*

PART V

Corel Paradox

Introducing Corel Paradox

25

Y ou can jump right into most programs and start working, learning as you go. Paradox is a bit different. Before using Paradox, or any database management program for that matter, you should first understand a little about databases themselves.

Anatomy of a Database

A database is just a collection of information, nothing more. So whenever you collect related information together you are creating a database, whether it's an index card file, an address book, or just a series of sheets where you've recorded information. Of course those databases aren't computerized. As an example, consider an index card box full of name and address cards. For each person you deal with you have two cards, one by their last name, another by their company name. If a company changes their address or phone number, what do you have to do? You have to pull both cards out of the box and make the change to both of them.

When you computerize a database, all of that work is easy. All you need is one copy of the information, and you can display it in any order you want. Using the computer, you can locate the telephone number you have to change by any piece of information you have—the number, the company, or the person you deal with. And you just have to change it once.

The computerized "card" that contains all of the address information is called a *record*. So in any database, there is a record for each object—whether it is an address, a video in your collection, or a member of your club. Each piece of information in the record is a *field*. So the address record will have a field for the company, address, city, street, zip code, telephone number, and maybe two or more fields for the person's name—at least one for the first name and one for the last name. You give each field a name to identify the information within it. In Paradox, every record of every database contains a special field called the *record number*. Paradox uses this number to keep track of your records.

Tables and Relations

When you computerize a database, you are not concerned with how the information is physically stored on your disk. All you really care about is getting to the information when you need it. Paradox stores all of the records that you've collected into files called tables. Each table contains the records about one common entity.

For example, your business might have one table that contains the names and address of clients, another table containing the same information on vendors, and a third table containing information about your inventory.

Paradox also uses a table to display the information onscreen. The table appears as a series of rows and columns, just like a page from a Quattro Pro notebook. Each row in the table is a record, and each column a field. The record numbers correspond to the row numbers in a spreadsheet, the field names correspond to the column letters.

Now all of the tables, along with related items such as forms, reports, and other objects, represent the database. So a Paradox database is just a collection of separate files that all relate to the same general entity, such as your company. It's best to place all of these files in the same directory on your disk so they are easy to access. Paradox even makes it easier by letting you assign an alias to the directory. The alias becomes the database name, and a shortcut to its directory, just like a shortcut on the Windows 95 desktop.

Dividing all of your information into tables makes it easier to organize and work with large amounts of data. As an example, look at the database shown here:

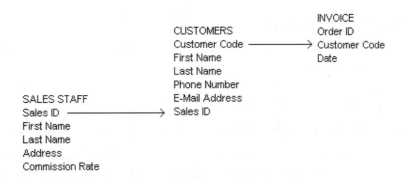

One table lists information about your sales staff. It contains each person's name and address, an ID or employee code, and commission information. Another table lists information about your customers—their names and addresses, a customer code, phone numbers, e-mail address, and the employee code of the salesperson you have assigned to that customer.

The two tables are related because the salesperson's code is contained in both tables. If you need to know the e-mail address of a client's salesperson, you find the client's record in the table. The record will contain the salesperson's ID. You then use the ID number to locate the e-mail address in the salesperson's table. Of course, using Paradox, you don't physically have to look up anything. The whole process of going from one table to the other one can be almost instantaneous. The field that

25

connects the table is called the link field. So in our example, the two tables are connected, or linked, on the salesperson's ID field.

The relation between the salesperson and client tables is called one-to-many. That's because we set up the company so each salesperson can have many clients, but a client can only have one salesperson. The salesperson table is on the *one side* of the relationship, the client table on the *many side*. So a salesperson can be linked to more than one client, but a client can only be linked with one salesperson. In this relationship, the salesperson's table is also called the parent table, and the client table is called the child table.

The invoice table contains a record for every client order. It includes the date of the order, the order number, and the code number of the client who placed the order. The client and invoice tables are related, linked by the customer code field. Each client can have one or more invoices, but each invoice can be from only one client. So in this case, the client table is on the one side and is the parent table, while the invoice table is the many side and is the child table. The invoice table doesn't need the salesperson's ID because it can be found by linking back through the Customer table.

Database Objects

In addition to tables, a Paradox database contains other objects that you'll use to work with information.

- *Custom* objects are special objects created by advanced users.

- *Applications* are other programs that you want to run from within Paradox.

- *Forms* let you display, enter, and edit information in other arrangements than the rows and columns of a table. You can even create form with information from several tables.

- *Queries* let you access information in any combination, on the fly, as you need it.

- *Reports* let you print information from your database, even from related tables.

- *SQL* objects are queries written in the Structured Query Language to access data in the database.

- *Scripts* are programs in the ObjectPAL programming language that let you automate and customize Paradox.

- *Libraries* are objects in which you store commonly used scripts.

- *Data Models* define the relationship between two or more tables, used to create forms and reports with information from multiple tables in the database.

- *INIs* are Windows configuration files.

Starting Corel Paradox

Paradox is usually installed automatically when you install the Corel WordPerfect Professional Suite. If you chose not to install Paradox, however, just insert the Corel CD in your drive, then choose Corel WordPerfect Suite 8 Setup from the Corel WordPerfect Setup & Notes menu, and follow the directions on the screen to add Paradox or any other component.

Once Paradox is installed, starting it is as easy as pointing and clicking:

1. Click on the Start button in the Windows 95 taskbar.

2. Point to Corel WordPerfect Suite 8.

3. Click on Corel Paradox 8.

You can also start the program by clicking on its icon in the Corel DAD bar in the taskbar.

 NOTE: *You can use a feature called the Launcher Expert to create a shortcut on the Start menu that starts Paradox and opens a database.*

In a few moments the Corel Paradox screen will appear with two windows—the Project Viewer window and the Startup Expert, as shown in Figure 25-1. The Project Viewer offers an easy way to open databases, tables, and other Paradox objects using their names or aliases. We'll look at that soon.

The Startup Expert lets you create or open a database. The Expert has four options:

- Use Database Expert to create a new database from ready-to-use templates.

- Create a new database and a table using Table Expert to help.

- Create an alias for an existing database.

- Open an existing database.

25

Project Viewer   Startup Expert

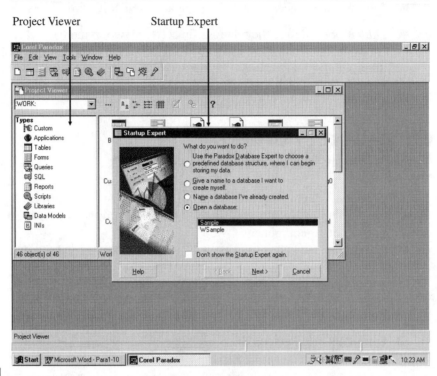

Initial
Paradox
window

FIGURE 25-1

TIP: *When you start Paradox, the last database you used will be opened by default. To use the same database again, click on Cancel in the Startup Expert dialog box.*

Database Expert

The Database Expert takes you step-by-step through creating a database using ready-made templates that include tables, forms, and reports. There aren't templates for every type of database you might need, but what's available is great to use for typical tasks and to learn about Paradox. As an example, we'll create a contact management database.

1. Click on the first option in the Startup Expert and then click on Next. A message appears telling you that you're ready to start.

2. Click on Finish.

The first of three Database Expert dialog boxes appears. In this dialog box, shown here, you choose the template that you want to use. The two tabs, Business and Personal, determine the names of the databases listed.

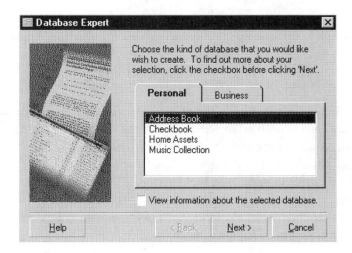

TIP: *To find out more about a database, click the checkbox labeled View Information About the Selected Database. When you click Next, a dialog box will appear with three tabs describing the tables, forms, and reports included in the database. Read the information in the dialog box, then click on Next.*

3. Click on the Business tab.

4. Click on the Contact Management database.

5. Click on Next.

The second Expert dialog box, shown here, gives you the opportunity to delete fields from or add fields to the tables that are part of the database.

25

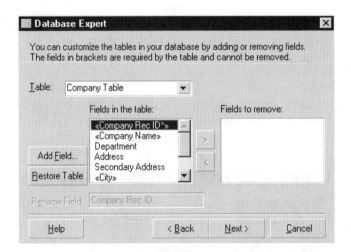

In the Table list, choose the table whose fields you wish to change. The fields in that table will appear in the list labeled Fields in the Table. The fields enclosed in chevrons are required and cannot be deleted. To delete a field, click on the field and then on the > button.

To add a field, click on the Add Field button. A dialog box appears listing all of the tables that are contained in all of the database templates. Select a table to see the fields it contains, then select the field you want to add and click on OK. Paradox adds the field to the Fields list in the table.

 NOTE: *Click on the Restore Table button to remove any added fields and to restore removed fields.*

6. Click on Next to accept the default fields. The final Expert dialog box lets you name the database and specify its location. By default, all databases are stored in the Paradox\Samples folder.

7. Click in the Database Location box, and then press the END key.

8. Type **\Contacts** to add the subfolder to the path.

9. Click on Finish. A message appears asking if you want to create the directory.

10. Click Yes. Paradox creates the database and displays a message that it has been created.

11. Click OK.

The database launcher window appears with three tabs—Tables, Forms, and Reports, as shown here.

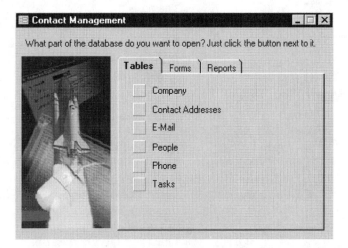

Click the Forms tab, and then click on Contacts Form. Paradox minimizes the launcher window and displays the form. This particular form includes fields from six different tables. Click on the form's Close button to close the form and restore the database launcher. Click on Company Form.

Now close the form and the Contact Management launcher window by clicking on their Close buttons.

The Paradox Screen

The Paradox screen is called the desktop because it can hold all of the tools and documents you need to work with your database. The desktop has all of the standard Windows features, such as the title bar, menu bar, and toolbar. The buttons in the toolbar depend on the task you are performing in Paradox, but the buttons shown now are explained in Table 25-1. Click on any of the Open buttons to open an existing object; right-click on the button to choose to either open an object or create a new one.

The Application Bar under the Paradox window lists the names of all open windows. Switch to a window by clicking on its name in the Application bar or by selecting it from the Window menu.

The status bar under the Application Bar displays information about the current state of Paradox, and about the task you are performing. When you open a table, you'll see the number of the current record and the total number of records.

25

Button	Name	Description
	New	Displays the Corel Perfect Expert dialog box, similar to choosing New from the File menu. Use this to select a Corel Project, work on an existing database, or create new database objects.
	Open Table	Open an existing table, or right-click to create a new table.
	Open Form	Open an existing form, or right-click to create a new form.
	Open Query	Open an existing query, or right-click to create a new query.
	Open SQL File	Opens a SQL query script, or right-click to create a new SQL query.
	Open Report	Open an existing report, or right-click to create a new report.
	Open Script	Open an existing script, or right-click to create a new script.
	Open Library	Opens program libraries, or right-click to create a new library.
	Open Data Model	Opens an existing data model, or right-click to create a new data model.
	Project Viewer	Opens the Project Viewer, if it is closed.
	Corel Web Site	Launch your Web browser to connect to the Corel Corporation.
	Perfect Expert	Displays the Perfect Expert dialog box with Experts to perform Paradox tasks.

Paradox
Toolbar

TABLE 25-1

The Project Viewer, shown in Figure 25-2, provides a convenient way to locate database objects. Use the buttons on top of the Project Viewer to change the way fields are displayed, change the working directory, or run an application.

The text box on the top of the Viewer shows the current working directory. The working directory is the default directory where Paradox opens and saves files. Paradox creates a directory called WORKING when it is installed, and this becomes the default directory. The notation :WORK: in the Project Viewer is the *alias* for the directory, an abbreviation that refers to the full directory path. To change the working directory, pull down the list next to the text box and choose one of the directories or aliases listed. You can also click on the Set Current Directory as Working Directory button in the Project Viewer toolbar, or you can choose Working Directory from the File menu.

Down the left of the Viewer are the types of objects contained in the database. Click on a type to display the objects that are in the working directory. For example, click on Tables to list just the tables in the directory, or on Forms to list just forms. Right-click on an item for the choice to open an existing object or to create a new one. Click on the word "Types" at the top of the list to display all objects in the directory.

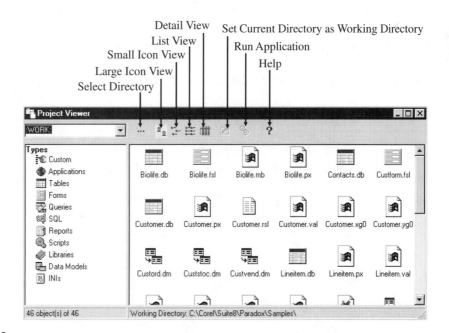

Project
Viewer

FIGURE 25-2

25

> *n*   **NOTE:**   *Paradox also has a private directory, which stores temporary files and objects. The default is called PRIVATE below the main Paradox directory on your hard or network drive.*

Now pull down the arrow next to the working directory and scroll the list to see :Contact Management:, the alias for the Contacts folder where Database Expert placed your database. Click on :Contact Management: to see a list of objects in Contacts.

Creating a Database

A database is a collection of tables and other objects. Store all of the objects in one folder, used exclusively for the database, and assign it an alias for easy access. If you've already created a database using Database Expert, you can add your own tables and other objects to it. You'll learn how to do that later. For now, let's see how you can create an entirely new database from scratch.

Close Paradox now, then restart it to see the Startup Expert. Click on the second option (Give a name to a database I want to create myself) to choose a name for a new database, then click on Next. A dialog box appears where you enter the name for your database and choose a location. In the Type a Name for the Database box, enter **My Company**. In the Type a Location for the Database box, add **/MyCompany** to the path, then click on Next. Click Yes when you see the message asking if you want to create the directory to display these options.

The last dialog box in the Startup Expert, shown here, will appear. Now we're ready to add the first table to the database using the Paradox Table Expert.

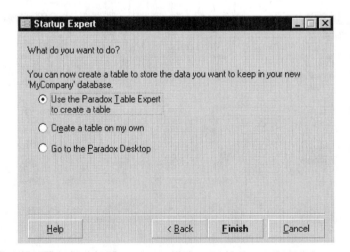

Using Table Expert

Table Expert is to tables what Database Expert is to databases. You can create a table manually by defining each field, but Table Expert will create a complete table for you, letting you select from various purposes and fields.

In the last Startup Expert dialog box (shown earlier), make sure the first option button (Use the Paradox Table Expert to create a table) is selected, then click on Finish. The first Table Expert dialog box, shown in Figure 25-3, will appear. The list on the left shows some sample tables. Under the list are the option buttons Business and Personal to select the type of table you want to create.

Click on Business for typical business tables.

Now scroll the Tables list to see the types of tables available. When you select a table, suggested fields appear in the list box in the center. Click on Customer List because we're going to create a clients table for our company database.

The trick now is to move the fields you want to use from the list box in the center into the list box on the right. Fields shown in brackets, such as [Full Name], contain several fields within them. The Full Name field, for example, includes First Name, Middle Name, and Last Name. To move an individual field, click on its name in the list and then on the > button. If you want to use all, or almost all of the fields, just click on >> —you can then remove the individual fields that you do not want included. We want all of the fields so click on the >> button.

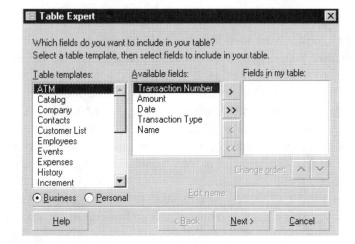

Selecting a
template
from the
Table Expert

FIGURE 25-3

To remove a field from the list, select it in the Fields in My Table list and click on <. Click on << to remove all of the fields. To change the order of a field, click on it in the Fields in My Table list, then click on the up or down arrow next to the Change Order prompt.

 TIP: *You can mix and match fields from any number of sample tables. Move the field from one table into the list box on the right, then choose another table, from either category, and select additional fields, as you want.*

When the list box on the right contains all of the fields that you want, click on Next to see the dialog box shown here.

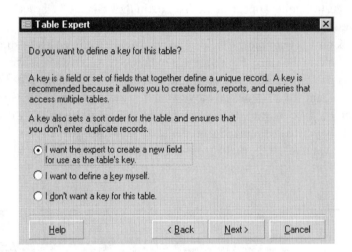

Here you choose if you want Paradox to create a new key field for you or if you want to define your own or have none. As you'll learn later, Paradox uses the key field to keep records in order and to relate the table to others.

We want to use the Customer ID field as the key, so click on the I Want to Define a Key Myself option, and then on Next see a list of the fields in the table. Double-click on the Customer ID field and then on Next.

In the next Expert dialog box you choose how you want the records sorted. The fields you select will be used for indexes, which help Paradox locate records. Click on the checkboxes for the Last Name and Account Number fields, and then click on Next.

You now enter a file name and location for the table, and select what you want to do after Paradox creates it. You can choose from these options:

- View the table and add data to it

- Add data to the table using a form that Paradox will create for you

- Change the table's structure

Type **Clients** as the table name. Because you created the table directly from the Startup Expert, it will be saved in the database folder that you created. Leave the View the Table and Add Data option button selected and click on Finish. Click on OK when you see the message that the table has been selected. The Clients table appears onscreen.

NOTE: *You can have more than one table or other object open at a time, but only one can be active. The menu options and toolbar buttons will depend on which object is active.*

Entering and Editing Data

The new, empty table appears as a row of field names and one blank record row, with a new toolbar, as shown in Figure 25-4. In addition to the familiar New, Open, Save, Print, Cut, Copy, and Paste buttons, the toolbar contains those described in Table 25-2.

A highlight bar appears in the current field. Click in the field you want to enter or edit, or use the appropriate toolbar buttons to move the highlight bar to it. Press the LEFT or RIGHT ARROW, the ENTER key, and the TAB or SHIFT-TAB combination to move the highlight bar to other fields in the record. Press the up and down arrow keys to move the highlight bar between records.

You enter and edit data using a combination of Field View and Edit Data modes.

To enter or edit information in the table, you have to enter Edit mode. Edit mode is on when the Edit Data button is pressed down—either click on the button or press the F9 key. When you start to type, the highlight bar disappears. There will be an insertion point on the field but pressing an arrow key will move the highlight bar to another field, not let you edit within the field. You can press BACKSPACE to delete what you type but not edit it in any other way. Normally Paradox is in Overwrite mode, so whatever you type replaces the contents of the field under the highlight bar.

NOTE: *To enter information in a memo field, press SHIFT-F2 to display the memo window. Enter or edit the text and press SHIFT-F2 to return to the table.*

25

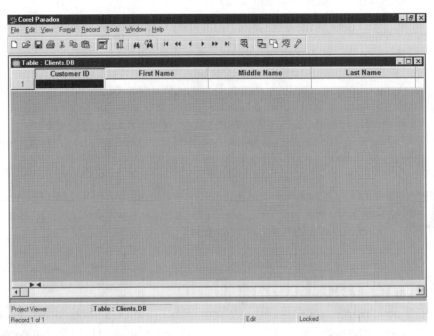

A new
Paradox
table

FIGURE 25-4

To edit within a field you have to enter Field View. Enter Field View by selecting Field View from the View menu or by pressing the F2 key. You can now move the insertion point with the field to insert and delete characters, and you type without deleting what's already there. In Field View, the RIGHT and LEFT ARROW keys only move the insertion point within the field, not to other fields.

Moving to another field, however, turns off Field View automatically. To keep Field View turned on you press CTRL-F2 or select Persistent Field View from the View menu. Press CTRL-F2 again to turn the feature off.

TIP: *Before you leave a field, you can cancel your changes by pressing ESC. Before you leave the record, you can cancel all of your changes to it by selecting Undo from the Edit menu.*

When you're ready to add another record into the table, press the DOWN ARROW key, or select Next from the Record menu to display a new blank record. To insert a record elsewhere in the table, press the INS key or select Insert from the Record menu. To delete a record, click in it to make it active, then press CTRL-DELETE, or

Button	Name	Description
	Edit Data	Toggles between being able to edit the field and only selecting it
	Restructure	Changes the structure of the table
	Locate Field Value	Lets you search the table for information that you specify
	Locate Next Value	Finds the next occurrence of information previously specified
	First Record	Moves the highlight bar to the first record in the table
	Previous Set	Scrolls up one screen-full of records
	Previous Record	Moves the highlights bar to the previous record
	Next Record	Moves the highlights bar to the next record
	Next Set	Scrolls down one screen-full of records
	Last Record	Moves the highlight bar to the last record in the table
	Filter	Lets you restrict the records that are displayed to those meeting certain criteria
	Data Model	Lets you create a relationship between tables
	Project Viewer	Displays the Project Viewer window

Table Toolbar Buttons

TABLE 25-2

25

Button	Name	Description
	Corel Web Site	Launches your Web browser and connects to the Corel Corporation Web site
	Perfect Experts	Displays the Experts window

Table Toolbar Buttons (*continued*)

TABLE 25-2

select Delete from the Record menu. Just remember that you must be in Edit mode to enter, insert, or delete records.

TIP: *Press CTRL-D to insert the same information in the field from the record above.*

If the table contains a key field, Paradox automatically keeps the records in key order, rearranging the records for you. If you are at the end of the table and select Next from the Record menu, the record you just entered will move to its position according to the key, even if it means it is moved off of the displayed set. The key value must be unique, so Paradox will not let you enter a key value that already exists in the table. In a table without a key, the records appear in the order in which you type them.

Paradox saves your record as soon as you move to another or close the table. You don't have to use the Save command in the File menu or manually save the table in any other way.

Now turn on Edit mode, and enter the information shown in Figure 25-5. We've only shown information for some of the fields—you may want to make up the entries for the others. If you want to edit within the record, turn on Field View. When you're done, close the table by clicking on its Close button or by selecting Close from the File menu.

The Project Viewer window appears but MyCompany is not yet shown as the working directory. Pull down the directory list and click on MyCompany. You'll see the objects in the directory that were created as part of the Clients table:

Clients.DB   Clients.PX   Clients.VAL   Clients.X04   Clients.X05   Clients.Y04

Clients.Y05

```
Customer ID:  AMCH              Street: 765 Lock Road
First Name: Adam                City: Margate
Middle Initial:  M             State/Prov::  NJ
Last Name: Chesin              Country: USA
Account Number: 101            Zip/Postal Code: 08402
Contact: Adam Chesin          Phone: 609-822-8765

Customer ID:  AWOODIN         Street: 24 N Madison Ave.
First Name: Alan              City: Margate
Middle Initial:  W            State/Prov::  NJ
Last Name: Woodin            Country: USA
Account Number: 102          Zip/Postal Code: 08402
Contact: Alan Woodin         Phone: 609-345-9845

Customer ID:  EKANE          Street: 87 Lyndon Lane
First Name: Erica             City: Llandview
Middle Initial:  J           State/Prov::  PA
Last Name: Kane              Country: USA
Account Number: 103         Zip/Postal Code: 19087
Contact: Erica Kane         Phone: 215-876-0987

Customer ID:  HSWEIG        Street: 98 Ontario Way
First Name: Harvey           City: Lawrenceville
Middle Initial:  K          State/Prov::  NJ
Last Name: Sweig            Country: USA
Account Number: 104        Zip/Postal Code: 08654
Contact: Harvey Sweig       Phone: 609-235-6789

Customer ID:  WWAT          Street: 654 Oak Drive
First Name: William          City: Margate
Middle Initial:  W         State/Prov::  NJ
Last Name: Watson           Country: USA
Account Number: 105        Zip/Postal Code: 08402
Contact: Billy Watson       Phone: 609-823-9984
```

Client records to be entered in the fields

■ FIGURE 25-5

Creating a Form

A table is just one way to look at your information—a form is another. With a form, you see one record at a time, which may make it easier to enter and edit data. Although you can create custom forms with the fields arranged any way you want, you can quickly create a form using Form Expert.

In Chapter 27 we'll look at creating custom forms and combining forms from more than one table. To quickly create a form for the Clients table, follow these steps:

1. Right-click on the Form button in the toolbar or on the Form icon Project Viewer, and select New from the menu that appears.

2. In the box that appears, click on Expert to see the first Form Expert dialog box where you can choose to create a form from a single table or from multiple tables.

25

3. Click on Data From One Table and then click on Next to see the dialog box shown here:

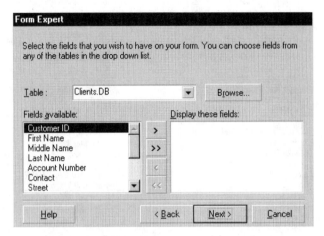

4. Click on >> to add all of the fields to the form. You can also select individual fields if you do not want to make them all available for display or entry into the table. Click on Next. You now select the form's overall layout. You can choose to display a single record with the fields in columns, multiple records in a row, or multiple records in a table format.

5. Select the first option to display one record, then click on Next. In the next box, shown here, you'll select from a series of styles.

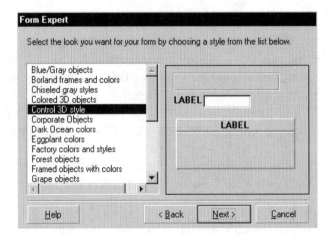

Each style includes the color of text, backgrounds, and the frame around labels and field values. When you click on a style, its format will appear in the Sample panel. Select a style that you like and click on Next.

6. In the final box, type **Clients** as the name of the form. You can select to run the form, displaying the data, or to open the form in a design view so you can customize it.

7. Click on Finish, then on OK when you see the message that the form has been created.

Paradox creates a form listing all of the fields in the current record, as shown in Figure 25-6.

The Form toolbar contains some new buttons. In place of the Restructure Table button, you'll see the Run Form and Design Form buttons. Use these to switch between displaying the form with information from the table and displaying the form in design view so you can change the form's layout.

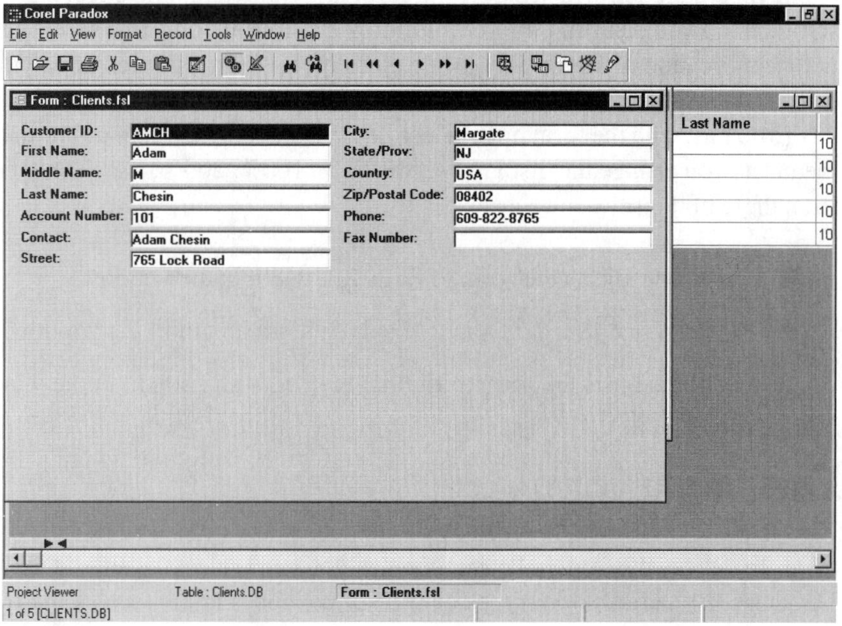

Paradox form

FIGURE 25-6

25

Editing in the Form

You edit, add, insert, and delete records directly on the form just as you do in tables. Using a form more closely resembles the "paper" form you may be familiar with.

- Use Edit mode, Field View, and Persistent Field View to change data in the table.

- Select and display records using the toolbar and Record menu.

- Insert and delete records just as you do in tables, except by pressing the DOWN ARROW key.

To print the form displayed on the screen, click on the Print button, or select Print from the File menu. Close the form by clicking on its Close button or by choosing Close from the File menu.

Zooming the Form Display

If your table has many fields, you may not be able to see all of the fields onscreen at one time. Paradox will separate the form into more than one page, and display a scroll bar so you can bring more of it into view. If you don't like scrolling, reduce the magnification of the display to see more of the form onscreen at one time. You can also enlarge the magnification to make forms easier to see and read.

To do this, with the form open select Zoom from the View menu. The drop-down menu lets you change the display to 25%, 50%, 100%, 200%, and 400%, or choose from these options:

- Fit Width adjusts the form to fit its full width in the window.

- Fit Height adjusts the form to display its full length in the window.

- Best Fit adjusts the form to fit both the width and height in the window.

Opening a Form

Now that you've created the form, you can open it any time to access the data in the table. To display the form in Project Viewer, you must select the alias in the Working Directory list and click on Types or the Forms icon. Paradox saves the form with the FSL extension, so the form you just created will be shown as Clients.fsl. Then use either of these techniques:

- Double-click on the form.

- Right-click on the form name and select Open or Run from the shortcut menu.

To open any form, even one not listed in the Project Viewer, click on the Open Form button in the toolbar or select Open from the File menu and click on Form. Paradox displays the Open Form dialog box, listing the forms in the working directory. Change to the directory where the form is located, then double-click on the form name.

 NOTE: *The Open Form dialog box also gives you the options to edit the form's design, and to open the form as a report.*

You do not have to open the table used to create the form first. When you open the form, Paradox automatically accesses the information in the table.

Querying the Data

You can use a query whenever you find yourself thinking "I need to know," or when you're asking who, what, when, where, and how questions. Who owes me money? What is Bob's telephone number? When was my fourth divorce granted? Where's my copy of the *Star Wars* video? How much do I still owe the IRS? A query lets you see just the specific fields and records you're interested in, and you can group together fields from multiple tables.

Normally, the output of a query is a special table called the Answer table, and it includes just the fields you asked for and the records that meet any conditions that you establish. You can also choose to create a *live* query. This is a subset of the actual table, so any changes you make to the information in the result set are actually made to the table.

You create a query using these steps:

1. Open a new query window.

2. Indicate the table, or related tables, that contain the information.

25

3. Specify the fields you want to display.

4. Indicate the criteria for selecting records.

5. Run the query.

You can edit, print, or restructure the Answer table using normal Paradox commands. However, the Answer table is temporary; a new table will replace it when you run another query. If you want to keep the data presented in the table, you must rename it before exiting.

Now let's create a few queries to use with our Clients table.

1. Right-click on the Query button in the toolbar or on the Queries icon in Project Viewer, and select New from the shortcut menu. Paradox displays a list of tables in the working directory.

2. Double-click on the Clients table.

You'll see the query window showing the fields in the table, each field in a separate column, as shown in Figure 25-7. Paradox calls this the *query image*.

 TIP: *Maximize the query image window if you find the background distracting.*

You now have to select the fields that you want to display, and enter criteria to select records. Each column in the query window contains a checkbox and a blank area to its right called the *query field*. You use the checkboxes to determine which fields to display, and you use the query fields to determine which records to display.

3. Click in the checkbox for the Last Name field.

4. Click in the checkbox for the State/Prov field. The query image will appear as shown here:

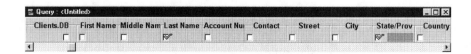

New   Run Query   Show SQL
   Open   Join Tables   Add Table
     Save   Query   Remove Table
      Cut   Properties Data Model
        Copy   Sort   Project Viewer
          Paste   Answer   Corel Web Site
                 Table   Perfect Expert

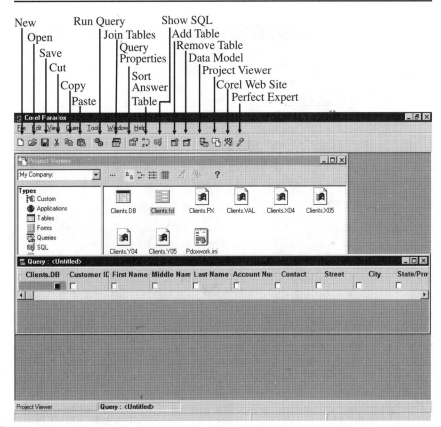

The query
image and
Query
toolbar

FIGURE 25-7

5. Click on the Run Query button, or select Run from the Query menu.
   Paradox creates the temporary answer table, ANSWER.DB, displaying
   only the fields that you checked, as shown in Figure 25-8.

6. Click on the Close box in the Answer table window. Now let's try
   something else.

7. Click in the checkbox for the Last Name field to remove the check mark.

8. Click in the checkbox for the City field.

25

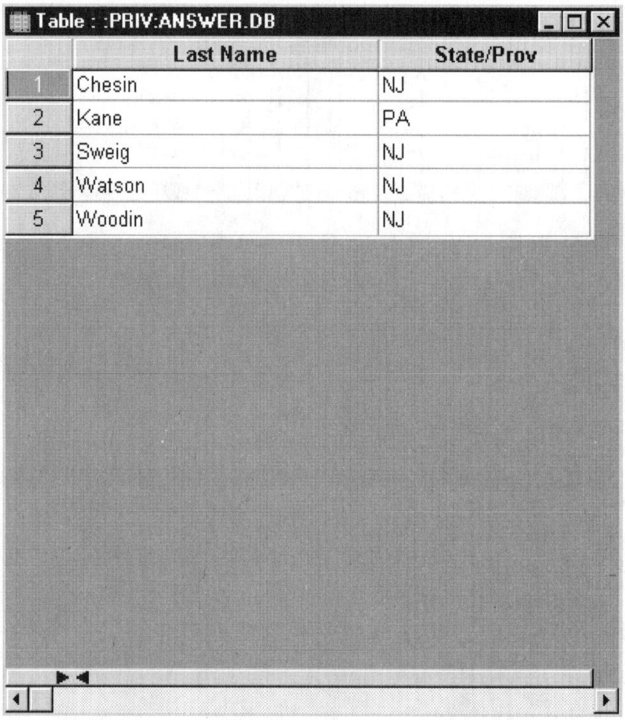

Table : :PRIV:ANSWER.DB

	Last Name	State/Prov
1	Chesin	NJ
2	Kane	PA
3	Sweig	NJ
4	Watson	NJ
5	Woodin	NJ

The Answer table displaying the results of the query

FIGURE 25-8

9. Click on the Run Query button. The Answer table only shows one row for Margate, NJ, even though we have three clients in that location. You'll learn why shortly.
10. Close the Answer table.

Selecting Fields

The check mark that appears when you click on the checkbox tells Paradox to display only unique values. It will not display more than one copy of records that have the same values on all of the displayed fields. To have more control over which records are displayed, right-click on the checkbox to see these options:

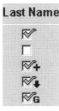

Table 25-3 explains how each option is used. Click on the check mark for the type of operation you want to perform.

Right-click on the checkbox for the City field and choose the Check Plus icon. Run the Query. Now both records for clients in Margate, NJ, are listed. Close the Answer table.

 NOTE: *If you want to use all of a table's fields in a query, click the checkbox beneath the name of the table in the first column. This will automatically check all of the fields.*

Selecting Records

You determine which records appear in the Answer table by typing a criterion in the Query Field. Try it now.

1. Click on the empty space following the checkbox in the State/Prov field.

Operation	Description
Check	Includes only unique values
Empty Check Box	Does not display the fields
Check Plus	Displays all records, even those with duplicate field values
Check Descending	Displays only unique records, but in descending order
Check By Group	Lets you define a group of records in a Set query

Select the Check Mark for the Function You Want to Perform

TABLE 25-3

25

2. Type **NJ**.

3. Click in the checkbox for the Last Name field.

4. Click on the Run Query button. Paradox now displays records for only clients in New Jersey.

5. Close the Answer table.

To use a field for criteria but not display it in the table, enter a condition into the query field but do not check the field's checkbox.

When you type a specific value in the query field, such as a name or number, Paradox displays records whose field exactly matches the value. Here are some other ways to enter criteria:

- If you are not certain of the exact spelling, use the LIKE operator, as in *LIKE chasin*. This locates words that sound alike and start with the same letter, regardless of case. Do not use LIKE in combination with wildcard characters.

- To exclude a value, use the NOT operate as in *not PA* or *not like chasin*.

- For records that do not have a value in the field, enter the word **BLANK.**

- Use operators for comparisons, such as *> 50*. The operators are = (equal), > (greater than), < (less than), >= (greater than or equal to), and <= (less than or equal to).

- In date fields, enter dates in the mm/dd/yy format. Use the TODAY operator to indicate the current date. Enter **<TODAY-30,** for example, to select records that contain a date over 30 days before the current date.

Multiple Conditions

When you enter criteria in more than one field, Paradox treats it as an AND operation. This means that all of the conditions must be met for the record to appear. You can also use the comma (,) to represent an AND condition in a single field. The criterion *>=5,<=10*, for example, displays values between 5 and 10. To create an OR condition, use the word "or", as in *PA or NJ*, to display clients in either Pennsylvania or New Jersey. With an OR condition, only one of the conditions must be true for the record to be selected.

To create an OR condition using more than one field, you have to add another field row. For example, suppose you want to list all PA clients as well as the record for the client named Smith. If you place Smith in the Name field and PA in the State field, Paradox will only list clients named Smith in PA.

To add a new row when you are in the last, press the DOWN ARROW key. To insert a new row elsewhere, press INS. (Press CTRL-DELETE to delete a row.) You can only insert a row when the current one has at least one field checked.

When using more than one row of query fields, you must have the same fields checked in each row; only the criterion differs. Otherwise, Paradox will display a message that tells you that you're asking unrelated questions.

Using Wildcards

You can also use wildcards in the query field when you do not want to limit a match to an exact match. These are the Paradox wildcards:

- Two periods (..) represent any number of characters. For example, G.. will match any word starting with the letter G, the pattern g..v.. will match gravy and Gorbachev.

- The @ symbol represents a single character, one for each @ in the pattern. The pattern sm@th would match Smith and Smyth, while g@@n matches gain and glen, but not gin.

You can combine the wildcards in the same criterion. Using sp@@d... would match speed, speeding, and speeds.

NOTE: *Many other programs use the ? and * symbols in place of the @ and .. symbols.*

25

Using the Answer Table

The Answer table is just like any other table in Paradox, but with two major exceptions. It is stored in the Private directory, and it is automatically overwritten when you run another query.

If you want to save the Answer table for use later, you must rename it. You can also change the query properties before running the query to an Answer table with a different name. To select a different name click the Properties button in the Query toolbar, then click in the Answer tab to see the dialog box shown in Figure 25-9.

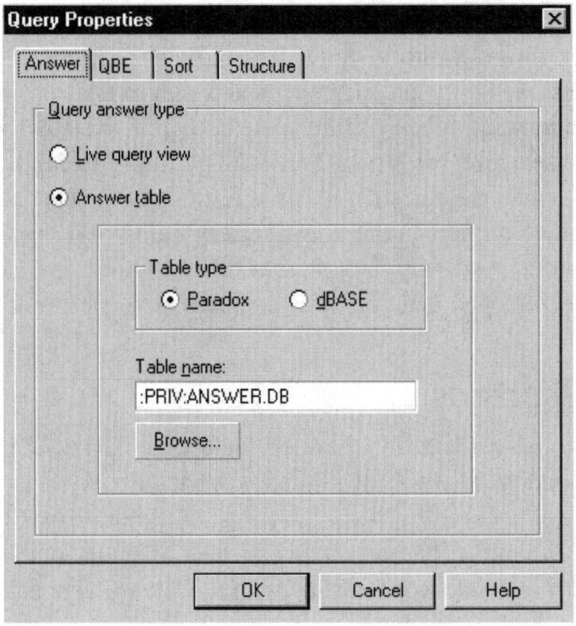

Query
properties

FIGURE 25-9

In the Table Name box, enter the name you want to give the Answer table, use the Browse button to choose a new location, then click on OK. When you run the current query, the results will be saved under the new name and location, leaving any existing ANSWER.DB table unchanged. The name and location you pick only affect the current query—the next query that you create will use the default.

Saving and Opening Queries

Saving an Answer table has limited value. If the data in your table changes, the saved Answer table no longer reflects the up-to-date information in your table. Rather than save the table, save the query itself. Each time you open and run the query, Paradox obtains the results from the current information in the database.

When the query window is active, choose Save from the File menu. Type a name for the query and then click on Save.

To later run the query, click on the Open Query button, then double-click on the Query name. Paradox opens the query and displays the query image—click on Run query to see the results. You can also right-click on the query name in Project Viewer and select Run Query to both open and run the query.

Creating a Live Query

The Answer table created by a query is separate from the table that it is based upon. Changing the information in the Answer table does not change the original table. When you create a live query, however, the Answer table is an actual subset of the source table. Any changes you make to the live query table are also made to the source table.

To create a live query, display the Answer tab of the Query Properties dialog box, click on Live Query View, and then on OK. Design the query using the CheckPlus option and then run the query. You'll see live field indicators next to the names of fields that you can edit.

Live field indicators

	City		State/Prov
1	Margate		NJ
2	Margate		NJ
4	Lawrenceville		NJ
5	Margate		NJ

Query View : <Untitled>

Creating Filters

A filter is similar to a query but it lets you select records that are displayed in a table or form. However, you cannot select to display specific fields, and there are certain restrictions on the use of wildcards.

- You cannot use the @ operator.

- You cannot use the .. in numeric or date fields.

- You can use the comma as the AND operator in simple conditions, but must use the word AND in more complex ones, such as (>456 AND <1456) OR (>1 AND <4).

- You cannot use the LIKE operators.

25

The fastest way to filter is to display the table or form that you want to view the information, right-click on the field that you want to use, then select Filter from the shortcut menu. A box will appear where you enter a condition for the field. When you type the condition and click on OK, Paradox applies the filter showing only those records meeting the condition. To create an AND condition using multiple fields, apply another filter to another field. To remove a filter, right-click on the field and select Filter. Delete the condition from the box and click on OK.

You can create more complex filters on more than one field using the Filter dialog box. To create a filter, open the table or form, and then click on the Filter button in the toolbar to see the dialog box shown in Figure 25-10.

The Order By list shows the available indexes to use for the order of the records. The primary key is indicated with an asterisk. To use a different index, click on an index to list the order of fields in the Filter on Fields list. If you are using an index, and the Order By checkbox is checked, you can click on Range and set the range of values.

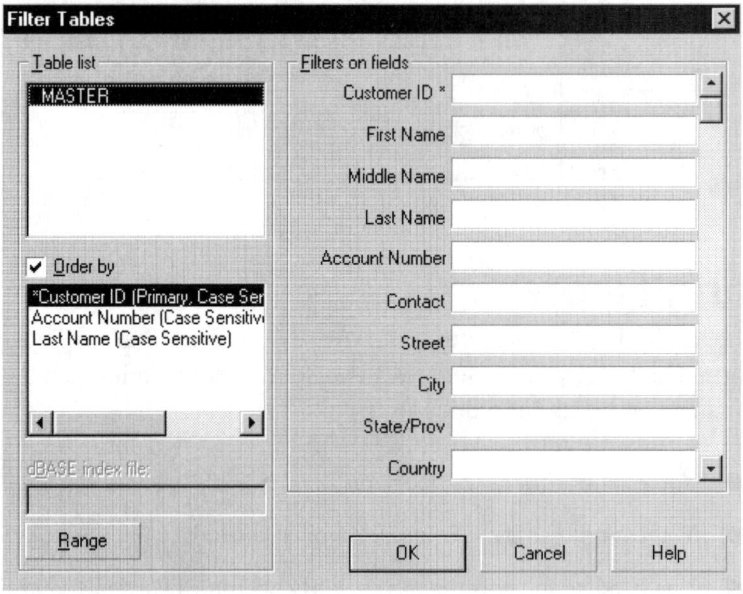

Filter
Tables
dialog box

FIGURE 25-10

The Filters On Fields list shows all of the fields in the table. For each field that you want to use for a criterion, type the criterion in the field's text box. When you are done, click on OK.

Unlike a query, the filter affects the view of the table itself, it does not create a new table. To remove the filter, display the Filter dialog box and clear the conditions.

 NOTE: *The two types of filters are related. Any criteria that you've applied using the shortcut menu will appear in the Filter dialog box, and vice versa.*

Creating a Report

Forms are great for displaying and editing one record at a time, or when you want to print records individually. When you want to print more than one recordcreate a report. As with forms, you can create a report using Paradox Expert, and you can create custom reports for documents such as mailing letters, labels, and invoices.

The Report Expert is similar to Form Expert. Here's how to use it to create a basic report from a single table.

1. Right-click on the Report button in the toolbar and select New from the menu that appears.

2. In the box that appears, click on Expert to see the first Report Expert dialog box.

3. Click on Data From One Table and then click on Next.

4. Select the fields you want to include on the report, then click on Next. In this next dialog box you can choose one or more fields in which you want to group the data in the report. By grouping, for example, you can organize clients by their location or products by type.

5. Choose the fields you want to group by, if any, then click on Next.

6. Select the style to use for the report, and if you want to display individual or multiple records, then click on Next to see the dialog box shown here:

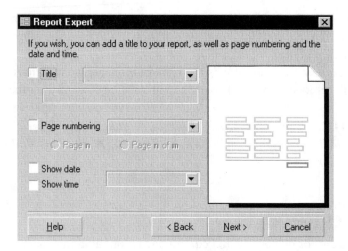

7. To add a title to the report, click on the Title checkbox, then select a position from the list that appears and enter the title text.

8. To add page numbers, click on the Page Numbering checkbox, then select a position and format.

9. To add the date or time, click on the appropriate checkboxes, then select a position. Click on Next.

10. In the final box, enter the report name, and optionally select to print the report immediately after it is created, click on Finish, then click on OK when you see a message telling you that the report has been created.

Paradox creates and displays the report as shown in Figure 25-11. Most of the buttons in the report toolbar are similar to those in the form toolbar. Use the navigation buttons to move between pages of the report:

Click on the Print button to print the report. The Print dialog box, shown in Figure 25-12, offers a number of options. You can print the entire report or just selected pages, print up to 32767 copies, indicate the starting page number, and choose to collate multiple copies into sets.

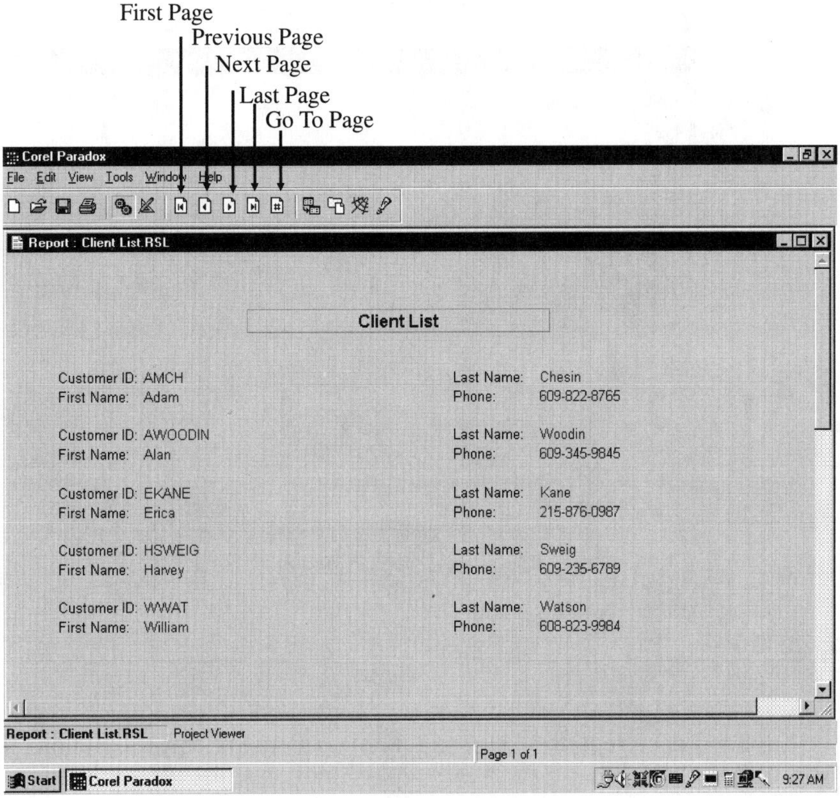

First Page
Previous Page
Next Page
Last Page
Go To Page

A Paradox
report

FIGURE 25-11

Because report pages can be quite large, the Overflow Handling section lets you select how to handle pages too wide to fit on one page:

■ *Clip to Page Width* just ignores material that doesn't fit between the margins.

■ *Create Horizontal Overflow* Page prints the extra material on a separate page, immediately following the page it extends.

■ *Panel Vertically* prints a second page for every page in the report, as long as at least one page has some overflow material.

25

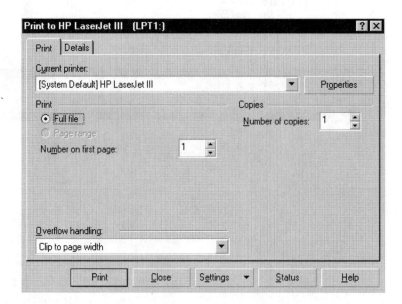

Print dialog
box

FIGURE 25-12

Save and open reports just as you do other Paradox objects. Reports are saved
with the RSL extension.

Finding and Replacing Data

When your table is small, you can easily scroll through it to find information. But
as your tables get larger, scrolling is just not very efficient. To locate information,
or to automatically replace data when you find it, use the Locate option from the
Report menu. The menu has four options:

- *Field* moves the highlight bar to the field that you specify, in the
  current record.

- *Record Number* moves the highlight bar to the record you specify, in the
  current field.

- *Value* moves the highlight bar to the next occurrence of a value
  you specify.

■ *Replace* locates and replaces the value you specify.

  NOTE: *Use the Find and Replace command in the Edit menu to locate or change text in a memo field.*

The Field and Record Number options are self-explanatory, but let's look at the other two. When you select Value, Paradox displays the dialog box shown here:

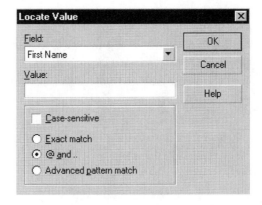

Use the box like this:

1. Pull down the Field list and choose the field that you want to search.

2. Enter the value you are looking for in the Value box.

3. Choose if you want to make the search case-sensitive.

4. Choose if you want an exact match. This means you will not use wildcards and Paradox will not locate text if it is just part of a larger word (such as locating microcomputer when searching for micro).

5. Choose @ and .. if you use the wildcard characters.

6. Choose Advanced pattern match to use a more robust series of wildcard characters.

When you click OK, Paradox searches for the first occurrence of the text in the table, regardless of the location of the highlight bar. To locate the next occurrence of the text, press CTRL-A, or select Locate Next from the Record menu.

25

Using Wildcards in Advanced Searches

When you choose the @ and .. option, you can use wildcards in the search phrase to locate text. When you perform an advanced pattern search, you can use the additional wildcards shown in Table 25-4.

Wildcard	Description
^	Locates the text only when it comes at the beginning of the field, as in ^*text*.
$	Locates the text only when it comes at the end of the field, as in *text$*.
*	Match text that has at least one or more of the characters before it. The string plan* will locate *plan* as well as *planning*.
+	Match text that has at least two or more of the characters before it. The string *plan+* will match *planning*, but not *plan*.
?	Match one or none of the expressions before the ? character.
|	Match either the characters before or after the vertical bar.
[abc]	Match any of the characters within the brackets.
[^abc]	Match any characters not within the brackets.
(abc)	Creates a group of literals.
\	Treats the wildcard character that follows as a regular non-wildcard character.
\r	Matches a carriage return.
\n	Matches a line feed.
\t	Matches a tab.
\f	Matches a form feed.

Advanced
Wildcards

TABLE 25-4

Finding and Replacing Values

The Values option just locates text in the table. The Replace option lets you locate text and replace it with something else. The dialog box has the same options as Value, but with an additional text box labeled Replace With. Type the information you want to replace in the Value box, and the information you want to insert in its place in the Replace With box.

 NOTE: *You can only select the Replace option if you are in Edit mode.*

When you click on OK, Paradox searches the table for the matching value. On each match it displays these options:

- *Skip this occurrence*—Paradox will not make the replacement, but will continue to the next match.

- *Change this occurrence*—Paradox makes the replacement then continues to the next match.

- *Change all occurrences*—Paradox makes the replacement and all others in the table without further prompts.

Select the function you want to perform, then click OK.

Changing the Appearance of Your Table

Paradox tables are not designed for onscreen presentations, but you can format how the screen and characters appear. To change the appearance of a table, open the table and then select Properties from the Format menu for three categories for formatting.

- *Data*—The color of the background, alignment of text, the font and color of text, and numeric format of text.

- *Grid*—The color and shape of the grid lines and the color and shape of a line indicating the current record.

- *Heading*—The color, alignment, and font of row and column headers.

Selecting an option displays the Properties dialog box for formatting the active cell, grid line, or header. You can also change the same options by right-clicking on an object and selecting Properties from the shortcut menu. Once one of the Properties dialog boxes appears, however, clicking on any object will change the Properties dialog box, making it appropriate for that object.

Changing Column Width

To change the width of a column, point to the grid line to the right of any cell in a column (except the column name) so the pointer appears as a two-headed arrow, then drag the mouse to the left or right. If a series of asterisks appear in a numeric column, then you've made the column too narrow—widen the column to see the values.

Changing Row Height

To change the height of the rows, point to the line under any record so the mouse appears as a two-headed arrow. Drag the mouse down to widen rows, up to make them narrow. All of the rows will become the same height.

To change the height of the header row, drag the line on top of the blank box to the left of the first field name.

Changing the Order of Columns

Paradox positions the columns in the same order as the fields in the structure of the table, but you can change a column's position onscreen by dragging. Point to the header of the column you want to move so the pointer appears as a small box. As you drag the mouse, the pointer changes to a dark two-pointed arrow and a dark vertical line will appear onscreen. Release the mouse when the line is in the position where you want the column to appear.

Data-Dependent Formats

When you set the format of data, Paradox applies the format to the entire column. By choosing a data-dependent format, you can designate a format that will be applied only when certain conditions are met. So, for example, you can display all positive numbers in one color, and all negative numbers in another.

Right-click on the column that you want to apply a data-dependent format to, then select Data Dependent from the shortcut menu. You can only apply data-dependent formats to alphanumeric, number, date, and money fields. In the dialog box that appears, click on the New Range button so you see the options shown in Figure 25-13.

You now can enter one or more conditions, and the properties to use when each condition is met. For each condition, select an operator and enter a value in the Range Includes Values section. To include a range of values, select the operator in the And section and then enter the other value. For example, to set the color of all values between 0 and 50, select the > operator and enter **0** as the first value, then select the <= operator and enter **50** in the AND section.

Next, click on the Set Properties button and set the background color of the column, the font and font color, and other properties that you want the text to have when it meets the condition. Click OK to close the Properties dialog box, then click on Apply Changes. Paradox adds the range and format to the Ranges list.

In the same way, create other ranges or conditions that you want to apply to the field. When you're finished, click on OK.

Saving and Restoring Properties

In order to save the properties, you must save the table. When you close the table, Paradox will ask if you want to save the changes that you've made to it—click on Yes.

To save the changes without closing the able, pull down the Format menu, point to Properties, and click on Save. Paradox stores the properties for the table in a file with

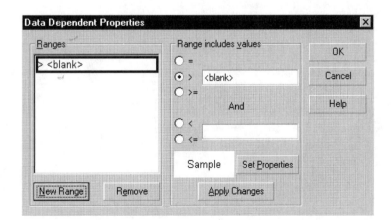

Setting data-dependent formats

FIGURE 25-13

the table name but with the TV extension. Select Delete from the Format Properties menu to delete the associated TV file, restoring the default settings to the table.

NOTE: *If you haven't yet saved the table, use the Restore option in the Format Properties menu to return to the previous settings.*

Working with Databases

26

Database Expert and Table Expert are useful, but they cannot anticipate every task for which you'll need a database. When you can't find the right combination of fields in the experts, create your own tables. In this chapter, you'll learn how to create custom tables, work with database objects, and protect your database with passwords.

Creating Custom Tables

When creating tables and databases it pays to plan ahead. Start by thinking about the type of information you want to get out of the database, either on the screen or in a printed report. Then decide what data you have to put into the computer to get that output.

For each table, you'll need to know the name you want to give each field, the type of data it will contain, and if there are any special limitations or requirements for the information, such as a minimum or maximum number.

Creating databases that can automate an entire business can be a complicated process, and there are scores of rules that should be followed. For creating basic tables, however, there are two that are important.

First, avoid what's called *repeating fields*. These are fields in a table that basically contain the same type of information. For example, in a table of friends it would be nice to include the names of their children, but what do you call the fields? You could name them Child1 and Child2, but what do you do for families with more children? How many Child fields should you add to the table to be safe? The answer is none, because these are repeating fields—they repeat the same type of information. In a professionally designed database, the children's names will be in a separate table linked to the parent's table.

The other warning is not to include fields that can be calculated from other fields in the table. For example, if you have Quantity and Price fields, you do not need a field called Total that is their product. You can always multiply the two fields and display their product in a form, report, or query. Storing the product in the table is a waste of space, and the value would have to be changed every time you change either of the Quantity or Price fields.

Creating a new table takes three steps:

1. Select the format of the table.

2. Describe the fields.

3. Save and name the table.

As an example, let's create a table to store information about our client's orders. First, start Paradox, close the Startup Expert, and change the working directory to :My Company: if it is not already selected.

Now right-click on the Open Table button on the toolbar and select New from the shortcut menu. In the New Table dialog box, click on Blank to display the Create Table dialog box in which you choose the format of the table you want to create. You can select from several versions of Paradox and a program called dBASE. Use the older versions of Paradox or a dBASE option if you want the table to be compatible with these other programs. For now, click OK to accept the default Paradox 7 & 8 table type, and to see the Create Paradox 7 & 8 Table dialog box shown in Figure 26-1. Here is where you define the names and types of your fields.

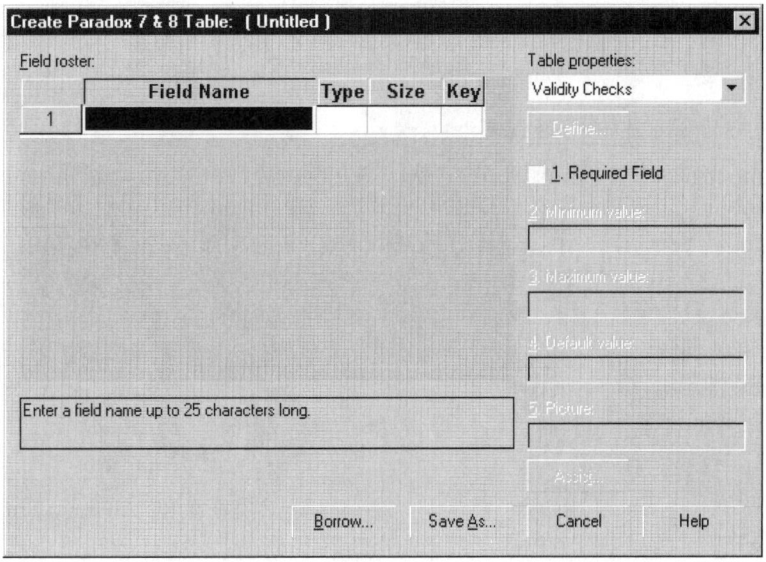

Define
the fields
and table
properties
for your
table

FIGURE 26-1

26

Field names can be up to 25 characters long, using any characters except [ ], { }, ( ), and the combination ->. The names can contain spaces but not as the first character. The names must be unique; you cannot have the same name twice in a table, although a name can be duplicated in the database. Paradox will automatically number each field.

Move from one field to another by clicking with the mouse, or by pressing the TAB or ENTER keys.

In the Field Name column for the first field type **Order Number**. To select the field type, right-click in the Type column, then select the type from the list that appears. You can also just type the symbol that represents the type instead of pulling down the list. The field types are shown in Table 26-1. Click on the +AutoIncrement

Symbol	Type	Size	Description
A	Alpha	1–255	Any characters
N	Number		Any number, up to 15 digits.
$	Money		Any number, automatically formatted with decimals and dollar sign.
S	Short		Any number in the range -32,767 to 32,767.
I	Long Integer		Any whole number in the range -2147483648 to 2147483647.
#	BCD	0–32	Numbers in Binary Coded Decimal format.
D	Date		A date between January 1, 9999 BC to December 31, 9999 AD. Use the format mm/dd/yy.
T	Time		A time, in the format hh:mm:ss followed by AM or PM.
@	Timestamp		Enter the current date and time by pressing the SPACEBAR repeatedly until the date you want appears.

Paradox Field Type

TABLE 26-1

Symbol	Type	Size	Description
M	Memo	1–240	Text strings of any length; the size just indicates how many characters Paradox stores with the table, the full memo is stored in a separate file. To use a memo field, click on the field in the table and press SHIFT-F2 to display a memo window. Type the text, and press SHIFT-F2 again.
F	Formatted Memo	0–240	A memo field that allows you to format the text.
G	Graphic		Graphic files in the BMP, PCX, TIF, GIF, and EPS file formats.
O	OLE		Objects linked from other applications.
L	Logical		Valid entries are either "True" or "False".
+	AutoIncrement		Paradox automatically increments the field by 1 for each record. You cannot edit this field, but you can specify a starting value.
B	Binary		Binary numbers.
Y	Bytes	1–255	Bytes.

Paradox Field Type (*continued*)

TABLE 26-1

option, so Paradox will automatically number each order for us starting with the number 1. You do not have to enter a Size for an AutoIncrement field.

Most tables will have a key field. When you specify a key, Paradox automatically keeps the records on key order, and prevents you from having two records with the same key value. A table can have only one key, although you can designate multiple fields to comprise the key. Double-click in the Key column for the first field. Paradox inserts an asterisk indicating it is the key field.

26

Table Properties

On the right side of the dialog box is where you further define your fields by setting the table properties. You can set the properties when you create the table or any time after by using the Restructure command.

There are seven categories of table properties:

■ *Validity Checks* lets you control the value and format of data entered. Depending on the type of field, you can specify the minimum and maximum value, a default value that will appear automatically, and a picture field that specifies the format.

■ *Table Lookup* lets you fill in a field by selecting from a list of values from another table.

■ *Secondary Indexes* help speed up queries and other operations by having Paradox maintain a special listing of the records in an order other than the key.

■ *Referential* ensures that relationships between tables are maintained.

■ *Password Security* lets you create passwords to prevent access by unauthorized users.

■ *Table Language* determines the sort order and character set.

■ *Dependent Tables* lets you define tables that depend on the current table for referential integrity. This option is only available when referential integrity is defined.

Rather than numbering orders beginning with 1, start with a higher number. That way, your customers won't think that you just opened for business. Make sure that Validity Checks is selected in the Table Properties list, then enter **150** in the Minimum Value text box. Paradox will now start numbering orders at 150.

Now create a second field to store the ID of the customer placing the order. We'll define the field so it matches the Customer ID field in the Clients table, and we'll set the properties to make it a required field, so every order must be associated with a client.

1. Click in the row for the Order Number field, then press the DOWN ARROW key to start the next field.

2. Type **Customer ID**.

3. Click on the Type column and type **A** to designate the field as an Alpha type to store alphanumeric information.

4. Click in the Size column and type **20** as the field size.

5. Click in the Required Field checkbox.

Creating an Index

We will be linking the Clients table with this table on the Customer ID field. To use Customer ID as the link field it has to be indexed. An index tracks the position of data in the table.

Pull down the Table Properties list and select Secondary Indexes. Click on the Define button to display the Define Secondary Index dialog box, as shown in Figure 26-2. Double-click on Customer ID to move it to the Indexed Field list.

We'll be accepting the default settings in this box, but first let's look at the options:

■ *Unique* limits the table to only one record for each value in the index field; no two records can have the same value in the index.

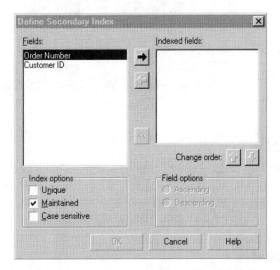

Creating a
secondary
index

FIGURE 26-2

- *Maintained* specifies whether Paradox updates the index automatically as you add records or only when you perform an action that uses the index.

- *Case Sensitive* specifies if Paradox recognizes capitalization when sorting.

Click on OK. In the box that appears type **Customer** as the index name and then click OK.

Now add two other fields.

1. Click in any column of the second field and press the DOWN ARROW key until Paradox inserts a new field row.

2. Type **Order Date** as the field name, and select the Date type.

3. Using the procedure just learned, create a secondary index named Date for the field Order Date, so we can list orders by their date. (You'll have to select Secondary Indexes from the Table Properties menu again, even if it is already shown in the box, so you can click on the Define button.)

4. Add another field called Rush Order using the Logical field type.

5. The four fields should appear defined as shown here:

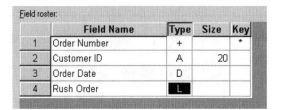

Field roster:

	Field Name	Type	Size	Key
1	Order Number	+		*
2	Customer ID	A	20	
3	Order Date	D		
4	Rush Order	L		

Table Lookup

When you add an order for a client, you have to enter the Customer ID number. Rather than trying to remember which numbers have been assigned to clients, you can create a *table lookup*. This lets you select the client number by picking it from a list of those in the Clients table. But more importantly, this lets you only select numbers that have been assigned to clients.

Follow these steps.

1. Click in the Customer ID field.

2. Pull down the Table properties list and click on Table Lookup.

3. Click on the Define button to see the dialog box shown in Figure 26-3. The field selected in the field roster should be shown in the Field Name box. If this is not the field you want to use for a lookup, double-click on the field in the Fields list.

4. Double-click on Clients.db in the Lookup Table list. This is the table containing the information we want to look up. Paradox inserts the table's key field in Lookup Field.

5. Make sure that Just Current Field is selected in the Lookup Type section. This setting inserts the matching value in the Lookup Table field. If you select All Corresponding Fields, Paradox will insert any other information from the client table in fields in the Orders table that have the same name.

6. Make sure that Help and Fill is selected in the Lookup Access section. With this setting, you cannot enter a value that is not in the lookup table. If you select Fill, No Help, you can enter any number and Paradox just warns you if there is no match.

7. Click on OK.

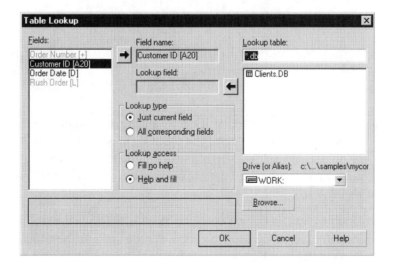

Creating a table lookup

FIGURE 26-3

You'll learn how to use a lookup table field later.

Referential Integrity

Referential integrity ensures that the relationship between two tables is enforced. For example, we would not want to add an order for a nonexistent client. Doing so would create an invalid order, a mistake that database designers call an *insertion anomaly*. We also would not want to delete a client record if there are any outstanding orders for that client. This would create what's called a *deletion anomaly*.

You can avoid these errors by specifying referential integrity, which tells Paradox what field the two tables have in common. Follow these steps.

1. Pull down the Table properties list and click on Referential Integrity.

2. Click on the Define button to see the dialog box shown here:

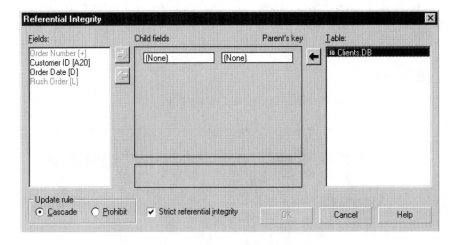

3. Double-click on Customer ID in the Fields list. Paradox inserts the field in the Child Field text box. The Child Field is the field that you should not be able to add unless there is a matching field in another table, called the *parent table*. Advanced databases can have several fields in the Child Field's list.

4. Double-click on Clients.db in the Table list. This is the table containing the information we want to match. Paradox inserts the table's key field into the Parent's Key box.

You can also select from several options.

- *Cascade* ensures that any changes in the parent table will automatically affect the matching field in the child table. This means, for example, that if you change a client's ID number, the same field in associated orders would be updated to match.

- *Prohibit* will not allow you to change the matching field if there are any related records in the tables.

- *Strict Referential Integrity* prevents users of earlier versions of Paradox that do not recognize Referential Integrity from updating your records.

5. Click on OK.

6. In the box that appears, type **My Customers** as the name for the property, then click on OK.

Saving the Table

It is now time to save the table. Save it in the same location as the Clients table because they are going to be part of the same database.

1. Click on Save As to display the Save As dialog box.

2. Type **Orders** as the table name.

3. Pull down the Alias list and select My Company.

4. Click on the Display Table box. This will display the empty table after it is saved.

5. Click on Save.

Entering Information into the Table

The empty Orders table now appears on your screen, so click on the Edit Mode button to start entering information.

NOTE: *If you did not select the Display Table box, double-click on Orders.DB in the Project Viewer to open the table.*

26

The highlight bars move directly to the Customer ID field. You can't type in the Order Number column because Paradox automatically inserts the number into that field when you move to another record.

Now you can type a value into the Customer ID field, or you can select it from the Clients table. To select it, press CTRL-SPACEBAR to display the Lookup Help window, as shown here:

Lookup Help		
	Customer ID	**First Name**
1	AMCH	Adam
2	AWOODIN	Alan
3	EKANE	Erica
4	HSWEIG	Harvey
5	WWAT	William

OK   Cancel   Help

You can scroll through the fields using the horizontal scroll bar, but the key field will always appear—it is locked in the first column position. Click on the record for the Customer ID you want to add to the order, scrolling the window as needed to display the record, then click on OK to add the Customer ID to the table.

Now enter the information into the table as shown in Figure 26-4. You can enter a T (for true) or F (for False) in the Rush Order field. You can enter the year by typing just the last two digits. To account for the turn of the century, Paradox will add 20 to the digits 00 through 50 (so entering 1/2/04 will result in 1/2/2004) and add 19 to the digits 51 to 99. To override this for dates such as 1945, type all four digits.

TIP: *If you type a customer ID that does not have a match in the Clients table, Paradox displays a warning in the status bar. Reenter a valid Customer ID or press CTRL-SPACEBAR to select one from the lookup table. Paradox will also display a warning if you enter an invalid date in the Order Date field, or a character other than T or F for the Rush Order field.*

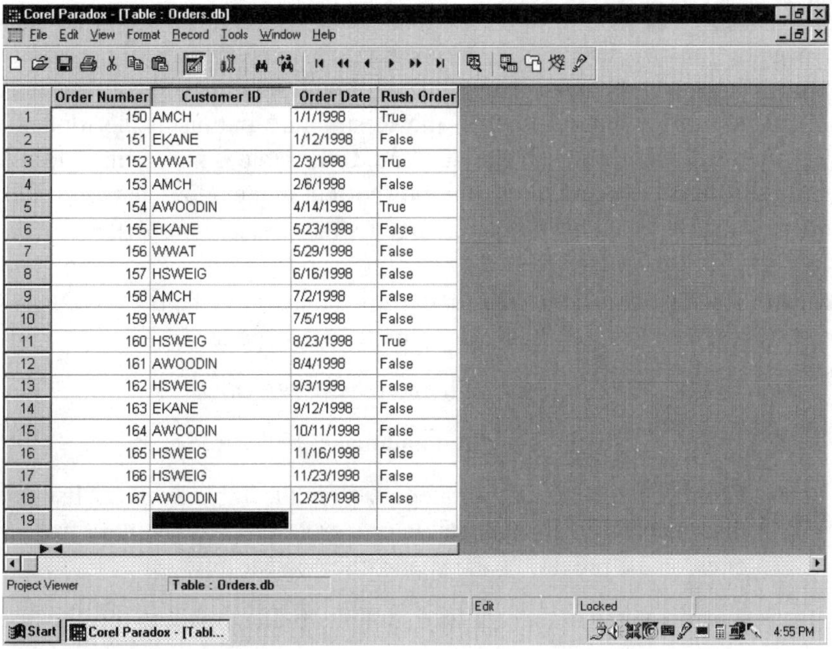

Corel Paradox - [Table : Orders.db]
File Edit View Format Record Tools Window Help
Order Number Customer ID Order Date Rush Order
1 150 AMCH 1/1/1998 True
2 151 EKANE 1/12/1998 False
3 152 WWAT 2/3/1998 True
4 153 AMCH 2/6/1998 False
5 154 AWOODIN 4/14/1998 True
6 155 EKANE 5/23/1998 False
7 156 WWAT 5/29/1998 False
8 157 HSWEIG 6/16/1998 False
9 158 AMCH 7/2/1998 False
10 159 WWAT 7/5/1998 False
11 160 HSWEIG 8/23/1998 True
12 161 AWOODIN 8/4/1998 False
13 162 HSWEIG 9/3/1998 False
14 163 EKANE 9/12/1998 False
15 164 AWOODIN 10/11/1998 False
16 165 HSWEIG 11/16/1998 False
17 166 HSWEIG 11/23/1998 False
18 167 AWOODIN 12/23/1998 False
19
Project Viewer
Table : Orders.db
Edit
Locked
Start
Corel Paradox - [Tabl...
4:55 PM

Information to be entered into the Orders table

FIGURE 26-4

Viewing a Table's Structure

You can review and change the structure of any table, even one created by Database Expert or Table Expert; however, when you review the structure, you won't be able to make any changes to it.

If the table is open, select Table Structure from the View menu. If the table is not open, right-click on the table's name in Project Viewer and select Info Structure from the shortcut menu.

You'll see a dialog box much like the one you used to create a table. To see details of a lookup table or referential integrity, select it from the Table Properties list, click on the name in the list box, and then click on the Detail Info button.

When you're finished examining the structure click on Done. You can also click on Save As to save a duplicate of the structure under a new table name.

Modifying a Table

Changing the structure of a table is called *restructuring*. You can add and delete fields, change their names, types, and sizes, and set or change table properties.

If the table is open, click on the Restructure button in the toolbar or select Restructure Table from the Format menu. If the table is not open, right-click on the table and choose Restructure from the shortcut menu. Now just as you learned for creating a table, add, delete, and change fields and table properties as you want:

- To add a new field to the end of the table, press the DOWN ARROW past the last field. To insert a field within the table, press INS.

- To delete a field, click on it and press CTRL-DELETE.

- To change a field, click in it and make the desired changes.

- To add a table, select the category from the Table Property list, and define the property. To change a table property, select its category from the list, click on the property's name and click on Modify.

- To change the order of a field, drag its field number to the new location.

Be careful when changing a table's structure because you can make changes that will delete data from the table, such as making an alpha field smaller, adding validity checks that current data violates, or changing a field type. When you save the table, Paradox will display the Restructure Warning dialog box shown here:

Restructure Warning	✕
Should the new and modified validity check(s) be enforced on existing data? ⦿ Yes ○ No	OK / Cancel / Help
Field trim ☐ Trim fields ○ Trim all fields ○ Trim no fields	
Validity checks ☐ Validity checks ○ Apply to existing data ○ Do not apply	
☐ Skip confirmation for each deleted field	

First select if you want the changed validity checks to be applied to existing data, then choose from these options:

- *Field Trim* determines how Paradox handles data that will be lost because it no longer fits in the field. Select Trim All Fields to simply delete the excess information or select Trim No Fields to save the excess information in a table named Problems.db.

- By default, if any fields will be deleted because of your changes, Paradox will display a confirmation message. Choose the Skip Confirmation for Each Deleted Field option to bypass the confirmation.

- *Validity Checks* determines how they will be applied. Select Apply to Existing Data to check your information. Values that no longer meet the validity test will be saved in a table called Keyviol.db. Select Do Not Apply to not enforce the validity checks on the data, retaining current information even if it violates the validity rules.

When you click on Save, Paradox makes the changes, displaying the KeyViol table if any violation were found.

Using Picture Clause

One of the validity check properties that you can set for some fields is called the *Picture*. The Picture is a template that controls which characters you can enter into the field. You create the template by entering one or more symbols that represent each character you can enter. You can also use the Picture Assistant to help you. Table 26-2 shows the picture symbols.

For example, suppose you assign an inventory code to each item in your stock. The code is always two uppercase letters followed by four numeric characters. This would be an alpha field six characters in size. To restrict the value to a code matching the specifications, use the picture &&####. To accept a Canadian postal code, use the picture #&#&#& (for values such as 3G6B1C).

Any other character in the picture is taken to be a literal, which means it must be entered in that position. If we want all of our inventory codes to begin with the letter G, for example, use the picture G@####. Now you must enter the letter G as the first character. To format a zip code, use the picture #####[-####]. The first five digits are required, the hyphen and last four digits are optional.

26

Symbol	Represents
#	Any numeric digit.
?	Any letter.
&	Any uppercase letter—Paradox will automatically change to uppercase any lowercase letter you enter.
~	Any lowercase letter—Paradox will automatically change to lowercase any uppercase letter you enter.
@	Any character at all, no restriction.
!	Any character, but Paradox will automatically change to uppercase any lowercase letter you enter.
;	Paradox will use the picture symbol that follows as itself, not interpret it as a picture-string character.
*	Allow multiple entries of the character that follows.
[xxx]	Entering the characters for the symbols enclosed in brackets is optional
{a, b, c}	The user must enter one of the characters enclosed in the braces when adding information to the field.

Symbols for Field Pictures

TABLE 26-2

Picture Assistance Dialog Box

For help in creating a picture clause, click on Assist to display the Picture Assistance dialog box shown in Figure 26-5.

To select from some common pictures, pull down the Sample Pictures list. Click on a sample to read a brief description of it in the box above the list. If you find a sample you want, click on it and then on the Use button. Paradox adds the picture to the Picture text box.

If you can't find a sample picture you want, try typing it in the Picture box. To make sure it is a valid picture, click on the Verify Syntax button. Paradox will display a message telling you that the picture is correct or warning you of an error in the box above the Sample Picture list.

 NOTE: *If you change your mind about the changes you have made to the picture click on Restore Original.*

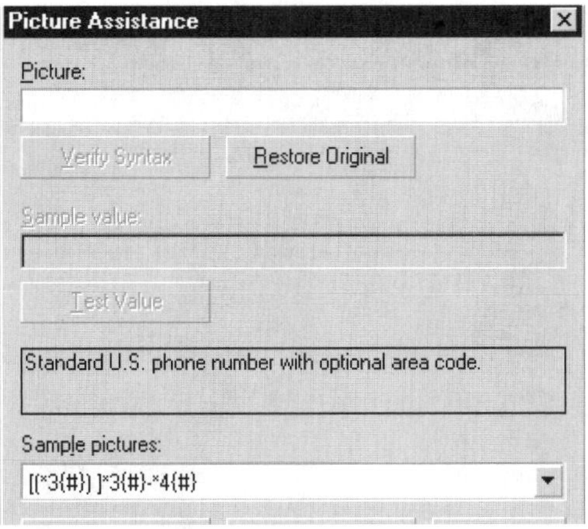

Picture Assistance

Picture:

[   ]

[Verify Syntax]   [Restore Original]

Sample value:

[   ]

[Test Value]

Standard U.S. phone number with optional area code.

Sample pictures:

[[(*3{#})]*3{#}-*4{#}   ▼]

Picture
Assistance

FIGURE 26-5

After you enter or select the picture clause, type a sample entry in the Sample Value box. If you enter an invalid character, you'll hear a beep and a message will appear telling you that picture does not accept the value. Even if you do not hear a beep, click Test Value to have Paradox check the entry for you.

If you create a custom picture, you can save it so it later appears in the Sample Pictures list. Click on the Add To List button. In the box that appears type a brief description of the picture and then click on OK.

To delete a custom picture from the list, select it in the list and click on the Delete From List button.

Sorting a Table

If you assigned a key to the table, your records will automatically appear in order of the key value. The only way to change their order is to create a new table with the same records, but in a different order. When there is no key, the records appear in the order you enter them, and you can enter them in any order you choose.

To sort the table, open it, then choose Sort from the Format menu to see the dialog box shown in Figure 26-6.

Click on the Same Table option button to rearrange the records in the current table or select New Table to save the rearranged records in another table. The Same Table option will be dimmed if the table has a key.

26

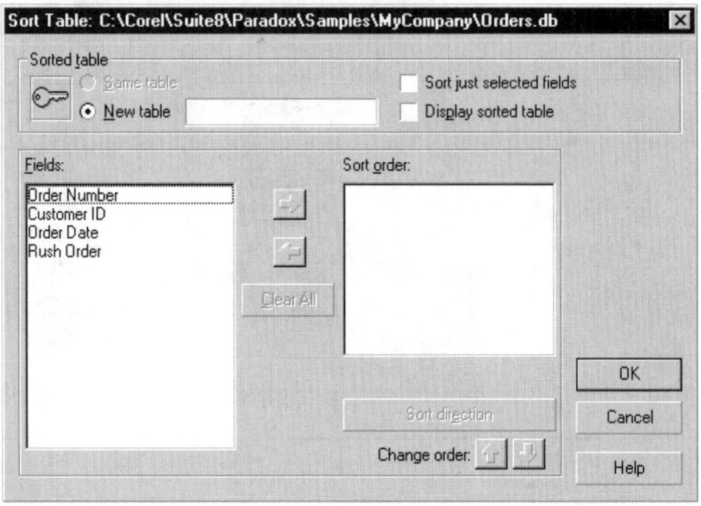

Sorting a table

FIGURE 26-6

Select Sort Just Selected Fields to sort only the fields you select. If you do not select this option, Paradox will sort on all of the fields, from left to right across the table.

Select Display Sorted Table to show the sorted records when the process is done.

To specify the fields to sort on, double-click on the field in the Fields list to add it to the Sort Order list or select the field then click the right arrow button. Use the left arrow button to remove a field from the Sort Order list, or click on Clear All to remove all of the fields. Once you have the fields in the Sort Order list you can change their order using the up arrow or down buttons next to the Change Order label in the Sort dialog box.

By default, Paradox sorts fields in ascending order. This is indicated by a small plus sign next to the field name in the Sort Order list. To change the direction for a field, click on the field in the Sort Order list and click on the Sort Direction button. Clicking the button toggles between ascending and descending order. A descending order is indicated by a minus sign before the field name.

Manipulating Table Objects

Windows 95 gives you many ways to work with files. You can easily copy, delete, and rename files, for example, from the desktop or from the Explorer. If you want to work with Paradox table files, however, you should perform file management functions from within Paradox itself.

For example, depending on your table's field types and properties, Paradox may create a number of files in addition to the actual table itself. If you have a table named MEMBERS.DB, you might also have MEMBERS.MB that contains the memo fields, MEMBERS.PX containing the primary index file, and MEMBERS.VAL that contains the validity checks and referential integrity. If you use Windows 95 to delete MEMBERS.DB, the other auxiliary files will still be on your disk, wasting space.

Suppose you rename MEMBERS.DB without renaming its auxiliary files. When you try to open the renamed table, Paradox will try to find the related file under the same name and will report an error when it can't.

If you delete MEMBERS.DB with Paradox, however, all of the related files will be deleted as well. If you rename MEMBERS.DB, Paradox will automatically rename all of the auxiliary files.

Perform file management functions in Paradox using either the Utilities option in the Tools menu, or by right-clicking on a table name in Project Viewer and choosing from the shortcut menu. If you use the Tools menu, you'll have to select the table from a dialog box.

 NOTE: *No shortcut menu will appear when you right-click on an auxiliary table file.*

The shortcut menu and the Tools Utilities menu contain these functions:

- *Add*—Adds records from one table to another. Both tables must have the same structure, although number and money fields are interchangeable, and you can add an AutoIncrement field to a long integer field.

- *Copy*—Makes a copy of the selected table and its associated table files.

- *Delete*—Deletes the selected table and its associated table files.

26

- *Empty*—Deletes all of the records from the selected table.

- *Info Structure*—Displays the structure of the selected table.

- *Rename*—Renames the selected table and its associated table files.

- *Sort*—Sorts the selected table.

- *Restructure*—Lets you change the structure of the selected table.

- *Subtract*—Deletes records from a table that have matching records in another table. You can only use this command on a keyed Paradox table.

From the shortcut menu, you can also select Open and Run to display the table, or Export to save a copy of the table in the formats listed here:

- Delimited or fixed-length text files

- Quattro Pro for Windows, version 1, 5, 6, and 7

- Quattro and Quattro Pro for DOS

- Excel, versions 3, 4, and 5

- Lotus 1-2-3, versions 1 and 2

- dBASE, versions III+, IV, and 5

- Paradox, versions 3, 4, 5, and 7

- WordPerfect document or merge file format

Other options on the shortcut menu let you save versions of the table using the Corel Versions feature, create a shortcut, or display table properties.

Working with Other Paradox Objects

When you copy, delete, or rename a table, only the table's auxiliary files are affected. The command will not affect forms, queries, reports, and other object files that you are using as part of the database. So, you'll need to perform file management tasks on these other Paradox objects individually.

Using either the shortcut menu or Tools Utilities menu, you can copy, delete, and rename forms, reports, queries, scripts, libraries, SQL files, text files, data models, and style sheets.

For Forms, the shortcut menu also offers the options to change the design of the form. The shortcut menu for reports has choices to design or print the report. The shortcut menu for queries lets you run and open the selected query.

Protecting Your Database with Passwords

Whether you are on a network, an intranet, or just a stand-alone computer, there's always a chance that someone can access your database without your permission. Even if you're not worried that someone will see your data, you should be concerned that someone can accidentally or maliciously change it. By specifying password security, you can limit access to your tables to those individuals who have a right to be there.

You create password protection as a table property, so you have to do so either when you create the table or by restructuring it afterward. If you have already created the table, right-click on it in the Project Viewer and select Restructure from the shortcut menu to display the Restructure dialog box. If you already have the table open, click on the Restructure button on the toolbar.

 NOTE: *If you have parent and child tables created with a lookup table or referential integrity, add the password to the child table before the parent table.*

Pull down the Table Properties list and select Password Security. Then click on the Define button to see the Password Security dialog box, shown here:

In the Master Password text box, type the password you want to use for the table. It can up to 31 characters, including spaces. As you type, Paradox displays an asterisk for each character, just in case someone is watching as you type. Then click in the Verify Master Password text box and type the same password again, and click on OK. Paradox will warn you if the two passwords don't match, and give you a chance to reenter them. Click on Save to save the table structure.

The next time you start Paradox and try to open the table, a dialog box will appear as shown here:

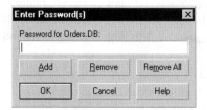

The box lets you enter the master password so you can use the table, or run a form, report, or query that accesses its data. Enter the password and then click on OK.

The box also gives you the opportunity to remove or add passwords to the password list. For example, suppose you specified a different password for each of ten tables in the database. Rather than have Paradox display the Enter password(s) dialog box for each one as you use it, enter all of the passwords in this box, clicking on Add after each. Paradox will not display the box again when you open a table that was protected by a password that you added to the list.

Use the Remove option to delete a password from the list. Type the password and click on Remove. You will then be prompted for the password when you try to access a table that was protected by it. Click Remove All to delete all of the passwords from the list, again protecting them.

NOTE: *You can display the Enter Password(s) dialog box at any time by selecting Security from the Tools menu and clicking on Passwords.*

Protecting Fields

The master password limits access to opening a table. If you want to allow users some limited access to a table, such as to insert but not delete records, then assign an auxiliary password. You can also use an auxiliary password to protect specific fields, allowing a user to enter or edit one field but not others, for example.

To set these passwords, click on the Auxiliary Passwords button in the Password Security dialog box. The Auxiliary Passwords dialog box is shown in Figure 26-7. In this dialog box, you specify a password, then assign certain table and field levels of security. You can add any number of passwords to provide different levels of use.

In the Current Password text box, type a password, then select a level of table rights:

- *All*—The user can do anything to the table.

- *Insert & Delete*—The user can insert, delete, or edit data, but not delete or restructure the table.

- *Data Entry*—The user can edit and insert data, but not delete records or restructure the table

- *Update*—The user can edit non-key fields, but not edit key fields or insert and delete records.

- *Read Only*—The user can open and view the table, but not change it in any way.

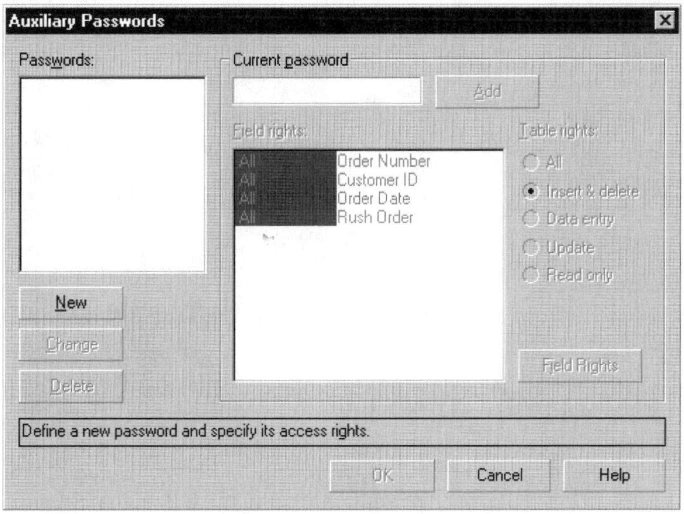

Setting
auxiliary
passwords

FIGURE 26-7

Selecting Read Only makes all of the fields read only; selecting All or Insert & Delete makes all of the field All. If you select Data Entry or Update, you can then assign individuals rights to the fields.

To set a field right, click on the field in the list, then click on the Field Rights button to toggle between these options:

- *All*—The user can perform any action allowed by the table rights.

- *Read Only*—The user cannot change the data in a field.

- *None*—The user cannot view or change the data. The column for the field will not appear in the table.

For example, suppose you want a user to be able to edit and enter all of the fields in a table except one. Set the table rights to Data Entry, then select the field and change its field rights to either None or Read Only.

Click on Add after setting the table and field rights for the password. Paradox inserts the password in the Passwords list. Click on New to enter another auxiliary password.

To change the rights assigned to a password, click on it in the Passwords list and click on Change. To delete a password, select it in the list and click on Delete.

Customizing Databases

27

The previous two chapters presented the fundamentals of using Paradox. With what you've learned in these chapters, you can create databases and tables of all types, including forms, reports, and queries. By incorporating lookup tables, referential integrity, and other features, your databases can be quite powerful and sophisticated. In this chapter, you'll learn more about Paradox, and about some of its special and custom features.

Working with Tables

So far, we've concentrated on using text and numbers in fields. Paradox tables can contain much more than that, such as clipart, scanned pictures, WordPerfect documents, Quattro Pro spreadsheets, and other objects linked to Windows applications.

Using Graphics

The Graphic field type lets you insert a graphic image into your table. You can use any graphic, even scanned photographs, that are in the BMP, PCX, TIF, GIF, or EPS format. Once you enter the graphic into the field, Paradox converts and stores it in the BMP format.

To create a graphic field, use the Graphic type when you define the field. You don't need to enter a field size because Paradox doesn't really save the graphic with the table but in a separate file. To enter the graphic into the table, click on the field in Edit Mode, pull down the Edit menu, and select Paste From. In the dialog box that appears, locate the graphic using the usual file management techniques, then double-click on the graphic file.

 TIP: *If the graphic is already in the Windows clipboard, click on the Paste button.*

When you are not in the graphic field, Paradox displays the notation <BLOB graphic> in the table. When you click in the field, you'll see as much of the graphic as can fit in the column. To see the entire image in a special window, double-click on it or press F2. Press F2 or click on the window's Close box to return to the table.

 **TIP:**   *To paste the graphic directly into the graphic window, turn on Field View.*

Inserting Linked Objects

You can also insert graphics and other objects into a field using the OLE field type. The object is inserted while maintaining a link with its source application, so double-clicking on the field opens the application you used to create the object and displays it for editing.

The application used to create the object must be OLE compliant. Use this technique, for example, to add a graphic file that you may be updating, a WordPerfect document, or a Quattro Pro worksheet.

Importing and Exporting Tables

Paradox can directly read tables that have been created by dBASE or saved as SQL database files. If you have a dBASE table, for example, just open it as you would any Paradox table. If you have a database in some other format, however, you may still be able to use it in Paradox without retyping the same information.

When you *Import* a table, Paradox reads the information and converts it into its own format. You can import the data into an existing table, create a new table with it, or replace information in a table.

 NOTE: *When you create a new table, Paradox assigns field types and sizes for you. You can later restructure the table if you want to customize the assignments.*

Paradox can import files in the following formats:

- Fixed-length or delimited text

- dBASE

- Quattro Pro for Windows

- Quattro and Quattro Pro for DOS

- Lotus 1-2-3

- Excel, version 3.0, 4.0, or 5.0

27

To import data, select Import from the File menu to see the following options:

- Use the Import button if you want to import a file that is not plain text. In the dialog box that appears, locate the file and double-click on it.

- Use the Text Expert option to import a delimited or fixed-length file, and then follow the Expert dialog boxes as they appear.

- Use the HTML Expert option to import a table that is formatted as an HTML document.

Select an option, then follow the directions that appear onscreen in the Expert dialog boxes. When you import a table, for example, you can choose to create a new table with the imported information, to overwrite an existing table, or to add the information to an existing table. Problems encountered during the import operation will be stored in a file called PROBLEMS.DB.

When you *export* a Paradox file, Paradox converts it to a format that some other program can understand. To export a table, right-click on the table in Project Viewer and select Export from the shortcut menu to see the dialog box shown in Figure 27-1. Pull down the To Type list and select the format that you want to export the table into. Paradox will dim all but the appropriate tab in the dialog box, based on the

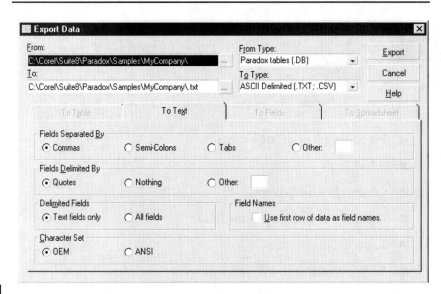

Exporting a
Paradox
table

FIGURE 27-1

type. Figure 27-1, for example, shows the options when exporting to a text file. Select options from the dialog box and then click on Export.

Creating Custom Forms

As you learned in Chapter 25, it is easy to create a form from a single table using the Form Expert. You can also use Form Expert to create forms from multiple tables or you can design the form yourself completely from scratch.

NOTE: *To create a form from scratch, right-click on the Open Form button in the toolbar or on the Form icon in Project Viewer, select New from the menu, then click on Blank. Design the form using the techniques discussed in the " Customizing Forms" section later in this chapter.*

Multiple Table Forms

In many instances, you'll want to view information from two or more tables at a time, or enter information into two tables. For example, when looking at a customer's orders, it would be helpful to view the customer information from the Clients table at the same time you're reading the information from the Orders table. A form with information from both tables, in fact, would look much like an order form on paper.

Form Expert lets you easily create a form from multiple tables, but the tables should already be linked on a key field. The Clients and Orders tables, for instances, are linked on the Customer ID fields in both tables using referential integrity. This means that the resulting form will display the orders for the customer being displayed on the form.

To create a multiple table form, right-click on the Open Form button in the toolbar or on the Form icon in Project Viewer, select New from the menu, then click on Expert. In the first Form Expert dialog box, select the Data From Two Tables option, then choose options from the series of dialog boxes that appear.

NOTE: *To use the Data from Multiple Tables option from Form Expert you must have already created a data model. Choose this option to create a form from two or more tables. In the next Expert dialog box that appears, choose the data model and then the fields to include in the form. See the "Using a Data Model" section next.*

27

- Select the master (parent) table.

- Select the detail (child) table.

- Select the fields from the tables.

- Choose the arrangement of the form—to show the master data in columns and the child in a table, both in tables, or multiple master and child data in tables.

- Select the style of text and labels.

- Enter the form's name.

Paradox creates the form and displays a message when it is complete. Click on OK to display the form, as shown in Figure 27-2. Each time you enter a number in the Customer ID field, Paradox displays the orders for that customer in the table. Click where you want to enter or edit information. Using this form, you are actually working on two tables at one time.

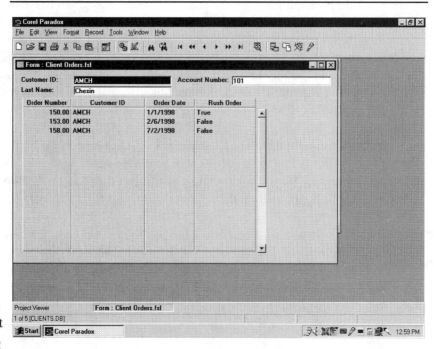

Multiple table form created with Form Expert

FIGURE 27-2

Using a Data Model

If the tables are not already related, you can create a multiple table form by first designing a data model. A *data model* is a graphic representation of the relationships between tables.

To create the form, right-click on the Open Form button in the toolbar, select New, and then click on Data Model. Paradox displays the dialog box shown in Figure 27-3.

The list box on the left shows the files in your working directory. The panel on the right shows the data model that you create. To create a data model, you indicate the tables you want to relate, then drag a line between the tables showing the parent-to-child relationship.

TIP: *Even though we're discussing multiple table forms here, you can use the Data Model option to create forms from single tables as well. Just insert one table into the design and click on OK.*

For example, to create a multiple table form for our sample database, double-click on Clients.DB and then on Orders.DB to add the tables to the design

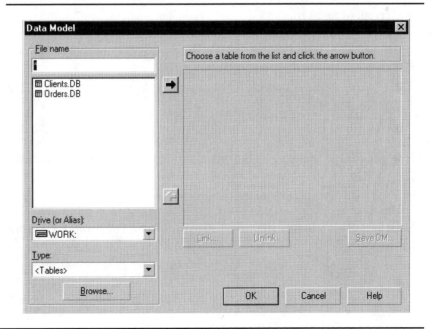

Creating a
data model

FIGURE 27-3

27

panel. Click on Clients.DB in the design panel and drag the mouse to Orders.DB. Paradox will draw a line between the tables indicating the type of relationship, from the parent to the child, as shown here:

The double-headed arrow pointing to Orders.DB indicates that it is a child table with a one-to-many relationship to the clients table.

NOTE: *If you want to change how the tables are related, click on the child table, then click on the Link button. In the dialog box that appears, you can choose the fields that you want to use for the table relation.*

Next save the data model so it is available for use with other forms and reports. Click on the Save DM buton to display the Save File As dialog box. Type a name for the model, then click on Save. Paradox saves data models with the DM extension. To use the data model when creating another form, pull down the Type list in the Data Model box and select <Data Models>, then double-click on the model name.

When the data model is complete, click on OK. Paradox displays the Design Layout dialog box shown in Figure 27-4. In this box, you choose options for the basic layout of the form.

The panel on the left of the box displays options that you can select. The three tabs on the top right of the form let you choose the options that are listed:

- *Layout* displays options for changing the layout of the parent table information.

- *Detail Tables* displays options for the child table layout.

- *Fields* lets you change the order of fields, and remove fields from the form.

The Layout options let you select to display the parent table fields by columns (down the page) or in rows (across the page). The Style options let you choose how to arrange the fields:

- *Single-Record* shows one record at a time—you can deselect the Fields Before Tables option to display the child fields before the parent fields.

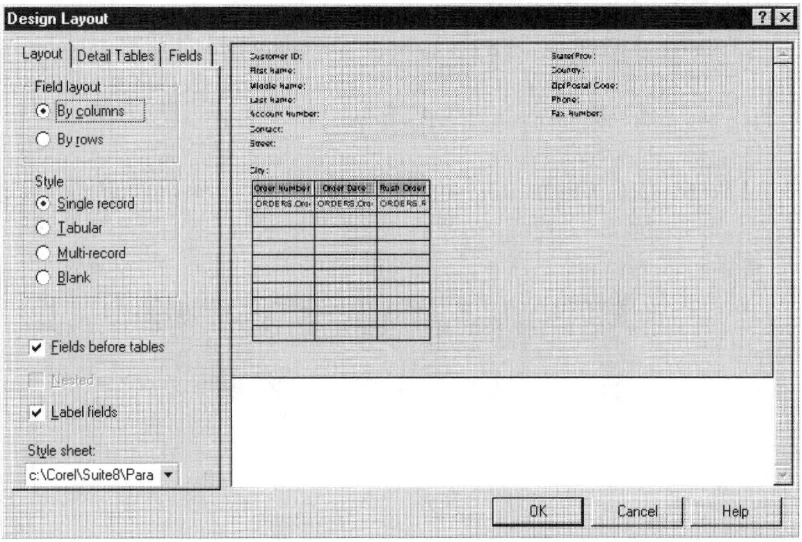

Designing
the layout
of a
multiple
table form
using a data
model

FIGURE 27-4

■ *Tabular* shows multiple master records in a table.

■ *Multi-Record* displays multiple records in columns—you can choose the Nested option and Paradox displays the child records within the box showing the parent record.

■ *Blank* removes all of the fields from the layout, but lets you add them manually in the design window using the Field tool.

If you deselect Label Fields, Paradox removes the field labels. The Style Sheet list contains predefined form designs. Pull down the list and select a design to see how it appears in the preview panel.

The Detail Tables page of the dialog box lets you show the detail fields as a table or in record format, with multiple records per page. If you choose record format you can also choose how the records are arranged: horizontally across the page, vertically down the page, or both across and down.

When you're pleased with the sample layout, click on OK to display the form in design view, then customize the form as you want.

27

Data Model Designer

Paradox also lets you create a data model separate from the process of designing a form as you just learned. You can then save the data model, and retrieve it when you need it for the design process. Here's how:

1. Select Data Model Designer from the Tools menu to see the dialog box shown here.

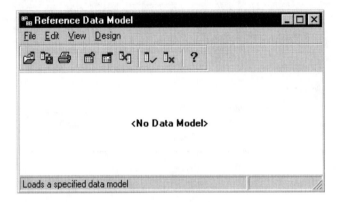

2. Click on the Add Table button to see a list of tables in the working directory

3. Click on the first table you want to add.

4. Hold down the CTRL key and click on any other tables.

5. Click on Open.

6. Click on the parent table, and drag to the child table. Paradox will draw a line between the tables indicating the type of relationship, from the parent to the child.

7. Click on the Save Data Model button to display the Save File As dialog box.

8. Type a name for the model, then click on Save.

Customizing Forms

Even though Form Expert offers a number of options, it may still not produce the exact layout that you want. Fortunately, Paradox lets you manually create and modify forms in a special design window.

To modify the design of a form, right-click on the form's name in Project Viewer and choose Design from the shortcut menu. If the form is open, click on the Form Design button on the toolbar. The design of the form appears, as shown in Figure 27-5, along with the form design toolbar with these buttons. Table 27-1 describes the design form toolbar.

NOTE: *When you start with a blank form, this same window and toolbar appear but without any form displayed.*

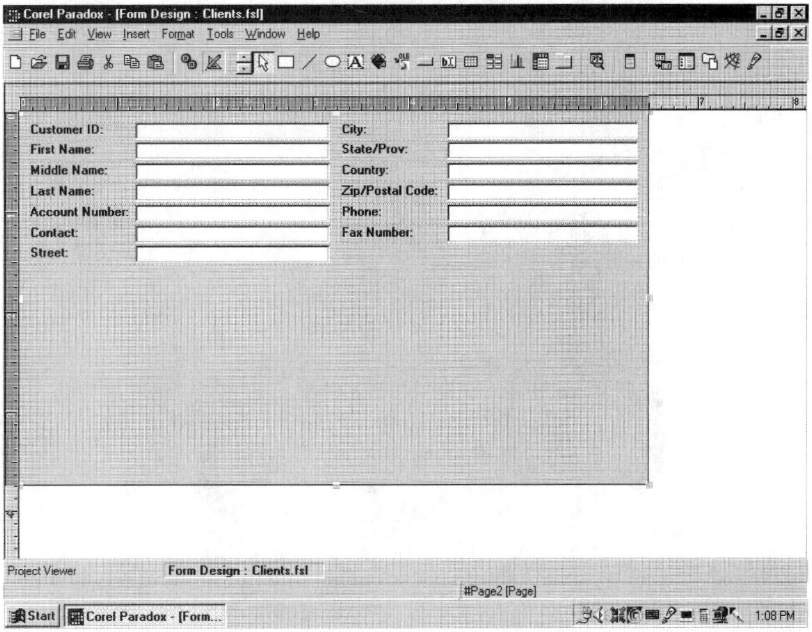

Design
window for
customizing
a form

■ **FIGURE 27-5**

27

Button	Name	Description
	New	Displays the New dialog box.
	Open Form	Lets you open another form into the design window.
	Save Form	Saves the current form.
	Print	Prints a copy of the form design.
	Cut	Deletes the object and places it in the clipboard.
	Copy	Places a copy of the object in the clipboard.
	Paste	Inserts the contents of the clipboard into the form.
	Run Form	Shows the form with the table data.
	Design Form	Displays the form in the design window.
	Scroll Bar	Scrolls additional tools into view.
	Selection Arrow	Selects object.
	Box	Draws squares and rectangles.
	Line	Draws straight lines.

The Design
Form
Toolbar

TABLE 27-1

Button	Name	Description
	Ellipse	Draws circles and ellipses.
	Text	Adds text labels.
	Graphic	Inserts a graphic.
	OLE	Inserts objects from other applications.
	Button	Inserts pushbuttons, radio buttons, and checkboxes.
	Field Tool	Insert an object that can display field values and other information.
	Table Frame	Inserts a table into the form.
	Multi-Record	Inserts an object for displaying multiple records.
	Chart	Begins Chart Expert.
	Crosstab	Inserts an empty cross tabulation object.
	Notebook	Inserts a tabbed object for storing text, fields, and objects.
	Filter	Lets you specify a filter for selecting records.
	Field Palette	Lets you add a table field to the form.

The Design Form Toolbar (*continued*)

TABLE 27-1

27

Button	Name	Description
	Data Model	Displays a dialog box for relating tables.
	Object Explorer	Displays a window listing the object's properties.
	Project Viewer	Opens the Project Viewer.
	Corel Web Site	Launches your Web browser and connects to Corel Corporation.
	Experts	Lets you select a Paradox Expert.

The Design Form Toolbar (*continued*)

TABLE 27-1

When you click on the scroll bar in the toolbar, Paradox displays these buttons:

- *List Box*—Inserts a list box object.

- *Combo Box*—Inserts a combo box, a text box with a drop-down list.

- *Spin Box*—Inserts a spin box, a text box with Up and Down buttons to increment or decrement the value.

- *Progress Bar*—Inserts a progress indicator to track the percent-finished of a process.

- *Trackbar*—Inserts a slider control to drag to select values.

- *Corel Web Server Control*—Inserts controls for performing Web server functions.

Each field on the form is surrounded by a border. Inside the border are two elements—the label that identifies the field and an empty box that will contain the field value. You can select the entire field, just the label, or just the field value. To select the entire field, click on it once. To select the field value area or the field name area, first select the field and then click on the specific area, or point to the specific area and double-click. The selected area will be surrounded by handles.

■ To move the selected object, drag it with the mouse.

■ To change the size of the object, drag one of the handles.

■ To change the label, select it and edit the text. Changing the label does not affect the contents of the field.

Every object in the form has a series of properties assigned to it, such as its color, style, and background. To change a property, right-click on it and choose Properties from the shortcut menu. Paradox displays the dialog box shown in Figure 27-6 with options for the type of object selected. Click on the tab for the properties you want to set, then select options.

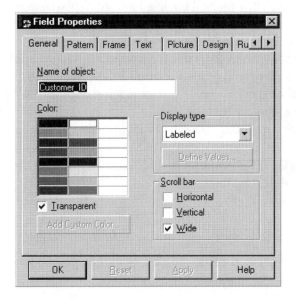

Setting
form object
properties

FIGURE 27-6

27

The Run Time properties let you control how the object behaves when the form is displayed. The properties include:

- *Visible*—Deselect to hide the object when the form is displayed.

- *Tab Stop*—Deselect to skip the field when pressing the TAB key.

- *Enabled*—Deselect to skip the field when entering data.

- *Complete Display*—Displays the full text of Memo and formatted memo field types.

- *No Echo*—Select to hide the information as you enter it, as in a password.

- *Read Only*—Select to prevent the field from being changed.

- *Choose The Next Tab Stop*—Choose the name of the next design object that you want to receive focus when the user presses TAB.

Special Fields

Most of the fields that you will use in a form are displayed as *labeled edit fields*—text boxes that let you enter or edit information into the table. But in addition to these, you can create special types of fields that make data entry easier or that perform calculations.

For example, the Orders table we created has a logical field called Rush Order. Rather than making us type the word true or false, we can display this as a checkbox field, one of the special types. Then we can just click on the checkbox to indicate a true, or leave it empty for false.

These are the special data entry types available when you define a field:

- *Labeled* is the default type with a text box to store the data and a label identifying the field.

- *Edit* is a field without an identifying label.

- A *list field* displays a list of values, from which you must select.

- A *combo box* contains a list to select from as well as a text box in which you can directly enter data.

- A *checkbox* lets you indicate only one of two possible field states—checking the box usually means that the field is selected or turned on; unchecking the box means the field is not selected or turned off.

■ A *radio button field* displays the possible values you can enter into the field—click on the button for your choice.

To change a field type, right-click on the field in design view and choose Properties. In the General tab, pull down the Display Type list and choose the type.

If you select a List, Radio Button, or Checkbox type, click on the Define Values buttons, then specify the values you want the field to offer. For example, with a check box you enter the values the field will have when the box is checked or unchecked. For lists and radio buttons you enter the items in the list or displayed with each button, as shown here. You'll learn more about these options next.

Creating a New Field

You can add new fields to a form to help in data entry or to provide additional functionality. For example, you can add a field that displays a clock when you have a table field that requires the time—just look at the clock to see the time.

TIP: *Use the Field Pallet tool on the toolbar to add an existing table field to the form. Click on the Field Pallet button, then drag the field from the list that appears onto the form.*

To create a new field, click on the Field tool, then drag in the form where you want the field to appear. When you release the mouse, Paradox displays the first of the Field Expert dialog boxes, shown here, from which you choose the type.

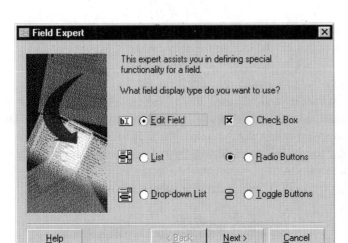

In addition to edit, list, checkbox, and radio button options, you can also choose these types:

- A *drop-down list* is an edit field that contains a text box with an arrow on its right indicating that it has a drop-down list. Either type the value into the text box or click on the arrow to display the list of choices.

- *Toggle buttons* operate much like radio buttons, but are rectangular. Clicking on one turns off any other button that is on.

 NOTE: *The Edit option in Field Expert creates a labeled text box.*

The next Expert dialog box asks if you want the field to be attached to a field in the table. If you select Attach Field, you then choose the field you want to attach it to. By attaching it to a table field, the value you enter or select in the special field will be inserted into the attached field. If you do not attach it to a field, the value you enter only appears on the form. It is not saved with the table or with the record. Use fields like this when you want to print a value with the record, and do not mind if the value is lost afterward.

The next Expert dialog box depends on your choice of type. For each button, type the label you want to appear with it and press ENTER. You can also sort the items, manually change their order, and edit or delete an item. When your list or other selects are done, click on next. If you selected a list or drop-down list, Expert asks if you want to enter the list yourself, take the list from the current data in a table, or load the list when you use the form. Choosing to load the list when you use the form ensures that the most current data available will be listed, creating a lookup-type function.

In the next Expert dialog box you enter the label for the field and choose an initial value. If you select an edit field, you can also choose from standard functions, such as the clock. For a drop-down list field, you can choose from these options:

- Wrap-around scrolling

- Drop list on arrival

- Require values to exit

- Disable editing of field

- Windows browser behavior

- Auto-select closest match

The final Expert dialog box lets you pick the size and style of the frame that surrounds the objects. The options are 8 or 10 point, with no frame, raised, recessed, shadowed, or Windows 3D frame, and an LED readout style.

 NOTE: *Most of the special functions for edit fields are for advanced uses to program in ObjectPal, the Paradox macro language.*

Using a Defined Field

A defined field is one that performs some mathematical operation or displays a value generated by a Paradox function.

One of the rules of creating a database is not to include a field in the table that contains a value that can be calculated from other fields. If you have fields called *Quantity* and *Cost,* you do not need a field to store their product to show the value of the stock on hand. Instead, whenever you want to display this type of information, you perform the calculations in a form, report, or query.

To add a calculated field, click on the Field tool and drag on the form where you want the field to appear. When you release the mouse, the first Field Expert dialog

27

box appears. Click on Cancel to close the Expert, right-click on the field, and choose Define Field from the shortcut menu. Paradox displays the Define Field Object dialog box, shown here:

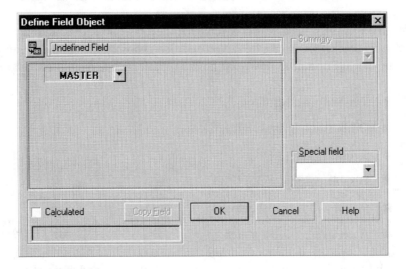

- If you created the form from a single table with Form Expert, the word "Master" on the drop-down list indicates that the list contains the fields in the master (parent) table.

- If you are creating a form from two tables created with the Data From Two Tables option of Form Expert, you'll see lists labeled Master for the parent table and Detail for the child table, as well as a line showing the relationship between the tables.

- If you created the form using a data model and the Data From Multiple Tables option from Form Expert, the table name will appear on each list.

To simply display a value from a table field in the special field, pull down the field list for the table containing the field and click on the field name. At the bottom of the field list you can also choose to display the table name, the record number, the total number of records, or the total number of fields. You choice will replace the term "Undefined Field."

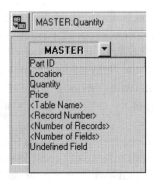

To perform a summary operation on a field, select the field from the list, then pull down the Summary list and choose from these options:

- *Sum* calculates the total of all values in the field.

- *Count* displays the number of records that have a value in the field.

- *Min* displays the smallest value in the field for the entire table.

- *Max* displays the largest value in the field for the entire table.

- *Avg* displays the average of all of the values, ignoring blank fields.

- *Std* displays the standard deviation.

- *Var* displays the variance.

To display a special field, make sure that the Calculated checkbox is clear, pull down the Special Field list, and choose from these options:

- *Today* to display the current date.

- *Now* to display the time.

- *Timestamp* to display the time and date.

- *Page Number* to display the number of the page.

- *Number of Pages* to display the total number of pages.

The Now and Timestamp functions display a running digital clock.

27

To perform a calculation on field values, click on the Calculated checkbox. In the box below the Calculated checkbox you enter a formula that performs the calculation in the field. To represent a field's value, use the syntax [TableName.Field]—the table and field names separated by a period, and enclosed in brackets. Using the same inventory example, the formula to compute the value of stock when only the inventory table is used would be [Master.Quantity] * [Master.Cost].

You must use the table name shown on the list. If the lists are labeled Master and Detail, you must use those names instead of the table name itself. If you created the form from a data model and the table names appear on the lists, use the table name itself in the expression, as on [Inventory.Quantity]*[Inventory.Cost].

Instead of typing the table and field names into the formula, you can copy them from the field list. Pull down the list next to the table name, click on the field you want to add to the formula, then click on the Copy Field button. Click in the text box and add any operators or literal values.

Although we generally think of calculated fields for use with numbers, you can also perform calculations with dates and alpha fields. The calculation [Master.Order Date] + 30, for example, displays the date 30 days from the order. With alpha fields, you can combine fields and literals in a process called *concatenation.* For example, the Clients table has fields called First Name, Middle Name, and Last Name. To display the client's full name on the form, use the calculation [Master.First Name]+" "+[Master.Middle Name]+" "+[Master.Last Name]. You've concatenated the three name fields into one.

You need to explicitly add a space between the names. The string " " is a space between two quotation marks. Any literal that you want added to the expression must be in quotes, including spaces, as in "My best friend "+[Master.First Name]. In this case, there is a space between the word *friend* and the closing quotation mark so a space appears between the word and the field value.

Customizing Reports

Paradox lets you create custom reports in much the same way that you created custom forms.

If you right-click on the Open Report button and select New, you'll see similar choices. You can start with a blank report, use Expert to take you step-by-step through creating a single table or multiple table report, and you can select Data Model. The Data Model option, by the way, works *exactly* the same for reports as it does for forms. There is one other option, Label Expert, that we'll look at next.

Label Expert

You use the Label Expert in much the same way as creating labels in WordPerfect. The Expert boxes offer these options:

- Select from a list of standard label formats or design your own.

- Select the table or query that contains the fields to be included.

- Choose font, type size, and style to use for the label text.

- Select the order in which labels will be filled with the data, as shown here.

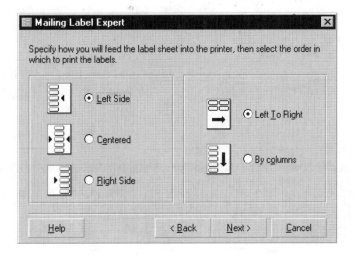

- Layout the fields and other text or punctuation on the label form.

- Name the report, and choose to display the labels on screen, print the labels immediately, or display the report in design view.

The Report Design Window

Because reports are typically more than one page long, they contain more elements than forms. These elements are divided into bands that divide the report into sections, as shown in Figure 27-7.

- The report header band appears only at the start of the report.

- The page header band appears at the top of every page.

27

- The record band contains the body of the report.

- The page footer band appears at the bottom of every page.

- The report footer band appears only at the end of the report.

The default report header includes the Today field that prints the current date, the name of the report title, and the page field to print the page number. You can also add group bands. Group bands divide the records into groups, so you can create and display subtotals and totals.

All of the techniques that we discussed for forms, such as adding special fields and changing the layout, apply to reports as well.

Custom Queries

Using queries to simply display fields and records only touches on their potential. With queries, you can perform calculations on fields, and even change, insert, and

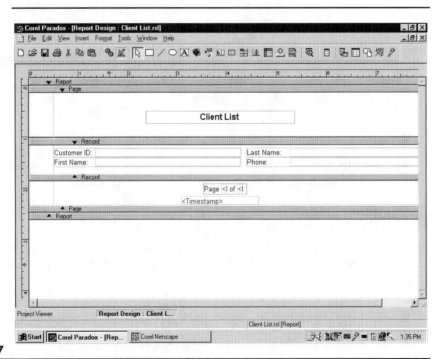

The Report design window

FIGURE 27-7

delete information from your tables. The query is really an alternative way to interact with your table, especially if you create live queries rather than simply display and use the Answer table.

Performing Calculations in Queries

You can use calculations in a query for much the same purpose as on a form—to display information that is derived from data already in the table. To use fields for calculations, you have to create one or more *example elements*. An example element is simply a name that you assign the field. You then use that name in the formula. To create an example element, click in the query field, press F5, then type the example element name. Paradox displays the name in color to differentiate it from other elements in the query field, such as criteria.

NOTE: *An example element name can contain any alphabetic or numeric characters, but no other characters or spaces. Invalid characters will appear in the normal text color and will not be part of the example element name.*

You enter the calculation in the query field of any field in the query image, using the CALC keyword and typing example elements by pressing F5 before each name. For example, this query image would calculate and display the cost of inventory:

Inventory.DB	Part ID	Location	Quantity	Price
☐	☑ ▓▓▓▓	☐ CALC qty * cost	☐ qty	☐ cost

The example elements *qty* and *cost* were entered into the appropriate fields, then the calculation entered. When you run the query, Paradox creates a new column at the end of the Answer table and displays the results:

	Part ID	Quantity * Price
1	HG765	$870.00
2	JB960	$138.00
3	JK654	$130.41
4	TY876	$1,120.00

The title of the result column, however, is the formula. For a more meaningful name use the AS keyword, as in CALC QTY * PRICE AS Total Cost. The text following the AS keyword is used as the column label.

27

TIP: *You must be in Edit Mode to edit the contents of a query field.*

You can type the calculation to any field, even one that has a criteria or example element—just enter a comma before typing the CALC keyword.

As an example, let's create a calculation for the Orders table. The calculation will display the number of days that have elapsed since each order.

1. Right-click on the Queries icon in Project Viewer and select New.

2. Double-click on the Orders table.

3. Click on the checkboxes for the Order Number, Customer ID, and Order Date fields.

4. Click on the query field for Order Date.

5. Press F5 and type **ODATE** as the example element name, and then type **,** (a comma).

6. Type **CALC** and press the SPACEBAR.

7. Type **today**, the keyword that represents the current date.

8. Type a minus sign (hyphen).

9. Press F5 to create an example element and type **odate**.

10. Press the SPACEBAR and type **AS Days Since Order**. The query field is now this:

Orders.DB	Order Numb	Customer IC	Order Date	Rush Order
☐	☑	☑	☑ ODATE, CALC today - odate AS Days Since Order	☐

11. Click on the Run Query button. Paradox performs the calculation and displays the Answer table.

12. Close the Answer table to return to the query image.

NOTE: *You must use a comma to separate the example element, which names the field, from a keyword that follows the element.*

You can also use calculations to concatenate alpha fields. Use example elements in the First Name and Last Name fields, for example, to display the full name with the expression CALC First + " " + Last AS Full Name.

Summary Operators

The word *today* is a built-in keyword that tells Paradox to use the current date. There are other keywords that you can use in queries to perform summary operations:

- *Average* calculates the average of the values in a group.
- *Count* displays the number of items in a group.
- *Max* displays the largest value in a group.
- *Min* displays the smallest value in a group.
- *Sum* calculates the total of values in a group.

When you use the plan check mark in a field, Paradox does not display duplicate records. The record that does appear is a group record because it represents all of the records that have those values. For example, if you create a query with the Orders table and just click on Customer ID, the Answer table will list one record for each client that has placed an order. The only Customer IDs that do not appear are for clients who have not yet ordered. If we want to display the number of orders for each client, we'd use the Count operator.

Now suppose you were interested in when clients place orders. You want to see if certain days of the week are more busy than others. In this case, you'd only check the date field and use the COUNT operator.

The trick is to limit the fields in the query to those that will display group records. If you select both the Customer ID and Date fields, you probably will see a record for every order. The count for each will be one, because there is only one order for each client on a specific day.

Try this now. The query image should still be on your screen. Delete the example elements and calculation from the query, and deselect all of the fields except Customer ID. Click in the query field for Order Date and type **CALC count AS Number of Orders**. The query image should appear like this:

Orders.DB	Order Numk	Customer IC	Order Date	Rush Order
		☑	CALC count AS Number of Orders	

27

Run the query. Paradox displays one record for each client who places an order. It counts the number of records that contain dates for each client. Close the Answer table to return to the query image.

Creating MultiTable Queries

Just as forms and reports can get information from more than one table, so can queries.

If you are starting a new query, hold down the CTRL key and click on each of the tables in the Select File dialog box. When you click Open, the query window appears with query images for all of the tables. If you already started the query, click on the Add Table button in the query toolbar, then select the other table from the dialog box that appears. In the query images, you select fields, enter criteria, and insert example elements and calculations just as you would for a single table.

 NOTE: *To delete a table from the query window, click on the Remove Table button and double-click on the table name in the dialog box.*

However, before running the query you must tell Paradox which fields to use to link the tables by entering the same example element in the linked fields. You can use the F5 key to type the example element names, or you can use the Join Tables button.

Let's try this now. Suppose you want to list the last name and telephone number of each client and the dates of their orders. The order date is in the Orders table and the last name is in the Clients table, so we need two tables for the query. The Orders table should already be on your screen. Follow these steps.

1. Delete the calculation from the Order Date field and remove the checkmark from the Customer ID field.

2. Click on the Add Table button to display the Select File dialog box.

3. Double-click on the clients.db table to add its query image.

4. Click on the checkboxes for the Last Name and Phone fields in the Clients table.

5. Click on the Order Date checkbox in the Orders table.

6. Click on the Join Tables button in the toolbar. When you point to a field in the query image, the mouse pointer will appear with an icon of two tables.

7. Click in the Customer ID field in the Orders table. Paradox inserts an example element named Join1.

8. Click in the Customer ID field in the Clients table. Paradox inserts the same Join 1 example element.

TIP: *To join the tables on more than one field, click on the Join Tables button again and repeat the process. The example elements will be numbered consecutively.*

9. Run the query.

Paradox shows the selected fields from the tables. Now close the Answer table and the query window without saving.

Changing Tables with Queries

Paradox provides three special types of queries that let you actually change the contents of the table when you run the query:

■ An *Insert* query adds records to a table.

■ A *Delete* query removes records from a table.

■ A *Changeto* query changes the values in a table.

When you run these queries, Paradox makes the changes to the table but displays the inserted, deleted, or changed records in a temporary table. If you made a mistake, you can restore the original records before exiting Paradox.

To create an Insert or Delete query, right-click in the box under the table name in the query image, then choose Insert or Delete from the shortcut menu that appears, as shown here.

27

The menu also contains the Set command that lets you group records together. To create a Changeto query, you must type **CHANGETO** in the query field that you want to change.

 NOTE: *Do not check any fields when creating an insert, delete, or changeto query.*

Inserting Records

An Insert query lets you add records to a table in two ways. You can type the information that you want to add into the query image or you can insert records from another table.

To insert a record yourself, right-click under the table name in the query image and choose Insert. Next, in the query fields, type the values that you want to insert in the new record. When you run the query, Paradox will create a new record in the table with the information you typed. What's different is it will also display an Answer table called Inserted.DB that shows you which records were actually inserted into the table.

To insert a record from another table, you must add both tables to the query image. The tables do not have to have the same structure. The table that you are taking the record from is called the *source table*. The table to which you are adding the record is called the *destination table*. Add the two tables to the query image then use this procedure:

1. Right-click below the destination table's name and select Insert.

2. In the source table, enter criteria in the query fields. Paradox will use the criteria to select the records that it will insert into the destination table.

3. Enter matching example elements in the fields that you want to insert. Use either the F5 key or the Join Tables button as you learned how to do to create multiple table queries. The example elements must be the same in matching fields, but the field names do not have to match.

4. Run the query.

For example, this query image selects records from a table called Prospects that have a value of TRUE in the Returned Card field, and inserts them into the Clients table:

Prospects.DB	Customer IC	Returned C;	First Name	Middle Nam	Last Name	Account Nu	Contact	Street	City	
■	□ join1	□ True	□ join2	□ join3	□ join4	□ join5	□ join6	□ join8	□ join9	

Clients.DB	Customer IC	First Name	Middle Nam	Last Name	Account Nu	Contact	Street	City	State/Prov
Insert ■	□ join1	□ join2	□ join3	□ join4	□ join5	□ join6	□ join8	□ join9	□ join10

Deleting Records

A delete query works the same as a regular query that selects records. The difference is that it deletes the records that match the criteria rather then merely displaying them in an Answer table.

To create a delete query, create and run a regular query (without choosing Delete from the shortcut menu in the query image) using criteria to select the records that you'll want to delete. When the Answer table appears, confirm that it contains only records that you want to delete. If it does not, return to the query image and modify the conditions. When the Answer table contains only records you want to delete, return to the query image, right-click under the table name, and select Delete from the shortcut menu. Finally, run the query again, this time to actually delete the records. Paradox will display a temporary Answer table called Deleted.DB showing the deleted records.

Changing Records

A Changeto query lets you change the values in a table. Although you can always edit the table in a table window or using a form, a query lets you perform a mass update. This means that you can change any number of records at one time, such as increasing all prices by 10 percent.

To create a Changeto query, enter an example element in the field you want to change followed by a comma. Type the keyword **Changeto**, then the value you want to insert in the field. For example, to replace the phone number for the client named Adam Chesin, you'd use this query image:

Clients.DB	Customer IC	First Name	Middle Nam	Last Name	Phone	Account Nu	Con
□	□	□ Adam	□	□ Chesin	□ tele, changeto 555-5555	□	□

We've changed the order of the field in the query image so you can see the fields that we've used. The query locates the record using the information in the First Name and Last Name fields. The change was made by using an example element and the Changeto keyword in the field we are changing. You must use an example element in the changed field. When you run the query, Paradox displays the temporary Answer table called Changed.DB showing the original contents of the changed records.

 NOTE: *You can change more than one field by using an example element and the Changeto keyword in each field you want to change.*

Here's another example. This time we are using the field we are changing as the criterion as well. It locates all records in the 19006 zip code, and changes the code to 19006-1234:

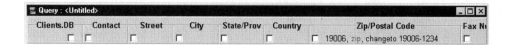

You can also use a calculation to modify a value. This query, for instance, increases the cost of all items by 5 percent.

Notice that the field starts with an example element which is then used in a formula following the Changeto keyword.

Creating Charts

Sometimes the best way to get a point across is to use a chart. A chart can graphically show a trend or relationship that would be difficult to explain in words. Each of the Corel WordPerfect Suite 8 major applications has a charting feature. Although those from WordPerfect, Quattro Pro, and Presentations are similar, Paradox uses its own brand of charting tool. You create a chart as part of a form or report.

TIP: *To create a chart directly onto a new form or report, use the Chart Expert. Refer to the section "Paradox Experts" later in this chapter to learn how to access the Chart Expert.*

To start, open the form or report in design view. Then in design view, click on the Chart Tool button, and drag in the design window where you want the chart to appear. When you release the mouse, Paradox displays the first Chart Expert dialog box shown in Figure 27-8. Let's review the series of Expert dialog boxes.

■ In the first box you select the table or query that contains the data that you want to chart. By default, the table on which the form is based will be listed, but you can also choose from any other table or query in the working directory.

 TIP: *If you already have both a form and report open, the first Expert dialog box may ask if you want to place the chart on a new form or a new report. To insert the chart on an open design window, close the other window where you do not want to insert the chart.*

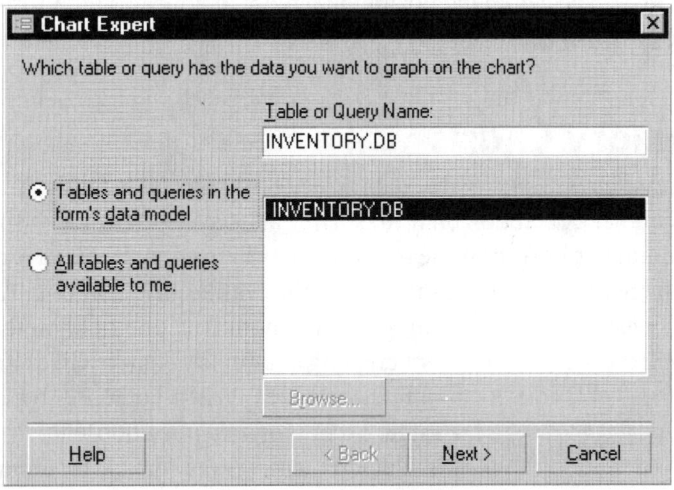

Creating a chart in a form or report

FIGURE 27-8

Chart Expert ✕

Which table or query has the data you want to graph on the chart?

Table or Query Name:

INVENTORY.DB

⦿ Tables and queries in the form's data model

◯ All tables and queries available to me.

INVENTORY.DB

Browse...

Help   ‹ Back   Next ›   Cancel

27

- In the second box you choose whether to create a tabular or summary chart. A *tabular chart* displays the values of one field along the X-axis and one field along the Y-axis. A *summary chart* plots summary values along the X-axis and only shows unique values.

The Expert dialog boxes that follow depend on the chart type. We'll assume for now that you selected the tabular chart.

- In the third box you choose the design of the chart—the options are two- and three-dimensional area, bar, column, line, pie, rotated bar, and stacked bar charts.

- In the fourth box you select the field to use for the X-axis.

- In the fifth box you choose one or more fields to plot their values on the Y-axis. Each field you choose becomes another series plotted in the chart. Multiple fields will appear as a separate pie chart.

- In the sixth box you may enter the chart title and subtitle, and the axis titles. If you do not enter a title, Paradox will use the name of the table.

When you click on Finish in the final box, Paradox displays a general interpretation of the chart on the form or report in the design window, as shown in Figure 27-9. The actual data from the table will appear on the form or report when you view it onscreen.

Summary Charts

Summary charts do not use the data directly from the table for the Y-axis, but perform some summary operation on it first. They also group the values used for the X-axis. A summary chart can be either one-dimensional or two-dimensional. A one-dimensional chart summarizes the values in just one field, whereas a two-dimensional summary can group on more than one field on the X-axis.

The Expert dialog boxes for creating a summary chart in Chart Expert are similar, but with several additional options or boxes. When you choose a one-dimensional summary, the boxes are the same, except for how you choose the Y-axis field. When you add a field to the Y-axis, Paradox asks you to choose a summary operation— Sum, Max, Min, or Average. When you create a two-dimensional chart, you will be asked for the X-axis field and then for an additional field to use for grouping, called the Group By field.

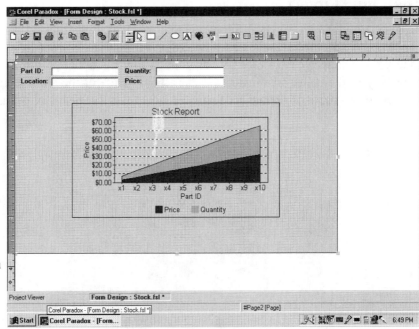

A representation of the chart in design view

FIGURE 27-9

Customizing Charts

When you are done with Chart Expert, your chart appears on the form or report in design view. You can now modify every element of the chart, even change the chart type and select different fields.

The best way to modify the chart is by *object inspection*. Picture the chart as being composed of a series of separate elements, or objects, such as the X-axis, Y-axis, titles, background, legend, as well as the individual slices in a pie chart, bars in a bar chart, and the walls of three-dimensional charts.

When you point to an object in the chart in design view, the mouse pointer will appear as a straight up-pointing arrow. To customize an object point to it and right-click to display a shortcut menu. The options that appear when you right-click depend on the object. The shortcut menu will have a title showing the name of the object. For example, when you right-click on the background of the chart area, the menu will be titled Background and you can change its color and pattern. The shortcut menus for other objects offer quite a few options, so let's review the most commonly used.

27

The Chart Object

To select options for the overall appearance of the chart, right-click on an area that is not any other object. You'll know you're pointing in the correct area when the mouse pointer changes to look like a diagonal arrow, not an up-pointing one. This is usually in the blank area inside the chart but outside of the charted area. The shortcut menu contains options for formatting the overall appearance of the chart.

- *Properties* set color and pattern surrounding the charted area, type of frame surrounding the chart, and design and run-time properties.

- *Object Explorer* opens a separate window displaying object properties.

- *Define Chart* displays the Define Chart dialog box for changing the data type and fields.

- *Data Type* lets you select from tabular, one-dimensional, and two-dimensional charts.

- *Chart Type* lets you change the chart type.

- *Min X Values* is the minimum number of values on the X-axis.

- *Max X Values* is the maximum number of values on the X-axis.

- *Options* lets you show or hide the title, legend, grid, axis, and labels.

- *Cut, Copy*, and *Paste* together allow you to make copies of the chart.

- *Copy to Toolbar* saves the properties of the chart as the default settings for new charts.

Formatting Axis

The shortcut menu options for the X-axis and Y-axis options are almost the same. For both, you can choose a new field to chart and edit the title. With the X-axis, you can choose to alternate the labels on two lines. The Y-axis menu lets you change the scale of values along the axis, and change their number format.

Formatting a Series

Each field that you plot along the Y-axis is a series. The series is identified by the bars, area, or lines that represent its values. If you have two fields on the axis, then you'll have two series—each represented by a number of bars or an area or line. If you have a bar or column chart, right-click on any bar or column in the series to format the entire series.

For each series, you can change the field used to create it, the color and pattern of its display, or remove it from the chart.

NOTE: *With a pie chart, the entire pie represents one series. You can right-click on an individual slice to change its color or pattern, and to explode it away from the rest of the pie.*

Formatting Text

To modify the title or subtitle, right-click on the chart title so the shortcut menu is titled Title Box. In addition to the Define Chart area, you can change the text, color, font, and style of the title and subtitle. The Use Default option will quickly return to the default table name as the title, and remove any subtitle that you've entered. You can also change the background color and pattern of the text.

Paradox Experts

You've been using various Experts throughout these chapters. To make the Experts easier to access, you can display a dialog box of them all by clicking on the Perfect Expert button on any toolbar. You'll see the Paradox Experts box shown in Figure 27-10. In addition to all of the experts that you've used so far, you can select the Merge, Launcher, and the Crosstab experts.

The *Merge Expert* lets you merge data from a Paradox tab with a word processing document created by programs such as WordPerfect and Microsoft Word that you have installed on your system.

The *Launcher Expert* creates a tabbed form from which you can open tables, forms, queries, or reports that you specify. The form is much like the tabbed form

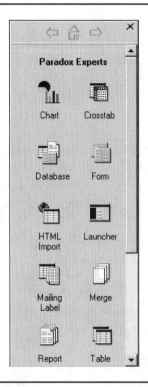

Paradox
Experts

FIGURE 27-10

that appears when you create a database with Database Expert. In addition, it can create a shortcut that you can access directly from the Windows 95 start menu under the option Paradox Launchers. Selecting the options from the start menu launches Paradox and displays the tabbed form.

The *Crosstab Expert* creates a cross tabulation much like the crosstab feature of Corel Quattro Pro discussed in Chapter 20. Figure 27-11, for example, shows a cross tabulation showing the number of orders for each client by date.

Publishing Your Data to the Internet

Paradox offers you two ways to publish your database information to the Internet:

- *HTML Table Expert* converts a table to an HTML document.

- *HTML Report Expert* converts a report to an HTML document.

To create a Web page from a table, open the table then select Publish to HTML from the File menu to display the first HTML Table Expert dialog box. In this

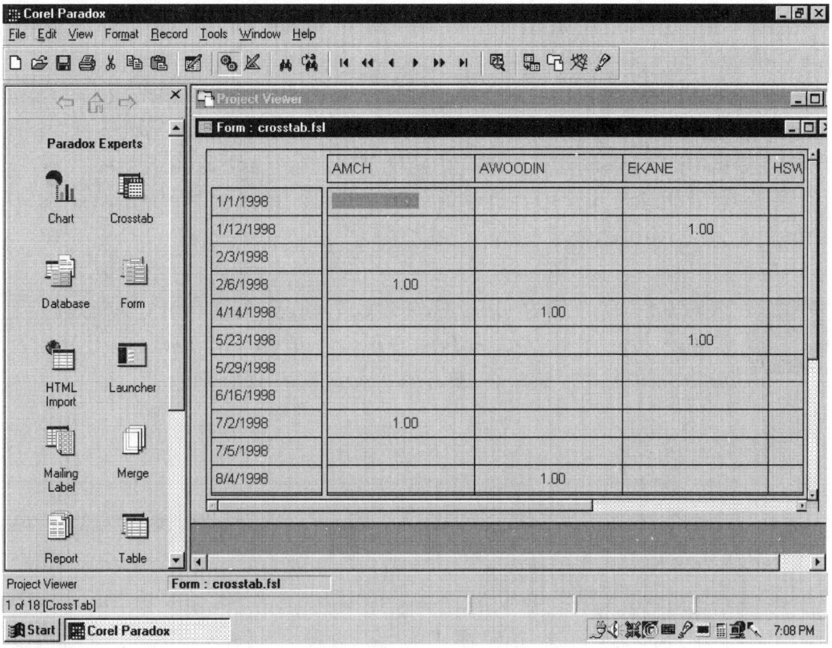

A Paradox
cross
tabulation

FIGURE 27-11

dialog box, you select the fields that you want to include in the Web page, and then click on OK.

The second Expert dialog box, shown here, lets you enter a Web page title, select to place a border around the table, center it on the page, and choose text and background colors.

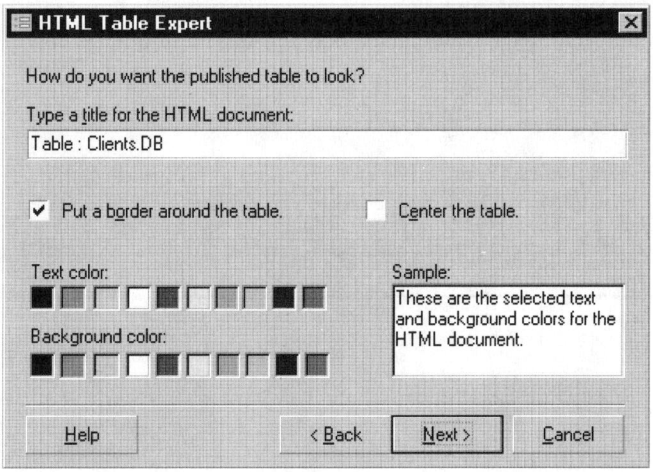

The third Expert dialog box lets you choose to create a static document or a dynamic document. A *static document* means that any information you see on the Web page that you create will also appear on the screen when the page is accessed in the Net. The Web page will not reflect any changes you make to the table after creating the page. A dynamic page takes advantage of Corel Web Server by updating the page to the current information each time the page is accessed.

The final dialog box asks if you want to launch your Web browser to display the same page, as shown in Figure 27-12.

NOTE: *HTML Report Expert operates the same way except it does not display the first dialog box. The resulting Web page displays the fields included on the report used to create the Web page.*

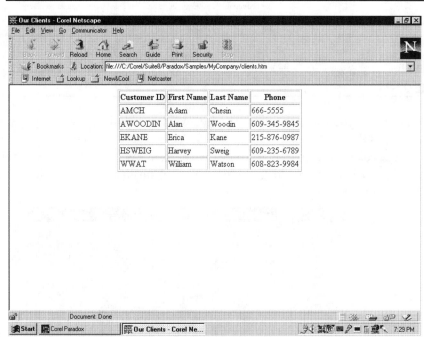

Sample
Web page

FIGURE 27-12

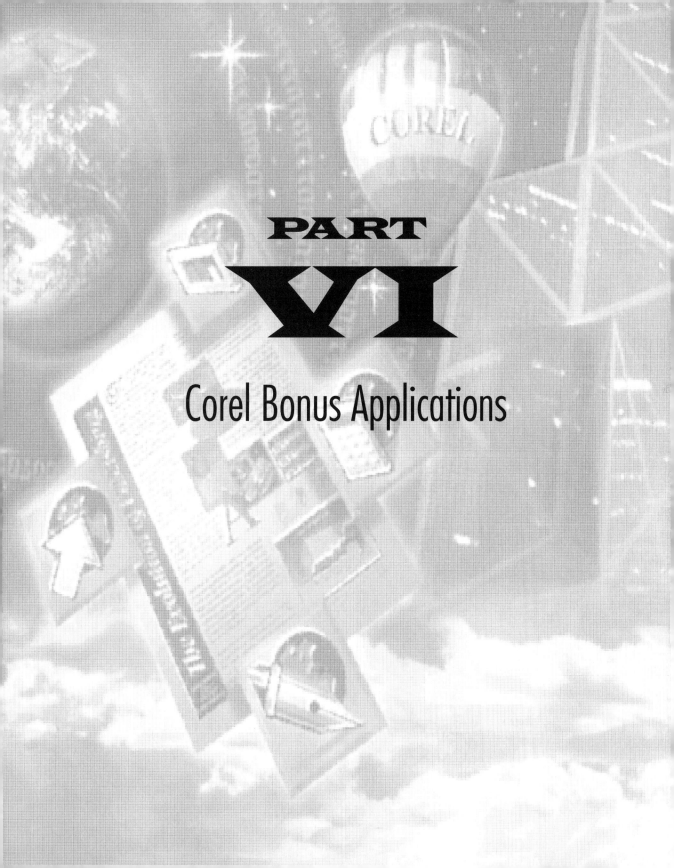

PART VI

Corel Bonus Applications

Introducing Time Line

28

Corel Time Line is a *project management* program. Project management involves organizing, scheduling, and coordinating a set of *tasks*. A task is a specific action that, together with the rest of the set of tasks, is aimed at completing a specific job, called a *project*.

Every project has a specific number of tasks, and there is a definite starting and ending point. For example, suppose your company is planning to move into a new building. That's the project, and it involves a large number of tasks, such as selecting the new location, packing equipment, moving to the new location, and unpacking. There will be a start date, when you begin planning for the move, and an end date, when you have to be moved in, unpacked, and back to business.

In general, the project management effort has three distinct phases.

You start by *gathering information* to determine the specific tasks involved, any constraints that exist, the resources available, and the relationship between tasks. Time Line won't gather the information for you, but it helps you determine what information you need.

Then, you *schedule* the tasks to find the best way to allocate resources. You have to determine, for example, in what order the tasks must be performed and what resources are available for each.

Finally, you *track* your progress as you perform the tasks, adjusting the flow of tasks and use of resources as needed, and reporting your progress to decision makers.

Time Line helps in all three phases of the project management process. While it cannot actually perform the tasks for you, it helps you get the job done on time and make the best use of your resources—personnel, hardware, and budget. It does so by letting you organize the project, schedule tasks and resources, and track your progress by developing these items:

- A *task list* that records the name, duration, start and end time, resources, and cost of every task.

- A *resource list* containing the name, type, availability, and cost rate of all resources allocated to the project.

- *Calendars* that determine the availability of personnel and other resources. There are two types of calendars—a master calendar that records the hours, days, and weeks that are available, and resources calendars that determine when each resource is available. You can also use calendars to define work shifts and day types (different hours for different days).

■ *Layouts* that let you view your project, including Gantt and PERT charts.

Projects can also be divided into subprojects to help organize your work. As an example, consider the project to move a large company to another location. The tasks of finding a location, designing, and constructing a new building are three separate projects just in their own right, carried out by people with very different skills. So, you may want to divide the project into four distinct phases—finding a location, designing the new building, constructing the new building,and actually moving into it.

You store all of the information about the project in a database, and you can use the database to record any number of projects. For example, as part of the project management process, you must record information about the personnel available for the tasks. If the same personnel will be used for more than one project, create both projects in the same database. This way, you'll be able to allocate the personnel between projects, and watch for conflicts in assignment.

To create the Time Line database, you follow seven basic steps.

1. Establish the tasks that are required to complete the project.

2. Estimate the length of time that each task takes.

3. Schedule the tasks in relation to each other.

4. Determine the resources that are available to the project.

5. Allocate the resources among the tasks.

6. Determine the cost of each task based on the resources allocated to it.

7. As the project progresses, adjust the duration, resource allocation, and task flow to meet your needs.

NOTE: *Time Line is a sophisticated management tool that can be used to plan and schedule major and complex projects. In this book, you'll learn the fundamentals of this powerful program. For additional information on Time Line, refer to the online Help system and the Corel Reference Center. You can also click on the TLSC Web Site button on the Time Line toolbar for additional information, support, and upgrades.*

Creating a Time Line Database

When you start Time Line, you'll have the opportunity to automatically create a new database. A database is actually just a file in which projects and project information are stored. Create a new database with these steps.

1. Click on Start in the Windows 95 taskbar, point to Corel WordPerfect Suite 8, point to Accessories and then click on Corel Time Line. The Welcome to Corel Time Line dialog box appears.

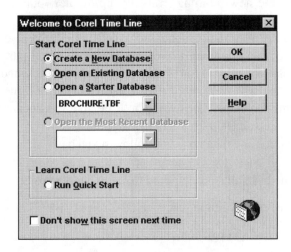

From this you can create a new database, open an existing database, open a sample database (called a Starter database) provided by Corel, or open a recently used database. You can also run Quick Start, which takes you step-by-step through the process of creating a project.

2. Click the option button labeled Create a New Database, then click on OK.

 TIP: *If you've already started Time Line, create a new database by selecting New Database from the File menu.*

You'll see the opening Time Line window, shown in Figure 28-1 with three cascaded windows—the OverView, Resource View, and Gantt View. The Time Line window also includes a toolbar.

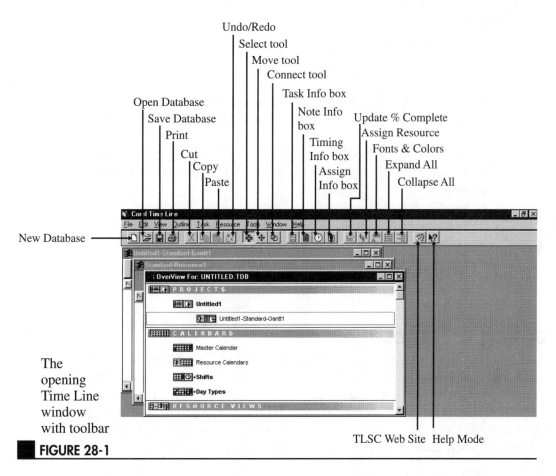

New Database

The
opening
Time Line
window
with toolbar

FIGURE 28-1

The Resource View window is a table listing information about the resources available. The Gantt View displays information about the tasks, graphically showing the flow of tasks and the relationship between them. The OverView window serves as an index to the categories of information in the database. You use this window to select, add, and delete categories of information, and to access the categories. The categories include:

- *Projects*—a list of the projects and subprojects in the database

- *Calendars*—access the Master Calendar, resource calendars, shifts, and day types.

28

- *Resource Views*—access information about the resources that are available.

- *Layouts*—lists the layouts defined for all views in the database.

- *Conditions*—criteria used to determine how tasks and resources are listed.

- *Custom Columns*—lets you define your own columns of information for the spreadsheet-like tables in which tasks and resources are displayed.

The OverView window title bar shows that the default name given the database is UNTITLED.TDB. You'll be able to change the name when you save the database, which we'll do later.

TIP: *If you perform a function that might cause a scheduling problem, Time Line will display the Co-Pilot help window. Select options from the Co-Pilot window to complete or cancel your action so Time Line can help you keep track.*

Creating a Project

Now that you've started a new Time Line database, the next step it to create a project. The new database actually has a blank project called Untitled1, as shown in the Projects section of the Time Line window. Before adding tasks to the project, however, you should give it a more meaningful name, and if you're not starting the project immediately, assign it a starting date. Time Line will use the start date to determine where tasks are displayed in the Gantt chart and other views.

1. Click on the word Unitled1 that appears in boldface in the Projects category of the OverView window.

2. Type **Company Move** as the project name.

TIP: *To add other projects to the database, use the New Project command from the File menu.*

3. Pull down the Tools menu and select Project Information to see the dialog box shown here. The current date will automatically appear in the Project Start Date box.

Project Information

General Information

Project **N**ame: | Company Move

Manager: |

Project **S**tart Date: | 7/22/1997

OK

Cancel

Help

Project Statistics

Tasks: 0   Resources: 0

	Baseline	Current Project
Start:		7/22/1997
End:		7/22/1997
Duration:		0d
Effort:		0d
Cost:		

4. Double-click in the Project Start Date box and type **11/16/98**, the date we plan to start our project. You can also enter the project manager's name. You'll learn about the Project Statistics panel later.

5. Click OK. Notice that your own project name replaces Untitled in the Project category area.

Entering Tasks

It is now time to enter tasks using the Gantt window, shown in Figure 28-2. The window has two sections. The Spreadsheet pane on the left lists information about the tasks, in columns labeled Task Name, Resources, Start Date, Effort, Duration, End Date, and Total Cost. The right-pointing triangle on the left of each row is called the row selector, which you use to select one or more rows in the spreadsheet. The Time Scale pane on the right graphically shows the duration, starting, and ending dates of all tasks.

NOTE: *You can display a Graph pane in the Gantt layout that illustrates resource and effort information, and you can add additional columns to the Spreadsheet pane.*

28

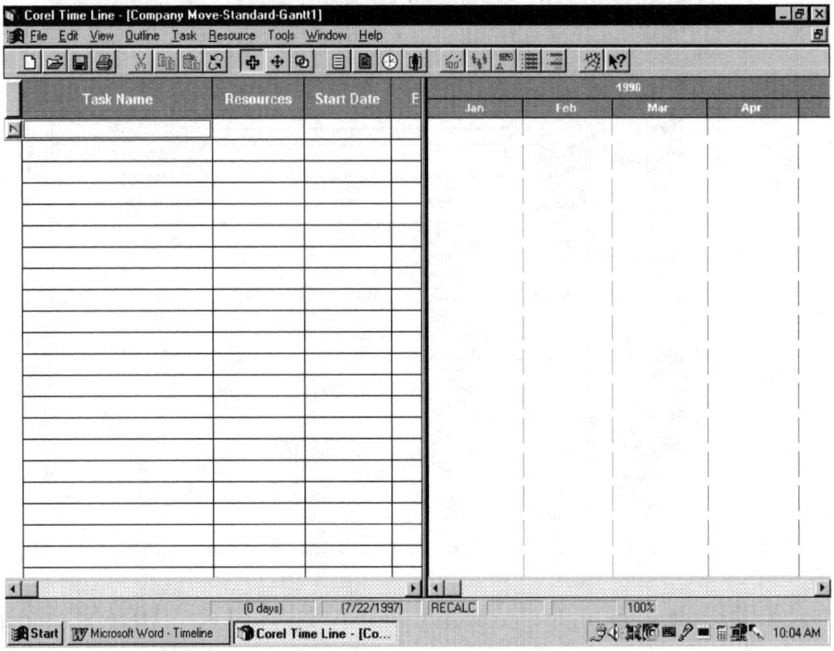

The Gantt
layout
window

FIGURE 28-2

Let's enter a number of tasks as well as two *milestones*. A milestone is not a task, but a point in the project's progress. For example, you may divide your project into phases, and mark the date that each phase ends with a label such as End of Phase 1. There is no activity involved with End of Phase 1, it only marks a goal's completion. You mark a milestone by entering 0 for the duration.

1. Double-click on Company Move-Standard-Gantt1 in the Project category. You can also click on the Gantt1 window or pull down the Window menu and select Company Move - Standard - Gantt1.

2. Maximize the window.

3. Click in the first empty cell in the Task Name column. You can also select Insert Task on the Edit menu.

4. Type **Begin the Project** and press ENTER to move to the next task.

5. Type **Select Site** and press ENTER.

6. Enter the following tasks in the same way.

> **Prepare Site**
> **Pack Equipment**
> **Move Equipment**
> **Unpack Equipment**
> **Setup Computers**
> **Move Complete**

Don't worry if you enter tasks in the wrong order, you can easily move tasks within the list, or insert and delete tasks.

- To move a task, click on it in the Task Name list, then press CTRL-UP to move the task up, or CTRL-DOWN to move the task down. You can also choose Move Up or Move Down from the Task menu, or click on the Move tool in the toolbar and drag the task up or down.

- To delete a task, click on it and press DEL, or select Delete Task from the Edit menu.

- To insert a task, click on the task that you want to precede the new one, then press INSERT, or select Insert Tasks from the Edit menu.

Entering Estimated Effort and Duration

Once your tasks are entered, you estimate how much time each task takes to complete. Time Line lets you use two methods—fixed-duration and effort-based.

Fixed-duration tasks are those that take a specific amount of time regardless of the resources that you allocate to it. For example, if you are planning a three-day seminar, the actual duration of the seminar is fixed. You must complete it in three days, no more and no fewer.

Effort-based tasks are those that can be accomplished faster by applying additional resources, or slower by removing resources. Installing cable for a new computer system, for example, may take one week if you use one installer, or just three days if you use two installers.

When you enter a duration, you can designate the amount of time in hours (h), days (d), weeks (w), months (m), and years (y). The default value is days. If you just enter 4, for example, Time Line assumes you mean 4 days.

For both types of tasks, begin by entering the time in the Effort column of the Gantt spreadsheet. You enter the duration of fixed-duration tasks using whatever time the task has been allocated. For an effort-based task, however, enter the total time the task takes in hours, days, weeks, or months. If you use hours, for example, assume that you have one person working on the task. Don't worry that you may have more people actually assigned to the task—Time Line will figure everything out for you. For instance, suppose a certain effort-based task requires 24 hours of work if only one person were assigned to it. Type **24h** in the Effort column. If you later assign three people to the task, Time Line computes that the task's duration is actually just one day. Three persons working together for one eight-hour day accomplish 24 hours of work.

Before you enter the duration for each task, look at how Time Line displays the information in the Gantt chart.

1. Drag the line between the Spreadsheet and Time Scale panes to the right to see the Effort and Duration columns.

2. Scroll the Time Scale pane to see November 1998, as shown in Figure 28-3.

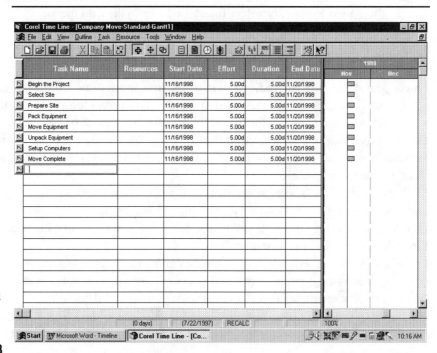

Task bars in the Gantt chart

FIGURE 28-3

Time Line has added task bars to the Gantt chart. The size of the bar indicates the duration of the tasks, currently set at the default 5 days each. When you view a Gantt chart, keep in mind that the bars indicate the number of calendar days, not just working days. If a tasks takes 7 days, for example, the bar will appear nine days long—two of the nine days are non-working weekend days. You will learn in the next chapter how to modify the calendar to adjust working and non-working days, including holidays and vacation days.

 NOTE: *The solid vertical line down the Gantt chart in the middle of November indicates the project start date.*

Now enter the duration for each task.

1. Click in the Effort column for the Begin the Project task.

2. Type **0** and press ENTER to move to the next task. The zero duration indicates that the task is a milestone, and Time Line marks it on the Gantt chart with a triangle.

3. Type **2w** (for two weeks), and press ENTER to move to the next task. Excel inserts 10.00d in the Duration column. Time Line converts all units entered in the Effort column to days for the Duration column.

4. Type **4w** for the Prepare Site task and press Enter.

5. Type **10d** for the Pack Equipment task and press Enter

6. Type **2d** for the Move Equipment task and press Enter

7. Type **10d** for the Unpack Equipment task and press Enter.

8. Type **2d** for the Setup Computers task and press Enter.

9. Type **0** for the Move Complete task to enter the last milestone, and press Enter.

We've created all of the tasks as effort-based, but let's now assume that the company we've hired to set up the computers has contracted for two days of work. This means that the task will take two days, regardless of the resources that we allocate to it. So, we have to change this tasks to a fixed duration.

1. Click in any column for the Setup Computers task.

2. Click on the Task Information button on the toolbar to display the dialog box shown here. You can always use this dialog box to enter duration information.

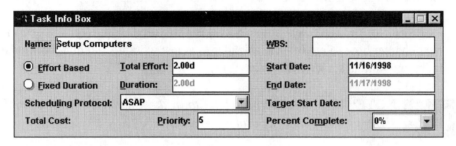

3. Click on the Fixed Duration option button. Time Line changes the Total Effort to 0d indicating that effort will not affect the duration of the tasks.

4. Click on the Close button of the dialog box.

The Effort is now shown as 0d, but the duration as two days. This means that Time Line will keep the task duration at two days regardless of the amount of resources applied to it. Notice that the task bars now correspond to the task's duration, and milestones are indicated by triangles rather than bars.

TIP: *You can leave the Task Info box onscreen and click on another task to display or change its task information.*

Setting Relationships Between Tasks

Although the current Gantt chart shows that every task starts on the same day, this is just not practical. There is no sense in packing the equipment if you haven't yet selected the site, for example, and you can't move the equipment until you've packed it. Starting every task on the same day also means that you have enough staff to work on all of the tasks at the same time. This is not likely, so the next step is to establish the flow of the tasks by defining the relationships between them. Time Line calls these relationships *dependencies*.

Each task except the first has a predecessor (a task that comes before it), and each task except the last has a successor (a task that comes after it). In defining a relationship, you specify how the start and finish date of each task is related to its predecessor and successor. Excel defines the default dependency as Finish-to-Start, which means that one task must end before the next begins. That is, a task's predecessor must be completed before it can start.

There are three other types of dependencies that can be defined, which Time Line classifies as *partial dependencies*:

■ Start-to-Start means that two tasks must start at the same time, but not necessarily end at the same time.

■ Finish-to-Finish means that two tasks must finish at the same time, regardless of when they started.

■ Start-to-Finish means that one task must start before another can finish.

In addition, there can also be some overlap between tasks called *lead time* when a task is being performed while its predecessor is still running; and some gap between tasks called the *lag time*.

 NOTE: *A task can have multiple predecessors or multiple successors. For example, there may be two or more tasks that can begin concurrently when one task ends.*

You should start by assigning the standard finish-to-start dependency to all of the tasks. Here's how.

1. Drag over the row selectors of all of the tasks.

2. Select Set Dependencies from the Task menu.

3. Select Recalculate Now from the Tools menu to let Time Line calculate the dates.

Each of the tasks now follows the other, as shown here:

Task Name	Resources	Start Date	Effort	Duration	End Date	1998	
						Nov	Dec
Begin the Project		11/16/1998	0d	0d	11/16/1998		
Select Site		11/16/1998	2.00w	10.00d	11/30/1998		
Prepare Site		12/1/1998	4.00w	20.00d	12/29/1998		
Pack Equipment		12/30/1998	10.00d	10.00d	1/13/1999		
Move Equipment		1/14/1999	2.00d	2.00d	1/15/1999		
Unpack Equipment		1/18/1999	10.00d	10.00d	1/29/1999		
Setup Computers		2/1/1999	0d	2.00d	2/2/1999		
Move Complete		2/2/1999	0d	0d	2/2/1999		

28

The status bar shows the number of days the project takes and its ending date. If you point to the number of days in the status bar, a box appears showing the project duration in hours, calendar days, workdays, weeks, and months, as shown here.

Total length of project	
Hours:	1,880
Calendar days:	78.33
Work days:	54
Weeks:	11.19
Months:	2.57

54 days	2/2/1999

TIP: *After making changes to any part of the schedule or task flow, you should use the Recalculate Now command. If you're not sure, check for the notation RECALC in the status bar. If you see the notation, then you should recalculate the schedule.*

We want to make one change to the flow of tasks. There is no need to wait until the site is prepared to begin packing equipment. Because we'll have different personnel performing the tasks, we can have the equipment being packed while the site is being completed. This way we can make the move as soon as the site is ready.

1. Click on the Pack Equipment Site task.

2. Click on the Timing Info Box button on the toolbar to see the dialog box shown here. The box shows the predecessor of the selected task.

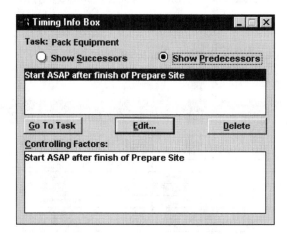

3. Click on Edit to display the following dialog box.

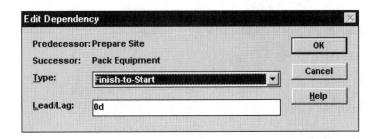

Here you select the type of dependency and enter any lag or lead time. Enter a positive for lag or a negative for lead time.

4. Pull down the Type list and choose Finish-to-Finish.

5. Click OK.

6. Close the Timing Info box. You can leave this box onscreen and click on any other task that you want to edit.

7. Select Recalculate Now from the Tools menu.

The task bars now show that the two tasks end at the same time:

	Task Name	Resources	Start Date	Effort	Duration	End Date	1998	
							Nov	Dec
	Begin the Project		11/16/1998	0d	0d	11/16/1998		
	Select Site		11/16/1998	2.00w	10.00d	11/30/1998		
	Prepare Site		12/1/1998	4.00w	20.00d	12/29/1998		
	Pack Equipment		12/15/1998	10.00d	10.00d	12/29/1998		
	Move Equipment		12/30/1998	2.00d	2.00d	12/31/1998		
	Unpack Equipment		1/4/1999	10.00d	10.00d	1/15/1999		
	Setup Computers		1/18/1999	0d	2.00d	1/19/1999		
	Move Complete		1/19/1999	0d	0d	1/19/1999		

Setting Constraints

Sometimes factors other than dependencies control when a task must start. For example, often you must schedule your tasks around the availability of outside resources, such as your construction crew or architect only being available during

28

specific stretches of time. These types of factors are called *constraints*, and Time Line offers five constraint options:

- ASAP (As Soon As Possible)

- ALAP (As Late As Possible)

- Start No Sooner Than

- Start No Later Than

- Must Start On

As an example, suppose the company you've hired to move you to the new building will not be available until January 6, 1999. According to the dependencies we've established, however, the move date is December 30, 1998. To make the date of the move coincide with the moving company's schedule, set a constraint.

1. Click on the Move Equipment task.

2. Click on the Task Info Box button on the toolbar.

3. Pull down the Scheduling Protocol drop-down list and select Must Start On.

4. In the Target Start Date text box type **1/6/1999**.

5. Close the Task Info box.

6. Select Recalculate Now from the Tools menu.

The Gantt chart now indicates a lag time between the completion of the Pack Equipment task and the start of the Move Equipment task.

Task Name	Resources	Start Date	Effo	1998		1999	
				Nov	Dec	Jan	Feb
Begin the Project		11/16/1998					
Select Site		11/16/1998	2				
Prepare Site		12/1/1998	4				
Pack Equipment		12/15/1998	1				
Move Equipment		1/6/1999					
Unpack Equipment		1/8/1999	1				
Setup Computers		1/22/1999					
Move Complete		1/25/1999					

> **TIP:** *When you create a project using dependencies and constraints, the finish date of the project is calculated by Time Line. You can see the number of days the project takes, and its finish date, on the status bar. Sometimes, however, the calculated end date may be too late for your needs. If this occurs, consider making the start date earlier, reducing the duration of some tasks, or changing dependencies or constraints.*

Printing a Gantt Chart

You can print a copy of the spreadsheet and time scale for a hardcopy reference or to distribute to those working on the project. Before printing the Gantt view, however, check the page setup, then preview the printout onscreen.

Setting Up the Page

To set up the page, select Page Setup from the File menu. In the dialog box that appears, you can set the margins, the page orientation, and the border style. You can also choose to print titles and a legend on each page. The legend explains the symbols that Time Line uses to represent various activities, milestones, and other features.

To customize the headers and footers that print on each page, click on Edit in the Page Setup dialog box to see the box shown here. In this box, you edit the header and footer text.

Edit Header and Footer

Header Text:

&n|

    OK

    Cancel

    Help

Footer Text:

Printed: &d
Page &p

By default, the header includes the name of the project, indicated by the symbol &n. The footer contains the word "Printed" followed by the date, and the word

"Page" followed by the page number. You can add your own text to the header and footer, and insert other information using these symbols:

Symbol	Prints
&p	Current page number
&m	The name of the manager in the Project Information dialog box
&a	The date from the As-of Date field in the Calculations dialog box
&d	The current date
&u	The user names from the System Preferences dialog box
&n	The project name
&w	The layout name
&h	From the Task Name field of a task that represents a group of included subtasks
&H	From the Task Name field of a summary of a group task
&F	The name of the applied filter

Previewing the Printout

Before actually printing the chart, preview how it will appear onscreen. Select Print Preview from the File menu to see a screen such as that shown in Figure 28-4.

The preview shows one page of the printout at a time, organized and numbered from left to right and from top to bottom. Use the arrow buttons to move from page to page. The current page, and the total number of pages are shown, as well as the number of pages across and down.

Click on the Zoom command to toggle between the reduced view and 100% magnification. You can also toggle the display by clicking on the page display.

Printing the View

When you are ready to print the chart, select Print from the File menu, or from the Print Preview window. From the Print dialog box that appears you can choose to print every page, selected pages, or a range of pages, and to scale the printout to one page, to fit a specific number of pages, or by a percentage.

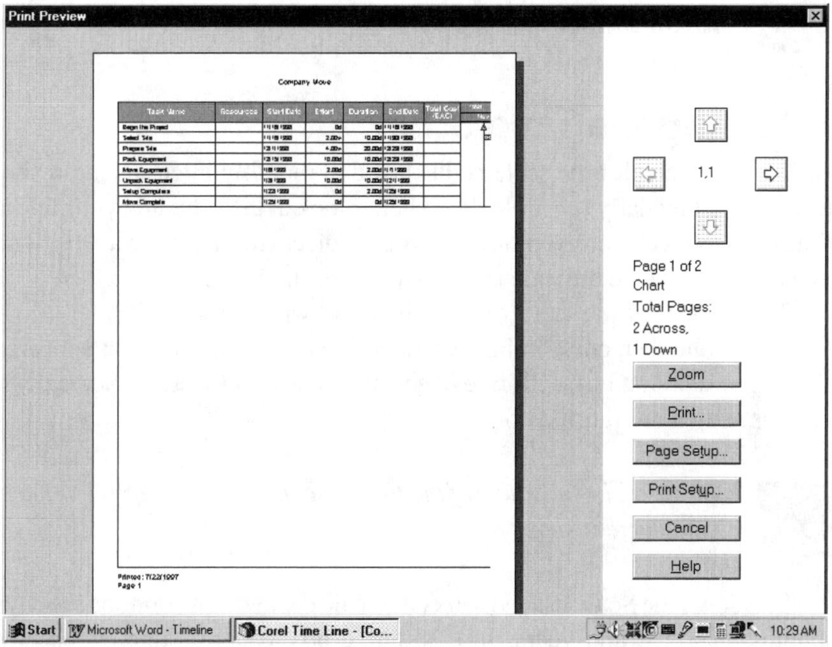

Previewing
a printout

FIGURE 28-4

You can also choose to print the view in color (if you have a color printer), print
a draft copy if your printer has a faster draft mode, or to replace the onscreen colors
with black and white.

Saving the Database

The OverView window title bar shows that the default name given the database is
Untitled1.TDB. You can give the database your own name when you save it. Click
on the Save Database button in the toolbar, then type the name **BigMove** as the
database name.

You can save your database in one of two formats. If you save it as a database
file (with the TDB extension) you can access the information in the database to
import and export to other applications, use with ODBC functions, and for Time
Line Reports. If you save it as a binary file (with the TBF extension) the database
will be faster to open and save, and take up less disk space.

28

TIP: *You can always change the format using the Save As command and selecting the other format options.*

Adjusting the Time Scale

Because the default time scale is displayed in monthly intervals it may be difficult to see the actual daily schedule. For a better look at the schedule you can change the timescale to weeks or even days. If your project extends over a very long period, you can also change the time scale to quarters and years.

To change the time scale, display the Gantt window, select Preferences from the Edit menu and then click on Format Gantt Layout. In the box that appears, click on Edit to see a dialog box with five pages, then click on the Time Scale tab to see the options shown in Figure 28-5.

 NOTE: *The full name of the Format command in the Preferences depends on the current view.*

Pull down the Scale list and select the scale desired. The options are days, weeks, months, quarters, and years. In this dialog box you can also choose what other

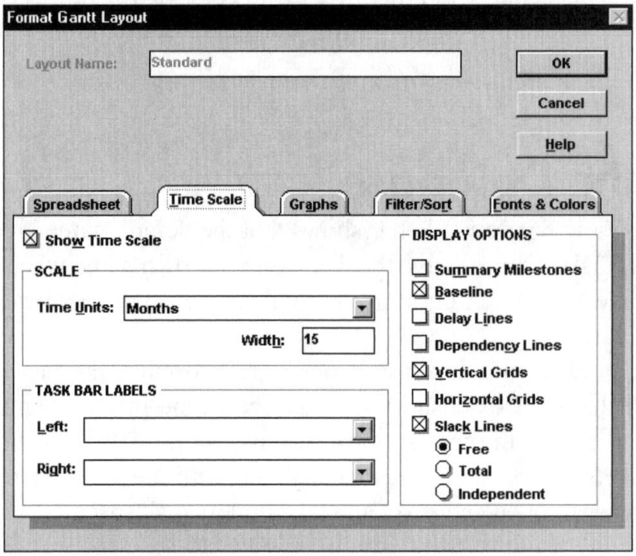

Adjusting
the
timescale

FIGURE 28-5

elements are displayed on the chart. For example, click on Dependency Lines to show lines that graphically show the connection between tasks.

Setting Other Preferences

In addition to the Format preference, there are other preference settings that you can make in Time Line. Many of the preferences are for advanced users, but we'll summarize the options.

- *System* allows you to customize the working environment, including the user name, the order that dates appear in drop-down menus, the date format and date separator character, and the time format. You can also determine whether to show the time in a drop-down list that shows the date, the month in which the fiscal year begins if you're not using a calendar year, the day the week starts on, and where new rows are added when you insert items in the OverView. Choose whether the Co-Pilot is on or off, the default task duration and task effort, and the default scheduling protocol, whether the status bar is displayed, the hours in a work day, the days per week, weeks per month, to make a backup when you save a database, and the currency symbol.

- *Calculation Settings* set the As-Of Date that Time Line uses to mark the division between past and future as a vertical red line in the Time Scale, or to use the current date as the As-Of Date every time the project is opened. You can choose to perform Automatic Recalculation whenever a change is made, to calculate negative total slack time, and to honor priorities that have been assigned to tasks.

- *Fonts & Colors* lets you choose the fonts, size, styles, and colors used for various Time Line views.

- *Holidays* establishes non-working holidays for all calendars in the database.

- *Task Bar Symbols* sets the symbols and patterns for task bars in the Gantt and Time-Scaled PERT views.

- *Highlights* determines how highlights appear to mark tasks that meet criteria that you establish.

- *Graph Patterns* sets the patterns issued in graphs, such as histograms, off time, and cost graphs.

- *Task Columns* determines the default formatting for task columns.

28

Displaying the PERT View

Time Line offers several ways to look at your project in addition to the Gantt chart. One of the most popular is the PERT chart, in which each task is displayed in a rectangle, called a *node*, that shows the task name, and the starting and ending dates, as shown in Figure 28-6. The chart also shows lines between nodes to indicate the dependencies.

To display the PERT chart, select New View from the View menu and click on PERT.

TIP: *There is also a Time-Scaled PERT view that resembles a Gantt chart with dependency lines and the task names on a time scale, as well as a Crosstab view that displays project and task cost over time.*

Viewing the Critical Path

Project planners often rely on the *critical path* to help manage their project. The critical path is the sequence of tasks in which any delay will affect the project end

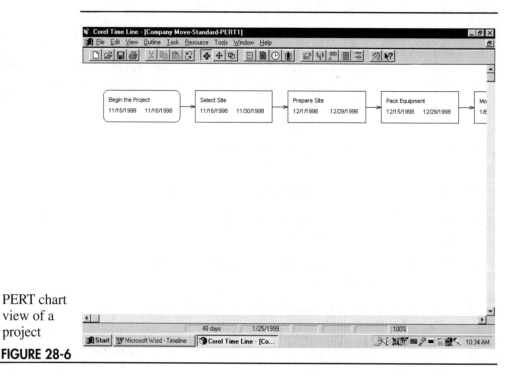

PERT chart
view of a
project

FIGURE 28-6

date. For example, we've set our move so the packing can occur while the site is being prepared. As long as packing ends at the same time as preparing the site, taking an additional two days to pack would not affect the end date.

NOTE: *Use of the critical path is referred to as a the Critical Path Method (CPM).*

In fact, even if it takes a few extra days to prepare the site, the end date is still not affected because of the lag time between packing and moving while you're waiting for the movers to arrive. Therefore, preparing the site and packing the equipment are not on the critical path.

However, if it takes more than two days to make the move, or more than four days to unpack, the end date is pushed back. So these tasks are on the critical path.

To display critical path information on the chart, you can add two columns to the Gantt spreadsheet. Add the Critical column to display the word "Yes" for tasks on the critical path, and add the CPM Start Date column to show the earliest date the task can start.

To display these, and other columns, display the Format Gantt Layout dialog box. From the Gantt window, select Preferences from the Edit menu, click on Format Gantt Layout, and then on Edit. Click on the column that you want to precede the added column, then click in Insert. Pull down the list associated with the new column and select the information that you want to appear.

Outlining

A complex project can have a large number of tasks, and it is often useful to group some tasks under a common objective. For example, when making a major real estate acquisition, the Select Site task might be subdivided into a number of individual jobs, such as determining your company's needs, survey sites, negotiating contracts, and arranging financing. Because these jobs are part of the Select Site effort, they can be grouped together to help organize your project.

The individual tasks in the group are called *detail tasks*, while the group heading is called the *summary task*. The summary task indicates the total accumulated time and costs of the detailed tasks that are within it.

To create detail tasks, enter a summary task name followed by the detail tasks to be included within it. Select the detail tasks, then choose Indent from the Outline menu. Time Line indents the task names and displays the name of the summary task in boldface. When you recalculate the project, the total duration of the detail tasks is inserted into the duration column of the summary task, as shown in Figure 28-7. Choose Move Up or Move Down from the Outline menu to change the position of a detail task, or choose Outdent so the task is no longer a detail under the summary.

You can collapse and expand a Time Line outline to display various levels of tasks using the Collapse, Collapse All, Expand, and Expand All options from the Outline menu. To view just a selected summary task and its details, hiding all other tasks of the project, click on the summary task and choose Hoist from the Outline menu. Select Dehoist from the Outline menu to redisplay the other tasks. The Hoist command collapses an outline to show just the summary tasks. Dehoisting displays the details.

TIP: *Double-click on a summary task to expand or collapse it.*

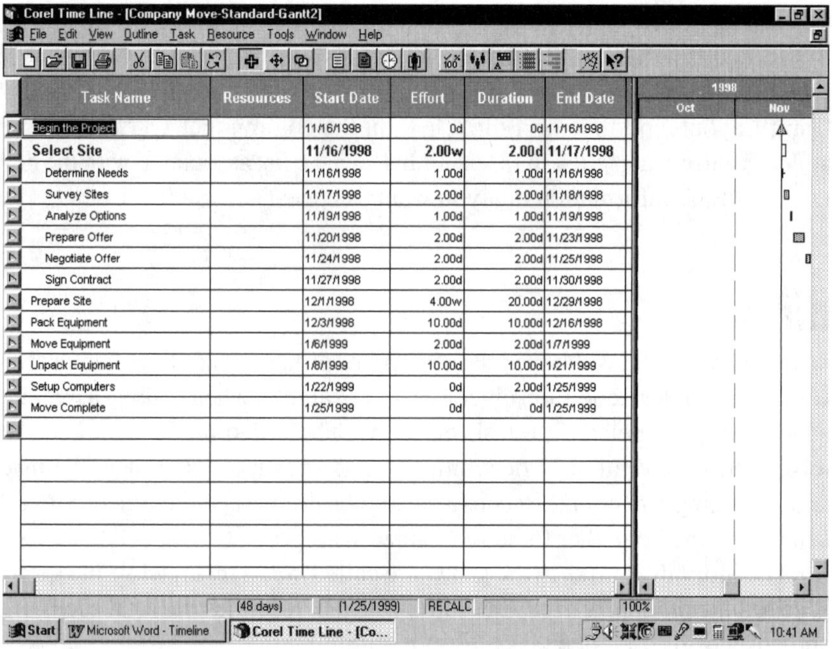

Summary and detail tasks in an outline

FIGURE 28-7

Calendars and Resources and Costs

29

Organizing the tasks of your project, as you learned to do in the last chapter, is really just the beginning of project management. You have to assign resources to each task. A resource is a person, piece of equipment, material, or any other object that is required to complete a task. The availability of resources determines when your tasks begin, how long they take to complete, and the costs involved. If you do not have enough resources, for example, a task may take longer to get done—if it is completed at all. It is only by assigning and scheduling resources that you can tell if your schedule is practical and possible.

Setting Up Calendars

In order to assign resources to a project, you have to know when those resources are available. To schedule people, equipment, and facilities, you create one or more calendars. You start with the master calendar, which serves as the overall calendar for the project. You then develop calendars for shifts and resources as they are needed. A shift calendar records the availability of various work shifts, whereas resource calendars are maintained for individual resources.

Holidays

The first step in developing your master calendar is to ensure that all non-working holidays are accounted for. Select Preferences from the Edit menu and click on Holidays to see the dialog box shown here:

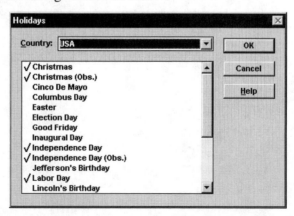

The non-working holidays are shown with a checkmark. Click on a holiday to toggle it between working and non-working.

Time Line keeps track of national holidays by country. If you're planning a project for your subsidiary in New Zealand, for example, choose New Zealand from the Country pull-down list. You will then be able to choose from New Zealand holidays, such as Auckland Anniversary Day, Boxing Day, and the Queen's birthday.

Click on OK when you have chosen the holidays for your company. You can later override a holiday (from within a resource's calendar) to make it a working day, as you'll learn in the section "Resource Calendars" later in this chapter.

Setting Up the Master Calendar

The next step is to create the master calendar, which defines regular workdays and non-working days, such as weekends and company-wide vacation days. You also use the calendar to indicate *exceptions*—days that do not conform to the regular schedule, such as a half-day of work on New Year's Eve.

Double-click on Master Calendar in the Calendars section of the OverView to see the calendar as shown in Figure 29-1. You can also select Master Calendar from the View menu. Days are color coded on the calendar to represent regular workdays, vacation days, weekends, holidays, and exception days. Exception days are workdays with irregular hours.

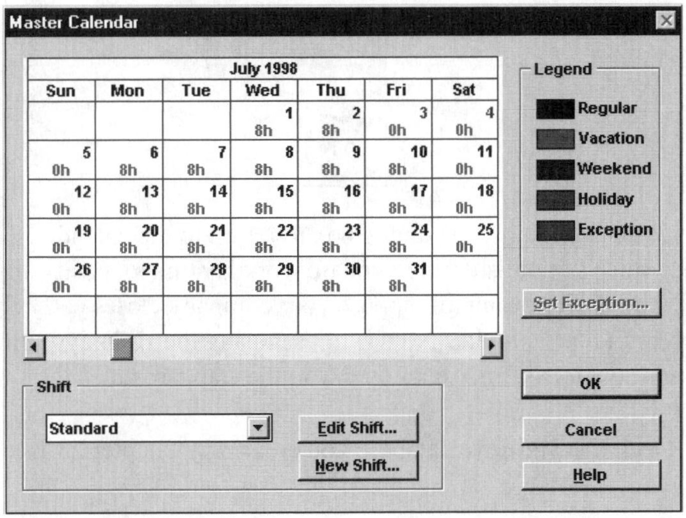

Master calendar for the project

FIGURE 29-1

You start by checking the hours and days for the standard shift. For example, suppose your workday ends at 4:30 instead of 5 PM, or say you want to allow for a one-hour lunch break, or work just half a day on Fridays. Make sure that Standard is selected in the Shift list, then click on Edit Shift to see the Edit Weekly Shift dialog box shown here:

Select the day of the week you want to change, then edit the start and stop time in the Work Time section. Time Line will calculate the total daily and weekly hours for you. To add a block of time, move to a row in the Work Time section or click on Insert. Click on Off All Day to make the day a non-working day. For example, here is the Work Time section for a Friday, assuming a one-hour lunch break and ending the day at 3:30 PM:

Start	Stop
9:00 AM	12:00 PM
1:00 PM	3:30 PM

When you're done, close the dialog box to return to the calendar.

Once you've established the standard workday times, specify any exceptions for particular days. For example, suppose your company closes early on December 24. This day isn't a legal holiday so it is not set using the Holidays command.

Here's how to add an exception day to the standard calendar:

1. Open the BigMove database you created in Chapter 28.

2. Double-click on Master Calendar in the OverView.

3. In the Master Calendar dialog box, scroll the bar under the calendar to see December 1998. Click on the scroll bar to move one year at a time, or on the arrows at the ends of the bar to change a month at a time.

4. Click on December 24, 1998.

5. Click on Set Exception to see the dialog box shown here.

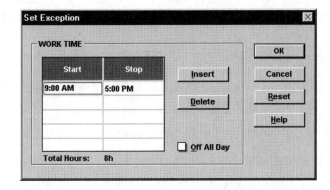

In this box, you can change the hours of work for the day or make it a non-working day by selecting the Off All Day box.

6. In the Stop box, enter **1 PM**.

7. Click on OK. The day will now be color coded as an exception day.

Creating Shifts

Not every resource is on the standard calendar. Your company may have a night shift, for example, that works from 12 AM to 8 AM. Time Line includes three predefined types of shifts for the master calendar:

- *Standard shift* is available from 9:00 AM to 5:00 PM, Monday through Friday. Use this as the general master calendar for your project.

- *7 day/24 hour shift* is available 24 hours a day, 7 days a week.

- *Swing shift* is available from 3:00 PM to 11:00 PM, Monday through Friday.

You can edit the work hours and days of these shifts, and you can create your own custom shifts. When you create a new shift, it will be based on whatever calendar is selected in the shift list. So, for example, if you start with the Standard calendar selected, your new shift will begin with the same holidays and vacation days.

1. Click on New Shift in the Master Calendar box. A box appears in which you type the name of the shift. You can also create a weekly or a custom calendar here, which we'll learn to do later. A custom shift lets you define individual *day types* which define special types of schedules, such as shifts that work one 12-hour period, have a day off, then work two 8-hour days.

2. Type **Night Shift**.

3. Click OK. You'll see the Edit Weekly Shift dialog box for the Night Shift calendar.

4. If Mon is not selected in the Weekday column, click on it now.

5. In the first row under Start Time, where is says 9:00 AM, type **12 AM**.

6. In the Stop box type **8 AM**.

7. Click on Tues in the Weekday column.

8. Type **12 AM** and **8 AM** as the Start and Stop times.

9. In the same way, enter the same start and end times for Wednesday, Thursday, and Friday.

10. Click on Saturday to accept your changes to Friday, then click on OK to return to the master calendar.

11. If Standard is not displayed in the Shift list, pull down the list now and select Standard. Time Line uses the current calendar as the default calendar for resources.

12. Click on OK.

13. Select Company Move-Standard-Gantt1 from the Window menu. Notice that the ending dates of the Prepare Site and Pack Equipment tasks are both 12/29. Also notice the word Recalc in the status bar. This means that you have to recalculate the Gantt chart to adjust to changes that affect the project schedule.

14. Select Recalculate Now from the Tools menu.

The ending dates of those two tasks are now 12/30 because of the half day vacation on December 24. The end date of the final project does not change, however, because of the lag time later in the schedule.

Adding Resources

Before you can go any further, you have to assign resources to each task. Although most resources will be personnel, either employees or contractors, a resource can also be a piece of equipment, a facility, or any other item that you must have to complete a task. For example, you may have to rent a truck or lease a warehouse to perform one or more project tasks. These are also resources that must be assigned to tasks.

Start by deciding which resources are needed, then enter them in the Resource View. Click on the Resource window or double-click on Standard-Resource1 in the OverView window. You can also choose the Standard Resource option from the Window menu. A blank resource window appears as shown in Figure 29-2. Maximize the Time Line and Resource windows so you can see all of the columns.

The Resource name can be the name of an individual or a generic name, such as Movers, Carpet Installers, or Night Shift Workers. There are four resource types that you can choose from a pull-down list. The types indicate the way costs are assigned:

- *Resource* is used for personnel when their availability must be taken into account when scheduling tasks.

- *Fixed Cost* means that that there is a one-time expense applied to a task, such as the purchase of equipment or a contractor's charge.

- *Time Cost* means that there is an hourly, daily, weekly, or other charge applied, such as renting a truck or piece of equipment, or hiring a contractor on an hourly basis.

- *Unit Cost* means that the cost depends on the number of items, regardless of the time it's used, such as the cost of each unit of material.

Use the Availability column to indicate the quantity of the resource that is available. If the resource is Night Shift Workers, and there are 10 people on that shift, for example, you'd enter 10 in the column.

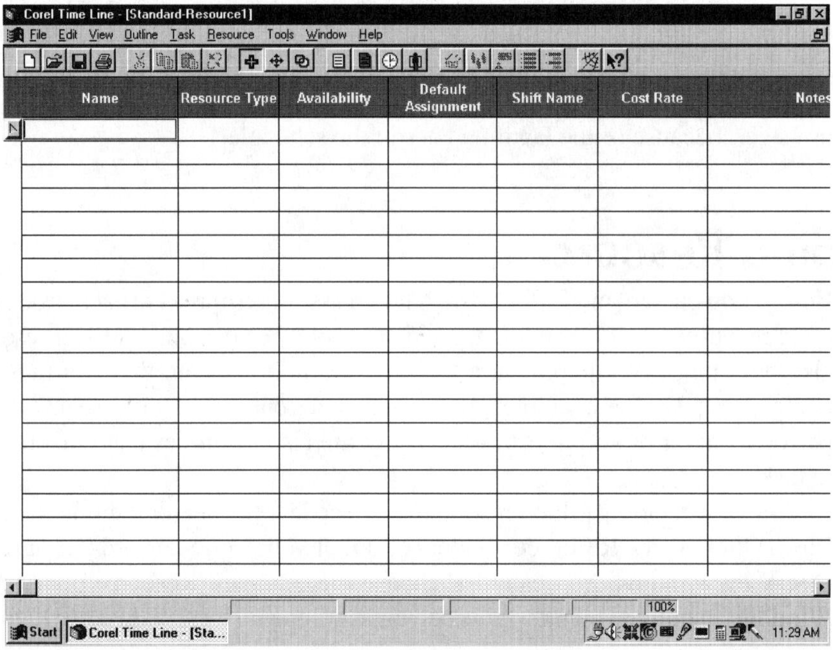

Enter
resources
for the
project

FIGURE 29-2

Use the Default Assignment column to indicate the amount of the resource initially assigned to each task. You can't change this setting for a Fixed Cost resource because the number of units assigned won't affect the cost. The Shift Name is the calendar applied to the resource, and the cost rate is either a periodic rate (such as hourly or daily), the fixed cost, or the unit cost.

In the Cost Rate column you can enter the cost for Resource and Time types using a time unit, such as

50000/Year
5000/Month
500/Week
50/Day
5/Hour

If you leave out the unit, Time Line assumes hours.

For the Unit type, enter just the cost per unit. If desired, you can specify a unit, such as 50/box. Time Line will simply multiply the dollar amount times the number of units assign to a task. It cannot, for instance, know that there are 144 units per box, and calculate a box cost on its own.

Now enter these resources for our company move project:

Name	Resource Type	Availability	Default Assignment	Shift Name	Cost Rate
John Mundy	Resource	1.00	1.00	Standard	$80,000.00/Year
Day Shift Workers	Resource	1.00	1.00	Standard	$12.50/Hour
Night Shift Workers	Resource	1.00	1.00	Standard	$14.50/Hour
Peters Construction	Fixed Cost		1.00		
Johnson Movers	Time Cost		1.00		$50.00/Hour
Paulson Computers	Fixed Cost		1.00		

Profiles

Sometimes, availability and costs are not constant. For example, the hourly rate of a contractor or the unit cost of a supply may increase on July 1st. Likewise, a resource's availability may vary with time. When you need to account for a change of cost or resource availability over time you create a *profile*.

To create a profile, click on the resource, pull down the Resource menu, and select the Cost Rate Profile option to see a dialog box like the one shown here. In each row, enter the starting date for each new rate, then enter the cost in the rate column. For a unit cost type of resource you enter the type of unit in the Unit text box. For a resource or time type of resource, the dialog box contains a list labeled Per. Pull down the list to select a unit of time in which the cost rate will be measured.

Cost Rate Profile for Wigits

Effective Date	Rate	
<Start>	$0	

Unit [   ]

OK   Cancel   Insert   Delete   Help

To create an availability profile, click on a resource-type resource, pull down the Resource menu, and select the Availability Profile for option. You'll see the dialog box shown here:

Availability Profile for Day Shift Workers			
Effective Date	**Total Avail**	**Company Move**	OK
<Start>	1.00		Cancel
			Insert
			Delete
			Help

RESOURCE TYPE
◉ Shared   ◯ Project Specific

Leave the Resource Type set at Shared if you want Time Line to allocate the resource's availability over multiple projects. Choose Project Specific if you want to assign the availability yourself. When you select Project Specific, you will be able to enter the availability amount in the columns listing the current projects in the database.

In the Effective Date column, enter the dates when the resource's availability changes, then enter the units of availability in the Total Avail column.

Resource Calendars

By default, each resource is assigned to the standard calendar, as shown in the Shift Name column of the resource window. That calendar also becomes the resource calendar that Time Line uses to track the resource's availability for each task.

You can select another calendar for the resource, such as a shift calendar, and you can customize the resource calendar as needed. For example, in our sample project, we've created the Night Shift calendar. Let's now assign that calendar to the employees designated as the Night Shift Workers resource.

1. In the Resource View, click on the Night Shift Workers row.

2. Pull down the Resource menu and select the Calendar option. The option will show the name of the selected resource, as in Calendar for Night Shift Workers. The Calendar window appears.

3. Pull down the Shift list and select the Night Shift calendar.

4. Click on OK.

You can personalize a calendar for a class of workers, such as an entire shift, or for a specific worker named as an individual resource. As an example, let's assume that the office manager has a vacation day scheduled for November 27, 1998. You have to mark that day as non-working on that resource's calendar.

1. Click on the row for John Mundy.

2. Pull down the Resource menu and select the Calendar for John Mundy option.

3. Scroll the bar under the calendar to see November 1998.

4. Click on the 27th.

5. Click on Set Exception.

6. Click Off All Day.

7. Click on OK twice.

When you return to the OverView, you'll see three calendars listed under the Resources calendars option—one for each of the resource-type resources:Day Shift Workers, Night Shift Workers, and John Mundy. You can edit the a resource's calendar by double-clicking on its calendar in the OverView window.

Assigning Resources to Tasks

Once you have resources defined, you assign them to tasks. Assigning resources helps Time Line compute the cost of the project, determine the start and end date of tasks, and account for an over allocation of resources. Let's look at some examples.

■   Time Line computes the cost of the project based on the cost rate information and task duration. If you have a manager who makes $1000 a week assigned to a task for three days, Time Line records that the task costs $600.

- Suppose you scheduled a five-day task for a manager during a period when the manager has a two-day vacation. Time Line will extend the task two days, taking up nine calendar days but still five working days—the five days it takes to complete the project, the two vacation days, and the weekend. This will, of course, push back the completion date by two days.

- You have two tasks that you scheduled to run concurrently, perhaps with a Finish-to-Finish relationship. You assign six employees to each but only have a total of ten available. In a process called *leveling*, Time Line can reallocate resources or change duration to match the resources that you have available.

There are three ways to assign a resource to a task:

- You can use the Connect tool to drag between a task and a resource with the mouse. The major drawback is that you have to tile and arrange multiple windows, and you later have to edit the assignment if you need to customize it.

- If you are in the Gantt view, you can use the Assign Resources command. Click on the task, and then on the Assign Resources button. A list of resources appears. Click on the resource to assign to the task and then on OK. Time Line will assign the value in the Default Assignment column.

- For more control over task assignments use the Assignments Info box. This lets you assign resources to tasks and customize their allocation.

Let's use the Assignments Info box now to assign resources to the tasks in our sample project.

1. Switch to the Gantt view by selecting Company Move-Standard-Gantt1 from the Window menu.

2. Click on the Select Site task.

3. Click on the Assign Info box tool in the toolbar, or select Assignments Info box from the Task menu. You'll see the dialog box shown here:

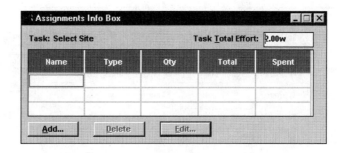

4. Click the Add button to see a list of resources in the database.

5. Click on John Mundy, and then on OK. The Edit Resource Assignment dialog box appears as shown in Figure 29-3.

6. Click on the Required checkbox. This tells Time Line that this resource must be allocated to the task. You can also change the requested and minimum quantities.

7. Click on OK.

The Effort section of the dialog box offers these settings:

■ *Total*—The total effort the resource must apply to this task. You can only change this item when the resource is required.

■ *Spent*—Enter the amount of effort already applied to this task.

■ *To Go*—Time Line calculates the amount of effort remaining.

■ *Overtime*—Enter any additional effort.

The Estimated Cost section shows the cost breakdown for the task based the resources cost rate.

If the resource is required, the Permit Allocation Splitting lets Time Line cease the task if there are insufficient resources to complete it. Choose Yes to allow the task to be interrupted until resources are available. Choose No to postpone the start of the task until there are enough resources to complete it continuously. Choose Around Vacations Only to allow the task to be interrupted only if a resource is scheduled for vacation time.

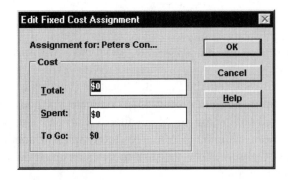

Specifying
resource
allocation

FIGURE 29-3

Click on OK to redisplay the Assignments Info Box. Leave the box displayed
so you can assign additional resources to the same task and to other tasks.

1. Click on the Prepare Site task, then click on Add to display the resource list.

2. Click Peters Construction Company, and then OK. Because this is a fixed
   cost resource, the Edit Fixed Cost Assignment dialog box appears as
   shown here:

3. In the Total box, type **10,000**, then click on OK.

4. Click on the Pack Equipment task, then click on Add.

5. Click on Day Shift Workers, and then on OK. The Default Availability was set at 1 and the effort 10 days. Let's make it go faster by assigning two workers to packing.

6. In the Requested Quality text box, enter **2**, then click on OK.

7. Drag the Assignment box out of the way to see the duration for the Pack Equipment task. Notice it is now 5d.

8. Leave the Pack Equipment task selected, and click on Add to assign an additional resource to it.

9. Click on Evening Shift and then OK.

10. In the Requested Quantity field, enter **3** and then click on OK.

11. Assign Johnson Movers to the Move Equipment task. Time Line will calculate the costs as $800 based on the $50 per hour charge.

12. Assign five Day Shift Workers to the Unpack Equipment task. The task will then be two days duration.

13. Assign Paulson Computers to the Setup Computers tasks, with a total cost of $1600.

14. When you have finished making the assignments, close the Assignment Info box.

15. Select Recalculate Now from the Tools menu.

16. Time Line adjusts the Gantt chart to account for the assigned resources.

Setting the Baseline

An important part of the project management process is to compare the actual time line of the project to the estimate schedule that you had created. Time Line lets you do this by setting the estimated schedule as a *baseline*, a schedule against which you track the actual duration of tasks. You can then change the schedule as necessary during the project and compare the new schedule to the baseline. In the Gantt chart, the baseline for each task appears as a shadow behind the bar, as shown next.

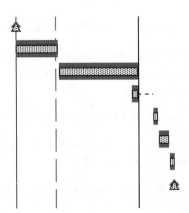

To establish the baseline, first recalculate the project using the Recalculate Now command from the Tools menu, then select Set Baseline from the Tasks menu. In the dialog box that appears, select All Tasks and then click on OK. The baseline shadows appear under each taskbar.

 TIP: *If the baseline is not displayed, select Preferences from the Edit menu and click on Format Gantt Layout. On the Time Scale tab, click the Baseline checkbox and then click on OK.*

Tracking Progress

As you perform your project, you may have to modify the duration of tasks or the dependencies between them, comparing the actual progress with the baseline. If it takes more time than expected to complete a task, the taskbar will extend past the baseline on the Gantt chart, as shown here:

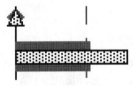

Keeping track of progress includes updating the chart to show the percent completed, or adjusting the start date or duration of tasks.

Updating Percent Complete

As you perform a task, indicate on the taskbar the amount of it that has been completed. You can then see your progress at a glance. The percent completed is indicated by filling in the relative portion of the taskbar. In this illustration, for example, a task has been marked as 50 percent completed, so half of the taskbar if filled in.

As usual, there are several ways to update the percent completed.

■ Select the task in the Gannt chart, then click in the Task Info box button. Enter the percentage in the Percent Completed box, or pull down its list and choose from the options shown.

■ You can also update all of the tasks, or just selected tasks, in one step. Select Update Percent Complete from the Task menu to display the dialog box shown here:

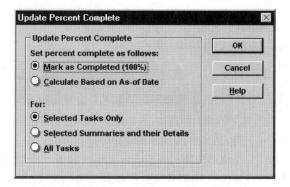

You can choose to mark the tasks as 100 percent complete, or have Time Line calculate the percentage for you from the As-Of Date. The As-Of

Date is usually the current date, although you can change it in the Calculating Settings dialog box (you'll learn about this later). You can also choose to update just the selected task, a summary task and its details, or all of the tasks.

Changing Start Date and Duration

You should adjust the Gantt chart to reflect the actual start date and duration of tasks. To change the start date, just enter the actual date the task was begun in the Start Date column, or in the Start Date text box of the Task Info box. Time Line will adjust the position of the taskbar, but leave the baseline unchanged. In this illustration, for instance, the task was started one week late:

If a task takes more or less time than expected, change the value in the Effort column (for effort-based tasks) or in the Duration column (for fixed-duration tasks). You can also change the corresponding settings in the Task Info box. Time Line will adjust the taskbar, again leaving the baseline unchanged. In this example, one task took more time to complete than expected, another less time:

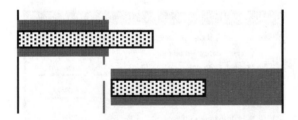

As an alternative to entering dates and times, you can use the mouse to drag the bar directly onscreen. To change the start date, point to the taskbar so the mouse appears as a two-headed arrow, then drag. Drag to the right to move the start date back, to the left to move it ahead. As you drag, a box appears showing the start and end dates:

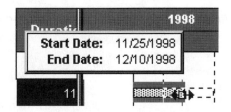

When you release the mouse, the start and end dates will adjust in the Start Date and End Date columns. You still have to select Recalculate from the Tools menu to update the entire chart to account for dependencies to other tasks.

To change the effort or duration of a task, point to the right end of the taskbar so the mouse appears as a right-pointing arrow, and then drag. As you drag, a box appears showing the resulting end date and the amount of effort (for an effort-based task) or duration (for a fixed-duration task).

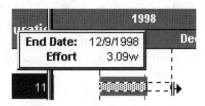

Release the mouse to update the columns in the chart, then recalculate the tasks.

When you drag bars that have certain constraints or dependencies, Time Line will display Co-Pilot for additional information on how to adjust the chart. For example, if you adjust a task that has a relationship with a predecessor, you'll see the Co-Pilot box shown here:

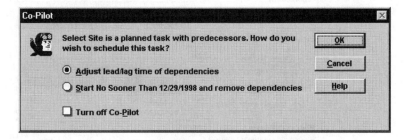

Choose an option from the dialog box, and then click on OK.

NOTE: *To turn off Co-Pilot, select the Turn off Co-Pilot checkbox.*

Printing Reports

In Chapter 28, you learned how to print a copy of your Gantt and PERT charts. For more detailed information about your project, select from the report formats that Time Line has provided.

Select Reports from the Files menu to display the dialog box shown in Figure 29-4.

The list on the left shows the names of reports. Click on a report then read a description of it in the Report Description box on the right. Select if you want to report on all of the projects in the database, or click on a specific project on the list. You can also specify the start and end date of the tasks to include.

Then, select Print Report from the File menu to display the report as a preview, as shown in Figure 29-5. Click on the Print button to print the report, or either of the Export buttons to save the report in another format, such as a text file, Lotus 1-2-3, Excel, or Quattro Pro worksheet.

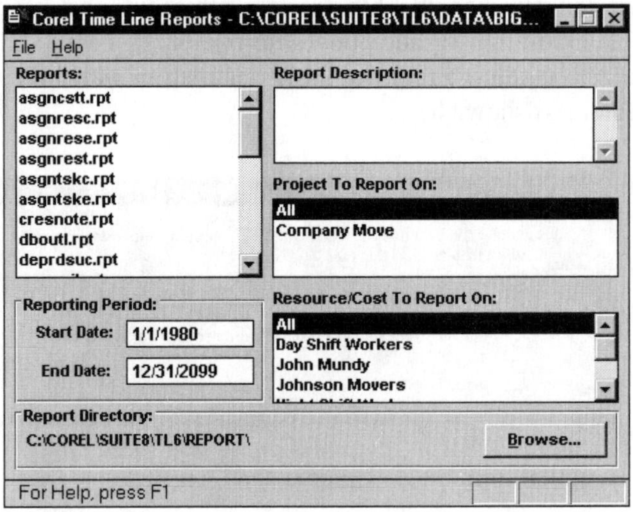

Select a
report for
printing
project
details

FIGURE 29-4

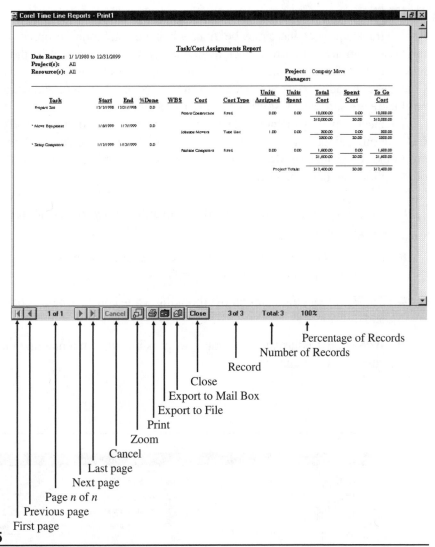

29

Preview of
report to be
printed

FIGURE 29-5

NOTE: *You can also use options in the File menu to print a calendar and to publish the project to Envoy, as an HTML file, or to Corel Barista.*

Leveling

As you track a project, there may be times when there are more resources assigned to a task than are actual resources available. When you recalculate the project, however, Time Line does not adjust for these situations by default. To have Time Line make the adjustment you need to turn on *leveling*. Leveling will delay a task until there are sufficient resources for it to be accomplished.

To select a leveling method, select Preferences from the Edit menu, and click on Calculation Settings to see the dialog box shown in Figure 29-6. The leveling options are in the Recalculation Method section. The default setting is No Leveling. The other options are described here:

■ *Quick Leveling* only considers the availability of resources, not priorities assigned to tasks.

■ *By Target Date* allows over allocation of resources when needed to meet a target completion date that you specify.

■ *Full Leveling* eliminates all overbooking while considering all constraints and priorities.

■ *Within Slack* adjusts tasks as much as possible while maintaining the current project end date.

Select leveling options for over allocation of resources

FIGURE 29-6

Adding a Graph to a Layout

In addition to the Spreadsheet and Time Scale panes, the Gantt chart layout can also contain one or more graphs. To add a graph, display the Gantt view, pull down the Edit menu, point to Preferences and choose the Format Gantt Layout options. Click on Edit in the dialog box that appears, then click on the Graphs tab to see the dialog box shown in Figure 29-7.

Pull down the list in the Resource Name column and select the resource that you want to graph. Click in the Graph Type column, pull down the list, and select the type of chart—Period Cost, Cumulative Cost, or Histogram.

 TIP: *To add another graph to the same layout, click on Insert, then choose another resource or graph type.*

In the Show section of the dialog box, make sure that the Graphs checkbox is selected. You can also choose the Totals on Graphs and then Off-Time on Histograms

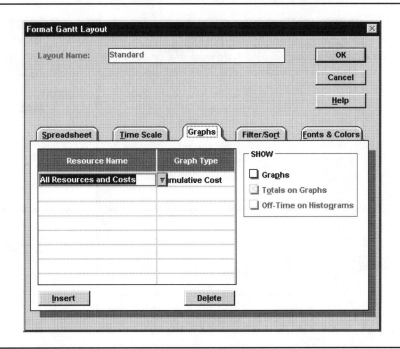

Adding a graph to the layout

FIGURE 29-7

options. Totals on Graphs displays the y-axis value for each bar. Off-Time on Histograms displays the time off for each resource.

Click on OK to display the graphs. Time Line displays the graphs in additional panes of the chart with scroll bars when necessary, as shown in Figure 29-8.

To change the patterns on the graph bars, choose Graph Patterns from the Edit Preferences menu, then select patterns from the dialog box shown here:

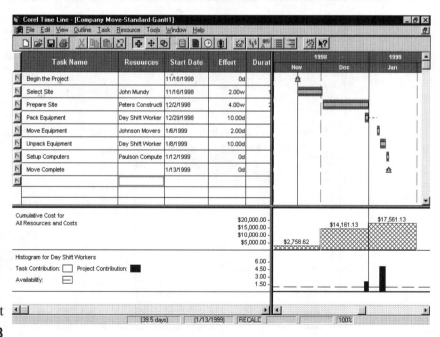

Graphs in a
Gantt layout

FIGURE 29-8

Importing and Exporting Project Information

If you also use another project management program, such as Microsoft Project, or want to share information with another user who does, you can export information from a Time Line project. Exporting converts your Time Line project to another program's format. Importing converts a project created by another program to Time Line's format. You can also export or import task information only to and from ASCII, dBase, DIF, and Lotus 1-2-3 formats.

To export or import information, close Time Line, then select Corel Time Line Import-Export from the Corel WordPerfect Suite 8 Tools menu from the taskbar. The Import-Export program begins and you'll see the dialog box shown in Figure 29-9.

Use the first two options in the dialog box to import or export an entire project. Selecting Import Project Management, for example, will display the dialog box shown in Figure 29-10. In this box, you select the file you want to import and the format in which it is currently stored. You also choose the Time Line database that you want to add the project to, and other options that affect how the information is inserted.

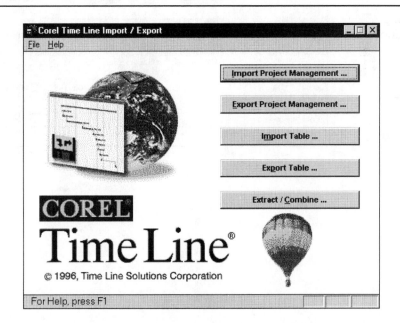

Importing and exporting Time Line information

FIGURE 29-9

The Import Table and Export Table options let you save task information from a Time Line project to another format, or load information into a task table. The Extract/Combine option lets you copy a project from one Time Line database to another, and combine two projects.

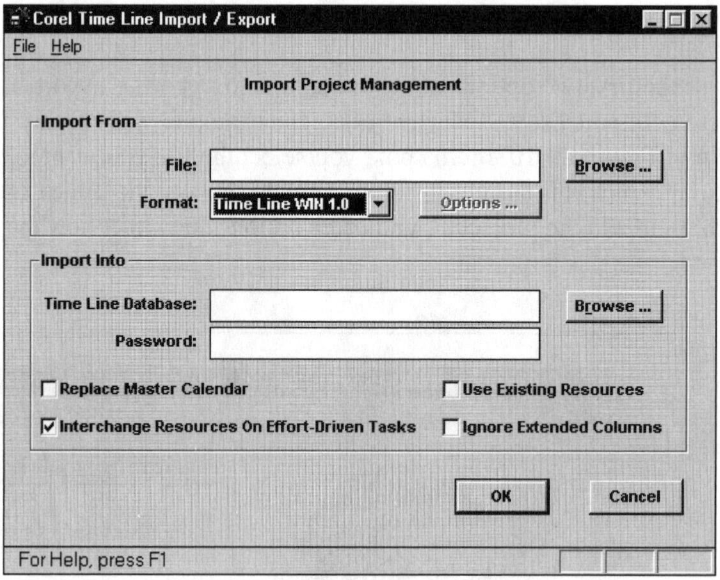

Importing
information
from
another
project
management
program

FIGURE 29-10

Corel WEB.SiteBuilder

30

943

Corel WEB.SiteBuilder helps you build professional-looking Internet or intranet Web sites. A *Web site* contains a series of linked Web pages. SiteBuilder helps you create the individual pages, as well as organize and maintain the links between them. Use SiteBuilder to create marquees and banners, import graphics (even animated GIFs), add lists, tables, frames, forms, and sound. You can then publish your Web site to the Internet through your Internet Service Provider or your own site using Corel Web Server software, or make your computer a server on your company's intranet using Corel WEB.IntraServer. Both Corel Web Server and WEB.IntraServer software come with Corel WordPerfect Suite 8.

You can import into your Web site HTML pages that you've created with Corel WordPerfect, Corel Quattro Pro, Corel Presentations, and other software.

Starting SiteBuilder

To start Corel WEB.SiteBuilder, click on its icon in the DAD bar, or click on Start, point to Corel WordPerfect Suite 8, and click on Corel WEB.SiteBuilder. When the program starts you'll see the two windows shown in Figure 30-1 with a blank Web site.

As shown in Figure 30-1, the SiteBuilder window contains a toolbar and a property bar. Here, the buttons on the SiteBuilder toolbar are identified:

30

New HTML page
New Web site
Open
Save
Print

Show/Hide Site Manager
Show/Hide Content Gallery
Object List
Clipart

Web Browser
Perfect-
Expert

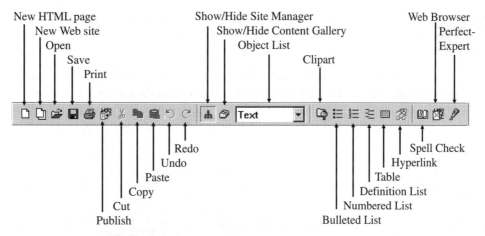

Redo
Undo
Paste
Copy
Cut
Publish

Spell Check
Hyperlink
Table
Definition List
Numbered List
Bulleted List

Site Manager toolbar
Site Manager window
SiteBuilder toolbar
SiteBuilder property bar
SiteBuilder window

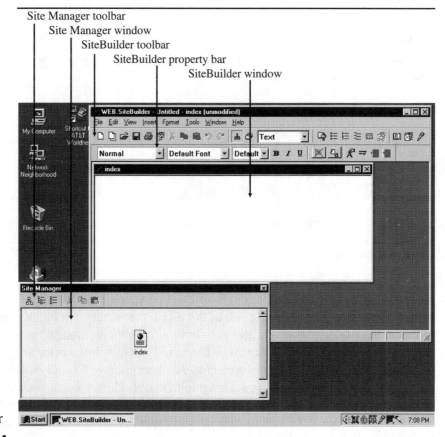

WEB.
SiteBuilder

FIGURE 30-1

 TIP: *Enlarge the SiteBuilder window if you do not see the Perfect Experts button on the toolbar.*

As with other Corel applications, the buttons on the SiteBuilder property bar depend on the object selected in the window. These buttons are identified here:

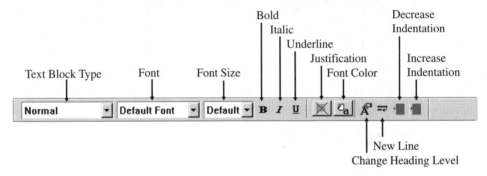

Use Site Manager to view and change the overall structure of your Web site. The Site Manager toolbar is shown here:

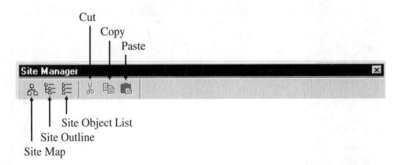

Use the toolbars to format text and add items such as tables and lists. Format text using styles by selecting options from the Text Block Type list in the property bar. The style you select applies to all of the text in the current text block. Pressing ENTER in SiteBuilder, however, does not start a new block (paragraph) as it does in other applications. It inserts a line break command that moves the insertion point to the next line but retains the same formats as the previous line. To apply a new style, press CTRL-ENTER or choose New Paragraph from the Insert menu after the line before. The next line will begin a new text block that can be formatted separately from the text before it. To add another item to a numbered or bulleted list, choose New Item from the Insert menu.

Each site contains an index. The index is a Web page that serves as a home page for the site, with general information and links to the other pages. You'll see the Index page in its own window in SiteBuilder and as an icon in Site Manager. You create a site by designing the index page, then adding other pages as needed.

 NOTE: *Closing the Index page will also close the Web site.*

When you add a page to the site, its window appears in SiteBuilder, and its icon in the Site Manager. SiteBuilder inserts links to the other pages in the index automatically. For example, SiteBuilder includes a complete Web site example called Personal Website, shown in Figure 30-2. The Site Manager window shows the HTML pages that are part of the site and the links between pages. You display and edit the pages in the SiteBuilder window.

 TIP: *To see the HTML tags that actually create the Web site, select HTML View from the View menu, or right-click on the page and choose HTML Source from the menu that appears.*

Creating a Web Site

The initial default SiteBuilder window includes a blank Web site ready for you to create. Once you design a site it will be opened by default when you next start SiteBuilder.

You create a new site using these steps:

1. Pick a theme.

2. Add pages, text, graphics, and other page elements.

3. Set up for publishing.

4. Publish the Web site.

 TIP: *To start a new Web site, choose New from the File menu, then double-click on Blank Website. You can also choose to create a blank Web page, use a Personal Web Page template, or a Resume Web Page.*

SiteBuilder's
Personal
Website
template

FIGURE 30-2

Selecting a Theme

When designing the site, you'll be able to add backgrounds, buttons, lines, and other graphic elements from the Content Gallery. You can choose the theme (the overall design) of the available graphics before you start, or change the theme at any time.

Choose Change Theme from the Format menu to display the dialog box shown here. Choose the category of the theme from the buttons on the left. Click on the theme you want and then click on Apply.

You cannot mix images from more than one theme in the same site. If you change a theme, SiteBuilder replaces those already in your page with the corresponding image from the new theme.

 TIP: *You can download additional themes from the Corel Web site. Select Corel Web Site from the Help menu to launch your browser.*

Content Gallery

You are now ready to design your Web site. You can use the tools in the toolbars to format text and add elements to a page just as you do with Internet Publisher in Corel WordPerfect. To add pages and other elements to the site, click on the Show/Hide Content Gallery button in the toolbar, or select Content Gallery from the View menu to see the dialog box shown here. You drag and drop Web page templates or page elements from the Content Gallery into the Web page.

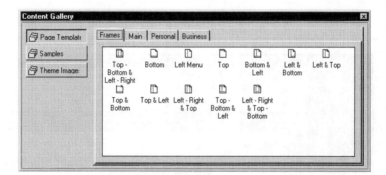

Adding Pages

The Page Template category contains complete predesigned Web pages. Drag and drop a page from the Content Gallery to the location in an existing page where you want the link to occur.

When you release the mouse, you'll see the options shown here.

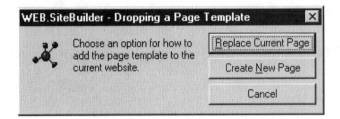

Click on Create New Page. SiteBuilder inserts a link at the drop position and opens a window with the template. For example, Figure 30-3 shows a Web site after the Alphabetical Index template was added to the index page. From the index page of your Web site, the user just clicks on the link to display the Alphabetical Index page.

NOTE: *Use the Windows menu to change windows, and to tile or cascade windows to see multiple windows at one time.*

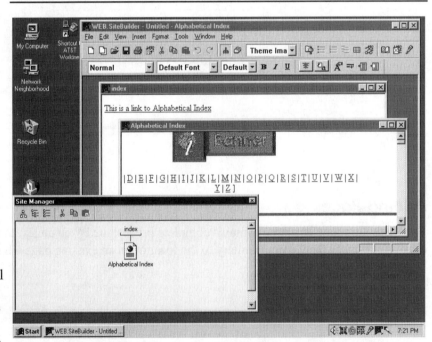

Alphabetical
listing page
added to the
site

FIGURE 30-3

The link text is generic, such as This is a link to Alphabetical Index. Drag over the link text and type the text that you want to appear on your Web page. To see that the link works correctly, right-click on it and choose Follow Link from the QuickMenu. SiteBuilder will open the window of the linked page.

If you choose the Replace Current Page option when you drop a template into the Web site, a box will appear asking you to confirm the action and reporting that it cannot be undone. Click on Replace. SiteBuilder replaces the contents of the current window with that of the new template but does not change the window name or the hyperlink text.

 You can add HTML pages to a Web site that you've already created with other Corel applications. Choose HTML File from the Insert menu.

Most of the pages contain headings and sample text that you replace with your own. To automate adding your own text, select Replace Sample Text from the Tools menu to display a PerfectExpert panel and to highlight the first text as shown in Figure 30-4. Type the text that you want to replace the highlighted text, then click on Next in the Perfect Expert Panel to move to the next text to replace. (Click on

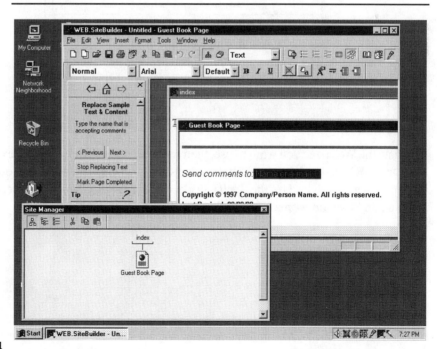

Replacing the default text

FIGURE 30-4

Previous to move back through the page.) Click on Stop Replacing Text to close the Perfect Expert panel if you want to continue replacing at some other time. Click on Mark Page Completed to accept the page as it is—the Replace Sample Text option will then be dimmed in the Tools menu for that page.

When Perfect Expert reaches a hyperlink to be replaced it displays a dialog box asking for the URL of the site. Enter the URL and click on OK.

 NOTE: *The Frames tab contains various combinations and shapes of frames within a blank page. You'll learn more about frames in the "Working with Frames" section later in this chapter.*

You can also use Web pages from the Internet as the basis for a page in your site. Select Retrieve Page from the File menu. In the dialog box that appears, click on OK to launch your Web browser and display the options shown here:

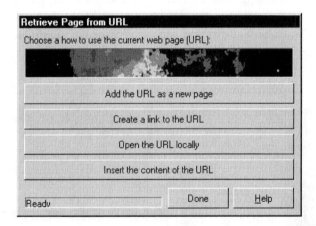

Navigate the Web page you want to use, then select an option from the Retrieve Page from the URL dialog box. Use SiteBuilder's tools to edit the site with our own information and images. Use the Spell Check option in the Tools menu to check your spelling, and look up words by choosing Thesaurus from the Tools menu.

NOTE: *To delete a page, click on its icon in Site Manager, press DELETE and select Yes from the box that appears. Then, delete any links to the page from other pages in the site.*

Adding Page Elements

30

The *Samples* category of the Content Gallery contains typical Web page elements that you can drag and drop into an existing page, such as a bulleted or numbered list of links, a link to your home page, and an e-mail link. Dragging an item from the Samples tab does not start a new page, as with the Page Templates, but inserts the item into the current page.

The Samples category contains five tabs, as shown here:

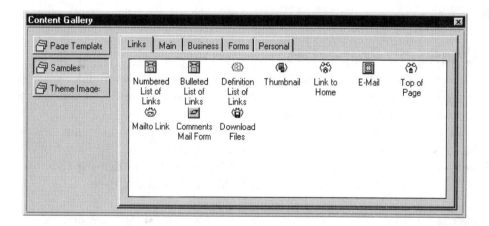

Click on the tab for the type of item you want to insert, then drag an item to the page where you want it to appear. If the element contains sample text, use the Replace Sample Text command from the Tools menu to replace it.

Theme Images

The *Theme Images* category includes buttons, bullets, horizontal bars, and backgrounds that are coordinated with your selected theme, as shown here. Drag and drop an element where you want it in your Web page.

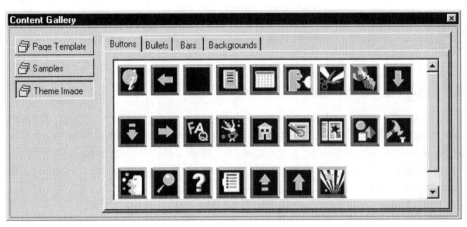

Changing Properties

Pages and objects that you insert are formatted according to SiteBuilder's default properties. You can change the properties to customize how the object appears and acts when viewed by a Web browser.

The page properties affect the overall look of the page, including its title, background color, and link colors. To change the properties, choose Page from the Format menu to see the dialog box shown in Figure 30-5. (You can also right-click on the page, point to Properties in the QuickMenu, then choose Page.)

 NOTE: *If the page contains frames, click on the Page tab of the dialog box that appears to set page properties.*

The Title is the text that appears in the title bar when the page is displayed. The Filename is the name under which the page is stored on your disk. Avoid changing filenames because they are used by hyperlinks to locate and open the page. If you change a page's filename, you'll have to edit all of the links to that page. The main reason to change a filename, however, is to avoid overwriting existing Web pages with the same name.

Use the properties to choose a background color, image, or sound. You can also choose to have the sound play more than once or play continuously while the page is open. When you use an image or sound that is not already in your current Web site directory, a message appears reporting that SiteBuilder will move it there for you so it can access the file.

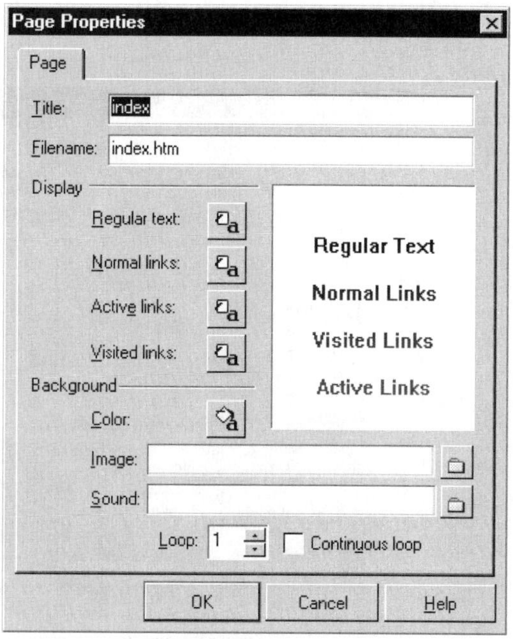

Setting page
properties

FIGURE 30-5

Using Images

In addition to the graphics available in Content Gallery, you can insert a graphic that
you have on disk. SiteBuilder can use graphics in the GIF (static or animated), JPEG,
BMP, and PCX formats. Choose Graphic From File from the Insert menu to see the
Image Properties dialog box shown in Figure 30-6. Enter the path and name of the
file in the Image Source box, or use the Browse or Web Browse buttons to locate
the file. The other options in the dialog box define the image properties.

Setting Image Properties

You can define the image's properties when you insert it into the page or at any time
later. Double-click on the image, button, bullet, or graphic line that you've inserted
to display the Properties box.

   In the Alternate Text box, enter text you want to appear in those cases where the
reader's Web browser is unable to display the graphic. You can also change the

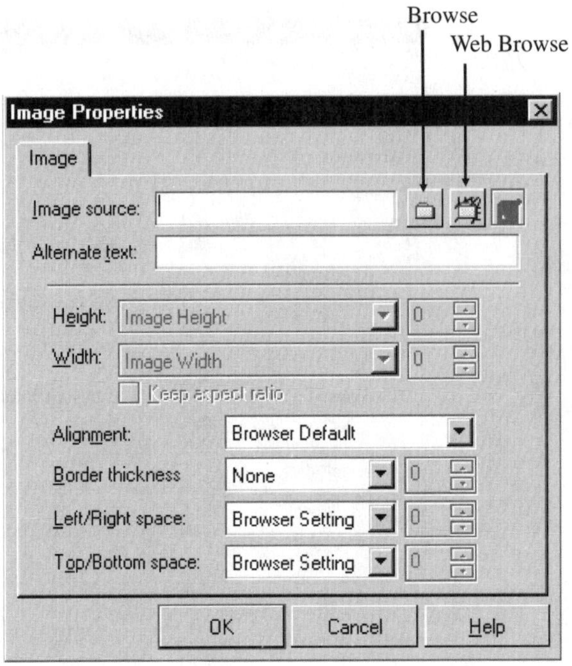

Browse
Web Browse

Inserting a
graphic
from the
disk

FIGURE 30-6

image's height and width, its alignment, the thickness of the border around it, and the spacing between it and text.

TIP: *You will soon learn how to use an image for a hyperlink and how to create an image map.*

Creating Hyperlinks

You can also insert hyperlinks in addition to those inserted automatically by SiteBuilder when you add another page. A hyperlink can be text or an image. To create a hyperlink, select the text or image that you want to use for the link, then click on the Hyperlink button in the toolbar to see the dialog box in Figure 30-7.

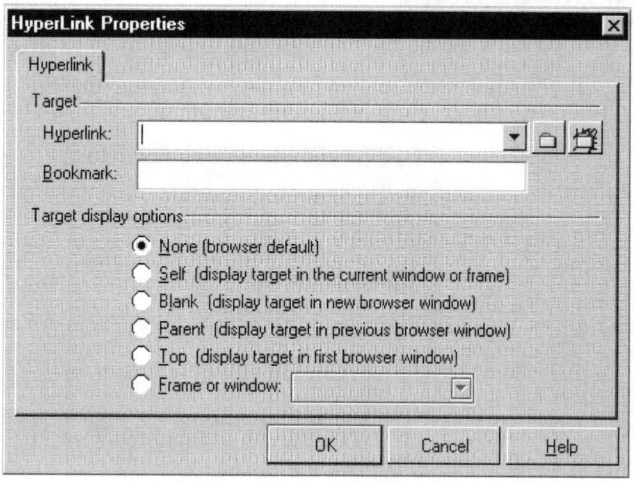

Creating a
hyperlink

FIGURE 30-7

  TIP: *To create a bookmark to use for the destination of the link, select the text or image, then choose Bookmark from the Format menu. In the dialog box that appears, type a name for the bookmark that is not currently being used, then click on OK.*

In the Hyperlink text box, enter the complete URL of the site you want to jump to. You can pull down the list associated with the text box to select to jump to the index page, or to enter a prefix such as ftp://, gopher://, and others used by the Internet. To jump to a site on the current page, choose [current page] from the list, then choose the bookmark name from the Bookmark drop-down list. Use the Target Display Options section to determine how the hyperlink appears.

TIP: *Used links appear in red in SiteBuilder but not in your Web browser.*

Creating Image Maps

When you double-click on an image, the Image Properties dialog box also contains the Image Map tab, shown here:

By using an image map, you can define different hyperlinks for various areas of a graphic. Which link is jumped to depends on the area of the image clicked.

There are two types of maps that can be created:

- A server-side image map sends the coordinates of the insertion point to the server, which then computes the URL of the hyperlink.

- A client-side image map contains the coordinates directly on the page by defining a hotspot for each link. Unfortunately, client-side image maps are not supported by all Web browsers.

SiteBuilder automatically creates both types of image maps for you. To use or create an image map, enable the Use Image Map checkbox, then click on Create Map to display a dialog box like the one shown in Figure 30-8.

The notation "Default (background)" represents areas of the image not separately defined for a link. In the Target URL box type the URL that you want to jump to when you click on a background area of the graphic.

Next, click on the shape tool for the area of the image you want to map. For example, if you want to map a rectangular area of the image as a hotspot, click on the rectangle shape tool. Drag the tool on the image to draw the shape, then enter the URL for that area. The Elements list will show the shape and names of all of the defined areas. Continue designating areas and the URLs for all of the other

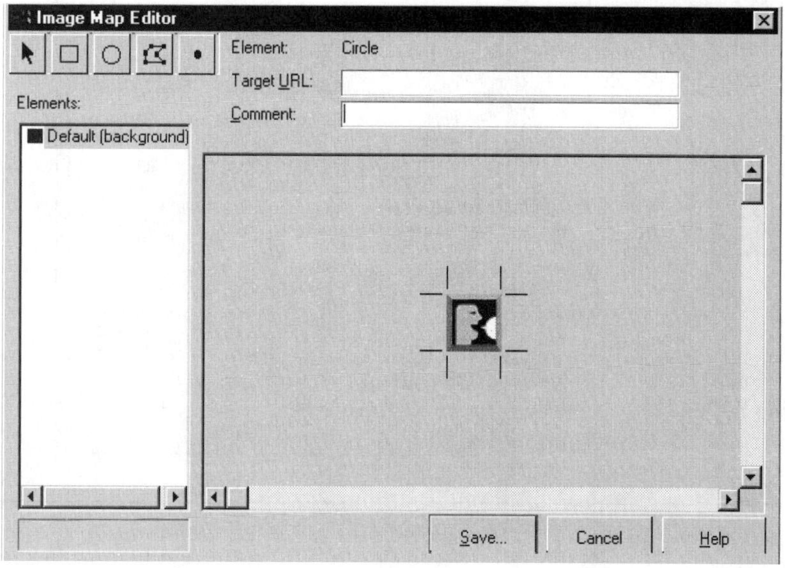

Creating an
image map

FIGURE 30-8

hyperlinks you want to create. When you're done, click on Save, then enter an image
map name.

Creating a Marquee

A marquee is text that scrolls across the screen when your Web site is viewed in a
browser. Select Marquee from the Insert menu to display the dialog box shown in
Figure 30-9.

TIP: *Not all Web browsers support the scrolling of the marquee.*

Type the text that you want to appear in the marquee and choose a background
color. Select the alignment of the marquee in relation to other text on the line, set its
height and width, and its horizontal and vertical spacing.

The setting in the Behavior list determines how the text scrolls across the screen.
Your options are to have the text scroll left or right, slide left or right, or alternate
its starting direction. Choose an option and whether to loop the movement
continuously or a specific number of times.

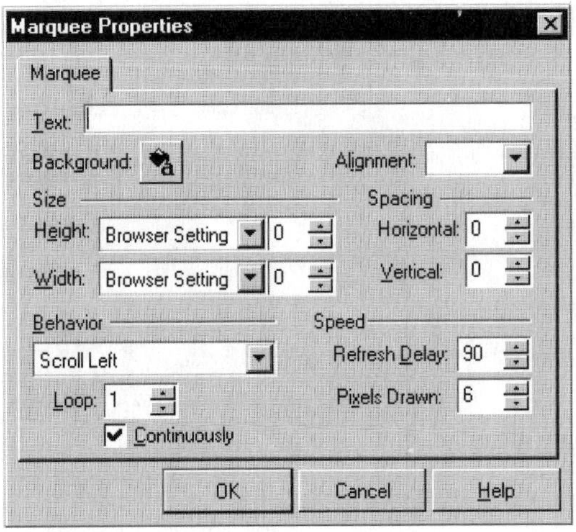

Designing a
marquee
FIGURE 30-9

The Refresh Display setting determines the time between each scroll across the page. The Pixel Drawn setting sets the number of pixels to present on each scrolling move.

Inserting a Banner

A banner is a rectangular text box with an icon from the current theme, such as shown here. Unlike a marquee, the banner text does not scroll, but you can choose the icon that appears and change the font, size, and color of the test.

Select Banner from the Insert menu to display the dialog box shown in Figure 30-10. Choose the icon to appear on the banner from the drop-down list, the alignment, and enter the banner text. Click on Update Preview to see how the banner will appear.

To change the font of the text, select the checkbox labeled Use a Font From Your Own computer, then select a font from the pull-down list, choose the text size, and the text color.

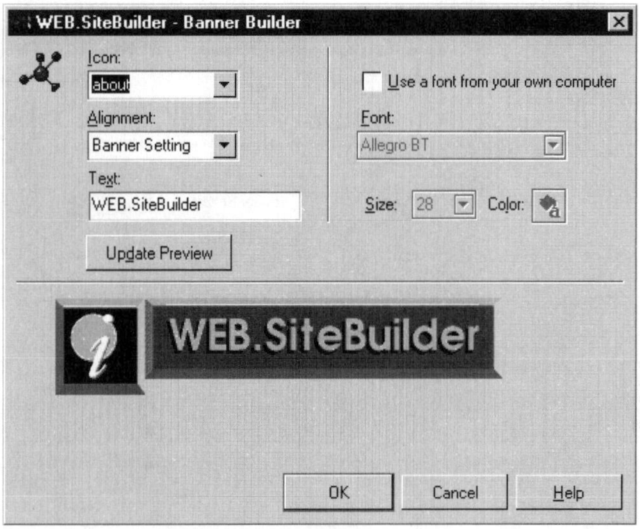

Adding a
banner to
the page

FIGURE 30-10

> **NOTE:** *The icons and default banner text and style are determined by the selected theme.*

Working with Frames

A framed Web page is divided into two or more windows. Use frames to display information in easy-to-read sections. The windows are independent, so scrolling the information in one window will not affect the others. Use the Content Gallery to select the layout of the page you want, then add and format text with the frames.

To set frame properties, right-click on the frame, point to Properties, and then click on Page/Frame. Click on the Frame tab of the dialog box that appears to see the options shown in Figure 30-11. Each frame is assigned a unique URL name. You can change the name or enter an URL to use for the frame contents. You can also select to display a border, choose if you want the user to be able to resize the frame, and specify the margin and frame size. In the Scrolling list, choose if you want the user to be able to scroll the frame, or have it scroll automatically (the Browser Setting option).

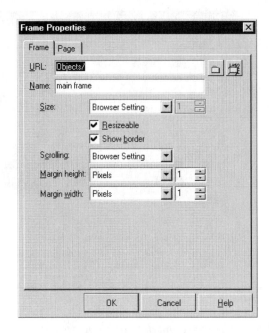

Frame
options

FIGURE 30-11

NOTE: *The Frames option in the Format menu lets you split, combine, and delete frames.*

Creating Forms

You can add forms to your Web site to accept information from readers, such as order forms and questionnaires. Forms can contain text boxes, checkboxes, radio buttons, drop-down lists, and other elements to display and accept information, as shown in Figure 30-12.

   To use a form on your Web site, you also have to create a CGI (Common Gateway Interface) script. The script allows your Web site to deal with the information entered into the form. SiteBuilder can create a CGI script for you that records the responses to the form and displays the form entries onscreen on your Web site.

NOTE: *Beyond using SiteBuilder to create scripts, CGI is well beyond the scope of this book.*

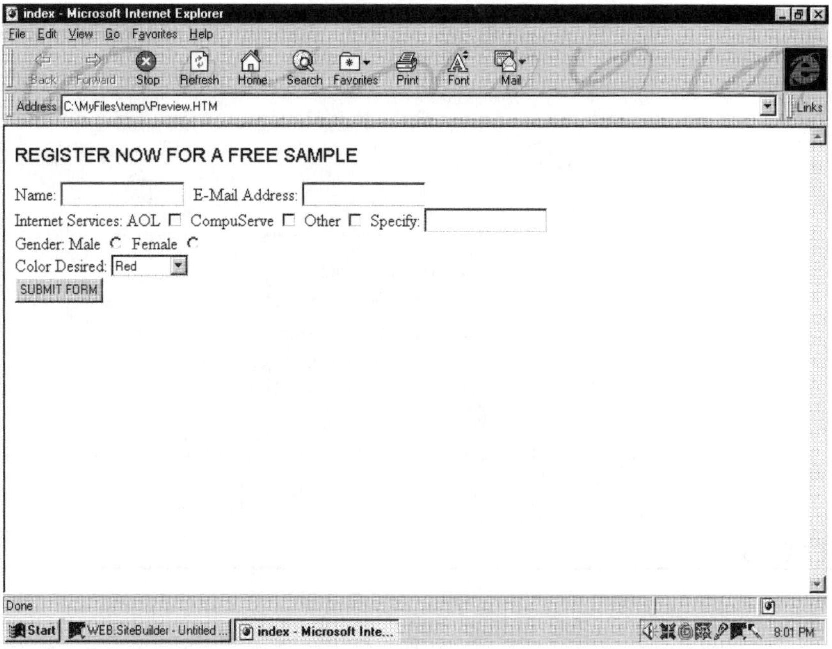

A SiteBuilder form

FIGURE 30-12

To create a form, click in the Web page where you want the form to appear, then select Form from the Insert menu to display the dialog box shown in Figure 30-13. Type the URL of the CGI script (if there is one) that will control the form, then choose a Target Display Option to determine how the form appears.

TIP: *Use PerfectExpert to help create forms.*

If you do not have a CGI script, just leave the CGI Script text box empty. You can still create the form, although it will not actually function in the browser window. You can later designate the CGI script by double-clicking on the form's border (or right-clicking on the form and choosing Properties) to redisplay the Form Properties dialog box.

Click on OK in the dialog box to display a blank form indicated by a dashed rectangular border.

Next, insert text and form objects to the form. Place the insertion point where you want the object to appear, then select Form Element from the Insert menu to

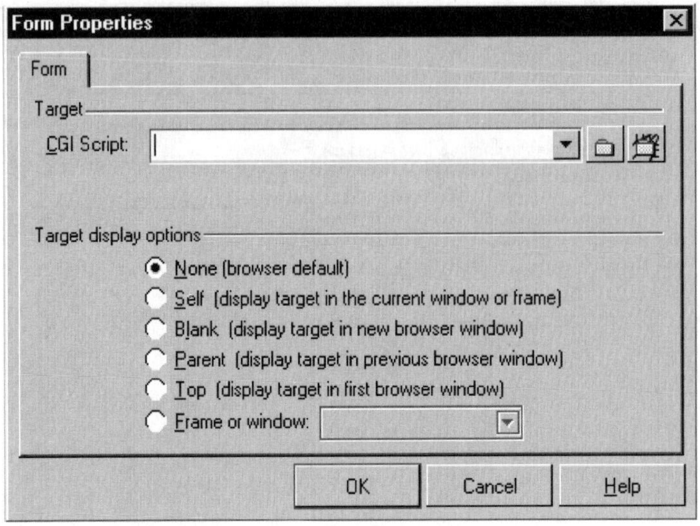

Form Properties

Form

Target
CGI Script:

Target display options
- ⦿ None (browser default)
- ○ Self (display target in the current window or frame)
- ○ Blank (display target in new browser window)
- ○ Parent (display target in previous browser window)
- ○ Top (display target in first browser window)
- ○ Frame or window:

[OK] [Cancel] [Help]

Creating a
form

FIGURE 30-13

display these options: Text Field, Button, Check Box, Radio Button, and List/Menu.
Click on the object you want to insert.

Double-click on the object to display its properties box. The options shown in
the box depend on the object:

- *Text Field*—Field name, type (single line, multiple line, or password
  field), fixed width, maximum length, and initial value.

- *Button*—Field name and label, and type (submit the form contents to
  URL, reset form with the default values, or normal).

- *Check box*—Field name, value sent to script when checked, and
  initial setting.

- *Radio button*—Field name, value sent to scripts when selected, and
  initial setting.

- *List/Menu*—Field name, choose a drop down list or displayed list, number
  of items in the displayed list, and if user can select multiple items, and the
  label, value, and initial states of the items. You can create, edit, and delete
  list items.

TIP: *You must include a button object set to submit the form contents to the URL.*

Creating a CGI Script

When the form is complete, you can generate the CGI script files necessary to store responses in a database and display the user's entries on screen. Make sure that the insertion point is within the form and choose Generate Script from the Tools menu to see the first of several CGI Expert dialog boxes, shown in Figure 30-14.

 NOTE: *You'll be warned if you still need to set any form properties to create a meaningful script.*

In this first box, enter the base name for the necessary files. Your entry will serve as the name for DAT (database), HTML, and CGI files generated by SiteBuilder.

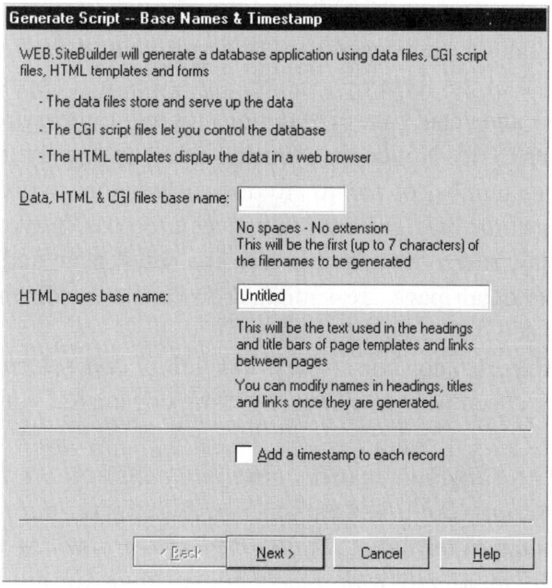

Generate Script -- Base Names & Timestamp

WEB.SiteBuilder will generate a database application using data files, CGI script files, HTML templates and forms

- The data files store and serve up the data

- The CGI script files let you control the database

- The HTML templates display the data in a web browser

Data, HTML & CGI files base name: [   ]

No spaces - No extension
This will be the first (up to 7 characters) of the filenames to be generated

HTML pages base name: [Untitled   ]

This will be the text used in the headings and title bars of page templates and links between pages

You can modify names in headings, titles and links once they are generated.

☐ Add a timestamp to each record

‹ Back   Next ›   Cancel   Help

Generating
a CGI script

FIGURE 30-14

You should also enter the base name for other HTML files to be generated, and select to time stamp each record stored in the database.

Click on Next to display the second Expert dialog box. In this box, you choose which files SiteBuilder should create:

- To convert the form into a form page template for storing information.

- A summary page that lists all of the responses in list or table format.

- A detail page that shows each user's response per page.

Check the checkboxes for the forms you want to create, then click on Next to select the type of feedback—what happens when the user submits the form. You can have feedback represented by any of these choices:

- A template created by the script, with a title and message that you enter.

- A specific page that you select from your site.

- A message that you specify is added to the form page.

- No feedback.

The next dialog boxes depend on the forms you selected SiteBuilder to create. If you chose all of the form options, dialog boxes will appear for the form page, summary page, and detail page. The options for the summary page, for example, are shown in Figure 3-15. Notice that you can select to display the records in either a list or table, the number of records to display, whether to display them in reverse order, and to include links for moving between records. You can also choose which fields to display, and to include a link to the detail page and a mail-to page. The options for the detail page are similar. You can later edit the appearance of the summary and detail pages in SiteBuilder.

The final Expert dialog box displays a review of your selections. Read the review, selecting Back if you want to change a setting or Finish if you are done.

NOTE: *SiteBuilder uses something called the Perl 5 Interpreter to run CGI scripts. Both Perl 5 and Corel IntraServer must be installed on your computer to test your scripts. Perl is not installed when you perform a "typical" installation, only with a custom one. Your ISP must also have Perl and several Perl library files that can be obtained from Corel.*

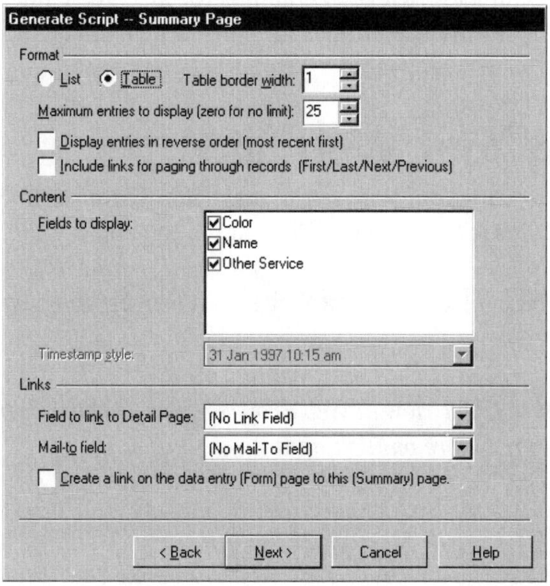

Generate Script -- Summary Page

Format
○ List   ● Table   Table border width: 1
Maximum entries to display (zero for no limit): 25
☐ Display entries in reverse order (most recent first)
☐ Include links for paging through records (First/Last/Next/Previous)

Content
Fields to display:
☑ Color
☑ Name
☑ Other Service

Timestamp style: 31 Jan 1997 10:15 am

Links
Field to link to Detail Page: (No Link Field)
Mail-to field: (No Mail-To Field)
☐ Create a link on the data entry (Form) page to this (Summary) page.

< Back   Next >   Cancel   Help

Summary
page options

FIGURE 30-15

Using Site Manager

You use Site Manager to view and change the overall organization of your Web site. Site Manager displays your Web site in three views. You choose which view you'd like but selecting one of the first three buttons on the Site Manager toolbar.

- Site Map shows the overall structure of your site. It is much like an organization chart, but illustrates where each page is linked from. Double-click on a page icon to open the page. You can also drag and drop a page icon, automatically inserting a link to it in the page where you drop the icon.

- Site Outline shows the structure of your site, much as your disk contents are displayed in Windows Explorer. As with Explorer, you can double-click on a site to collapse and expand its structure, and you can move a page to change its position.

■   The Site Object List displays the page, image, and script files much like a details directory view, in columns for the page name, title, and type. This view is mostly used for sorting the files that make up the site.

Publishing Your Web Site

You have to publish your Web site to make it available to Internet users. Publishing places the HTML pages of your Web site in the appropriate folder of your disk or server.

Before you publish your first Web site, however, you have to set up your system for publishing.

TIP: *Select View in Web Browser from the View menu to see how your site appears before publishing it.*

Setting Up for Publishing

The setup procedure saves a set of specifications describing how to publish Web sites. You can create more than one set, then switch between them depending on the Web site.

To set up SiteBuilder for publishing, save your site, then choose Publish from the File menu or click on the Publish Project button in the toolbar to see the Publish dialog box. In the Publish dialog box, click on the Setup button to see the dialog box shown here:

Type a name to identify the setup information site, then choose a protocol from the Type list. The Type options are File Copy, Ftp, HTTP, and WEB.IntraServer.

Use the File Copy option to publish the site to a connected drive or server, then enter the path where the files should be stored. Use the WEB.IntraServer option to publish the site to a computer using Corel WEB.IntraServer intranet.

To publish the site to your ISP, use the HTTP or FTP options, enter the full http:// or the ftp:// address, and specify the user name and password in the Security section of the dialog box.

Click on the Save button, then repeat the procedure for any other sets of setup specifications.

Publishing

After you've created the setup specifications you're ready to publish the site. Choose Publish from the File menu, then pull down the Setup Name list and choose the specifications to use. When publishing with the HTTP or FTP protocol, enter your username and password. Your ISP can tell you what specifications to use.

 TIP: *If you selected the Remember Username and Password checkbox when creating a setup specification, you do not have to enter the username and password when publishing the site.*

Select an option in the Pages and Other Files to Publish section—all of the files, only selected files, or only new and updates files. If you select Only Selected Files, click on the Select Files button to see a dialog box listing the files in the Web site. Check the files you want to publish, and uncheck the files you do not want to publish.

Finally, click on Publish.

Choosing SiteBuilder Settings

You can customize some of SiteBuilder's settings. Select Settings from the Tools menu to see the dialog box shown in Figure 30-16.

In the Environment section of the dialog box, set the default folder for your Web sites, the Internet browser you use, and the image editor for working with graphics. In the Startup section, enter the default name you want to use for your site home pages, and choose a new default theme.

By default, SiteBuilder will open with your last open Web site displayed. Deselect the Start With Last Open Website button if you want SiteBuilder to open with a blank Web site. You can also choose not to show a confirming prompt when you add a new file to the site.

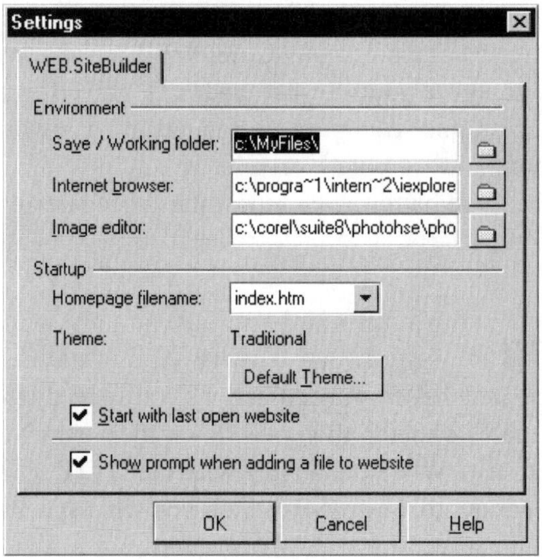

Customizing
SiteBuilder
settings

FIGURE 30-16

Corel WEB.IntraServer

If your company has a network or intranet, you can use Corel WEB.IntraServer to use your computer as a Web server. An intranet offers Internet-like capabilities on your company's network. When you publish your Web site to the WEB.IntraServer option, the site will then be available to anyone browsing on the network or intranet. Users just need to know your computer's name or IP address.

NOTE: *You may need to configure the TCP/IP interface of your operating system to put your Web server online. Consult your system administrator if you need additional information.*

After you publish to the WEB.IntraServer, start the server by running it from the Corel WordPerfect Suite 8 Accessories menu. The server window shows a list of the files that make up your site, as shown in Figure 30-17, and your site is now accessible in the intranet.

To publish HTML pages to the server that you created with other applications, such as Corel WordPerfect or Corel Presentations, just drag its file or folder to the

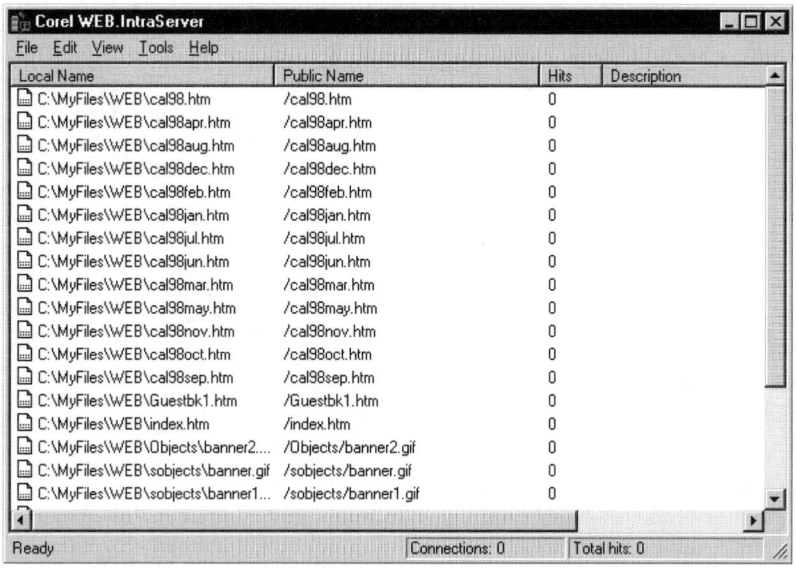

Local Name	Public Name	Hits	Description
C:\MyFiles\WEB\cal98.htm	/cal98.htm	0	
C:\MyFiles\WEB\cal98apr.htm	/cal98apr.htm	0	
C:\MyFiles\WEB\cal98aug.htm	/cal98aug.htm	0	
C:\MyFiles\WEB\cal98dec.htm	/cal98dec.htm	0	
C:\MyFiles\WEB\cal98feb.htm	/cal98feb.htm	0	
C:\MyFiles\WEB\cal98jan.htm	/cal98jan.htm	0	
C:\MyFiles\WEB\cal98jul.htm	/cal98jul.htm	0	
C:\MyFiles\WEB\cal98jun.htm	/cal98jun.htm	0	
C:\MyFiles\WEB\cal98mar.htm	/cal98mar.htm	0	
C:\MyFiles\WEB\cal98may.htm	/cal98may.htm	0	
C:\MyFiles\WEB\cal98nov.htm	/cal98nov.htm	0	
C:\MyFiles\WEB\cal98oct.htm	/cal98oct.htm	0	
C:\MyFiles\WEB\cal98sep.htm	/cal98sep.htm	0	
C:\MyFiles\WEB\Guestbk1.htm	/Guestbk1.htm	0	
C:\MyFiles\WEB\index.htm	/index.htm	0	
C:\MyFiles\WEB\Objects\banner2....	/Objects/banner2.gif	0	
C:\MyFiles\WEB\sobjects\banner.gif	/sobjects/banner.gif	0	
C:\MyFiles\WEB\sobjects\banner1...	/sobjects/banner1.gif	0	

Corel WEB.IntraServer

Ready   Connections: 0   Total hits: 0

Putting your
site online
in an
intranet

FIGURE 30-17

file list box of the Corel WEB.IntraServer window. You can also use the Add File
command from the WEB.IntraServer Edit menu.

NOTE: *Corel WordPerfect Suite 8 also includes Corel Web Server
software for using your computer as an Internet server or as a Paradox
Integration Server. Run it from the Corel WordPerfect Suite 8
Accessories menu.*

Using CorelCENTRAL

31

CorelCENTRAL is a handy set of desktop tools—the same type of resources that you'd keep handy on your actual desk, such as a calendar and address book. CorelCENTRAL is also integrated with Netscape Communicator to provide e-mail, messaging, and online help features. So, for example, you can schedule a meeting, add it to your calendar, then e-mail a notice of the event to add it to the calendars of other CorelCENTRAL users.

In this chapter, you'll learn the basics of using CorelCENTRAL. This first step is to select the CorelCENTRAL option from the Reference Center in the Corel WordPerfect Suite Setup & Notes menu.

> **TIP:**   *Not all of the CorelCENTRAL functions described in this chapter will be available if you did not install Netscape Communicator. If some of your dialog boxes appear different than those shown here, then you do not have Netscape Communicator installed. See the section "CorelCENTRAL Lite" at the end of this chapter.*

Introducing CorelCENTRAL

CorelCENTRAL includes these features:

- A *calendar* for keeping track of appointments, calls, and things you have to do—with daily, weekly, monthly, or yearly views. You can also schedule multi-day activities and a special occasions list for recording birthdays, anniversaries, and other events.

- An *activity log* that summarizes your activities, and which is integrated with your calendar, card file, and phone dialer.

- An *address book* for recording names and addresses, which shares its information with the Corel Address Book 8 accessory.

- A *card file* for creating databases of all types.

- A *phone dialer* for calling persons listed in your card file or address book.

- A *mailbox* for sending, receiving, and managing e-mail and discussion group messages.

- A *help desk* with links for online support on Corel applications.

The best way to learn the features of CorelCENTRAL is to start the program and look at its window. To start CorelCENTRAL, click on the CorelCENTRAL button in the DAD bar, or click on the Start button, point to Corel WordPerfect Suite 8, and click on CorelCENTRAL.

TIP: *The first time you start CorelCENTRAL or Netscape Communicator, you'll have to create a user profile. Refer to Chapter 3 for additional information on creating and using profiles.*

Now look at the CorelCENTRAL window shown in Figure 31-1. The initial screen shows the Calendar view. CorelCENTRAL provides six views—ways of looking at information. Each view contains a menu bar and a toolbar whose buttons depend on the view displayed. Below the toolbar is the View bar. Click on the icon in the View bar for the view you want to display:

NOTE: *You can also change views by selecting Main View from the View menu, then selecting the view to display.*

Your selection from the View bar becomes the *main view*, which occupies most of the screen. You can also select an *additional view*, displaying two CorelCENTRAL features at one time. To display an additional view, choose Additional View from the View menu, or pull down the list on the lower right of the screen, and choose the view to add. The additional view appears in the lower right of the screen. To remove the additional view, choose Additional View from the View menu and click on Close Additional View.

Planners

When you first start CorelCENTRAL, it will contain a *planner* for the default user's profile. A planner contains a calendar, address book, and card file that you can use immediately. You can also create additional planners to manage specialized calendars or card files. Whenever you open CorelCENTRAL, it will automatically

Card File   Activity Log

Address Book   Mailbox

Calendar   Help Desk

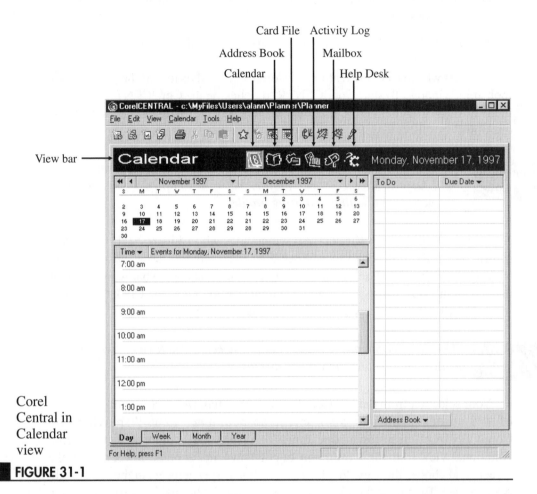

View bar

Corel
Central in
Calendar
view

FIGURE 31-1

open the last planner you were working with. You can have only one planner open at a time, but a planner can contain more than one card file. All changes you make to the planner, such as adding a calendar event or card, are saved automatically—you do not have to select a save action.

The default planner, called simply Planner, is stored in the \MyFiles\Users folder, under a subfolder of the profile name, as in c:\myfiles\users\alann\planner\planner. The folder contains the overall planner files, as well as subfolders storing calendar, address book, and card file information. The main planner file has the CCP extension.

CAUTION: *The default location for planners may be changed with your release of Corel WordPerfect Suite.*

To create a new planner, select New from the File menu. Click on the Create New tab of the New dialog box, then make sure that [CorelCENTRAL 8] is chosen in the categories drop-down list. Click on [CorelCENTRAL Planner] and then on Create. In a series of dialog boxes, enter the required information, clicking Next when you are done with each box:

- The planner name

- The default card files—Personal, Memo, and Reference

- Where to store the file—in the default CorelCENTRAL location or another location of your choice

When you select Finish in the last dialog box, the planner is saved and opened into the CorelCENTRAL window. If you select to use the default location, the planner is stored in the \MyFiles\Users folder, under a subfolder of the profile name, as in c:\myfiles\users\alann\planner\planner1.ccp.

 TIP: *Calendars, address books, and card files created in CorelCENTRAL planners can become corrupted by computer glitches. Use the Maintenance option in the File menu to rebuild the indexes or otherwise clean up files that CorelCENTRAL has problems using.*

To open a planner, choose Open Planner from the File menu. If the planner CCP file is not listed, navigate to the location it is stored in, then double-click on the planner name.

Now let's look at the components of a CorelCENTRAL planner.

NOTE: *The Mailbox feature of CorelCENTRAL is discussed in Chapter 3.*

Using the Calendar

Use the calendar to schedule appointments, and to keep track of special occasions. If you're connected to the Internet, you can also schedule events and give assignments to others. If they use CorelCENTRAL, the event can be added directly to their own calendars; otherwise, it appears as a message on their e-mail system.

The calendar window contains the toolbar and items shown in Figure 31-2. To display the calendar if it is not already on screen, click on the Calendar icon in the View bar.

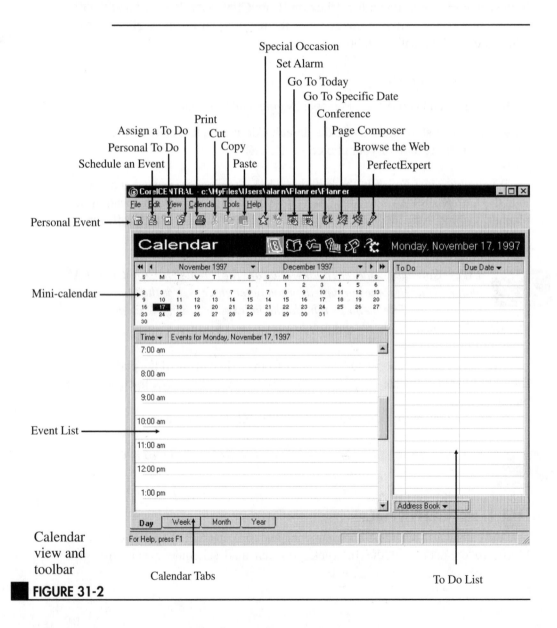

Special Occasion
Set Alarm
Go To Today
Go To Specific Date
Conference
Print
Assign a To Do   Cut   Page Composer
Personal To Do   Copy   Browse the Web
Schedule an Event   Paste   PerfectExpert

Personal Event

Mini-calendar

Event List

Calendar
view and
toolbar

Calendar Tabs

To Do List

FIGURE 31-2

You can enter information into the appointment book and add a To Do item. To see your appointments for another day, just click on the date in the mini-calendar. Scroll the month and year bars or pull down the Month list to change months.

NOTE: *Use the Calendar tabs to change to day, week, month, or year calendars. Double-click on a date in the week, month, or year calendars to display the date in day view.*

31

Scheduling a Personal Event

CorelCENTRAL lets you record two types of events—personal and group. A personal event is the same as an appointment, an event that you'd add to your personal calendar. A group event is one that involves one or more persons that you want to notify of the event. We'll look at scheduled events later in this chapter.

To add a personal event, follow these steps:

1. Select the month and year of the appointment.

2. Click on the day in the mini-calendar.

3. Click on the time in the Event List, scrolling the times if necessary.

4. Type information about the appointment.

5. Click elsewhere or press ENTER.

The event appears in a colored box, representing the default one-hour duration. An event icon appears before the text and an icon of an alarm clock appears next to the appointment, as shown here:

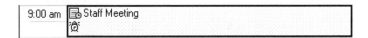

Here are some ways to work with events in the calendar:

■ To delete an event, click on it and press the DELETE key.

■ To edit the text of the event, click on its description, then edit it as you would other text.

- Drag and drop the event by the Event icon of the calendar to change its starting time. As you drag, CorelCENTRAL highlights the time where the event will be placed when you release the mouse.

- Drag the top border of the selected event to change its start time, increasing its duration.

- Drag the bottom border of the selected event to change its ending time, decreasing its duration.

Setting an Alarm

By default, CorelCENTRAL sets an alarm to sound ten minutes before each event, as indicated by the Clock icon in the events list. There is also a "snooze" option that repeats the alarm every five minutes until you turn off the alarm. You can turn off the alarm, change its timing and snooze amount, and even change the sound that plays when the alarm goes off.

TIP: *To quickly set or remove an alarm, right-click on the event and select Alarm from the QuickMenu.*

Click on the appointment in the Events List, then click on the Set Alarm button in the toolbar, or choose Set Alarm from the Calendar menu, to see the dialog box shown here:

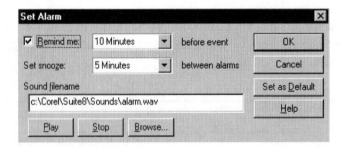

Deselect the Remind Me checkbox to remove the alarm from the event. To change the timing, pull down the first list and select the lead time that you want— *lead time* is how long before the time of the appointment the alarm will sound. Change the snooze time from the Set Snooze list. Use the Sound Filename box to change the sound that plays, or use the Browse button to locate a sound file on your disk.

When the alarm time occurs and CorelCENTRAL is running, the alarm sound is played and a dialog box appears listing the events. Click on the event in the list and then on OK or Snooze.

Special Occasions

A special occasion is an event, such as a birthday or anniversary, that you want to be reminded of. CorelCENTRAL has a set of special occasions already defined for holidays in your country, but you can add your own occasions to the list.

To display a special occasion, choose Special Occasions from the Calendar menu to display the Special Occasions dialog box. To place holidays on the calendar, click on the Holiday Sets button in the box, choose your country in the box that appears, and then click on OK. The holidays will appear in the Special Occasions box as shown here. Delete a holiday from the list using the Delete button, or change its date using the Edit button in the dialog box.

To add your own special occasion, click on Add to display the dialog box shown in Figure 31-3, then type a name for the event in the Name text box. If the day always falls on the same date, such as a birthday, use the Day of Month tab. Choose the Month from the pull-down list, then click on the date. Deselect the Repeat Annually box if you only want to schedule the event for the current year. Use the Day of Week tab if the event falls on a certain week, such as the first Monday of March. In the tab, choose the month, the number of the week the event occurs, and the day of the week.

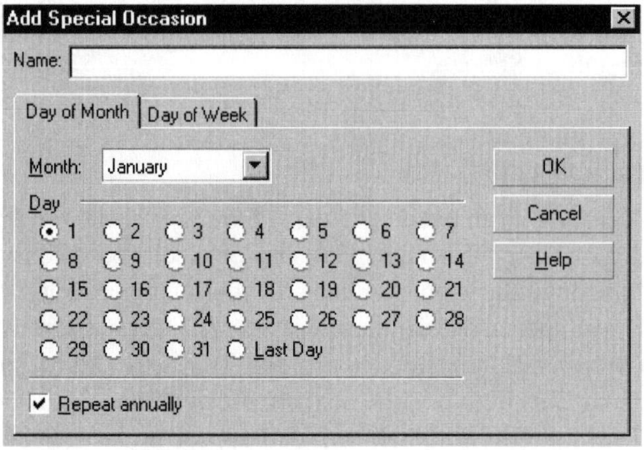

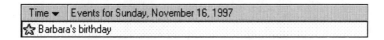

Add a
custom
special event

FIGURE 31-3

Click on OK, to add the event to the Special Occasions list, then close the Special Occasions dialog box.

Special Occasions appear in day, week, and month views with a star icon, as shown here.

Time ▾	Events for Sunday, November 16, 1997
☆ Barbara's birthday	

TIP: *To delete or edit a special occasion, right-click on it in Day view and select Edit or Delete from the QuickMenu.*

Customizing Personal Events

Each appointment can be associated with additional information, and you can change an event's duration or make it a recurring event. Double-click on the appointment to display the dialog box shown in Figure 31-4.

TIP: *You can also display the dialog box by clicking on the Personal Event button in the toolbar or by choosing Personal Event from the Calendar menu. Use the dialog box to edit the selected event or to create a new one.*

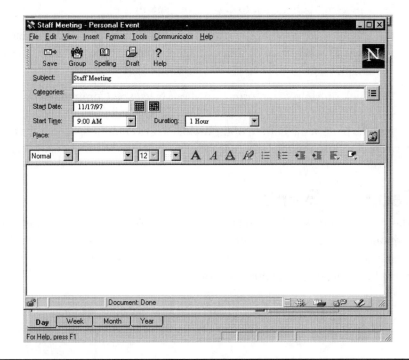

31

Entering
appointment
information

FIGURE 31-4

- Change or set the day, time, and duration of the task. To create a multiple day event, select the number of days from the duration list, or enter the number of days followed by the letter "d", as in 6d. Multiple day events are shown at the top of the calendar for each day—double-click on it to edit it.

- Choose a category, such as business or personal by clicking on the Categories button. To create a new category, type it in the Category text box, then select Yes when you are asked if you want to save the new category when closing the event window.

- Select a date by clicking on the Pop-up Calendar button.

- Locate a place for the meeting from the address book by clicking on the Address Book button.

- Click on Save to save the event to the calendar.

- Click on Group to change the message to a scheduled event.

- Click on Spell Check to check your spelling.

- Click on Save as Draft to save the text to the Drafts folder of the Mailbox view. Double-click on the message in Mailbox view to edit or complete the message.

- Click on Help for information about Netscape Communicator.

Use the pane at the bottom of the dialog box to enter notes about the event, using the page composer buttons as you learned in Chapter 3 to format using HTML styles.

Recurring Events

Many appointments, calls, and tasks you have to perform are recurring—they occur at regular intervals, such as every week or the first day of every month. You can set a recurring event from the Personal Event dialog box by clicking on the Recurring Event button to see the options shown here:

Choose the tab that represents when and how often you want the event to occur:

- *Weeks of Month* sets an event for the same day of the week each month, or for a certain number of months, such as on Monday of the first week of every month.

- *Days of Month* sets an event the same day of the month or any number of months, such as the 15th of every other month.

- *Weeks* sets an event the same day of every week or any number of weeks, such as every other Friday.

- *Days* sets the event for every day or any number of days, as in every 15 days.

Next, enter or select from the pop-up calendar the from and to dates for which to set the event—the default is one year. Chose options from the dialog box to set the recurring dates, and click on OK. The notation "Recurring Date" will appear in the Start Date text box, which will now be dimmed. When you save the event, CorelCENTRAL adds the event to each of the days that are determined by your selections.

Group Events

A group event is one that involves the calendars of more than one person. When you create a group event, you can e-mail it to others over the Internet. To create a group event, click on the Schedule an Event button in the toolbar. If you are already creating a Personal Event, click on the group button. The Event dialog box is shown in Figure 31-5.

This is similar to the standard e-mail window—the toolbar is the same, you can enter the recipient's e-mail addresses, add attachments, set message options, and enter and format a message. It also includes the features to schedule an event, just as you learned for a personal event. When you've completed the event, however, click on Send to transmit to the other users via e-mail.

When the event is received by the recipient, it is placed in their Inbox. When they click on the message, it appears along with a calendar noting the event date, as shown in Figure 31-6. They can then click on either the Accept or Decline button in the toolbar.

Clicking on Accept adds the event to their own calendar. Clicking on Decline simply leaves the item in their Inbox.

Using the To Do List

A *To Do list* contains reminders of things you have to do. You add items to the list and associate them with additional information, similar to appointments. You can

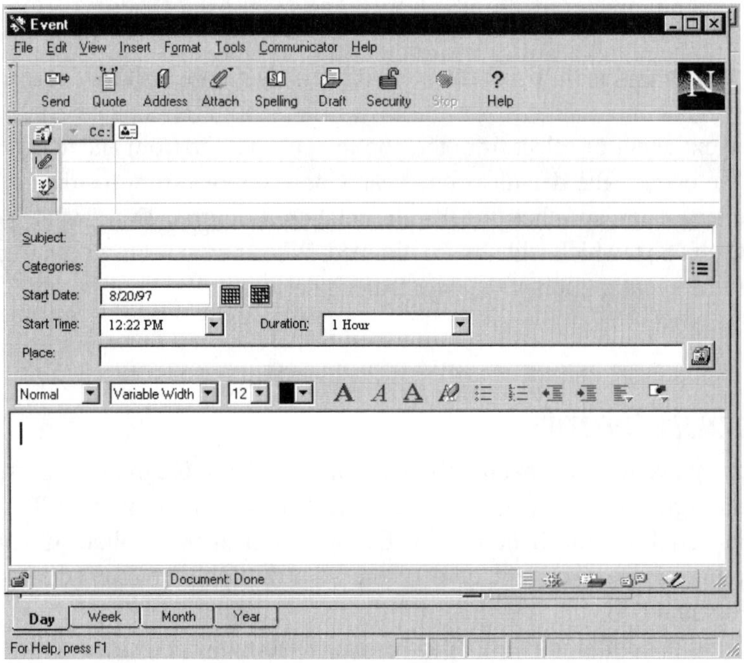

Scheduling
an event

FIGURE 31-5

create a personal to do item for yourself, or assign a to do item to others. Here's how to create a personal to do item by typing directly in the To Do list.

1. Click on an empty line in the To Do list.

2. Type a reminder or message, and press ENTER. A small Page icon appears next to the item and the current date in the Due Date column.

3. Double-click on the Page icon or the Due Date column to see the dialog box shown in Figure 31-7.

TIP: *You can also create a new personal to do item in the dialog box by clicking on the Personal To Do button on the toolbar.*

4. Select or enter a category.

5. Change Start Date or Due Date, using the pop-up calendars to select a date if needed. Deselect the Due Date button if there isn't any.

Accept

Decline

```
CorelCENTRAL - c:\MyFiles\Users\alann\Planner\Planner                    _ □ ✕
File  Edit  View  Message  Tools  Help
```

Mailbox   Wednesday, August 20, 1997

Name	Unre...	Total		Subject		Sender	Date ▽	Prio...
Local Mail				Welcom...	◦	Marc Andreessen	06/02/9...	Nor...
Inbox		4		Outstand...	◦	PressmanR@aol...	08/14/9...	
Unsent Mess...				Welfare r...	◦	PressmanR@aol...	08/14/9...	
Drafts				Chesin c...	◦	Alan Neibauer	08/20/9...	Nor...
Sent		1						

1997 November 1997

S	M	T	W	T	F	S
						1
2	3	4	5	6	7	8
9	10	11	12	13	14	15
16	17	18	19	20	21	22
23	24	25	26	27	28	29
30						

Start Date: 11/23/1997
End Date: 11/23/1997
Classification: PUBLIC

Event
14:00 - 15:00 : Chesin contract
meeting

```
Document: Done                                    Total: 4   Unread: 0
```

Receiving a
scheduled
event

▌ FIGURE 31-6

6. Enter or select the percentage complete, if you've already performed some of the task.

7. Select a priority.

8. Enter the text of any message.

9. Click on Save. Your item will be added to the To Do list and to the To Do folder in the mailbox.

If you entered a percentage complete greater than zero, but less than 100 percent, the item will have a green dot in the left-most column indicating it is a job in progress.

You can mark your actions as completed when they are done, and choose how you want them sorted in the To Do list. When you complete an activity, click on the

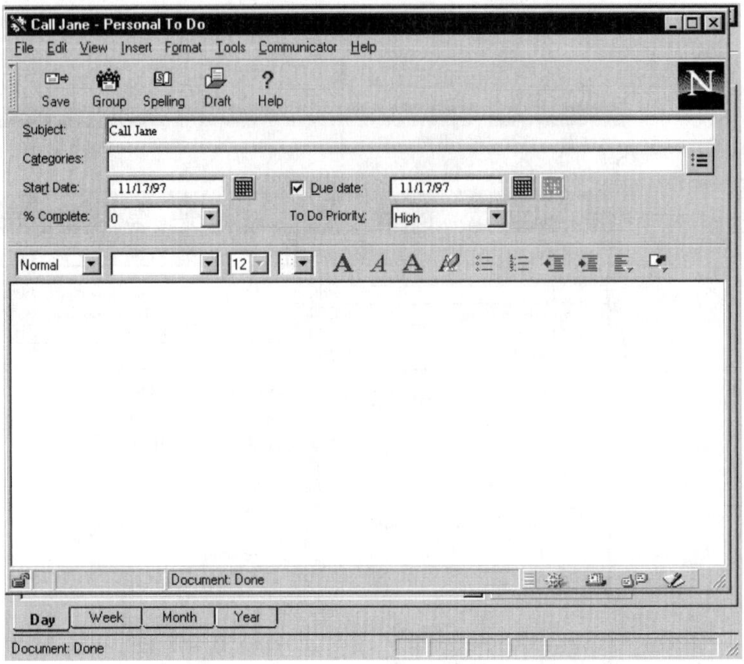

Entering
To Do
information

FIGURE 31-7

empty box to the left of the item in the To Do list. CorelCENTRAL will place a check mark in the box and strike out the item.

To sort the lists of items, pull down the Due Date list and select from these options: Due Date, % Complete, and Start Date. The items will be sorted by your selection, displaying the selected information in that last column.

You can also change the item properties using a QuickMenu. First, select the to do item by clicking on the Due Date. Then right-click on the Due Date and select options from the QuickMenu. You can change the sort order, the priority, and the percentage complete.

Assigning To Do Items

In addition to creating a personal to do item, you can assign a "to do" to someone else and transmit the item through e-mail. To assign a "to do", click on the Assign a To Do button in the toolbar. The dialog box that appears lets you create the to do item, as you learned previously, as well as enter the recipient e-mail addresses, attach documents, and change message settings. Complete the dialog box, then click on Send to e-mail the item.

When the to-do item is received by the recipient, it is placed in their Inbox. When they click on the message, it appears along with a calendar showing the period between the start and due dates. They can then click on either the Accept or Decline buttons in the toolbar, as they can for a received scheduled event. If the recipient accepts the item, it appears in their To Do list.

Printing a Calendar

You print a calendar using standard Windows techniques, although the dialog box is not the same as those in other Corel WordPerfect Suite applications. To print your calendar, click on the Print button in the toolbar, or select Print from the File menu to display this dialog box:

Choose to print a day, week, month, or year calendar, then enter the starting and ending dates to print. The default will be the current day, week, month, or year depending on your selecting in the Print section. Designate the number of copies to print, then click on the Print button.

Publishing a Calendar to HTML Format

If you want to display your calendar on a Web site, you can publish to HTML format. Select Publish to HTML from the File menu to see the dialog box shown in Figure 31-8.

- On the Calendar page of the dialog box, select the items you want to include, then choose the range of days.

- On the Banner/Signature page, add the text for the banner across the page, and choose items for the signature block, such as the copyright and name, the date the page was updated, and a return e-mail name and address.

- On the Location page, specify where to store the HTML file and the filename prefix.

Click on OK to create the Web page.

Using Card File

Card File is a mini database manager. Although it cannot perform the advanced database functions of Paradox, Card File can be used to store, display, and report information in much the same way as a database program. You can use Card File as an enhanced address book, or to record almost any type of information.

Like a Paradox database, each card is divided into fields, but CorelCENTRAL allows both global and local fields. A global field is one that appears in every card in a group of cards. A local field appears in individual cards. For example, suppose you have one client who has a Web site. You can add a field to just that client's card

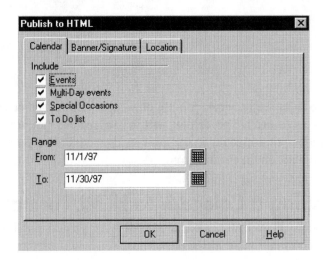

Publishing a calendar to the Internet

FIGURE 31-8

in the file containing a link to the Web site URL. All of the fields in a card file are indexed to help you find information quickly.

The cards can be organized into groups, and fields can be linked to other cards, to start the phone dialer, surf the Web, and even start applications.

There are two primary ways to use groups. If you have a large number of fields that you want to store, you can divide the fields into groups. The cards in a group are then related to the corresponding cards in other groups using a linked field. This is very much like creating related tables and using key fields in Corel Paradox or another database management program. Another way to use groups is simply to divide the cards according to some common objects. You may, for example, group the cards for your wine collection into red, white, rosé, and sparkling. A card can be contained in more then one group. For example, you may have a group called All Wines. Each wine in your collection will be in the All Wines group as well as the group for its type—red, white, rosé, or sparkling.

To display the card file, click the Card File icon in the View bar, or select Main View from the View menu and click on Card File. The default card file is designed to store personal information, and may contain one or more sample cards to demonstrate how the file can be used, as shown in Figure 31-9. The Card File toolbar is shown here:

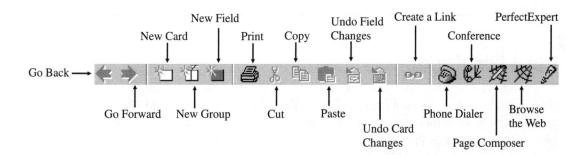

The power of CorelCENTRAL card file view is that you can create or customize card files, adding and deleting fields, creating links, and changing field properties. To get you started with card file, we'll begin by looking at using the default card files in the planner. We'll be looking mostly at the Personal card file which contains nine groups that store a wide range of information about persons. You can use all of the same techniques for working with your own custom card files.

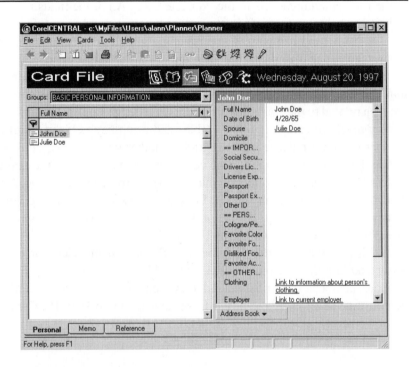

Card file
view

FIGURE 31-9

Card File Window

You can have more than one card file open at a time. The names of the files are shown in tabs at the bottom of the card file window. The three default card files that you'll learn about in this chapter are Personal, Memo, and Reference. Click on the tab to display the cards in the file.

On the left of the card file window is the Card List, which displays an index of the cards in the file. Use the arrows on the right of the column heads to scroll additional fields into view.

Above the Card List is the Group pull-down list. Pull down the list to select which group you want to display.

Groups: **BASIC PERSONAL INFORMATION** ▼

Click on a card in the list to display it in the Card Detail area on the right of the card file window. You can also double-click a card in the card list to display it in a separate window. To see more than one card at the same time, double-click on each card in the card list, then arrange their windows.

 NOTE: *The card title is taken from the contents of the first global field.*

31

The left side of the Card Detail list is the field name column, with global and local fields separated by a horizontal line—global fields above the line, local fields below the line. To change the order of fields, just drag and drop the field to the new position in the field list. Dragging a global field below the horizontal line converts it into a local field, and vice versa. A field can be global (or local) in one group, and local (or global) in another.

You can change the sizes of the panes by dragging the vertical line between them. Drag the line to the right of the field name column to change the size of columns in the Card Detail pane. Drag the line between column heading in the Card List pane to adjust the width of columns.

Adding Information to Cards

To add information to a card, you have to show it in the Card Detail. First pull down the Group list and choose the group where the card is contained. Then, scroll the Card List and click on the card's listing.

In the Card Detail, click where you want to enter data and then type. Do not press ENTER after the text, unless you want to add a new line of information in the field, such as when entering a two-line address. To move to another field, click in the field or use the UP ARROW, DOWN ARROW, TAB, or SHIFT-TAB keys.

CorelCENTRAL features QuickType. When you type, CorelCENTRAL looks at the other cards in the file for information in the same field beginning with the same characters. If it finds a match, it displays it in the field selected. To accept the entry, just move to another field. To reject the QuickType suggestion, just keep typing—CorelCENTRAL will continue to look for matching entries using the additional characters that you type. To edit the suggested QuickType entry, press the LEFT ARROW or RIGHT ARROW keys, edit the entry, and then move to another field.

 NOTE: *You can also click on a field to change its name. If you change the name of a global field, the name is changed for all cards in the group.*

Searching for a Card

Rather than scrolling the list to find a card, you can search for it or create a filter. Searching for a card scrolls the list to display a card that matches the text that you enter. Filtering the list temporarily hides all of the cards that do not contain the text that you type. You perform both operations by entering the text you are looking for in the search boxes—the empty boxes under the field names in the Card List.

However, start by selecting either the search or filter operation. When the icon next to the first search box appears as shown here, the list will be filtered.

Click on the icon to change it to the image shown here when you want to perform a search.

Next, enter the text you are searching for, or filtering by, in the empty search box under the field name that contains the text. CorelCENTRAL will scroll or filter the list as you type. You can also use the > and < operators, although CorelCENTRAL treats the > operator as "equal to or greater than" and the < operator as "equal to or less than."

NOTE: *To remove a filter, displaying all of the cards again, delete the text in the search boxes.*

Enter text in more than one search box to locate cards based on more than one field. CorelCENTRAL treats the condition as an "and" operation, displaying cards that contain all of the search text.

With filters, you can also use operators within the search box to perform AND and OR operations. Use the character "+" to perform an OR operation, and the character "&" to perform an AND operation.

Adding Cards

To add a card, first pull down the group list and choose the group you want to add the card to, then click on the New Card button in the toolbar. You can also right-click in the card list and choose New Card from the QuickMenu. The new card will contain all of the global fields from that group. Click in the Card Detail area and enter the information to the card.

To add a duplicate of a current card to the file, click on the card in the Card list, then choose Duplicate Card from the Cards menu, or right-click and choose Duplicate Card from the QuickMenu.

> **TIP:** *To delete a card, right-click on the card in the Card List, choose Delete Card from the QuickMenu, then click on OK in the box that appears. Select several cards by holding down the CTRL key as you click, or use the SHIFT key to choose a range of cards.*

31

Sorting Cards

The order of the cards depends on their order in the Card List. The name of the field in which the cards are sorted will contain a triangle icon:

```
Full Name                                    ▽ ◀ ▶
```

The direction of the triangle indicates the direction of the sort. The cards are in ascending order when the triangle is pointing down, and descending when the triangle is pointing up. Click on the field name that you want to sort by—click it again to toggle between sort directions.

Working with Fields

Card File fields are just like fields in a Corel Paradox database. Each field represents a piece of information in the card file, and you can set its properties to determine the type of information allowed. You can also add and delete fields to customize a card file.

Adding Fields

If you want to insert a global field to a card, you can start with any card in the group. To add a local field to a specific card, display that card in the Card Detail pane. Click on the field that you want to precede the next one—a global field to create a new global field, or a local field to create a new local field. Then select New Field from the Card menu, or click on the New Field button in the toolbar to insert the field, and type the field name in the text box that appears.

NOTE: *If you want to add the first local field to a card, scroll the field list, then click under the horizontal line—then just type the field name.*

To add a duplicate of a current field, click on the field in the Card Detail, then choose Duplicate Field from the Cards menu, or right-click on the field and choose Duplicate Field from the QuickMenu. To delete a field, right-click on the field then choose Delete Field from the QuickMenu. Deleting a global field removes it from all of the cards in its group.

Add Comment Fields

You use a comment field to store additional information about the object. You add one or more comment fields to existing global or local fields, then decide if you want the comments to appear onscreen.

To add a comment field, right-click on the field you wish to add a comment to, then choose New Comment Field from the QuickMenu. The new field will appear under the current field as shown here:

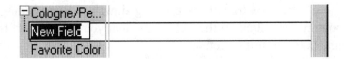

Type the name for the field, then click to its right and enter the field information. When you're done, the field will be displayed, with a minus sign next to the field that contains the comment. The minus sign indicates that the field contains comments that are displayed—that the field is expanded, much like an outline in Corel WordPerfect or a folder in Explorer. Click on the minus sign to collapse the field, hiding the comments—the icon changes to a plus sign. Click on the plus sign to redisplay the comment fields.

The comment field is added only to the current card, even if the field it is attached to is global. To delete a comment field, right-click on it and choose Delete Comment from the QuickMenu.

Adding Links

A link lets you click on a field to perform one of these actions:

- Display another card in the file

- Display a card in the address book

- Dial a number using the Phone Dialer

- Jump to a Web site

- Open a file or run an application

- Open a folder

- Send e-mail

As an example, look at the card shown in Figure 31-10. The card contains a link in the Spouse field. When the user clicks on the link, CorelCENTRAL opens the card for Julie Doe, the spouse of the person in the current card. Julie's card will also contain a link back to her spouse. There are also links that display cards showing employer, medical, and other information about Mr. Doe. To see Mr. Doe's medical information, for example, just click on the link next to the medical field.

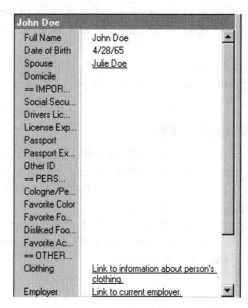

Links to cards in other groups

FIGURE 31-10

To add a link, click on the field where you want to insert a link, then click on the Create a Link button in the toolbar to display these options:

Link to Card File...
Link to Address Book...
Link to Phone Dialer
Link to Web Site...
Link to File/Application...

You can also select Link To from the Cards menu to display the same choices, along with Folder and Send E-Mail. When you choose the type of link you want to insert, CorelCENTRAL opens a dialog box in which you complete the link information. For example, if you choose to link the field to another card, a dialog box appears with a duplicate of the Card List. Select the card you want to link the field with, then click on OK.

When you add a link that displays another card, CorelCENTRAL adds to that card a return link as a local field. This lets you jump to the card by clicking on the link, then return to the original card by clicking on the local field that CorelCENTRAL inserted.

A link is shown in the same color as the title bar and underlined. Links to other cards or to the address book are shown as information in the field itself. Links of all other types, such as to the phone dialer or to a Web site, are added as a comment field.

To edit a link, right-click on it and choose Edit Link from the QuickMenu. To delete a link, right-click on it and choose Remove Field from the QuickMenu.

Setting Field Properties

You can set properties for Card File fields to define their type, size, and the way they are displayed. By default, all fields that you add are alphanumeric (they can contain text and numbers) and are displayed as text boxes. You can leave the fields blank or enter as much into a field as you want.

You can change a field's properties to help control the information entered into a card. Right-click on the field and choose Properties from the QuickMenu to see the dialog box shown in Figure 31-11.

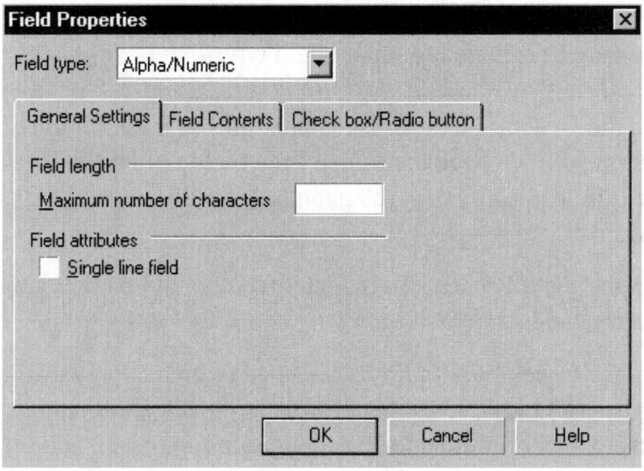

Setting field
properties

FIGURE 31-11

Pull down the Field Type list and choose from these types:

- Alpha/Numeric
- Check Box
- Currency
- Date/Time
- E-mail address
- Internet URL
- Mailing address
- Numeric
- Radio Button
- Separator
- Telephone

The dialog box has three pages: General Settings, Field Contents, and Check box/Radio button. Not all pages are available for every field type, and some options on a page may be dimmed for some field types.

- In the General Settings page, enter the maximum number of characters allowed, and check the Single Line Field option to allow only one line of text in the field. For a Telephone type field, select the type: Call, Fax, Modem, or Pager.

- In the Field Contents page, enter the default text that you want to appear in the field.

- In the Check box/Radio button page (which is only available for those types of fields), enter the information you want to appear next to each check box or radio button in the group (up to 10), and set the default status of each box or the selected radio button.

The type of field determines the characters that you can enter, the number of lines, and the way the field appears. After completing the Check box/Radio button page of the dialog box, for example, a Check Box field might appear like this:

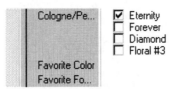

Fields of the telephone, e-mail address, and Internet URL types appear as links. Use the telephone type, for instance, when you want to be able to automatically dial the phone number in the card using the Phone Dialer. The separator type creates a horizontal line across the field information column. Use the field type to divide fields into groups for easy reference.

Working with Groups

As you know, there are two reasons to create groups:

- To divide the card file into logical groups of fields
- To divide cards into groups based on type

CorelCENTRAL lets you create as many groups as you want. You can also delete and rename groups, and assign cards to more than one group.

For example, the default Personal card file contains the groups shown here:

```
BASIC PERSONAL INFORMATION
CLOTHING INFORMATION
EMERGENCY MEDICAL INFORMATION
EMPLOYMENT -- PAST & PRESENT
FAMILY CONTACTS
FAMILY HISTORY
GIFT LIST
INSURANCE
RESIDENCES -- PAST & PRESENT
```

31

Each of these groups contains a set of related fields, with the cards to be linked to the appropriate card in the basic personal information group.

You can create a new empty group to which you then add fields, or you can base a new group on an existing one, using its fields and optional information from one or more of its cards.

To base the new group on an existing one, pull down the Group list and choose the group. Next, select any cards that you want to place in that group. Don't bother selecting cards if you want to place them all in the new group. Then click on the New Group button in the toolbar to display the New Group dialog box. (You can also display this dialog box by selecting New Group from the Cards menu, or right-clicking on the card list and selecting New Group from the QuickMenu.)

Enter the name for the new group, then choose an option from the Contents section:

- *Empty* creates a new group with no information from the current group, even if they are selected

- *Include selected cards* adds the selected cards along with their fields to the new group

- *Include all cards from [current group]* adds all of the cards to the new group

- *Include fields from [current group]* adds all of the global fields from the current group to the new group

When you include existing cards in the new group, the cards are not actually duplicated, but are synchronized in both groups. If you make changes to a card in one group, the changes will be displayed when viewing the same card in other groups.

To delete or rename a group, pull down the Group list and select the group. Right-click on the card list, then choose Delete Group or Rename Group from the QuickMenu. Deleting a group removes all the cards in the group, but does not remove duplicated cards in other groups.

To move or copy a card between groups, right-click on it in the card list, then choose Cut or Copy from the QuickMenu. Open the destination group, right-click in the card list and choose Paste. When you cut the card, it is removed from the original group and added to the destination group.

Working with Card Files

CorelCENTRAL lets you use more than one card file in each planner. You can create your own card file, and you can select a CorelCENTRAL project for a ready-made file to perform useful everyday functions. Each CorelCENTRAL project includes global fields and many contain groups.

To create a new card file, select New from the File menu, then choose CorelCENTRAL 8 from the pull-down list in the Create New tab to see the options shown in Figure 31-12. To start with a blank card file, click on [CorelCENTRAL Card File] and then on Create. To use a CorelCENTRAL project, such as the Finance Card File, select it from the list and then click on Create.

NOTE: *Some sample card files are only installed if you select them when performing a custom installation of the Corel WordPerfect Suite.*

The New Card File dialog box appears in which you enter the name that will appear on the card file tab, and the file name and location in which to store the file on your disk. The default name will be taken from the project (such as Finance), or will be called Empty if you choose to create a new blank file. If you do not want to use the default name, enter a new one for both the tab and as the filename. It is best to accept the default path, however.

Click on OK to create the card file and display it in the CorelCENTRAL window. A new tab will appear at the bottom of the window showing the name of the new file.

Managing Card Files

You can delete and rename card files, and change their order in the card file tabs. Pull down the cards menu and point to Card File to see these options:

■ *New* lets you create a new card file, just as the New command from the File menu does.

- *Insert* lets you insert an existing card file into the planner.

- *Rename* lets you change the name of a card file.

- *Reorder* displays a list of the current files in the order of their tabs. Select a file and then click on the Move Up or Move Down buttons in the dialog box to change its position.

- *Delete* displays a list of the current files. Select the file you want to delete, click on OK, and then on Yes to confirm the deletion.

- *Close* lets you remove a card file from the planner, but not delete it from the disk. You can later use the Insert option to insert the file into a planner.

Importing and Exporting Card Files

CorelCENTRAL offers some capability to share card files with other applications.

If you already have a data file in ASCII, InfoCENTRAL, Netscape, or Sidekick format, or saved as a Corel WordPerfect Merge file, you can import it into

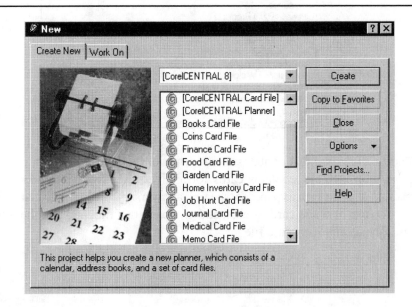

Using
CorelCENTRAL
projects

FIGURE 31-12

CorelCENTRAL. Pull down the File menu, point to Import, and choose the format of the existing file. Choose the file in the dialog box that appears, then click on OK.

To save a CorelCENTRAL card file in another format, choose Export from the File menu, then select either the ASCII or WP Merge options. Although only those two formats are allowed, you should be able to open the exported file, and even convert it to additional formats from within other programs.

The Memo File

The Memo file in Card File is used to record messages and notes. There is one default group, Notes to Self, and two fields, Subject and Comments. You can add cards, fields, and groups to the file, just as you can to any card file. In fact, use the Memo file just as you learned to do for the Personal card file.

The Reference File

The Reference file is a handy source of information, divided into these groups:

```
Anniversary Gifts (Traditional)
Birthstones
Calories - Dairy Products
Calories - Meat/Fish/Poultry
Conversions - Linear
Conversions - Temperature
Conversions - Volume
Conversions - Weight
International System of Units
Mileage - U.S. Cities
Mileage - World Cities
Telephone Codes - Country/City
```

Choose the group that contains the information you need. The Anniversary Gifts group, for example, contains cards for anniversaries from 1 to 60, showing the traditional gifts (such as paper for the first anniversary) and a suggested modern gift.

You can also add cards, fields, and groups to this file, and edit the information just as you can in any card file.

Printing Cards

Because of the number of groups and fields that a file can contain, printing a card file presents some new challenges. Before printing the file, first use the Page Setup command to determine which fields print out, and how they appear.

Start by selecting the card file and the group that you want to print, then choose Page Setup from the File menu to see the dialog box shown in Figure 31-13. Choose the page size, orientation, paper source, and then set the margins as desired.

Next, use the options in the Format tab to choose the font used for the page title, column headings, the contents of the fields, and the header and footer. Click on the Fonts button for the element you want to format, then choose the font, font style, size, effects, and color in the dialog box that appears.

Use the Headers and Footers tab to enter the page title and select its justification, and to enter the text of a header and footer. The header and footer are divided into three areas—the left, center, and right of the page. For the title, header, and footer, you can also choose to insert the page number, date, and time.

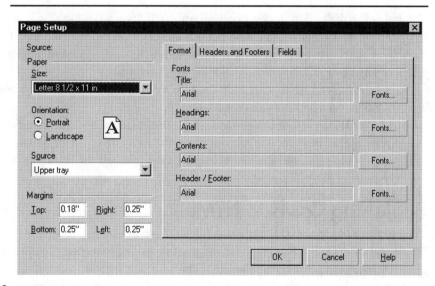

Setting up the page for printing cards

FIGURE 31-13

Use the Fields tab of the dialog box, shown here, to determine which fields print and how they appear.

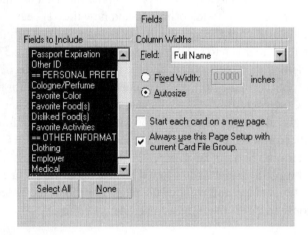

The fields highlighted in the list box will print. Click on a field to select or deselect it, or choose the Select All or None buttons to act on all fields in the list. Then, for each field, select its name in the Column Widths list and designate either a fixed width or have CorelCENTRAL adjust the width for you.

You can also choose to start each card on a new page, and to always use these settings whenever you print the group again.

Click on OK to close the Page Setup box, then select Print from the File menu. In the print dialog box, choose to print the cards in a table or list format, choose a range of cards to print, the number of copies, then click on the Print button.

Publishing Cards to HTML

You publish a card file to HTML in much the same way as you learned for Calendars. When you select Publish to HTML from the File menu, however, the options in the dialog box appear as shown in Figure 31-14.

In the Entries page of the dialog box, select how you want the Web page to appear (as a table or a separate Web page for each card) and if you want to include an index page. Choose the range of cards to include, then select the fields in the Fields list. Check the Include Field Names option to publish the field names along with the field information.

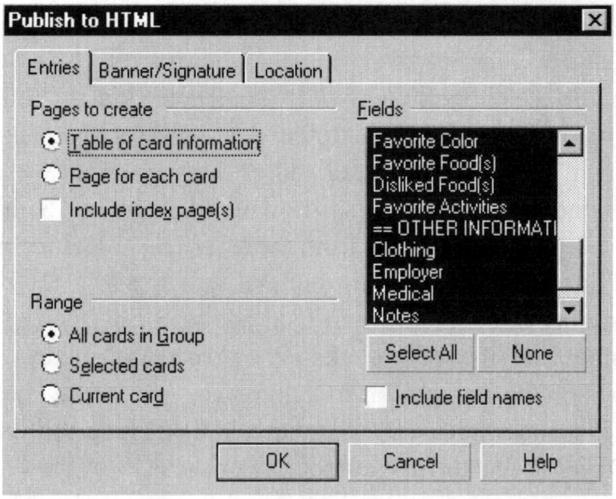

Publishing a
card file to
HTML

FIGURE 31-14

> **NOTE:**   *The Banner/Signature and Location pages of the dialog box are the same as you learned for Calendars.*

The Address Book

The CorelCENTRAL Address Book view is essentially the same as Card File. To display the address book, click the Address Book icon in the View Bar, or select Main View from the View menu and click on Address Book. Unlike a card file, all fields in the address book are global. There are two tabs—My Addresses and Frequent Contacts—and the groups are All, Person, Organization, and Resource.

The address book includes the same entries and books as Corel Address Book 8 that you leaned about in Chapter 1. They share the same file, so information you enter in one program will be available to the other. However, links that you insert when in CorelCENTRAL will not appear in the Corel Address Book 8.

Using the Phone Dialer

Use the *phone dialer* feature to dial your telephone. You can enter the number you want to call or use a number that you've entered into a card file. The program can even record information about the call into the activity log.

NOTE: *You must have a modem installed to use the phone dialer.*

You can start the phone dialer from the calendar, address book, or card file views by clicking on the Phone Dialer button in the toolbar or choosing Phone Dialer from the Tools menu. From the card file or address book, you can also click on a telephone link. The phone dialer appears, as shown in Figure 31-15. It will automatically display any telephone type fields from the selected card, along with the card title. If you clicked on a telephone link, the number will appear in the Number to Dial box.

If the number in the Number to Dial box is correct, click on Dial. Otherwise, select a number from the list or click on the phone number keys to enter the number, and then click on the Dial button.

If there is no answer or a busy signal, click on Hang-up. Use the Redial button on Phone Dialer to dial the last number again.

Pick up your telephone and talk. To time the call, click on the Start button—use the Reset button to reset the timer to 0. When the call is done, click on the Stop button (which replaced Start) to stop the time, and then click on Call Notes to insert a note about the call.

Phone
Dialer

FIGURE 31-15

To save a record of your call, click on the Save to Activity Log button. The activity log will include the date and time of the call, the name of the person called if from an address book or card file card, the phone number, duration of the call if you timed it, and the call notes.

TIP: *Use the Setup button in the phone dialer to configure your modem.*

Activity Log

The Activity Log conveniently lists all your events, To Do items, notes from the Calendar, and call information from the Phone Dialer in separate logs. To display the Activity Log, shown in Figure 31-16, click on its icon in the View Bar, or select Main View from the View menu and click on Activity Log.

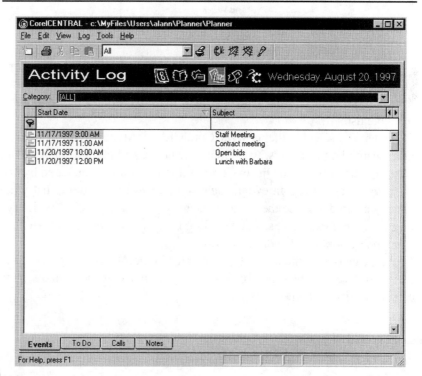

Activity Log

FIGURE 31-16

Click on the tab for the type of activity you want to list, then choose All or another category from the Category list.

You can scroll the column headings and sort the list just as you learned for Card File. Click on the arrows on the right of the column headings to scroll the list, and click on a column heading to sort the list by it. Click again to change the sort order.

The Activity List also contains search boxes that let you find or filter information, just as you leaned for Card File. Click on the icon on the left of the first heading to choose a filter or find operation, then enter criteria in the search boxes.

You can also filter activities based on the date and time of the call, or the start date of an event, to do item, or note. Pull down the Filter Criteria list in the toolbar, which contains the items shown here as well as additional choices:

For example, to display just the phone calls that you made the current week, click on the Calls tab, pull down the Filter Criteria list and choose This Week. To see events scheduled for the next day, click on the Events tab, then choose Tomorrow from the list.

When you select a filter criteria, CorelCENTRAL inserts the criteria to the Start Date search box of events, to do items, or notes, and to the Date and Time search box for calls. It filters the list even if the find operation is indicated by the icon.

If you want to log an event, such as a personal to do item, that you have not already entered, choose the tab and category, then select New Log Entry from the Log menu. For example, select New Log Entry when viewing the To Do page will open the Personal To Do dialog box.

You cannot edit the contents of an entry in the Activity Log list. To change an entry, however, double-click on it to display it in a separate window in which you can change its content.

CorelCENTRAL Lite

The integration of CorelCENTRAL with Netscape Communicator makes it a powerful application for managing your time and contacts. However, if you are not interested in coordinating events over the Internet, browsing the Web, or using the mailbox, conference, or help desk features of CorelCENTRAL, you can switch to CorelCENTRAL Lite.

NOTE: *If you did not install Netscape Communicator when you installed the suite, you'll be using CorelCENTRAL Lite automatically.*

CorelCENTRAL Lite does not include the Netscape Communicator features of the program. You'll still be able to create personal events and to do items, but you will not be able to use Page Composer to format notes, create group events, or assign to do items.

To switch to CorelCENTRAL Lite, start CorelCENTRAL, pull down the Tools menu, and click on Use CorelCENTRAL Lite. (If there is a check mark next to the option, you are already using the Lite version.) Select Use CorelCENTRAL Lite again from the Tools menu to use the full version again.

Using Envoy

32

Envoy is a program that lets you share your Corel WordPerfect Suite and other Windows 95 documents with other users, even if they do not have the Suite. This means that they can read your documents, worksheets, and presentations fully formatted, just as if they had the application that you used to create it. They can even print pages, add annotations and bookmarks, and use links to move to other parts of the document, or to sites on the World Wide Web.

Users can read your documents whether or not they have Envoy themselves. If they do not have Envoy, you can create a runtime version of your document, which is similar to a runtime version of a Corel Presentations slide show. You can alternately create a copy of the Envoy Viewer, a special limited version of Envoy that lets user read and annotate documents, but not create new Envoy documents themselves.

NOTE: *If you have the Standard version of the Suite, you can only use Envoy to read and annotate documents already in Envoy format, such as the documents included in the Corel WordPerfect Suite Reference Center.*

Running Envoy

When you install Corel WordPerfect Suite on your computer, Envoy is installed as a Windows 95 printer driver. This means that any program that can use the Windows 95 printers can send a document to be saved or annotated in Envoy. So you can start Envoy from the Windows 95 desktop as you can start any application, or from directly within an application, such as Corel WordPerfect, Corel Quattro Pro, Corel Presentations, Corel Paradox, or even Microsoft Word and other Windows 95 programs. Starting Envoy from one of these programs automatically inserts the current document—whether a letter, worksheet, or slide show—into the Envoy window. It is easy to use because you'll find it as an option under the File menu.

When you launch Envoy from an application, your program will actually generate an electronically "printed" copy of the document. The copy has been converted into a format that Envoy understands so it can be displayed in the Envoy window.

 NOTE: *There is also a Netscape plug-in for Envoy that will let you launch Envoy from within the Netscape window with a Web document.*

Here's how to use Envoy directly from a Corel application.

1. Prepare your document, worksheet, or slide show just as you want to print or display it.

2. Pull down the application's File menu, point to Sent To, and click on Envoy in the submenu.

Because the application must create a special printed version of the document for Envoy, it will behave similarly to when you are actually printing a document. From Corel WordPerfect, for example, you'll see a box reporting that the program is preparing the document for printing. From within Corel Quattro Pro, the Print dialog box appears—click on the Print button in the dialog box to continue. From within Corel Presentations, you'll also see a dialog box reporting that the slide show is being printed.

Don't worry. In all of these cases, the program is preparing the document to be displayed in Envoy, and in a moment or so, the Envoy application will open with your document displayed as shown in Figure 32-1.

Use the menu bar and toolbar to customize how the document appears onscreen and to add bookmarks, annotations, and hyperlinks. The buttons on the toolbar are shown in Table 32-1.

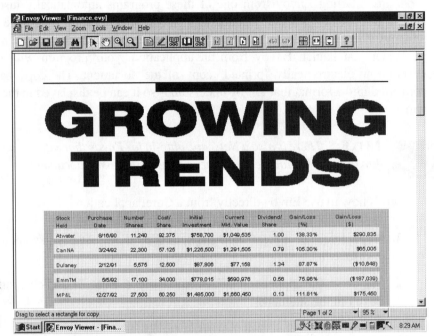

A document in Envoy

FIGURE 32-1

Button	Name	Function
	New	Opens a blank Envoy window
	Open	Retrieves an existing Envoy file
	Save	Stores the current document onto a disk
	Print	Prints the current document on paper
	Find	Searches the document for text, a QuickNote, highlight, OLE-embedded object, hypertext link, or bookmark

Envoy Toolbar

TABLE 32-1

Button	Name	Function
	Select	Selects text, notes, or other objects
	Scroll	Moves the document by dragging
	Zoom In	Enlarges the display
	Zoom Out	Reduces the display
	QuickNote	Inserts a QuickNote
	Highlight	Lets you highlight text or graphics
	Hypertext	Creates a hypertext link to move to another location in the document
	Bookmark	Inserts a bookmark
	Web Links	Creates a link to a Web site or to another document
	First Page	Displays the first document page
	Previous Page	Displays the previous page
	Next Page	Displays the next page
	Last Page	Displays the last page in the document

Envoy
Toolbar
(*continued*)

TABLE 32-1

Button	Name	Function
	Previous View	Returns to the previous view, such as the magnification or page
	Next View	Returns to the next view
	Thumbnails	Displays or hides the thumbnail views
	Fit Width	Adjusts the magnification so the page fills the screen width
	Fit Height	Adjusts the magnification so you can see the full height of the page
	Help	Displays the Envoy Help system

Envoy
Toolbar
(*continued*)

TABLE 32-1

The status bar shows a hint or tip about the function you are performing on the left, followed by the page number and total pages, and the current magnification. Click on the page number to display a dialog box to move to a specific page. Click on the magnification indicator to select another magnification. If you set bookmarks, there will be a bookmark at the right of the status bar. Click on the button to select a bookmark to go to.

NOTE: *For users of the Standard suite, when you select an option from the Corel Reference Center or double-click on an Envoy file—one with the EVY extension—Envoy is launched and the document appears onscreen.*

Opening and Importing Envoy Documents

Although it is easy to start Envoy from within a Corel application, you can also start it as a separate program from the Windows desktop. Click on Start in the Windows taskbar, point to Corel WordPerfect Suite 8, then on Tools, and click on Envoy 7 Viewer. A blank Envoy window will appear.

You can now open an existing Envoy document to read or annotate it, or you can import a file. Importing a file, such as a Corel WordPerfect document, converts it into Envoy format and displays it on the screen. To import a file, use these steps:

1. Pull down the File menu and point to Import.

2. Click on File.

3. In the dialog box that appears, select the file, and then click on OK.

NOTE: *Envoy does not use the same file management boxes as the major Corel applications.*

Saving Files in Envoy

The reason why you publish a document to Envoy when using the Professional version of the Suite is so you can save it in a format that others can view and annotate. From Envoy, you can save your document in three formats:

- *Envoy format* requires that the user have Envoy itself or a program called the Envoy Distributable Viewer. The Viewer is a special program that lets the user read but not create an Envoy document.

- *Runtime format* is an executable program file with the .EXE extension. Like the Viewer, this lets the user read the file, but it does not require the special Viewer file.

- *Text format* saves just the text of the document without any of its formats.

CAUTION: *An Envoy and Envoy Runtime file created in Windows 95 cannot be used in Windows 3.1.*

Follow these steps when you are ready to save the file.

1. Select Save As from the File menu to see the Save As dialog box.

2. Pull down the Save As Type list and choose a format.

- Select *Envoy Files (*.EVY)* if the person you are sharing the file with also has Envoy or you will provide the Distributable Viewer.

- Select *Text Files (*.TXT)* to save the document as plain text without any formatting.

- Select *Envoy Runtime Files (*.EXE)* so users can run the executable program file to display your document.

3. Enter a name for the Envoy document in the File Name box. Make sure the name ends with .EXE if you are saving it as a runtime file, or in *.EVY if you are saving it as an Envoy file.

4. Click on Save.

 TIP: *You can create an Envoy Runtime file from within Corel WordPerfect, Corel Quattro Pro, and Corel Presentations by choosing the Envoy printer driver when you print the document.*

Using Security

The Security option in the Save As dialog box lets you assign the document password protection and a security level. Click on the Security button in the Save As dialog box to see the Security Settings dialog box.

To require that users input a password to open the document, click on the Password check box and then type the password in the text box—the password appears as asterisks as you type. Next, select the type of access you want to provide:

- *Unrestricted* allows the user to view, print, and annotate the document.

- *View and print only* does not allow the user to annotate the document.

- *View only* does not let the user print or annotate the document.

Click on OK. A box will appear asking you to reenter the password. Type the password again and click on OK.

Using Envoy Files

If you saved the file as a runtime, anyone can display the file by running it from the Run option in the Start menu or by double-clicking on it in Windows Explorer. The document will appear in an Envoy window.

A Macintosh user, by the way, will not be able to run an Envoy runtime file. Sharing documents with a Macintosh user requires that the user have the Envoy 7 Viewer for Macintosh, available from Corel. Save your files in the Envoy format with a .EVY extension.

If you save the file in Envoy format, either the user must have Envoy or you must supply the user with a copy of the Distributable Viewer files. To do so, from the WordPerfect Suite Setup & Notes menu, select Distribute Envoy 7 Viewer, then click on Accept to accept the message that appears. In the dialog box that opens, enter the path where you want the viewer to be saved, then click on OK.

 NOTE: *The Distributable Viewer files are too large to fit on a single 1.44 MB floppy disk.*

Annotating Documents

While the document is in the Envoy window, you cannot edit or format text, but you can annotate it in a number of ways. An *annotation* is a way to give the reader more information than is in the actual document. There are five ways that you can annotate text:

- Highlight text with the Highlighter tool.
- Insert a sticky note.
- Insert a bookmark.
- Create a hypertext link to somewhere else in the document.
- Create a link to the World Wide Web or to another local file.

 NOTE: *Use the Insert Object command from the Edit menu to insert a graphic or other OLE object into the document.*

Highlighting Text

Highlighting text calls attention to it on the screen. You already learned how to use the Highlighter tool in Corel WordPerfect. It works just the same way in Envoy.

1. Click on the Highlight tool on the toolbar, or select Highlight from the Tools menu.

2. Point to one end of the text that you want to highlight.

3. Hold down the mouse button, drag to the other end of the text, and release the mouse.

4. Drag over any other text that you want to highlight.

5. Click on the Highlight tool or press ESC to turn it off.

To remove the highlighting from text, click on the Highlight tool, right-click on the highlighted text, and select Clear from the menu that appears. Press ESC or click on the Highlight tool again to turn it off.

 TIP: *Use the Annotations option from the File Import menu to copy the annotations from one Envoy document to another. The annotations will be copied to the same page number as they are in the source file.*

Changing the Highlight Properties

The default setting displays the highlight as a solid color over the text. You can change the color used for the highlighter, and you can set it to strike out the text with a single line. Use a strikeout highlighter, for example, when you want to indicate text that you feel should be deleted.

Follow these steps:

1. Click on the Highlight tool.

2. Right-click on any highlighted text.

3. Select Highlight Properties to see this dialog box:

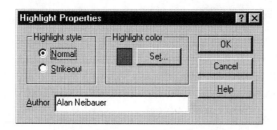

4. To change the color, click on Set, choose a color from the palette that appears, and then click on OK.

5. To highlight text with a color line, rather than a solid block of color, click on Strikeout.

6. Click on OK.

Adding a QuickNote

Although you cannot edit the text of the document in Envoy, you can add your own messages. Certainly you've seen those yellow stick-on notes that can be stuck to a printed document. A QuickNote works the same way, but onscreen:

ald-producing mines. (The Brazilian Whispering Grotto mine alone steadily produces 5,000,000 carats of emeralds annually.) However, one of the four mines, the Shadow Mine, located in Norway, has failed to produce a significant discovery in four years. This mine will be sold to Miserile Industries.

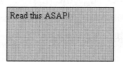

1. Click on the QuickNote icon on the toolbar, or select QuickNote from the Tools menu.

2. Click in the Envoy document window to insert a standard-size note about 2" by 3", or drag the mouse to create a note any size you want. You'll see an insertion point inside the note.

3. Type the text of the note.

4. Click outside of the note when you're done.

To later edit the text of the note, double-click on it to position the insertion point within it. You can also copy text from the document into a note. Here's how to create a new note with text from the document:

1. Drag over the text in the document.

2. Choose Copy from the Edit menu.

3. Choose Paste from the Edit menu to turn on the QuickNote feature.

4. Click or drag in the document to create a note containing the text from the document.

5. Edit or add to the text as desired.

6. Click outside of the note.

To add text from the document to an existing note, select the text and choose Copy from the Edit menu. Double-click on the note, and choose Paste from the Edit menu.

To delete a note, click on it so it appears surrounded by eight handles, and then press DELETE. To change the position of a note, click on it, point inside of it so the mouse appears as a four-headed arrow, and then drag the mouse. Change the size of a note by dragging one of the handles.

Customizing QuickNotes

You can reduce the note to a smaller icon, and you can even change its color and the way text appears in it. These functions are chosen from the QuickMenu that appears when you right-click on a QuickNote.

To change the note to a small icon, right-click on the note and choose Close QuickNote from the menu that appears. The note will now appear as shown here.

To open the closed note so you can read it, double-click on it, or right-click on it and choose Open QuickNote from the menu.

 TIP: *You can also toggle the note on and off by selecting it or the icon and pressing F2.*

To change the appearance of a note, right-click on it and choose QuickNote Properties from the QuickMenu to see the dialog box shown in Figure 32-2. In this dialog box, you can change:

■ The *alignment* of text in the note—left, centered, right, or fully justified

■ The *font* and *font size* of the text in the note

■ The *icon* that appears when you close the note

■ The *text color*

■ The note *background color*

32

Creating a Bookmark

You've already learned how to use bookmarks in Corel WordPerfect documents and in Netscape. A *bookmark* is simply a way to hold a place in a document. Set a bookmark at a location that you may want to quickly return to.

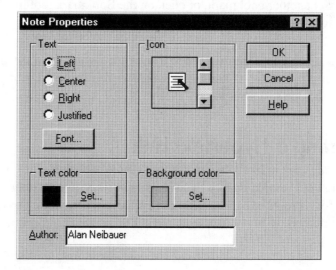

Changing
QuickNote
properties

FIGURE 32-2

To set a bookmark, follow these steps:

1. Click on the Bookmark tool in the toolbar, or choose Bookmark from the Tools menu.

2. Click on the text where you want the bookmark to appear, or drag over selected text. Envoy will display the Bookmark Properties dialog box.

3. Type a name for the bookmark in the Bookmark Name text box.

4. If you selected text in step 2, you can also choose the Select Bookmark Content After Jump box. This will highlight the same text when you move to the bookmark.

5. Choose a bookmark style. This determines how the bookmark appears when you move to it.

   ■ Select *Center Bookmark in Window* to show the bookmark in the center of the window.

   ■ Select *Fit Bookmark to Window* to enlarge the bookmark so it fills the screen.

6. Click on OK.

7. Set another bookmark, or click on the Bookmark tool in the toolbar to turn it off.

Now when you want to move to a bookmark, pull down the Bookmarks list in the lower-right corner of the Envoy window. You'll see a list of your bookmarks; click on the one you want to see.

Creating a Hypertext Link

A *hypertext link* is like a bookmark, but you just click on it to move to a specific location. For example, suppose you have a reference in your document such as "See page 3 for more information." You can create a hypertext link so the user can click on the reference to jump directly to page 3.

To create a hypertext link, follow these steps:

1. Click on the Hypertext tool on the toolbar or select Hypertext from the Tools menu.

2. Position the insertion point at the start of the text that you want the user to click on so the mouse pointer appears with the same icon as on the Hypertext tool along with an I-beam.

3. Drag over the text that you want the user to click on to move to another location. The text will be highlighted in the default color.

4. Move to the location where you want Envoy to go when the link is clicked, and then drag over the area that you want to display.

5. Click on the Hypertext tool or press ESC to turn the feature off.

To go to a hypertext link, point to the text that you marked as the link so the pointer appears as a small hand, and then click.

Changing Hypertext Properties

Envoy displays the link in the default color and when you click on it, the linked area is displayed centered on the screen. You can change the appearance of the link and the linked area by changing the hypertext properties. Here's how:

1. Click on the Hypertext tool on the toolbar.

2. Right-click on the link, and select Properties from the QuickMenu to see the dialog box shown in Figure 32-3.

3. Choose an option in the Source Text Style section to select how the hypertext appears.

4. To change the color, click on Set and select a color from the palette that appears.

5. Choose an option from the Link Style section to select how the linked area appears when displayed.

6. Click on OK.

7. Click on the Hypertext tool or press ESC to turn the feature off.

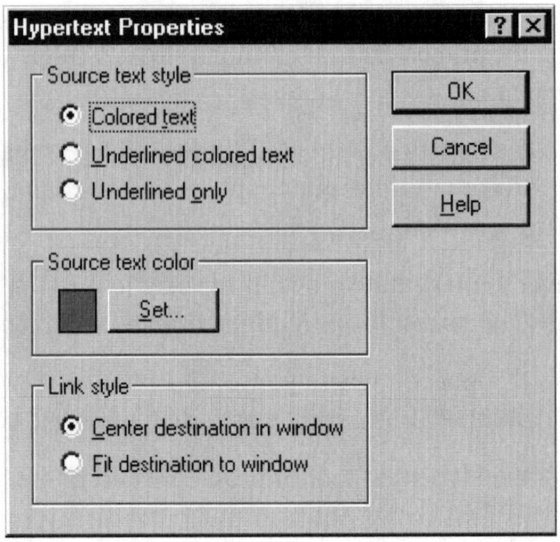

Hypertext Properties   [?] [X]

Source text style
- ⦿ Colored text
- ○ Underlined colored text
- ○ Underlined only

OK

Cancel

Help

Source text color

[ ] Set...

Link style
- ⦿ Center destination in window
- ○ Fit destination to window

Changing
hypertext
properties

▪ **FIGURE 32-3**

Creating a Hypertext Button

To add a little sparkle to your hypertext links, create a Link button rather than just selecting text. The button can be a plain rectangle with or without a fill color, or it can contain a graphic image, as shown in the margin.

Follow these steps to create the button:

1. Click on the Hypertext tool on the toolbar.

2. Drag in the document to create a rectangle that you want to be the button.

3. Move to the location in the document where you want the link to move.

4. Drag to set the location.

5. Click on the Hypertext tool or press ESC to turn the feature off.

The default rectangle is just an empty box. To add a fill pattern or graphic to the button, use these steps:

1. Click on the Hypertext tool on the toolbar.

2. Right-click on the box and select Properties from the QuickMenu to see the dialog box shown in Figure 32-4.

3. To add a color to the box, click on Set and choose a color from the palette that appears.

4. To add a graphic to the box, click on the Button option. Scroll the list and choose one of the graphics provided by Envoy.

5. Click on OK.

6. Click on the Hypertext tool or press ESC to turn the feature off.

Linking to the Internet

Whereas the Hypertext tool creates a link within the document, the Web Links tool creates a link to a site on the Internet or to another document. Click on the Web Links tool in the toolbar, and then drag over the area you want to use for the link. When you release the mouse, you'll see the Create Web Link dialog box.

To link to the Internet, type in the Destination text box the Web address or URL that you want to jump to. You can also click on the Browse Web button to launch your Web browser to locate the address. To jump to another document, enter its path

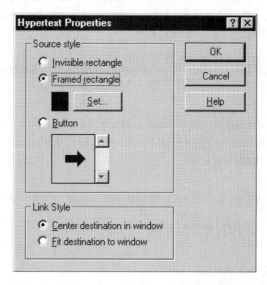

Hypertext
button
properties

FIGURE 32-4

and filename in the Destination box. If you want to move to a specific bookmark in the document, enter the bookmark name in the Bookmark text box.

TIP: *You can also drag to create a Web Link rectangle and add a color fill or graphic as you learned to do for hypertext links.*

Using Thumbnail Mode

Although you cannot edit the text of a document in Envoy, you can add, delete, and rearrange pages. You work with pages using *thumbnails*, miniature versions of every page in the document.

CAUTION: *If you want to add, delete, or change pages, do so before you set any bookmarks or links.*

To create thumbnails, click on the Thumbnail button on the toolbar. Click on the button once to see the thumbnails on the top of the window, as shown in Figure 32-5. Click on it a second time to place the thumbnails on the left, and a third time to remove the thumbnails. You can select the same options by choosing Thumbnails from the View menu.

To change the arrangement of pages, drag the thumbnail of the page to the position where you want it in the document. To delete a page, click on its thumbnail and press DELETE. This only deletes the page from the Envoy document, not from the original file.

CAUTION: *Delete with care—you cannot undelete the page!*

You can also add a page from another document. To do this, you need to open the other document into a second Envoy window. With one of the documents already open, follow these steps:

1. Click on the Open tool on the toolbar, or select Open from the File menu.

2. Enter the path and name of the other Envoy file, or select it from the list boxes.

3. Click on Open.

4. Select Tile Top to Bottom or Tile Side by Side, from the Window menu. This displays both documents on screen at the same time, in two separate windows.

5. Display the thumbnails on the top if you tiled the documents Top to Bottom. If you tiled them Side by Side, display the thumbnails on the left.

6. Click on the thumbnail of the page you want to insert into the other document.

7. To copy the page from one document to the other, hold down the CTRL key and drag the page to the thumbnail section of the other document. You do not have to hold down the key if you want to move the page, deleting it from its original document.

8. Save and close each of the windows.

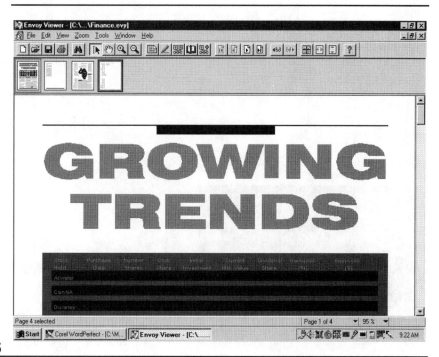

Thumbnail view

FIGURE 32-5

Corel Photo House

33

The Corel WordPerfect Professional Suite contains almost all of the elements of the Standard Suite—and more. The one missing ingredient is Corel Photo House—a program that lets you retouch and add special effects to photographs and other graphics. If you are using the Standard Suite or have Corel Photo House "left over" from the Standard Suite, then this chapter will show you how to use it. It's easy to use and fun to play with, so enjoy. Sorry—Corel Photo House just doesn't come with the professional version of the suite.

Using Corel Photo House

With Corel Photo House, you don't have to settle for the image that comes out of your camera, is generated by your scanner, or comes from your collection of clipart.

 Before you insert a graphic into a Corel WordPerfect document or other project you're working on, use Corel Photo House to enhance it in ways not possible with other Corel applications.

With Corel Photo House you can open and edit graphics in most of the common graphic formats, including these:

JPEG, BMP, PCX, GIF, TIF, CPT, PSD, PCD, CMX, WMF, EMF, FPX, and WPG

This wide range of formats means you can work with graphics from almost any source—graphics downloaded from the Internet or from any of the popular online services, scanned images, and clipart collections.

To start Corel Photo House, click on the Start button in the taskbar, point to Corel WordPerfect Suite 8, and click on Corel Photo House.

The Corel Photo House Desktop

When you start Corel Photo House you'll see the window shown in Figure 33-1. There's a lot to this desktop, so take some time to become familiar with it.

You use the *toolbox* to select or erase parts of the graphic, and to add and change colors. The toolbox contains the buttons shown here.

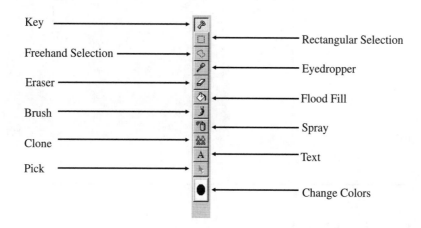

Key — Rectangular Selection

Freehand Selection — Eyedropper

Eraser — Flood Fill

Brush — Spray

Clone — Text

Pick — Change Colors

Use the Key tool to display the Key page of the notebook when you need help on what to select from a menu of options. You'll use the other tools to select and delete segments of your graphic, and to add your own elements.

The *toolbar* contains the usual array of buttons, including tools to zoom in, zoom out, and display the full page. There are also these buttons on the right of the toolbar:

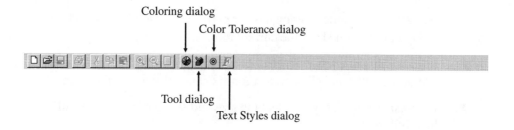

Coloring dialog

Color Tolerance dialog

Tool dialog

Text Styles dialog

Toolbox

Toolbar ⟶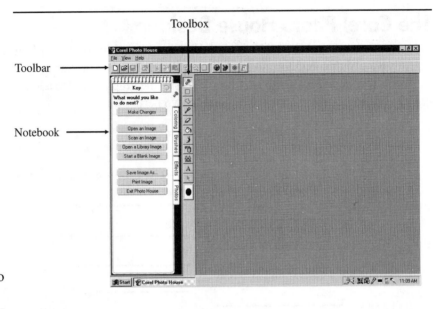

Notebook ⟶

Corel Photo
House

FIGURE 33-1

Using the Notebook

The *notebook* is the notepad on the left of the desktop. As with PerfectExpert, the notebook will change depending on the task you are performing or the tool you are using. You use the notebook to perform Corel Photo House functions, select colors, brush shapes, and photographs, and to add special effects.

Select a page of the notebook by clicking on its tab. You can also click on the Key tool to display the Key page.

The notebook includes five pages:

■ The *Key page* includes commands for performing useful tasks, and it will display information about the current tool.

■ The *Coloring page* lets you select colors to apply with the Brush tool. Hold down SHIFT and click on a color to change the color of the page.

■ The *Brushes page* lets you select the size and shape of the Brush and Flood Fill tools.

■ The *Effects page* lets you apply special effects to photographs.

■ The *Photos page* displays a catalog of photographs on the Corel CD.

When you select an option on some pages, an additional page of choices may appear. Next to the name of the page at the top is the Back button. Click on the button to go back to the previous page of that tab.

Retouching Photographs

Corel WordPerfect Suite 8 comes with a variety of sample photographs on the CD to help you get started. They are located in the Photos folder and organized into categories such as Cars, Landmarks, and Lifestyles. To access the photographs, click on the Open button in the toolbar, use the Look In list to display the contents of the folder on your CD, and then double-click on the photograph of your choice.

33

 NOTE: *Use the Open button if you cannot access your CD with the Photos page of the notebook.*

If you have a scanner, you can also scan a graphic directly into Corel Photo House using the Acquire Image command from the File menu. The Acquire Image command offers two options, Select Source and Acquire. The Select Source command lets you choose your scanner device if you have more than one installed on your system. The Acquire Image command launches your software, such as a Twain-compatible scanning program, so you can input the image and display it on the Corel Photo House desktop. Once the photograph is displayed, apply Corel Photo House tools and effects to edit it.

Adding Colors

Use the Brush, Flood Fill, and Spray tools in the toolbox to add your elements to the photograph, selecting colors and brush shapes from the notebook. Use the Eraser tool to remove elements.

To use the Brush tool, click on it and then drag around the graphic, "painting" as you do. The Spray tool works the same way, but leaves a trail similar to using a can of spray paint. The Flood Fill tool fills an area with the current color. Click on the tool to change the mouse pointer to an icon of the Flood Fill can. Place the tip of the can—which looks like paint pouring out—in the area you want to fill and then click.

The Brushes page of the notebook lets you choose the shape and size of the brush and spray. It includes a wide range of round and square brushes in various shapes, as well as patterns and symbols, such as those shown here.

Click the one you prefer.

Click the Brush on the photograph to paste one copy of the shape. For example, to insert a musical note on the graphic, click on the music-note brush shape in the notebook; then click where you want the note to appear on the image. Drag the mouse to leave a trail of notes.

As an alternative to using the notebook, select and customize brush shapes by clicking on the Tool Dialog button on the toolbar to see the dialog box shown in Figure 33-2. Choose from the available tools by pulling down the list box under the Preview area, then customize it by specifying the Size and Angle settings. Set a size between 1 and 100 pixels, and an angle from 0 to 360 degrees. The angle determines the shape of the image, much like you can by holding a paint brush at various angles.

You can also set the transparency, edge fading, and ink flow rate of the tool:

- *Transparency* determines the opacity of the color, ranging from most opaque (0) to transparent (100). Use a transparent tool, for example, to let background colors show through.

- *Edge Fading* determines the hardness of the edge. Values range from hard edges (0) to soft edges (100) more reminiscent of actual brush strokes.

Tool

Preview

Size [10]
Angle [0]

Transparency [0]
Edge Fading [80]
Ink Flow Rate [0]

OK   Cancel   ?

Tools
Dialog
button
opens this
dialog box

FIGURE 33-2

- *Ink Flow Rate* determines the amount of ink left on the page when you
  click the mouse button. Values range from a clean brush (0) to a wet brush
  (100). For example, imagine painting with a very wet brush. When you
  touch the paper with the brush, the excess paint bleeds around the contact
  area. If you use a high setting, more color will bleed on the page as you
  hold down the mouse button.

To customize the action of the Flood Fill tool, click on the Color Tolerance Dialog
button on the toolbar to see the dialog box shown here:

Color Tolerance

Few colors   Many colors

RGB [10]

OK   Cancel   ?

The *color tolerance* determines the range of colors that will be affected by the Flood Fill tool. Setting a low tolerance, for example, will cause the tool to affect just the colors that you click on with the tool. Selecting a higher tolerance will cause the tool to affect other colors as well. For example, when tolerance is set to the far left, using the Flood Fill tool on a red area of the graphic will only affect red pixels. Setting a higher tolerance will affect other colors, such as reds, pinks, browns, and oranges.

Selecting Colors

Corel Photo House offers you several ways to select drawing colors. The current colors are indicated in the Change Colors tool in the toolbox—the *paint color* (the foreground) is shown in the center oval, the *page color* (the background) around the oval.

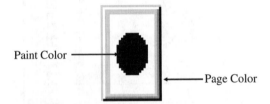

Paint Color ——————

—————— Page Color

The paint color determines which color is applied when you drag the brush and spray tools, or click with the Flood Fill tool. The page color is applied when you drag the Eraser tool.

To use the Coloring dialog box, shown here, click on the Coloring Dialog button on the toolbar or click on the Change Colors tool in the toolbox. Pull down the list at the top of the box, select either Paint Color or Page Color, and then click on the color of your choice in the palette.

TIP: *The section of the tool that you click on determines whether Paint Color or Page Color options are shown when the dialog box opens. Click on the Paint Color portion of the Change Colors tool, for example, to open the dialog box with the Paint Color options shown.*

To use the Coloring page of the notebook, click on the tab to display a palette of colors. Click on the color to use for the paint color, or hold down the SHIFT key and click on the color to use for the page color.

You can also use the Eyedropper tool in the toolbox to pick colors from those already in the graphic. This lets you match colors, or select a custom color that is not in the Corel Photo House palette. To use the Eyedropper, just click on the color that you want to use as the paint color, or hold down the SHIFT key and click on the color to use as the page color.

Cloning Objects

For special effects, use the Clone tool. This tool lets you copy an image on the photograph to another location, even to another photograph. By opening two photographs and tiling their windows, you can use the Clone tool to copy an image from one to the other. Figure 33-3, for example, shows a young girl's face cloned on Rembrandt's portrait. The photographs were reduced using the Zoom Out tool to display the full image. The results are, of course, dependent on your artistic ability and steadiness of hand.

Here's how to use the Clone tool:

1. If you are copying an image from one graphic to another, open both files and use the Window menu to tile them. Scroll the windows so you see the area you want to copy and the area you want to replace at the same time.

2. Click on the Clone tool. The mouse pointer appears like a large crosshair.

3. Point the crosshair on the center of the area that you want to copy, then click the mouse. The crosshair will remain in that position. For example, if you want to copy a person's head from one body to another, click the Clone tool in the center of the head.

4. Point the mouse to the center of the area where you want to insert the section. If you are copying a head from one person to another, click in the center of the head you want to replace.

5. Watching the crosshair in the image you want to copy, drag the mouse. As you drag, the mouse pointer and the crosshair at the original location will remain synchronized. Whatever is under the crosshair will be "painted" under the mouse pointer, copying the image from one location to the other. If you need to reset the origin point of the Clone tool, hold down the SHIFT key and click. When the crosshair appears, click a new origin point.

Adding Text

Use the Text and Pick tools in the toolbox to add and manipulate text on the graphic. Add text using the Text tool, then select the text with the Pick tool to change its size, position, proportions, and to rotate text.

To add text, click on the Text tool, click where you want the text to appear on the image, then type. To add a paragraph of text, click on the text tool, then drag in

Using the
Clone tool

FIGURE 33-3

the image to create a text box. As long as the blinking insertion point is in the text area, you can edit the text, or use the Text Tools dialog button to change fonts and other text properties.

NOTE: *Once you leave the text area, so the insertion point does not appear there, the text is merged with the image as a bitmap and can no longer be edited.*

To change the position, size, or rotation of the text bitmap after you type it, click on the Pick tool so the text is surrounded by handles. Drag the handles to change the images size or proportion. Click directly on the text to display handles for rotating or skewing the image.

33

Adding Special Effects

The Effects page of the notebook offers a variety of special visual effects that you can apply to a photograph. There are two general categories, Touch Up and Cool & Fun.

TIP: *You can also select effects from the Image menu.*

The Touch Up effects let you enhance and color-correct images. For example, correct overexposed or underexposed photographs using the Brightness/Contrast/ Intensity effect, or remove defects from old or damaged photographs using the Remove Dust & Scratches effect. These are the Touch Up effects:

- Brightness/Contrast/Intensity

- Deskew

- Reduce Speckles

- Remove Dust & Scratches

- Remove Red Eyes

- Replace Colors

- Sharpen

- Simplify Colors

NOTE: *You can apply multiple effects to the same photograph.*

To use an effect, double-click on it or drag it into the photograph. A dialog box will open showing Before and After panels, along with options for applying the effect, as shown in Figure 33-4. Select and set options in the dialog box, then click on Preview to see the effects in the After panel. When you're pleased with the results, click on OK.

While you are using the dialog box, you can click on Reset to remove the applied effect. Once you exit the dialog box, however, the effects are applied. If you then select the same or any other effect, the photograph as it appears becomes the new Before image, and clicking on Reset will not remove the effect. If you do change

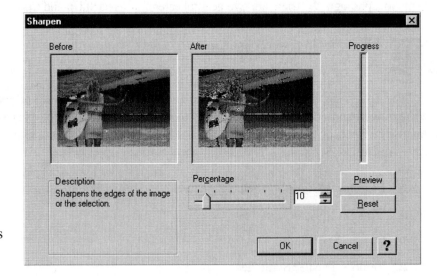

Check Before and After panels when using a special effect

FIGURE 33-4

your mind, use the Undo command from the Edit menu to remove the effect before selecting another. You can also choose Revert to Last Saved from the File menu to reload the last saved version of the file.

The Cool & Fun effects let you add textures, change colors, apply three-dimensional effects, and distort the image of photographs. Figure 33-5, for example, shows Page Curl and Texture effects applied to a photograph.

As with Touch-Up effects, you can control the amount of effect applied by choosing from a dialog box. To apply an effect, select Cool & Fun from the initial Effects page of the notebook, then double-click on the effect you want or drag it to the photograph. In the dialog box that appears, select and set options, using the Preview button to see the effects on the After panel.

33

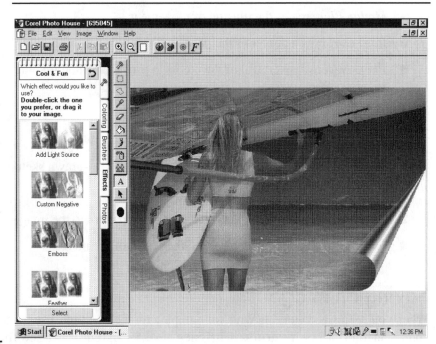

Special
effects

FIGURE 33-5

NOTE: *Not all effects can be applied to all types of images. For a description of the current image, select Image Properties from the Image menu.*

Here's a recap of the Cool & Fun effects:

- *Add Light Source* applies a spot of light that appears as the refraction of light through a camera lens.

- *Custom Negative* transforms the colors to a photographic negative.

- *Emboss* applies a carved-stone three-dimensional appearance.

- *Feather* blurs the edges of the photograph, or of a selected portion of it.

- *Impressionist* transforms the photograph into an impressionist-style painting.

- *Motion Blur* creates the illusion of movement.

- *Page Curl* rolls a corner of the page.

- *Photo Negative* inverts all of the colors to produce a photographic negative effect.

- *Psychedelic* applies bright, electric colors.

- *Ripple* adds an effect similar to a ripple in a pool of water.

- *Sketch* makes the image appear as though it's a hand-drawn sketch.

- *Swirl* rotates and drags an image.

- *Texture* applies a paper, linen, rock, or marble pattern to the image.

- *Vignette* adds an oval frame around the center of the image.

Saving an Image

When you're finished working with your graphic for the first time, use the Save As command from the File menu to save it. Using Save As, and entering a new filename, retains the original version of the image if you later change your mind about the applied effects. Use the Save As Type list in the Save As dialog box to select the image format. The options are JPEG, Windows Bitmap, PaintBrush (PCX), TIFF Bitmap, and Corel's own Photo-Paint format with the CPT extension.

If you select the TIFF format, a dialog box will appear after you click on Save, asking if you want to store the image in CIELab format. If you select JPEG, you'll see the dialog box shown here. Choose the type of JPEG format and subformat, and the quality factor, then click on OK.

JPEG Export

JPEG Format: Interchange Format (JPEG/JFIF)

Sub-format: Standard (4:4:4)

Quality Factor (2-255)

10

High Quality
(Large File)

Low Quality
(Small File)

OK   Cancel   Help

Creating a Graphic

Although Corel Photo House is not designed as a drawing and painting program, such as CorelDraw, you can use it to create graphics. When you select New from the File menu, you'll see the dialog box shown in Figure 33-6.

In the Color Mode section select a mode suited to how you want to create, print, or display your graphic. Select one of these options:

- Black & White
- Grayscale
- Color
- Million Color
- CMYK

Creating a
new graphic

NOTE: *"CMYK" represents cyan, magenta, yellow, and black, the inks used in four-color printing.*

From the Paper Color drop-down list, choose the default page color. Then select the checkbox to use a transparent background, if desired. With a transparent background, the area surrounding the graphic will be transparent so background images can be seen.

These are your choices in the Type drop-down list of the Image Size area:

- Custom
- Full Page
- Post Card
- Post Card (Large)
- Side Half Folded Card

- Side Quarter Folded Card

- Top Half Folded Card

- Top Quarter Folded Card

You can then change the size of the project, or set a custom size, by changing the width and height into either inches, millimeters, or pixels. Setting the Maintain Aspect Ratio checkbox will maintain the height-width ratio if you resize an image.

Under Resolution, the Horizontal and Vertical settings determine the resolution of the image in dots per inch. Select the Identical Values checkbox to use the same horizontal and vertical resolutions if you resample the image at a later time.

NOTE: *The Image Size value indicates the size of the resulting file in kilobytes.*

33

Click on OK to display a blank window on the desktop, and then use the image tools to create your graphic.

G

JUST THINK HOW MUCH MORE
YOU COULD DO WITH THE HELP OF
WORDPERFECT SUITE MAGAZINE

RGFD

80 timesaving macros to create impressive WordPerfect® documents.

80 Macros for WordPerfect® 8

FOR WINDOWS '95

TO INSTALL THIS DISK:
- Choose Start, Run from the taskbar
- Type a:\80macros and choose OK
- Choose OK in the dialog box that appears
- Choose Unzip when ready to install the disk
- Follow instructions in the Readme file

from **MAGAZINE WordPerfect**

Here are just a few of the macros you'll receive!

▶ **(8PRIORITY.WCM)**
Prioritize your tasks!

▶ **(8CNVTFILE.WCM)**
Convert multiple files from one file format to another!

▶ **(8INDXTAB.WCM)**
Create index tabs for hanging file folders!

▶ **(8YEAR.WCM)**
Produce a sharp, full-year calendar!

▶ **(8INVEST.WCM)**
Shows you how an investment can grow!

▶ **(8LOGENTRY.WCM)**
Track and log your incoming mail!

Supercharge Corel WordPerfect 8 by combining it with these customized macros

We've compiled 80 of the most popular, useful macros for WordPerfect 8 from the editors of WordPerfect Suite Magazine. All on one high-density diskette. **Continue to enjoy instant automation** of dozens of daily business communications tasks such as thank-you cards, resumes and calendars. Each macro has been carefully edited for seamless WordPerfect 8 integration **including various graphics** and readme files. **Work easier, faster and better** by ordering your 80 Macros disk today. (Requires WordPerfect 8 for Windows 95)

MAGAZINE WordPerfect SUITE AN IVY PUBLICATION
Helping you use Corel WordPerfect Suite Easier, Faster and Better

Only $19.95*

Call Today
1-800-228-9626

About the CD

The CD that comes with this book contains templates, sample Web sites, HTML pages, and other goodies to make your work with the Corel WordPerfect Suite 8 Professional even easier. For example, rather than download the Corel Presentations Show-It! plug-in, just install it directly from the CD!

For a complete index and to learn how to use the CD contents, insert the CD into your computer and double-click on these items: "My Computer" on the Windows 95 desktop, the icon for your CD-ROM, and then the icon labeled "Index." As an alternate, click on the Start button in the task bar, and then on Run. In the dialog box that appears, type **D:\index.htm** (using the letter for your CD drive, of course), then click on OK.

Your Web browser will start, and you'll see an index of the CD contents on the left of the window. Click on an item to learn more about it. The interface we've used for this CD, by the way, was created with Corel WEB.SiteBuilder.